EXCEL

IN BUSINESS

M000102869

SECOND EDITION

EXCEL

IN BUSINESS

Completely updated — covers version 2.2

The Cobb Group
Douglas Cobb
Allan McGuffey

Microsoft
PRESS
®

MAC VERSION

PUBLISHED BY
Microsoft Press
A Division of Microsoft Corporation
One Microsoft Way, Redmond, Washington 98052-6399

Library of Congress Cataloging in Publication Data

Cobb, Douglas Ford.
   Excel in business.

    1. Microsoft Excel (Computer program)   2. Macintosh (Computer)—Programming.
3. Business—Data processing.
I. McGuffey, Allan.   II. Title.
HF5548.4.M523C63   1989   650'.028'55369   89-14530
ISBN 1-55615-238-8

Printed and bound in the United States of America.

  2 3 4 5 6 7 8 9 FGFG 3 2 1 0

Distributed to the book trade in Canada by General Publishing Company, Ltd.

Distributed to the book trade outside the United States and Canada by Penguin Books Ltd.

Penguin Books Ltd., Harmondsworth, Middlesex, England
Penguin Books Australia Ltd., Ringwood, Victoria, Australia
Penguin Books N.Z. Ltd., 182-190 Wairau Road, Auckland 10, New Zealand

British Cataloging in Publication Data available

Apple®, Macintosh®, ImageWriter®, LaserWriter®, HyperCard®, and MacTerminal® are registered
trademarks and Finder™, MultiFinder™, and MPW™ are trademarks of Apple Computer, Incorporated.
dBASE®, dBASE II®, and dBASE III® are registered trademarks of Ashton-Tate Corporation. IBM® is a
registered trademark of International Business Machines Corporation. 1-2-3®, Symphony®, and Lotus®
are registered trademarks of Lotus Development Corporation. Helvetica® is a registered trademark of
Linotype AG and its subsidiaries. Microsoft® and Multiplan® are registered trademarks and Windows™
is a trademark of Microsoft Corporation.

Acquisitions Editor: Marjorie Schlaikjer   **Project/Technical Editor:** Online Press Incorporated

Dedication to the First Edition

To my son, Westray Stewart Cobb II
DFC

To Art
JLM

To my wife, Michelle
SSC

Dedication to the Second Edition

To Amy, for graduating,
and to Bonnie Raitt for ''Nick of Time''
A.McG

Contents

Acknowledgments

Our most sincere thanks to the following people, without whom this book would not have been possible: Mike Pizzo for his support; Dan Boone for diligent, eleventh-hour response to our macro questions; Shane Kim; Online Press, especially Pat Kervran, for marathon editing sessions; Marjorie Schlaikjer for being the generous and patient liaison in all this business; and at the Cobb Group for sharing the experience: Linda Baughman, Doug Been, Julia Bennett, Tara Billinger, Toni Bowers, Jenny Camacho, Teresa Codey, Gordon Colby, Tom Cottingham, Mark Crane, Rose Fairfax, Donald Fields, Luanne Flynn, Patty Flynn, Jody Gilbert, Laura Heuser, Lori Houston, Lori Junkins, Ginger Kepple, Tim Landgrave, Kathleen Fitzgerald Lane, Becky Ledford, Tracy Milliner, Elayne Noltemeyer, Beth Ording, Maureen Pawley, Joe Pierce, Jonathan Pyles, Beth Riggle, David Schmitt, Ann Sgt. Rockers, Raven Sexton, Patricia Shields, Duane Spurlock, Julie Tirpak, Margaret Walz, Jeff Warner, Linda Watkins, Teri Whitelaw, Kellie Woods, Jim Wooldridge, Jeff Yocom, Peggy Zeillmann, and Clyde Zellers.

Preface

In early 1984, Apple introduced the Macintosh—the computer "for the rest of us." The Mac was unique in the history of computing because it was the first computer that didn't require its user to think like a computer. The Mac's graphics interface, pull-down menus, and icons made it easy for even computer novices to get up and running.

There was only one thing missing: powerful business software. Although some programs, such as Microsoft Corporation's Multiplan and Chart, were introduced for the Macintosh in 1984, there was no software for the Mac that could challenge the power of the most popular IBM PC program: Lotus 1-2-3. The Macintosh languished, awaiting software that would convince serious business users to buy it.

With the introduction of Excel in 1985, the wait was over. Excel, an integrated spreadsheet program from Microsoft, is and has been the most powerful piece of business software available for the Macintosh.

What is Excel?

Excel is an integrated spreadsheet and graphics software package for the Apple Macintosh. It features three work environments—a worksheet (which can also be used to store databases), graphics, and macros—all bundled into one easy-to-use package. This combination of features makes Excel a powerful tool that allows you to perform a variety of tasks for business, science, and engineering.

Although Excel's business graphics and macro capabilities are very powerful, at heart Excel is a spreadsheet program. As you'll discover in a few pages, the first thing you see when you load Excel is a worksheet. Excel's worksheet offers many features and capabilities, such as user-defined formats, that are not available in any other spreadsheet program.

Excel's worksheet is an electronic replacement for traditional planning tools: the pencil (and eraser!), the accountant's ledger sheet, and the calculator. In fact, the electronic spreadsheet is to these tools what a word processor is to a typewriter. In addition, the Excel worksheet can be used as a database manager. Now, you can store basic information within easy reach—only a worksheet away. Because

Excel holds your reports, analyses, and projections in your computer's memory, making changes to them is as easy as typing a few characters and pressing a key or two. In fact, one of the most important reasons for building a projection in Excel or any other spreadsheet program is so that you can play "what if" games, varying assumptions and measuring their effects on "the bottom line."

On top of this worksheet, Excel offers the best business graphics available in an integrated program. Excel's chart capabilities, which are very similar to those of the stand-alone graphics program Microsoft Chart, allow you to create six basic types of charts—area, bar, column, line, pie, and scatter—and even combine two of these types. The program also offers tools that you can use to add titles, legends, arrows, and other enhancements to your charts.

Finally, Excel also offers a macro programming capability, which gives you the ability to create "scripts" that automate routine or tedious tasks. Excel's macros could even be used by more experienced users to write sophisticated applications programs in the Excel worksheet. Probably the most exciting aspect of Excel's macros is that they enable you to create user-defined functions—your own personal supplements to Excel's extensive library of built-in functions.

Excel 2.2

In 1989, Microsoft introduced Excel 2.2. With dozens of improvements and new features, this latest version of Excel signals a significant advance in business computing on the Macintosh. Although some of the changes offered in Excel 2.2 are relatively minor, others—such as a new, more efficient memory management system and a greater worksheet formatting capability—add a tremendous amount of power and flexibility to an already outstanding program. This book focuses on this new, more powerful version of Excel.

About this book

This book is a user's guide and tutorial for Microsoft Excel. It is designed to help you, the Excel user, gain the deepest possible understanding of Excel in the shortest time.

The book has six sections. The first section, which contains only Chapter 1, introduces Excel. In this chapter, we cover the basics of using Excel, give you a tour of the Excel screen, and show you how to save and open files.

The second section, which contains Chapters 2 through 9, covers the Excel worksheet. This section begins by showing you how to make entries in the worksheet, then covers such topics as formatting entries, using functions, and editing the worksheet.

The next section contains Chapters 10 through 13 on Excel's business-graphics capabilities. Chapter 10 walks you through the process of creating and enhancing a simple chart. The next chapters show you how to add more data to your charts, then how to use each of Excel's types of charts. The last part of this section shows you how to print charts.

The fourth section discusses Excel's database capabilities. A brief discussion of the general principles of database management in Chapter 14 is followed by a discussion of working with a database—locating and manipulating the data—in Chapter 15. Chapter 16 takes up a particularly useful kind of database manipulation, sorting.

The fifth section, which contains Chapters 17 through 20, explains macros. After introducing macros and describing Excel's macro functions in Chapters 17 and 18, we show you how to build user-defined functions in Chapter 19. Finally, in Chapter 20, we discuss the various ways you can customize Excel to suit your needs.

The sixth section contains three appendices. The first appendix explains how to use Excel in conjunction with other programs. The other two appendices cover Excel's keyboard shortcuts and the program's ability to work with Microsoft Mail.

If you're new to Excel, we want you to know that Excel 2.2 is not for power users only. Although you might not want to dive into the chapters about macros and custom menus and dialog boxes right away, you can start with the chapters about worksheets and printing and file management. Then, as you grow comfortable with the basics of Excel 2.2, you can move on to the sections of the book that seemed advanced to you when you bought it.

Now you're ready to enjoy an Excel experience.

SECTION ONE

INTRODUCTION

1

Introducing Microsoft Excel

In this chapter, we show you how to get started with Microsoft Excel. We describe the program's hardware requirements, then walk you through loading Excel and saving and retrieving files. If you are a first-time Excel user, we suggest that you read this chapter carefully before you move on to Chapter 2, "Worksheet Basics."

We assume you have used your Apple Macintosh with other programs and that you are familiar with the hardware components of the Macintosh and concepts like menus, windows, dialog boxes, pointing, dragging, and clicking. Instead of covering these concepts in detail, we concentrate on explaining concepts that are specific to Microsoft Excel. If you don't feel comfortable with these terms, please refer to Chapters 1, 2, and 3 of your Macintosh manual before you proceed.

Hardware requirements and memory considerations

Microsoft Excel 2.2 requires that your computer have at least 1 megabyte of random access memory (RAM). At more than 700 KB, Excel is a large program, requiring at least two 800 KB disk drives to operate. With only two disk drives, however, you may encounter storage problems because you will need to use one disk drive for your System Folder and the other for your Excel program.

Excel 2.2 makes more efficient use of your computer's memory than Excel 1.5 does. Version 2.2 can access a 4 megabyte "heap space." (*Heap space* refers to the area in RAM where Excel stores formulas and floating-point numbers.) For those of you who still want to use version 1.5 on occasion, the documents you create in version 2.2 might be too large to open in version 1.5. To remedy this problem, you can save your large 2.2 worksheets as smaller, linked worksheets.

Because memory is an important consideration with a program as powerful as Microsoft Excel 2.2, you should be aware of how Excel uses memory and how you can conserve memory. The amount of free memory for your work depends, of course, on several factors:

☐ The memory in your Mac.

☐ How much memory your desk accessories and printer network are using.

☐ The length and complexity of your documents.

☐ The fonts used in your documents.

☐ If you are using MultiFinder, the other programs that you are running concurrently with Excel.

You can reduce the amount of memory that Excel uses by closing documents you aren't using; reducing the number of fonts in your documents; and reducing the size of large documents by breaking them into smaller, linked worksheets. (For instance, blank spaces in the middle of documents use memory.)

To run Excel easily, you should have a Macintosh Plus or Macintosh SE with a hard disk and one floppy drive or with three floppy drives, or a Macintosh II with a hard disk and one floppy drive. If you choose hardware that includes a hard disk drive, Excel runs more quickly. Once you've loaded Excel, however, the hardware differences are indistinguishable. All your Excel windows look the same, and the commands and dialog boxes don't change; that is, the hardware you run Excel on doesn't affect the appearance on the screen of the worksheet window, dialog boxes, and so on. (Throughout this book, we address the SE with a hard disk as the most common configuration, because two disk drives severely limit the amount of space available for saving documents.)

If you plan to print your Microsoft Excel documents, you also need an Apple ImageWriter or Apple LaserWriter printer. These are the only two printers designed specifically for the Macintosh. Although there are other printers that will work with your Mac, they require external networking links, and you'll find it's more difficult to print graphics and to take advantage of Excel's font styles. We discuss Excel's various printer options in more detail in Chapter 9, "Printing the Worksheet."

The Microsoft Excel disks

The Microsoft Excel package is stored on three master disks: the program disk, the tour disk, and the help/examples disk. The program disk contains the actual program and the Dialog Editor. Most of the information you need to build your worksheets and charts is stored on this disk. The tour disk contains a HyperCard Tour of Excel's worksheet, charting, and database capabilities. The help/examples disk contains the Excel Help file, the Macro Library, and examples that help teach you the program.

Copying Excel

Before you load Microsoft Excel, make sure you create at least one working copy of each master disk. (You can make as many copies as you wish. If you have a hard disk, simply copy the files from your Excel package onto the hard disk. Never work from the original disks.)

To copy the program disk onto your hard disk, insert it into one of the drives of your Macintosh, open the program disk icon on the Finder desktop, and drag the Excel icon into the window of your hard disk or onto your hard drive icon. To copy the program onto another floppy disk, insert the program disk into one of the drives of your Macintosh and insert a blank disk into the other drive. When you insert a blank disk, you see the dialog box shown in Figure 1-1 on the next page. To initialize the new disk, click the Two-Sided button, then the Initialize button. The system prompts you to name the disk. Type a name, like *Excel Program Backup*, and click OK.

To copy the contents of the Microsoft Excel program disk onto this new disk, drag the Excel program disk icon until it overlays the icon of the blank disk. In a few moments, your Macintosh presents a dialog box telling you that it is about to replace the contents of the blank disk with the contents of the program disk. When you click the OK button, the system proceeds with the copy process. A status box appears, telling you how many files remain to be copied. When the copy process is successfully completed, the status box disappears.

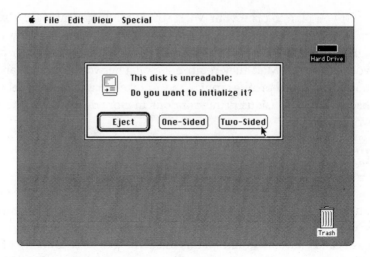

FIGURE 1-1. *This is the Initialize dialog box.*

Loading Excel

To load Microsoft Excel into an SE with a hard disk, double click the Excel icon. Your Mac's disk whirrs for a moment as it loads Excel into memory. If you have a Mac without a hard disk, insert the disk with your System Folder into the internal drive. Then, insert your copy of the program disk into the external drive. These disk drives also whirr while the Macintosh loads information about the contents of each disk. When you are ready to load Excel into memory, open the Excel program window, shown in Figure 1-2.

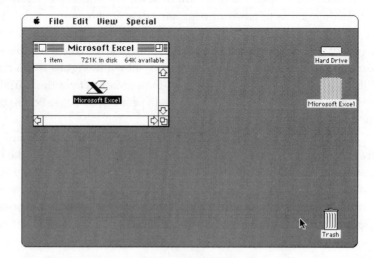

FIGURE 1-2. *The Finder desktop looks like this with the Microsoft Excel program disk loaded.*

Note: Always start Excel with a *copy* of the program disk. Then, if you experience a mechanical or system failure that damages the information on your disk, you will be able to use your master disk to make a fresh copy of the program. Be sure to store the original program and companion disks somewhere safe.

Now, you are ready to start Excel. Click the Excel logo symbol in the program window, then choose Open... from the File menu. To open the file automatically, double click the Excel logo symbol. A wristwatch symbol appears while the Mac is loading the program and collecting information from the System file.

When all of the necessary files are loaded, a Microsoft Excel copyright box briefly appears, then Excel constructs a blank worksheet. When the program has finished, your screen looks like Figure 1-3.

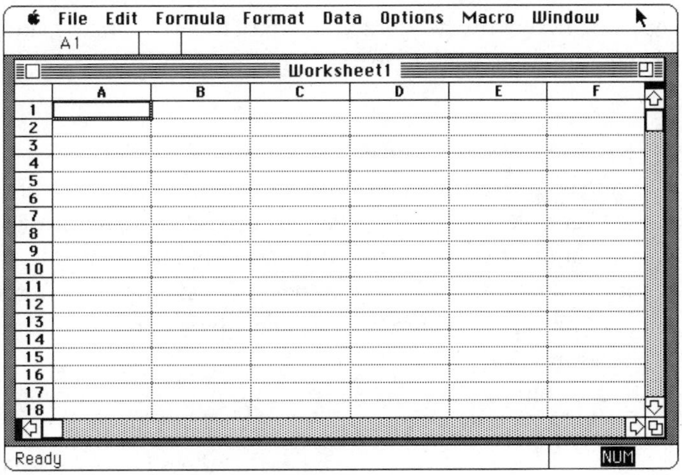

FIGURE 1-3. *This is Excel's initial worksheet screen.*

When you open the Excel program file, Excel automatically creates a new worksheet document for you. This document is called *Worksheet1*. Excel names any subsequent worksheet documents that you create *Worksheet2*, *Worksheet3*, and so on. (Of course, you can save the document under any name you like. We show you how to do that later in this chapter.)

There are actually three different types of windows in Excel: worksheet windows, like the one shown in Figure 1-3; chart windows; and macro windows. For the first nine chapters of this book, you'll be working only with worksheet windows. Once you've learned how to build a worksheet, we'll show you how to plot your worksheet data in a chart window and how to use macros to perform advanced worksheet functions.

A tour of the screen: The worksheet

When you start Microsoft Excel, your screen looks like Figure 1-3. Notice that the screen is divided into four major areas: the menu bar at the top, the formula bar just below the menu bar, the worksheet itself, and the status bar beneath the worksheet. All of these areas are viewed through a window. We explain windows below. For now, let's examine what appears on the screen.

The bulk of the screen is occupied by the worksheet itself. Like a paper accounting ledger, the worksheet is divided into a grid made up of columns and rows. A letter assigned to each column appears in the column header just above the worksheet grid. The column letters range from A to IV. (After column Z comes column AA, after AZ comes BA, and so on, up to IV.) A number assigned to each row appears in the row header to the left of the worksheet grid. The rows are numbered sequentially from 1 to 16,384.

Cells

At the intersection of each column and row is a cell. Cells are the basic building blocks of every worksheet. Each cell occupies a unique location on the worksheet where you can store and display information, and each cell is assigned a unique set of coordinates, called the *cell reference*. For example, the intersection of column A and row 1 has the cell reference A1. The intersection of column Z and row 100 has the cell reference Z100.

With 256 columns and 16,384 rows, your worksheet contains more than four million individual cells. Before you try to unravel the mysteries of the universe on a single worksheet, however, remember that the number of cells you can use at any one time is limited by the memory capacity of your Macintosh. Even though the program uses a sparse matrix system for efficient memory management, you probably won't be able to fill all the cells in one worksheet. (In a sparse matrix system, memory is allocated only to "active" cells—those with data in them.) Like most spreadsheet programs, Excel was created in anticipation of the day when microcomputers will be able to toss around megabytes of memory effortlessly. In fact, Excel 2.2 lets you create spreadsheets up to 12 megabytes in size.

Windows

In the worksheet shown in Figure 1-3, only about 100 cells are visible. Because the worksheet is so large, you can see only a small percentage of your worksheet on your 9-inch Macintosh screen at any given time. For this reason, you always view the Excel worksheet through windows. A window is like a porthole that lets you look at a limited portion of the worksheet.

To illustrate, suppose you were to cut a small, square hole in a piece of cardboard and then place the cardboard over this page. At any given time, you could see only a portion of the page through the square. By moving the cardboard around on the page, however, you could eventually read the entire page through the "window" in your piece of cardboard.

With a large worksheet, you might soon find it tedious to move the window back and forth across the "page" every time you wanted to see a different set of cells. Fortunately, Excel lets you create multiple windows for different views of your worksheet. By creating two windows, you can, in effect, use two pieces of cardboard at once. You can move the "holes" or windows independently to compare different parts of the worksheet simultaneously.

The status bar

The status bar displays the condition of the workspace as well as the function of the currently selected command. For example, most of the time, the status bar displays the word *Ready* at the left of the bar. This means that the worksheet will accept new information. As you type new information into a cell of the worksheet, the status bar displays the word *Enter*. To return to the Ready mode, you need to "enter" the information you just typed. To do this, simply press Enter or Return on the keyboard.

Another function of the status bar is to let you know what the currently chosen command does. When you scroll through the commands on a menu, you'll notice that the function of each command is explained briefly in the status bar. This is a helpful feature in case you forget the function of a command you use infrequently.

The scroll bars

To change the position of your window over the worksheet, move the worksheet past the window using the scroll bars located along the right and bottom sides of the screen.

The scroll arrows at either end of the scroll bars allow you to move one row or column at a time through the worksheet. If you click the up or down arrow in the vertical scroll bar, the worksheet scrolls up or down one row at a time. Similarly, if you click the right or left arrow at either end of the horizontal scroll bar, the worksheet scrolls one column to the right or left.

You can move a new screenful of information into view by clicking the shaded area of the scroll bar. If you click below the scroll box in the vertical scroll bar at the right side of the window, the window moves down one screen. If you click above the scroll box, the window moves up one screen. If you click in the shaded area to the right of the scroll box in the horizontal scroll bar at the bottom of the window, the window moves one screen to the right. Similarly, if you click in the shaded area to the left of the scroll box, the window moves one screen to the left.

The number of columns or rows that scroll into view when you click in the scroll bars is determined by the size of the worksheet window, the font size you are using, and the width of the columns. We talk more about creating and sizing windows in Chapter 5, "One Worksheet, Many Windows." For now, just keep in mind that you shift one entire screenful of cells when you click the gray areas of the scroll bars.

If you need to move a large distance through the worksheet you've created, you can drag the scroll boxes in the scroll bars to the desired position. The position of the scroll boxes in the scroll bars corresponds to the position of the window over the worksheet. For example, if you drag the scroll box in the vertical scroll bar to the middle of the scroll bar, the window ends up roughly halfway through your active worksheet.

When you drag the vertical scroll box to the bottom of the scroll bar, Microsoft Excel scrolls the bottommost row of the active area of the worksheet to the top of the window. Similarly, when you drag the horizontal scroll box to the far-right position in the scroll bar, Excel scrolls the rightmost column of the active area of the worksheet to the left edge of the window. When you drag the scroll box to the middle of the scroll bar, Excel moves the center of your active area into view. While you are dragging a scroll box, Excel flashes row numbers or column letters in the far-left portion of the formula bar, where the contents of the reference are displayed. This allows you to see which part of the worksheet you're bringing into view and can help you position the scroll box more precisely. When you stop scrolling, the far-left portion of the formula bar again displays the active cell.

Suppose your worksheet entries extend from cell A1 to cell S75. If you drag the vertical scroll box to the bottom of the scroll bar, row 75 appears at the top of your window. If you drag the vertical scroll box to the middle of the scroll bar, row 37 appears at the top of your window. Similarly, if you drag the horizontal scroll box to the right edge of the scroll bar, column S appears at the left edge of your window. When you drag the scroll box to the middle of the horizontal scroll bar, column J appears at the left edge of your window.

If you would like to move beyond the active area of the worksheet, you have several methods at your disposal. First, you can press the Shift key while you drag the scroll boxes. For example, holding down the Shift key and dragging the vertical scroll box to the bottom of the scroll bar brings the last row of the worksheet—row 16384—into view. Similarly, pressing the Shift key and dragging the horizontal scroll box to the far-right edge of the scroll bar brings column IV into view.

Second, you can use the scroll arrows to move beyond the active area of the worksheet. As always, clicking these arrows brings one new row or one new column into view.

Third, the Goto... command on the Formula menu offers a way to bring any cell of the worksheet into view. The Goto dialog box is easy to use. Simply type the cell location you want into the Reference field, then click OK or press Enter. Excel closes the dialog box and highlights the specified cell. Goto... can be faster than clicking the scroll arrows and more precise than pressing the Shift key as you drag the scroll boxes.

You will probably find it difficult to pinpoint a specific area of your worksheet by dragging the scroll boxes. If you need to move a large distance, however, you can use the scroll boxes to move the window to the general area of the worksheet, and then use the scroll arrows to zero in on the desired cells.

It is important to note the difference between scrolling through cells and selecting cells in your worksheet. Scrolling changes only the position of your window over the worksheet. If you have selected a cell to make an entry, that cell stays selected, no matter where you move the window. (We talk more about selecting cells and making entries later in this chapter.)

The size box

In the bottom-right corner of the window, at the intersection of the two scroll bars, is the size box. You can drag the size box to control the size of the window. The smaller the window, the less you can see of the worksheet; but because Microsoft Excel lets you create multiple windows to get different views of your worksheet, you may find it more convenient to view different parts of the worksheet side by side in two small windows rather than scrolling one large window back and forth.

The title bar

Just above the column headers on your worksheet is the window's title bar, which identifies the worksheet and window you are working in. When you first load Microsoft Excel, the title bar always displays the name *Worksheet1*, unless you load Excel by opening a previously saved document. When you create new windows, the names of the worksheets in those windows appear in their title bars.

On the left side of the title bar is the close box, which you can use to close the window you are currently working in. If only one window is open, Excel assumes that you want to close the entire worksheet file when you click the close box.

The window you are currently working in has black stripes in its title bar, indicating that it is the active window. You can reposition the active window on your screen by dragging its title bar.

The formula and menu bars

Just above the window is the formula bar and above that is the menu bar. These bars are not actually part of the worksheet window; they appear even if there is no window visible on the screen.

The formula bar

We mentioned earlier that worksheet cells are Microsoft Excel's building blocks. They store and display the information you enter into an Excel worksheet and allow you to perform worksheet calculations. However, you don't enter information directly into the worksheet. The formula bar, shown in Figure 1-4, is your link to the worksheet. You enter information into the worksheet through the formula bar. The contents of the active cell always appear in the formula bar.

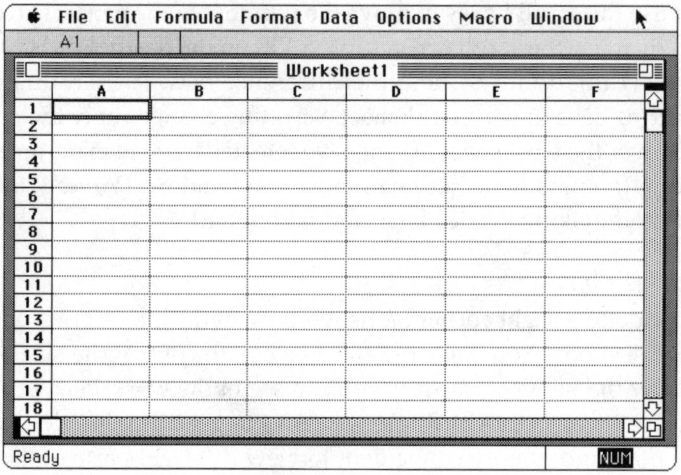

FIGURE 1-4. *This is the formula bar.*

If you move the pointer into the formula bar and click, you'll notice that two boxes appear to the left of the formula bar. The box containing the check mark is called the *enter box*. The box containing the *X* is called the *cancel box*.

When you click the enter box, you "lock in" the information you have typed and tell Excel to transfer that information to your worksheet. If you make a mistake while typing in the formula bar, you can click the cancel box to tell Excel to delete the information you typed.

To the left of the cancel and enter boxes is the *cell reference box*. This box contains the "address" of the cell or cells you are working on. At the moment, it probably contains the reference A1, telling you that cell A1 is your active cell; that is, A1 is the cell you have selected to work on.

The menu bar

Above the formula bar is the menu bar. Here, you select from the Microsoft Excel bill of fare to manipulate the information you have entered into your worksheet. In addition to the Apple symbol, which appears on the menu bars of all Macintosh programs, there are eight menus in Excel's menu bar: File, Edit, Formula, Format, Data, Options, Macro, and Window.

In our examples, we use Excel's Full Menus instead of the Short Menus. Excel offers more commands on its menus when you use the Full Menus option. You can toggle between Full Menus and Short Menus by choosing the appropriate command from the Options menu.

You pull down Excel's menus just as you pull down those of any Macintosh program: Simply point to the menu you want to pull down, then press the mouse button. When you pull down a menu, you'll notice that some commands are displayed in black, while others are displayed in gray; that is, they are dimmed. Excel monitors the status of your worksheet and only allows you to select those options that are applicable at any given time. The black options are choices that are currently available for use; the dimmed options are those choices that are currently unavailable.

You'll also notice that some of the commands in the menus have an ellipsis (three dots) after them, indicating that you must supply more information before Excel can carry out the command. You supply this information in a dialog box, which is basically another menu level where you direct Excel to take a specific action on the cells in your worksheet. Think of the menus, commands, and dialog boxes as a hierarchy of selections. Each time you make a selection you narrow down your instructions to Excel.

When you pull down Excel's menus, you also notice that some commands are followed by the Command-key symbol (⌘) and a letter. For example, notice the list of Command-letter combinations in the Edit menu shown in Figure 1-5. These Command-letter combinations sometimes offer you an alternative to using the Excel menus.

FIGURE 1-5. *This is the Edit menu.*

Instead of pulling down the menu and choosing the command, you can simply press the Command key and the appropriate letter at the same time. For example, to choose the Clear... command, you can press Command-B.

We talk more about Excel's commands in the next few chapters. For now, we'll briefly mention an important command that is new with Microsoft Excel version 2.2: the Workspace... command.

The Workspace... command on the Options menu, which we discuss again in Chapter 2, "Worksheet Basics," and Chapter 3, "Formatting the Worksheet," contains two useful options, Alternate Menu Key and Command Underline. These options let you display Excel's menus and then use the numeric and arrow keypads to choose commands. They provide an alternative for people who don't like using a mouse.

Accessing the menu bar using the keyboard

In addition to using the command key on your keyboard to choose commands, you can choose commands by using the slash (/) key. Pressing this key lets you pull down the menus using the keyboard. When you press the slash key, Excel highlights *File* on the menu bar. Pressing the down arrow key at this point pulls down that menu. If you want to access a menu other than File, you can press either the left or right arrow key. Excel displays each menu, one by one. Once the menu you need is displayed, you can press the down arrow key to highlight the command you want, and press Enter or Return to choose the command.

For example, if you want to use the keyboard to choose the Workspace... command from the Options menu, you can press the slash key, press the right arrow key five times until Excel highlights *Options* in the menu bar, then press the down arrow key to pull down the menu, and finally, press the down arrow key again to highlight the Workspace... command. To tell Excel to display the Workspace dialog box, press Enter or Return.

There is a second way to access the menus with the slash key. When you press the slash key, you'll notice that an underline appears under one letter in each of the menu names on the menu bar. This underline designates a letter you can press to open that particular menu. For instance, after you press the slash key to activate the menu bar, you can press the letter *O* to display the Options menu. To choose a particular command, such as Workspace..., press the down arrow key until Workspace... is highlighted, and then press Enter or Return, or press the letter *W* on your keyboard—the underlined letter in *Workspace...*—to open the Workspace dialog box.

The Alternate Menu Key option

If you prefer, you can assign the slash key's menu-accessing function to any other key on your keyboard. Simply choose Workspace... from the Options menu and type the key you want to use in the Alternate Menu Key field. Until you change the function key again, that key allows you to access the menu bar using the keyboard, just as the slash key did before you replaced it.

The Command Underline option

The Command Underline option in the Workspace dialog box determines whether Excel displays underlines under the menu and command names. This option has three mutually exclusive settings: On, Off, and Automatic. If you select On, the underlines appear constantly. If you select Off, they never appear. If you select Automatic (the default), they appear only when you press the slash key or the current Alternate Menu key. If you turn off the underlines, you can still press the letters that were underlined to pull down a menu or choose a command. Turning off the underlines does not deactivate the function of the letters as keyboard shortcuts.

The pointer

You should already be familiar with the basic technique of using the mouse to move your pointer around the screen. As you've probably already guessed, the pointer serves different functions in different areas of your worksheet.

When you move the pointer to the menu bar, Microsoft Excel automatically changes the pointer's shape to an arrow so that you can point to the command you want. When you move the pointer to the formula bar, the pointer changes to an I-beam shape. As you'll see in the next chapter, the I-beam lets you select an insertion point when you are editing information in your worksheet.

When you move your pointer back into the worksheet grid, the pointer changes to a plus sign. If you move the plus sign over cell C5 in your worksheet and click the mouse button, you'll notice that a gray border appears around the cell, and the cell reference box at the left end of the formula bar now contains the cell reference C5, indicating that you have selected this cell to work on.

You'll see the pointer take on other shapes as you begin using it to manipulate the worksheet and its window. We explain the significance of each pointer function as we address those topics in the next few chapters.

Now that we've taken a quick tour of the screen, let's get down to work and see how you go about entering information into the worksheet.

The File menu

You use the Microsoft Excel File menu to save and retrieve your worksheet, chart, database, and macro documents. To access the File menu, simply point to the word *File* in the menu bar at the top of the screen and hold down the mouse button. You see the menu shown in Figure 1-6 on the next page.

```
 File
  New...            ⌘N
  Open...           ⌘O
  Close             ⌘W
  Links...

  Save              ⌘S
  Save As...
  Save Workspace...
  Delete...

  Page Setup...
  Print...          ⌘P

  Quit              ⌘Q
```

FIGURE 1-6. *This is the File menu.*

The first two commands on this menu have to do with opening files. However, because you already have a worksheet open, we begin our discussion of the commands on this menu with those that save files. (We're going to bypass the Links... command for now, because linking is an advanced topic that we cover in detail later.) For the rest of the chapter, we use worksheet files as examples, but keep in mind that the techniques discussed here also apply to chart and macro files.

Saving files

Microsoft Excel has four commands—Save, Save As..., Close, and Quit—that allow you to save your Excel files. Each of these commands works in a slightly different way. When you save a document with the Save or Save As... command, Excel leaves the saved file on the desktop. When you save a file with the Close or Quit command, Excel removes that file from the screen as soon as it is saved.

When Excel saves a file, it also saves worksheet settings such as window size, type and display characteristics, formulas, functions, formats, fonts, and styles, in addition to saving its contents.

Saving a file for the first time

To save a file for the first time, you can choose either Save, Save As..., Close, or Quit from the File menu. If you choose Save or Save As..., Microsoft Excel presents the dialog box shown in Figure 1-7.

To save the document, you must give Excel two pieces of information: the name of the document and the name of the disk on which you want to store the document file. Notice that Excel automatically displays the name of the disk in the upper-right corner of the dialog box and the file name, *Worksheet1*, in the Save Worksheet As field. Those of you without hard disks will usually want to save your files on a data disk, because of limited space on your program disk.

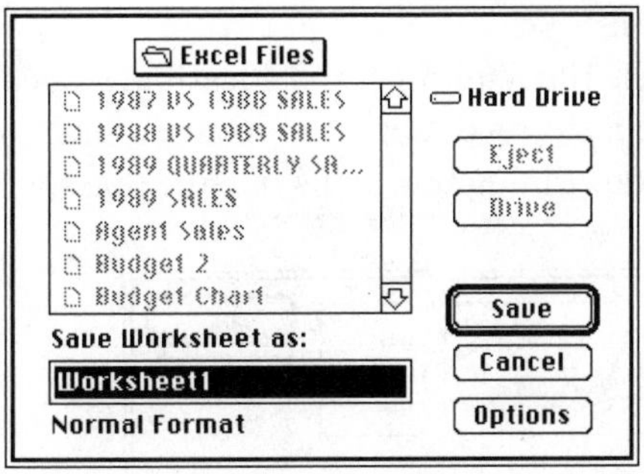

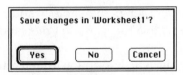

FIGURE 1-7. *This is the Save As dialog box.*

To save a file to a third disk, begin by clicking the Drive option in the dialog box until the name in the upper-right corner changes to the name of the data disk. (Of course, you can eject the Microsoft Excel program disk and place the disk on which you want to save your file in the external drive; but because Excel needs certain information on the program disk to save and load files, you'll find yourself swapping disks a number of times every time you want to save or retrieve a file.) If you insert a new disk, Excel may ask if you want to initialize it (following the same process we described in the section on copying disks). If you have already initialized and formatted the disk, Excel simply displays the disk name.

When you have selected the disk you want to save to, type a name for your document. Excel will automatically replace the default name, *Worksheet1*, when you begin typing. The file name can contain any character on the Macintosh keyboard except the colon (:) and must be shorter than 32 characters in order for Excel to display the entire name on the file's title bar. After typing the name, click the Save button or press Enter or Return to save the file. When Excel has finished saving the file, the window remains on the desktop, and Excel displays the worksheet's new name in the title bar.

If you choose the Close or Quit command to save a file for the first time, Excel displays a dialog box like the one shown in Figure 1-8. This dialog box lets you tell Excel whether to save the active window. If you click the No button, Excel will not save the file. If you click Yes, however, Excel presents the same dialog box shown in Figure 1-7 and allows you to save the file. In either case, Excel removes the window from the desktop.

FIGURE 1-8. *This is the Close dialog box.*

File formats and options

In addition to providing the file name and disk location, you can specify a number of different options in the Save As dialog box. To access these options, choose the Options button. The Options dialog box looks like the one shown in Figure 1-9.

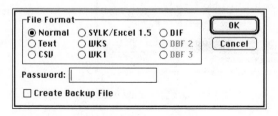

FIGURE 1-9. *This is the Options dialog box.*

You can save your files in nine formats. The default is Normal, and you'll almost always use this option. If you want to export your Microsoft Excel file to another program, however, you may need to use one of the other options to convert the file into a format that is readable by that program.

The Normal format (the standard Microsoft Excel format) saves your worksheet with all the formatting intact. The Text format saves only the text and values you entered into your worksheet and allows you to transfer your file to and from a word processor. The CSV format is similar to the Text format. However, instead of saving the worksheet with columns separated by tabs as the Text format does, the CSV format uses commas.

Clicking SYLK/Excel 1.5 saves the worksheet in a format that allows you to transfer data to another Microsoft spreadsheet program. Saving in WKS format allows you to transfer data to Lotus 1-2-3, version 1A, and saving in WK1 format lets you transfer data to Lotus 1-2-3, version 2, and Symphony. The DIF format saves your worksheet in Data Interchange Format and stores only values, not formulas. The remaining two formats, DBF 2 and DBF 3, are used for saving Excel worksheets that you plan to use with dBASE II or III. These last two formats are available only if you have set up all or part of your worksheet as a database. We cover databases in Chapter 14, "Excel Database Management."

You can also protect your documents by typing a password in the Options dialog box Password field. When you assign a password to a document, Excel prompts you to supply that password before it allows you to reopen the file. Your password can be up to 16 characters long, and capitalization matters. Thus, if you've assigned the password *Secret* to a file, you can't reopen that file by typing *SECRET* or *secret*.

Finally, you can use the Create Backup File option to create a duplicate copy of your file on disk. This duplicate file carries the same file name as your original, but preceded with the words *Backup of*. If this is the first time you've saved the file, the backup file and the worksheet file are identical. If you've previously saved the file with the Create Backup File option selected, Excel renames the last-saved version of your file by attaching the *Backup of* prefix and overwrites the existing backup file. Keep in mind that Excel always uses *Backup of* when creating backup files, regardless of file type. The benefit of using this option is that you always have the two latest versions of your Excel file, in case you want to verify a change you have made or in case something goes wrong with one of the files.

Resaving a file

The Save, Close, and Quit commands work differently when you use them to save a file that you have already saved at least once before. If you choose Save to resave a worksheet, Excel does not ask you to name the file. Instead, it automatically overwrites the contents of the file with the current contents of the worksheet and leaves the window on the desktop.

If you choose Close or Quit to resave a file, Excel again displays the dialog box shown in Figure 1-8. If you click No, Excel does not save the new version of the file. (The old version is still stored on the disk.) If you click Yes, Excel overwrites the previous contents of the file, just as if you had chosen Save. Whether or not you resave the file, Excel removes the window from the desktop.

If you make no changes to a file from the time you open it to the time you use the Save, Close, or Quit command, Excel doesn't resave the file. Excel always removes the window from the desktop when you choose the Close or Quit command.

The Save As... command allows you to resave a file under a new name. When you choose Save As..., Excel displays the same Save As dialog box shown in Figure 1-7. Within this box, Excel displays the name under which you last saved the file. If you press Return or click Save without changing that name, Excel overwrites the old file, just as it would if you had chosen Save. If you type a new name before pressing Return or clicking Save, however, Excel saves the current worksheet under that new name and leaves the old file intact under the old name. It then displays the new name in the active window's title bar.

The close box

The close box in the upper-left corner of every Microsoft Excel window works much like the Close command. Whenever you click a window's close box, Excel behaves as if you had chosen Close from the File menu. If you have never saved the file before, Excel displays the Save As dialog box and prompts you to supply a name. If you have already saved the file, Excel allows you to specify whether you want to save the current version of the file. If you click Yes, Excel overwrites the contents of the file. If you click No, Excel does not resave the file. In either case, however, Excel removes the window from the desktop.

Opening files

Saving Microsoft Excel worksheets in files would not be of much use without a
way to reopen those files in windows on the Excel desktop. Although there are
four commands that you can use to save a file, Open... is the only command you
can use to retrieve files while you are working in Excel.

To open a file in Excel, pull down the File menu and choose the Open... command. Excel displays an Open Document dialog box something like the one shown
in Figure 1-10.

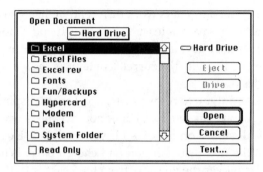

FIGURE 1-10. *This is the Open Document dialog box.*

As with the Save As dialog box, you must give Excel two pieces of information:
the name of the file you want to open and the name of the disk on which it is stored.
And, as when you are saving a file, you can, if necessary, use the Drive and Eject
buttons to exchange the program or data disk for the disk containing the file you
want. We suggest that you exchange the data disk, because opening a file from the
data disk is faster and requires less disk swapping.

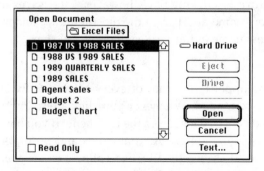

FIGURE 1-11. *This Open Document dialog box displays
the names of some Excel files.*

When you eject the data disk and insert the disk containing your file, Excel displays a list of the names of the Excel files you have stored on that disk, something like Figure 1-11. To open a file, you can double click its name in the list, or click the file name once and then click the Open button. No matter which of these techniques you use, Excel reads the file from disk and opens it onto the desktop.

The Read Only option

You use the Read Only option in the Open Document dialog box when you want to be sure you don't accidentally make changes to the file and then save them on disk. When this box is checked, you can view—and edit—the file you've opened. But you can't save the file under its current name, even if you've made no changes to the file. If you try to save the file using the Save command, Microsoft Excel displays the Save As dialog box and requires you to specify a new file name.

The Read Only option is most useful when you're using Excel on a network, because the option allows several network users to read the same Excel document at the same time. Each user can access the file as long as he or she selects the Read Only option when opening the file. If a user opens a document without selecting Read Only, no one else on the network can open that document until the original user closes it. The Read Only option thus prevents two users from altering the file at the same time.

Opening several files at once

Microsoft Excel 2.2 offers a unique new command: the Save Workspace... command. (This command, which creates a file called a *workspace file*, replaces the Resume Excel feature in Excel 1.5.) A workspace file contains a list of all the documents you have open in Excel at the time you choose the Save Workspace... command. If you frequently work with more than one document open on the screen, then the Save Workspace... command allows you to save the entire set of documents so that you can open them all at the same time when you next need them. This saves you some time and keystrokes when you load your files into Excel.

In addition to the set of documents you saved, the workspace file includes the following items:

- ☐ The size and position of all windows you saved.
- ☐ The options you selected in the Options Workspace dialog box.
- ☐ The preferred chart type.
- ☐ The global calculation settings.
- ☐ The Full or Short Menus settings.
- ☐ The Info window settings.

We discuss all of these items later in the book.

A workspace file lists only documents. It doesn't contain them but makes them accessible to being opened simultaneously. However, Excel opens only those documents you saved after working in them, even if they were open when you saved the workspace. Any change you make in a document that is part of a workspace file is retained (if you save it) the next time you open the workspace file. Also, you can still open separately any document listed in the workspace file.

To save a workspace file, choose the Save Workspace... command from the File menu. As you can see in Figure 1-12, Excel suggests the name *Resume* for the worksheet file. If you want to use a more specific name, simply begin typing. Excel then uses that name to identify your workspace file.

FIGURE 1-12. *This is the Save Workspace dialog box.*

EXCEL

Opening multiple files

Excel allows you to open as many files at one time as your computer's memory allows, simply by selecting either the Open... or New... command from the File menu. However, you may find that RAM constraints prevent you from opening several large documents at once.

In order to preserve the maximum amount of free memory for your work, Excel stores part of its code in RAM and leaves the rest on disk to be called in when needed. Each file you open onto the desktop occupies memory, regardless of the amount of data it contains. As we mentioned at the beginning of this chapter, for reasons of memory consumption, you should try to limit the number of files you have open on the desktop at any one time. This is especially true if some of them contain large amounts of data (such as a worksheet in which you have filled thousands of cells).

Starting Excel and opening a file simultaneously

You can load Microsoft Excel and open a file simultaneously. By double clicking the icon of the file you've saved, you can both start Excel and open the worksheet's window on the Excel desktop.

Creating a new file

Whenever you need to create a new Microsoft Excel file, simply choose New... from the File menu. Excel displays the dialog box shown in Figure 1-13 to find out what kind of file you want to create.

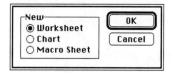

FIGURE 1-13. *This is the New dialog box.*

Notice that the Worksheet option is already selected in this dialog box. If you want to create a new worksheet file, simply click the OK button. If you want to open a chart or macro file, double click that option. If you select Worksheet, Excel displays a new, empty worksheet window on your screen. If another worksheet is already open, Excel displays the new worksheet's window on top of the existing one, as shown in Figure 1-14. You can use the Window menu commands to switch

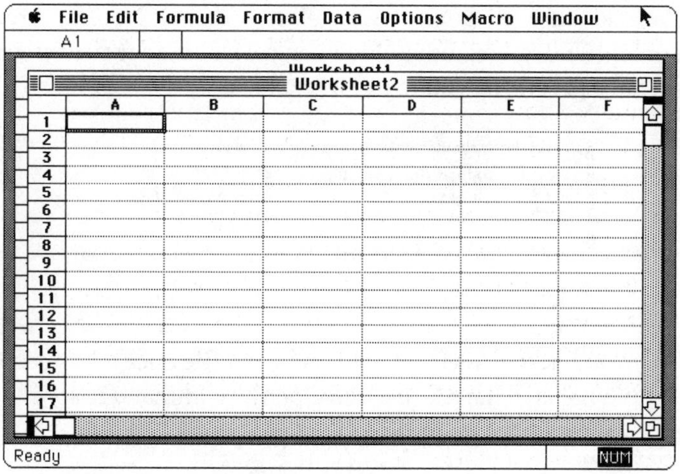

FIGURE 1-14. *The New... command opens a new file, which appears in a new window displayed on top of any existing windows.*

from one worksheet to another. We talk more about Excel's windows in Chapter 5, "One Worksheet, Many Windows."

Deleting files

You should already be familiar with the technique for deleting files using the Trash icon on the Finder desktop. However, you can also delete files while you are working in Microsoft Excel. To delete a file, choose Delete... from the File menu. Excel displays a dialog box like the one in Figure 1-15. Use the Drive and Eject buttons to access the disk containing the file you want to delete, then double click the name of the file or select the file name, then click Delete.

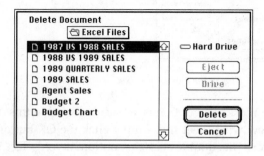

FIGURE 1-15. *This is the Delete Document dialog box.*

When you select a file for deletion, Excel displays the dialog box in Figure 1-16. If you are sure you want to delete the file specified in this dialog box, click Yes. If you are not sure, click No or Cancel. If you click No, Excel returns to the Delete Document dialog box, where you can select another file for deletion. If you click Cancel, Excel returns you to the worksheet.

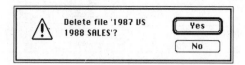

FIGURE 1-16. *This dialog box asks you to confirm deletion.*

Remember, there is no way to recover a file once it has been deleted. If you are not sure what is in the file, use the Open... command to look at the file before you use the Delete... command.

Exiting Excel

When you finish a work session, you usually want to leave Microsoft Excel and either turn off your Macintosh or load another program. To exit Excel, choose the Quit command from the bottom of the File menu. If you have changed any of the files on the desktop since you last saved them, Excel displays a dialog box like the one shown in Figure 1-8 for each altered file. If you click Yes, Excel saves the new version of the file. If you click No, Excel does not save the document, and any changes you've made since you last used the Save or Save As... command are lost when you exit Excel. Clicking the Cancel button cancels the Quit command and returns you to the program.

Once all of the active files are closed, Excel returns you to the Finder desktop, previously shown in Figure 1-2. Here, you can load another program or shut down your Macintosh.

Getting help

When you are using Microsoft Excel, help is never more than a moment away. If you become confused, or forget exactly what a certain command does, or forget the order of the arguments in a function, you can get help by pulling down the Window menu and choosing the Help... command. When you make this selection, Excel displays a dialog box like the one in Figure 1-17. Notice the list of help topics at the left side of this dialog box. To get help on any topic, simply select that topic from the list. When you do this, Excel displays a help screen that contains information about the selected topic.

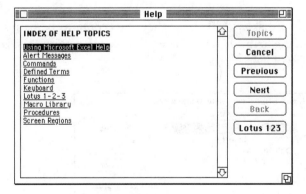

FIGURE 1-17. *This is the Help dialog box.*

For example, to get help on the Close command, you select Commands from the list of help topics, then scroll down to File Close and click. Figure 1-18 shows the result. Once your chosen topic is displayed, you can view the next or the previous help screen by clicking Next or Previous. You can retrace your steps through the levels of help screens by clicking Back. The Lotus 123 button displays a dialog box that allows you to type the key sequence you would use to choose a command in Lotus 1-2-3. When you click the OK button in the dialog box, the Help dialog box tells you the Excel-equivalent command. When you have answered your questions, you can click Cancel to return to the worksheet.

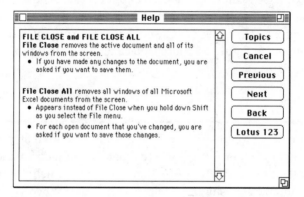

FIGURE 1-18. *This is the help screen for the Close command.*

If the Excel Help file is not on your hard disk, you see the alert box in Figure 1-19 when you choose the Help... command. From this box, select the correct folder in which the help file is located on your hard disk, or click Drive (if necessary) to make the data disk the active disk and click Eject to eject that disk. Then, replace the data disk with the disk that does contain the help file. Finally, click Open to open the help file on the new disk. When you do this, Excel displays the familiar listing of help topics.

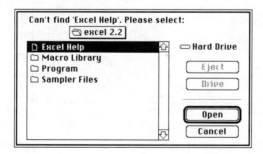

FIGURE 1-19. *This alert message appears when Excel cannot locate the help file.*

Incidentally, Excel allows you to open the Help dialog box from the keyboard without using the Window menu. Simply press Command-/. The same Help dialog box that appears when you choose the Help... command is displayed on your screen.

Microsoft Excel also allows you to obtain help without going through the Help dialog box. This type of help is called *context-sensitive* help, because it allows you to select the topic about which you want help directly from the worksheet.

To use context-sensitive help, simply press Command-Shift-/. When you do this, the pointer changes to a question mark, as shown in Figure 1-20. Now, you can use this pointer to choose the command about which you want help. When you make a selection, Excel displays the help screen that applies to the selected command.

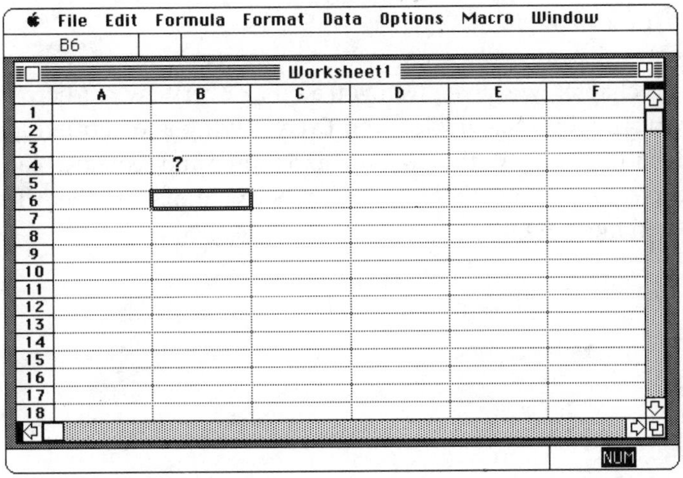

FIGURE 1-20. *The pointer changes to a question mark when you press Command-Shift-/.*

For example, suppose you want to erase the contents of a group of cells and you think you need to use the Clear... command, but you're not quite sure. To get help about the Clear... command, you simply press Command-Shift-/, pull down the Edit menu, and choose the Clear... command. Figure 1-21 on the next page shows the result. To return to the worksheet, click Cancel.

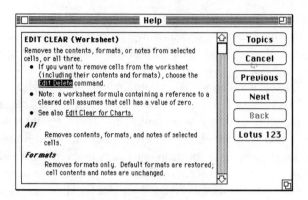

FIGURE 1-21. *This is the help screen for the Clear... command.*

Conclusion

In this chapter, we have given you a quick overview of Microsoft Excel, including hardware requirements, loading Excel, saving and retrieving files, getting help, and exiting Excel. With this information in mind, you are ready to proceed to the next chapter, "Worksheet Basics," where we discuss the Microsoft Excel worksheet in more detail.

SECTION TWO

WORKSHEETS

2

Worksheet Basics

*I*n the previous chapter, we introduced you to Microsoft Excel. We told you what hardware you need to use Excel, showed you how to load the program, and gave you a tour of the Excel screen. In this chapter, you'll learn to select cells, make cell entries, and correct errors. We also discuss how Excel calculates your worksheets, and we explain the concept of memory management. If you are a first-time Microsoft Excel user, we suggest that you follow along with the examples in this chapter, experimenting as you read. Once you feel comfortable with the basic techniques described here, you'll be ready to move on to the more advanced worksheet topics in Chapters 3 through 8.

Selecting cells

Before you can enter information into or perform any other operation on the cells in your worksheet, you must tell Microsoft Excel which cells you want to work with—a process called *selecting* cells. In Excel, you can select one cell at a time, or you can select ranges of cells.

Selecting single cells

To select a single cell, you simply point to the cell and click. Clicking a cell selects that cell and makes it the active cell in the worksheet. Once you have selected a cell, you can make an entry in that cell, or you can use Excel's commands to copy, move, erase, format, or otherwise manipulate the entry in the cell.

For example, to select cell C5, begin by pointing to that cell and clicking. When you do this, a border appears around cell C5, and the cell's reference appears in the cell reference box at the left end of the formula bar. Figure 2-1 shows the screen at this point.

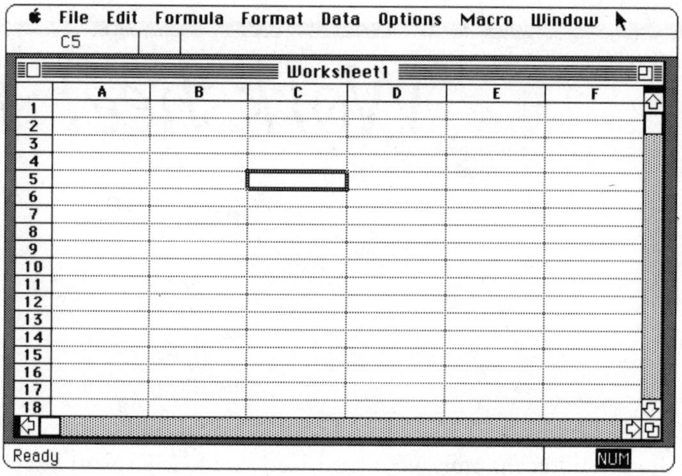

FIGURE 2-1. *This is the worksheet after selecting cell C5.*

When you select a single cell, that cell becomes the active cell in the worksheet. There can be only one active cell in the worksheet at any time. You can identify which cell is active in two ways: First, the cell reference box at the left end of the formula bar always displays the reference of the active cell; second, Excel always puts a heavy border around the active cell. (We call this border the *active cell border.*)

Whenever you make an entry in the worksheet, that entry is stored in the currently active cell. Once you have activated a cell, you can make an entry in it by typing. We show you how to do this later in this chapter.

Selecting ranges

Although only one cell at a time can be active in your worksheet, you can speed up the process of making entries, formatting entries, erasing entries, and so on, by selecting rectangular groups of cells called *cell ranges*. To select a range, you point to the cell that you want to be in the upper-left corner of the range, press the mouse button, drag to the cell that you want to be in the lower-right corner of the range, and then release the button.

For example, suppose you want to select the range of cells from A1 through B6 of your worksheet. To do this, you point to cell A1, press the mouse button, and drag to cell B6. Notice the rectangular area that grows as you drag the pointer down and to the right. Figure 2-2 shows this rectangular area, which helps you to identify the cells you are selecting.

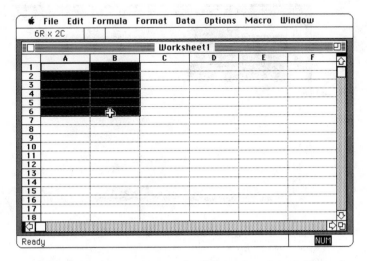

FIGURE 2-2. *The rectangular area that follows the pointer indicates the range of cells you are selecting.*

Excel uses the references of the cells in the upper-left and lower-right corners of a range to describe the range. For example, the range you just selected is written as A1:B6, which can be read *A1 through B6*.

When you release the mouse button, your worksheet looks like Figure 2-3 on the next page. Notice that the entire range A1:B6 is now highlighted and that cell A1—the first cell you selected—is the active cell. This cell appears in white, with a heavy border. The remaining cells in the range appear in black. Also notice that the cell reference box now reads A1. When you select a range, the first cell you select is always the active cell when you release the mouse button.

While you are selecting a range of cells, Excel displays the dimensions of the range in the cell reference box at the left end of the formula bar. For example, while you were selecting the range A1:B6, the message in the cell reference box might have changed from 2R X 1C (meaning that a block of cells two rows deep by one column wide had been selected) to 3R X 2C to 6R X 2C. When you released the mouse button, however, this message changed to the active cell's reference, A1.

Once you select a range, you can scroll through your worksheet without changing the selection. The range you have selected remains highlighted until you click another cell or drag through another range.

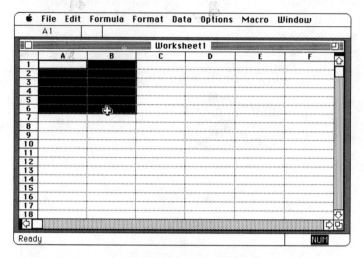

FIGURE 2-3. *The worksheet looks like this after you select the range A1:B6.*

You can make entries in the cells of a selected range, one cell at a time. We show you how to do this later in this chapter.

Extending a selection with the Shift key

The Shift key lets you quickly select large ranges of cells without dragging. All you need to do is select a cell that will be in any corner of the range you want to select, hold down the Shift key, then click the cell at the opposite corner. This technique is called *extending a selection.*

For example, suppose you want to select the range A1:C12. To do this, click cell C12, hold down the Shift key, and click cell A1. As you can see in Figure 2-4, Excel automatically extends your selection to include cells A1 through C12. Notice that cell C12, which you selected to begin the range definition, is the active cell in this range.

Instead of starting with cell C12, you could have started by selecting cell A1. Then, you could have held down the Shift key and clicked cell C12 to define the range. If you had defined the range in this way, cell A1 would be the active cell.

This shifting technique comes in handy when you need to select a large range of cells and some of those cells are not visible on your screen. For example, suppose you want to select the range A1:C38. Since C38 is out of view, click cell A1 and then scroll the window until cell C38 is in view. (By this time, A1 is out of sight.) You can then press the Shift key and click cell C38. As soon as you click C38, Excel selects the range A1:C38, with A1 as the active cell.

You can also use the Shift key in conjunction with the arrow keys to extend your selection. Suppose you want to select the range A1:C12, as you did in Figure 2-4, except that this time you want to use the arrow keys. To do this, select cell A1, hold down the Shift key, and press the right arrow key twice and the down arrow key 11 times. Your screen resembles the screen in Figure 2-4; however, because you began with cell A1, that cell is the active cell in the selected range. If you want, you can begin with cell C12, hold down the Shift key, press the left arrow key twice and the up arrow key 11 times to select the same range.

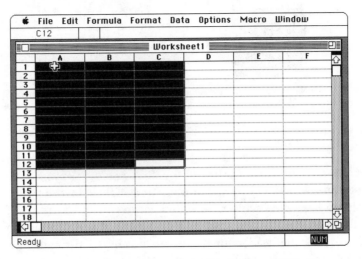

FIGURE 2-4. *You select the range A1:C12 by clicking cell C12, then clicking cell A1 while holding down the Shift key.*

Dragging beyond the window border

If your selection is relatively small, you may prefer to scroll beyond the borders of the current window by dragging to the edge of the window. For example, suppose you want to select the range A18:A25. To do this, you can select cell A18, then drag the pointer straight to the bottom of the screen. (Notice the rectangular area that appears as you begin dragging the pointer.) When the pointer reaches the horizontal scroll bar at the bottom of the window, the window begins scrolling down one row at a time. When cell A25 comes into view, point to that cell and release the mouse button. Figure 2-5 on the next page shows the screen at this point.

Now, suppose you want to select the range A3:A9, beginning from the screen shown in Figure 2-5. To do this, you select cell A9, then drag the pointer to the title bar. This time, the window scrolls up one row at a time. When cell A3 comes into view, point to that cell and release the mouse button. Cells A3:A9 are now selected, and cell A9 is the active cell.

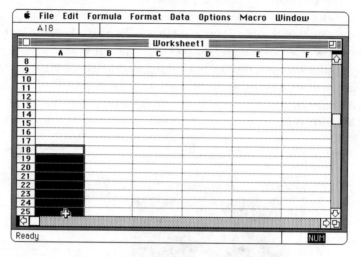

FIGURE 2-5. *The worksheet looks like this with the range A18:A25 selected.*

Selecting rows and columns

You can select an entire row or column of cells in one step by clicking the row or column header. When you select an entire row or column, Excel makes the first cell in the row or column that is visible in the window the active cell. For example, if you click the header for row 6 when cells A1 through F19 are visible on the screen, Excel selects cells A6 through IV6, and cell A6 becomes the active cell. If cells E1 through J19 are visible when the row header is clicked, Excel still selects the range A6:IV6, but cell E6 is the active cell.

Similarly, you can select an entire column of cells simply by clicking the header for that column. For example, if you click the header for column B, Excel selects cells B1 through B16384, and cell B1 becomes the active cell. If cell B1 is not in view when you click the header, Excel makes the first visible cell in the column the active cell.

You can select more than one adjacent row or column at a time by dragging through several row or column headers at once. For example, to select columns B, C, and D, you point to the header for column B, press the mouse button, drag to the right to the header for column D, and release the button. This action selects cells B1 through D16384 and makes cell B1 the active cell.

Selecting multiple ranges

Microsoft Excel allows you to include several different rectangular areas in a single range. For example, suppose you have already selected the range A1:B6. You want to add cells C7:E10 to this range without eliminating cells A1:B6 from the range selection. To do this, simply hold down the Command key and drag through cells C7:E10. Excel adds the new area to your selection without deselecting the original range. When you press the Command key and drag through a new area, the first cell you click in the new area becomes the active cell.

Multiple-area ranges are also called *discontinuous ranges* because they do not encompass a single rectangular area. You can select any combination of cells when you select discontinuous ranges. For example, you can drag through cells A1:A5, hold down the Command key, drag through cells B6:C8, then, continuing to hold down the Command key, click cell E8. Your worksheet looks like Figure 2-6.

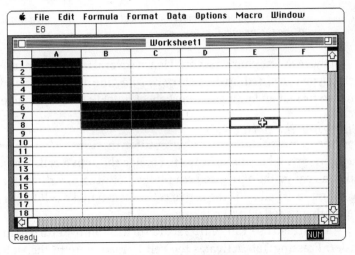

FIGURE 2-6. *You use the Command key to select discontinuous ranges.*

Moving a selected range

Once you have selected a range, you can move the entire range across your worksheet by pressing the Command and Tab keys simultaneously. For example, if you press the Command and Tab keys while cells A1:B6 are selected, Excel changes the selected range to C1:D6, as shown in Figure 2-7 on the next page.

Similarly, you can move the entire range down by pressing the Command and Return keys simultaneously. You can press Shift-Command-Tab and Shift-Command-Return to move the selected range backward through the worksheet. You'll find these techniques particularly helpful when you begin using the editing commands described in Chapter 4, "Editing the Worksheet."

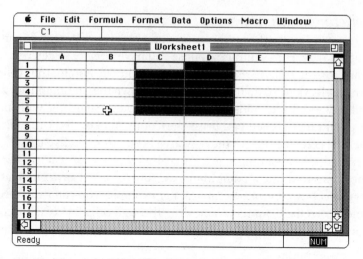

FIGURE 2-7. *You have moved the selection from one range to another using Command-Tab.*

In the next few chapters, you'll learn several uses for ranges. As we mentioned earlier, you can speed up data entry by selecting a range of cells to work with. You can also format and edit your worksheet quickly by using range selections.

Changing the active cell

There are several different ways to change the active cell. You already know that you can change the active cell simply by pointing to a different cell and clicking. For example, if cell A1 is the active cell, you can make cell B2 the active cell simply by pointing to cell B2 and clicking.

You can also use Tab, Shift-Tab, Return, or Shift-Return to move the active cell border. Pressing Tab activates the cell immediately to the right of the currently active cell. For example, if cell B2 is active, pressing Tab activates cell C2. Pressing Shift-Tab activates the cell immediately to the left of the currently active cell. For example, if cell C2 is active and you press Shift-Tab, cell B2 becomes the active cell again.

Pressing Return activates the cell below the currently active cell. For example, if cell B2 is the active cell and you press Return, Excel moves the active cell border to cell B3. As you might expect, pressing Shift-Return activates the cell above the currently active cell. For example, if cell B3 is active and you press Shift-Return, cell B2 becomes the active cell again.

Moving the active cell in a range

If you select a range of cells, you can also use the Tab, Shift-Tab, Return, and Shift-Return keys to move the active cell around in that range. These keys move the active cell up or down, or left or right, one cell at a time, just as they do when you select a single cell. When you are working in a selected range, however, Excel restricts the active cell's movement to that range. When you reach the end of a column or row, Excel automatically moves to the next column or row in the range.

For example, we have selected cells B2:D4 in the worksheet in Figure 2-8. Cell B2 is the active cell. As you might expect, if you press Return, the active cell moves to cell B3. If you press Return again, cell B4 becomes the active cell. However, if you press Return yet again, the active cell, as shown in Figure 2-9 on the next page, moves to cell C2 instead of B5. As you can see, Excel has restricted the movement of the active cell to the range of selected cells.

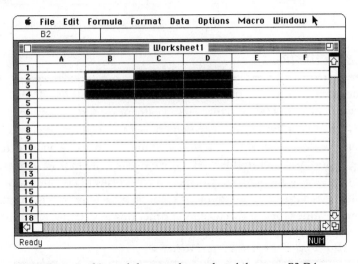

FIGURE 2-8. *In this worksheet you have selected the range B2:D4.*

Now, if you press Tab, cell D2 becomes the active cell. If you press Tab again, however, the active cell border moves to cell B3. Once again, Excel has restricted the movement of the active cell to the range of selected cells.

You can also use Tab, Shift-Tab, Return, and Shift-Return to move the active cell around in discontinuous ranges. When the active cell reaches the end of one area, pressing one of these keys moves the active cell to the first cell in the next area.

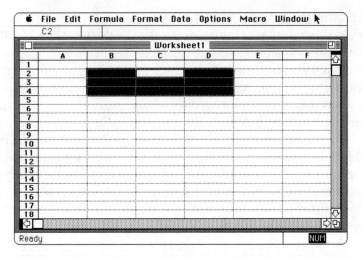

FIGURE 2-9. *Pressing Return has moved the active cell from B4 to C2.*

Cell entries

There are two basic types of cell entries in Microsoft Excel: *constant values* and *formulas*. Constants fall into three main categories: *text values*, *numeric values*, and *date and time values* (which are represented as a special type of number). In this discussion, we start with text and numeric values, then move on to techniques for building formulas. Later in this chapter, we take a brief look at date and time values.

Excel also recognizes two special categories of constants, called *logical values* and *error values*. We address error values a little later in this chapter, but we'll save logical values for our discussion of functions in Chapter 6, "Built-in Functions."

Simple text and numeric values

In general, any entry that includes only the numerals 0 through 9 or one of a select group of special characters is a numeric value. For example, the entries 123, 345678, 999999, and 1 are all numeric values. An entry that includes almost any other character is a text value. In other words, any cell entry that can't be interpreted as a number is treated as a text value by Microsoft Excel. The entries

Sales

Hello

A Label

123 Main Street

are all text values. (We sometimes refer to text values as *labels* or *strings*.)

The distinction between numbers and text is an important one. As you will see, Excel allows you to create formulas that link number cells to number cells and text cells to text cells. However, Excel does not allow you to create a formula that links a number cell directly to a text cell. Any formula that attempts to do this returns a #VALUE! error. However, the distinction between text and numeric values is less important in Microsoft Excel than in some other spreadsheet programs, because you can perform the same mathematical operations on numeric text entries that you can on numbers.

If you aren't sure whether Excel will treat a value as text or as a number, check the way the value appears in the cell after you press Enter. Unless you use a formatting command (described in Chapter 3, "Formatting the Worksheet") to change the cell display, Excel always aligns numbers at the right side of the cell and text entries at the left side of the cell. For example, cells C5 and D5 in Figure 2-10 contain numeric values. Cells A1, B2, C6, and A10 contain text values.

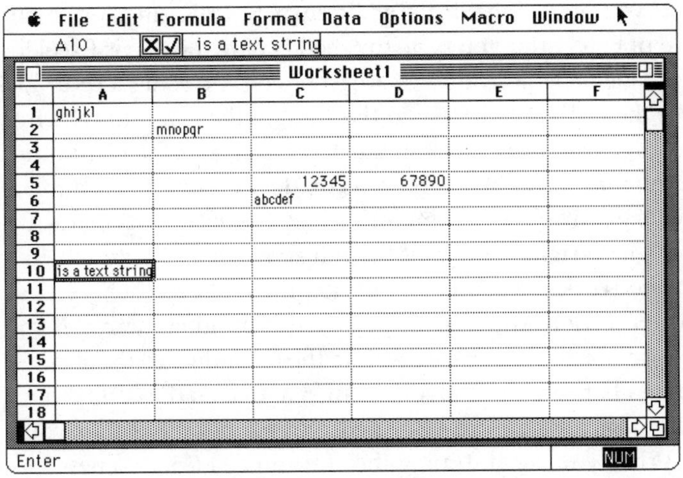

FIGURE 2-10. *The default format for numeric values is right-aligned and for text values is left-aligned.*

Making number entries

You can enter a label or number in your worksheet simply by selecting a cell and typing the label or number. For example, suppose you want to make the number entry 100 in cell C5 in your worksheet. First, point to cell C5 and click. When you do this, cell C5 becomes the active cell, and the cell's reference appears in the cell reference box.

Once you have selected a cell, you can make an entry in that cell by typing. To enter the number 100 in cell C5, simply type *100*. As you type, the number 100 appears in the formula bar; it also appears in cell C5.

Notice the flashing vertical bar that appears in the formula bar when you begin to type. This bar is called the *insertion point*. The insertion point moves in front of the characters as you type them in the formula bar. For example, as you typed the number 100, the insertion point moved to the right. Later in this chapter, you'll see how to move this insertion point to edit cell entries.

Locking in the entry

When you are finished typing, you must *lock in* the entry. Locking in the entry stores it permanently in the selected cell.

There are several ways to lock in an entry. The simplest is to press the Enter key. When you press Enter, the insertion point disappears from the formula bar, and the entry you typed is stored in cell C5, which remains the active cell.

If you press Tab, Shift-Tab, Return, Shift-Return, or any of the arrow keys instead of Enter after you have finished typing the entry, Excel locks in the entry and simultaneously activates an adjacent cell. Pressing Tab to lock in the entry activates the cell immediately to the right of the cell into which the entry was made. Pressing Shift-Tab to lock in the entry activates the cell immediately to the left of the cell into which the entry was made. Pressing Return to lock in the entry activates the cell below the cell into which the entry was made. Pressing Shift-Return to lock in the entry activates the cell above the cell into which the entry was made.

The Workspace... command on the Options menu contains a useful option: Move Selection After Return. When this option is active, if you press Return after typing a text or numeric value into the formula bar, Excel enters the contents of the formula bar into the active cell, then activates the cell below. If this option is not active, the cell that receives an entry remains active after you press Return.

When you began typing the entry in cell C5, two new boxes appeared on the screen: the enter box and the cancel box (we mentioned these briefly in Chapter 1, "Introducing Microsoft Excel"). The enter box—the box with the check mark—is another way to lock in your entry when you are finished typing. For example, to lock in the entry in cell C5 and keep cell C5 active, you can click the enter box instead of pressing Enter.

The cancel box—the box with the *X*—allows you to cancel an entry before you lock it in. If you make a mistake while typing in the formula bar, you can click the cancel box to tell Excel to delete the information you typed. After you click the cancel box, the formula bar is no longer active.

Other numeric characters

In addition to the numerals 0 through 9, numeric values can sometimes include the characters

$$+ - E\ e\ \$\ ,\ .\ \%\ (\ )$$

You can begin any number entry with a plus sign (+) or a minus sign (–). If you begin a number entry with a minus sign, Excel interprets that entry as a negative number and retains the minus sign. If you begin a number entry with a plus sign, Excel drops the plus sign.

The characters *E* and *e* can be used to enter a number in scientific notation. For example, if you click a cell and make the entry

1E6

Excel interprets that entry as the number 1,000,000 (or 1 times 10 to the 6th power).

Numbers enclosed in left and right parentheses are interpreted as negative numbers by Excel. Representing negative numbers this way is a common practice in accounting, to ensure that negative cash amounts are not overlooked. If you make the entry

(100)

in a cell, Excel interprets that entry as –100.

The decimal point can be used as you normally use it. Similarly, you can use commas to separate the hundreds from the thousands, the thousands from the millions, and so on, as you normally would in number entries. For example, if you type the entry

1,234,567.89

Excel interprets that entry as the number 1234567.89. When Excel stores this number in the selected cell, it removes the commas, unless you have specifically formatted the cell to display them.

If you begin a number entry with a dollar sign, Excel automatically assigns one of its currency formats to the cell. (We explain more about formats in the next chapter.) For example, if you select a cell and enter the number

$123456

Excel assigns a special dollar format to that cell, and displays the number as

$123,456

Note that, in this case, commas are added by Excel.

Similarly, if you end a number entry with a percent sign (%), Excel interprets the entry as a percentage and assigns one of its percentage formats to the cell that contains the entry. For example, if you type the number

23%

Excel interprets that number as .23, and assigns a percentage format to the cell. (In the formula bar, you'll see the number as a decimal value.)

Displayed values versus underlying values

A cell entry in Microsoft Excel can be up to 255 characters long. Because the standard column width in Excel is just 10 characters, it should be clear that Excel needs some rules for displaying long entries. If you enter a number that is too wide to be displayed in the active cell, Excel converts the number into scientific notation so that it can be displayed in a single cell. For example, if you select cell A3 and enter the numeric value

1234567890123

Excel displays this number in scientific notation, as shown in Figure 2-11, rather than letting the number overlap into the next cell. If you look at the formula bar, you'll see that Excel has stored the number the way you entered it, even though the cell displays the value 1.2346E+12. Although Excel has changed the appearance of the entry in cell A3, the actual contents of cell A3 have stayed the same.

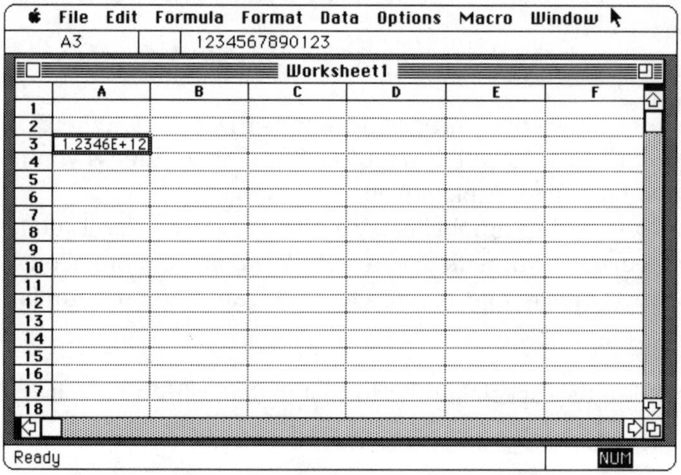

FIGURE 2-11. *The number 1234567890123 is too long to display in cell A3, so Excel displays the number in scientific notation.*

This is the first example we've shown of an important Excel concept: What you see in a cell and what is actually in the cell may be two different things. The values you see when you look at the worksheet are called *displayed values*. The values that appear in the formula bar are called *underlying values*. Keep in mind that unless you tell it otherwise, Excel always remembers the underlying values in your cells, no matter how those values are displayed. When you build formulas, Excel uses the underlying values rather than the displayed values, so your calculations are always correct.

The number of digits Excel displays in this sort of situation depends on the width of the column that contains the long number. If you change the width of a column that contains long entries, Excel changes the displayed value according to the width of the cell. Keep in mind, however, that the column width affects only the displayed values of numbers on your worksheet. Column width has no effect on the actual numbers stored in the cells.

We come back to this concept again in Chapter 3, "Formatting the Worksheet," and Chapter 4, "Editing the Worksheet," where you will learn to control the way cell entries are displayed by changing the formats and column widths that are assigned to cells.

Making text entries

The process of making a text entry is nearly identical to that of making a number entry. All you do to enter a text value into a cell is select that cell and type. When you are finished typing, you can use any of the techniques discussed earlier to lock in the entry. If you make an error while typing, you can cancel the entry by clicking the cancel box.

For example, suppose you want to enter the label *Sales* in cell C4 of your worksheet. To do this, you click cell C4, type *Sales*, and press Enter, Return, or one of the other keys that you can use to lock in an entry. Figure 2-12 on the next page shows the result.

Long text entries

A few pages ago, you saw that Microsoft Excel converts long numbers into scientific notation for display purposes. Excel treats long text values somewhat differently. If you create a label that is too long to be displayed in a single cell, Excel allows the label to overlap into adjacent cells.

For example, click cell A1 in a new worksheet and enter the label

This is a text value

Your worksheet looks like Figure 2-13 on the next page. Notice that this text entry overlaps the right border of cell A1 and spills into cell B1.

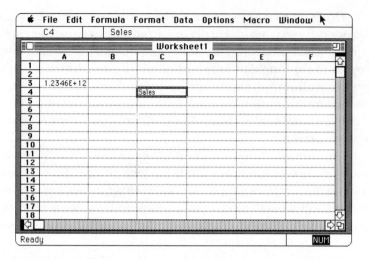

FIGURE 2-12. *You have entered the text value* Sales *in cell C4.*

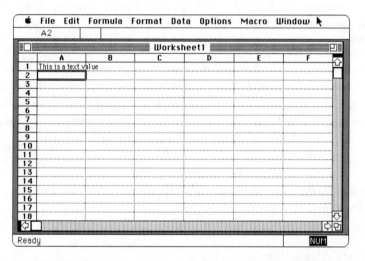

FIGURE 2-13. *This text entry appears to occupy two adjacent cells but it is in fact stored only in cell A1.*

However, don't let this display confuse you. The entire label is still stored in cell A1. If you select cell B1 and look at the formula bar, you'll see that the cell is empty. The characters that seem to be contained in cell B1 are really in cell A1 and only overlap B1 for display purposes.

Now, select cell B1 and type

This is another text value

As you can see in Figure 2-14, this new entry makes it impossible for Excel to display all of the long text value in cell A1. Again, this change affects only the way the label is displayed and has no effect on the contents of either cell. If you move back to cell A1 and look at the formula bar, you'll see that the entire label is still stored intact.

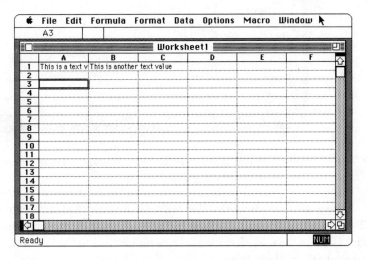

FIGURE 2-14. *When the cell to the right contains an entry, long text values cannot spill over and appear to be truncated.*

Numeric text entries

There will be times when you'll want to create text entries that are made up partly or entirely of numbers. If you want to enter a text value like

1234 Main Street

into the worksheet, you need only select a cell, type the entry, and press Enter. Because this entry includes non-numeric characters, Excel automatically assumes that it is a text value.

However, sometimes you may want to create text entries that are made up entirely of numbers. For example, suppose you are developing a price list like the one shown in Figure 2-15 on the next page. Column A in this worksheet contains a series of part numbers. If you want Excel to treat these part numbers as text entries rather than numbers, you must enter them into the worksheet as *literal strings*. For example, part number 1234 in cell A4 was entered as

="1234"

Unless you treat all the part numbers this way, Excel left-aligns the entries that are text and right-aligns those that are purely numbers.

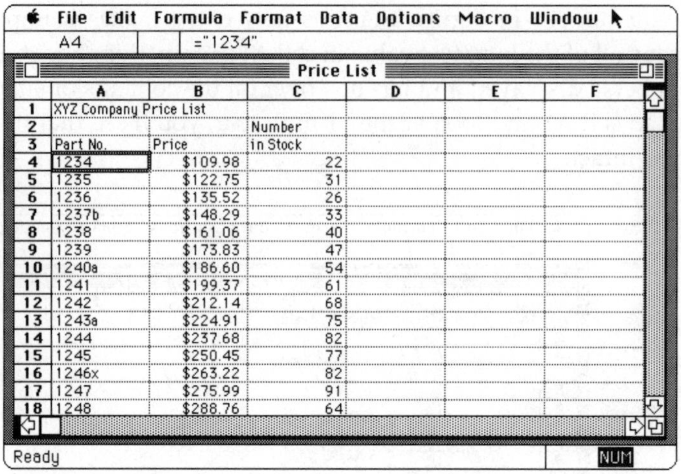

FIGURE 2-15. *These part numbers have been entered as literal strings rather than as numeric values.*

The distinction between this numeric text entry and the simple number entry 1234 is very small. In fact, about the only important difference between the two entries is, as we've said, that Excel aligns text values to the left of the cell and numeric values to the right of the cell.

Making entries in ranges

Suppose you want to make a number of entries in a range of adjacent cells. If you select those cells before you begin making entries, you can use Return, Tab, Shift-Return, and Shift-Tab to move the active cell from cell to cell within the range. Because Excel does not allow the active cell to move out of the range of selected cells, you can devote your attention to making entries, without worrying about the location of the active cell.

For example, suppose you want to make some entries in the range B2:D4. To begin, select the range (drag from B2 to D4 so that cell B2 is the active cell). Type the number *100* and press Return. When you press Return, cell B3 automatically becomes the active cell. Now, if you type the number *200* and press Return again, cell B4 becomes the active cell. If you type the number *300* and press Return yet again, cell C2—the first cell in the next column of the range—becomes the active cell, as shown in Figure 2-16. You can continue like this—making entries and pressing Return—until the entire range is filled. As you might expect, you can also use the Shift-Return, Tab, and Shift-Tab keys to lock in entries and move about in a range.

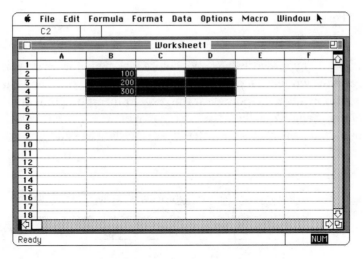

FIGURE 2-16. *This figure shows how to make entries in a range.*

Correcting errors in entries

No matter how good a typist you are, you will sometimes make mistakes when you make cell entries. Fortunately, Excel makes it easy to edit your cell entries in the formula bar.

Correcting errors before you lock in the entry

If you make simple typing errors as you are making an entry, you can correct them by pressing the Delete key. For example, suppose you have selected cell A1 and are entering the text

This is a label

As you make the entry, you type

This is ala

To correct this error, you can press Delete twice to erase the *a* and *l*, then type the space you forgot the first time and complete the entry. When you are finished making the entry, you can press Enter to lock it in.

The Delete method is good for correcting errors if you catch them quickly. However, Delete actually erases characters, so if you don't catch the error until you've done quite a bit more typing, you're better off not using Delete. If you discover an error before you lock in an entry, but too late to use Delete, you can simply reposition the insertion point in the entry and erase, insert, or replace characters from this new location.

For example, suppose you enter the text

This is a label

in cell A1 of your worksheet and, before locking in the entry, you realize you want to add the words *rather long* just before the word *label*. To add characters to the entry, simply click the pointer at the desired insertion point and begin typing. The pointer changes into the I-beam, as shown in Figure 2-17. Excel pushes the insertion point—and any characters after it—to the right as you type.

I-beam pointer

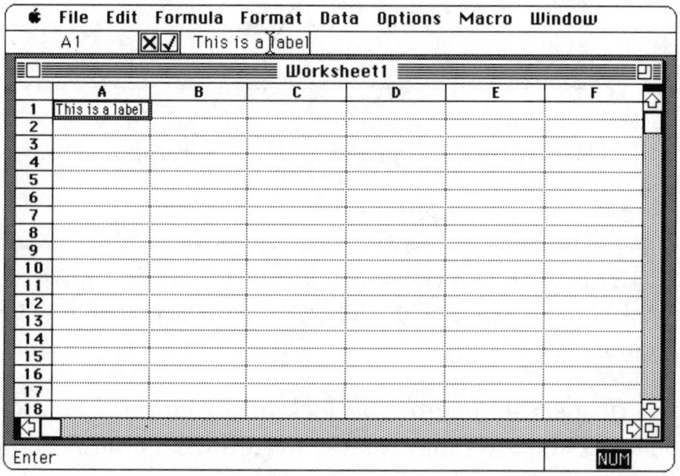

FIGURE 2-17. *The pointer changes to an I-beam in the formula bar.*

To add the words *rather long* to the entry in cell A1, you first point to just before the first letter *l* in the word *label* in the formula bar. When you click the mouse button, Excel moves the insertion point to the indicated spot in the entry—in this case, just in front of the letter *l*. Now, to add the words *rather long* to the label, you simply type *rather long*, followed by a space. Figure 2-18 shows the result. If the entry is now correct, you can press Enter to lock it in.

If you want to delete several adjacent characters, you can drag across all of the characters you want to delete and press Delete once. For instance, to erase the word *rather*, you can position the pointer just before the first *r* in *rather*, press the mouse button, and drag to the right until the entire word plus one space is highlighted. Figure 2-19 shows the screen at this point. Now, you can delete the word *rather* by pressing Delete once.

If you want to replace one set of characters with another, drag across the characters you want to replace and type the new characters. Excel automatically deletes the selected characters as you type the replacement characters. When you finish making the change, press Enter or click the enter box to lock in the entry.

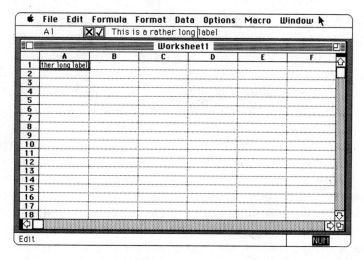

FIGURE 2-18. *You have added the words* rather long *to this text entry.*

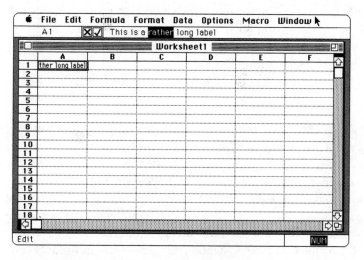

FIGURE 2-19. *You have selected the word* rather *before deleting it by pressing Delete.*

For example, suppose you want to replace the word *label* with the words *text entry*. To do this, you can drag through *label* to select it, then type *text entry* without pressing Delete. As soon as you begin typing, Excel automatically deletes the selected characters.

Correcting errors after you lock in the entry

If you have already locked in the entry, you must select the cell before you can correct any errors. When you select a cell that already contains a value or formula, the formula bar is not active; that is, there is no blinking insertion point in the bar.

To erase the entire contents of a cell, select the cell and press the Delete key. You do not have to create an insertion point to do this. Once you have pressed Delete, you must press Enter or click the enter box to lock in the change. If you press Delete accidentally, simply click the cancel box to restore the contents of the cell.

If you want to replace the entire contents of a cell with another entry, you can simply select the cell and type. Excel erases the previous entry as soon as you begin typing. For example, suppose you want to enter the label *Sales* in cell A1, but instead you type *Purchases*. To correct this error, you can simply select cell A1, type *Sales*, and press Enter. If you decide that you want to retain the original contents of the cell, you can simply click the cancel box to revert to the original entry.

If the entry you want to change is relatively short and simple—like most labels and almost all numbers—it is probably easier to replace the erroneous entry with a new entry. If, however, the entry you want to change is long or complex—like some labels and most formulas—you're probably better off editing the entry instead of replacing it. To edit an entry, simply select the cell that contains the entry and begin editing its contents.

For example, suppose cell A1 contains the label

This is a long label

If you want to edit this label, you first select cell A1, and then you activate the formula bar by moving the pointer to the formula bar and clicking or by pressing Command-U. In the formula bar, the pointer changes its shape to the I-beam, indicating that you can use the pointer to position the insertion point anywhere in the formula bar. Once the formula bar is active and the insertion point is in place, you can insert, delete, or replace characters, just as we did in the previous examples.

You can also use the Edit-menu commands, which we discuss in Chapter 4, "Editing the Worksheet," when you want to edit individual cells or ranges of cells in your worksheet.

Building formulas

Excel would be of little value if it allowed you to enter only simple numbers and text values into the worksheet. Excel's strength lies in its ability to calculate new values from existing ones. Armed with a few mathematical operators and rules for cell entry, you can turn your Excel worksheet into a powerful calculator.

Now, let's walk through a series of simple formulas to see how they work. If you've been following along with the examples in this chapter, you'll want to move to a blank area of your worksheet before you begin. We use cells A20 through A26 in the following examples.

Begin by selecting cell A20 and typing the simple formula

=10+5

As soon as you press Enter or click the enter box, Excel displays the value 15 in cell A20. If you look at the formula bar, however, you'll see that Excel also remembers the underlying formula you typed.

Now, move down to cell A21 and type

=10−5

When you lock in this entry by pressing Enter or clicking the enter box, Excel displays the value 5 in cell A21. Now, enter the formula

=10∗5

in cell A22 and the formula

=10/5

in cell A23. When you lock in these formulas, Excel displays the values 50 and 2 in cells A22 and A23, respectively. Your screen now looks like Figure 2-20.

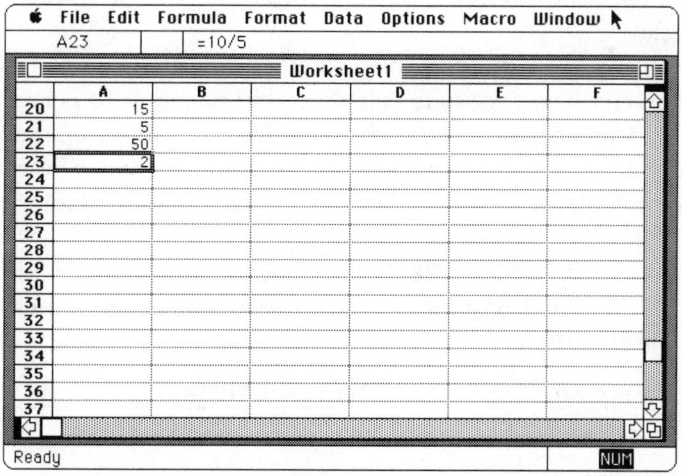

FIGURE 2-20. *Here, the results of formulas were entered in cells A20:A23.*

Notice that each of the formulas you have entered began with the equal sign (=). Every formula must begin with an equal sign, which serves as a flag to Excel that a formula follows. If you forget to begin the formula with an equal sign, Excel interprets the entry as text, unless it's a simple numeric value.

Each of the formulas in Figure 2-20 uses one of the program's mathematical operators: the plus sign (+); the minus sign (–); the asterisk (*), which tells Excel to multiply; and the slash (/), which tells Excel to divide.

Precedence of operators

As you begin building complex formulas that use more than one operator, you'll need to consider the precedence that Microsoft Excel assigns to each operator. You may remember warnings about the precedence of operators from high-school math classes. The term *precedence* simply refers to the order in which Excel performs calculations in complex formulas. For example, the formula

    =4+12/6

returns the value 6. When Excel evaluates this formula, it calculates the value 12/6 first, then adds 4. The formula

    =4*12/6

returns the value 8. In this case, Excel calculates the value 4*12 first, then divides by 6. Excel multiplies and divides before it adds and subtracts. If two operations are of the same level, as in the previous example, Excel processes them from left to right.

When you are building long, complex formulas, it can often be difficult to predict exactly how Excel will calculate your formula. To get around this problem, you can use parentheses to override Excel's built-in operator precedence and specify the order in which you want the elements of your formula to be evaluated. Excel calculates formula elements in parentheses before it calculates other operations.

For example, all of the formulas below use the same values and operators. Only the use and positions of the parentheses change. However, the results are completely different.

If you enter...	The result will be...
=3*6+12/4–2	19
=(3*6)+12/(4–2)	24
=3*(6+12)/4–2	11.5
=(3*6+12)/4–2	5.5
=3*(6+12/(4–2))	36

Whenever you use parentheses in your formulas, make sure you include a closing right parenthesis for each opening left parenthesis. Otherwise, Excel displays the message *Error in formula.*

Using cell references in formulas

While simple formulas like the ones you've built so far are convenient for quickly calculating values, the program's real magic lies in its ability to use references to other cells in formulas. When you create a formula that contains cell references, you link the formula to other cells in your worksheet. As a result, the value of the formula always reflects the values in the source cells. You'll find this capability enormously valuable when you begin using your worksheet for financial planning or other calculations.

For example, select cell A20 in the last worksheet and type *15*, then select A24 and type the formula

    =A20

As you probably guessed, the formula in cell A24 returns the value 15. So why not simply type the value *15* in cell A24?

To see why, select cell A20 and change the entry there to 100. (Excel automatically overwrites the existing entry as you type.) Now, look at the displayed value in cell A24. When you changed the value of cell A20, Excel automatically updated cell A24 as well. The formula in cell A24 links cell A24 to cell A20, so that the value of cell A24 always equals the value in cell A20. If you make a change to A20, the value of A24 also changes.

Now, select cell A25 in your worksheet and type the formula

    =A20+A21–A22*A23

As you can see in Figure 2-21 on the next page, Excel returns the value 5. Of course, you can create more complex formulas in Microsoft Excel, using cell references or even references to large ranges of cells. When we discuss Excel's many worksheet functions in Chapter 6, "Built-in Functions," you'll discover a number of applications for cell references in your worksheet.

Pasting cell references You can save time and avoid typographical errors by clicking the cells you want Excel to include in your formulas rather than typing their references. This technique is called *pasting a cell reference into a formula.*

For example, suppose you want to create a formula in cell A26 that totals the values you have entered in cells A20:A24. To do this, click cell A26 and type an equal sign (=). Next, click cell A20, then cells A21, A22, A23, and A24. Notice that Excel surrounds each cell with a flashing border as you click it, as shown in Figure 2-22 on the next page. This border is called a *marquee.* More importantly, notice that as you click each cell, Excel places a plus sign (+) in the formula and adds a reference to that cell to the formula. Your finished formula is

=A20+A21+A22+A23+A24

When you lock in the formula, Excel displays the value 257.

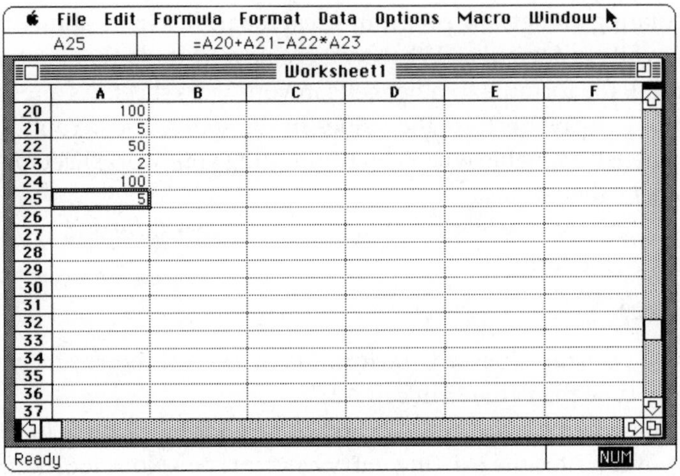

FIGURE 2-21. *The formula in cell A25 links that cell to cells A20:A23, so if any of them change, cell A25 also changes.*

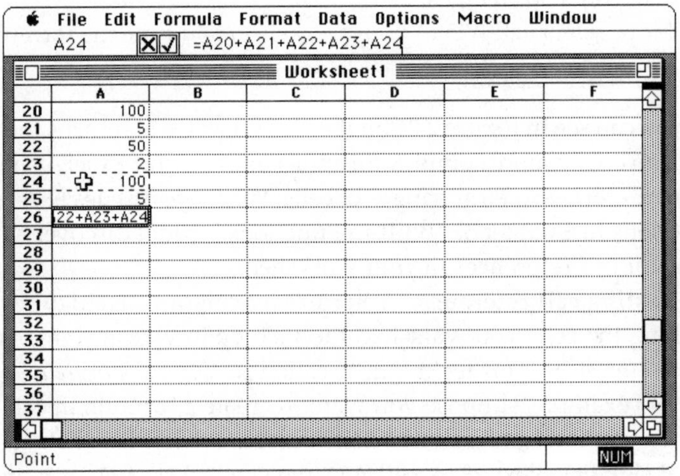

FIGURE 2-22. *Excel surrounds with a marquee cells you are pasting into a formula.*

If you want to create a formula that uses operators other than the plus sign, you'll have to type those operators. For example, to create the formula shown in Figure 2-21, you select cell A25, type an equal sign (=), click cell A20, then click cell A21. Next, type a minus sign (–), click cell A22, type a multiplication symbol (∗), and click cell A23. The result is identical to the one displayed in Figure 2-21.

When you finish entering formulas, make sure you lock in your entry—by clicking the enter box or by pressing Enter, Tab, Shift-Tab, or Shift-Return—before you attempt to select another cell. Any time you click a cell while the formula bar is active, Excel assumes that you want to paste in a cell reference.

For example, suppose you complete the formula in Figure 2-22, then you click cell B20 and type the formula *=A20–A21*. If you forget to lock in the formula in cell A26 before moving to cell B20, your formula bar looks like the one in Figure 2-23. When you lock in this formula, Excel returns the value FALSE in cell A26, assuming that you are attempting to perform a logical test. (We discuss logical values in Chapter 6, "Built-in Functions.")

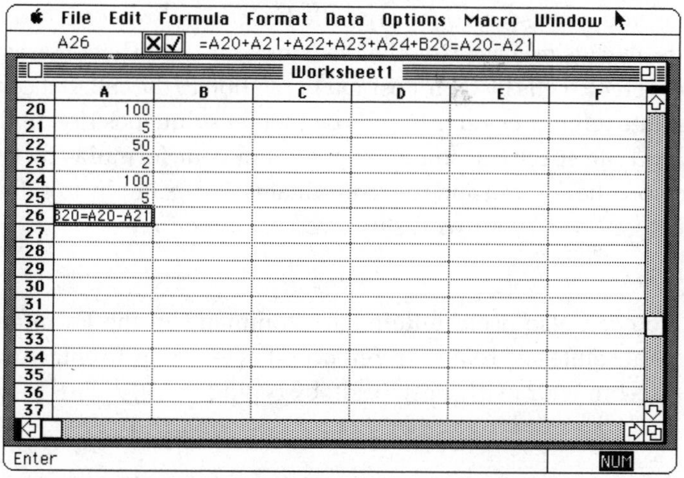

FIGURE 2-23. *Two formulas have been merged because the first formula was not locked in before the second formula was typed.*

Long distance is just as good as being there A cell does not have to be visible in the current window in order for you to make an entry in that cell. As we mentioned earlier, you can scroll through the worksheet without changing the currently selected cell. For example, suppose you want to look at another part of your worksheet while you make a cell entry. You can click the cell in which you want to make the entry, then scroll to the area you want to view. The active cell does not change. After you have looked at the remote portion of the worksheet, if you begin typing the entry, Excel automatically brings the active cell back into view.

You can also use this technique to point to cells in remote areas of your worksheet as you are building formulas. For example, suppose you want to enter a formula that calculates the sum of your first- and second-quarter sales in cell M50. You know the totals for first-quarter sales are located somewhere in column G of your worksheet, but you don't remember the exact cell reference. You can simply activate cell M50, scroll through your worksheet, find the correct cell in column G, and click it. Excel includes this cell reference in the formula in cell M50.

If you do want to see the active cell as you're entering information, you don't have to scroll back through the worksheet. Simply choose the Show Active Cell command from the Formula menu, and Excel immediately displays the selected cell. The Show Active Cell command appears on the Formula menu when you choose the Full Menus command from the Options menu. As we said in Chapter 1, our discussions presume that you've done this.

Absolute and relative references The cell references used in the sample formulas you have seen so far are called *relative references*. Excel also allows you to create *absolute references* to other cells in your worksheet. Basically, relative references refer to cells by their position in relation to the cell that contains the formula. Absolute references refer to cells by their absolute position in the worksheet.

You can specify absolute references in your formulas by typing a dollar sign ($) before the column and row coordinates. For example, to enter an absolute reference to cell A1 in your worksheet, you can type

    =$A$1

You can also use the Reference command in the Formula menu to quickly define absolute and relative references. For example, to enter an absolute reference to cell A1 in your worksheet, begin by typing

    =A1

then choose the Reference command from the Formula menu. Excel changes the reference to the left of the insertion point to an absolute reference, so that the formula appears as

    =$A$1

If you choose the Reference command again, Excel changes your entry to a mixed reference, with a relative column coordinate and an absolute row coordinate. The formula now appears as

    =A$1

If you choose Reference a third time, the reference will be changed to

=$A1

Here, the column coordinate is absolute and the row coordinate is relative.

The difference between absolute and relative references will not mean very much to you at this point. However, absolute and mixed references will become very important when you begin moving and copying cells around your worksheet. We cover this concept again in Chapter 4, "Editing the Worksheet."

The R1C1 option As you've seen throughout this chapter, formulas in Excel usually refer to cells by a combination of their column letter and row number, like A1 or Z100. However, you can use the R1C1 option in the Workspace dialog box to cause Excel to refer to cells by row number and column number, instead. (The Workspace... command is on the Options menu.) The cell reference R1C1 means *row 1, column 1*, so cell R1C1 is the equivalent of cell A1. When you select this option, Excel automatically converts all of the cell references in your formulas to R1C1 format. For example, cell M10 becomes R10C13, and cell IV16384, the last cell in your worksheet, becomes R256C16384.

When you use R1C1 notation, Microsoft Excel displays relative cell references in terms of their relative location to the cell that contains the formula, rather than displaying them in terms of their actual coordinates. For example, suppose you want to enter a formula in cell R10C2 (B10) that adds cells R1C1 and R1C2. After selecting cell R10C2, you type an equal sign and then click cells R1C1 and R1C2. Excel displays

=R[–9]C[–1]+R[–9]C

This formula can be read as follows: *Add the cell nine rows up and one column to the left to the cell nine rows up in the same column.* Negative row and column numbers indicate that the pasted cell is above and to the left of the formula cell, while positive numbers indicate that the pasted cell is below and to the right of the formula cell.

To type a relative reference to another cell, you must include square brackets around the reference. If you do not include the brackets, Excel assumes that you are using absolute references. For example, the formula

=R9C1+R8C1

uses absolute references to the cells in rows eight and nine of column 1.

Although some spreadsheet programs, like Microsoft Multiplan, use the R1C1 style, we recommend that you stick with the A1 format. The A1 format requires fewer keystrokes and makes your formulas substantially shorter. For example, which of the formulas on the next page is easier to type?

=(B10−C10)∗($E$16+$F$16)

or

=(R[−7]C[−3]−R[−7]C[−2])∗(R16C5+R16C6)

As you can see, even in a simple formula the R1C1 format requires 14 more characters than the A1 format. You may also find that long, complex formulas are harder
to interpret in R1C1 format. Often, though, relative row and column relationships
are clearer in this format, particularly for those with experience in Multiplan.

When you select the R1C1 option, Excel checks the box preceding the option in
the Workspace dialog box. If you want to change back to standard notation, you
can select this option again, to uncheck the box.

Editing formulas

You can edit formulas just as you would text entries. To delete a cell reference or
other character from a formula, you simply click to the right of the reference and
delete each character in turn, or drag through the reference and then press Delete.
For example, suppose cell A10 in your worksheet contains the formula

=A1+A2

You decide that this formula should read

=A1+A3

To correct the formula, you can simply drag through the characters A2, then type
A3. When you start typing, Excel deletes the reference to cell A2 and replaces it
with the characters you type.

Alternatively, you can select the portion of the entry you want to replace, point
to the replacement cell, and click. As soon as you click the new cell, Excel replaces
the old reference with the new one.

Of course, if you want to undo your changes and you haven't yet locked in the
new formula, you can click the cancel box. If you have locked in the entry but
haven't selected another cell or chosen a command, you can use the Undo command on the Edit menu.

You can also insert additional cell references in a formula. To insert additional
references, click the insertion point in the desired location—to the left of a plus
sign (+)—then click the cell you want to add to the formula. Of course, you can
also type the cell reference. For example, suppose you want to change the formula
in cell A10 to

=A1+B1+A3

To do this, you click the insertion point just after the reference A1, type +, and then
either type *B1* or point to cell B1 and click.

You can delete cell references and other characters from formulas just as you would from text entries: Click to the right of the reference and delete it, or drag through the reference and then press Delete.

You can also use the Edit commands, which we discuss in Chapter 4, "Editing the Worksheet," to edit formulas in your worksheet.

Using numeric text in formulas

Unlike most other spreadsheet programs, Microsoft Excel allows you to use numeric text values to perform any mathematical operation, as long as the numeric string contains only the characters

0 1 2 3 4 5 6 7 8 9 + − E e .

You can use five other number-formatting characters

$, % ( )

with numeric text, but if you do, you must enclose the numeric string in quotation marks. For example, the formula

=$1234+123

causes Excel to display an alert box stating *Error in formula*. However, the formula

="$1234"+123

causes Excel to display the result 1357. In effect, Excel translates the numeric text entry into a value when it performs the addition.

Text values

Throughout this section, we have referred to text entries as text *values*. The concept of using alphabetic characters as values may seem a bit confusing, until you begin using formulas to manipulate text entries.

Microsoft Excel allows you to perform many of the same manipulations on text values as on numeric values. For example, suppose cell A1 in your worksheet contains the text entry *abcde*. If you enter the formula

=A1

in cell A10 of your worksheet, that cell also displays *abcde*. Because this type of formula treats a string of text as a value, it is often called a *string value*.

Concatenating text values You can use a special concatenation operator (&) to *concatenate*, or string together, several text values. For example, suppose cell A2 in the same worksheet contains the text entry *fghij*. You can use the formula

=A1&A2

to produce the text value *abcdefghij*. You can also include a space between the two strings by changing the formula to

   =A1&" "&A2

This formula would return the string *abcde fghij*.

Notice that this formula uses two concatenation operators. The formula also includes a literal string, or *string constant* (a space enclosed in quotes), to separate the two halves of the string value. When you use literal strings in a worksheet formula, you must include a double quotation mark before and after the string.

You can also use the concatenation operator (&) to concatenate a string of numeric values. For example, suppose cell A3 in your worksheet contains the numeric value 123, and cell A4 contains the value 456. The formula

   =A3&A4

produces the string value *123456*. This string value appears left-aligned in your worksheet cell, indicating that Excel considers it a text value. (Keep in mind that you can use numeric text values to perform any mathematical operation, as long as the numeric string contains only the numeric characters listed earlier.)

You can also use & to concatenate numeric and text values. For example, if cell A1 contains the text entry *abcde* and cell A3 contains the numeric value 123, the formula

   =A1&A3

produces the value *abcde123*.

Of course, the string values we have created so far are meaningless, but there are several real-world applications for the concatenation operator in your worksheet. For example, suppose cell A1 in your worksheet contains the first name of a client, *Gena*, and cell B1 contains her last name, *Woods*. You can use the formula

   =A1&" "&B1

to produce the string value *Gena Woods*. Alternatively, you can use a formula like

   =B1&", "&A1

to produce the value *Woods, Gena*.

Using functions: A preview

The formulas we have built thus far perform relatively simple mathematical calculations. In Chapter 6, "Built-in Functions," you'll see a special set of operators, called *functions*, that help you build more sophisticated formulas.

Many of the Microsoft Excel functions are shorthand versions of tedious formulas that are used often in worksheets. For example, earlier in this chapter we showed you how to calculate the sum of a range of cells by pasting each cell reference individually into a formula. Although this is fine when you are adding the values in only two or three cells, imagine pasting 20 or 30 cells into a formula! Excel's SUM function lets you add together a series of cell values simply by dragging through a range. For example, compare the formula

=A1+A2+A3+A4+A5+A6+A7+A8+A9+A10

with the formula

=SUM(A1:A10)

Obviously, the SUM function makes the formula a lot shorter and easier to create.

Other Excel functions let you perform extremely complex calculations that would be difficult, if not impossible, to perform with standard mathematical operators. For example, Excel's NPV function lets you calculate the net present value of investments.

There are other advantages to using functions and references to cell ranges rather than individual cells, as you'll see in Chapter 6, "Built-in Functions."

Naming cells in your worksheet

So far, we have shown you how to build formulas using references to cells in the worksheet. However, Microsoft Excel also allows you to assign English-language names to cells and use those names in your formulas.

To name a cell, first select it, then choose the Define Name... command from the Formula menu. When you choose this command, you see a Define Name dialog box like the one shown in Figure 2-24. (You can also quickly access the Define Name dialog box by pressing the Command and L keys simultaneously.)

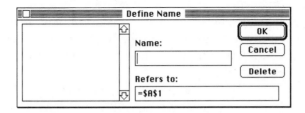

FIGURE 2-24. *This is the Define Name dialog box.*

When you select a cell and choose the Define Name... command, Excel looks at the selected cell, then at the cells to the left of and above the one you have selected to see if they contain labels that might serve as cell names. For example, suppose you want to assign a name to cell B5 in Figure 2-25. First, click cell B5 and then choose Define Name… from the Formula menu. The Define Name dialog box looks like the one shown in Figure 2-26.

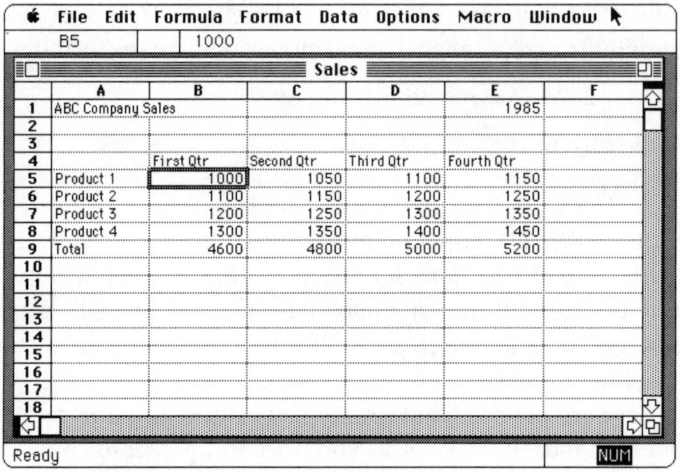

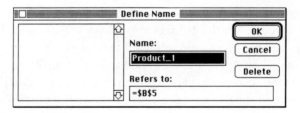

FIGURE 2-25. *You have selected cell B5 in order to assign it a name.*

FIGURE 2-26. *This Define Name dialog box refers to cell B5.*

Notice that Excel displays the name *Product_1* in the Name field and that the name is automatically highlighted. Notice also that Excel automatically adds the underline character (_) to indicate a blank space in the name, because spaces are not allowed in reference names.

If you want to accept Excel's suggested name, simply click the OK button or press Enter. Of course, you can also type your own cell name or edit Excel's suggested name. To enter your own cell name, simply type the name you want. When you begin typing, Excel automatically deletes the existing contents of the Name field. For example, you might want to use the name *First_Qtr* instead of *Product_1*.

To do this, you simply type over Excel's suggested name with your own, then press Enter or click the OK button.

The coordinates of the selected cell appear in the Refers To field, in the form of an absolute reference. Excel assumes that you want to use absolute references when you name cells in your worksheet.

You can edit the cell reference in the Define Name dialog box as you would edit the contents of the formula bar. Begin by clicking in the Refers To field, then use the techniques described earlier to add, delete, and replace characters.

You can also assign names to continuous and discontinuous ranges of cells in your worksheet. For example, suppose you want to name the range B5:B9 in Figure 2-27. To do this, you select cells B5:B9, then choose Define Name... from the Formula menu. The Define Name dialog box looks like Figure 2-28.

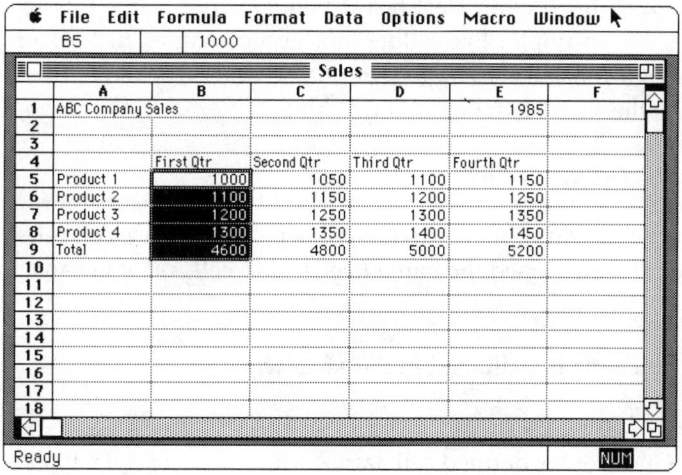

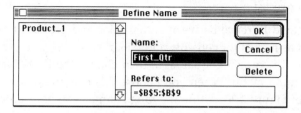

FIGURE 2-27. *You have selected cells B5:B9 to assign them a name.*

FIGURE 2-28. *This Define Name dialog box refers to cells B5:B9.*

Notice that the Refers To field contains the reference of the range you selected, not just the reference of the active cell, and that Excel suggests the name *First_Qtr* for the range. To accept Excel's suggested name, simply click the OK button.

Range name rules

There are a few rules to remember about range names. First, the name must begin with a letter. You can use numbers and some special symbols within the name, but Excel does not accept a name that begins with a number, period, dollar sign, and so on. Excel also returns an error message if you enter blank spaces in the name. For example, Excel does not accept the names *1st Quarter* or *Region A*. If you want to indicate a blank space in your cell name, use the underline character (_), as in *Quarter_1* and *Region_A*.

Excel displays an alert box if you specify a name that looks like a cell reference. For example, Excel does not accept names like *A1* or *R2C1*. In addition, although you can use single-letter names like *A*, *B*, and *C*, Excel does not allow you to use the single letters *R* and *C*.

Using range names

You can use range names in formulas just as you use cell references. For example, if you have assigned the name *Region_1* to cell A10, you can create the formula

    =Region_1–21

This formula is evaluated in the same way as

    =A10–21

Once you've defined cell names, you can paste cell names into your formula in much the same way as you paste cell references. For example, cell B18 in Figure 2-29 uses the formula

    =Actual–Projected

to calculate the difference between actual sales and projected sales, which have been defined as names for cells B16 and C16, respectively. To create this formula, you click cell B18, type an equal sign, then choose the Paste Name… command from the Formula menu. When you choose this command, you see a dialog box like the one in Figure 2-30, listing the range names you have created. To paste the name *Actual* into your formula, simply double click the name. Now, type a minus sign (–) and choose the Paste Name… command again. To select the next name, double click *Projected* in the Paste Name dialog box.

	A	B	C	D	E	F
1	Sales Projections					
2						
3	Date	Actual	Projected			
4	1/1/88	$1,230	$1,000			
5	2/1/88	$1,309	$1,079			
6	3/1/88	$1,388	$1,158			
7	4/1/88	$1,466	$1,236			
8	5/1/88	$1,545	$1,315			
9	6/1/88	$1,624	$1,394			
10	7/1/88	$1,703	$1,473			
11	8/1/88	$1,781	$1,551			
12	9/1/88	$1,860	$1,630			
13	10/1/88	$1,939	$1,709			
14	11/1/88	$2,018	$1,788			
15	12/1/88	$2,096	$1,866			
16	Total	$19,959.00	$17,199.00			
17						
18	Difference	2760				

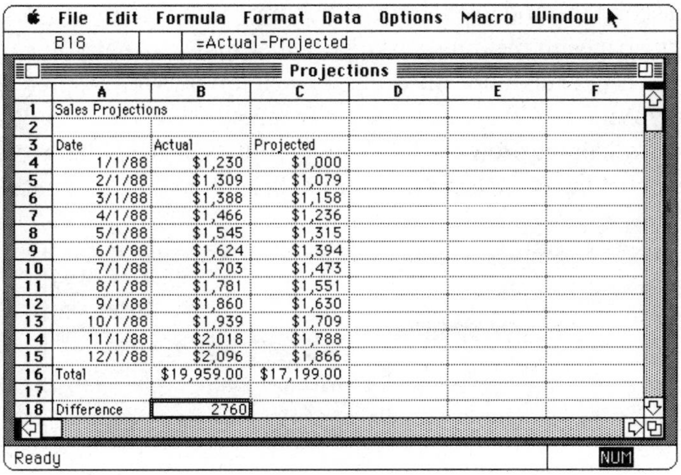

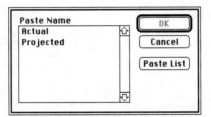

FIGURE 2-29. *You have created a formula that uses range names.*

FIGURE 2-30. *This is the Paste Name dialog box.*

Editing range names

You can edit the contents of the Refers To field to change the cells associated with a range name at any time. Simply choose the Define Name... command, select the name of the range whose reference you want to edit, and click the Refers To field. For example, suppose you have assigned the name *Sales* to cells B5:E8 in your worksheet and you want to change the named range to include cells B5:E9. Begin by choosing Define Name..., then select *Sales* from the list of names in the Define Name dialog box, as shown in Figure 2-31 on the next page. Excel immediately displays the cell reference for the range with that name in the Refers To field.

To edit the cell reference $B$5:$E$8 in Figure 2-31, you can click to the right of the 8, press Delete, and type *9*, or you can drag through the reference $E$8 and click cell E9 in your worksheet. However, cell E9 is not visible in Figure 2-31, because the dialog box covers the entire range of cells named *Sales*. If you want to use the second method to edit the range, simply drag the dialog box out of the way. The black stripes in the dialog box's title bar indicate that you can drag it around on the screen. (For more on dragging windows, see Chapter 5, "One Worksheet, Many Windows.") For example, in Figure 2-32 we have simply dragged the Define Name dialog box toward the bottom of the screen so that we can point to cell E9. After clicking cell E9, press Enter or click OK to lock in the new range reference.

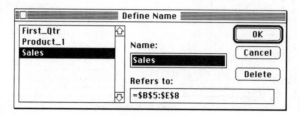

FIGURE 2-31. *You have selected the Sales range from the list in the Define Name dialog box in order to edit it.*

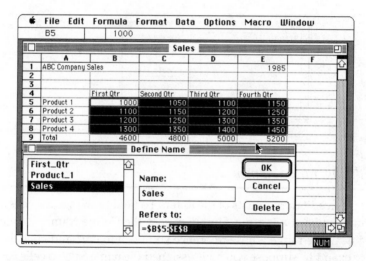

FIGURE 2-32. *You have moved the dialog box so that you can paste a cell into the range reference.*

To delete a range name, simply select the name in the list in the Define Name dialog box and click Delete, but be careful. When you delete a range name, every formula in the worksheet that refers to that name returns the #NAME? error message. For example, suppose cell A1 in a worksheet has the name *Test_Case* and that cell A2 contains the formula

=Test_Case

If you choose the Define Name... command, select the name *Test_Case*, and click Delete, Excel deletes the name. However, the formula in cell A2 remains

=Test_Case

Because the name *Test_Case* no longer exists, the formula returns the error message #NAME?.

The Create Names... command

Excel's Create Names... command lets you name several individual cells or continuous cell ranges at once. It allows you to use the labels in the top or bottom row or left- or right-most column of a range to name the other cells in the range.

For example, the simple worksheet in Figure 2-33 contains a series of labels in column A and a series of values in columns B and C. Suppose you want to assign to each of the values in columns B and C names that correspond to the labels in column A. To do this, you drag through cells A1:C5 and choose the Create Names... command from the Formula menu. When you choose this command, Excel displays the dialog box shown in Figure 2-34 on the next page. Next, select Left Column from the Create Names dialog box. When you click OK or press Enter, Excel assigns the name *First* to the range B1:C1, the name *Second* to the range B2:C2, and so on.

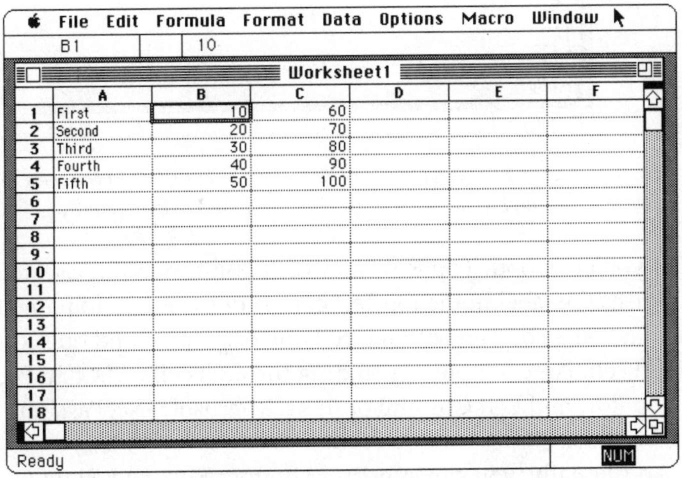

FIGURE 2-33. *The labels in column A can be assigned to the cells in rows 1 through 5 using the Create Names... command.*

Similarly, you can use the labels in cells A1:C1 in Figure 2-35 on the next page to name cells A2:C5. To begin, you drag through cells A1:C5, then choose Create

Names... from the Formula menu. When you select Top Row from the Create Names dialog box, Excel assigns the name *First* to cells A2:A5, *Second* to cells B2:B5, and *Third* to cells C2:C5.

FIGURE 2-34. *This is the Create Names dialog box.*

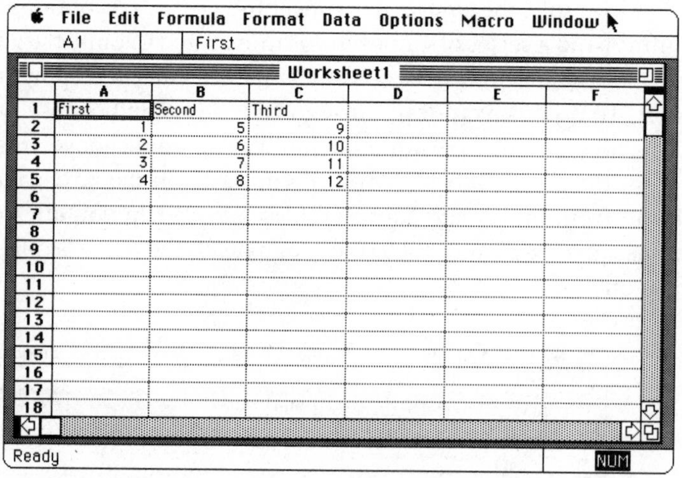

FIGURE 2-35. *The labels in row 1 can be assigned to the cells in columns A through C, also using the Create Names... command.*

If you click both Top Row and Left Column in the Create Names dialog box, Excel uses the label in the top-left corner of the range to name the entire group of cells. The range begins with the cell one row down and one column over from the top-left cell. For example, if you drag through cells A1:C5 in Figure 2-36 and select the Top Row and Left Column options, Microsoft Excel assigns the name *Summary* to cells B2:C5.

Additionally, you can substitute Bottom Row and Right Column for Top Row and Left Column. In this case, Excel uses the entry in the bottom-right cell to name the range. This named range will begin one row up and one column to the left of the bottom-right cell. The Create Names... command allows you to use any combination of the four choices it presents you in its dialog box.

However, there's one hitch. You cannot use the Create Names... command to name discontinuous ranges of cells. For example, if you attempt to use the Left Column option in the Create Names dialog box to name the selected cells in Figure 2-37, Excel returns the alert message *Selection is not valid* (although you could use

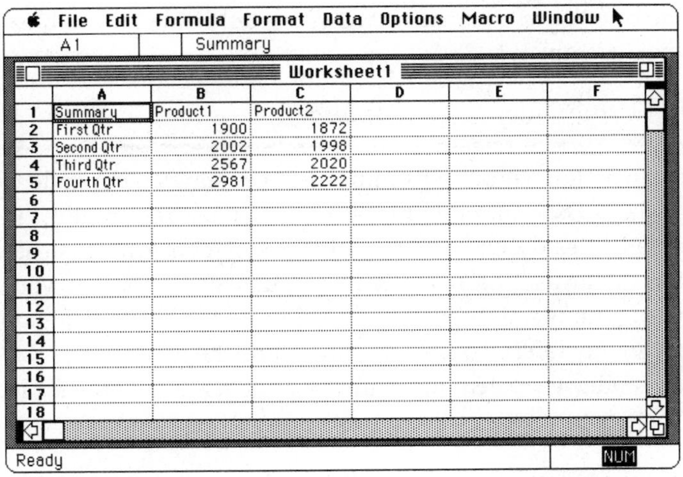

FIGURE 2-36. *The label in cell A1 is assigned to cells B2:C5 when you select both Create Names options.*

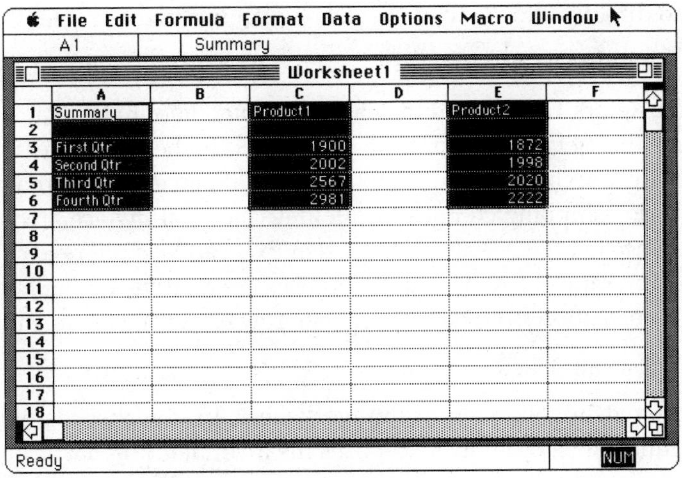

FIGURE 2-37. *The Left Column option of the Create Names... command cannot be used with these selected cells.*

the Top Row option to name the cells in the column below each row entry). If you need to name a discontinuous range of cells, you have to use the Define Name... command.

The names you create with the Create Names... command appear in the Define Name dialog box when you choose the Define Name... command. You can delete or edit these names just as you would a name you created with the Define Name... command.

The Define Name... command

You can assign names to formulas and constants independent of the cells in your worksheet. For example, suppose you often use the value 5% in your worksheet to calculate sales tax on products sold by your company. Instead of typing 5% or .05, you want to use the name *Tax* in your calculations. If you choose the Define Name... command, type the name *Tax* into the Name field, and type .05 or 5% directly in the Refers To field, Excel assigns the name *Tax* to the constant value 5%. Once you have created this name, you can use a formula such as

    =Price+(Price∗Tax)

to calculate the cost of items with sales tax.

If you enter a formula in the Refers To field that refers to a cell in your worksheet, Excel updates that formula whenever the value in the worksheet cell changes. In other words, Excel treats named formulas just as it does formulas entered directly into the worksheet. For example, you can enter the formula in cell E6

    =C6−($B$2∗C6)+D6

in the Refers To field and the name *Amount_Billed* in the Name field in the Define Name dialog box. This formula, when used in the worksheet in Figure 2-38, calculates the purchase amount, subtracts the 10 percent preferred-customer discount, and adds shipping charges to calculate the total invoice amount. Notice that the reference to cell B2 is absolute, so that Excel always refers to cell B2 for the correct discount rate. The remaining references are relative, telling Excel to draw the billing information from the appropriate row each time the formula

    =Amount_Billed

is entered in column E of the worksheet. In other words, when you enter this formula name in cell E9, Excel uses the formula

    =E9−($B$2∗E9)+D9

to calculate a total billing amount of $429.34.

```
 ⬛  File  Edit  Formula  Format  Data  Options  Macro  Window ▶
     E9              =Amount_Billed
```

	A	B	C	D	E	F
1						
2	Discount:	10%				
3						
4						
5		Client	Amount	Shipping	Total	
6		ABC	$101.23	$2.45	$93.56	
7		XYZ	$1,200.00	$57.45	$1,137.45	
8		LMN	$1,300.00	$43.98	$1,213.98	
9		JKL	$457.45	$17.63	$429.34	
10						
11						
12						
13						
14						
15						
16						
17						
18						

```
Ready                                              NUM
```

FIGURE 2-38. *You can increase your efficiency by defining names for often-used formulas.*

The Paste Name... command

After defining one or more names in your worksheet, you can use the Paste Name... command on the Formula menu to paste those names into your worksheet formulas. For example, suppose you've assigned the name *Discount* to cell B2 and the name *Amount* to the cells in C6:C9 of the worksheet shown in Figure 2-38. You want to use these values in a formula, such as

=Discount∗Amount

To create this formula, you can type *Discount* and *Amount* directly into the formula bar. Alternatively, you can use the Paste Name... command to paste the names into the formula. Paste Name... not only saves time when you need to enter several names, it also helps reduce typographical errors and serves as a memory aid when your worksheet contains many name definitions.

To use the Paste Name... command, first select the cell in which you want to enter the name. If the name is to appear at the beginning of the formula, choose the Paste Name... command to display the dialog box shown in Figure 2-39 on the next page, then select the name you want to paste and click OK or press Enter. Excel enters an equal sign in the formula bar, followed by the selected name. The formula bar remains active so that you can type the remainder of the formula. If the name is to appear in the middle of the formula, select the cell that is to contain the formula, type an equal sign and the first portion of the formula, and then, at the spot where you want the name to be included, choose the Paste Name... command and select the desired name. The name you selected appears to the left of the insertion point so that you can continue typing the formula. You can also paste names into an existing formula by clicking the insertion point at the spot where you want the name to appear and choosing the Paste Name... command.

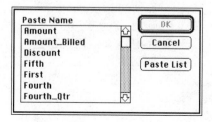

FIGURE 2-39. *You have used the Paste Name dialog box to enter names into your formulas.*

The Paste List option

To help you keep track of the names you've created in your worksheet, Microsoft Excel provides a Paste List option in the Paste Name dialog box. When you select Paste List, the program creates a list of the names in your worksheet, similar to the one shown in Figure 2-40. The list occupies two columns. The first column contains the names and the second column contains their definitions. The cell that is active when you select the Paste List option becomes the first cell in the list.

	D	E	F	G	H	I
1				Amount	=$C$5	
2				Amount_Billed	=E2-($B$2*E2)+F2	
3				Discount	=$A$2	
4				Fifth	=$C$6:$E$6	
5	Shipping	Total		First	=$C$3:$E$3	
6	$2.45	$93.56		Fourth	=$C$5:$E$5	
7	$57.45	$1,137.45		Fourth_Qtr	=$A$1:$A$5	
8	$43.98	$1,213.98		Product1	=$C$3:$C$6	
9	$17.63	$429.34		Product2	=$E$3:$E$6	
10				Second	=#REF!	
11				Summary	=$A$3:$A$6	
12				Third	=$C$4:$E$4	
13						
14						
15						
16						
17						
18						

FIGURE 2-40. *You have used the Paste List option to create a list of the names and definitions in your worksheet.*

(In a macro window, you must allow room for four columns to hold the list created by the Paste List option. There, Excel pastes not only the names and their definitions, but also the macro types and the keyboard shortcuts you can use to run the macros. We talk more about macros in Chapter 17, "Macro Basics.")

The Apply Names... command

When you create names in your worksheet, Microsoft Excel does not automatically apply those names in your worksheet formulas. Continuing with the sample worksheet in Figure 2-38, suppose you enter a series of formulas similar to

=$B$2*C6

and

=$B$2*C7

in cells F6:F9, then use the Define Name... command to assign the name *Discount* to cell B2. The formulas in cells F6:F9 do not automatically change to read

=Discount*C5

and so forth. You can use the named reference *Discount* in your formulas in three ways. First, you can edit the formulas by typing over the current reference to cell B2 with the name *Discount*. Second, you can select the characters $B$2 in the formula bar and use the Paste Name... command to paste the name *Discount* over the cell reference. And third, you can use the Apply Names... command on the Formula menu to instruct Excel to replace the reference with the appropriate name. You are already familiar with the first two techniques. Let's look at the Apply Names... command.

The Apply Names... command searches through the formulas in your worksheet and locates cell and range references for which you've defined names. If you've selected a range in your worksheet, Microsoft Excel applies those names to the selected cells only. However, if only one cell is selected when you issue the command, Excel applies the names throughout the worksheet.

When you choose the Apply Names... command, you see a dialog box like the one shown in Figure 2-41 on the next page. (The last three options appear only if you click the Options button to expand the dialog box.)

The Apply Names list box contains all the cell and range names you've defined in the worksheet. (Named values and formulas do not appear in this list.) To select more than one name, press the Shift key as you click. Excel highlights all the names from the first one you selected to the one you are pointing to.

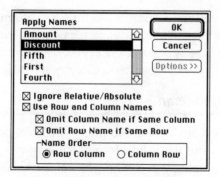

FIGURE 2-41. *You use the Apply Names... command to substitute names for cell and range references in your formulas.*

The Ignore Relative/Absolute option indicates whether you want to replace references with names regardless of the type of reference—relative or absolute—you've used in your name definitions or your worksheet formulas. Generally, you'll want to leave this option selected, because most of your name definitions will use absolute references (the default when you use the Define Names... and Create Names... commands), and most of your formulas will use relative references (the default when you paste cell and range references into the formula bar). If you deselect this option, however, Excel replaces absolute, relative, and mixed references in your worksheet only if your name definitions use the corresponding reference style.

The Use Row And Column Names option determines how Excel applies range names in formulas. If this option is deselected, Excel applies the range names in your formulas only if the name definition refers to the exact range referenced by the formulas. If this option is selected, however, Excel attempts to build a substitute from existing name definitions.

For example, in Figure 2-28 back on page 65 we assigned the name *First_Qtr* to cells B5:B9. Suppose you enter the formula

    =B5*4

in cell I5 of the worksheet. If you then select the Use Row And Column Names option, Excel changes the formula in cell I5 to

    =First_Qtr*4

This formula tells Excel to look to the cell in the range named *First_Qtr* that lies in the same row as the cell containing the formula.

If a formula refers to a cell in a different row and column from the cell containing the formula, the reference, such as A5:B5 B4:B5, is replaced with the row-oriented and column-oriented names that contain the reference. These names are separated by a blank space, indicating that you want Excel to locate the cell at the intersection of the two ranges. (If Excel cannot locate both a row-oriented and a column-oriented range, it doesn't replace the reference with a name.) If you enter the previous formula in a row other than row 5, Excel changes the reference to cell A5 to

=Product_1 First_Qtr*4

This formula tells Excel to look to the cell that lies at the intersection of the range named *Product_1* and the range named *First_Qtr*.

If a formula refers to a cell in the same row as the cell containing the formula but in a different column, the reference is replaced with the column-oriented name (if any). If a row-oriented range also contains the referenced cell, Excel adds that name to the reference as well, creating a reference to the intersection of the two named ranges. Similarly, if a formula refers to a cell in the same column as the cell containing the formula but in a different row, the reference is replaced with a row-oriented name (if any). If a column-oriented range also contains the referenced cell, Excel adds that name to the reference as well.

If you click the Options button in the Apply Names dialog box, the Omit Column Name If Same Column and Omit Row Name If Same Row options appear. These options, which are available only if you have selected Use Row And Column Names, tell Excel not to use the intersection referencing technique described above. In other words, if the referenced cell is in the same column as the cell that contains the formula but in a different row, Excel uses the name of the row-oriented range only, ignoring any column-oriented ranges that may intersect the row-oriented range. By the same token, if the referenced cell is in the same row as the cell that contains the formula but in a different column, Excel uses the name of the column-oriented range only, ignoring any row-oriented ranges that may intersect the column-oriented range.

The last set of options in the Apply Names dialog box is Name Order. These options appear only when you click the Options button, and they are available only if you have selected Use Row And Column Names. The Name Order options let you determine which range is listed first when a reference is replaced by a combination of row-oriented and column-oriented range names. The Row Column option lists rows first (*Product_1 First_Qtr*). The Column Row option lists columns first (*First_Qtr Product_1*).

The Goto... command

The Microsoft Excel Goto... command on the Formula menu allows you to move around your worksheet and select cells quickly. For example, suppose cell A1 is currently selected and you want to select cell M50. Rather than scrolling over and down to cell M50, simply choose Goto... from the Formula menu. When you choose this command, Excel displays the Goto dialog box shown in Figure 2-42. In the Goto dialog box, type *M50*, then click OK or press Enter. Immediately, Excel moves the window so that cell M50 is in its lower-right corner and makes M50 the active cell.

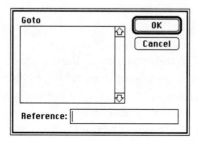

FIGURE 2-42. *This is the Goto dialog box.*

If you have created range names in your worksheets, those names appear in the list at the left side of the Goto dialog box. To select one of these ranges, simply double click the range name in the dialog box. For example, suppose you have assigned the name *Subtotals* to cells C5:F5 in your worksheet. If you choose the Goto... command and double click the range name *Subtotals*, Excel highlights cells C5:F5. The first cell in the range, C5, is the active cell.

Error values

On occasion, a set of rather unfriendly looking codes will pop up in your worksheet. These flags, which are called *error values*, indicate that Microsoft Excel is unable to resolve one of your formulas.

One of the most common error values is #DIV/0!. As you might have guessed, #DIV/0! indicates that you have attempted to divide a number by zero. This error usually shows up when you create a division formula with a divisor that refers to a blank cell. For example, suppose cell A1 contains the formula

    =32/A2

As long as a numeric value other than zero appears in cell A2, Excel can resolve the formula correctly. If A2 is blank, or if you erase cell A2 or change its value to zero, Excel cannot resolve the formula and returns the #DIV/0! error value. To correct the problem, you must either edit the formula or enter a value in cell A2.

The #N/A error value indicates that you have entered into a formula a reference to a cell that holds no information. If, while building a worksheet, you need to reserve some empty cells for information that you will receive at a later date, you can enter #N/A into those cells. When you create formulas that refer to those cells, Excel returns the #N/A, reminding you that you still need that information. When you finally enter the information in those cells, Excel displays the correct results of the formulas.

The #NAME? error value indicates that you have entered into a formula a name that Excel could not find in the Define Name dialog box listing. If you see this error, check to see whether you have mistyped the name reference or included a reference to a deleted name.

This error sometimes pops up when you are attempting to enter a literal string in a formula, rather than a name, but forget to put double quotation marks around the string. For example, if you enter

=Hometown, USA

Excel assumes you want to refer to a range or cell name. To correct the problem, add a set of double quotes around the text string, as in

="Hometown, USA"

You may also see the #NAME? error if you leave out the colon in a range reference. For example, when Excel runs into formulas like

=SUM(A1C4)

or

=SUM(A1.C4)

it tries to interpret the range reference as a name. To correct the problem, you must change the formula to

=SUM(A1:C4)

The #NUM error value indicates that you used an unacceptable argument in a formula that requires a number. For example, if you use a negative number where a positive one is expected, such as

=SQRT(–1)

in your worksheet, Excel displays a #NUM error value.

The #VALUE! error value usually means that you have entered a mathematical formula that refers to a text entry. For example, if you enter a formula such as

=A1*A2

in your worksheet, and cell A1 contains a text string, the formula returns the #VALUE! error value.

You will see a #REF! error value if you use the Delete… command to eliminate a range of cells whose references are included in a formula. For example, suppose you enter the formula

    =A1+A2+A3

in cell A5 of your worksheet. If you delete row 3 from the worksheet, the formula changes to

    =A1+A2+#REF!

and cell A5 displays the #REF! error value.

The last, and least common, error value is #NULL!. This error value appears if you enter a formula like

    =SUM(A1:C1 A6:F6)

The blank space between the two sets of references tells Excel to find the value of the cell at the intersection of the ranges A1:C1 and A6:F6. Because these two ranges have no common cells, Excel returns the #NULL! error value.

Calculating the worksheet

As you have already seen, you can enter formulas into your worksheet that refer to other cells in the worksheet. When you change the values in the cells that these formulas refer to, Microsoft Excel automatically updates the value of the formula as well. This process of updating the values of formulas to reflect any new values entered in the cells that the formulas refer to is called *calculation*, or *recalculation*.

In most spreadsheet programs, the entire worksheet is recalculated every time you make a cell entry. This can be quite time-consuming and frustrating, particularly when you're making minor editing changes in a large spreadsheet. Microsoft Excel, on the other hand, performs *smart recalculation*. When you add or edit a cell in Excel, only those cells that are affected by the entry are recalculated. For example, if you enter the formula

    =A1*B2

in cell C1 of your worksheet and then make a change to cell A1, Excel automatically recalculates cell C1. The remaining cells in your worksheet are not recalculated. However, if there are other formulas in the worksheet that refer to cell A1, or to cell C1, then those cells—and only those cells—are also recalculated.

Because Excel doesn't recalculate every cell in the worksheet each time you make a change, you'll spend a lot less time waiting to make your next cell entry and a lot more time being productive.

Manual recalculation

When you are working with a large worksheet containing many interdependent formulas, Excel may still need several seconds to recalculate your worksheet. To save time, you may prefer to change the method of recalculation to Manual while you enter data. When calculation is set to Manual, Excel does not recalculate every time you make an entry. Instead, it does not recalculate until you tell it to do so.

To set calculation to Manual, choose Calculation... from the Options menu. When you choose this command, Excel displays a dialog box like the one in Figure 2-43. Next, click the Manual option in the dialog box, then click OK.

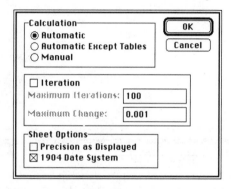

FIGURE 2-43. *This is the Calculation dialog box.*

With calculation set to Manual, you can enter values and formulas in your worksheet without waiting for Excel to recalculate dependent cells after each entry. When you are ready to see the effects of your cell entries, simply choose Calculate Now from the Options menu or press Command-=. When you choose this command, Excel calculates all of the cells in the worksheet that are affected by the changes you've made since you last recalculated.

You can also tell Excel to recalculate all of the cells in your worksheet automatically except for your data tables. (We talk more about data tables in Chapter 8, "Other Worksheet Topics.")

The order of recalculation

When Microsoft Excel recalculates a group of cells, it starts with the most basic cell in the group—the cell that must be calculated first if the others are to be recalculated properly—then the next most basic cell, and so on, until all of the cells in the group have been recalculated. The order of recalculation resembles an inverted pyramid with the most fundamental cells on the bottom and a hierarchy of dependent cells above.

For example, look at the formulas in Figure 2-44. We've formatted this worksheet to display the underlying formulas in each cell by selecting the Formulas option in the Display dialog box. If you make a change to cell A1 in this worksheet, Excel recalculates cell A4, then A3, then A2. Even though cell A2 comes before the other formula cells in Figure 2-44, it is recalculated last.

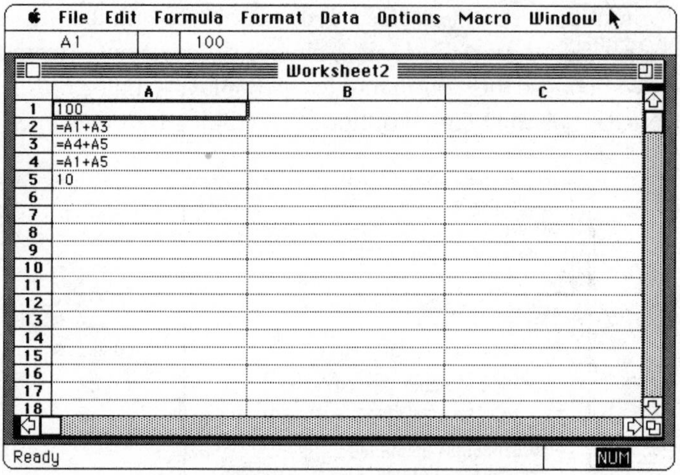

FIGURE 2-44. *If a change is made to cell A1, the formulas in this worksheet are recalculated in the following order: A4, A3, then A2.*

Unlike some spreadsheet programs, Microsoft Excel does not allow you to change the order of recalculation. However, because natural recalculation is by far the preferred order, you probably won't miss the ability to alter the order.

Changing formulas to values with the Calculate Now command

You can also use the Calculate Now command (or Command-=) to change one or more of the cell references in your formulas from cell references into values.

For example, cell A6 in Figure 2-45 contains the formula

    =A1+A2+A3

Notice that cell A1 contains the value 100. If you drag across the cell reference A1 in this formula and choose Calculate Now from the Options menu, Excel converts the formula to

    =100+A2+A3

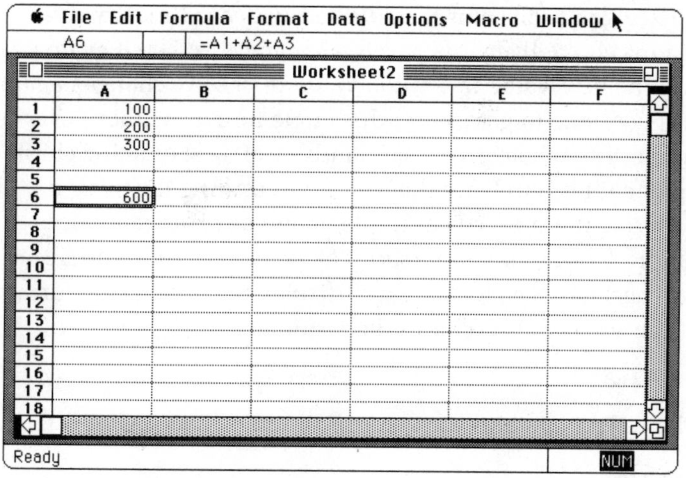

FIGURE 2-45. *This is the formula in cell A6, before you selected the cell reference A1 and chose Calculate Now.*

If you select the entire formula and choose the Calculate Now command, Excel computes the sum of the values and displays

=600

Keep in mind that you can't retrieve the original cell references after you lock in the entry, unless you immediately choose Undo Entry from the Edit menu. This means, in this example, that after this point Excel cannot update the value in the formula cell if the values in cells A1:A3 change. In other words, once you change the cell references to values with Calculate Now, the formula in cell A6 is no longer linked to the values in the range A1:A3.

Circular references

Circular references occur when two or more cells in a worksheet are dependent on each other. When this happens, Excel cannot resolve the formula in either cell correctly. The most obvious type of circular reference occurs when you create a formula in a cell that contains a reference to that same cell.

For example, if you enter a formula such as

=C1–A1

in cell A1 of your worksheet, Excel will display an alert box with the message *Can't resolve circular references*. When you click OK or press Enter to acknowledge the error, the formula returns the value 0.

Excel can't solve this formula because each time it arrives at a value for the formula in cell A1, the value of cell A1 changes. When it evaluates the formula in A1 using the new value in A1, the value in cell A1 changes again. Obviously, Excel could continue to go around this circle forever without ever really resolving the formula. The whole process reminds us of a cat or a dog chasing its own tail, running in endless circles and never quite catching the thing it is chasing.

Unlike the previous example, many circular references can be resolved. For example, look at the simple series of formulas in the worksheet in Figure 2-46. This worksheet has been formatted to display the underlying formulas in each cell. As you can see, cell A1 contains the formula

=A2+A3

while cell A2 contains the value 1000, and cell A3 contains the formula

=.5∗A1

This set of formulas is circular because the formula in A1 depends on the value in A3, and the formula in A3 depends on the value in A1.

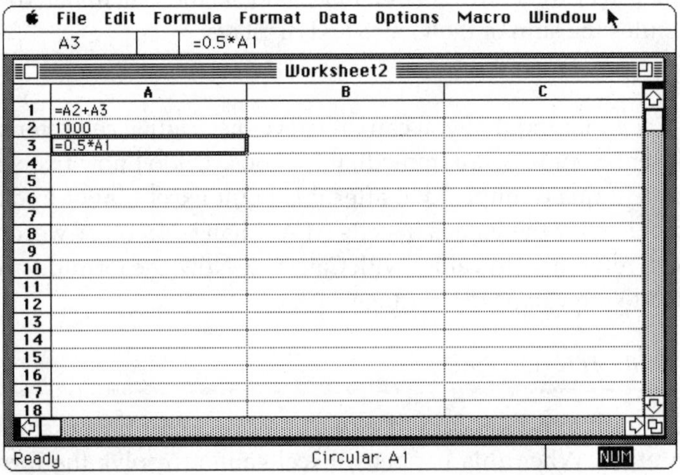

FIGURE 2-46. *This is an example of a circular reference.*

When you enter this circular reference, Excel displays the value 1000 in cell A1 and the value 0 in cell A3, even though the value in A3 should equal one half of the value in cell A1—assuming, of course, that the Formula option in the Display dialog box is turned off. The *Can't resolve circular references* alert message appears as soon as you enter these formulas.

You can use the Iteration option in the Calculation dialog box to resolve this kind of circular reference. When this option is selected, Excel recalculates the cells that contain the circular reference a specified number of times. Each time the formulas are recalculated, the results in each cell of this example get closer and closer to the correct values.

To resolve the circular reference in the example, you can click OK in the alert box, then choose Calculation… from the Options menu. Next, click the Manual button and the Iteration box in the Calculation dialog box and click OK to close the dialog box. Now, select the cell with the circular reference (A3) and choose the Calculate Now command.

When you click the Iteration option in the Calculation dialog box, Excel automatically sets the Maximum Iterations option to 100 and the Maximum Change option to 0.001. These settings tell Excel to recalculate the cells involved in the circular reference up to 100 times, or until the values in these cells change less than 0.001 between iterations, whichever comes first.

The table in Figure 2-47 on the next page shows how the values in cells A1 and A3 change as Excel recalculates the circular reference. (We've rounded these figures to three decimal places.) Notice that the values in cells A1 and A3 change less with each iteration as Excel closes in on the correct answer. The final results in cells A1 and A3 are very close to correct, because 999.999 is almost exactly half of 1999.999. The recalculation stops after 21 iterations because the change in the values in cells A1 and A3 in that iteration is less than 0.001.

Unfortunately, Excel does not repeat the *Can't resolve circular references* message if it fails to resolve the circular reference within the specified number of iterations. Instead, it displays the values of the formulas as of the last iteration. You'll have to rely on your common sense to determine whether the value that Excel comes up with is really the answer you're looking for.

In many spreadsheet programs, iterative calculations are very time-consuming, because every cell in the worksheet must be recalculated for each iteration. Excel's ability to perform smart recalculation is a real timesaver when you are using the Iteration option. Because only those cells needed to resolve the circular reference are recalculated, Excel can perform 100 iterations in a matter of seconds. When you are using iterative calculation, however, make sure the recalculation option is set to Manual; otherwise, Excel attempts to recalculate the circular references every time you press the Enter key.

In some spreadsheet programs, you can specify only 50 iterations. Excel lets you set Maximum Iterations as high as 32,767. However, you'll probably find that the default 100 iterations is enough to resolve most intentional circular references in your worksheet. Similarly, you can set Maximum Change to any number greater than zero, though you'll probably find that the 0.001 default is adequate for most applications.

Iteration number	A1	A3	Iteration number	A1	A3
	(=A2+A3)	(=.5*A1)	11	1999.023	999.023
1	1000	0	12	1999.512	999.512
2	1500	500	13	1999.756	999.756
3	1750	750	14	1999.878	999.878
4	1875	875	15	1999.939	999.939
5	1937.5	937.5	16	1999.969	999.969
6	1968.75	968.75	17	1999.985	999.985
7	1984.375	984.375	18	1999.992	999.992
8	1992.188	992.188	19	1999.996	999.996
9	1996.094	996.094	20	1999.998	999.998
10	1998.047	998.047	21	1999.999	999.999

FIGURE 2-47. *The values of cells A1 and A3 change through successive iterations (A2=1000).*

Although there are occasions when you may want to build circular references into your worksheet, Excel's circular-reference warning usually indicates that you have made an error in one of your formulas. Sometimes it takes a little detective work to track down these errors. To correct the problem, click OK in the alert box and look back at the formula you just entered. You may have inadvertently included the formula cell in your calculation.

For example, when you are calculating the sum of a series of values, it's easy to click one cell too many and inadvertently include the total cell itself in the formula. This kind of error is easy to correct: You simply edit the formula to remove the formula cell reference.

If the circular reference is not immediately obvious, check the cells that are referenced in the formula. Those cells may contain references to the formula cell itself. For example, look at the series of formulas in Figure 2-48. Notice that the formula in cell A1 refers to cell A3 and that the formula in cell A3 refers to cell A1. This kind of error might result if you made the entry in cell A3 without checking the contents of cell A1.

By the way, this circular reference is impossible to resolve, no matter how many iterations you specify. Excel begins by calculating the value of A1+A2, then assigns that value to cell A3. When the value in cell A3 changes, Excel updates the value in A1 as well. As soon as A1 changes, Excel again recalculates the value of cell A3. No matter how many times the worksheet is recalculated, cell A3 always equals the value in cell A1 plus 100.

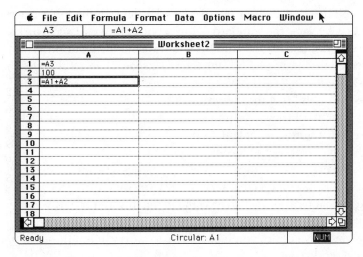

FIGURE 2-48. *This example of a circular reference cannot be resolved.*

Precision of numeric values

Microsoft Excel stores numbers with up to 14 digits of accuracy. If you enter an integer that is longer than 14 digits, Excel converts any digits after the 14th to zeros. If you enter a decimal fraction that is longer than 14 digits, Excel drops any digits after the 14th. In addition, as you saw earlier in this chapter, Excel automatically converts any numbers that are too long to be displayed in their cells into scientific notation.

For example, if you enter a number like 123456789123456789 in a cell, Excel displays that number as 1.2346E+17. In addition, Excel retains only the first 14 digits of this number in the cell. The remaining digits are converted to zeros, like this: 123456789123460000. You'll be able to see this in the formula bar as soon as you enter the number in the cell.

The following table shows several other examples of how Excel treats integers and decimal fractions that are longer than 14 digits when they are entered into cells with the default column width of ten characters.

If you enter...	Excel displays...	Excel converts the underlying value to...
123456789012345678	1.2346E+17	123456789012340000
1.23456789012345678	1.23456789	1.2345678901234
1234567890.12345678	1234567890	1234567890.1235
123456789012345.678	1.2346E+14	123456789012340

Notice that each of the displayed values in the table is ten characters wide. This is because the standard column width in your Excel worksheet is ten characters. If you change the column width (using the Column Width... command, described in Chapter 4, "Editing the Worksheet"), Excel changes the displayed value to 11 digits, such as 1.23457E+17, but doesn't necessarily fill the width of the cell. Keep in mind that the column width affects only the displayed value of numbers on your worksheet. Column width has no effect on precision. In other words, Excel still stores and calculates numbers with up to 14 digits of accuracy, no matter what the displayed value is.

Excel is able to calculate positive values as large as 1.798E+307 and as small as 2.25E–308. If you create a formula that results in a value greater than 1.798E+307, Excel assigns a #NUM! error value to the formula cell. If you create a formula that results in a value less than 2.25E–308, Excel assigns a *0* value to the formula. However, we doubt you'll ever have to worry about these limitations in a typical Excel worksheet.

With 14 digits of accuracy and the ability to use numbers in the zillions, you should be able to perform just about any kind of calculation in your Excel worksheets. In fact, you'll generally want to use numbers less precisely than Excel's standards. For example, when you are performing financial calculations, you'll probably want to round numbers to two decimal places.

There are two more options, called *sheet options*, in the Calculation dialog box: Precision As Displayed and 1904 Date System. In Chapter 3, "Formatting the Worksheet," where we show you how to format the cells in your worksheet to display currency, percentages, fixed decimal places, and other numeric formats, we also discuss how to use the Precision As Displayed option. This option allows you to use displayed values rather than underlying values in your calculations. In Chapter 7, "Date and Time," where we explain how Excel interprets, displays, and manages dates and times, we also discuss the 1904 Date System option.

Memory management

The amount of RAM (random-access memory) Microsoft Excel uses is highly variable and is influenced by a number of factors. The size of your Mac's memory is a major factor, as is the number and content of all the worksheets open during a session and how much data they contain. As you might expect, every entry you make in your Excel worksheet uses memory. However, all entries are not created equal: Some require more memory than others. Here are a few guidelines.

Integer values use less memory than floating-point values. Text values require 1 byte per character. For example, the entry *This is a text string* requires 21 bytes.

(Blank spaces count!) Formulas also require more memory than simple numeric values. Although the number of bytes used depends on the length and complexity of the formula, you can roughly estimate about 20 bytes for every formula in your worksheet.

The windows you use to view different areas of the worksheet use memory. If you find yourself running out of memory, you might close a few windows and revert to using the scroll bars to move around the worksheet.

You can determine the amount of memory that is free at any time by choosing the About Excel... command from the Apple menu. As you can see in Figure 2-49, Excel displays the percentage of memory that is free just below the copyright information.

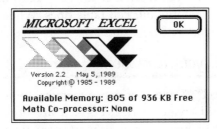

FIGURE 2-49. *This is the About Excel dialog box.*

When you're working with floppy drives and you're creating a large worksheet, you should make it a point to keep track of the amount of free memory available. If it gets low, you should start looking for ways to trim down the file before you make any more additions. After checking the amount of free memory, simply click the OK button to get back to your worksheet.

Excel's sparse matrix memory management system

Although the program code for Microsoft Excel 2.2 occupies more RAM than Excel 1.5, you can create larger worksheets and hold more worksheets in RAM at one time with version 2.2. One reason for this increased capability is that, unlike previous versions of Excel, version 2.2 can address up to 8 MB of RAM. The other reason is that version 2.2 uses a sparse matrix memory management system, allocating memory only to cells that either contain entries or are formatted.

Chances are you'll never use the entire 8 MB of available RAM while you are working in Excel. Here's why. Excel divides the 8 MB among three separate areas: a *heap space*, an *application heap*, and a *cell table*.

Excel allocates up to 2 MB of RAM to the heap space, using it to collect all of the complex formulas and formats in an Excel document. The application heap consumes up to 2 MB of RAM and contains all of the program code. (As a user, you have no access to the application heap.) Together, these two areas form the 4 MB heap space we mentioned in Chapter 1.

Finally, the cell table assigns 6 bytes of memory to each cell that contains an entry or is formatted. In earlier versions of Excel, a worksheet could consume more memory than users expected because Excel assigned 6 bytes of memory to every cell that lay in the rectangle between the upper left-most cell of the worksheet (cell A1) and the cell at the intersection of the lowest row containing an entry and the right-most column containing an entry. All cells in this rectangle, even empty cells, used memory in earlier versions of the program. Excel 2.2 assigns memory only to cells with entries in them.

Rarely will you use all 8 MB of available RAM, because your heap space and application heap will fill up before your cell table does. When the heap is full, Excel effectively is out of memory.

Managing the entries in your worksheets

Even though Microsoft Excel 2.2 does not waste memory by assigning bytes to empty cells, you still should create worksheets that are organized efficiently. Don't scatter entries randomly throughout your worksheet. If your cell entries are unnecessarily spread out, you may have problems locating the cells you need to refer to.

There may be times when you'll find yourself with a number of complex documents open simultaneously on the desktop. To free up available memory, you may want to make adjustments to cells that serve no purpose or use memory unnecessarily. For example, you may want to delete empty, formatted cells; enter the results of formulas as literal values; and enter a range of formulas as one array formula. You'll learn how to make these adjustments in the chapters that follow. Unfortunately, you won't realize any immediate memory savings. You need to save the worksheet before Excel will free up memory.

Conclusion

In this chapter, you have learned how to select cells and enter text, numbers, and formulas in the worksheet. You have also learned how Microsoft Excel calculates the worksheet and manages memory.

Still, we've just scratched the surface. In the next chapters, you'll learn to format and edit the entries you make in the worksheet. You'll also learn how to use functions, how to print a worksheet, and how to use special commands, such as Tables and Find.

3

Formatting the Worksheet

*I*n Chapter 2, "Worksheet Basics," we introduced you to the basics of Microsoft Excel and you learned how to make entries in the worksheet. You may have noticed that all of the entries you have made so far have the same format: All numbers (and the results of formulas) are right-aligned in their cells and have what is called the General format. All labels (text entries) are left-aligned. In this chapter, you'll learn how to use Microsoft Excel's formatting commands to change the format, alignment, and style of the entries in your worksheet.

Why use formats?

The Microsoft Excel Format-menu and Options-menu commands give your worksheets a professional appearance and make them easier to read and use. Take a look at the unformatted worksheet in Figure 3-1. Although this worksheet provides a lot of valuable information, the data is very hard to interpret. The reader has few visual clues about what is being presented. Important totals and key headings blend into the background, and many of the columns appear to be misaligned.

Now, look at the formatted worksheet in Figure 3-2. The contents of this worksheet are identical to Figure 3-1, but the worksheet looks better and is easier to read.

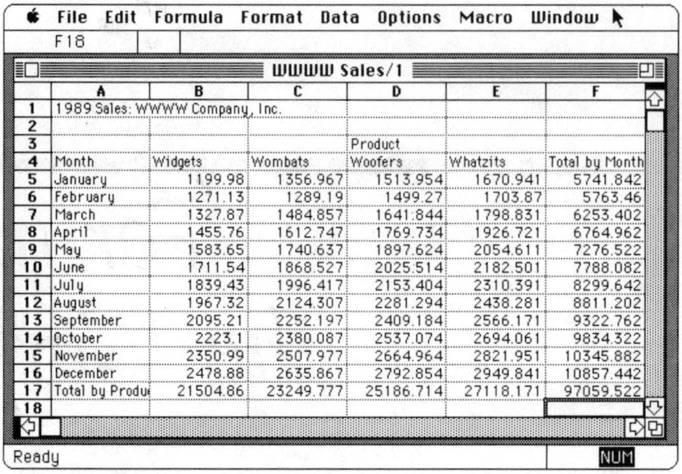

FIGURE 3-1. *An unformatted worksheet looks like this.*

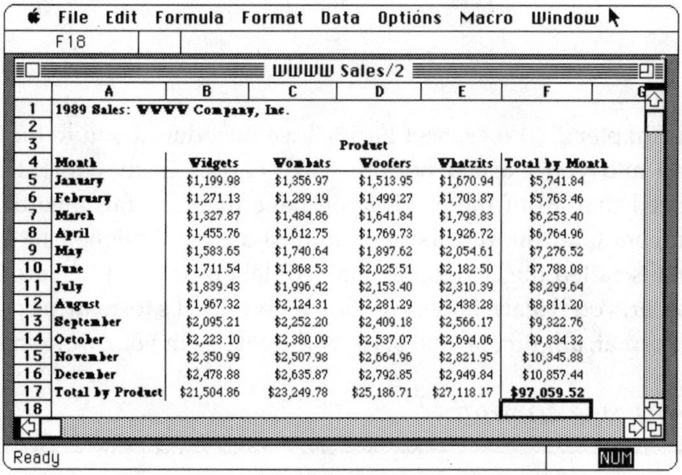

FIGURE 3-2. *This is the same worksheet with formatting.*

As you would expect, most of Excel's formatting commands are found on the Format menu, shown in Figure 3-3. We cover the Number…, Alignment…, Font…, Border…, Row Height…, and Column Width… commands in this chapter, the Justify command in Chapter 4, "Editing the Worksheet," and the Cell Protection… command in Chapter 8, "Other Worksheet Topics." Three other important formatting commands are found on the Options menu: the Standard

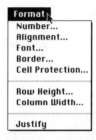

FIGURE 3-3. *These commands are available on the Format menu.*

Font..., Display..., and Workspace... commands. We also cover those commands in this chapter. (We'll postpone our discussion of the Font... command until after we discuss the Standard Font... command.)

Assigning formats

Assigning a special format to a cell or range of cells is easy. You begin by selecting the cells you want to format, then you use the appropriate format commands. You can select a single cell, a block of cells, a discontinuous range, a named range, an entire column or row, or the entire worksheet. (Chapter 2, "Worksheet Basics," offers more information on selecting cells.) You can even assign a format to cells that do not yet contain entries, although most of the Format-menu commands do not have any visible effect until you make entries in those cells.

Normally, you select a range of cells to work with, make your cell entries, then—while the range of cells is still selected—choose the desired commands from the Format menu to assign a format to this range of cells. However, Excel accepts your commands in any sequence, so you can assign a format to a cell, or change the existing format of a cell, at any time.

For example, in column C of Figure 3-4 on the next page, cells C4 through C18 are unformatted. Suppose you want to add a dollar sign and commas to the values in these cells and round each value to two decimal places. You drag through cells C4:C18 and choose Number... from the Format menu. Then, you double click the $#,##0.00 option in the Format Number dialog box. Figure 3-5 shows the result.

Now, suppose you want the values in column C to appear in bold type. Highlight cells C4:C18, then choose Font... from the Format menu and select the Bold option. The results appear in Figure 3-6.

Once you have formatted a cell, that cell remains formatted, even if you make a new entry in the cell. For example, suppose you notice an incorrect entry in cell B6 of your worksheet. You have already formatted this cell to display a percentage with no decimal places. To correct the error, you need only to click cell B6, retype the number or formula, and click the enter box. There is no need to reformat the cell; the new number is also in the percentage format.

Keep in mind that numeric formats do not apply to text cells. If you are working with a range of cells that contain both text and numbers, you can assign a numeric format to the entire range without affecting your text entries.

	A	B	C	D	E	F
1	Expense Account Statement					
2						
3	Date	For	Amount			
4	4/10/89	Air Fare	542.77			
5		Meals	37.98			
6		Taxi	15.5			
7		Tips	9			
8		Misc	27.76			
9	4/11/89	Meals	42			
10		Taxi	13			
11		Tips	6			
12		Misc	19.99			
13	4/12/89	Hotel	298.91			
14		Meals	49.66			
15		Taxi	14.5			
16		Tips	11.5			
17		Misc	9.78			
18	Total		1098.35			

FIGURE 3-4. *This expense-account worksheet has no custom formatting.*

	A	B	C	D	E	F
1	Expense Account Statement					
2						
3	Date	For	Amount			
4	4/10/89	Air Fare	$542.77			
5		Meals	$37.98			
6		Taxi	$15.50			
7		Tips	$9.00			
8		Misc	$27.76			
9	4/11/89	Meals	$42.00			
10		Taxi	$13.00			
11		Tips	$6.00			
12		Misc	$19.99			
13	4/12/89	Hotel	$298.91			
14		Meals	$49.66			
15		Taxi	$14.50			
16		Tips	$11.50			
17		Misc	$9.78			
18	Total		$1,098.35			

FIGURE 3-5. *This is the expense-account worksheet after it has been formatted for currency with two decimal places.*

File Edit Formula Format Data Options Macro Window

	A	B	C	D	E	F
			Expense Report			
1	Expense Account Statement					
2						
3	Date	For	Amount			
4	4/10/89	Air Fare	$542.77			
5		Meals	$37.98			
6		Taxi	$15.50			
7		Tips	$9.00			
8		Misc	$27.76			
9	4/11/89	Meals	$42.00			
10		Taxi	$13.00			
11		Tips	$6.00			
12		Misc	$19.99			
13	4/12/89	Hotel	$298.91			
14		Meals	$49.66			
15		Taxi	$14.50			
16		Tips	$11.50			
17		Misc	$9.78			
18	Total		$1,098.35			

Ready   NUM

FIGURE 3-6. *This is the expense-account worksheet after selecting the Bold option.*

Deleting formats

To delete an assigned format, first select the cell or range of cells whose formats you want to delete, then choose Clear... from the Edit menu and select the Formats option in the Clear dialog box. Excel returns the selected cells to their default formats. The values in the cells are not changed.

You can also erase the contents of a cell without altering the assigned format. Suppose you have centered the contents of cells B5:C20. After formatting these cells, you discover a series of incorrect entries in cells B10:C20. To erase the contents of these cells without changing their format, drag through cells B10:C20, and

EXCEL

Format before you paste

You can take advantage of the fact that formats are copied along with cell contents by formatting your source cell before you choose the Copy, Fill Right, Fill Down, or Series... commands. For example, suppose you have entered the value 123 in cell A1 of your worksheet. You want to format this cell to display currency with no decimal places, and you also need to copy this value to several other cells. Be sure to assign any special formats, like currency, before you use the Copy and Paste commands. When you copy cell A1, the pasted cells automatically assume identical formats.

choose the Clear... command from the Edit menu. When you see that the Formulas option is selected, click the OK button or press Enter. The contents of the selected range of cells are erased, but any new entries you make in this range are automatically centered.

As you've probably guessed, if you select All from the Clear dialog box, Excel erases both the contents of the cell and the format you have assigned.

Copying and cutting formatted cells

When you use the Number..., Alignment..., Font..., and Border... commands, remember that formats are assigned to the contents of cells and not to the cells themselves. For example, when you cut a cell and paste it in another area of your worksheet, the pasted cell takes on the assigned special format, and the cut cell reverts to the General format. When you copy a formatted cell, both the original and the copy retain the format you have assigned.

Formatting numbers

You use the Number... command from the Format menu to tell Microsoft Excel how to display numeric values. Excel's numeric formats apply only to numbers and to the results of formulas; they do not affect text entries. These formats allow you to display numbers and formula results as integers, currency, percentages, and exponents. For example, the numeric format $#,##0.00 tells Excel to display values as currency with two decimal places, so that the number 1234.567 would be displayed as $1,234.57.

The Number... command offers a total of 21 formats. We look at ten of these numeric formats in this chapter: General, 0, 0.00, #,##0, #,##0.00, $#,##0 ;($#,##0), $#,##0.00 ;($#,##0.00), 0%, 0.00%, and 0.00E+00. Two more formats have provisions to display negative numbers in red. We note this capability when we get to it. (The remaining formats available with the Number... command apply only to date and time values. Before you can use these formats, you need a little more information about date and time functions and Excel's methods for calculating dates and times. We cover these formats in Chapter 7, "Date and Time.")

Microsoft Excel also allows you to supplement the offerings of the Number... command with your own numeric formats. We show you how to create custom formats a little later in this chapter.

The General format

In Excel, the default format is General. Unless you specifically change the format of a cell, Excel displays any numbers you enter in that cell in the General format. You can think of the General format as being the "what you see is what you get" format. In other words, the General format usually shows you exactly what you have entered in a cell. If you enter the number 1234.567 in a cell with the General format, that cell displays the number 1234.567. If you enter the number –654.3 in a cell, that cell displays the number –654.3.

There is one exception to this rule: If a number is too long to be displayed in a cell in its entirety, the General format either displays the number in scientific notation or displays only a portion of the number. If the number is an integer (a number with no decimals), it is displayed in scientific notation. For example, if you enter the number 12345678901234 in a standard-width cell, the General format displays it as 1.2346E+13. If the number includes decimals, however, the General format truncates the number, displaying only the portion of the number that fits in the cell. For example, if you enter the number 123456789.12345 into a ten-character-wide cell, the General format displays it as 123456789. If you enter the number 12345678.12345, it is displayed as 12345678.1. The following table shows several other examples of the General format:

If you enter...	Excel displays...
321	321
123.456	123.456
1234567.123456789	1234567.12
9876543219876543210	9.8765E+18

Note: The most important rule to remember about formats is that they do not affect the underlying values in your cells. For example, if you enter the number 12345678.12345 into a cell with the General format, Microsoft Excel displays that number as 12345678.1. When you perform calculations on that cell, however, Excel uses the underlying value, 12345678.12345. The formula or value you see in the formula bar when you select a cell is always the value Excel uses in its calculations. (Excel alters long numbers—that is, those over 14 digits long—when it displays them in scientific notation. In such a case, you may want to check the underlying value of that number by clicking on the cell and looking at the formula bar. For instance, if you enter 9876543219876543210 into a cell and Excel displays it in scientific notation as 9.8765E+18, the formula bar displays 9876543219876500000. Your underlying value is not as precise as the number you entered into the cell.)

The Integer, Fixed, and Punctuated formats

The next four options available with the Number... command are 0, 0.00, #,##0, and #,##0.00. We call the first option *Integer*, the second *Fixed*, and the last two *Punctuated* because these are the names of the same formats in popular IBM PC spreadsheets like Lotus 1-2-3 and Symphony.

The 0 (Integer) format causes numbers to be displayed as integers (numbers without decimals). For example, if you enter the number 1234.567 in a cell and then assign that cell the 0 format, the cell displays the number 1235. (Remember, though, that the actual contents of the cell are unaffected by the format.)

The 0.00 (Fixed) format fixes at two the number of decimal places that are displayed. For example, if you enter the number 1234.567 in a cell that has the 0.00 format, Excel displays that value as 1234.57. Notice that the number is rounded to two decimal places. If the number being formatted has only one decimal place, Excel adds a zero to the number for display purposes. For example, the number 1234.5 is displayed as 1234.50 under the 0.00 format. If the number is an integer, Excel adds a decimal point and two trailing zeros after the number. For example, the number 1234 is displayed as 1234.00.

The #,##0 and #,##0.00 formats are similar to the 0 and 0.00 formats, except that they display numbers with commas between the hundreds and thousands, thousands and millions, and so on. For example, the number 1234.567 is displayed as 1,235 under the #,##0 format and as 1,234.57 under the #,##0.00 format. Like the 0.00 format, the #,##0.00 format, if necessary, adds zeros to the number to display two decimal places.

The Currency formats

Excel offers two special Currency formats: $#,##0 ;($#,##0) and $#,##0.00 ;($#,##0.00). These two formats are identical except that the first displays the number with no decimal places and the second displays the number with two decimal places. Both formats cause Excel to place a dollar sign in front of the formatted number and use commas to separate hundreds from thousands, thousands from millions, and so on. (In addition, Excel offers two extra formats that allow you to display negative currency values in red. These appear in the Format Number list box as $#,##0 ;[RED]($#,##0) and $#,##0.00 ;[RED]($#,##0.00).

Notice that both of the Currency formats have two parts and that the parts are separated by a semicolon. The first part of each format is the form that is used for positive numbers; the second part is the form for negative numbers. As you can see from the following examples, both of the Currency formats tell Excel to enclose negative numbers in parentheses.

$#,##0 ;($#,##0) format

If you enter...	Excel displays...
12345.678	$12,346
12345	$12,345
−12345.678	($12,346)
−12345	($12,345)
345	$345
−345	($345)

$#,##0.00 ;($#,##0.00) format

If you enter...	Excel displays...
12345.678	$12,345.68
12345	$12,345.00
−12345.678	($12,345.68)
−12345	($12,345.00)
345	$345.00
−345	($345.00)

The Percentage formats

The next two choices available with the Number... command, 0% and 0.00%, are called the *Percentage* formats. These formats cause Excel to display numbers as percentages. When you select one of the Percentage formats, Excel automatically shifts the decimal point of the formatted number two places to the right and adds the percent sign (%) at the end of the number. For example, the number .1234 is displayed as 12% under the 0% format and as 12.34% under the 0.00% format.

When we say the Percentage formats shift the decimal point two places to the right, what we really mean is that these formats multiply the displayed number by 100. If you think about it, you'll realize that this makes sense—after all, .1234 and 12.34% are just two ways to express exactly the same number.

If you forget that the Percentage formats shift the decimal point two places to the right, you'll get some surprising results. For example, if you want a cell to display 33%, you might be tempted to enter the number 33 in the cell, then select the 0% option from the Format Number dialog box. Instead of displaying 33%, however, Excel displays 3300%!

One way to overcome this problem is to type the percent sign directly into the formula bar. For example, if you enter the number 33% (including the percent sign), Excel reads the entry as .33 and displays the number as 33% (more on this technique later).

The Scientific (Exponential) format

The next option in the Format Number dialog box, 0.00E+00, causes numbers to be displayed in scientific, or exponential, notation with two decimal places. This format is used to display large numbers in a form that is shorter and easier to read. For example, the Exponential format could be used to display the number 987654321 as 9.88E+08.

If you are not familiar with exponential notation, the number 9.88E+08 may be confusing. However, it's quite simple. The number 9.88E+08 can be read

9.88 times 10 to the 8th power

The symbol *E* stands for the word *exponent*, a synonym here for the words *ten to the nth power*. The expression 10 to the 8th power means *ten times itself eight times*, or 100,000,000. Multiplying this value by 9.88 returns 988000000, an approximation of the original number. (Of course, like the other numeric formats, the 0.00E+00 format alters only the appearance of a number, and not the actual number itself, as long as that number is 14 digits long or less.)

You can also use Exponential format to display very small numbers. For example, the number .000000009 could be displayed as 9.00E–09. The number 9.00E–09 can be read

9 times 10 to the –9th power

This time, the expression 10 to the –9th power is the reciprocal 1 divided by 10 to the 9th power, which means *1 divided by 10 nine times*, or .000000001. Multiplying this number by 9 returns the original number: .000000009.

Typing cell entries in a numeric format

Often, you can increase efficiency by entering numbers in your worksheet exactly as you want them to appear. If you include any special formatting characters like dollar signs or commas when you enter a number in a cell, Excel automatically assigns the appropriate numeric format to that cell. For example, suppose you type $45.00 in a cell of your worksheet. Excel interprets your entry as the value 45, formatted as currency with two decimal places ($#,##0.00) in the formula bar. Only the value 45 appears in the formula bar.

Keep in mind that when you type a "preformatted" number, you also format the cell containing the number. Any new entry you make in that cell will be formatted in the same way. Even though you did not actually choose the Number... command to format the cell, Excel treats that cell just as if you had. This can lead to some confusion. For example, suppose you enter $20.00 in a cell of your worksheet.

Later, you select the same cell and overtype your original entry with the new value 10%. Excel immediately changes your display to $0.10. Although the correct value (0.1) appears in the formula bar, Microsoft Excel displays your entry as currency. To change the format to percentage, you have to choose Number... from the Format menu and select the percentage formatting you want.

Sometimes, Excel has to guess which format you mean to use. If, for example, you enter the number $4444 in a cell, Excel assigns the $#,##0 format to that cell, even though the number you typed lacks a comma. However, if you enter the number 4,444.4 in a cell, Excel assigns the General format to that cell, because it cannot find a format in its Format Number dialog box to match your entry.

When you are working with only a few cells, it may be more efficient to type your entries "in format" than it is to enter the numbers and then choose the Number... command. If you are working with more than two or three cells, however, you can actually save keystrokes and avoid typing errors by using the Number... command. In general, it's better to let Excel do the work for you, so you don't have to edit for omitted or misplaced formatting characters.

Creating your own numeric formats

Microsoft Excel allows you to create your own numeric formats. You can create a format by modifying existing formats, or you can build them from scratch. The formats you design can be variations on the standard Excel formats, or they can differ radically. You're free to create almost any format you want. You can select from the symbols in Figure 3-7 on the next page (which we have adapted from the manual) to add your own formats to the list in the Format Number dialog box. Let's look at a couple of examples of user-designed formats.

Editing existing formats

You can use Excel's existing formats as a starting point for creating your own formats. To edit a format, just choose the Number... command from the Format menu and select the format you want to change from the list in the dialog box. The format you select appears in the Format field at the bottom of the dialog box. Now you can position the insertion point in the Format field and edit the format just as you would edit the contents of a cell in the formula bar.

For example, suppose you want to create a format to display percentages with three decimal places. You can simply click the 0.00% format, place the insertion point between the 0 and % sign in the Format field, add another 0, then click OK or press Enter. Excel adds your new format to the end of the list of built-in formats. The original 0.00% format is not affected.

Symbol	Meaning
0	Digit placeholder. If the number has fewer digits on either side of the decimal point than there are 0s on either side of the decimal point in the format, Excel displays the extra 0s. If the number has more digits to the right of the decimal point than there are 0s to the right in the format, Excel rounds the number to as many decimal places as there are 0s to the right. If the number has more digits to the left of the decimal point than there are 0s to the left in the format, Excel displays the extra digits.
#	Digit placeholder. Follows the same rules as for 0 above, except that Excel does not display extra 0s if the number has fewer digits on either side of the decimal point than there are #s on either side in the format.
.	Decimal point. Determines how many digits (0s or #s) Excel displays to the right and left of the decimal point. If the format contains only #s to the left of this symbol, Excel begins numbers smaller than 1 with a decimal point. To avoid this, use 0 as the first digit placeholder to the left of a decimal point instead of #.
%	Percentage. Excel multiplies by 100 and inserts the % symbol.
,	Thousands separator. Excel separates thousands by commas if the format contains a comma surrounded by #s or 0s. In addition, a *rounding agent*. One comma at the end of a format is used by Excel to tell it to round a number left to the nearest thousandth. Two commas tells Excel to round left to the nearest millionth.
E− E+ e− e+	Scientific format. If a format contains one 0 or # to the right of an E−, E+, e−, or e+, Excel displays the number in scientific format and inserts an E or e. The number of 0s or #s to the right determines the number of digits in the exponent. Use E− or e− to place a negative sign by negative exponents. Use E+ or e+ to place a negative sign by negative exponents and a positive sign by positive exponents.
:$−+ () space	Display that character. To display a character other than one of these, use a backslash (\) before the character or enclose the character in double quotation marks (".").
\	Display the next character in the format. Excel does not display the backslash.
*	Repeat the next character in the format enough times to fill the column width. You can have only one asterisk in a format.
"Text"	Display the text inside the double quotation marks.
@	Text placeholder. When text is in the cell, the text is inserted in the format where the @ appears.

FIGURE 3-7. *These are the symbols to use when creating your own numeric formats.*

Let's look at another example. Suppose you sometimes work with British currency and you want to create a format that uses the pound sign (£). To do this, select one of the cells you want to format and choose the Number... command. Next, select the $#,##0 ;($#,##0) format. Now, point to the space immediately after the first $ in the Format field at the bottom of the Format Number dialog box, click, and press Delete to erase the $ symbol. Now, type a double quotation mark ("), press Option-3 to enter a £ symbol in the Format edit field, then type another double quotation mark.

To complete the job, use the same steps to change the second $ symbol to £. When the job is finished, press Enter. Your screen should now look something like Figure 3-8. Now, if you enter a number into the selected cell, it is displayed as pounds sterling.

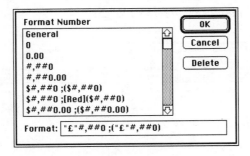

FIGURE 3-8. *You have edited an existing Currency format to create a British-pound format.*

Once you create a new format, it becomes a part of the Excel format list. When you choose the Number... command again, your new format appears at the end of the listing in the Format Number dialog box. This means that you can assign custom formats to many different cells in the worksheet without having to re-create the format each time.

When you save your worksheet, the new formats you have created are saved as well. However, Excel does not carry your special formats from one file to another unless you cut and paste a group of cells with the desired format between the worksheets. Otherwise, you add any special format you want to use to each of your worksheet files.

EXCEL *tip*

Using the Precision As Displayed option

When you format cells to display whole numbers or a fixed number of decimal places, the results of calculations that build on those cells sometimes appear to be incorrect. For example, suppose you enter the values 123.4 and 100.3 in cells A1 and A2 of your worksheet. Assuming that these cells have the General format, if you enter the formula

    =A1+A2

in cell A3, Excel returns the value 223.7. Now, suppose that you have formatted cells A1:A3 to be displayed as whole dollars (the $#,##0 format). The result of the same formula looks like this:

♣	File	Edit	Formula	Format	Data	Options	Macro	Window	▶
	A3		=A1+A2						

	A	B	C	D	E	F
1	$123					
2	$100					
3	$224					
4						
5						

Because you formatted the range A1:A3, the numbers in cells A1 and A2 are displayed as 123 and 100, and the total in cell A3 is displayed as 224. Although the actual values in these cells have not changed, the total no longer seems to make sense (123 plus 100 does not equal 224). This error occurs because Excel uses the underlying cell values in A1 (123.4) and A2 (100.3) in its calculations, but displays the numbers rounded to zero decimal places. The rounded sum of the actual values, 224, is different from the sum of the displayed values, 223.

Fortunately, Excel offers a way to get around this problem: The Precision As Displayed option in the Calculation dialog box. When you select this option, Excel uses the displayed values of cells, instead of their actual values, in calculations.

Going back to our example, if you select Calculation... from the options and then select the Precision As Displayed option after formatting cells A1 through A3, the warning *Data will permanently lose accuracy* appears. When you click OK, the problem of incorrect addition disappears. Because Precision As Displayed is being used, the formula in cell A3

    =A1+A2

adds the displayed values in cells A1 (123) and A2 (100) instead of the actual values in those cells (123.4 and 100.3). The result, 223, looks correct.

Here's how Precision As Displayed works. If you enter the formula

=1/3.71

into a cell, Excel computes the result to 14 decimal places, but displays 0.269541779 in the cell. Similarly, when you enter the PI function into a cell, Excel computes the result to 13 decimal places, but displays 3.141592654 in the cell.

The Precision As Displayed option, however, uses only as many digits as are displayed on the screen. If you use one of Excel's numeric formats to change the precision of the numbers in your worksheet, then select Precision As Displayed, Excel uses the displayed values of those cells, not the actual values of the cells, in calculations. For example, if Precision As Displayed is active and you format the result of the formula

=1/3.71

to be displayed with two fixed decimal places, Excel not only displays the result as .27, but also changes the actual result of the formula to .27.

Because the display of numbers in the General format is not fixed but varies with column width, Precision As Displayed does not affect numbers in the General format.

It is important for you to understand that, unlike the Format commands, the Precision As Displayed option can change the values in your worksheet. You may run into problems when you format numbers while the Precision As Displayed option is in effect. For example, suppose you enter the number 12345.678 in a cell and then format that cell to display currency with no decimal places. Excel changes the display to $12,346, as you might expect. If you now choose the Precision As Displayed option, Excel also changes the actual value of the entry from 12345.678 to 12346. As you've seen, when you select the Precision As Displayed option, Excel displays an alert box that says *Data will permanently lose accuracy*.

Now, suppose you want to reformat the cell to display two decimal places. You click the cell again and select $#,##0.00 in the Format Number dialog box. This time, instead of displaying $12345.68, Excel displays $12346.00. When you formatted the number the first time, Excel substituted

(continued)

continued

the formatted value (12346) for the actual value (12345.678). Because the Precision As Displayed option was active, the original numbers were permanently lost.

The same thing can happen when you enter a number "in format" while Precision As Displayed is in effect. For example, if you enter $12.009 in a cell when Precision As Displayed is active, Excel displays the number as $12.01 (assuming you meant the $##,##0.00 format) and changes the actual value in the cell to 12.009.

Building new formats from scratch

To create a new numeric format from scratch, select the cells you want to format, then choose Number... from the Format menu. Next, instead of clicking an option in the Format Number dialog box, type the format you want to use into the Format field. As soon as you begin typing, the highlighted characters in the field disappear and the characters you type appear. When you press the Enter or Return key or click the OK button, Excel displays the cells you have selected in the new format and adds your custom format to the list of numeric formats in the Format Number dialog box.

For example, suppose you decide that you want all of the entries in the range A5:A100 in a worksheet to appear in the form

Part XXX-XXXX

To assign this format to this range, you first drag through the range A5:A100, then choose the Number... command. Now, instead of selecting one of the standard options, you can type

"Part" ###-###0

When you are finished typing, press Enter. Now, you can begin making entries in column A. All you have to do is type the numbers for each part. Excel adds the word *Part* and the hyphen automatically. For example, if you click cell A10 and type 1234567, cell A10 contains

Part 123-4567

Similarly, to create a telephone number format for your worksheet, you might use the format (000) 000-0000. Then, when you enter 1234567890 into a cell having that format, Excel displays the entry as (123) 456-7890. (You will notice this entry is too long for the standard width cell. We discuss how to alter column width in Chapter 4, "Editing the Worksheet.")

The Precision As Displayed option also slows down recalculation, because Microsoft Excel rounds all of the formatted numbers as it recalculates the worksheet. This shouldn't be a problem in small worksheets, but it can be irritating in large worksheets that contain lots of formulas and formatted values.

As you can see, Precision As Displayed can be a tricky feature. However, it can also be an invaluable aid in overcoming the arithmetic problems that a worksheet's numeric formats can cause.

E X C E L

Using formatting templates

As we have said, Microsoft Excel does not carry your special formats from one file to another unless you explicitly cut and paste them between worksheets. One way around this problem is to create a blank worksheet template that contains all of the special formats you want to use. Each time you want to create a worksheet that uses these formats, you can open the template file, then use the Save As... command to save the template under a different name. By saving the template under a different name before making worksheet entries, you preserve the original template so that it can be used again and again.

You can also use this technique to create template worksheets with different "default" Font, Alignment, Column Width, and Display settings. Simply apply the formats you want to use and save them in the empty worksheet template file.

Four-way formatting

So far, we've assumed that formats apply only to positive and negative values in the cells of your worksheets. In fact, Microsoft Excel also allows you to control the display of zero values and text entries, as well as positive and negative values. In other words, Excel offers "four-way" formatting instead of just "two-way" formatting. To create a four-part custom format, you must separate the parts with semicolons (;) like this:

positive values;negative values;zero values;text values

If your custom format includes only one part, Excel applies that format to positive, negative, and zero values. If your custom format includes two parts, the first format applies to positive and zero values; the second applies only to negative values. Unless you explicitly include text-value formatting in your custom format, your instructions will have no effect on the text in cells that use your custom format. Text-value formatting instructions must always be the last formatting in your list.

For example, suppose you're creating a billing-statement worksheet and you want to format the entries in the Amount Due column to display different text, depending on the value in each cell. You might create a format like this:

"Amount Due: "$#,##0.00;"Credit: "($#,##0.00);"Let's call it even.";"Please Note: "@

The table below shows the effects of this format on various worksheet entries:

Entry	Display
12.98	Amount Due: $12.98
−12.98	Credit: ($12.98)
0	Let's call it even.
This is not a bill.	Please Note: This is not a bill.

If you want to specify a custom text-value format without changing the formats for your positive, negative, and zero values, simply enter the *text values* argument portion of the custom format alone. The @ symbol alerts Excel that the format applies only to text.

Formatting rules

As we've mentioned, Microsoft Excel does not require that you use all four formatting arguments when you define a new format. However, you need to be aware of how Excel applies the different formatting arguments when you choose to omit one or more arguments. Here are the general rules again: If you use three arguments in a format, Excel applies the first format argument to positive values, the second to negative values, and the third to zero values. If you use two arguments, the first format argument applies to positive and zero values, and the second applies to negative values. Finally, if you use only one formatting argument, Excel applies it to positive, negative, and zero values. In all of these cases, your format has no effect on text entries.

There is a method for skipping a format. If you want to skip a format, surround that argument's position in the format with semicolons. For example, if you want to prevent Excel from displaying zero values, all you need to do is to type the format argument for positive values, follow it with a semicolon, then type the format for negative values, followed by two semicolons. It's that easy. The second semicolon surrounds the position of the format argument for zero values and tells Excel to skip the display of zero values.

By using the @ symbol, you can specify a format that affects only text entries. For example, suppose you want to use the default General format for all the numbers in a column, but you want the word *Note* and a colon to precede each text entry in that column. Just create the one-part custom format

"Note: "@

and apply it to all the entries in the column. This format has no effect on your numbers.

When you want to assign a special format to text entries, you can leave out the other arguments. Again, your *text values* format argument must include the @ symbol. For example, suppose you want all your numbers to be displayed with three decimal places, and you want your text entries to be followed by the initials *ARH*. You could accomplish this with the custom format

0.000 @" ARH"

If you create a format that has all four arguments, it's not necessary to include the @ symbol in the *text values* argument. Excel assumes that the fourth argument in a format applies to text. However, when you want to include text as part of your *positive values*, *negative values*, or *zero values* format arguments, you must include the @ sign at the place in the value format argument where you want the text to appear. Otherwise, Excel displays the argument alone, without the text.

Hiding entries

If you want to hide a particular type of entry, you create a format that includes a semicolon as a placeholder for that entry type's argument. For example, the format

#,##0 ;(#,##0);;"Note: "@

uses a semicolon as a placeholder for the *zero values* argument. When you apply this format in your worksheet, Excel hides all zero values in the formatted range.

Since an extra semicolon causes Excel to hide certain entries, you cannot "skip" a format argument by entering an extra semicolon as a placeholder then entering the format argument for the next type of entry. Also, if you're creating a one-part, two-part, or three-part format, don't include a semicolon at the end of the format unless you want to hide some entries. For example, if you create a format with three arguments followed by a semicolon, such as

#.00 ;(#.00);0.00;

Excel hides any text entries in your formatted range. If you want to skip the *text values* argument of a format without affecting text entries in your formatted cells, simply omit the final semicolon.

The following table shows the different combinations of hidden and displayed values that you can create by including extra semicolons in your custom formats:

This format...	Tells Excel to hide...	Tells Excel to display...
;;;	Positive, negative, zero, and text values	No values
; or ;;	Positive, negative, and zero values	Text values only
;-0.00;;	Positive, zero, and text values,	Negative values only
;;0.00;	Positive, negative, and text values,	Zero values only
0.00;;;	Negative, zero, and text values	Positive values only
;;0.00	Positive and negative values	Zero and text values
;-0.00;	Positive and zero values	Negative and text values
;0.00;0.00;	Positive and text values	Negative (without minus signs) and zero values
0.00;;	Negative and zero values	Positive and text values
0.00;;0.00;	Negative and text values	Positive and zero values
0.00;-0.00;;	Zero and text values	Positive and negative values
;0.00;0.00	Positive values	Negative (without minus signs), zero, and text values
0.00;	Negative values	Positive, zero, and text values
0.00;-0.00;	Zero values	Positive, negative, and text values
0.00;0.00;0.00;	Text values	Positive, negative, and zero values

Formatting financial statements

Microsoft Excel 2.2 offers the ability to display numbers rounded to the nearest thousand, million, and so forth. Because financial statements for large organizations often display rounded numbers, this type of formatting is referred to as financial-statement formatting. You achieve this type of formatting in Excel by creating a custom format that ends with one or more commas. Each comma tells Excel to move the decimal point in a number three digits to the left and to display the rounded result.

For example, suppose your worksheet contains the number 2,345,678. You would like to display this number rounded to the nearest thousand. First, you must create a custom format that ends with one comma, such as

#,##0,

To create this format, select the cell or range you want to format and choose Number… from the Format menu. In the Number dialog box, click the #,##0 format to select it. Then, in the Format field, type a comma at the end of the format. Finally, click OK to close the dialog box. When you apply this format, Excel rounds the number you enter. For example, it displays the number 2,345,678 as 2,346.

If you would like to display this number rounded to the nearest million, simply add another comma to your custom format, like this

#,##0,,

This format causes Excel to display a 2 in the formatted cell. The following table gives several more examples of how you can use the financial-statement formatting feature to change the display of numbers in the worksheet:

This format...	Applied to this value...	Displays this result...
$#,##0.00,	2345678	$2,345.68
$#,##0.00,,	2345678	$2.35
$#,##0,,	2345678	$2
$#,##0,,,	2345678	$0

Notes about custom formats

Including one or more commas in a format is similar to using the ROUND function whose *decimal places* argument is a –3 (one comma), a –6 (two commas), or some other negative multiple of 3. Unlike the ROUND function, however, the comma formatting feature does not change the underlying value of your cell entries. Thus, with financial-statement formatting, you can display numbers in their rounded form without losing the precision of the number in its full form. For example, suppose you've used financial-statement formatting to display the value 3,659,780 as $3. If you click the cell that contains this formatted value, Excel displays 3659780 in the formula bar.

When you create a custom format that uses one or more commas, be sure that you include the comma in both the *positive values* and *negative values* format arguments. If you don't, Excel rounds some of your numbers and not others. For example, suppose you've created the custom format

$#,##0, ;($#,##0)

Notice that the second argument in this format does not include a comma at the end. When you apply this format in your worksheet, Excel displays all positive values rounded to the nearest thousand but continues to display negative values in their full form.

Deleting custom formats

To delete a format from the Format Number dialog box, click the format you want to erase and click Delete. You can delete only those formats that you have created. Excel does not allow you to delete the first 21 built-in selections in the Format Number dialog box.

Adding color to your formats

In addition to controlling the display of numeric values, the Number... command can change the color of selected cell entries. Excel gives you eight color options: red, green, blue, yellow, magenta, cyan, black, and white. This color capability gives you tremendous flexibility for emphasizing selected areas of your worksheet. For example, you might use different colors to help distinguish the categories of information in a worksheet model, or you might apply a color to the Total cells to make them stand out from the rest of your worksheet data.

To change the color of an entry, simply type the name of the color you want, in brackets, in front of the definition of the format. For example, suppose you want the totals in row 17 of the worksheet shown in Figure 3-2 to be displayed in blue. Because you also want these values to appear in the currency format with two decimal places, you can simply edit Excel's built-in $#,##0.00 format to create a custom format, like this:

    [Blue]$#,##0.00 ;($#,##0.00)

This format tells Excel to display positive values in blue. Text and negative values still appear in the program's default color, black.

Even if you want to use Excel's default General format to display your worksheet entries, you can specify color options for different types of entries by typing the colors you want to use in the Format field. For example, the custom format

    [Blue];[Red];[Yellow];[Green]

tells Excel to display positive values in blue, negative values in red, zero values in yellow, and text in green. Of course, you can add color to your own custom formats as well.

Although the color capability is designed primarily for those who use a color monitor, you can assign colors even if you use a monochrome monitor. Of course, with the exception of black and white, any colors you assign won't show up until you display your worksheet on a color monitor or print it with a color printer.

Aligning entries

The Alignment... command tells Microsoft Excel whether you want the contents of the cell to be right-aligned, centered, or left-aligned. This command also allows you to tell Excel to repeat a series of characters within the cell. Excel offers five cell-alignment options: General, Left, Center, Right, and Fill.

The General format

General is the default alignment option. When you use the General format, cells that contain numeric values are always right-aligned, and cells that contain text are always left-aligned.

The Left, Right, and Center formats

The Left, Right, and Center options do exactly what they say: They cause the contents of the selected cells to be aligned to the left side, the right side, or the center of the cell. For example, look at the eight entries in the worksheet in Figure 3-9. The entries in cells B3 and D3 have the General alignment: The number in cell B3 is right-aligned, while the text in cell D3 is left-aligned. The number in cell B4 is left-aligned, and the number in cell B6 is centered. The text in cell D5 is right-aligned, and the text in cell D6 is centered.

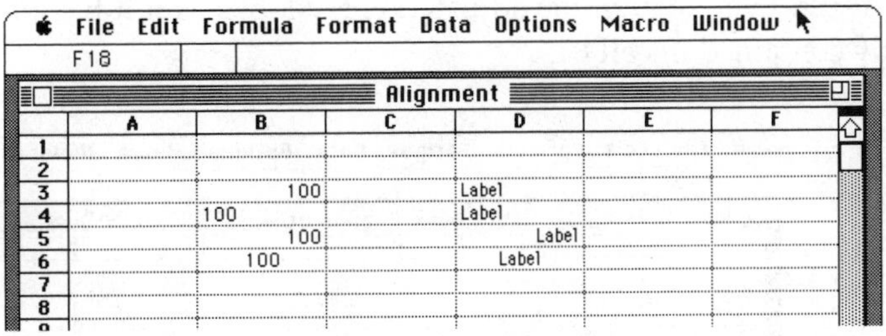

FIGURE 3-9. *We've formatted numbers and text with different alignment options.*

The Alignment... command has some interesting effects on long text entries. For example, look at the three text entries in Figure 3-10. All three entries have the default General alignment. Now, suppose you click cell B3, choose the Alignment... command, and select the Center option. Figure 3-11 shows the result.

Notice that, in order to center the entry in cell B3, Excel has shifted the text entry so that it appears to start in cell A3. In fact, the entry is still stored in cell B3.

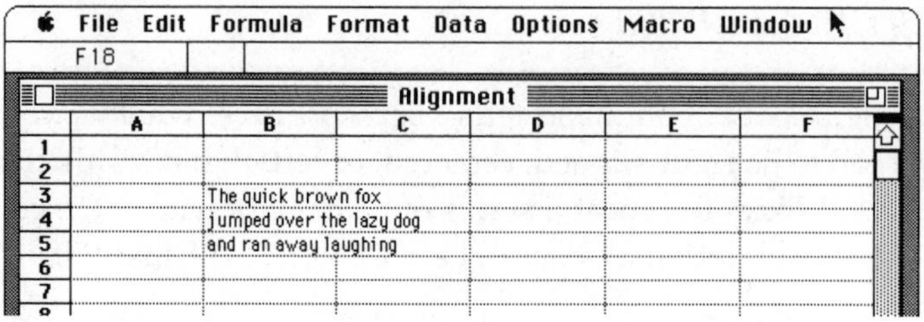

FIGURE 3-10. *We used the General format to align these text entries.*

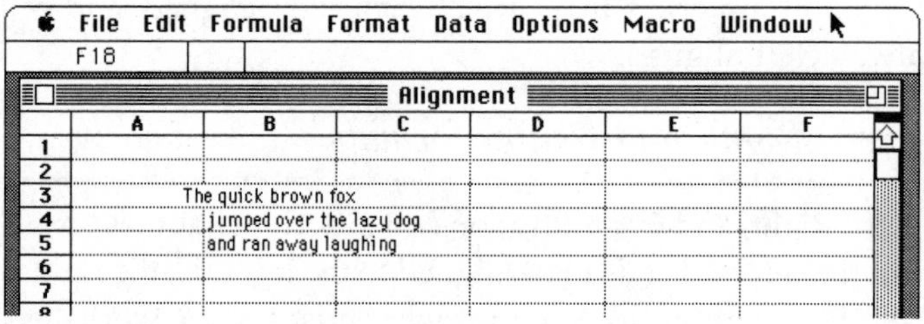

FIGURE 3-11. *We used the Center option of the Alignment... command to center the first line of text.*

Now, suppose you decide to right-align the text in cell B4. To do this, you click that cell and select the Right option in the Alignment dialog box. Figure 3-12 shows the result. Even though the adjusted entry looks as if it begins in cell A4, it is actually contained in cell B4.

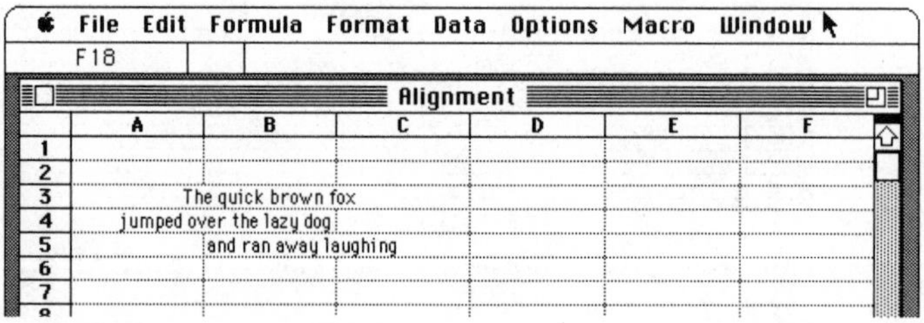

FIGURE 3-12. *We used the Right option of the Alignment... command to align the second line of text.*

Of course, the result of these two commands would be different if the cells to the left of B3:B5 also contained entries. For example, if cell A3 contained an entry, then Excel would not have been able to display the long, centered entry in B3 in its entirety. As shown in Figure 3-13, the entry in cell B3 would be centered, but the first few characters of text would not be visible.

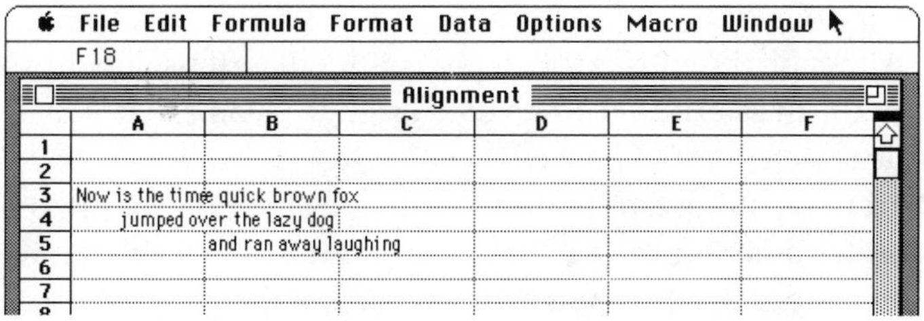

FIGURE 3-13. *The entry in B3 is truncated when there is an entry in A3.*

Microsoft Excel is the only spreadsheet program we know of that allows you this much flexibility in aligning text entries. The ability to center a text entry in a cell, without regard to the cell's boundaries, is very powerful and useful.

The Fill option

The Fill option tells Excel to repeat the entry you make in a cell until the repeated entry fills the entire cell. For example, suppose cell A12 of your worksheet contains a formula that totals the entries in cells A1 through A10. You want to enter a row of dashes (hyphens) in cell A11 to separate the values in cells A1:A10 from the total in cell A12. You can do this by typing a dash (-) in cell A11, pressing Enter, and choosing the Alignment… command. When you click the Fill option in the Alignment dialog box, Excel repeats the dash across cell A11. The resulting worksheet looks like Figure 3-14.

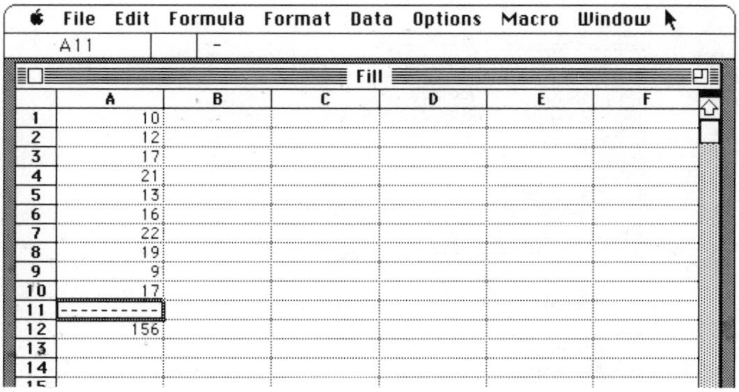

FIGURE 3-14. *We used the Fill option of the Alignment… command to repeat a character across a cell.*

Notice that, although cell A11 seems to contain a series of ten dashes, the formula bar at the top of the screen reveals that the actual entry in the cell is a single dash. Like the other options contained within Format-menu commands, the Alignment command's Fill option affects only the appearance, and not the actual contents, of a cell.

Although the entries you repeat with Fill will usually be single characters like a dash (-), an asterisk (*), or an equal sign (=), you can use this command to repeat multicharacter entries as well.

You may think that in many situations it would be almost as easy to type the dashes (or other repeating characters) as it is to use Fill. However, the Fill option has one important advantage: If you expand the width of column A of Figure 3-14, Excel automatically expands the dashes in cell A11 to fill the entire cell. You do not have to worry about adjusting filled cells to correspond to their column width.

Assigning borders

The Border... command lets you enhance the appearance of your worksheets by adding solid-line borders and shading to cells and ranges in your worksheet. Borders can be very effective tools for dividing your worksheet into defined areas or for drawing attention to important cells.

To assign a border format to a single cell, click the cell and choose the Border... command from the Format menu. You'll see the dialog box shown in Figure 3-15. As you can see, the Border dialog box offers six choices, Outline, Left, Right, Top, Bottom, and Shade, which you can combine to create any combination of borders. The effect of each of these options is what you would expect. The Outline option places a solid line on all four sides of the selected cell or range of cells. The Left, Right, Top, and Bottom options place solid lines across their respective edges. The Shade option adds shading to a cell or a range of cells.

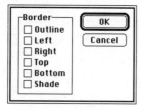

FIGURE 3-15. *This is the Border dialog box.*

To illustrate, let's add a set of double dividing lines beneath a row of cells, to set a group of worksheet totals apart from the data above. First, select the row you want to set apart, then choose the Insert command from the Edit menu, if necessary, to add a blank row between that row and the rows above it. Next, select the appropriate cell in the blank row, open the Border dialog box, and click both the Top and Bottom options. When you click OK to close the dialog box, you'll see a border above and below the row you selected. You may also want to decrease the height of the row to bring the border lines closer together. (In the section called "Controlling row height," later in this chapter, you'll learn how to alter the heights of the cells in your worksheets.)

Similarly, to create a double dividing line between columns in your worksheet, use the Insert... command to add an extra column (if necessary), select the appropriate cell in the blank column, and click the Left and Right border options to create a line on both sides of that column. Then, decrease the width of the column and bring the border lines closer together.

If you want to place a solid border around cell B10 of your worksheet, click cell B10, choose the Border... command, select the Outline option, and click OK. Figure 3-16 shows the result of the Border... command's Outline option: the solid-line border around cell B10.

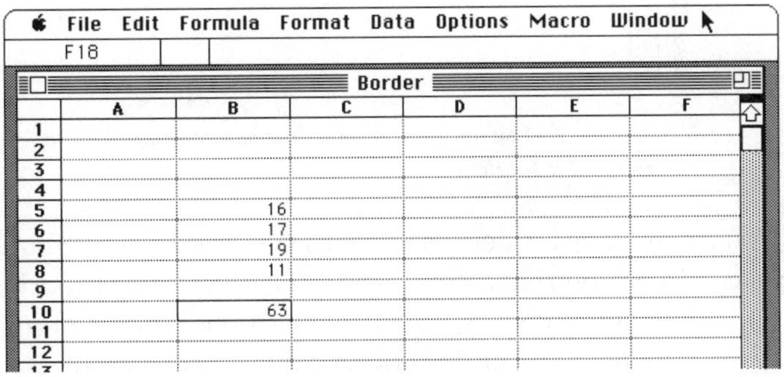

FIGURE 3-16. *You have used the Outline option of the Border... command to put a solid-line border around cell B10.*

If you rechoose the Border... command while cell B10 is still active, you'll see that Microsoft Excel has deselected the Outline option and has instead selected the Left, Right, Top, and Bottom options. The Outline option simply serves as a shortcut for outlining a cell or range without having to select each side of the border manually. This feature is particularly important when you want to place borders around a range.

For example, if you select cells B5:B10 in Figure 3-16, choose the Border... command, and then select Outline, Excel creates a solid line around the entire range of cells, as shown in Figure 3-17 on the next page. Notice that when you use the Outline option with a multicell range, Excel does not place border lines within the range. To do that, you'd have to select the Left, Right, Top, and Bottom options. Instead, Excel assigns the appropriate Border formats to each of the cells along the perimeter of the selected range: Cell B5 carries the Top, Left, and Right options; cells B6 through B9 carry the Left and Right options; and cell B10 carries the Bottom, Left, and Right options.

As you can also see in Figure 3-17, you can shade a cell to add emphasis to your worksheet. For example, you might use shading to set apart worksheet totals or to draw attention to cells in which you want the user to make an entry in a worksheet template. You apply the Shade option in the same way you apply the other border options.

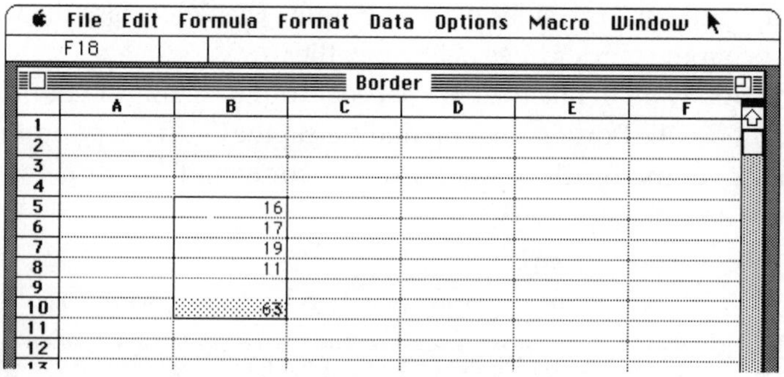

FIGURE 3-17. *You have put a solid-line border around a range of cells and shaded a single cell.*

You can remove borders as easily as you create them. Simply select the cell or range, choose the Border... command, and select the appropriate option to deactivate it. When you click OK, Excel removes the borders from the selected cells. However, to remove an Outline border, you need to vary the procedure. When you select an outlined range, you'll notice that several options in the Border dialog box determine the Border format in the range. The simplest way to remove the formats is to select the entire outlined cell or range, then choose the Clear... command, selecting the Format option that will remove all the border formats you applied earlier. Bear in mind, however, that any number, alignment, or font formatting you have applied with the Format-menu commands will also be lost. Use the Clear... command with caution.

You may have noticed that the borders in these examples are barely visible. As you'll see in a few pages, you can increase the effectiveness of cell borders by using the Display... command from the Options menu to turn off the dotted-line worksheet grid.

Controlling column width

Excel's default column width is ten numeric characters. However, this does not necessarily mean that each cell in your worksheet can display only ten characters. Because Microsoft Excel uses proportional fonts rather than fixed-pitch fonts, each character takes up a different amount of space in the worksheet. For example, an *l* takes up less room than an *M* or a *W*. Similarly, bold characters take up more space than plain characters. The ten-character standard width is simply an approximation of the number of numeric characters that will fit in each standard-width column.

Often, you'll find that the standard ten-character width is not wide enough to display the complete contents of a cell. When you make a text entry into a cell that is not wide enough, Excel simply lets the entry run over into the cell to the right. If there is an entry in the adjacent cell, however, Excel truncates the display of the text entry. For example, consider cells A1 and A3 in Figure 3-18. Both cells contain the text entry

This is an especially long label

Notice that the text entry in cell A1 overlaps cell B1, but the text entry in cell A3 is cut short because there is an entry in cell B3. Although the underlying label in A3 is not affected, important information is obscured.

When you enter a long number into a narrow column that has the General numeric format, Excel displays the number in scientific notation. For example, cell A5 in Figure 3-18 contains the numeric entry 12345678912345. Notice that Excel displays this number as

1.2346E+13

In addition, when you assign a format to a cell, its entry may become too long to be completely displayed. When this occurs, Excel displays a series of pound signs (#) to indicate that the formatted entry is too long to be displayed in its entirety. For

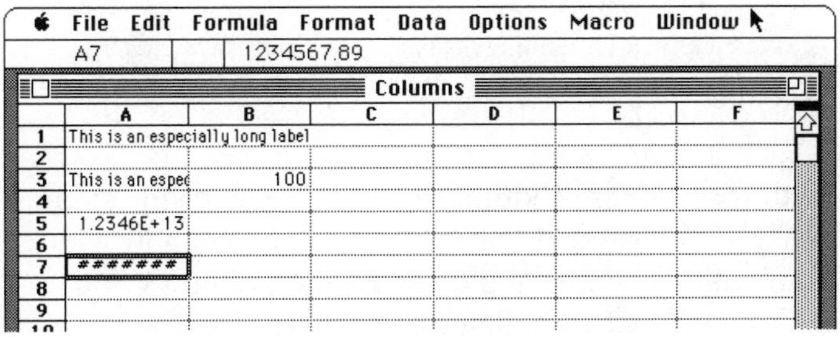

FIGURE 3-18. *This figure shows three ways Excel displays text and number entries that are too long to fit the width of the column.*

example, cell A7 in Figure 3-18 contains the number 1234567.89, which has been assigned the $#,##0.00 ;($#,##0.00) format. All you can see in cell A7, however, is a series of pound signs.

The best way to overcome these problems is to change the width of the column or columns that contain the long entries. Excel offers two ways to control the width of cells in your worksheet. The first method lets you modify column widths one column at a time; the second lets you change the widths of selected columns or set a new column width for the entire worksheet.

For example, suppose you want to change the width of column A in Figure 3-18. Just place your pointer on the vertical line in the column header between columns A and B. As you can see in Figure 3-19, the pointer changes shape when it nears the vertical line. The double arrows on this special pointer indicate that you can move the pointer to the right to widen the column, or to the left to narrow the column. To widen the column, hold the mouse button down and drag the pointer until the divider line between columns A and B falls to the right of the longest entry in column A (cells A1 and A3 in the example). When you release the mouse button, Excel automatically extends column A to the point that you indicated. Figure 3-20 shows the screen at this point. Notice that all of the entries in column A are now fully displayed, except the value in cell A5. To display in cell A5 the entire number 12345678912345 that appears in the formula bar, you need to assign the 0 number format to cell A5. The default number format, General, causes the number to appear in Scientific format.

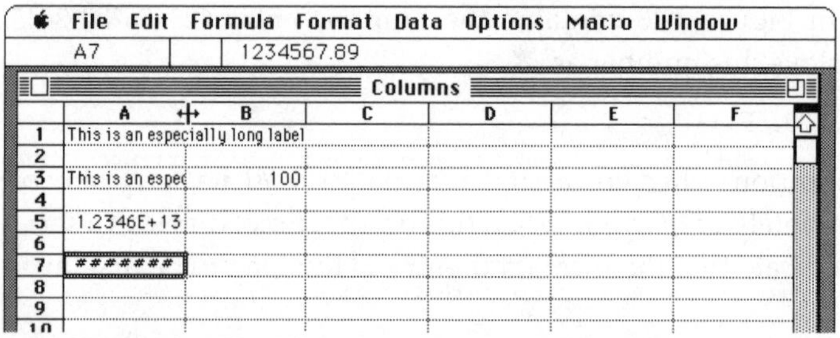

FIGURE 3-19. *Aiming the pointer at the vertical header bar causes the pointer to change shape, indicating that you can drag the bar to the right or left.*

With the Column Width… command, you can find out exactly how wide a column is in just one step. For example, to find out how wide column A is, you can click any cell in column A and choose the Column Width… command from the Format menu. You'll see a dialog box like the one shown in Figure 3-21. Notice that the column width setting for column A is now substantially wider than the default width of ten characters.

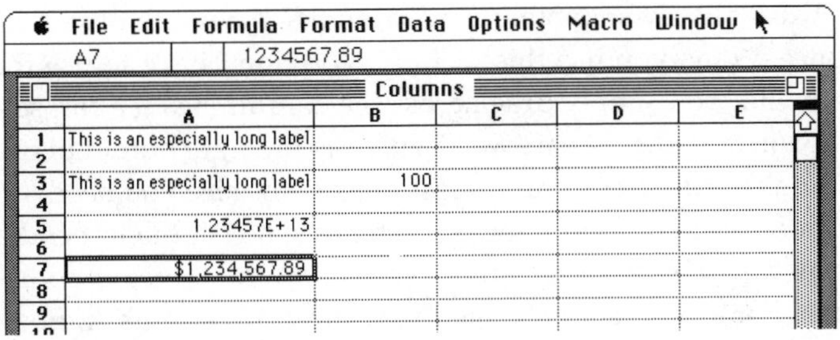

FIGURE 3-20. *The long text and number entries can now be displayed in their entirety.*

FIGURE 3-21. *This is the Column Width dialog box.*

You can also use the Column Width... command to change the width of a column. All you have to do is click any cell in that column, choose the Column Width... command from the Format menu, and specify the new width by typing the desired number of characters. You can use this command to set the width of any column to a number of characters from 0 through 255. You can also indicate a column width in decimal fractions.

For example, suppose you want to change the width of column A to 25. To do this, click any cell in column A and choose the Column Width... command. Excel displays the Column Width dialog box showing the current column width. To change the width of column A to 25, just type 25, and then click OK or press Enter. The old width setting is erased as soon as you begin typing.

If you want to restore the width of a column to the default, you can click any cell in that column, choose the Column Width... command, and click the Standard Width box. As soon as you click Standard Width, Excel enters the standard column width, 10, in the Column Width box. When you click OK or press Enter, Excel sets the width of the column to 10.

To change the widths of several adjacent columns at once, drag across any cells in the columns whose widths you want to change and use the Column Width... command. If all of the columns you select have the same width, Excel displays that width in the dialog box. If the columns you select have different widths, the Column Width field is blank. Either way, you can change the width of all of the selected columns by clicking the Standard Width option or entering a new column width, then pressing Enter or clicking OK.

Excel gives you another way to change the width of several adjacent columns at once. When you use this method, you don't have to use the Column Width... command. You simply drag across the column header bar, selecting the columns you want to widen or narrow. Then, drag the right border of one of the highlighted columns until the column corresponds to the size you need. (You can monitor the width of your column in the cell reference box at the left end of the formula bar.) When you release the column border, all the selected columns have the same width. For example, to change the widths of columns A, B, and C in your worksheet to 20, you select the headers for columns A, B, and C. Then, you drag the right column border for one of the columns—B's border will do—until the cell reference box indicates 20.00. Excel expands all three columns to 20 characters.

If you want to change the width of several nonadjacent columns at once, click any cell in the first column, hold down the Command key, and click cells in the remaining columns. Set the new column width just as you would for single or adjacent columns. For example, to change the widths of columns A, C, and E in your worksheet to 20, click a cell in column A, then, holding down the Command key, click a cell in each of columns C and E. Next choose Column Width... and type 20 in the Column Width dialog box, then click OK or press Enter. Excel expands all three columns to 20 characters each.

If you want to change the widths of all of the columns in the worksheet, you must select all of the columns in the worksheet. To select all of the columns, click one of the row headers at the left edge of the worksheet. Figure 3-22 shows the result of clicking the header for row 6. Once you have selected the columns, choose the Column Width... command and define the width you want. When you click OK or press Enter, Excel changes the width of every column in the worksheet.

Interestingly, there is no way to change the standard column width setting. Even if you change the width of every column in the worksheet, this new width does not become the standard width. The standard column width remains 10.

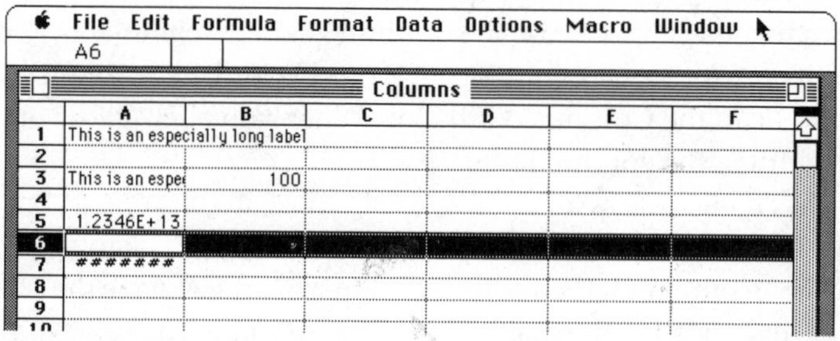

FIGURE 3-22. *Clicking one of the row headers automatically selects all of the columns in the worksheet.*

Controlling row height

Excel's default row height varies according to the default font you select for your worksheet. In addition, the size of the largest letter in a row determines the standard height for that row. For example, when a worksheet uses the default font, Geneva 10-point, the default row height is 13 points. If you apply the Helvetica 12-point font to a cell, however, the height of that entire row changes to 14 points.

Like font size, row height is measured in points. One point equals approximately $1/72$ inch. Thus, to make a row 1 inch high, use a row height setting of 72. To make a row $1/2$ inch high, use a row setting of 36.

Adjusting the height of a row is similar to adjusting the width of a column. When you point to the horizontal bar under a row header, the pointer takes on the double-arrow shape that allows you to drag the row header up or down, to make the row taller or narrower to suit your worksheet's needs.

As with the Column Width... command, you can use the Row Height... command to change the height of several adjacent or nonadjacent rows at once. Simply select at least one cell in each of the rows you want to change and choose the Row Height... command to access the dialog box shown in Figure 3-23. If you want to change the height of all the rows in your worksheet, click one of the row headers before you choose the Row Height... command. If all the rows you select are the same height, that height appears in the Row Height field. If the rows are different heights, the field is blank. Either way, you can change the height of all the selected rows by entering a new row height, and then clicking OK or pressing Enter.

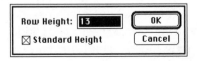

FIGURE 3-23. *You have used the Row Height dialog box to change the height of selected rows in your worksheet.*

To restore the height of a row to its default, select any cell in that row, choose the Row Height... command, and select the Standard Height box. As soon as you select Standard Height, Excel displays the standard row height for the font you're using in the Row Height field. At that point, click OK or press Enter.

Format commands versus Options commands

In addition to the formatting commands available on the Format menu, Excel's Options menu offers three other important formatting commands: the Standard Font... (which we discuss with the Font... command from the Format menu), the Display..., and the Workspace... commands.

You may find the relationship between the Format and Options commands a bit confusing at first. After all, it seems odd that Excel's formatting commands should be divided between two menus. However, the distinction between the Format commands and the Options commands is really very simple: Format commands control the appearance of individual cells, while Options commands control the overall appearance of your worksheet. In other words, Format commands are cell-specific, affecting only the cells you select. Options commands, on the other hand, are global, affecting every cell in your worksheet.

E X C E L *Tip*

Hiding a column or row

You may, on occasion, want to hide certain information in your worksheet. For example, suppose you are developing a departmental budget and you need to list employee salaries and benefits in your worksheet in order to forecast next year's personnel expenditures. You may want to display overall salary information without revealing sensitive information about individual employees. Unfortunately, Excel doesn't offer any built-in way to hide selected cells in your worksheet. (The Hidden option in the Cell Protection dialog box only hides formulas from display in the formula bar. A cell's displayed values are still visible.)

In order to hide information in a column on your worksheet, you must set the width of the column that contains the sensitive information to 0. You can do this by dragging the vertical bar between column headers to the left until you have narrowed the column to nothing, or by entering 0 in the Column Width dialog box. Once the width of the column is set to 0, the column is almost completely ignored by Excel. If you select a range that includes the hidden column, and then press Enter to move the active cell marker from cell to cell, the marker skips over the hidden column. In addition, the column letter disappears from the top of the worksheet. For example, if you hide column C in your worksheet, the column header line reads A, B, D, and so on.

Redisplaying a column you have hidden can be a bit tricky. Because

Using fonts

Microsoft Excel has two commands that allow you to customize the font types, sizes, styles, and colors in your worksheets. One command, the Standard Font... command on the Options menu, lets you change the default font for the entire worksheet. The other, the Font... command on the Format menu, lets you change the display of fonts in individual cells or in a range of cells. These two closely related commands give Excel a flexibility not available in other spreadsheet programs. In this section, we first focus on the worksheet as a whole with the Standard Font... command, then discuss the Font... command.

The Standard Font... command

The Standard Font... command, located on the Options menu, allows you to choose the font, type size, style, and color Excel uses to display your worksheet entries. As we've said, the Standard Font... command is global and affects every cell.

the column does not appear on the screen, there is no way to select it. This makes it impossible to use the Column Width... command or to reopen the column with the pointer. To open a column you have hidden, drag across the column headers on both sides of the hidden column. After the range is selected, you can use the Column Width... command to assign a width greater than 0 to the columns in the range. When you click OK, all the selected columns, including the hidden one, display the width you set in the Column Width dialog box. At this point, you can reset the columns surrounding the previously hidden one to their previous widths.

You use the same type of procedure to hide a row. To hide information in a row on your worksheet, set the height of the row that contains the sensitive information to 0. You can do this by dragging up the horizontal bar between row headers until you've narrowed the row to nothing, or by entering 0 in the Row Height dialog box.

Redisplaying a row that you have hidden is similar to the procedure for redisplaying a column. Because you can't select the row, you must select the rows on both sides of the hidden row. Then, you can use the Row Height... command to reset a uniform height for the three rows. After you reset the row height, click OK in the Row Height dialog box, and the hidden row reappears, you might find that you have to adjust the heights of the two rows surrounding the previously hidden one.

When you choose the Standard Font... command, Excel displays the dialog box shown in Figure 3-24. Notice that this box contains two list boxes: Font and Size. The Font list tells you which fonts are available; that is, the fonts that are installed in your System file. The Size list contains the recommended type sizes for the font selected in the Font list. Below each of these list boxes are fields that allow you to type in the font or size you want to use as the default in your worksheet. You can change the default font and size either by choosing the font and size you want to use from the lists or by typing the font name and the size into the fields.

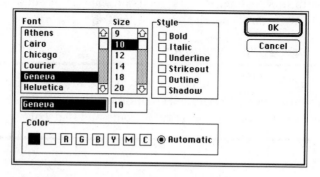

FIGURE 3-24. *This is the Standard Font dialog box.*

There can be only one default font and size in a given worksheet. If you want to use different fonts and sizes in different parts of your worksheet, you need to use the Font... command. In addition, whatever settings you select in the Standard Font dialog box apply only to the active worksheet. If the desktop contains several worksheets when you choose this command, the font changes in the active worksheet only.

Suppose you want to change the standard font in your worksheet from 10-point Geneva (the default) to 14-point New York. To do this, choose the Standard Font... command, then select New York from the list of fonts. Next, select the point size 14 from the available list. Finally, click OK.

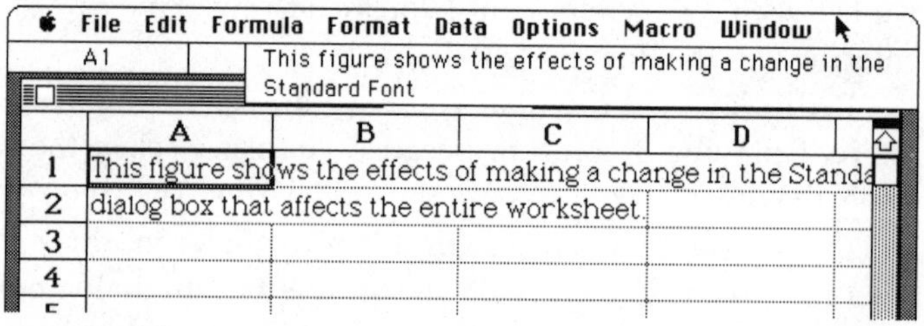

FIGURE 3-25. *You have used the Standard Font... command to change to the 14-point New York font.*

As you can see in Figure 3-25, Excel is now using the New York font instead of the Geneva font to display the contents of the worksheet. Notice that changing the font setting changes the appearance of every cell in the worksheet. Also, notice that the size of each cell has increased to accommodate the new, larger letters. Fortunately, you do not need to adjust your column width or row height to accommodate different font sizes. Excel automatically adjusts the size of your cells in proportion to the size you select. The only time the Standard Font... command won't adjust cell sizes to accommodate different font sizes is when you've previously set the Row Height to a specific height. If this is the case, your larger fonts may appear cut off.

The Style check boxes in the Standard Font dialog box allow you to use six different styles as the default styles for the entries in your worksheet. You can even combine these styles if you want. For example, the entries in your worksheet can be displayed both in bold and italic. To do this, you choose the Standard Font... command, click the Bold and Italic style check boxes, then click OK. Excel adds the bold and italic styles to the default style of the worksheet.

Suppose you want to change the standard font style in a worksheet from normal to italic. To do this, choose the Standard Font... command, then click the Italic style check box. Next, click OK. Figure 3-26 displays the new default style for the worksheet. The result is interesting. You'll notice that changes in the Standard Font dialog box do affect the entire worksheet. Selecting the italic style changes the display of the row and column headings as well as the entries in all the cells.

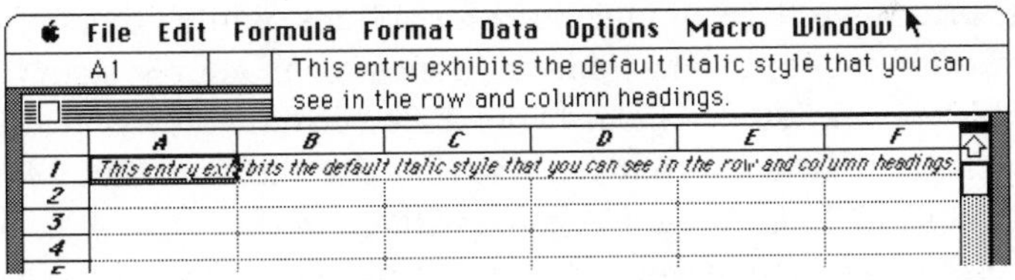

FIGURE 3-26. *This worksheet shows a default italic style setting.*

Usually you won't want to use any style other than normal as the default. Keep in mind that when you want to display important information, you are generally interested in the impact of your data. You don't want to call too much attention to your worksheet's style. You may want to vary the style of some cells or ranges but only to emphasize their importance in relation to the other cells. For that reason, it's better to use the Font... command to set the style of specific cells and ranges.

The Standard Font... command also allows you to select the default color Excel uses to display the text in your worksheet. You have six color choices plus black and white. Choosing a color in the Standard Font dialog box is as easy as choosing a style. You merely click the color you want, then click OK to close the dialog box. Excel adds your color choice to the display of your worksheet.

If you are working with a monochrome monitor, you see no colors on your screen; however, any color change you make is visible if you view the worksheet on a color monitor. If you select white for a worksheet displayed on a monochrome monitor, you see nothing.

Clicking the Automatic button applies the system font color to your text; that is, the color that works best with your system's color settings.

Points to remember

If you have already used the Font... command to format some cells in your worksheet before you use the Standard Font... command to change the default font and size, the Standard Font... command does not affect the entries in those cells. For example, suppose you have used the Font... command to assign the bold style to the entry in cell A10. If you later use the Standard Font... command to make the default style italic, the entry in cell A10 will not be displayed in italic but in bold. If you want to change the style of the entry in cell A10, you'll need to use the Font... command either to change the style of that cell or to return to the cell to the default style.

Remember that the Size list in the Standard Font dialog box contains the recommended font sizes for the font currently selected in the Font list. When you select different fonts in the Font list, Excel displays different font sizes in the Size list box. The list contains only sizes that are explicitly defined for each font. Some fonts offer several recommended size options, while others offer only a few, and some offer only one. (The fonts and font sizes in your System file determine what choices you see in the Standard Font dialog box. If you want to add or remove some fonts and sizes from your System file, use the Font/DA Mover on one of the Macintosh Utilities disks that came with your Macintosh.)

From time to time, you may want to use a size that has not been defined for the selected font. In fact, you can bypass Excel's size list and select any size between 1 and 127 for any font. Simply choose the Standard Font... command and make sure the font you want is selected. Then, instead of clicking one of the size options offered by Excel, type the size you want in the Size field and click the OK button or press Enter. When you use an undefined font size, Excel approximates the size as well as it can. However, the results might look a bit ragged. Because of this questionable quality, you're probably better off accepting Excel's suggested sizes in most situations.

For example, if you want to change the font in the previous example from 14-point New York to 10-point Athens, you can choose the Standard Font... command, select Athens from the Font dialog box, type 10 in the Size field, then click

OK. The result is shown in Figure 3-27. Notice that the characters in this figure are ragged compared to the characters in the previous example. This occurs because 10-point Athens is not a standard system font.

As we said before, you can type a font name into the Font field under the Font list box in the Standard Font dialog box. However, if you happen to type the name of a font that isn't installed in your System folder, Excel reverts to Geneva, the default font. Excel does not try to approximate a noninstalled font, nor does it leave your worksheet without an appropriate font in which to display your data.

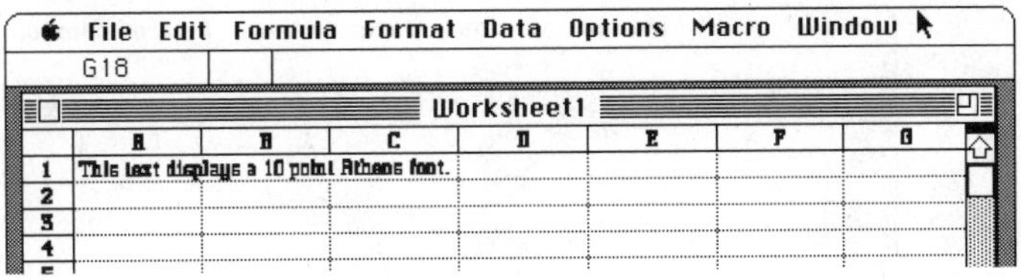

FIGURE 3-27. *This worksheet is displayed in 10-point Athens.*

The Font… command

The Font… command lets you control the font type, size, and style of worksheet entries in selected cells or ranges. You can use this command to change the font and size of selected cells in your worksheet to any that are stored in your System file and to display the contents of selected cells in bold, italic, underline, strikeout, outline, or shadow styles. Additionally, you can alter the color of selected cells to draw attention to important entries in the worksheet, such as column titles or totals. The Font… command is similar to the Standard Font… command we discussed in the previous section. In fact, when you first open the Font dialog box, the only difference you see between it and the Standard Font dialog box is one check box, Standard Font, under the Cancel button. (We explain this feature in a moment.)

It's very easy to understand the distinction between the Font… command and the Standard Font… command. The Font… command controls the font, size, style, and color of entries in a single cell or in a range of cells you've selected. The Standard Font… command, as we noted, governs the display of the same qualities, but for the entire worksheet—except in one case. When you choose the Font… command and change the font description for a cell or a range, the Font dialog box settings override the standard font settings; that is, the settings in the Font dialog box override the worksheet's default settings for the selected cell or range. To return the call or range to the standard font settings, select the cells, choose the Font…

command, then click the Standard Font check box. When you click OK, the cell or range returns to the worksheet's default settings selected in the Standard Font dialog box.

Let's consider how the Font... command works. Look at the five short sentences in column B in Figure 3-28. Suppose you want to assign the italic style to the entry in cell B2. To do this, select that cell, then choose Font... from the Format menu to bring the Font dialog box shown in Figure 3-29 into view. To select italic, click the Italic style option, then click OK.

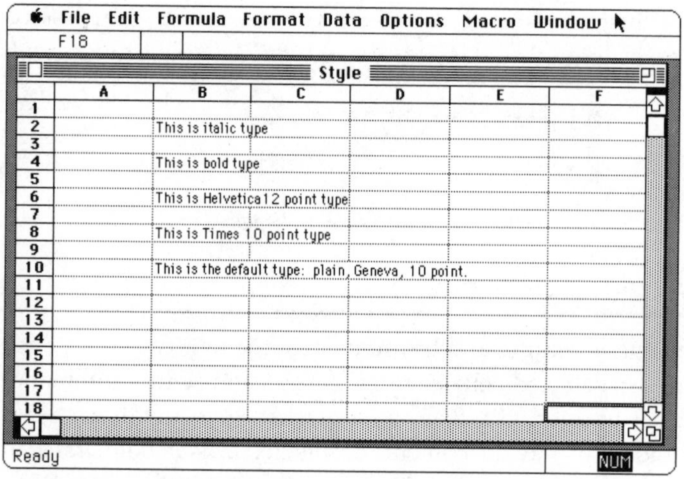

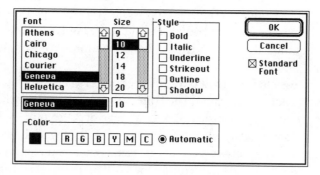

FIGURE 3-28. *These text entries have not been formatted.*

FIGURE 3-29. *This is the Font dialog box.*

Now, suppose you want to assign the bold style to the entry in cell B4 in Figure 3-28. First select cell B4, choose the Font... command, click the Bold style option, then click OK. The result is shown in Figure 3-30.

As you can see, you select options in the Font dialog box exactly the way you select them in the Standard Font dialog box. For example, to format the entry in cell B6 in Figure 3-30, you select the cell, choose the Font... command, click Helvetica in the Font list box, click 12 in the Size list box, then click OK. Figure 3-30 shows the results of these adjustments, as well as additional formatting to cell B8. (If you select a font size that is larger than the default worksheet cell size, Excel automatically adjusts the size of the row containing that cell, unless you've previously set that row's height with the Format menu's Row Height... command.)

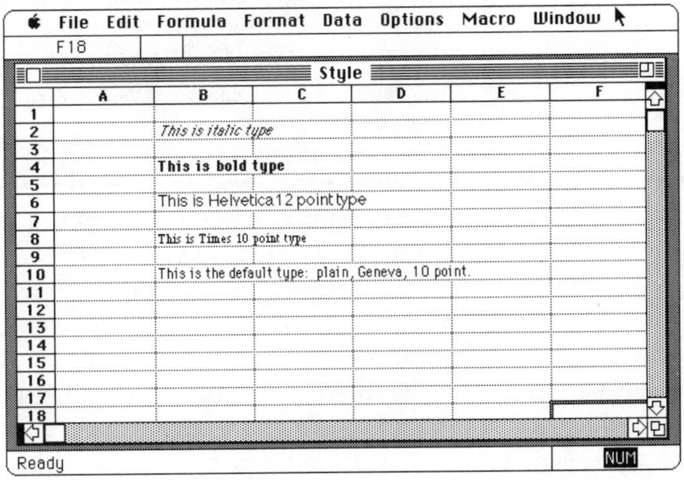

FIGURE 3-30. *These text entries have been formatted with the Font... command.*

Removing a style from a cell is as easy as assigning one. For example, to remove the bold style from the entry in cell B4, click that cell, choose the Font... command, and click the Bold option to deactivate the Bold check box. The result is shown in Figure 3-31 on the next page. The entry now matches the default entry in cell B10.

Although most of the time you will use Excel's Font... command to change the style of text entries, this command also works perfectly well on the display of numbers and the results of formulas.

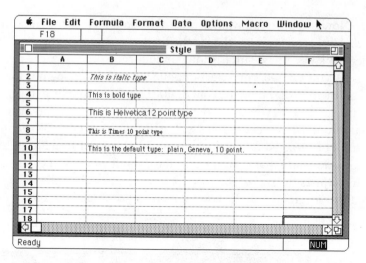

FIGURE 3-31. *You have removed the bold style from the entry in cell B4.*

Colors

You can use the color settings to emphasize special entries in a cell or range of your worksheet, such as bottom-line totals, titles, or legends. As we said in our discussion of the Standard Font... command, if you are working with a monochrome monitor, you'll see no color difference; however, any color change you make is visible when you view the worksheet on a color monitor. (Any color formatting that your number formats use takes precedence over color formats that you apply from the Font dialog box. For example, if you have selected yellow as the color for your cell or range, and you format your cell or range to display negative values in red and zero values in blue, your cell or range displays its contents in yellow except when a negative or zero value fills that cell or range.) Clicking the Automatic button applies the System font color to your selected cell or range.

We've discussed the similarities and differences between Excel's two font commands. Keep in mind that there is a fine but crucial distinction between them. The Standard Font... command sets the default for the entire active worksheet. The Font... command allows you to change the settings for a cell or a range. Suppose you are formatting a worksheet for the first time and you are using the Font... command to format selected cells throughout your worksheet. If, at some later time, you decide that the default font and size don't suit your worksheet, but you like the formats you applied to the selected cells, you can alter the font and font size of the worksheet by using the Standard Font... command, without disturbing the specific cells you formatted previously.

The Display... command

The Display... command allows you to control the display of formulas, gridlines, column and row headings, zero values, and gridline and heading color. When you choose this command, Microsoft Excel displays the dialog box shown in Figure 3-32. Notice that this dialog box offers four display choices: Formulas, Gridlines, Row & Column Headings, and Zero Values, as well as eight color options for gridlines and headings. (We discuss the color options at the end of this chapter, in a section called "Assigning color to gridlines, row headings, and column headings.") Let's look at how each of these options works.

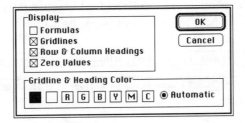

FIGURE 3-32. *This is the Display dialog box.*

The Formulas option

As you have seen, normally when you enter a formula in a cell, Excel displays the results of that formula, not the formula itself. Similarly, when you format a number, you won't usually see the underlying value. You'll only see the underlying values and formulas by selecting individual cells and looking at the formula bar.

The Formulas option makes it possible to see all of the underlying values and formulas in your worksheet at once. For example, suppose you want to see all of the underlying numbers and formulas in the worksheet shown earlier in Figure 3-6. To do this, choose the Display... command, click the Formulas check box, then click the OK button. Figure 3-33 on the next page shows the result. Notice that Excel is now showing you the actual contents of each cell.

In addition, notice that Excel has left-aligned all values and expanded the width of each column in the worksheet from 10 characters to 21 characters so that the underlying formulas can be better displayed. When you select the Formulas option from the Display dialog box, Excel expands all of the columns in the worksheet to twice their actual width setting, plus one character. This means that a column three characters wide becomes seven characters wide when you select the Formulas option, and a column 15 characters wide becomes 31 characters wide.

(This expansion is for purposes of display only. Excel still gauges a column's width according to its measurement in the Column Width dialog box when the Formulas option is deactivated.) When you cancel the Formulas option, Excel restores all of the columns to their former widths.

The Formulas option is particularly helpful when you need to edit a large worksheet. Suppose you have an error in a formula that is linked to several other formula cells. In order to find the error, you would have to click each cell that feeds into that formula in order to see the underlying value in the formula bar. By selecting the Formulas option, you can see the entire "flow" of cell references and debug your worksheet without searching out each cell that contains a formula.

The Formulas option can also be used to document your work. After you select Formulas, you can print your worksheet for historical purposes. (See Chapter 9 for information about how to print your worksheet.)

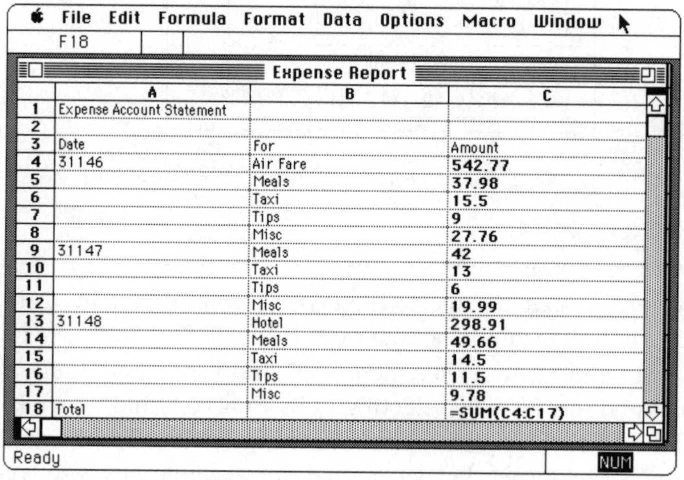

FIGURE 3-33. *You have used the Formulas option of the Display…*
command to view underlying values and formulas.

The Gridlines option

Typically, Microsoft Excel uses a dotted-line grid to mark the boundaries of each cell in the worksheet. Although this grid is usually a big help, there are times when you would rather not have it in view.

To suppress the display of these gridlines, select the Display… command from the Options menu. You'll notice that the Gridlines option in the Display dialog box is checked, because Excel normally displays grids. To turn off the gridlines display, click the Gridlines box, then click OK or press Enter. Figure 3-34 shows a sample worksheet without gridlines.

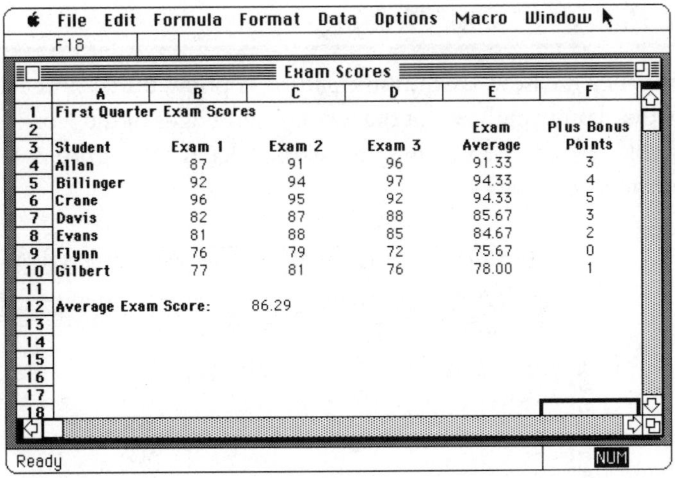

FIGURE 3-34. *This sample worksheet shows no gridlines.*

You can increase the effectiveness of your border formats dramatically by eliminating the gridlines in your worksheet. Figure 3-35 shows a worksheet with borders but without gridlines. Obviously, the borders are much more prominent in Figure 3-35 than they were in Figures 3-16 and 3-17.

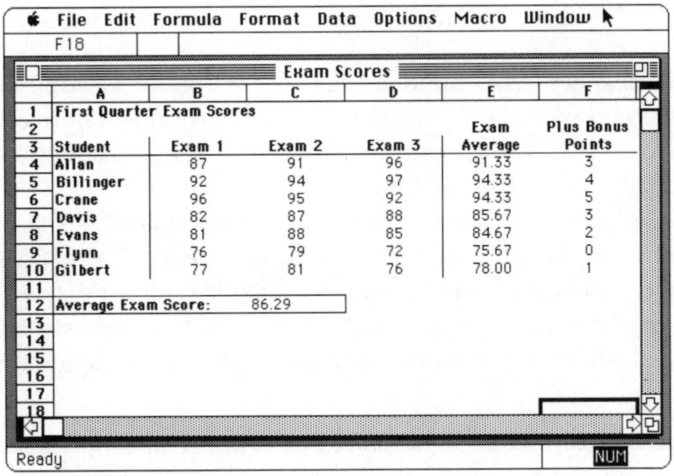

FIGURE 3-35. *Here, gridlines have been suppressed to increase the effectiveness of borders.*

If you want to print your worksheet without gridlines, you should deactivate them from the Page Setup dialog box. (We discuss printing in Chapter 9, "Printing the Worksheet.")

The Row & Column Headings option

If you click the Row & Column Headings option, the column letters and row numbers that you usually see at the top and left edges of the worksheet disappear. For example, Figure 3-36 shows the worksheet from Figure 3-35 without row and column headings.

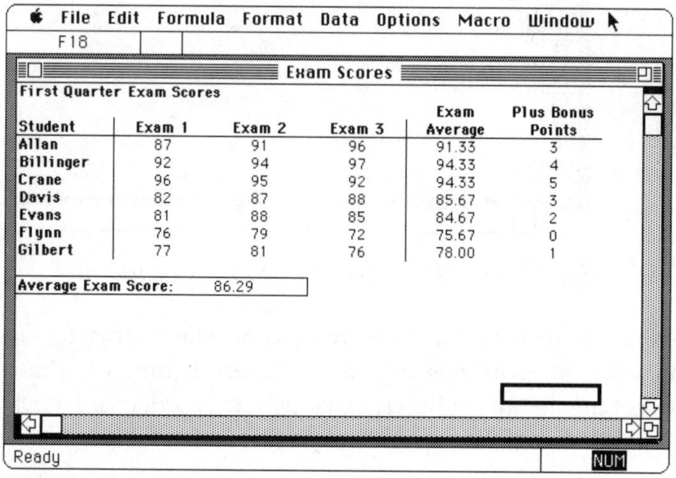

FIGURE 3-36. *You have suppressed row and column headings.*

Like other Display options, the Row & Column Headings option only affects the current worksheet. If you have several worksheets open on the desktop when you choose this command, the row and column headings disappear from the currently active worksheet only.

Generally, you'll want the row and column headings to be included in your worksheets. In fact, you may never deactivate the Row & Column Headings option, except perhaps to polish finished worksheets for display purposes. As with the Gridlines option, if you want to print your worksheets without row and column headings, you should deactivate them from the Page Setup dialog box.

The Zero Values option

Normally, zero values are displayed in your worksheet, but you can deactivate the Zero Values option to hide all those values. With Zero Values deactivated, any cells that contain zeros or formulas that result in zero values appear to be blank. However, the underlying entries are unaffected. If you edit an entry or if the result of a formula changes so that the cell no longer contains a zero value, the value immediately becomes visible again.

The sample worksheet shown in Figure 3-37 contains zero values. If you find these zeros distracting, you can suppress their display by deactivating the Zero Values option. Figure 3-38 shows the results.

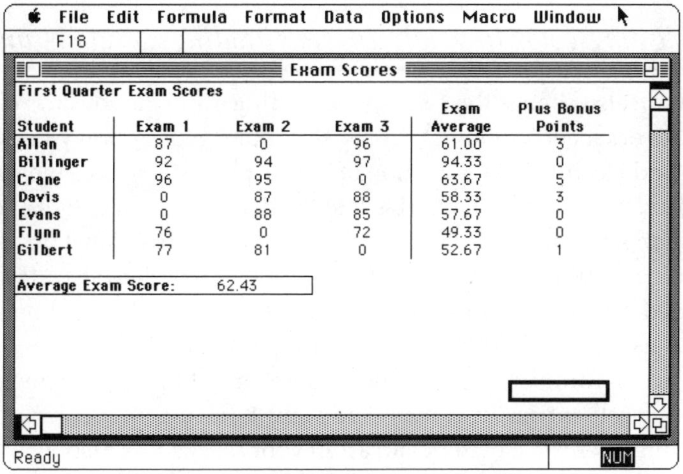

**   File   Edit   Formula   Format   Data   Options   Macro   Window**

F18

Exam Scores

First Quarter Exam Scores

Student	Exam 1	Exam 2	Exam 3	Exam Average	Plus Bonus Points
Allan	87	0	96	61.00	3
Billinger	92	94	97	94.33	0
Crane	96	95	0	63.67	5
Davis	0	87	88	58.33	3
Evans	0	88	85	57.67	0
Flynn	76	0	72	49.33	0
Gilbert	77	81	0	52.67	1

Average Exam Score: 62.43

Ready   NUM

FIGURE 3-37. *This worksheet contains several zero values.*

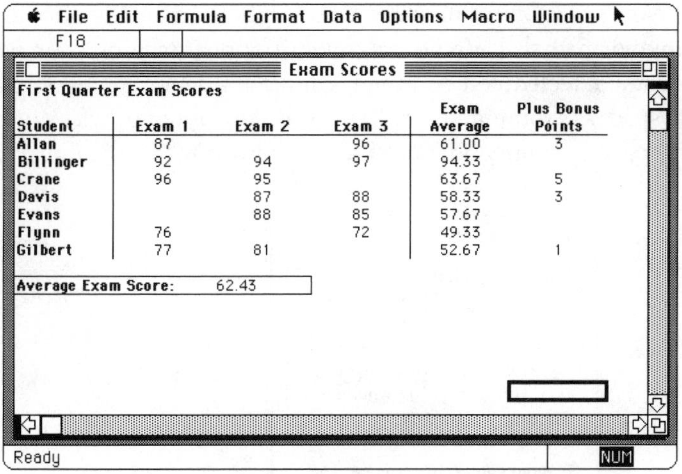

**   File   Edit   Formula   Format   Data   Options   Macro   Window**

F18

Exam Scores

First Quarter Exam Scores

Student	Exam 1	Exam 2	Exam 3	Exam Average	Plus Bonus Points
Allan	87		96	61.00	3
Billinger	92	94	97	94.33	
Crane	96	95		63.67	5
Davis		87	88	58.33	3
Evans		88	85	57.67	
Flynn	76		72	49.33	
Gilbert	77	81		52.67	1

Average Exam Score: 62.43

Ready   NUM

FIGURE 3-38. *Here, the Zero Values option has been deactivated to suppress the display of zeros.*

Keep in mind that when you suppress the display of zeros in the cells of your worksheet, you risk forgetting that there may be underlying formulas in those cells. If those zero values should change—that is, if they depend on a formula that produces a zero result only at the present time—and you have overwritten those apparently empty cells, you may skew the information in your worksheet.

If you have used the Format Number... command to format a cell for zero values, your format overrides the Zero Values option in the Display dialog box.

Assigning color to gridlines, row headings, and column headings

You can also change the color of the gridlines and the row and column headings in your worksheet windows. Simply select the color option you want from the Gridline and Heading Color portion of the Display dialog box, then click OK. Select the Automatic option to change back to the default screen colors. (For those with color monitors, the default color is defined in the Control Panel desk accessory.)

The Gridline and Heading Color option you select also affects the color of any shaded cells you've formatted in your worksheet. The shading is always the same color as the gridlines and row and column headings. Thus, if you've used the Font... or Number... command on the Format menu to change the color of some of your cell entries, you may also want to change the color of the gridlines and shading to create a better contrast in your worksheet display.

The Workspace... command

The Workspace... command on the Options menu is similar to the Display... command in that it affects the overall appearance of your worksheet window, not just a selected cell or range. Unlike the Display... command, however, the Workspace... command applies to all open windows. When you choose the Workspace... command, you'll see a dialog box like the one in Figure 3-39. We've

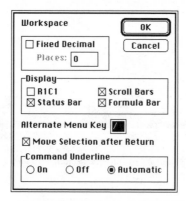

FIGURE 3-39. *This is the Workspace dialog box.*

already discussed three of the options presented here: Alternate Menu Key, Command Underline, and Move Selection After Enter. Here, we look at the other available options.

The Fixed Decimal option

The Fixed Decimal option is handy when you need to enter long lists of numeric values. For example, suppose you're entering data into an accounting journal. All your entries must contain two decimal places. Instead of typing the decimal point for each entry, select the Fixed Decimal option and, in the Places field, indicate the number of decimal places you want to use. (When you choose the Fixed Decimal option, the FIX indicator appears at the right side of the status bar at the bottom of the screen.) After you type each numeric value into your worksheet, Excel adds a decimal point at the specified position. For example, if you select Fixed Decimal, use the default Places option of 2, and then enter the number 12345 into a cell of your worksheet, your entry is converted to 123.45. If you enter a single-digit value, such as 9, it is converted to 0.09.

The Fixed Decimal option does not affect existing entries in your worksheet. The option applies only to entries you make after you select the option. Thus, you can select or deselect the option at any time or change the number of decimal places without altering existing data. The Fixed Decimal option only operates when you do not type a decimal point. If you type a number with a decimal point into a cell, then the Fixed Decimal option does not affect that cell.

The R1C1 option

Worksheet formulas usually refer to cells by a combination of column letter and row number, such as A1 or Z100. As we discussed briefly in Chapter 2, "Worksheet Basics," the R1C1 option causes Excel to refer to cells by row and column *numbers* instead. (Recall that the cell reference R1C1 means *row 1, column 1,* so R1C1 is the same as cell A1.) When you select this option, all the cell references in your formulas change to R1C1 format. For example, cell M10 becomes R10C13, and cell IV16384, the last cell in your worksheet, becomes R16384C256. Figure 3-40 on the next page shows a worksheet in R1C1 format.

When you use R1C1 notation, relative cell references are displayed in terms of their relationship to the cell that contains the formula rather than by their actual coordinates. For example, suppose you want to enter a formula in cell R10C2 (B10) that adds cells R1C1 and R2C2. After selecting R10C2, type an equal sign, then select cell R1C1, type a plus sign, select R1C2, and press Enter. Excel displays

=R[–9]C[–1]+R[–9]C

This formula can be read *Add the cell nine rows up and one column to the left to the cell nine rows up in the same column.* Negative row and column numbers indicate that the referenced cell is above and to the left of the formula cell. Positive numbers indicate that the referenced cell is below and to the right of the formula cell.

To type a relative reference to another cell, you must include square brackets around the reference. If you don't include the brackets, Excel assumes you're using absolute references. For example, the formula

=R9C1+R8C1

uses absolute references to the cells in rows 8 and 9 of column 1.

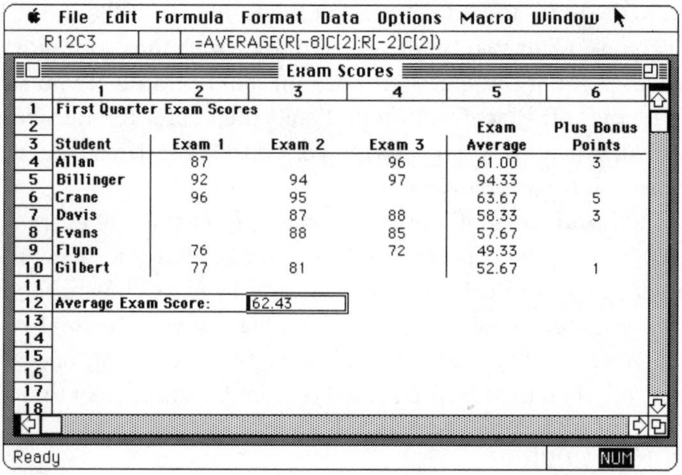

FIGURE 3-40. *You have used the R1C1 option to refer to cells by row and column numbers.*

The Status Bar, Scroll Bars, and Formula Bar options

The remaining three options in the Display portion of the Workspace dialog box let you suppress the display of the status bar, scroll bars, and formula bar on your screen. Figure 3-41 shows how your worksheet looks if you deactivate these three options. Because you need the status bar, scroll bars, and formula bar to navigate and edit your worksheet, you'll use these three options only when you complete a worksheet and want to hide these objects for display purposes. (For this example, we suppressed the display of gridlines and row and column headings, too.)

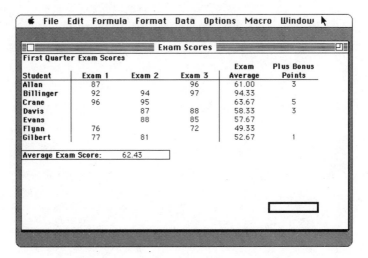

FIGURE 3-41. *You can suppress the display of the status bar, scroll bars, and formula bar.*

Conclusion

In this chapter, we discussed the many formatting options offered by Microsoft Excel to allow you to display your information exactly the way you want. We covered the various ways you can format cells to display numbers, including using number formats you have created to suit your particular needs. We showed you how to align number and text entries and how to set them off with borders, different fonts and type styles, and color. Finally, we looked at ways to tailor the appearance of your worksheets on the screen.

In the next chapter, we move on to discuss ways of editing and otherwise manipulating the information in your worksheets.

4

Editing
the Worksheet

*T*he Edit-menu commands of Microsoft Excel are real time-savers when you are constructing worksheets. These commands let you erase entries, copy entries from one cell or range into another cell or range, and move entries from one location to another in the worksheet. In fact, the Clear..., Delete..., Insert..., Cut, Copy, Paste, Paste Special..., Paste Link, and Fill commands take the place of old-fashioned erasers, scissors, and paste.

We start this chapter by explaining what may be the most important Edit-menu commands: Undo and Repeat. Then, we cover Clear..., Delete..., and Insert...—the simplest editing commands. Next, we explain how you can use Excel's Copy, Cut, and Paste commands to copy and move entries, and we explain the importance of relative, absolute, and mixed references, introduced in Chapter 2, "Worksheet Basics." Then we look at four shortcut commands: Fill Right, Fill Down, Fill Left, and Fill Up. We also cover the Series... and Justify commands in this chapter. We examine the Paste Link command in Appendix A, where we discuss linking Excel to other programs.

Most of the Edit-menu commands have shorthand Command-key equivalents. For your convenience, we've gathered these together into the table in Figure 4-1 on the next page as well as in Appendix B, where we list all the keyboard shortcuts.

Command	Keyboard shortcut	Excel action
Undo	Command-Z	Undoes last Edit command, as well as any typing; also undoes the following worksheet commands: Apply Names..., Replace..., Justify, Data Parse, Data Sort, and Paste List in the Paste Name dialog box
Repeat	Command-Y	Repeats the last command, including the options you changed in the dialog box
Cut	Command-X	Places a marquee around a selection; places a copy of the selection on the Clipboard
Copy	Command-C	Places a marquee around a selection; places a copy of the selection on the Clipboard
Paste	Command-V	Pastes the cut or copy area into the selected cells
Clear...	Command-B	Erases the contents of the selected cells
Delete...	Command-K	If the selection is an entire row or column, shifts all cells up or to the left; if the selection is a partial row or column, presents the Delete dialog box
Insert...	Command-I	If the selection is an entire row or column, shifts all cells down or to the right. If selection is a partial row or column, presents Insert dialog box
Fill Right	Command-R	Copies cells in left column into the remaining columns in a selected area
Fill Down	Command-D	Copies cells in top row into the remaining rows in a selected area

FIGURE 4-1. *These are editing-command keyboard equivalents.*

The Undo command

The first command on the Microsoft Excel Edit menu is Undo. Undo lets you recover from editing mistakes without having to re-enter data or patch information back in place. If you catch your mistake before you choose another command or make another cell entry, you can simply choose Undo to reverse the previous command. If you are new to Excel, Undo will be one of your most-used commands.

Undoing commands

You can use Undo to reverse any command on the Edit menu and to change any entry in the formula bar. For example, if you accidentally delete an important range of cells, you can choose Undo to paste the cells back in place. Similarly, if you edit the contents of a cell and discover that your changes are incorrect, you can use the Undo command to restore the original cell entry.

The name of the Undo command displayed on the Edit menu changes to reflect your last Edit command or cell entry. For example, suppose you choose the Clear... command to erase the contents of cells B4:B10 in Figure 4-2. After using the Clear... command, your worksheet looks like Figure 4-3. Now, suppose you discover that you have erased the wrong range of cells. As long as you catch your error before you use another command, you can easily recover from this mistake

	A	B	C	D	E	F
	Yellow Tree Publishers: 1989 Sales					
1						
2						
3						
4		Hopper's	National		Wall Street	
5		Bizarre	Trash	Miz	Jungle	Total
6	1st Qtr	$3,200	$3,932	$4,102	$2,310	$13,544
7	2nd Qtr	$4,501	$4,872	$5,432	$3,429	$18,234
8	3rd Qtr	$3,714	$4,321	$4,981	$3,012	$16,028
9	4th Qtr	$4,374	$5,012	$5,612	$3,001	$17,999
10	Total	$15,789	$18,137	$20,127	$11,752	$65,805
11						
12						
13	1989 Goal:			% of Goal:		
14	$91,000			55%		

FIGURE 4-2. *The worksheet looks like this before you choose the Clear... command.*

	A	B	C	D	E	F
1	Yellow Tree Publishers: 1989 Sales					
2						
3						
4			National		Wall Street	
5			Trash	Miz	Jungle	Total
6	1st Qtr		$3,932	$4,102	$2,310	$10,344
7	2nd Qtr		$4,872	$5,432	$3,429	$13,733
8	3rd Qtr		$4,321	$4,981	$3,012	$12,314
9	4th Qtr		$5,012	$5,612	$3,001	$13,625
10	Total		$18,137	$20,127	$11,752	$50,016
11						
12						
13	1989 Goal:			% of Goal:		
14	$91,000			55%		

FIGURE 4-3. *The worksheet looks like this after you choose the Clear... command.*

by choosing Undo Clear from the Edit menu. After you use the Undo Clear command, your worksheet again looks exactly like the one in Figure 4-2.

Undoing cell entries

If you are working in the formula bar—making a new cell entry or editing an existing cell, for example—and you make an error, you can use Undo to restore the entry to its original condition. If you pull down the Edit menu while you are still editing or making an entry, the Undo option reads Undo Typing. Once you press Enter or click the enter box, the Undo option reads Undo Entry. These options let you return the cell to its previous state.

For example, cell B10 in the sample worksheet in Figure 4-2 on the previous page contains the formula

=SUM(B6:B9)

Suppose you edit this formula to read

=SUM(B4:B10)

Excel immediately returns the error message *Can't Resolve Circular References*, indicating that you cannot include cell B10 in the formula. To correct this problem, just choose Undo Entry from the Edit menu. Excel immediately changes the formula in cell B10 back to

=SUM(B6:B9)

Actions that don't affect Undo

You can only undo an action in Microsoft Excel if you have not used another command or made another entry. Whenever you make an entry or choose a command, Excel's memory of the last state of the worksheet is updated so that you can undo that entry or command. If you don't discover an error before you make another entry or choose another command, you're out of luck.

There are, however, several actions you can take in the worksheet that do not affect the Undo command. For one thing, you can use the cell pointer and scroll bars to move through your worksheet without affecting Undo. You can even click other cells to display their contents in the formula bar, as long as you do not make an entry.

The Microsoft Excel commands that move the cell pointer, discussed in Chapter 2, "Worksheet Basics," are also safe. You can use the Goto..., Find..., Select Special..., and Show Active Cell commands on the Formula menu without affecting the Undo option. You can also move to other windows by selecting window names from the Window menu or by clicking the window itself.

The Redo command

When you use the Undo command, Excel changes its name on the Edit menu to Redo. Choosing the Redo command undoes the undo action, restoring the worksheet to the condition it was in before you used the Undo command.

For example, suppose you use the Clear... command to erase range B4:B10 as shown in Figure 4-3. As you know, if you use Undo Clear to undo that action, your screen looks like Figure 4-2 again, except that the range you cleared is now highlighted. If you now pull down the Edit menu, you'll see that the first command on the Edit menu has changed to Redo Clear. If you choose this command, your worksheet again looks like Figure 4-3.

You can take advantage of the Undo/Redo command to see the effects of an Edit command in remote areas of your worksheet. For example, suppose you want to edit a cell that is referred to in several formulas throughout your worksheet. To see the effects of your change, use the cursor-movement commands to move around the worksheet and view the other cells. If you don't remember what a cell looked like before, use Undo and Redo to get a "before-and-after" view.

When Undo won't work

You can undo only the following commands: the Edit-menu commands, Paste Name..., Paste Function..., Replace..., Justify, Series..., Sort, and Parse. After you choose any other command, Excel displays Can't Undo on the Edit menu. For example, if you format a range of cells to display percentages with two decimal places (the 0.00; format) and then pull down the Edit menu, the menu looks like Figure 4-4 on the next page. Notice that the Undo command has changed to Can't Undo. This choice appears in light gray, indicating that the Undo option is not currently available.

The loss of the Undo capability in these cases is usually not a problem, however, because these commands do not generally change the contents of your cells, but rather change the way the contents are displayed. You can usually undo the effects of these commands by choosing the command again and changing your selection. For example, if you format a range of cells to display percentages with two decimal places (the 0.00% format), you can always select the cells again and choose another format.

If you are working with a large range of cells, you may find that Excel cannot undo your mistakes for you. For example, suppose you try to use the Cut and Paste commands to move all of the cells in column A (cells A1:A16384) of an elaborately complex worksheet into column C (cells C1:C16384). Excel displays the alert box in Figure 4-5, indicating that the selection is too big. In other words, to move the selection strains Excel's memory. Your only options are to click the Cancel button or the

OK button, which erases the record of the previous state of the worksheet. You cannot undo your Cut and Paste procedure. Because of the power of Microsoft Excel 2.2, your range of cells needs to be full of formulas, formatting, and values that use a lot of memory before this happens. You will see the alert box shown in Figure 4-5 infrequently. The worksheet that uses so much of the Microsoft Excel 2.2 memory is rare.

FIGURE 4-4. *The Edit menu looks like this after you choose a command from another menu.*

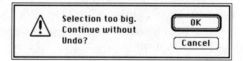

FIGURE 4-5. *This alert box might appear when you request an editing operation on a large cell range.*

An extra precaution

There are a few commands whose effects are irreversible. For example, the Delete... command on the File menu cannot be reversed. If you are not sure whether a file is needed, make it a point to open the file and take a look before you delete it. Similarly, you cannot reverse the Delete command on the Data menu. It's a good idea to save your worksheet before you enter these commands. If you later find that you have deleted cells incorrectly, you can always retrieve your original worksheet.

The Repeat command

The Repeat command on the Edit menu repeats the last command you chose. When you pull down the Edit menu, the Repeat command includes the name of the last command you chose. For example, if you just chose the Sort... command, the Repeat command becomes Repeat Sort. Any options that you selected in that command's dialog box are repeated as well. The Repeat command allows you to repeat tedious tasks, such as applying formats to different groups of cells, easily. If a command can't be redone, Can't Repeat appears in place of the Repeat command.

The Clear... command

The Clear... command allows you to erase the contents of a cell or range, the format assigned to that cell or range, or both. All you have to do is select that cell or range and choose the Clear... command from the Edit menu. When you choose this command, Microsoft Excel displays the dialog box shown in Figure 4-6.

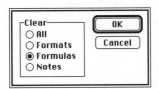

FIGURE 4-6. *This is the Clear dialog box.*

Notice that this dialog box offers four options: All, Formats, Formulas, and Notes. Often, you'll choose the All option, which instructs Excel to erase the contents of the selected cells, the formats that you have assigned to the cells, and any notes you've attached to those cells. If you choose the Formulas option, Excel erases the contents of the selected cells but leaves their formats and notes alone. If you choose Formats, Excel removes the formats from the selected cells but leaves their contents and notes in place. The selected cells then revert to the default General format. (We discuss the Notes option in Chapter 8, "Other Worksheet Topics," when we talk about cell notes.)

Let's consider the effects of the first three options—All, Formats, and Formulas—on our sample worksheet in Figure 4-2. To erase the contents of column B, you drag through cells B4:B10 and choose the Clear... command. If you select All from the Clear dialog box, Excel erases both the contents of the cells and the formats you have assigned to the cells, as shown previously in Figure 4-3.

If you select the Formulas option, Microsoft Excel erases the contents of the selected cells, but not the formats you have assigned. Although your worksheet still looks like Figure 4-3 after you select this option, if you make an entry in any of these cells, that entry is formatted to display in the existing format, which is currency with no decimal places. For example, Figure 4-7 shows the worksheet after you enter the number 12345.67 in cell B6.

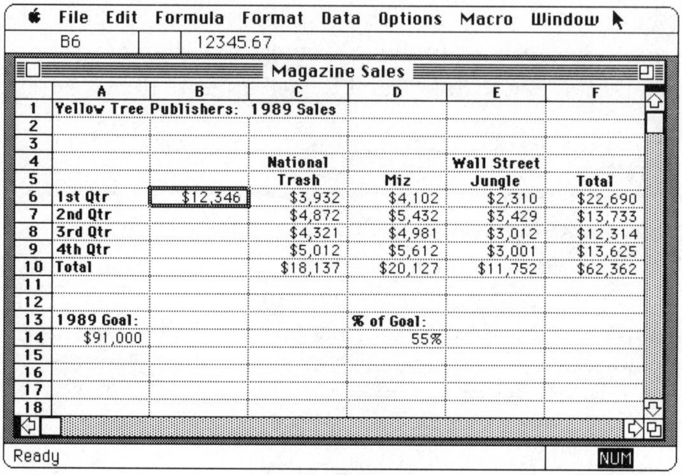

	A	B	C	D	E	F
1	Yellow Tree Publishers: 1989 Sales					
2						
3						
4			National		Wall Street	
5			Trash	Miz	Jungle	Total
6	1st Qtr	$12,346	$3,932	$4,102	$2,310	$22,690
7	2nd Qtr		$4,872	$5,432	$3,429	$13,733
8	3rd Qtr		$4,321	$4,981	$3,012	$12,314
9	4th Qtr		$5,012	$5,612	$3,001	$13,625
10	Total		$18,137	$20,127	$11,752	$62,362
11						
12						
13	1989 Goal:			% of Goal:		
14	$91,000			55%		
15						
16						
17						
18						

FIGURE 4-7. *You have entered a new value into a formatted cell after the Clear... command's Formulas option has been used to erase the cell's previous contents.*

If you choose Formats, Excel erases only the formats you have assigned to the cells. Figure 4-8 shows the result of the Formats option. Notice that the contents of the cleared cells are now displayed in the default General format. However, if figures were originally entered with decimal places, they revert to that format.

As we explained in the previous section, you can use the Undo command to undo the effects of the Clear... command. If you choose the Undo command after you have chosen the Clear... command (and before you make an entry in another cell or use another command), Excel restores the cleared entries and formats.

In the next section, we discuss the Delete... command. While the visual effect of the Clear... command is similar at times to the Delete... command, the two commands have one important difference: The Clear... command removes the contents of cells; the Delete... command removes the cells themselves. This difference matters when other cells refer to the deleted or cleared cells. When a formula refers to a cleared cell, the formula assumes the cleared cell has a value of 0. When a formula refers to a deleted cell, the formula will be unable to find the deleted cell and returns a #REF! error value.

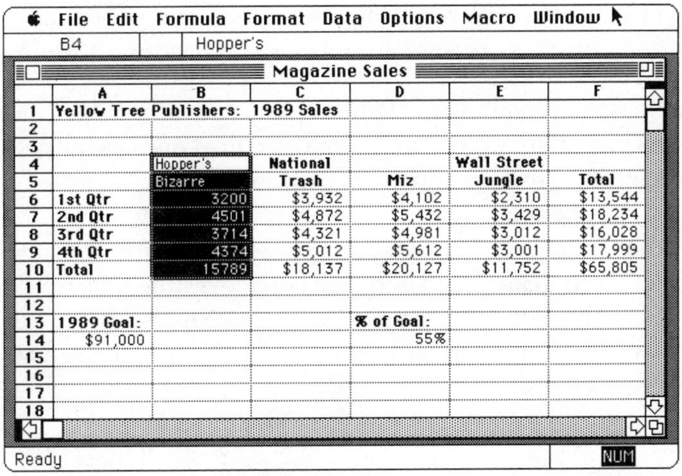

FIGURE 4-8. *You have used the Clear... command's Formats option to erase cell formats but not contents.*

The Delete... command

The Delete... command allows you to remove entire rows or columns—or partial rows and columns—from a worksheet. Unlike Clear..., which erases only the contents or formats of cells, Delete... actually removes rows, columns, partial rows, or partial columns from the worksheet. In other words, Clear... works like an eraser and Delete... works like a pair of scissors.

Deleting rows and columns

Let's consider a simple example of the Delete... command. Consider the worksheet in Figure 4-9 shown on the following page. Notice that there are three extra blank rows between the last items in the lists in columns A and C, and the total in row 15. You want to delete these blank rows from the worksheet.

We'll begin by deleting row 12. Click the row number 12 at the left side of the screen to select row 12, then choose the Delete... command from the Edit menu. Figure 4-10 on page 153 shows the result. As you can see, Excel has deleted row 12 from the worksheet and has shifted every entry in the rows below the deleted row up one cell, so the total that was in row 15 is now in row 14.

In addition to deleting a row from the worksheet, Excel has also adjusted the formula in cell C14 to account for the deleted row. For example, before you deleted the row, the function in cell C15 (which is now in cell C14) was

=SUM(C4:C14)

As you can see in Figure 4-10, however, cell C14 now contains the function

=SUM(C4:C13)

Excel has adjusted this function's argument to account for the deletion of row 12.

As you might expect, to delete more than one row or column, you need only select all of the rows or columns you want to delete, then choose the Delete... command. For example, suppose you now want to delete rows 12 and 13 from the worksheet in Figure 4-10. You drag across headers for rows 12 and 13, and choose the Delete... command. As before, Excel removes the selected rows from the worksheet and shifts all of the entries below those rows up—in this case, up two more cells as shown in Figure 4-11. In addition, the formula in what is now cell C12 is changed to

=SUM(C4:C11)

to reflect the deletion.

You can also use the Delete... command to delete columns from the worksheet. All you have to do is click the heading of the column or columns that you want to delete and choose the Delete... command.

You cannot delete discontinuous rows and columns in one operation. For example, suppose you want to delete rows 1, 8, and 9 in Figure 4-9. You might try to do this by clicking row 1, then holding down the Command key while you click rows 8 and 9, and finally choosing the Delete... command. When you choose this command, however, Excel beeps and displays the alert box shown in Figure 4-12. You have to click OK to close the alert box, then go back and delete row 1, then rows 8 and 9, in two separate operations.

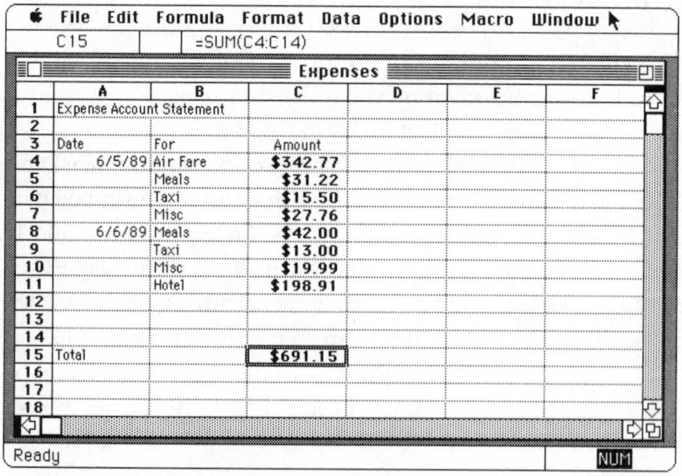

FIGURE 4-9. *This is an expense-account worksheet.*

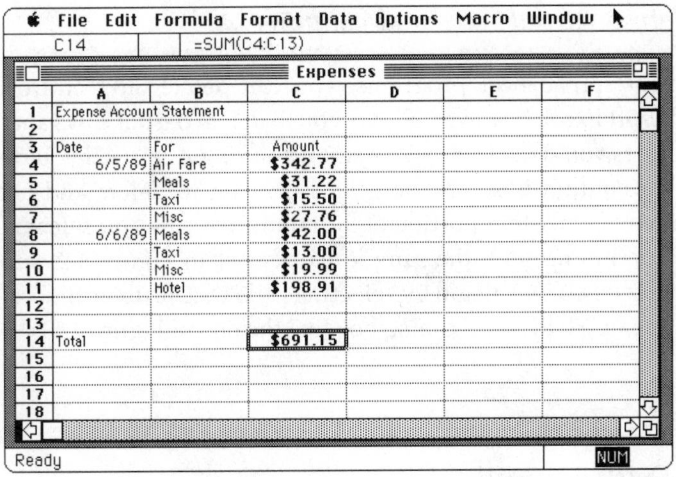

🍎 File Edit Formula Format Data Options Macro Window ⬉

C14		=SUM(C4:C13)				

Expenses

	A	B	C	D	E	F
1	Expense Account Statement					
2						
3	Date	For	Amount			
4	6/5/89	Air Fare	$342.77			
5		Meals	$31.22			
6		Taxi	$15.50			
7		Misc	$27.76			
8	6/6/89	Meals	$42.00			
9		Taxi	$13.00			
10		Misc	$19.99			
11		Hotel	$198.91			
12						
13						
14	Total		$691.15			
15						
16						
17						
18						

Ready   NUM

FIGURE 4-10. *The expense-account worksheet looks like this after deleting row 12.*

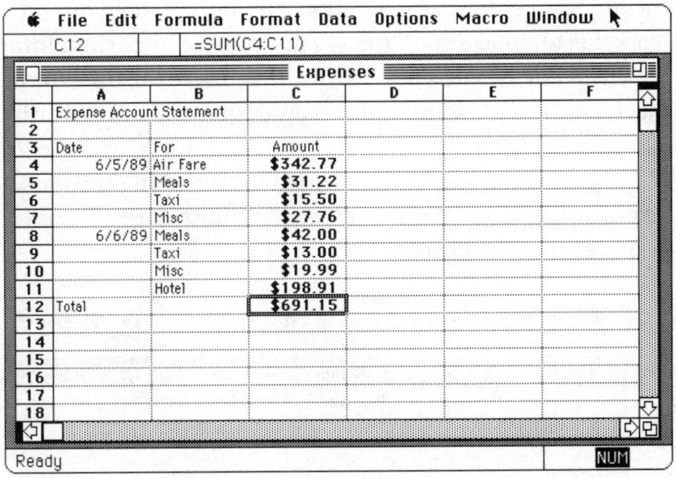

🍎 File Edit Formula Format Data Options Macro Window ⬉

C12		=SUM(C4:C11)				

Expenses

	A	B	C	D	E	F
1	Expense Account Statement					
2						
3	Date	For	Amount			
4	6/5/89	Air Fare	$342.77			
5		Meals	$31.22			
6		Taxi	$15.50			
7		Misc	$27.76			
8	6/6/89	Meals	$42.00			
9		Taxi	$13.00			
10		Misc	$19.99			
11		Hotel	$198.91			
12	Total		$691.15			
13						
14						
15						
16						
17						
18						

Ready   NUM

FIGURE 4-11. *The expense-account worksheet looks like this after deleting rows 12 and 13.*

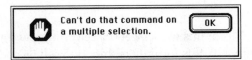

Can't do that command on a multiple selection.   [OK]

FIGURE 4-12. *This alert box appears when you try to delete discontinuous rows or columns.*

Deleting partial rows and columns

In most spreadsheet programs, you can delete only entire rows or columns. Microsoft Excel, however, allows you to delete partial rows and columns—in fact, Excel lets you delete a range as small as a single cell. All you do to delete a partial row or column is select the cells you want to delete and choose the Delete... command. Only that portion of the column or row you select is affected.

Continuing with the sample worksheet in Figure 4-2, suppose you want to delete cells D5:D10. Begin by selecting cells D5:D10, then choose Delete... from the Edit menu. You'll see a dialog box like the one in Figure 4-13.

E X C E L *tip*

Deletion pitfalls

Although you can usually use the Undo command to undo a deletion, there are still a few pitfalls you'll want to avoid. First, before you select an entire row or column for deletion, we suggest that you scroll through your worksheet to make sure you are not erasing important information that is not visible in the current window. If you take the time to check your worksheet, you will avoid making an error that you may not discover until it is too late to undo it.

If you delete a cell upon which formulas in other cells depend, Excel displays the #REF! error message in those formula cells. Consider, for example, this worksheet:

File	**Edit**	**Formula**	**Format**	**Data**	**Options**	**Macro**	**Window**

| B6 | | =B1+B2+B3+B4+B5 | | | | | |

	A	B	C	D	E	F
1		$100				
2		$123				
3		$182				
4		$93				
5		$91				
6		$589				
7						

Cell B6 contains the formula

    =B1+B2+B3+B4+B5

If you delete row 5 from this worksheet (by selecting row 5 and choosing the Delete... command), this formula is shifted to cell B5 and becomes

    =B1+B2+B3+B4+#REF!

```
┌─Delete──────────┐  ┌──────────┐
│ ⦿ Shift Cells Left │  │    OK    │
│ ○ Shift Cells Up   │  └──────────┘
│                    │  ┌──────────┐
│                    │  │  Cancel  │
└────────────────────┘  └──────────┘
```

FIGURE 4-13. *This is the Delete dialog box.*

As you can see, this dialog box offers two choices: Shift Cells Left and Shift Cells Up. These options tell Excel how you want the program to adjust the worksheet after it deletes the cells you have selected. If you select Shift Cells Left, Excel shifts all of the cells that are to the right of the selected cells to the left after

The result of the formula is also #REF!. As you can see here

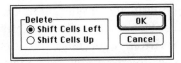

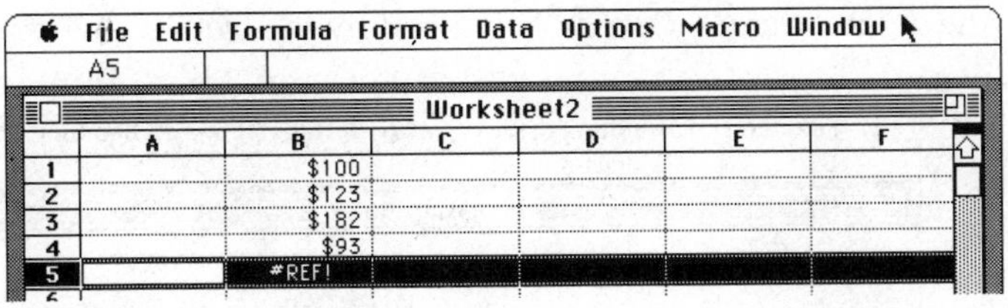

the results of deleting a row that contains cells that are referred to by formulas might well be disastrous. Of course, you could use Undo to undo this kind of deletion—but only if you catch the error before you choose another command.

Interestingly, functions behave different from pure formulas in this regard. When you delete a row or column that is referred to by an argument of a function, Excel modifies the argument if at all possible, to account for the deletion. For example, if cell B6 contained the function

=SUM(B1:B5)

and you deleted row 5, the function (which would have moved to cell B5) would be changed to

=SUM(B1:B4)

As you can see, Excel would adjust the function's argument to compensate for the deletion of row 5. This adaptability makes the case for using functions instead of formulas (where possible) even more compelling.

Excel deletes the selected cells. Similarly, if you select Shift Cells Up, Excel shifts up all of the cells that are below the selected cells after it deletes the selected cells.

When you select a partial row or column of cells to be deleted, Excel makes a "guess" at how you want to arrange the remaining cells in your worksheet. For example, if you select a horizontal range (one that is wider than it is deep), Excel assumes that you want to close up the range by moving up any cells in your worksheet that are below the selected range. If you select a vertical range (one that is longer than it is wide), Excel assumes that you want to close up the range by moving to the left any cells in your worksheet that are to the right of the selected range. To accept Excel's guess, simply click the OK button. If you do not want to accept Excel's guess, click the alternative option, then click OK.

Because the selected range in the example is taller than it is wide, Excel has selected the Shift Cells Left option. Because you want to shift the cells on the right of the deleted cells to the left, you can simply click the OK button. The results of the deletion appear in Figure 4-14. As you can see, Excel has deleted the contents of cells D5 through D10 and has shifted the contents of the cells on the right of the range D5:D10 to the left by one cell. Notice, however, that cells D13 and D14, just below the deleted range, were not changed by the Delete... command.

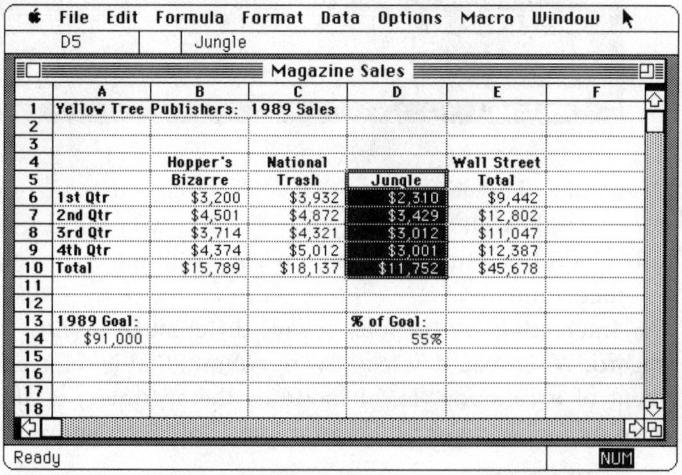

FIGURE 4-14. *You have used the Shift Cells Left option of the Delete... command when deleting cells D5:D10.*

When you delete a partial row or column of cells, it is very easy to misalign data. For example, in Figure 4-14, Excel did not move the label *Wall Street* in column E with the rest of the data in that column. As a result, the heading for column D now appears over the totals in the new column E. To avoid this problem, you should have selected cells D4:D10 before choosing the Delete... command, to make sure that the headings and data in column D were correctly aligned.

The Insert... command

The Insert... command lets you add blank cells or a range of cells to your worksheet. Suppose you have created the worksheet shown in Figure 4-15. Just as you are putting on your finishing touches, your boss tells you that your company has added a new product line. If you were working with a paper spreadsheet you might simply throw away the entire plan and start on a new set of calculations.

	File Edit Formula Format Data Options Macro Window					
	E17	=SUM(B17:D17)				

WWWW Sales

	A	B	C	D	E	F
1	1989 Sales: **VVVV Company, Inc.**					
2						
3			*Product*			
4	Month	Widgets	Wombats	Woofers	Total by Month	
5	January	$1,199.98	$1,356.97	$1,513.95	$4,070.90	
6	February	$1,271.13	$1,289.19	$1,499.27	$4,059.59	
7	March	$1,327.87	$1,484.86	$1,641.84	$4,454.57	
8	April	$1,455.76	$1,612.75	$1,769.73	$4,838.24	
9	May	$1,583.65	$1,740.64	$1,897.62	$5,221.91	
10	June	$1,711.54	$1,868.53	$2,025.51	$5,605.58	
11	July	$1,839.43	$1,996.42	$2,153.40	$5,989.25	
12	August	$1,967.32	$2,124.31	$2,281.29	$6,372.92	
13	September	$2,095.21	$2,252.20	$2,409.18	$6,756.59	
14	October	$2,223.10	$2,380.09	$2,537.07	$7,140.26	
15	November	$2,350.99	$2,507.98	$2,664.96	$7,523.93	
16	December	$2,478.88	$2,635.87	$2,792.85	$7,907.60	
17	Total by Product	$21,504.86	$23,249.78	$25,186.71	**$69,941.35**	
18						

Ready NUM

FIGURE 4-15. *This worksheet sets annual sales goals by product and by month.*

Fortunately, the Microsoft Excel Insert... command lets you add a new row or column to your worksheet without a lot of shuffling and recalculation. To insert a new column for a new product line in the sample worksheet, you can simply click the column heading B, C, or D (we'll use D) and choose the Insert... command from the Edit menu. Because you selected a column before choosing the command, Excel assumes that you want to shift cells to the right to create a new column. The contents of columns D and E move into columns E and F, leaving column D blank and ready for your new information. In addition to inserting a new row, the Insert... command also adjusts the formulas that are now contained in cells F5:F17 to account for the altered range.

You are now ready to enter the new product line's sales goals and have Excel add these goals to the totals in column F. Figure 4-16 on the next page shows the finished worksheet, with the data for Whatzits added in column D.

Similarly, suppose you want to add an extra row to the worksheet in Figure 4-16 so that you can add a series of dashed lines to separate the monthly sales data in rows 4 through 16 from the totals in row 17. You can simply click in the row heading for row 17 and choose the Insert… command from the Edit menu. Excel automatically shifts the contents of cells A17:F17 down one row. You can now add a series of dashes or equal signs to separate the monthly data and totals, as shown in Figure 4-17.

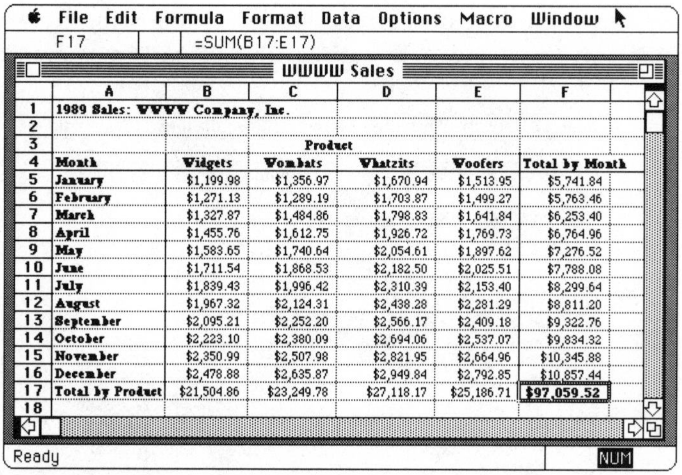

FIGURE 4-16. *You have used the Edit menu's Insert… command to create a column for a new product line.*

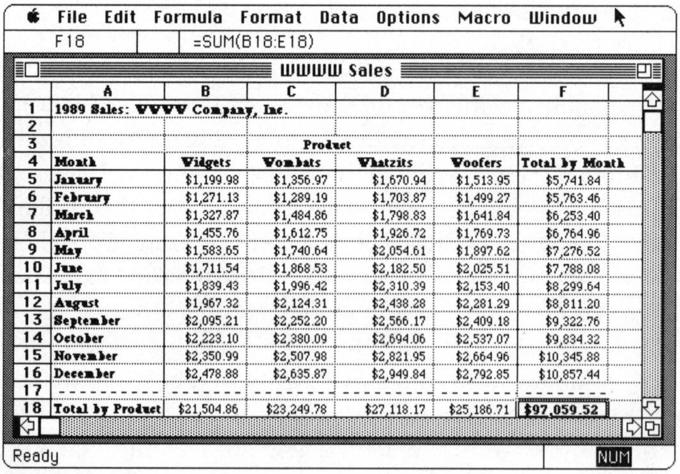

FIGURE 4-17. *You have used the Insert… command to create a new row to set off the totals.*

Although Excel has adjusted the totals in row 18 to account for the inserted row, notice that the dashed lines in row 17 have no effect on the totals.

There will be times when you'll need to insert just a partial row or column into the worksheet. For example, suppose rows 22 through 35 in our sample worksheet included information that would be damaged if you inserted a complete column all the way down the worksheet. You would therefore need to insert cells in column D only between rows 4 and 17.

Like the Delete... command, the Microsoft Excel Insert... command allows you to insert a partial row or column. For example, to make room for the fourth product line in Figure 4-15, you can drag through cells D4:D17 and choose the Insert... command from the Edit menu. If you do this, an Insert dialog box, like the one shown in Figure 4-18, appears so you can tell Excel whether you want to shift the remaining cells in your worksheet down or to the right.

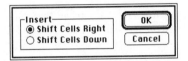

FIGURE 4-18. *This is the Insert dialog box.*

As with the Delete... command, when you choose the Insert... command, Excel makes a guess as to how you want to arrange the remaining cells in your worksheet. If you select a horizontal range, Excel guesses that you want to use the Shift Cells Down option. If you select a vertical range, Excel guesses the Shift Cells Right option. To accept Excel's guess, click OK in the Insert dialog box. If you don't want to accept Excel's guess, click the alternative option, then click OK.

In our example, you would accept Excel's guess, and after you clicked OK, the information in cells D4:E17 would move into cells E4:F17, leaving cells D4:D17 blank and ready to receive your new product-line information. None of the other cells in the worksheet would be disturbed.

Be careful not to misalign data when you are adding partial rows and columns. For example, if you had selected only cells D4:D16 in Figure 4-15 and then had chosen the Insert... command, your worksheet would look like Figure 4-19 on the next page. Notice that the totals in cells D17 and E17 are misaligned with the data in columns E and F.

Keep in mind that Excel moves *all* of the cells to the right of the selected range when you select Shift Cells Right in the Insert dialog box. Similarly, the Shift Cells Down option affects *all* of the cells below the range you select. It is possible to misalign a lot of entries very quickly with the Insert... command.

	A	B	C	D	E	F
1	1989 Sales: **VVVV Company, Inc.**					
2						
3			Product			
4	Month	Widgets	Vombats		Woofers	Total by Month
5	January	$1,199.98	$1,356.97		$1,513.95	$4,070.90
6	February	$1,271.13	$1,289.19		$1,499.27	$4,059.59
7	March	$1,327.87	$1,484.86		$1,641.84	$4,454.57
8	April	$1,455.76	$1,612.75		$1,769.73	$4,838.24
9	May	$1,583.65	$1,740.64		$1,897.62	$5,221.91
10	June	$1,711.54	$1,868.53		$2,025.51	$5,605.58
11	July	$1,839.43	$1,996.42		$2,153.40	$5,989.25
12	August	$1,967.32	$2,124.31		$2,281.29	$6,372.92
13	September	$2,095.21	$2,252.20		$2,409.18	$6,756.59
14	October	$2,223.10	$2,380.09		$2,537.07	$7,140.26
15	November	$2,350.99	$2,507.98		$2,664.96	$7,523.93
16	December	$2,478.88	$2,635.87		$2,792.85	$7,907.60
17	Total by Product	$21,504.86	$23,249.78	$25,186.71	$69,941.35	
18						

FIGURE 4-19. *This is an example of the misalignment that can result if you're not careful when inserting partial rows or columns.*

The Cut and Paste commands

The Microsoft Excel Cut and Paste commands let you move entries from one place to another on your worksheet. The Cut command puts a dotted-line marquee around any selected entries and places a record of the number of rows and columns within the marquee on the Clipboard. After you have selected the range to which you want to move the "cut" cells, the Paste command pastes them into their new location, then clears the contents of the cells within the marquee and erases that range of cells.

For your convenience, Microsoft Excel offers two kinds of shortcuts for its Cut and Paste procedures. The Command-key shortcuts are listed to the right of the commands on the Edit menu, and the Macintosh extended keyboard allows you to streamline this procedure to one keystroke for each stage in the operation. The F2 key cuts. The F4 key pastes.

When you use the Cut and Paste commands to move a range of cells, Excel automatically clears both the contents and formats of the cut range and transfers them to the cells in the paste range. For example, suppose you want to move the contents of the range A1:A5 in Figure 4-20 to cells C1:C5. You begin by dragging through cells A1:A5, then choose Cut from the Edit menu. When you choose Cut, a marquee appears around the cells you have selected, as shown in Figure 4-21. Next, you click cell C1 and choose the Paste command from the Edit menu. As you can see in Figure 4-22, both the contents and formats assigned to cells A1:A5 are transferred to cells C1:C5. Notice that cells A1:A5 are now blank.

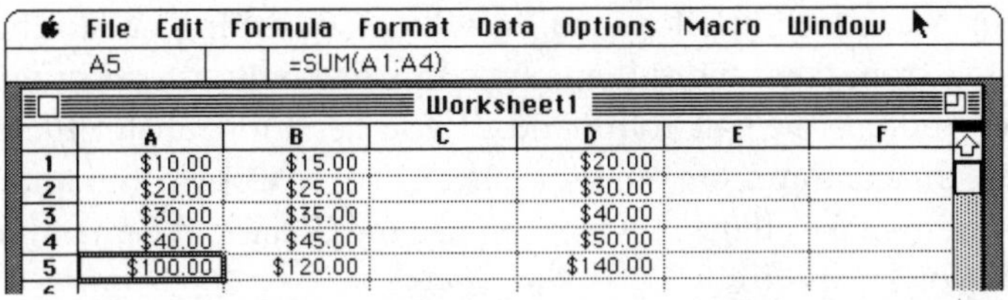

FIGURE 4-20. *This is a simple worksheet before cutting and pasting.*

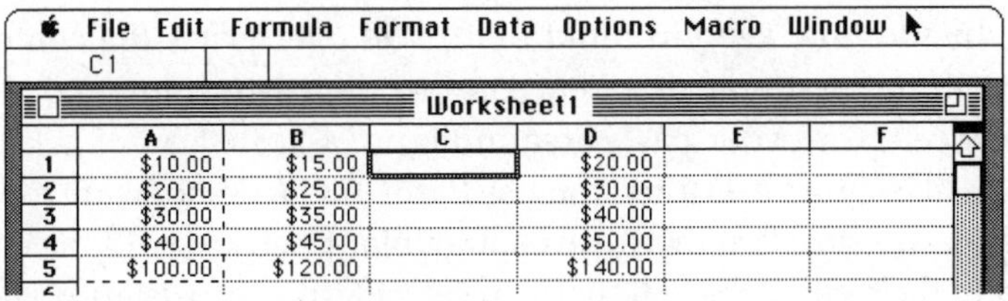

FIGURE 4-21. *You have selected cells for cutting.*

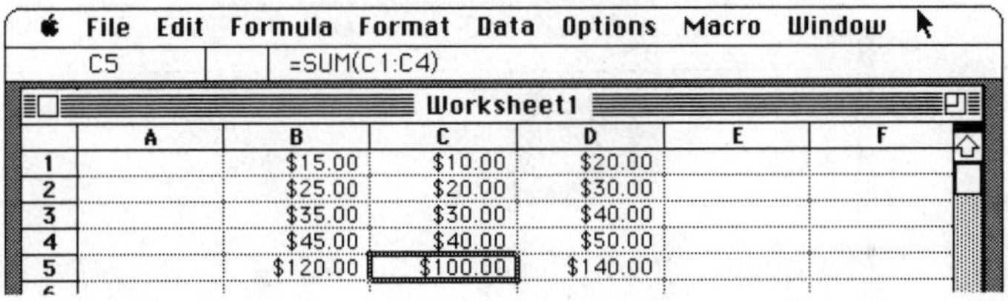

FIGURE 4-22. *This is the worksheet after cutting and pasting.*

Cut and Paste rules

There are a few rules to keep in mind as you use the Cut and Paste commands. First, the cut area you select must be rectangular in shape. You cannot select a discontinuous range of cells.

You do not have to select the entire paste range before you choose the Paste command. If you click a single cell, as you did in the example above, Excel automatically extends the paste area to match the size and shape of the cut area. The cell you select becomes the upper-left corner of the paste area.

If you do select the entire paste area, make sure that the range you select is exactly the same size and shape as the cut area. If the cut and paste areas are not identical in size and shape, Excel alerts you with the message *Cut and paste areas are different shapes*. To correct the problem, click OK in the alert box and select a new paste area.

The operation of cutting in Microsoft Excel is a little different from that of other Macintosh applications, in which something cut to the Clipboard can be pasted from there more than once. In Excel, you can specify only one paste area after you use the Cut command. If you need to transfer the contents of a cell to more than one area of your worksheet, use the Copy command, which is described below, to make all the moves, then use the Clear... command to erase the contents of the original cell.

As you saw in the previous example, when you cut a cell from one area of your worksheet and paste it in another area, you transfer both the contents and formats of this cut cell to the pasted cell.

In addition, keep in mind that Excel overwrites the contents of any existing cells in the paste range when you use the Paste command. For example, if you select cell B1 as your paste area in Figure 4-21 instead of cell C1, your worksheet looks like Figure 4-23 after you use Paste. If you do not want to lose existing cell entries, make sure that there are enough blank cells to hold the entire cut area below and to the right of the cell that you select as the upper-left corner of the paste area.

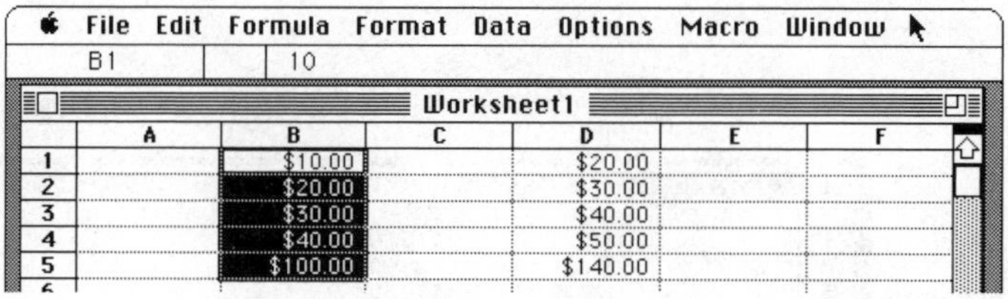

FIGURE 4-23. *Pasting into cells that already contain entries replaces the existing contents and formats with the pasted ones.*

Also, remember that when you move a cell, Excel automatically adjusts any formulas outside the cut area that refer to that cell. For example, in Figure 4-24, cell B1 contains the formula

=SUM(A1:A3)

Suppose you move cells A1:A4 into cells C1:C4. As you can see in Figure 4-25, the move has had no apparent effect on the cells' contents. Behind the scenes, however, Excel has done a lot of housekeeping to make sure the formulas remain correct. For example, Excel has changed the formula in cell B1 to read

=SUM(C1:C3)

Similarly, if the cells in the cut area contain references to other cells within the cut area, Excel adjusts those formulas accordingly when you choose the Paste command. For example, cell A3 in Figure 4-24 contains the formula

=A1+A2

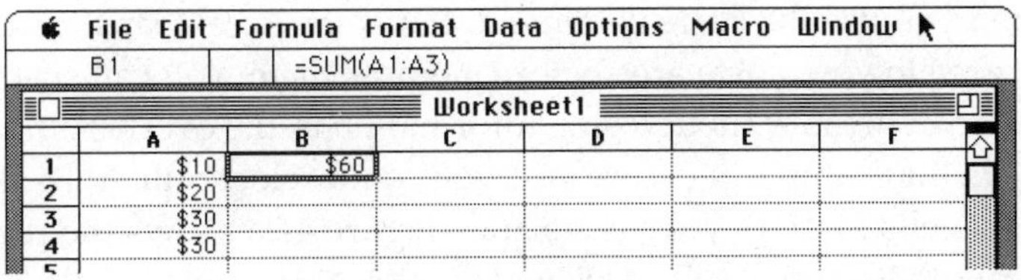

FIGURE 4-24. *The formula in cell B1 sums the cells in the range A1:A3.*

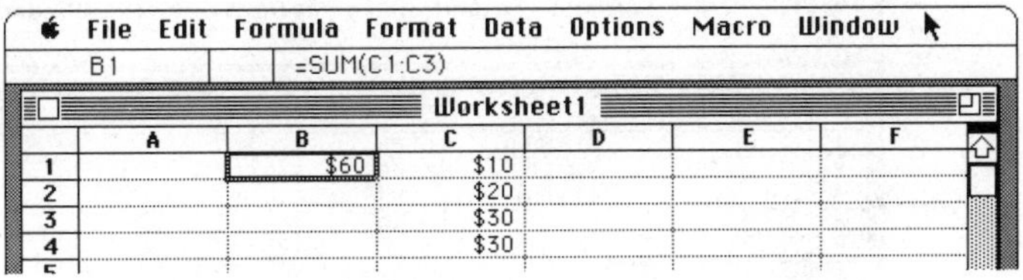

FIGURE 4-25. *Excel automatically adjusts the formula in cell B1 after referenced cells are moved.*

If you move the range A1:A4 into cells C1:C4, Excel automatically adjusts the formula in cell A3 to read

=C1+C2

If the cells in the cut area contain references to cells outside the cut area, those references remain unchanged. For example, in Figure 4-24, cell A4 contains the formula

=B1/2

When you move cells A1:A4 into cells C1:C4, the formula in cell A4 remains unchanged, but is moved to cell C4. References to cells outside the cut area still refer to that area when Excel pastes them to a new location.

References to the cut area from outside the cut area produce a #REF! error value if you decide to move the cut area to another worksheet. References to the paste area produce a #REF! error value if your paste overwrites existing entries.

Using overlapping cut and paste ranges

Suppose you want to move cells A1:B5 in Figure 4-20 into cells B1:C5. You could simply select cells A1:A5 and choose the Insert… command, but this would cause all of the cells in rows 1 through 5 to be shifted one column to the right. As a result, the remaining columns in the worksheet would move as well.

Fortunately, Microsoft Excel offers a way around this problem. We mentioned earlier that Excel overwrites any existing contents of the cells in the paste range when you use the Paste command. But since Excel transfers the contents of your cut area to your paste area before it erases them, you can specify overlapping cut and paste areas without losing information in the overlapping cells.

In the example in Figure 4-20, you could select cells A1:B5 as your cut area, then select cells B1:C5 as your paste area. Figure 4-26 shows the result. Notice that the entries that were in cells A1:B5 in Figure 4-20 are now in cells B1:C5, but that the entries to the right of column C in rows 1 through 5 have not moved.

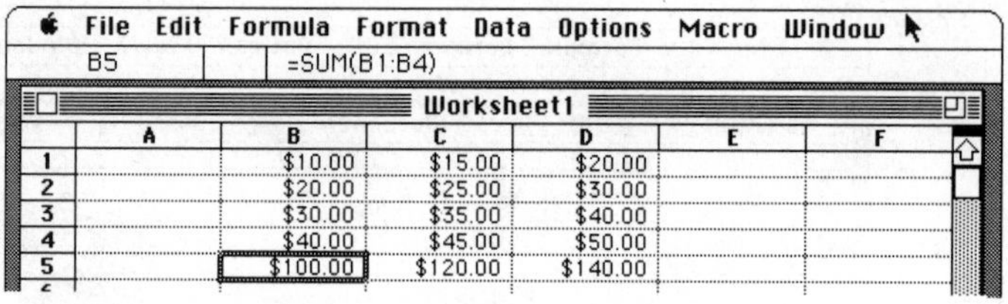

⌘ File Edit Formula Format Data Options Macro Window ▸					
B5		=SUM(B1:B4)			

▤▭▭▭▭▭▭▭▭▭▭▭▭ Worksheet1 ▭▭▭▭▭▭▭▭▭▭▭▭					
	A	B	C	D	E	F
1		$10.00	$15.00	$20.00		
2		$20.00	$25.00	$30.00		
3		$30.00	$35.00	$40.00		
4		$40.00	$45.00	$50.00		
5		$100.00	$120.00	$140.00		

FIGURE 4-26. *You can use overlapping cut and paste areas when moving information.*

E X C E L

The Show Clipboard command

As you probably know, most Macintosh programs use the Clipboard as a holding area for data when you use the Cut or Copy commands. In Microsoft Excel, you can choose the Show Clipboard command from the Window menu to bring the Clipboard onto the desktop.

In Excel, Show Clipboard does not display the contents of the cells you have selected to cut or copy. Instead, the proportions of the cut area or copy area appear in the Clipboard window. If you can't remember the size or shape of the cut or copy area when you are selecting a paste area, you can choose Show Clipboard from the Window menu to display the number of rows and columns in the cut or copy area.

The Copy and Paste commands

The Microsoft Excel Copy and Paste commands let you duplicate the contents and formats of cells in another area of your worksheet, without disturbing the contents of the original cells. You use the Copy command to indicate the range of cells you want to copy, and you use the Paste command to indicate where you want the copies to be placed.

Copying a single cell

For example, suppose you want to copy the contents of cell A1 of your worksheet into cell C1. You begin by clicking cell A1, then choose Copy from the Edit menu or use the F3 function key. As shown in Figure 4-27, a marquee appears around cell A1, the cell to be copied. Now, click cell C1 and choose Paste from the Edit menu or press the F4 function key. Figure 4-28 shows the result.

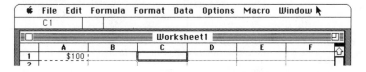

FIGURE 4-27. *You have copied the contents of one cell to another.*

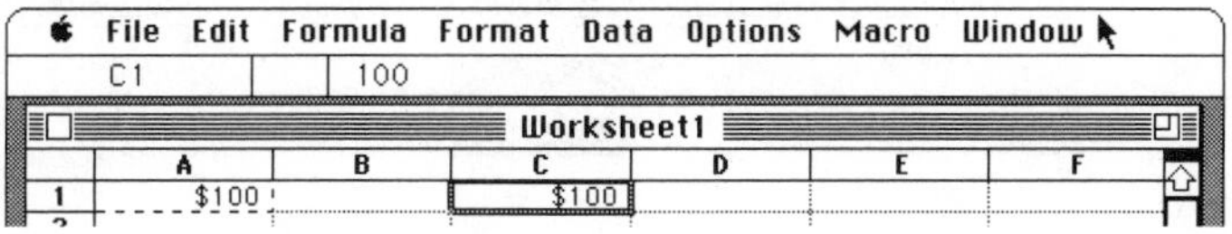

FIGURE 4-28. *The worksheet looks like this after copying.*

As you can see, the marquee around cell A1 does not disappear after you use the Paste command. The marquee indicates that your copy area is still "active." Although you can specify only one paste area when you use the Cut command, you can specify as many paste areas as you like when you are copying cells. Excel can retrieve the contents of the marquee until another Cut or Copy command changes its location.

You can even use the commands on the Window menu and the Open... and New... commands from the File menu to access other worksheets and windows without "losing" your copy area. For example, you might copy a range of cells into another area of your worksheet, then choose the File menu's Open... command in order to access a second worksheet. Excel allows you to copy the selected cells into the new worksheet as well.

By specifying paste areas of different sizes and shapes, you can create multiple copies of the contents of the copy area. For example, if you specify the range C1:D1 as the paste range, Excel copies the contents of cell A1 into both cells C1 and D1 as shown in Figure 4-29 on the next page. Similarly, if you designate the range C1:C2 as the paste range, Excel creates two copies of the copy range, one above another, in column C.

You can also specify multiple, discontinuous paste areas. For example, suppose you want to copy the contents of cell A1 into cells C1, C3, and D2. To do this, you click cell A1 and choose the Copy command. Next, you click cell C1 and, holding down the Command key, click cells C3 and D2. Then, you choose the Paste command. Figure 4-30 shows the result.

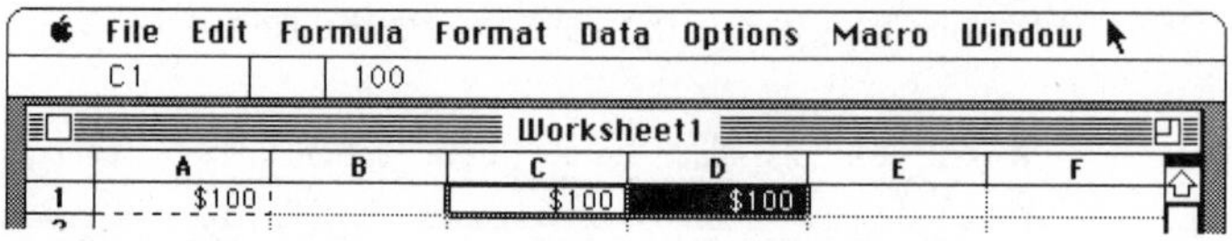

FIGURE 4-29. *You have created multiple copies of a cell.*

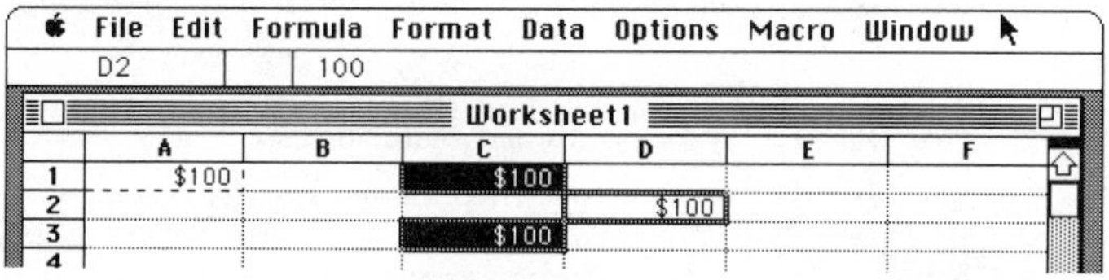

FIGURE 4-30. *You have copied into multiple, discontinuous paste areas.*

Copying ranges

As you might expect, you can use the Copy command to copy ranges as well as single cells. For example, to copy cells A1:A3 of your worksheet into cells C1:C3, you can begin by dragging through cells A1:A3, then choose Copy from the Edit menu. A marquee appears around the range of cells to be copied. Now, click cell C1 and choose Paste from the Edit menu to copy A1:A3 into C1:C3.

As with the Cut and Paste commands, you do not have to select the entire paste area when you copy cells. You need only indicate the upper-left corner of the range by clicking a single cell. You can, however, select the entire paste area. In the previous example, you could have selected cells C1:C3 before you chose the Paste command. The result would have been the same as selecting the single cell C1.

Microsoft Excel also allows you to create multiple copies of the copy range. For example, if you select C1:D1 as the paste range, Excel creates two copies of A1:A3, side by side, in columns C and D. The same result could be achieved by selecting the range C1:D3. Similarly, designating the paste range C1:C6 causes Excel to create two copies of the copy range, one above another, in column C. However, not every paste range works when you are copying ranges. For example, if you copy cells A1:A3, then designate the ranges C1:C2, C1:D2, C1:C4, or C1:E5, Excel alerts you that the copy and paste areas are different shapes.

Using overlapping copy and paste ranges

Although Microsoft Excel allows you to specify overlapping cut and paste ranges, you cannot specify overlapping copy and paste ranges quite so freely. For example, if you click the range A1:A3, choose the Copy command, then click cell A2 and choose the Paste command, you'll see the message *Selection is not valid.*

The only exception to this rule is that you can specify a paste range that contains the entire copy range. For example, Figure 4-31 shows the results of specifying cells A1:A3 as your copy range, then designating cells A1:C3 as your paste range. The contents of cells A1:A3 have not changed.

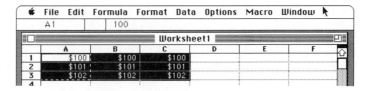

FIGURE 4-31. *Using overlapping ranges with the Copy command works only if the paste range contains the entire copy range.*

Using relative and absolute references with Copy

As we said in Chapter 2, "Worksheet Basics," Excel recognizes two different kinds of cell references: relative and absolute. These two types of references behave very differently when you use the Copy command.

Relative references

When you copy a cell that contains a formula that uses relative references, the cell references in that formula in the paste area do not refer to the same cells as the original cell references in the formula in the copy area. Instead, Excel changes the references in relation to the position of the pasted cell. Most of your cell references in Excel will be relative references.

For example, suppose you have created the worksheet in Figure 4-32 on the next page. You have entered the formula

=AVERAGE(B4:D4)

in cell E4. This formula tells Excel to average the test scores in the three cells immediately to the left of cell E4. Of course, you want to repeat this calculation for the remaining categories as well. Rather than typing a new formula in each cell in column E, you can click cell E4 and choose Copy from the Edit menu. Now, drag through cells E5:E10 and choose Paste from the Edit menu. The results appear in Figure 4-33 on the next page.

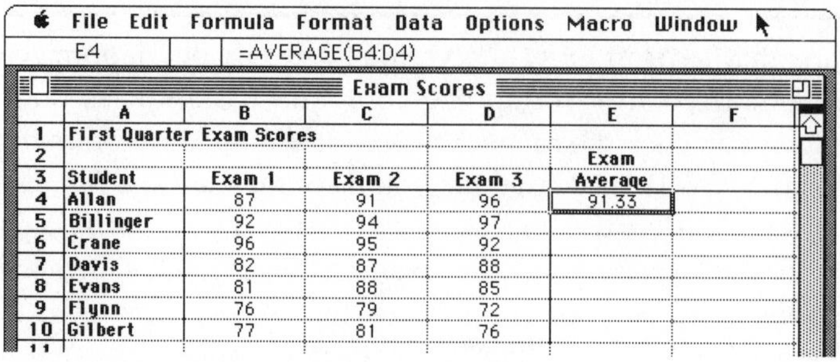

FIGURE 4-32. *This worksheet calculates average exam scores.*

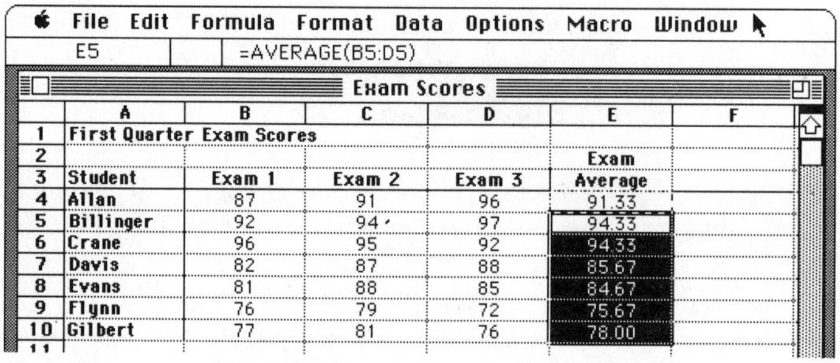

FIGURE 4-33. *This is the exam-score worksheet after copying and pasting a formula containing relative references.*

Because the formula in cell E4 contains a relative reference, Excel adjusts the cell references in each copy of the formula. As a result, each copy of the formula calculates the average of the three cells immediately to its left. For example, cell E6 contains the formula

=AVERAGE(B6:D6)

Absolute references

There will be many occasions when you want to create formulas that contain cell references that do not change when you copy them. In those situations, you'll want to use absolute references instead of relative references. Absolute references do not change when you copy them to another area of your worksheet.

For example, in the worksheet in Figure 4-34, cell C6 contains the formula

=B6*B2

Cell B2 contains the wage rate at which employees are to be paid. Now, suppose you want to copy this formula into the range C7:C9. Figure 4-35 shows what happens if you copy the existing formula into this range.

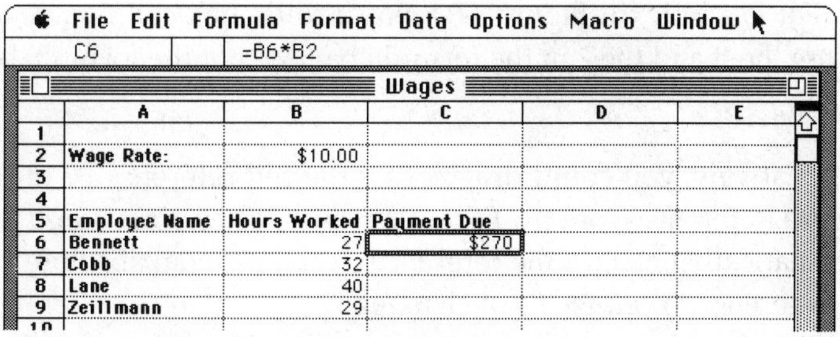

FIGURE 4-34. *The entry in cell C6 is a formula containing relative references.*

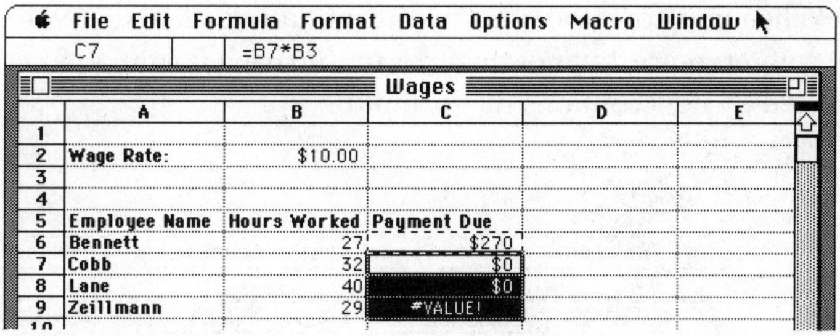

FIGURE 4-35. *This figure shows the result of copying the formula in cell C6 into the range C7:C9.*

Notice that the formulas in cells C7 and C8 return the value 0, while cell C9 contains the #VALUE! error value. If you look at the formulas in these cells, you'll see that none of them refers to cell B2. For example, the formula in cell C7 is

=B7*B3

Similarly, cell C9 contains the formula

=B9*B5

Because cell B5 contains a label rather than a value, the formula in cell C9 returns an error value.

Because the reference to cell B2 is relative, it changes as you copy this formula through the worksheet. Since you want to apply the wage rate in cell B2 to all of the calculations, you must change the reference to cell B2 to an absolute reference before you copy the formula.

There are two ways to change the reference style: by typing a dollar sign ($) in front of the row and column reference, or by using the Reference command from the Formula menu. The Reference command inserts dollar signs for you. The $ symbol tells Excel to "lock in" the reference.

For example, in Figure 4-34, you could click cell C6 and insert the $ symbol before the B and the 2 in the formula bar, so that the formula becomes

=B6*$B$2

Alternatively, you could drag across the cell reference B2 in the formula bar and choose Reference from the Formula menu. When you choose this command, Excel automatically changes the reference to cell B2 to an absolute reference. However, the reference to cell B6 is not changed.

You can also use the Command and T keys to change a cell reference from relative to absolute. This key combination is the shorthand equivalent of the Reference command. You simply select the cell reference you want to change and press Command-T.

When you copy the modified formula into cells C7:C9, Excel adjusts the second cell reference, but not the first, within each formula. As you can see in Figure 4-36, cell C9 now contains the formula

=B9*$B$2

É File Edit Formula Format Data Options Macro Window **k**
C9		=B9*$B$2

Wages

	A	B	C	D	E
1					
2	Wage Rate:	$10.00			
3					
4					
5	Employee Name	Hours Worked	Payment Due		
6	Bennett	27	$270		
7	Cobb	32	$320		
8	Lane	40	$400		
9	Zeillmann	29	$290		
10					

FIGURE 4-36. *This figure shows the result of changing the formula to make cell B2 an absolute reference.*

Mixed references

There will also be occasions when you want to use mixed references in your worksheet. In a mixed reference, the row or column portion of the reference is absolute and the other portion (column or row) is relative. When you copy mixed references, Excel anchors the row or column portion and adjusts the other portion in relation to the location of the copy cell.

In a mixed reference, a dollar sign appears in front of the absolute portion of the reference but not in front of the other portion. For example, the references $B2 and B$2 are mixed references.

Again, to create a mixed reference you can type the $ symbol in front of the row or column reference, or you can use the Reference command. Each time you choose Reference from the Formula menu or press Command-T, Excel cycles through the four combinations of absolute and relative references.

For example, if you select the $B$2 reference in the previous example and press the Command and T keys, Excel changes the formula to read

=B6*B$2

In this formula, the column reference is relative while the row reference is absolute. If you choose Reference a second time, Excel changes the formula to

=B6*$B2

Here, the column reference is absolute and the row reference is relative. Choosing Reference yet again restores the original B2 relative reference.

There are certain situations where you will use mixed references. The loan-payment table in Figure 4-37 shows one situation in which mixed references can be very convenient. Cell B5 uses the formula

=PMT($A5,10,B$4)

to calculate the annual payments on a $10,000 loan over a period of ten years at an interest rate of 7 percent. We have copied this formula into cells B5:D11 to calculate payments on three different loan amounts using several different interest rates.

	A	B	C	D	E
	Loan Payment Schedule				
1	Loan Payment Schedule				
2					
3		– – – – – –	LOAN AMOUNT	– – – – – –	
4	RATE	**$10,000**	**$15,000**	**$20,000**	
5	7.00%	($1,424)	($2,136)	($2,848)	
6	7.50%	($1,457)	($2,185)	($2,914)	
7	8.00%	($1,490)	($2,235)	($2,981)	
8	8.50%	($1,524)	($2,286)	($3,048)	
9	9.00%	($1,558)	($2,337)	($3,116)	
10	9.50%	($1,593)	($2,389)	($3,185)	
11	10.00%	($1,627)	($2,441)	($3,255)	
12					

FIGURE 4-37. *This loan-payment table uses formulas containing mixed references.*

The first cell reference, $A5, tells Excel that you always want to refer to the values in column A. The row reference remains relative, however, so that the copied formulas in rows 6 through 11 refer to the appropriate interest rates in cells A6 through A11. Similarly, the second cell reference, B$4, tells Excel that you always want to refer to the value in row 4. In this case, the column reference remains relative so that the copied formulas in columns B through D refer to the appropriate interest rates in cells B4 through D4. For example, cell D11 contains the formula

=PMT($A11,10,D$4)

Notice that only the row reference changes in the first cell reference. The column reference remains the same. By the same token, only the column reference changes in the second cell reference. The row reference remains constant. Without mixed references, you would have to edit the formula manually for each column or row of the calculations in cells B5 through D11.

Using Edit-menu commands in the formula bar

In addition to the Undo command, you can also use the Microsoft Excel Cut, Copy, Paste, and Clear... commands to edit entries in the formula bar. Often it is easier to re-enter a value or formula in a cell, but the Microsoft Excel Edit-menu commands can be convenient when you are working with a long, complex formula or label. Let's use the text entry

This is a very, very long label

as an example.

Suppose you want to add another *very* to this label. You can do this by placing the insertion point to the right of the first *very* and typing a comma, a space, and then the word *very*. Alternatively, you can drag through the word *very*, the comma, and the space after the comma in the formula bar, then choose the Copy command, place the insertion point just to the left of the *v* in the second *very*, and choose Paste from the Edit menu. Your label now reads

This is a very, very, very long label

To delete the word you just added, you can choose Undo Paste from the Edit menu, or you can drag across the characters, then choose the Clear... command. Excel erases the characters and closes up the resulting gap.

You can also use this capability to copy all or part of a formula from one cell into a formula in another cell. For example, suppose cell A10 contains the function

=IF(NPV(.15,$A$1:$A$9)>0,A11,A12)

You want to enter the function

=NPV(.15,$A$1:$A$9)

in cell B10. You can click cell A10, drag across the characters you want to copy—in this case, NPV(.15,$A$1:$A$9)—and choose Copy from the Edit menu. Now, press Enter, click cell B10, type an equal sign (=), and choose the Paste command. Excel inserts the contents of the copy range at the insertion point. You must press Enter after copying from the formula bar. If you don't, Excel inserts into the formula you're copying from a reference to the cell you plan to copy to.

The Paste Special... command

There may be times when you want to move or copy the value of a cell without carrying over the underlying formula on which the value is based. Or you may want to copy the formula, but not the format, of a cell. The Microsoft Excel Paste Special... command offers a convenient way to copy only selected "parts" of a cell.

For example, cell E4 in Figure 4-38 contains the formula

=AVERAGE(B4:D4)

Suppose you want to use the value from cell E4 in cell F4 of your worksheet, but you don't want to copy the formula from cell E4 to the new location. You can click cell E4 and choose Copy from the Edit menu, then click cell F4 and choose Paste Special..., instead of Paste, from the Edit menu. When you choose the Paste Special... command, Excel displays the dialog box shown in Figure 4-39.

	🍎 File Edit Formula Format Data Options Macro Window ▸

E4	=AVERAGE(B4:D4)

Exam Scores

	A	B	C	D	E	F
1	First Quarter Exam Scores					
2					Exam	
3	Student	Exam 1	Exam 2	Exam 3	Average	
4	Allan	87	91	96	91.33	
5	Billinger	92	94	97	94.33	
6	Crane	96	95	92	94.33	
7	Davis	82	87	88	85.67	
8	Evans	81	88	85	84.67	
9	Flynn	76	79	72	75.67	
10	Gilbert	77	81	76	78.00	

FIGURE 4-38. *This exam-scores worksheet shows the formula in cell E4.*

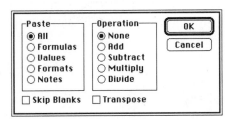

FIGURE 4-39. *This is the Paste Special dialog box.*

As you can see, the dialog box allows you to paste just the formulas, values, formats, or notes from the copy range into the paste range. For this example, you can double click Values. When you do this, Excel copies only the displayed value of the formula in cell E4 into cell F4. After the copy operation is complete, cell F4 contains the number 91.3333333. As you can see in Figure 4-40, the formula and numeric format of the original cell have not been copied, so even if you later change any of the values in cells B4:D10, the value in cell F4 remains unchanged.

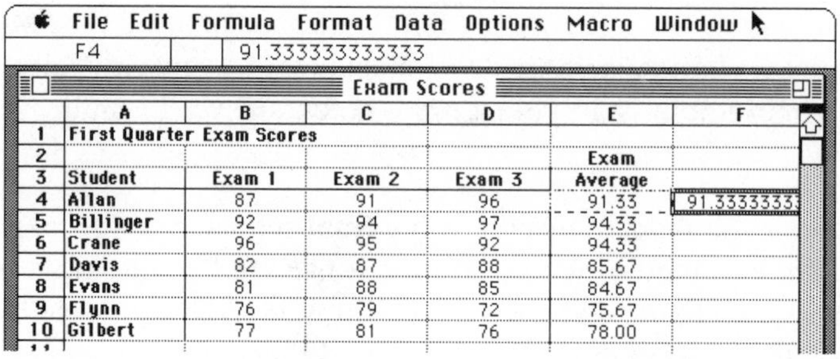

FIGURE 4-40. *This is the exam-scores worksheet, after using Paste Special... to copy the value of the formula in cell E4 into cell F4.*

Selecting Formats from the Paste Special dialog box transfers only the formats from the cells in the copy range to the cells in the paste range. This command has about the same effect as selecting a range of cells and choosing the appropriate options from the Format menu. Copying formats does not change the value of the cells in your paste area.

Selecting Formulas from the Paste Special dialog box causes Excel to copy the formulas in the cells in the copy range to the paste range without copying the formats you have assigned to those cells. For example, in Figure 4-41, cells A1:A5 are formatted to display currency with two decimal places (the $#,##0.00 format), while cells B1:B5 are formatted to display integers (the 0 format). If you copy cells A1:A5 into cells B1:B5 using the Paste Special Formulas option, the worksheet looks like Figure 4-42. Notice that the values in cells B1:B5 have changed, but the formats have not.

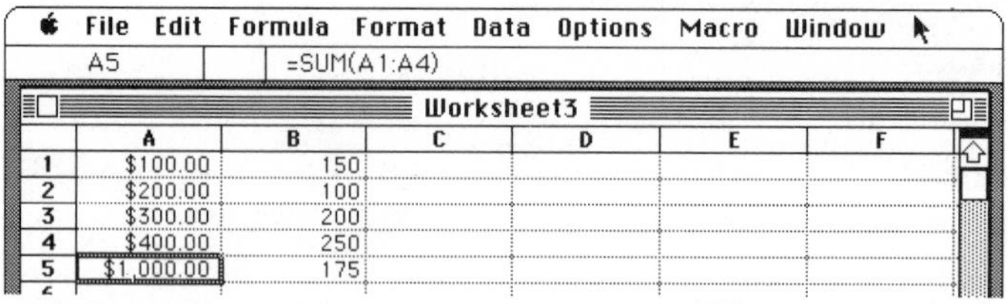

FIGURE 4-41. *The range A1:A5 is formatted to display currency with two decimal places; the range B1:B5 is formatted to display integers.*

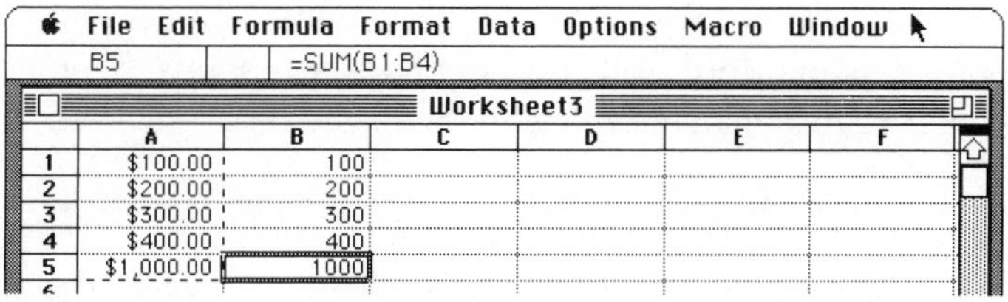

FIGURE 4-42. *You have used the Formulas option of the Paste Special…*
command to paste the formulas from A1:A5 into B1:B5 without
changing the latter's format.

If you select the Notes option, Excel pastes only the notes you've added to the cells in your worksheet. We discuss the concept of cell notes in Chapter 8, "Other Worksheet Topics."

If you select All in the Paste Special dialog box, Excel copies everything in the cell from the copy range to the paste range. Because selecting All has the same effect as selecting the regular Paste command, you may wonder why Excel offers this option. The answer has to do with the list of Operation options in the Paste Special dialog box.

The Operation options

The options in the Operation box allow you to combine the contents of the copy area with the contents of the paste area. When you select any option in this box other than None, Excel does not replace the contents of the paste range with the contents of the copy range. Instead, the contents of the copy range are combined with the contents of the paste range using the specified operator.

For example, you might add the average exam scores and bonus points in columns E and F of Figure 4-43 on the next page to calculate the final exam scores in Figure 4-44, also on the next page. Begin by dragging across cells E4:E10, then choose Copy from the Edit menu. Now, point to cell G4 and choose the Paste Special… command. Double click the Values option in the Paste Special dialog box to copy only the values in cells E4:E10 into cells G4:G10. Next, drag through the range F4:F10 and choose Copy again. Now, click cell G4 and choose the Paste Special… command. Click the Values and Add options in the Paste Special dialog box, then click OK. As you can see in Figure 4-44, Excel adds the values in cells F4:F10 to the values in cells G4:G10. Note that the resulting values appear in the default General format.

There's a reason why you didn't simply add the contents of cells E4:E10 directly to the contents of cells F4:F10. If you used the Paste Special… command to add the exam averages to the bonus points in column F, Excel would overwrite the original contents of column F with the combined values of columns E and F, leaving you with no record of each student's bonus points. In other words, you would no longer have had an audit trail by which to track each student's grades.

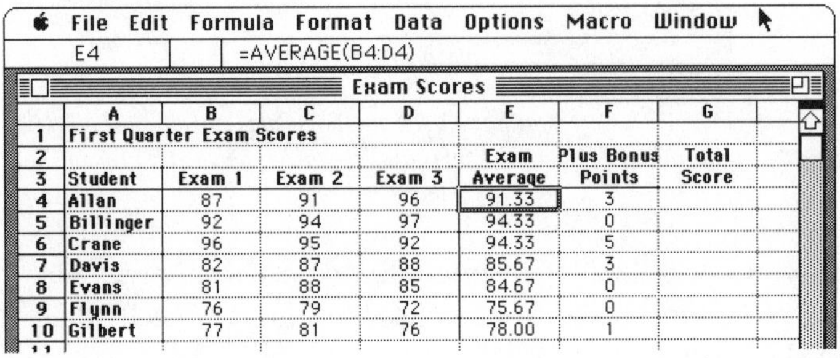

	A	B	C	D	E	F	G
1	First Quarter Exam Scores						
2					Exam	Plus Bonus	Total
3	Student	Exam 1	Exam 2	Exam 3	Average	Points	Score
4	Allan	87	91	96	91.33	3	
5	Billinger	92	94	97	94.33	0	
6	Crane	96	95	92	94.33	5	
7	Davis	82	87	88	85.67	3	
8	Evans	81	88	85	84.67	0	
9	Flynn	76	79	72	75.67	0	
10	Gilbert	77	81	76	78.00	1	

FIGURE 4-43. *The exam-scores worksheet shows average scores and bonus points.*

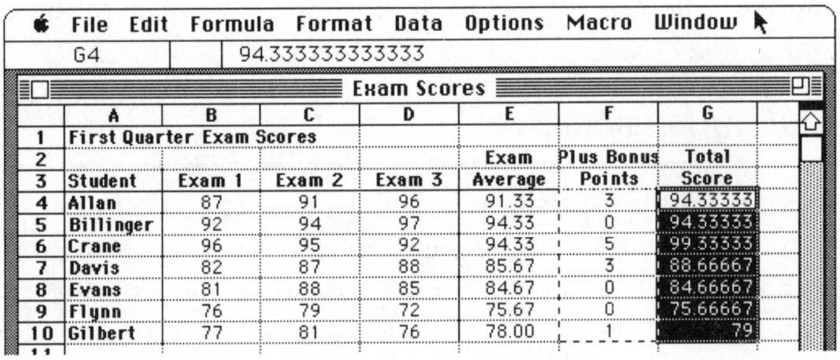

	A	B	C	D	E	F	G
1	First Quarter Exam Scores						
2					Exam	Plus Bonus	Total
3	Student	Exam 1	Exam 2	Exam 3	Average	Points	Score
4	Allan	87	91	96	91.33	3	94.33333
5	Billinger	92	94	97	94.33	0	94.33333
6	Crane	96	95	92	94.33	5	99.33333
7	Davis	82	87	88	85.67	3	88.66667
8	Evans	81	88	85	84.67	0	84.66667
9	Flynn	76	79	72	75.67	0	75.66667
10	Gilbert	77	81	76	78.00	1	79

FIGURE 4-44. *The exam-scores worksheet looks like this after you combine average scores and bonus points with the Paste Special... command's Values and Add options to produce a total score.*

The other options in the Operation box combine the contents of the copy and paste ranges using different operators. The Subtract operator subtracts the contents of the copy range from the contents of the paste range, the Multiply operator multiplies the contents of the ranges, and the Divide operator divides the contents of the paste range by the contents of the copy range.

Most of the time, you'll choose the Values option from the Paste portion of the Paste Special dialog box when you take advantage of the Operation options. When you choose Values, Excel combines the values from the copy range with the entries in the paste range, and does not copy the copy range formats to the paste range.

As long as the entries in the copy range are numbers, you can use the All option, instead of Values, to copy the numbers and the formats from the copy range to the paste range. If the copy range contains formulas, however, the result of using All may be a bit surprising.

For example, suppose that cell A1 contains the value 10, cell A2 contains the formula

=A1

which returns the value 10, and cell B2 contains the value 2. If you click cell A2, choose the Copy command, click cell B2, choose the Paste Special... command, click All, and click Add, Excel combines the formula from cell A2—adjusted, because it is a relative reference—with the entry in cell B2. The result is the formula

=2+(B1)

The same thing occurs if the cells in the paste range include formulas, even if you select the Values options. For example, if cell A2 contains the value 2, and cell B2 contains the formula

=B1

the result of copying A2 to B2 with Values and Add selected in the Paste Special dialog box is the formula

=(B1)+2

As a rule, you'll want to avoid using the All option with any of the Paste Special Operation options when the copy range includes formulas. In fact, you will probably want to avoid the Operation options altogether if the paste range contains formulas.

If the copy range contains text entries and you use the Paste Special... command with an Operation option, Excel does not copy those text entries into the paste range. For example, cells A1 and A3 in Figure 4-45 contain numbers, while cells A2 and A4 contain text. If you use the Multiply option to multiply the values in cells B1:B4 by the values in cells A1:A4, your worksheet looks like Figure 4-46 on the next page. Notice that the values in cells B2 and B4 did not change.

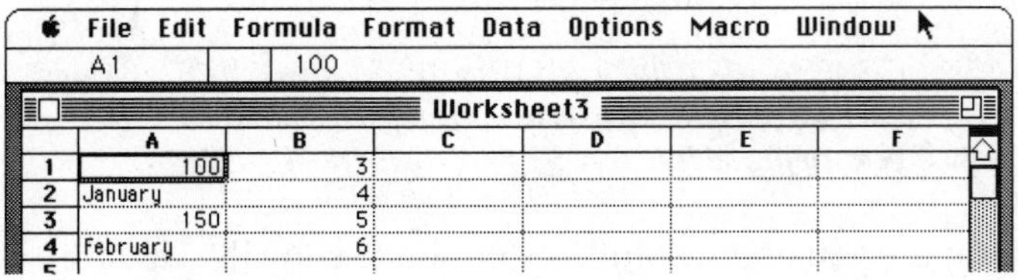

FIGURE 4-45. *This worksheet shows number and text entries.*

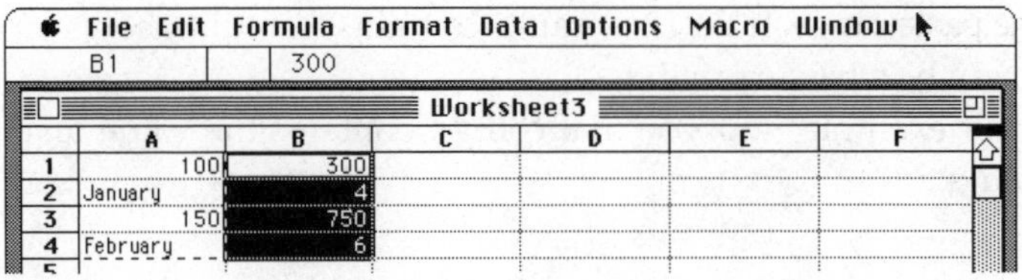

FIGURE 4-46. *Using the Multiply option of the Paste Special…*
command has no effect if one of the entries you are multiplying is text.

Blank spaces in the copy and paste ranges are assigned the value 0 if you select the Add, Subtract, Multiply, or Divide options. For example, suppose you use the Add option to copy the values in cells A1:A7 to cells B1:B7 in Figure 4-47. As you can see in Figure 4-48, Excel does not change the values in cells B2, B4, and B6, because cells A2, A4, and A6 have values of 0.

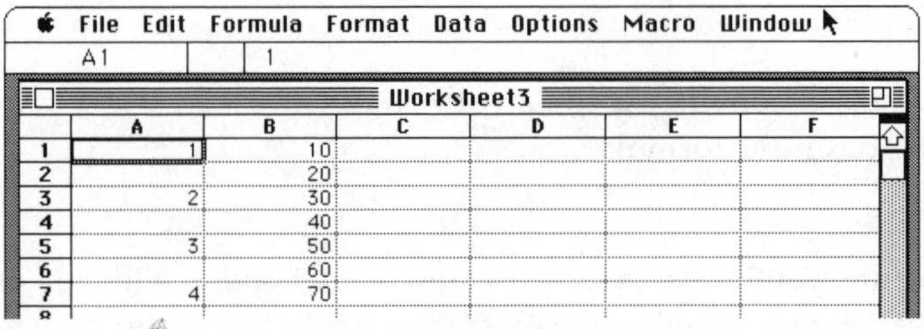

FIGURE 4-47. *Range A1:A7 has some blank cells.*

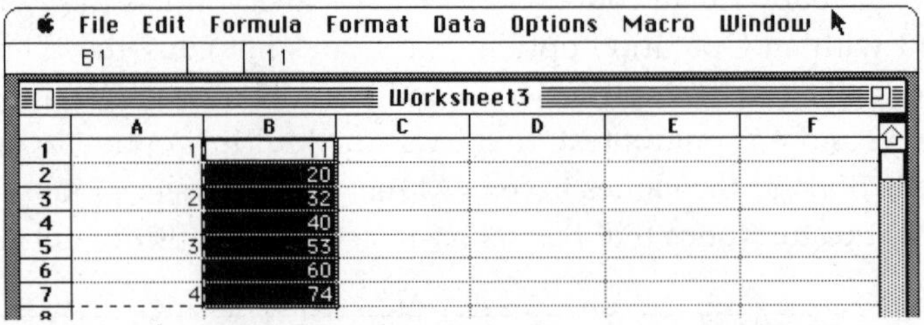

FIGURE 4-48. *Adding A1:A7 to B1:B7 leaves cells B2, B4, and B6*
unchanged because Excel assigns the value 0 to blank cells when
performing addition.

Suppose you use the Multiply option to copy the values in cells B1:B7 into cells A1:A7 in Figure 4-47. As you can see in Figure 4-49, the values in cells A2, A4, and A6 are equal to 0, because Excel assigns a value of 0 to the blank cells in column A.

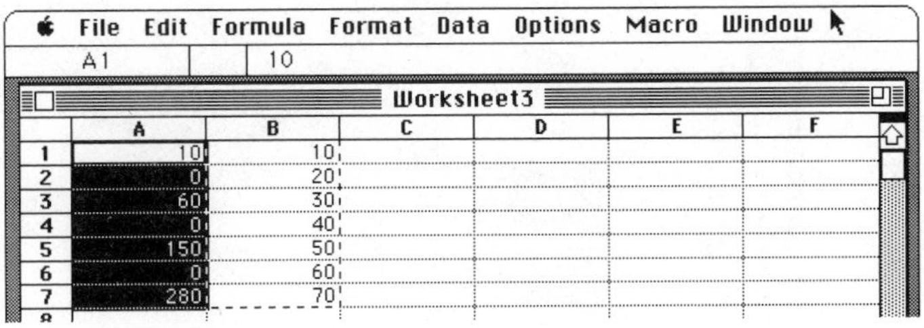

FIGURE 4-49. *Multiplying B1:B7 into A1:A7 makes A2, A4, and A6 equal to 0 because Excel assigns the value 0 to blank cells when performing multiplication.*

The Operation options can be particularly helpful when you are combining the contents of two or more worksheets into a single file. We talk more about linking one worksheet to another in Chapter 8, ''Other Worksheet Topics.''

Skipping blank cells

At the lower left of the Paste Special dialog box is a Skip Blanks check box. Use this option when you want Microsoft Excel to ignore any blank cells in the copy range. Generally, if your copy range contains blank cells, Microsoft Excel pastes those blank cells over the corresponding cells in the paste area. As a result, the contents, formats, and notes in the paste area are overwritten by the empty cell. When you use the Skip Blanks option, however, the corresponding cells in the paste area are unaffected.

For example, suppose you want to use the Skip Blanks option to copy cells A1:A7 into the range B1:B7 in Figure 4-50. As you can see in Figure 4-51 on the next page, the blank cells A2, A4, and A6 don't affect the entries in cells B2, B4, and B6. Instead, the entries from the two ranges are interwoven.

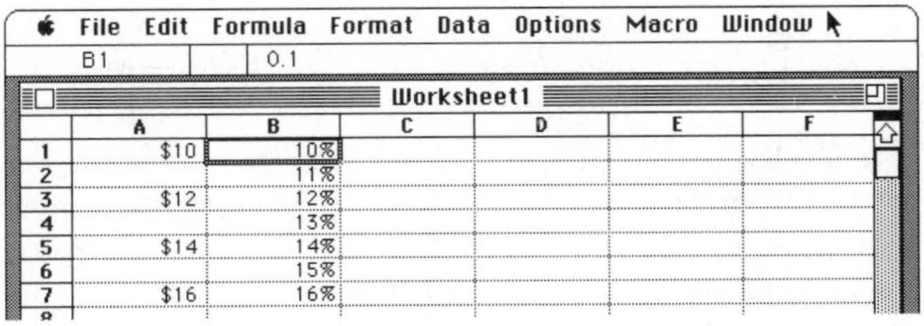

FIGURE 4-50. *Cells A2, A4, and A6 contain blank cells.*

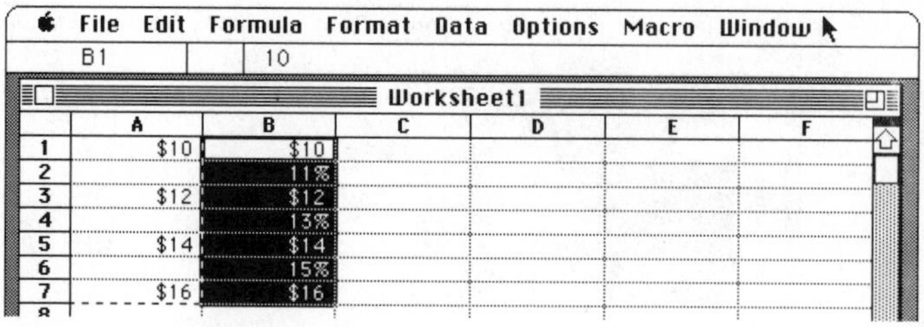

FIGURE 4-51. *When using the Skip Blanks option, the empty cells in the copy range don't affect corresponding cells in the paste range.*

Transposing entries

The last option in the Paste Special dialog box is Transpose, which lets you reorient the contents of the copy range in the selected paste range. When you use the Transpose option, entries in the top row of the copy area appear in the left column of the paste range, and entries in the left column appear in the top row. To illustrate, let's use the Transpose option to paste the contents of cells A1:B7 in Figure 4-50. If we specify cell C1 as the top-left corner of our Paste Special range, our worksheet looks like the one in Figure 4-52. Excel not only transposes the values from the copied cells, it also transposes the formats. (Notice that we've adjusted the column widths so that we can display the entire paste range.)

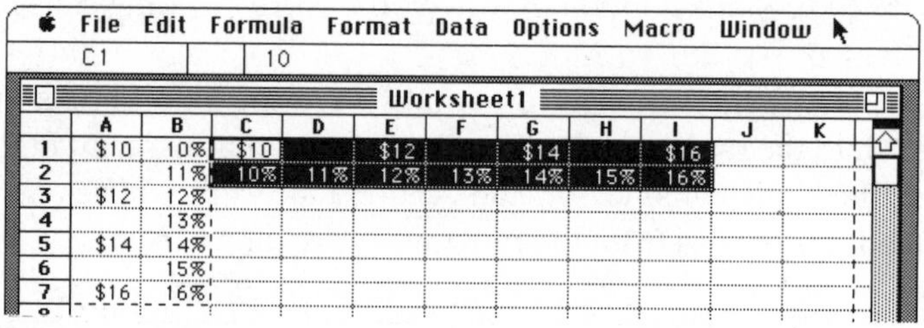

FIGURE 4-52. *The Transpose check box reorients a pasted selection.*

The Fill Commands

The Fill Right, Fill Left, Fill Down, and Fill Up commands are handy shortcuts that let you copy the contents of one or more cells into an adjacent set of cells. The Fill Right command copies the entries in the leftmost cells of a range into the rest of the cells in the range. Fill Down copies the entries in the top cells of a range down into the rest of the cells in the range. If you press the Shift key before choosing the Edit menu, Microsoft Excel changes the Fill Right and Fill Down commands to read the Fill Left and Fill Up commands. As you might have guessed, Fill Left copies the entries in the rightmost column of a range into the rest of the cells in the range, and Fill Up copies the entries in the bottom row of a range up into the rest of the cells in the range.

For example, in Figure 4-33 you used the Copy and Paste commands to copy the formula in cell E4 into cells E5:E10. You could have used Microsoft Excel's Fill Down command, instead of Copy and Paste, to copy this formula. To use Fill Down, you would simply have typed the desired formula in cell E4, dragged through cells E4:E10, and chosen Fill Down from the Edit menu. The resulting worksheet would have looked just like Figure 4-33.

Similarly, you can use the Fill Right command to copy a series of cells across your worksheet. Let's use the simple worksheet in Figure 4-53 as an example. Suppose you want to copy the contents of cells A1:A4 into cells B1:E4 of your worksheet. Simply drag through cells A1:E4 and choose Fill Right from the Edit menu. The results appear in Figure 4-54.

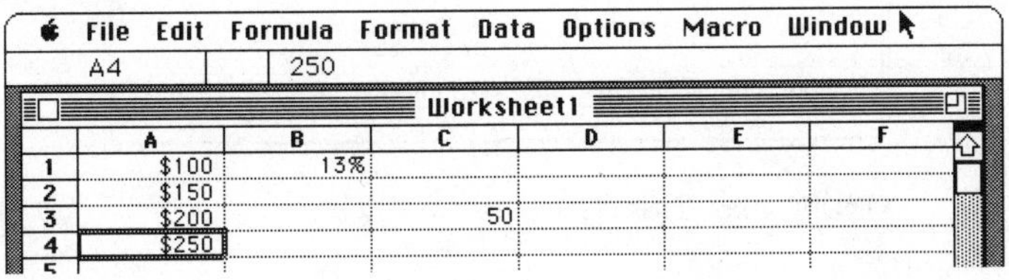

FIGURE 4-53. *This simple worksheet shows entries in A1:A4, B1, and B3.*

The results of the Fill commands are identical to the Copy and Paste commands. Any relative cell references in the copied cells are adjusted. As with the Copy command, Excel overwrites any existing entries in the fill area. Notice that the contents of cells B1 and C3 were overwritten when you used the Fill Right command. Whenever you use a Fill command, Excel copies the first cell in each row or column into the remaining cells. Any existing cell entries in the fill range are replaced with the value in the leftmost or top cell in the range.

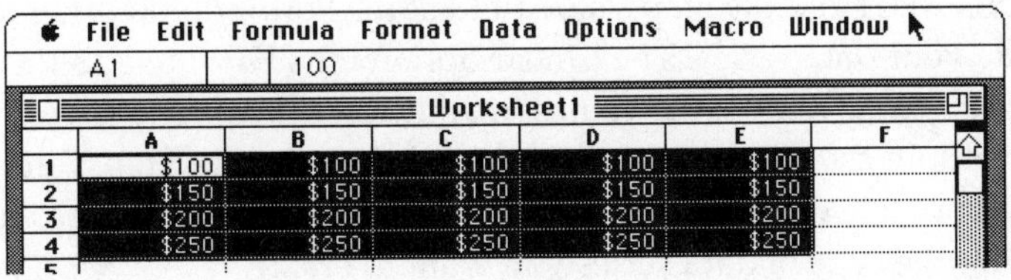

FIGURE 4-54. *The worksheet looks like this after you use the Fill Right command to copy the entries in cells A1:A4 into B1:E4.*

The Series... command

The Series... command on the Data menu is quite similar to the Fill commands, except that it allows you to quickly create an evenly spaced series of numbers in your worksheet. You supply a starting value, the range to be filled, an interval, and, if you wish, a maximum value for the range.

Let's take a look at the Series... command in action. Suppose cells A1 and B1 contain the values 10 and 100, respectively. Cell C1 contains the formula

    =A1*B1

If you drag through cells A1:C10 and choose Series... from the Data menu, Excel displays a dialog box like the one in Figure 4-55.

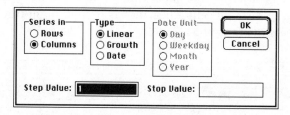

FIGURE 4-55. *This is the Series dialog box.*

To create a data series, you first need to tell Excel whether you want to create the series in rows or in columns. Like Fill Right, the Rows option tells Excel that you want to use the first value in each row to fill the cells to the right. Like Fill Down, the Columns option tells Excel that you want to use the first value in each column to fill the cells below. In this case, you want the Columns option, which is selected, because your range covers more rows than columns. If your range was the ten-column by three-row range A1:J3, you would have selected the Rows option in the Series dialog box.

Next, you need to tell Excel what type of data series you want to create: Linear, Growth, or Date. Excel uses the Type options in conjunction with the start values in cells A1:C1 and the Step Value field at the bottom-left corner of the dialog box to create your data series. The Linear option tells Excel to add the value specified in the Step Value field to the values in your worksheet. The Growth option tells Excel to multiply the start values in the worksheet by the Step Value. If you select the Date option, Excel also makes the options in the Date Unit box available to let you specify the type of data series you want to create.

We cover the Series... command in more detail in Chapter 7, "Date and Time," and Chapter 16, "Sorting the Database."

The Justify and Parse... commands

The Justify command on the Format menu lets you split a cell entry and distribute it into two or more adjacent rows of your worksheet. Unlike other formatting commands, Justify affects the contents of your cells, not just the way in which entries are displayed.

For example, cell A2 in Figure 4-56 contains a long label. Suppose you want to extend this label into cells A3 through A7 to make it more readable. If you select the range A2:A7 and choose Justify from the Format menu, the worksheet looks like the one in Figure 4-57. (For both Figures 4-56 and 4-57, we've adjusted the width of column A.)

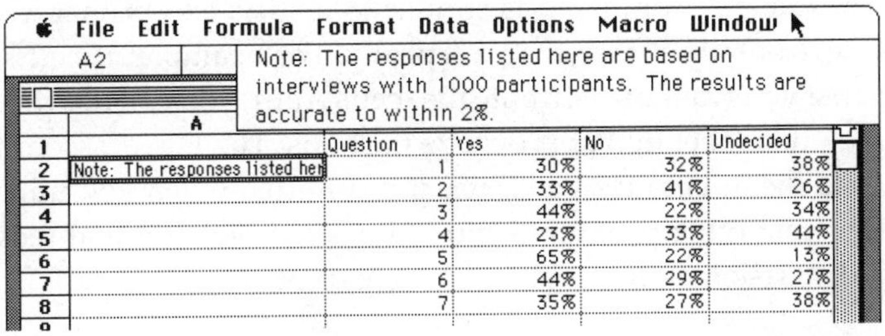

FIGURE 4-56. *Cell A2 contains a long label.*

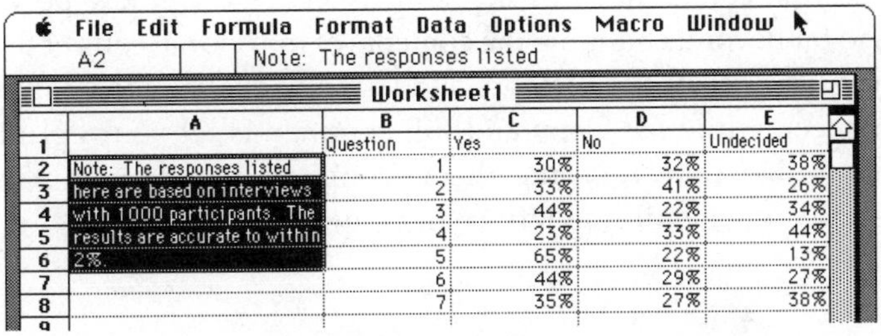

FIGURE 4-57. *You have used the Justify command to distribute the label from cell A2 into cells A2:A7.*

If the selected range isn't large enough to accommodate the long cell entry, Excel displays the message *Text will extend below range*. Clicking OK in the alert box causes Excel to extend the length of the selected range to the length required for justification, overwriting the contents of any cells within the extended range. To avoid this, click the Cancel button in the alert box, enlarge the column containing the range, and repeat the Justify command.

If you later decide to edit the entries in cells A2:A7, or to change the width of the column that contains those labels, you can use the Justify command to redistribute the text.

If you select a multicolumn range before choosing the Justify command, Excel justifies the entries in the leftmost column of the range, using the total width of the range you selected as its guideline for determining the length of the justified labels. The cells in adjacent columns are not affected by the command. As a result, you may find that some of your label displays are truncated by the entries in subsequent columns.

Any blank cells in the leftmost column of the selected range serve as "paragraph" separators; that is, Excel groups the labels above and below the blank cells when it justifies text entries.

The Parse... command is similar to Justify, except that it distributes cell entries horizontally rather than vertically. For example, if cell A1 contains a long label that you want to distribute into cells A1:E1, you can use the Parse... command to break that label into appropriate portions. The Parse... command is located on the Data menu because you'll use it most often when you import database information from other programs into Microsoft Excel. For that reason, we'll save our main discussion of the Parse... command for Appendix A.

Conclusion

The editing commands of Microsoft Excel are extremely powerful tools that let you go far beyond changing the contents of individual cells of the worksheet. Commands like Insert..., Delete..., and Cut make it easy to change the layout of the worksheet, while the Copy and Fill commands let you reproduce formulas and values rather than retyping them. You'll find these commands indispensable, especially when building large worksheets.

5

One Worksheet, Many Windows

*A*s we discussed in Chapter 1, "Introducing Microsoft Excel," windows are like portholes through which you view a small portion of your total worksheet. Microsoft Excel allows you to open a practically unlimited number of windows on the desktop at one time. The only limitation to the number of windows is the amount of available memory in your computer.

So far, we've considered windows and documents to be one and the same. When you choose New… from the File menu, Excel creates a new worksheet (or chart or macro sheet) and displays that new document in a window. Until now, it's been one window per worksheet.

In this chapter, we show you how to make working with Excel faster and easier by opening several windows that view the same worksheet. Then, you'll learn how to move among windows and how to move, size, and reposition them with the mouse and the keyboard.

All of the window techniques we describe here apply to macro sheets as well as to worksheets. The selection, sizing, and positioning techniques apply to chart windows as well; however, because the entire chart is visible in the window, you can open only one window with a chart document at a time.

Opening multiple windows

Suppose you have created a single worksheet window, called *Worksheet1*, like the one shown in Figure 5-1. To open a new window, simply choose the New Window command from the Window menu. Your screen then looks like Figure 5-2.

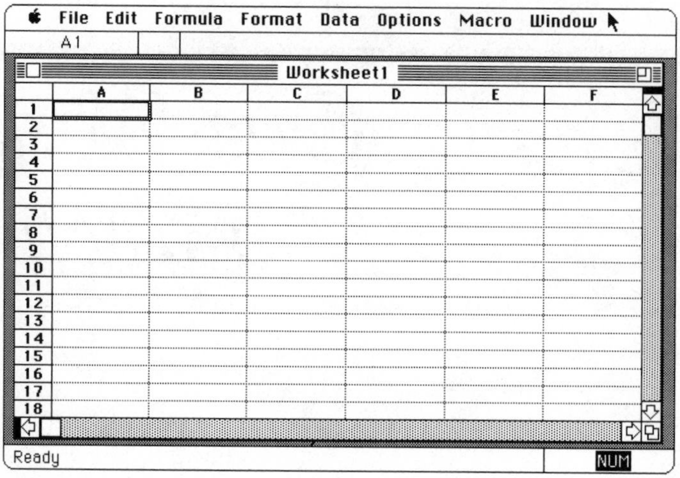

FIGURE 5-1. *This is a single worksheet window.*

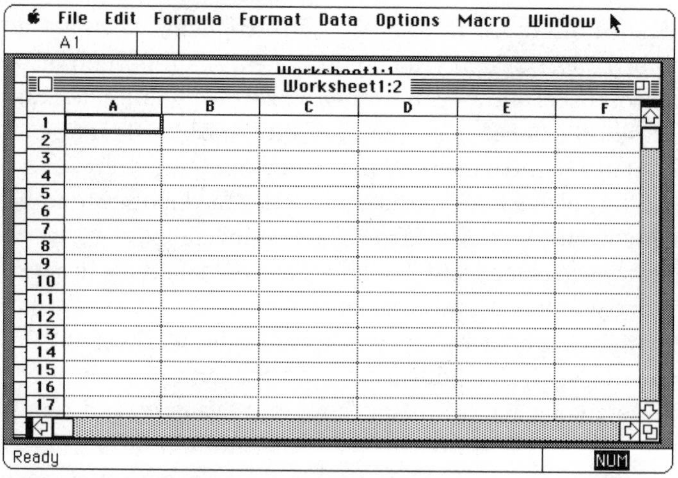

FIGURE 5-2. *You have used the New Window command to open a second window.*

Notice that Microsoft Excel automatically assigns the name *Worksheet1:2* to the new worksheet window and renames the original worksheet window *Worksheet1:1*. In addition, *Worksheet1:2* becomes the active window, as indicated by the black lines in its title bar. Because the top of the new window appears slighty lower on the screen, *Worksheet1:2* is one row smaller than *Worksheet1:1*.

It is important that you understand the difference between the File menu's New… command and the Window menu's New Window command. The File menu's New… command creates a worksheet (or chart or macro sheet), which it displays in a new window. The worksheet that results from the New… command is completely separate from any worksheets that existed before you chose the New… command.

The New Window command, on the other hand, does not create a new worksheet. Instead, this command simply offers a new "porthole" through which you may view an existing worksheet. If more than one document is open when you choose the New Window command, Microsoft Excel creates a new window for the active document only.

It is also important that you understand that any work you do in a window affects the underlying worksheet, and not just the worksheet as viewed through that window. For instance, when you make an entry in the worksheet displayed in one window, you can view that entry through any of the windows associated with that worksheet. By the same token, if you edit or erase the contents of a cell displayed in one window, you actually edit or erase the contents of the worksheet. If you look at the same cell through another window, you will see the change.

As you can see, the new window in Figure 5-2, *Worksheet1:2*, on the previous page, offers the same view of *Worksheet1* as the first window. Whenever you choose the New Window command, cell A1 always appears in the upper-left corner of the screen.

Of course, you can use the scroll bars in this window to look at another portion of the worksheet. For example, if you click the bottom and right scroll arrows in *Worksheet1:2* several times, you can position that window over cells K19:P35, as shown in Figure 5-3 on the next page. You can also use the Goto… command from the Formula menu to move the new window to a different location.

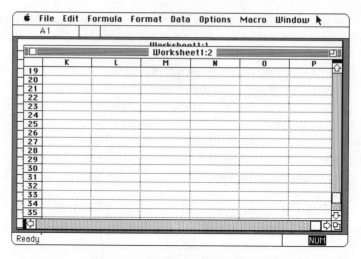

FIGURE 5-3. *You have altered the view in the second window by vertical and horizontal scrolling.*

Shuffling the stack

Whenever you choose the New Window command, Microsoft Excel adds the new window to the top of the "stack" of windows and makes it the active window. You can shuffle between windows, as you would shuffle a deck of cards, by clicking anywhere in the window that you want to view. As you can see in Figures 5-2 and 5-3, Excel staggers the windows slightly on the screen so that you can point to each window easily.

For example, suppose your screen looks like Figure 5-3. To select *Worksheet1:1*, you can position the pointer as shown in Figure 5-4 and click. After a moment, your screen shows only one worksheet window again, as in Figure 5-1, which is displayed on page 186.

When you bring *Worksheet1:1* to the top of the stack, you will notice that cells A1:F18 are visible in *Worksheet1:1*, even though we were just looking at cells K19:P35 in *Worksheet1:2*. When you change the view of a worksheet in one window, the views of the worksheet in other windows do not change. This brings us to one of the primary applications for windows. If you create more than one window for a worksheet, you can position those windows on different parts of the worksheet and move from one location to another just by jumping from window to window.

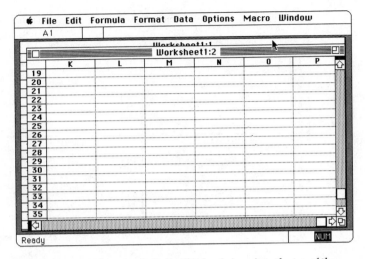

FIGURE 5-4. *Clicking a window's title bar brings it to the top of the stack of windows and makes it active.*

When you activate *Worksheet1:1*, you'll also notice that the *Worksheet1:2* window is no longer visible on your screen because the larger window, *Worksheet1:1*, covers it completely. If you can't point to a window, you can press Command-M to move through the windows in order or you can press Shift-Command-M to move backward through the stack. On an extended keyboard, you can also press Command-F6 to move forward through the stack and Command-Shift-F6 to move backward. Alternatively, you can select the window name directly from the Window menu to bring the window you want quickly to the top of the stack.

The Arrange All command

When you have several windows open and you need to see all of them at the same time, you can choose the Arrange All command from the Window menu to position the open windows more effectively on your screen. The Arrange All command tells Excel to resize and reposition all open windows so that they do not overlap on your screen. For example, if you have four windows open, Arrange All displays them with two on the top and two on the bottom, as shown in Figure 5-5 on the next page.

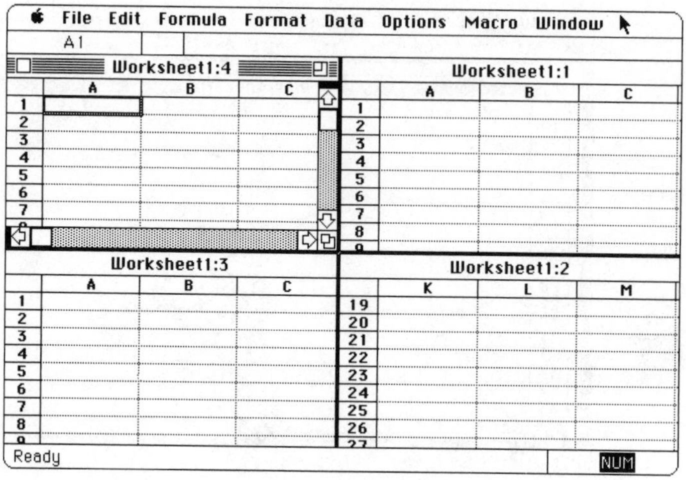

FIGURE 5-5. *The Arrange All command positions open windows more effectively on your screen.*

The Show Info command

The Show Info command, which appears on the Full Window menu, displays information about the active worksheet (or macro sheet). The information includes the active cell name, the formula, notes, formats, values, protection status, and other characteristics of a particular cell. You can open the Info window at any time or you can keep it displayed onscreen as you view your worksheet through a small window. To open the Info window, select a cell and choose the Show Info command from the Window menu. While the Info window is active, the menu bar displays four menus: File, Info, Macro, and Window. The Info menu allows you to choose what type of information you want displayed in the Info window. Figure 5-6 shows the Info menu and the Info window for cell A1 with the formats listed for that cell. The Info window lets you check the status of your active cell throughout your Excel session, in case you forget how many formats and other characteristics you've applied to the individual cells of your worksheet.

Initially, the Info window shows the cell reference, formula, and notes attached to the cell you have selected. These options are indicated by a check mark on the Info menu. You can toggle any of the Info-menu options on and off by clicking them. The Cell option gives the cell's location, and the Names option gives the named range to which it belongs. You can use the Formula option to display formulas, and the Precedents option to list the cells referred to by the active cell in its

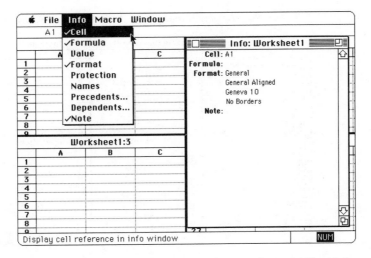

FIGURE 5-6. *This Info window appears when you choose the Show Info command.*

formulas. Other cells that refer to the active cell are listed in the Dependents option. To discover the status of the active cell—that is, whether the cell is locked and the formula is hidden—you can use the Protection option. Finally, as their names suggest, the Value option lists the value of the cell's contents, the Format option lists all the assigned formats, and the Notes option displays the text of the attached notes.

The following are two useful applications for the Info window when displayed with your active worksheet: The notes you attach to the cells of your worksheet can explain to other users how they should read or use the worksheet, and, if you create a macro, notes become very helpful in describing the actions each cell of the macro performs. (We discuss this application further in Section Five: "Macros.")

If you activate the Info window while you have four windows on your screen, then choose the Arrange All command from the Window menu, Excel reorders the windows on your screen to display the Info window neatly with all four of the other windows. Figure 5-7, on the next page, shows how your screen looks with four windows and the Info window displayed simultaneously on your screen. Notice that the active window is *Worksheet1:4*.

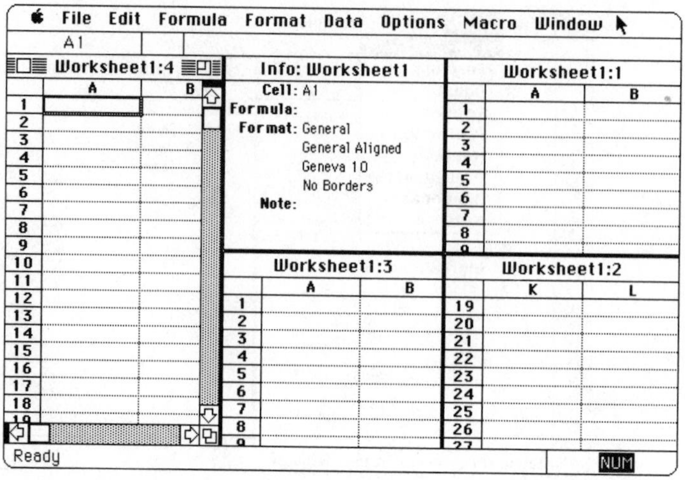

FIGURE 5-7. *The Arrange All command displays the Info window in a multiwindow display.*

Sizing and dragging

You can size and drag the worksheet windows you open with the New Window command just as you can size and drag other windows. To change the size of a window, point to the size box and drag the window.

If your worksheet windows overlap (as they usually do), the active window is always displayed on top of the other windows. If you want to view more than one window at once, simply size and drag the windows so that they no longer overlap. For example, to see both windows in Figure 5-3, click in *Worksheet1:1* and drag its size box to the left until the window is three columns wide. Your screen should look like Figure 5-8. Now, click in the *Worksheet1:2* window and drag that window's size box until three columns are visible. Finally, point to the title bar of *Worksheet1:2* and drag the window to the right side of the screen. As you can see in Figure 5-9, both windows are now visible.

You can make your windows any proportion you like, down to as small as about one inch square. For example, you might create a tiny window, like *Product Summary:2* in Figure 5-10, that displays only a few cells. Cell F35 contains the formula

=SUM(F4:F33)

Each time an entry is made in cells F4:F33, Microsoft Excel updates the sales total in cell F35. You can keep an eye on this running total in *Product Summary:2* as you enter data in column F.

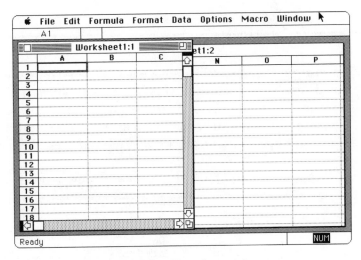

FIGURE 5-8. *This is the first window, after resizing.*

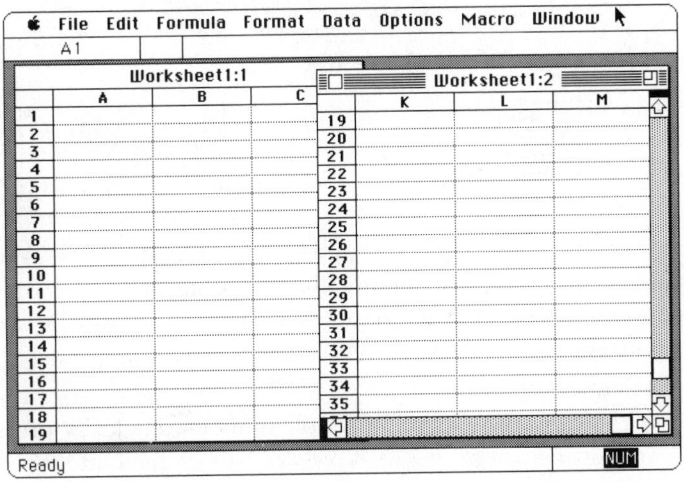

FIGURE 5-9. *This is the second window, after resizing and dragging.*

EXCEL

A shortcut for moving windows

You do not have to activate a window to reposition it. If you want to do some quick shuffling without activating the window on your screen, simply press the Command key as you drag the window's title bar.

For example, suppose you are working with these three windows:

		File	Edit	Formula	Format	Data	Options	Macro	Window	
	A26									

WWWW Sales:1

	A	B	C	D	E	F	G
1	1989 Sales: **VVVV Company, Inc.**						
2							
3			Product				

WWWW Sales:2

	A	B	C	D	E	F
6	February	$1,271.13	$1,289.19	$1,499.27	$4,059.59	
7	March	$1,327.87	$1,484.86	$1,641.84	$4,454.57	
8	April	$1,455.76	$1,612.75	$1,769.73	$4,838.24	
9	May	$1,583.65	$1,740.64	$1,897.62	$5,221.91	
10	June	$1,711.54	$1,868.53	$2,025.51	$5,605.58	

WWWW Sales:3

	A	B	C	D	E	F
10	June	$1,711.54	$1,868.53	$2,025.51	$5,605.58	
11	July	$1,839.43	$1,996.42	$2,153.40	$5,989.25	
12	August	$1,967.32	$2,124.31	$2,281.29	$6,372.92	
13	September	$2,095.21	$2,252.20	$2,409.18	$6,756.59	
14	October	$2,223.10	$2,380.09	$2,537.07	$7,140.26	
15	November	$2,350.99	$2,507.98	$2,664.96	$7,523.93	
16	December	$2,478.88	$2,635.87	$2,792.85	$7,907.60	

Ready							NUM

WWWW Sales:1 is active and you want to move *WWWW Sales:2* up on the screen so that more of its cells are visible. When you drag the *WWWW Sales:2* title bar, that window immediately becomes the active window. Once you have positioned *WWWW Sales:2*, you must click *WWWW Sales:1* to resume your work.

You can save yourself a couple of mouse clicks by pressing the Command key as you drag *WWWW Sales:2*. Once the window is positioned as you want it, release the mouse button. *WWWW Sales:1* remains active and you can resume work in that window without having to reselect it.

You cannot use this technique to change the size of windows because the scroll bar and size box do not appear until you activate or partially activate a window.

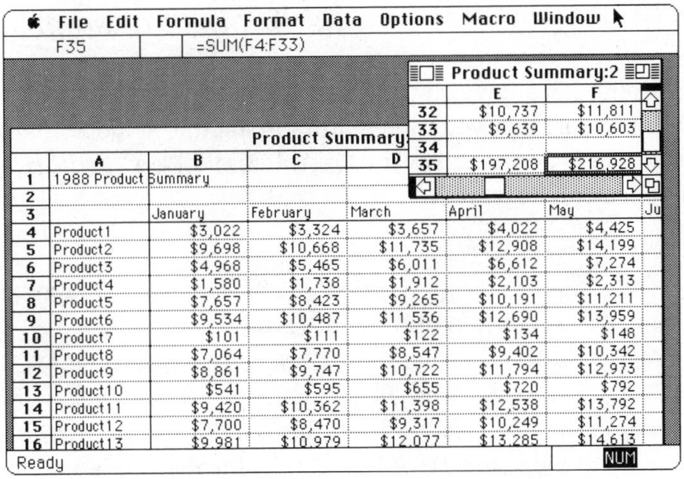

FIGURE 5-10. *You have used a small window to track sales totals.*

You'll find a lot of convenient uses for multiple windows as you build worksheet models. Keep in mind, however, that if a window is too small, Excel does not have room for complete scroll bars. If you want to be able to move around in a small window, make sure both scroll bars are visible.

Zooming in for a better look

When you are working with small windows, take advantage of the Microsoft Excel zoom feature to expand the window temporarily to full size. To expand a window, simply double click the title bar. To return the window to its previous size, double click the title bar again or select another window. You can also click the zoom box at the right corner of the title bar. The first click expands the window. The second click returns the window to its previous size.

When you use the zoom feature, Excel expands the window to fill the screen entirely. To select another window, you must press either Command-M or Shift-Command-M, or select the window name from the Window menu. You cannot click another window, unless you resize or reposition the zoomed window first.

You do not have to use the zoom feature each time you select a window. If you select another window without returning the expanded window to its original size, that window is still expanded when you select it again. This makes it easy to switch back and forth between windows as you are editing your worksheet. When you are through with your editing, simply double click the title bars in all of your expanded windows to return them to their original sizes.

Pasting references to cells in other windows

Microsoft Excel allows you to paste references to cells that are visible in one window into a formula you are creating in another window. For example, suppose *Worksheet1:1* is positioned over cells A1:F18, and *Worksheet1:2* over cells S19:X36. You want to enter the formula

=SUM(A11:A20)

in cell S25. You can easily paste a reference to cells A11:A20 into cell S25 without scrolling those cells into view in the active window.

Begin by selecting cell S25 in *Worksheet1:2*, then type =SUM(to start the formula. Now, select *Worksheet1:1* by clicking that window, using Command-M, or choosing the window name from the Window menu. Excel brings the selected window into view, but *Worksheet1:2* remains the active window. A glance at the formula bar and cell address block at the top of the screen tells you that you have not changed the status of S25, the active cell.

When you select *Worksheet1:1*, Excel partially activates that window. You can tell that a window is partially active when the scroll bars appear to let you move through the window but no black lines appear in the title bar. Once the window is partially activated, you can paste cell references into the formula bar by dragging through cells A11:A20—just as you would in a single-window worksheet. When you've pasted the cell references into the formula bar, be sure to type the closing parenthesis to complete your formula.

If the cells you need are not immediately visible, you can also scroll through the cells in *Worksheet1:1*, drag the window by its title bar, or use the size box to change the dimensions of the window. You can also use the Find..., Goto..., and Select Special... commands on the Formula menu to move around in the partially active window.

Copying and moving cells between windows

The Microsoft Excel windowing capability can be a real timesaver when you need to copy or move cells across a large worksheet. For example, suppose you are looking at cells A1:F18 through the *Worksheet1:1* window, and *Worksheet1:2* is positioned over cells Q1:V18. You want to copy the contents of cells A1:A5 into cells Q1:Q5. To do this, you can drag through cells A1:A5, choose Copy from the Edit menu, then click *Worksheet1:2* or press Command-M. Excel immediately activates *Worksheet1:2*.

The last cell you selected in *Worksheet1:2* is the active cell. However, you can select any cell or range of cells as your paste range. Again, you can use the scroll bars and the cell-selection commands on the Formula menu to bring cells Q1:Q5 into view in the active window. Select either cell Q1 or the range Q1:Q5 and choose the Paste command. When you choose the Paste command, Excel copies the contents of the range A1:A5 into cells Q1:Q5.

Saving and deleting windows

You do not have to save each window individually when you save your worksheet file. Microsoft Excel remembers all of your window settings. When you open the file again, your windows appear as you last saved them.

If you click a window's close box, however, Excel deletes that window permanently. The window name is deleted from the Window menu, and the remaining windows in your worksheet are renumbered. For example, suppose you open three worksheet windows, named *Worksheet1:1*, *Worksheet1:2*, and *Worksheet1:3*. If you click the close box to close *Worksheet1:2*, Excel deletes *Worksheet1:2* and assigns the name *Worksheet1:2* to *Worksheet1:3*.

If you delete one of these windows accidentally, don't panic: You have not lost any worksheet data. Keep in mind that there is still only one underlying worksheet, no matter how many windows you are working with. As we explained earlier, when you open multiple windows, you are simply creating new ports through which you can view different areas of the same worksheet. To recover from your error, simply choose the New Window command and re-create the closed window.

If you attempt to close the only window in your worksheet, Excel assumes you want to close the entire file. In that event, the program displays a dialog box asking whether you want to save the contents of the worksheet before you close it. If you did not mean to close the worksheet, simply click the Cancel button.

Hiding windows

At times, you might need to have several documents open simultaneously in your workspace. For example, you might want to have a supporting worksheet open so you can access information in that file for your dependent worksheets. Or you might want to keep a macro sheet open so that you can run macros from that worksheet. When you have several documents open at once, you can use the Hide command to conceal some of them and keep your workspace clear. Excel can still work with the information in the hidden documents, but the documents themselves won't clutter your workspace.

To hide an active window, simply activate the window and choose the Hide command from the Window menu. Excel removes the window display from your workspace, but the document remains open. If you want to bring the hidden window into view, choose the Unhide... command from the Window menu. Excel displays an Unhide dialog box, like the one shown in Figure 5-11, that lists all hidden windows. Select the window you want to see, then click OK or press Enter, and the hidden window appears and becomes the active window.

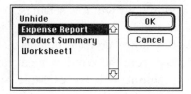

FIGURE 5-11. *Select the name of the window you want from the Unhide dialog box.*

If you've protected the hidden window by choosing the Protect Document... command (discussed in Chapter 8, "Other Worksheet Topics"), you must enter a password before you can hide or unhide the document window.

Splitting windows into panes

You can also use windowpanes to view different areas of your worksheet at the same time. Excel's windowpane feature lets you split any window on the screen vertically, horizontally, or both vertically and horizontally. Although several spreadsheet programs allow you to split a window only into halves or quarters, Microsoft Excel lets you create panes of any size. However, you'll find that the real advantage of Excel's windowpane feature lies in its synchronized scrolling capabilities.

Let's use the worksheet in Figure 5-12 as an example. Columns B through M and rows 4 through 33 in this worksheet contain monthly product summaries. Column O and row 35 contain product totals for the entire product line. Suppose you want to keep an eye on the totals in column O as you work with the monthly budget figures in columns B through M. You could accomplish this by splitting the window into two panes—one five columns wide and the other one column wide.

To create a vertical windowpane, point to the black bar on the left side of the horizontal scroll bar. This is the vertical split bar. When your pointer touches the split bar, the arrowhead instantly changes to a pair of smaller, horizontal arrows. Now, drag the split bar to the right so that it falls on the border between column E and column F. Your worksheet looks like Figure 5-13. Notice that you now have two horizontal scroll bars. Move your pointer to the horizontal scroll bar beneath the single-column pane, and scroll column O into view. Your worksheet looks like Figure 5-14 on the next page.

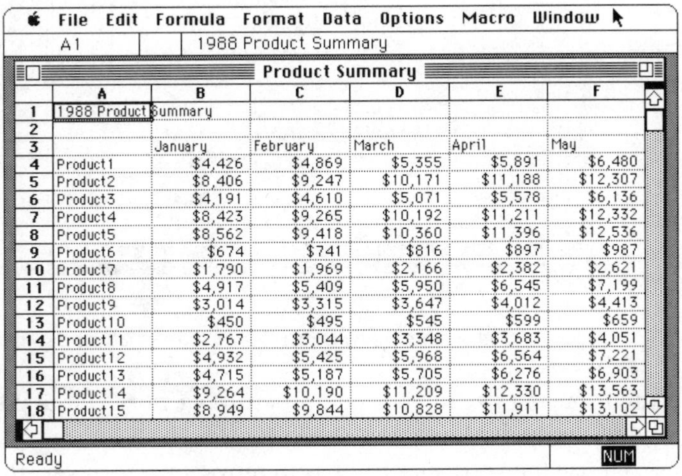

	A	B	C	D	E	F
1	1988 Product Summary					
2						
3		January	February	March	April	May
4	Product1	$4,426	$4,869	$5,355	$5,891	$6,480
5	Product2	$8,406	$9,247	$10,171	$11,188	$12,307
6	Product3	$4,191	$4,610	$5,071	$5,578	$6,136
7	Product4	$8,423	$9,265	$10,192	$11,211	$12,332
8	Product5	$8,562	$9,418	$10,360	$11,396	$12,536
9	Product6	$674	$741	$816	$897	$987
10	Product7	$1,790	$1,969	$2,166	$2,382	$2,621
11	Product8	$4,917	$5,409	$5,950	$6,545	$7,199
12	Product9	$3,014	$3,315	$3,647	$4,012	$4,413
13	Product10	$450	$495	$545	$599	$659
14	Product11	$2,767	$3,044	$3,348	$3,683	$4,051
15	Product12	$4,932	$5,425	$5,968	$6,564	$7,221
16	Product13	$4,715	$5,187	$5,705	$6,276	$6,903
17	Product14	$9,264	$10,190	$11,209	$12,330	$13,563
18	Product15	$8,949	$9,844	$10,828	$11,911	$13,102

FIGURE 5-12. *This figure shows a single-pane window.*

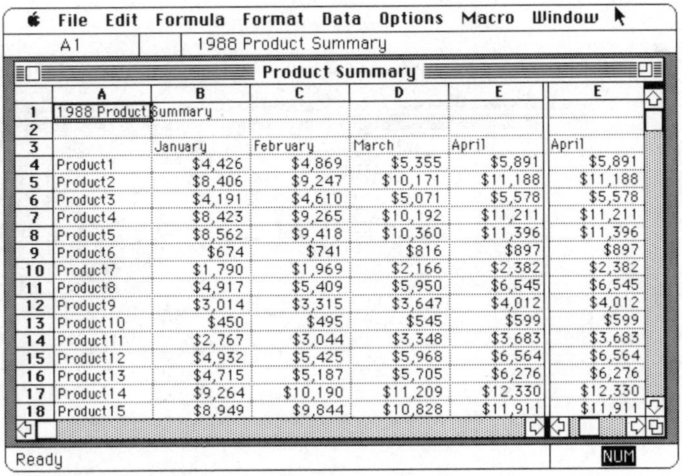

	A	B	C	D	E	E
1	1988 Product Summary					
2						
3		January	February	March	April	April
4	Product1	$4,426	$4,869	$5,355	$5,891	$5,891
5	Product2	$8,406	$9,247	$10,171	$11,188	$11,188
6	Product3	$4,191	$4,610	$5,071	$5,578	$5,578
7	Product4	$8,423	$9,265	$10,192	$11,211	$11,211
8	Product5	$8,562	$9,418	$10,360	$11,396	$11,396
9	Product6	$674	$741	$816	$897	$897
10	Product7	$1,790	$1,969	$2,166	$2,382	$2,382
11	Product8	$4,917	$5,409	$5,950	$6,545	$6,545
12	Product9	$3,014	$3,315	$3,647	$4,012	$4,012
13	Product10	$450	$495	$545	$599	$599
14	Product11	$2,767	$3,044	$3,348	$3,683	$3,683
15	Product12	$4,932	$5,425	$5,968	$6,564	$6,564
16	Product13	$4,715	$5,187	$5,705	$6,276	$6,276
17	Product14	$9,264	$10,190	$11,209	$12,330	$12,330
18	Product15	$8,949	$9,844	$10,828	$11,911	$11,911

FIGURE 5-13. *The window has been split into two vertical panes.*

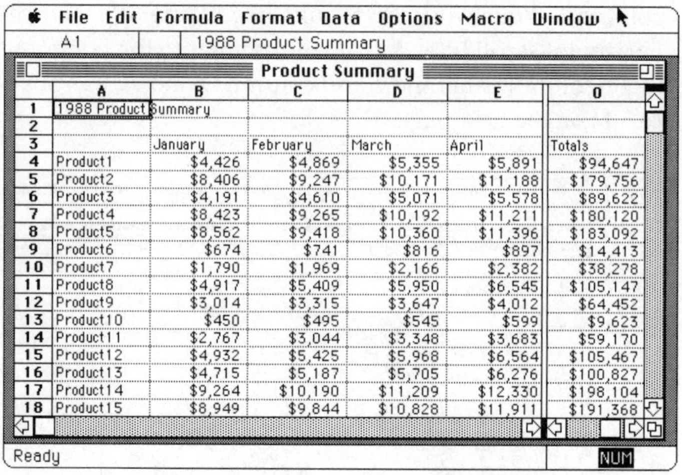

	A	B	C	D	E	O
1	1988 Product Summary					
2						
3		January	February	March	April	Totals
4	Product1	$4,426	$4,869	$5,355	$5,891	$94,647
5	Product2	$8,406	$9,247	$10,171	$11,188	$179,756
6	Product3	$4,191	$4,610	$5,071	$5,578	$89,622
7	Product4	$8,423	$9,265	$10,192	$11,211	$180,120
8	Product5	$8,562	$9,418	$10,360	$11,396	$183,092
9	Product6	$674	$741	$816	$897	$14,413
10	Product7	$1,790	$1,969	$2,166	$2,382	$38,278
11	Product8	$4,917	$5,409	$5,950	$6,545	$105,147
12	Product9	$3,014	$3,315	$3,647	$4,012	$64,452
13	Product10	$450	$495	$545	$599	$9,623
14	Product11	$2,767	$3,044	$3,348	$3,683	$59,170
15	Product12	$4,932	$5,425	$5,968	$6,564	$105,467
16	Product13	$4,715	$5,187	$5,705	$6,276	$100,827
17	Product14	$9,264	$10,190	$11,209	$12,330	$198,104
18	Product15	$8,949	$9,844	$10,828	$11,911	$191,368

FIGURE 5-14. *Column O has been scrolled into view in the right pane.*

Now, you can use the horizontal scroll bar in the large pane to scroll among columns A through M, without losing sight of the totals in column O. In addition, when you use the vertical scroll bar to move among rows 4 through 35, you'll always see the corresponding totals in column O. For example, if you scroll down until rows 20 through 35 are in view in the large window, as shown in Figure 5-15, those same rows are visible in the smaller windowpane.

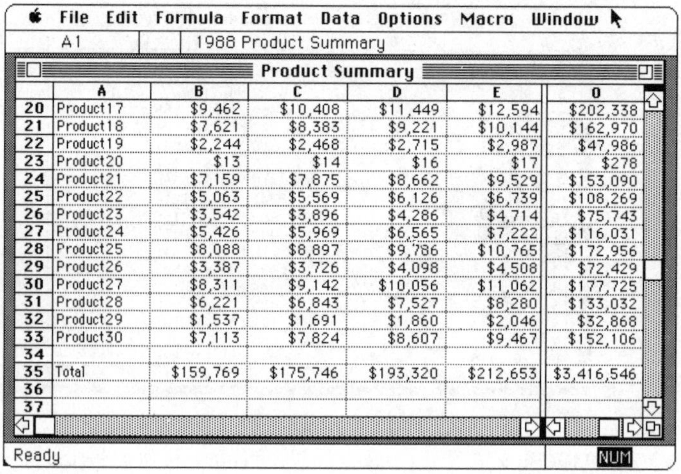

	A	B	C	D	E	O
20	Product17	$9,462	$10,408	$11,449	$12,594	$202,338
21	Product18	$7,621	$8,383	$9,221	$10,144	$162,970
22	Product19	$2,244	$2,468	$2,715	$2,987	$47,986
23	Product20	$13	$14	$16	$17	$278
24	Product21	$7,159	$7,875	$8,662	$9,529	$153,090
25	Product22	$5,063	$5,569	$6,126	$6,739	$108,269
26	Product23	$3,542	$3,896	$4,286	$4,714	$75,743
27	Product24	$5,426	$5,969	$6,565	$7,222	$116,031
28	Product25	$8,088	$8,897	$9,786	$10,765	$172,956
29	Product26	$3,387	$3,726	$4,098	$4,508	$72,429
30	Product27	$8,311	$9,142	$10,056	$11,062	$177,725
31	Product28	$6,221	$6,843	$7,527	$8,280	$133,032
32	Product29	$1,537	$1,691	$1,860	$2,046	$32,868
33	Product30	$7,113	$7,824	$8,607	$9,467	$152,106
34						
35	Total	$159,769	$175,746	$193,320	$212,653	$3,416,546
36						
37						

FIGURE 5-15. *Rows 20 through 35 are visible in both panes.*

If you also want to keep an eye on the monthly totals in row 35, you can create a horizontal windowpane. To create a horizontal pane, point to the black bar at the top of the vertical scroll bar and drag the horizontal split bar toward the bottom of the window, so that only about four rows appear in the bottom two panes. (You can make these panes small enough to display only one cell, but panes that display less than four rows lose their scroll bars and you cannot change your view of the worksheet in them.) Your screen looks like Figure 5-16.

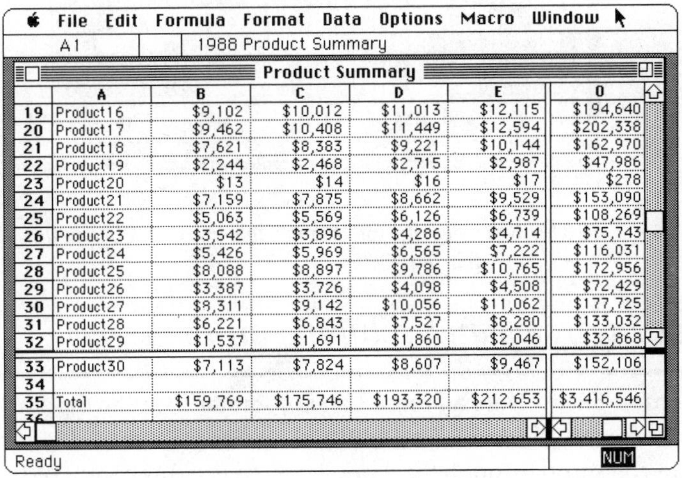

	A	B	C	D	E	O
19	Product16	$9,102	$10,012	$11,013	$12,115	$194,640
20	Product17	$9,462	$10,408	$11,449	$12,594	$202,338
21	Product18	$7,621	$8,383	$9,221	$10,144	$162,970
22	Product19	$2,244	$2,468	$2,715	$2,987	$47,986
23	Product20	$13	$14	$16	$17	$278
24	Product21	$7,159	$7,875	$8,662	$9,529	$153,090
25	Product22	$5,063	$5,569	$6,126	$6,739	$108,269
26	Product23	$3,542	$3,896	$4,286	$4,714	$75,743
27	Product24	$5,426	$5,969	$6,565	$7,222	$116,031
28	Product25	$8,088	$8,897	$9,786	$10,765	$172,956
29	Product26	$3,387	$3,726	$4,098	$4,508	$72,429
30	Product27	$8,311	$9,142	$10,056	$11,062	$177,725
31	Product28	$6,221	$6,843	$7,527	$8,280	$133,032
32	Product29	$1,537	$1,691	$1,860	$2,046	$32,868
33	Product30	$7,113	$7,824	$8,607	$9,467	$152,106
34						
35	Total	$159,769	$175,746	$193,320	$212,653	$3,416,546

FIGURE 5-16. *The window has been split into two vertical and two horizontal panes.*

Now, use the vertical scroll bar in the lower pane to scroll rows 32 through 36 into view. Notice cells A1:E13 and O1:O13 remain in view as you scroll through the rows in the bottom pane. Your worksheet should now look like Figure 5-17, on the next page. You can see the totals in row 35 of the worksheet, as well as the grand total in cell O35.

You can change the size of your windowpanes at any time by dragging the split bars. To get rid of a windowpane, drag the split bars to either end of their respective scroll bars.

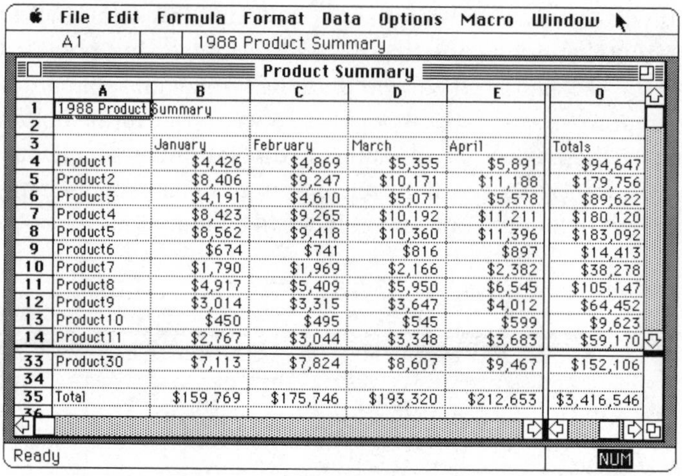

	A	B	C	D	E	O
1	1988 Product Summary					
2						
3		January	February	March	April	Totals
4	Product1	$4,426	$4,869	$5,355	$5,891	$94,647
5	Product2	$8,406	$9,247	$10,171	$11,188	$179,756
6	Product3	$4,191	$4,610	$5,071	$5,578	$89,622
7	Product4	$8,423	$9,265	$10,192	$11,211	$180,120
8	Product5	$8,562	$9,418	$10,360	$11,396	$183,092
9	Product6	$674	$741	$816	$897	$14,413
10	Product7	$1,790	$1,969	$2,166	$2,382	$38,278
11	Product8	$4,917	$5,409	$5,950	$6,545	$105,147
12	Product9	$3,014	$3,315	$3,647	$4,012	$64,452
13	Product10	$450	$495	$545	$599	$9,623
14	Product11	$2,767	$3,044	$3,348	$3,683	$59,170
33	Product30	$7,113	$7,824	$8,607	$9,467	$152,106
34						
35	Total	$159,769	$175,746	$193,320	$212,653	$3,416,546

FIGURE 5-17. *The row totals are visible in column O and the column totals are visible in row 35.*

Freezing rows and columns on the screen

Microsoft Excel offers a Freeze Panes command on the Options menu that allows you to freeze selected rows, columns, or both rows and columns on the screen while you scroll through the worksheet. To use this command, first drag the vertical split bar, the horizontal split bar, or each split bar in turn, to divide your window into panes. Then, scroll the upper windowpane, the left pane, or both panes, so that the information you want to freeze on the screen is in view. Next, choose Freeze Panes from the Options menu. Microsoft Excel now locks in view the row or rows that appear in the upper window and the column or columns that appear in the left window.

For example, the worksheet model shown in part in Figure 5-12 extends from cell A1 to cell O35. Products are listed in column A and months are listed in row 3. If you want to view the September sales figures for *Product5*, you can scroll to bring that cell into view. Unfortunately, it is impossible for you to view the cell *and* read the product names in column A and the month names in row 3 because they scroll out of view.

To avoid this problem, you can go back to the upper-left portion of the worksheet and divide the window into three panes. First, drag the horizontal split bar to divide the window between rows 3 and 4. Then, drag the vertical split bar to divide the window between columns A and B.

After making sure that rows 1 through 3 are visible in the upper windowpane and that column A appears in the left pane, choose Freeze Panes from the Options menu. When you choose this command, Excel replaces the double lines that appear between the windowpanes with a single line. In addition, the split bars disappear from the scroll bars and only one set of scroll arrows and one scroll box appear on each scroll bar. You can now scroll the lower-right windowpane to bring into view the sales information for *Product5* for the month of September. As you scroll, Excel displays the month names in the upper window and the product names in the left window, as shown in Figure 5-18.

	A	F	G	H	I	J
1	1988 Product					
2						
3		May	June	July	August	September
8	Product5	$12,536	$13,789	$15,168	$16,685	$18,353
9	Product6	$987	$1,085	$1,194	$1,313	$1,445
10	Product7	$2,621	$2,883	$3,171	$3,488	$3,837
11	Product8	$7,199	$7,919	$8,711	$9,582	$10,540
12	Product9	$4,413	$4,854	$5,339	$5,873	$6,461
13	Product10	$659	$725	$797	$877	$965
14	Product11	$4,051	$4,456	$4,902	$5,392	$5,931
15	Product12	$7,221	$7,943	$8,737	$9,611	$10,572
16	Product13	$6,903	$7,594	$8,353	$9,188	$10,107
17	Product14	$13,563	$14,920	$16,412	$18,053	$19,858
18	Product15	$13,102	$14,412	$15,854	$17,439	$19,183
19	Product16	$13,326	$14,659	$16,125	$17,737	$19,511
20	Product17	$13,853	$15,239	$16,763	$18,439	$20,283
21	Product18	$11,158	$12,274	$13,501	$14,851	$16,336
22	Product19	$3,285	$3,614	$3,975	$4,373	$4,810

FIGURE 5-18. *Using the Frozen Panes command, you can view any part of the model without losing sight of the month names or product categories.*

Notice that the row numbers in the left pane now read 1, 2, 3, 8, 9, 10, and so forth. The column letters in the upper pane are now A, F, G, H, I, and J. When you scrolled the worksheet horizontally, Excel scrolled the information in the upper window so that the data in the lower-right window was always aligned under the correct month name. Similarly, when you scrolled the worksheet vertically, Excel scrolled the labels in column A so that each product name was aligned with its corresponding data.

Notes

After you have chosen the Freeze Panes command, Excel no longer allows you to scroll the upper pane, the left pane, or the upper-left pane. You can, however, scroll the lower, the right, or the lower-right windowpane. As you scroll, you won't lose sight of the information in the "frozen" rows, columns, or both. However, Excel does not allow you to scroll beyond the rows or columns that appear in the frozen panes. For example, suppose you have frozen rows 2 and 3 in the upper window-pane and column B in the left windowpane. Row 1 and column A are out of view. Excel does not allow you to scroll row 1 or column A into view as long as the Freeze Panes command is in effect. You can still access these cells, however, by using the Goto… command or the arrow keys. For example, to activate cell A2, you could choose Goto… from the Formula menu, enter A2 in the Reference field, and click OK. Or, you could use the arrow keys to move the cell pointer to cell A2. In either case, you see the reference A2 at the left edge of your formula bar and, if cell A2 contains an entry, that entry appears in the formula bar as well. You can also make an entry in cell A2 as you normally would. But remember, you won't be able to see cell A2 in your worksheet window as long as it remains frozen and out of view.

You can include as many rows and columns as you want in your frozen panes. However, if you include more than a few rows or columns, you seriously limit the usefulness of the worksheet, because you won't be able to see much data in the window you are scrolling.

To unfreeze windowpanes, choose Unfreeze Panes from the Options menu. The split bars will then reappear in your scroll bars. You can drag the split bars to either end of their respective scroll bars to return to a full-screen window.

Conclusion

Windows offer a convenient alternative to scrolling around the worksheet when you need to access distant cells. When you are working with a large worksheet model, you'll often find it helpful to create multiple windows so that you can view and edit different areas of your worksheet without scrolling your life away.

6

Built-in Functions

Worksheet functions are special calculating tools built into the Microsoft Excel worksheet that allow you to perform complex tasks quickly and easily. You can think of functions as shortcuts that simplify computations that would be very difficult—and tedious—to perform with formulas.

You can use some functions, such as SUM, AVERAGE, and NPV, instead of mathematical formulas. Although you could use formulas to perform these computations, Excel's worksheet functions are simpler and easier to use. Other functions, such as IF and VLOOKUP, cannot be duplicated by formulas.

In a way, the Microsoft Excel worksheet functions are like the special function keys on sophisticated calculators. Just as many complex calculators have buttons that compute square roots, logarithms, and present values, Microsoft Excel has functions that perform these calculations—and many more. Once you begin using functions, we expect you'll find creating a budget or investment analysis without functions is like using an abacus to calculate the national debt.

The power of functions

Let's look at an example that demonstrates the power of the Microsoft Excel functions. The worksheet in Figure 6-1 on the next page shows monthly apple sales for a 12-month period. To find the total Winesap sales for the year, you could enter the formula

=B6+B7+B8+B9+B10+B11+B12+B13+B14+B15+B16+B17

in cell B18, but this formula is bulky and takes too long to enter. Now, consider the
shorthand formula

=SUM(B6:B17)

which also tells Excel to add the numbers stored in the range of cells B6 through
B17. The results of this formula and the longer version are identical: $4,628.

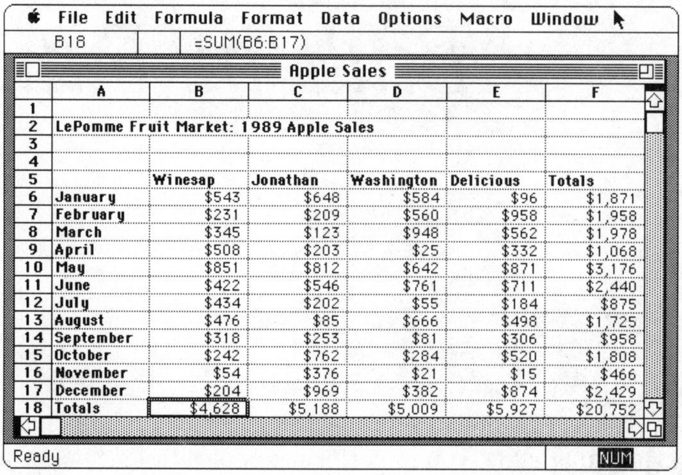

	A	B	C	D	E	F
1						
2	LePomme Fruit Market: 1989 Apple Sales					
3						
4						
5		Winesap	Jonathan	Washington	Delicious	Totals
6	January	$543	$648	$584	$96	$1,871
7	February	$231	$209	$560	$958	$1,958
8	March	$345	$123	$948	$562	$1,978
9	April	$508	$203	$25	$332	$1,068
10	May	$851	$812	$642	$871	$3,176
11	June	$422	$546	$761	$711	$2,440
12	July	$434	$202	$55	$184	$875
13	August	$476	$85	$666	$498	$1,725
14	September	$318	$253	$81	$306	$958
15	October	$242	$762	$284	$520	$1,808
16	November	$54	$376	$21	$15	$466
17	December	$204	$969	$382	$874	$2,429
18	Totals	$4,628	$5,188	$5,009	$5,927	$20,752

Menu bar: File Edit Formula Format Data Options Macro Window
Cell B18 = =SUM(B6:B17) — Window title: Apple Sales — Status: Ready NUM

FIGURE 6-1. *We used SUM to calculate apple sales for a 12-month
period.*

The more complex the formula you need to build, the more time you are likely
to save by using functions. For example, suppose you are considering a real-estate
purchase and you want to calculate the net present value of the purchase price to
determine whether the investment is worthwhile. To do this calculation without
functions, you would have to build a formula like

=(A1/(1+.15))+(B1/(1+.15)^2)+(C1/(1+.15)^3)+(D1/(1+.15)^4)

Fortunately, Excel's NPV function lets you perform the same calculation with just
15 keystrokes in the formula

=NPV(.15,A1:D1)

We cover the NPV function in more detail later in this chapter.

The form of functions

Worksheet functions have two elements: the function name and the argument. Function names are descriptive terms, like SUM and AVERAGE, that identify the operation you want to perform. The argument tells Microsoft Excel which cells you want the function to act on. For example, in the function

=SUM(C3:C5)

SUM is the function name and C3:C5 is the argument. This function tells Excel to sum, or total, the values in cells C3, C4, and C5. If cell C3 contains the number 4, cell C4 the number 100, and cell C5 the number 12, the result of the function is 116.

The equal sign at the beginning of this statement lets Excel know that the entry is a formula, not a text entry. If you were to leave out the equal sign, Excel would interpret this entry as the text *SUM(C3:C5)*.

Notice that the argument in the sample function above is surrounded by parentheses. In Excel, the argument of a function is always enclosed in parentheses. The left parenthesis marks the beginning of the function's argument. This delimiter must appear immediately after the function name, with no space before it. If you enter a space between the function name and the left parenthesis, Excel displays the #NAME? error value. If any other character appears between the function name and the parenthesis, Excel returns the same error message, indicating that it does not recognize the function name. You must use a right parenthesis to designate the end of the argument. Otherwise, you'll see the warning message *Error in formula*.

Using arguments

Although most Microsoft Excel functions require at least one argument, you can use more than one in many cases. If the function has more than one argument, the individual arguments are separated from each other by commas. For example, in the function

=SUM(C1,C2,C5)

commas separate the function's three arguments. This function tells Excel to total the numbers in cells C1, C2, and C5.

You can include up to 14 arguments in a function (as long as you don't exceed the 255-character limit for cell entries). However, a single argument can refer to any number of cells in your worksheet. For example, the function

=SUM(A1:A5,C2:C10,D3:D17)

has three arguments but totals the numbers in 29 cells. These cells, in turn, could contain numbers or formulas that refer to more ranges of cells. With practice, you can create a powerful hierarchy of calculations to perform many complex worksheet operations.

Different types of arguments

In the examples we've presented so far, all of the arguments have been cell references. You can, however, also use literal numbers, range names, other functions, and other types of entries as the arguments in functions.

Numbers

The arguments in a function can be literal numbers as well as cell references. For example, the function

    =SUM(327,209,176)

tells Microsoft Excel to sum, or total, the numbers 327, 209, and 176. Most of the time, however, you won't use functions to operate on literal numbers. Instead, you'll enter the numbers you want to use as arguments in cells, then use references to those cells as the arguments in your functions. By using cell references in your functions, you make them easier to understand and easier to modify.

Range names

You can also use range names as the arguments in functions. For example, if you use the Define Name... command from the Formula menu to assign the name *Test* to the range of cells C3:C5, you can use the formula

    =SUM(Test)

to tell Microsoft Excel to compute the sum of the numbers in cells C3, C4, and C5. (We covered range names in detail in Chapter 2, "Worksheet Basics.")

Other functions

You can even use other functions as arguments, using a technique called nesting. For example, in the function

    =SUM(ROUND(A1,0),ROUND(A2,0))

the ROUND(A1,0) and ROUND(A2,0) functions are arguments of the SUM function. Here, the ROUND function rounds the values of cells A1 and A2 to zero decimal points. We cover this function in greater detail later in this chapter.

Arrays

You can use arrays as arguments in functions. Some functions, such as TREND, GROWTH, and TRANSPOSE, require the use of array arguments. Other functions can accept array arguments although they do not require them. (For more information on arrays, see Chapter 8, "Other Worksheet Topics.")

Mixing argument types

You can also mix argument types within a function. For example, the formula

    =AVERAGE(Group1,A3,(5*3))

uses a named range of cells, a single cell reference, and an embedded formula to arrive at a single value. All three arguments are perfectly acceptable to Excel.

Functions without arguments

A few of Excel's functions, such as PI and TRUE, have no arguments. These functions are generally embedded, or nested, in other formulas or functions. You can nest as many as seven levels of functions within a formula.

Other types of arguments

So far you have seen five argument types for functions: cell references, numbers, range names, functions, and arrays. Excel accepts two other types of argument as well. Depending on the function you are using, the argument might also be a conditional test or a text string. The uses of conditional tests and text strings will become clear to you as you learn more about the Microsoft Excel functions.

Entering functions

There are two different ways to enter functions in your worksheet: You can type the function from the keyboard, or you can choose the Paste Function... command from the Formula menu.

Using the Paste Function... command

The Paste Function... command makes entering functions easy. When you click a cell and choose the Paste Function... command, Microsoft Excel provides you with a list of function names. Figure 6-2 on the next page shows part of this list. To select a function, you scroll through this alphabetical list and double click the function you want to use. Excel enters the equal sign (if you are inserting the function at the beginning of a formula), the function name, and a set of parentheses in the formula bar. The insertion point automatically appears between the parentheses. All you have to do is enter the arguments and separators.

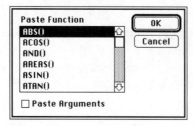

FIGURE 6-2. *Part of the list of function names is displayed when you choose Paste Function… from the Formula menu.*

Microsoft Excel 2.2 adds a new feature to the Paste Function dialog box. If you click the Paste Arguments check box, the function's form, or *syntax*, is displayed in parentheses following the function itself. This display is helpful if you are working with a relatively unfamiliar function and don't recall the sequence of arguments. In order for the function to work, you must replace the text Excel presents with the arguments you need.

There are a few functions that can accept different argument forms. For example, if you click the Paste Arguments check box and select the Index function, Excel presents you with a second dialog box containing a list of arguments. Select the one you want, then click OK. Figure 6-3 shows the dialog box that appears.

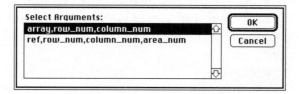

FIGURE 6-3. *These are the arguments that allow the Index function to operate.*

If you can't remember a function name, the Paste Function… command offers a convenient way to find the function you need. Once you become more familiar with Excel's function names, however, you'll probably find it faster to type the function name yourself.

Pasting cell references and range names

As with any other formula, you can also paste cell references and range names into your functions. For example, suppose you want to enter a function in cell C11 that totals the cells in the range C2:C10. Click cell C11 and either type *=SUM(* or use the Paste Function… command to select the function. Then move the cell pointer to cell C2 and drag through cell C10. A marquee appears around the selected cells to show your selection. If you typed the function name, be sure to add the closing right parenthesis. When you press Enter or click the enter box to lock in the formula, the marquee disappears and your selected cell range appears in the formula bar.

If you have defined range names in your worksheets, you can also paste them into your formulas. To paste a range name, choose the Paste Name... command from the Formula menu and select the desired range name from the list in the Paste Name dialog box. When you click OK, Excel places the range name in the formula bar at the insertion point. You can also select the desired range name from the dialog box by pointing to the appropriate name and double clicking.

Now that you're familiar with the basic structure of functions, you're ready to put Excel's functions through their paces. We start with the number-crunching functions: statistical, mathematical, trigonometric, and financial functions.

Statistical functions

The Microsoft Excel statistical functions are SUM, AVERAGE, MAX, MIN, COUNT, COUNTA, STDEV, STDEVP, VAR, and VARP. These functions allow you to calculate the sum (SUM) or average (AVERAGE) of the numbers in a range of cells, identify the high (MAX) and low (MIN) numbers in a range, compute the number of entries in a range (COUNT), count the number of values in a range (COUNTA), and compute both standard deviation (STDEV) and variance (VAR) based on a sample, as well as on a population (STDEVP and VARP). Microsoft Excel also offers the advanced statistical functions LINEST, LOGEST, TREND, and GROWTH, which we discuss later in this chapter. You'll probably use the Microsoft Excel statistical functions more than any other type of function.

The SUM function

You already know that the SUM function computes the total of a series of numbers. The SUM function has the form

=SUM(*numbers*)

The *numbers* argument can include any number, formula, or cell reference that results in a number. The SUM function ignores any arguments that refer to text strings, logical values, and blank cells.

As we mentioned earlier, SUM offers a quick method for adding a series of numbers. Several other advantages become obvious the first time you need to edit your worksheet. For one thing, it is much easier to expand a SUM range to include a new value than it is to change a regular formula. For example, cell B13 in Figure 6-4 contains the formula

=B4+B5+B6+B7+B8+B9+B10+B11+B12

Suppose you discover, after entering this formula, that you left out a $30 donation from Kellie Woods. To include this new name and donation, you can select cells A10 and B10, then choose the Insert... command from the Edit menu to add a row of cells.

Now, look at the total in cell B14 of Figure 6-5. Excel automatically keeps track of your cell movements by adjusting the formula you just entered to read

=B4+B5+B6+B7+B8+B9+B11+B12+B13

E X C E L

Using extra cells in your ranges

Although formulas that use the SUM function are more adaptable than those that use the addition operator (+), you will still run into problems if you add a cell to the beginning or end of a range. As an example, take a look at this worksheet:

♦ File Edit Formula Format Data Options Macro Window ▸

| A7 | =SUM(A1:A5) |

Worksheet

	A	B	C	D	E	F
1	100					
2	150					
3	210					
4	175					
5	200					
6						
7	835					
8						

Cell A7 contains the formula

=SUM(A1:A5)

Suppose you decide to insert a row in the worksheet below row 5. To do this, you can select cell A6 and choose the Insert... command from the Edit menu. Once the row has been inserted, you can enter the number 100 in cell A6.

Because the formula in cell A7 refers only to the range A1:A5, it is not

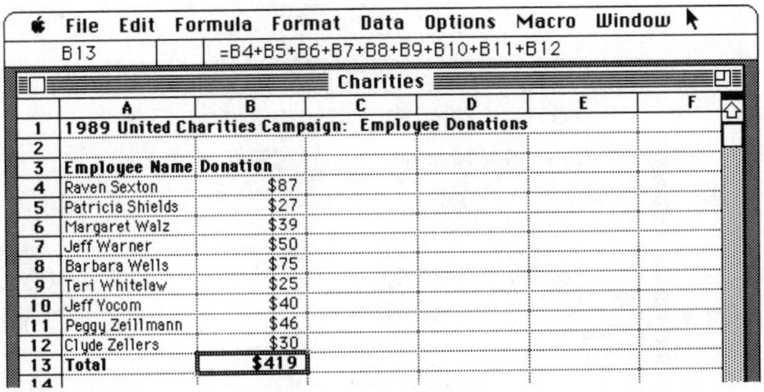

FIGURE 6-4. *You have used the + operator to calculate total employee donations.*

altered when you insert the new row. The formula, which is now in cell A8, is still

=SUM(A1:A5)

Obviously, the new number in cell A6 is not included in the total.

You can, however, use the fact that Excel ignores text entries and blank cells when it performs the SUM function to overcome this problem. Suppose the original SUM function in cell A7 had been

=SUM(A1:A6)

Because the SUM function ignores arguments that refer to blank cells, this function would return the same result as the previous version. However, when you inserted the new row in the worksheet below row 5, this new version of the formula would change to

=SUM(A1:A7)

As you can see, this function would include the new entry in cell A6.

This tip applies to all of the mathematical functions discussed in this section. Because you use these functions so often, this tip can save you a lot of time—and even more frustration. We suggest that you get into the habit of including an extra row or column in the arguments of these functions whenever you can.

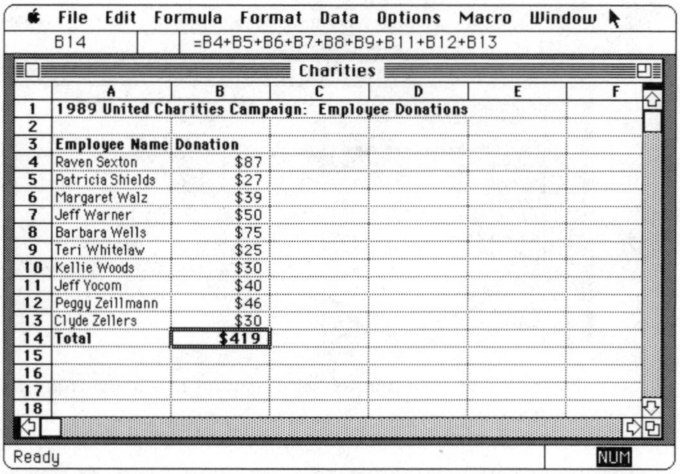

FIGURE 6-5. *The total does not change, even though a new donation has been added.*

But notice that Excel did not add the $30 donation in cell B10 to the total in cell B14. If you want to include this new number in your total, you have to edit the formula in cell B14. Imagine the confusion this would cause if your worksheet contained dozens of formulas with references to other cells.

The SUM function, on the other hand, is much more adaptable to changes in your worksheet. If you had used SUM to enter the formula

=SUM(B4:B12)

in cell B13 of Figure 6-4, Excel would have expanded the range of cells to include your addition. Because Excel always adjusts cell ranges when you insert or delete rows and columns within the range, cell B14 in Figure 6-5 would have been automatically updated to read

=SUM(B4:B13)

Keep in mind that the *numbers* argument does not have to refer to a continuous range of cells. Suppose you wanted to add a set of numbers located in cells A3, B12, and G13 through H15 of your worksheet. You could enter each of these cell references as separate arguments, to create the function

=SUM(A3,B12,G13:H15)

You could also assign a range name to this set of cells and use that name as the *numbers* argument. To assign a name to the cells in the above formula, click cell A3, then hold down the Command key and click cell B12. Then, without releasing the Command key, drag through cells G13 through H15. After selecting the eight cells in this range, use the Define Name… command to assign a range name, such as *Group1*, to this collection of cells, and enter the formula

=SUM(Group1)

in your worksheet.

The AVERAGE function

The AVERAGE function computes the arithmetic mean, or average, of the numbers in a range of cells. The form of this function is

=AVERAGE(*numbers*)

The AVERAGE function computes the average in the same way you would: It first computes the sum of a series of numeric values, then divides that sum by the number of values in the argument. Like SUM, AVERAGE ignores blank, logical, and text cells.

Like the SUM function, the AVERAGE function can be used instead of long formulas. For example, to calculate the average of the donations in cells B4 through B13 in Figure 6-6, you might use the formula

=(B4+B5+B6+B7+B8+B9+B10+B11+B12+B13)/10

to arrive at the number $44.90. Of course, this method has the same drawbacks as using the + operator instead of the SUM function: You have to edit the cell references and divisor each time you change the range of cells to be averaged.

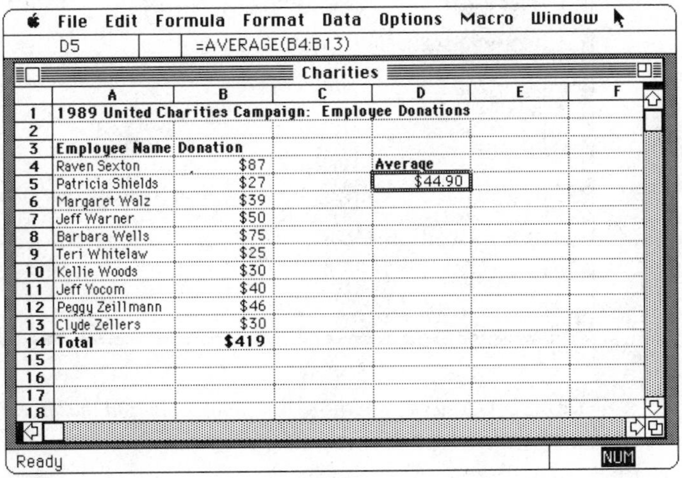

FIGURE 6-6. *You have used the AVERAGE function to calculate the average donation.*

The AVERAGE function makes life much easier by automatically calculating the sum and number of values for you. For example, cell D5 in Figure 6-6 contains the formula

    =AVERAGE(B4:B13)

to arrive at the arithmetic mean: $44.90.

The MAX function

Excel's MAX function computes the largest value in a range of cells. The form of this function is

    =MAX(*numbers*)

Like the SUM and AVERAGE functions, the argument of MAX is usually a range, like A1:A10 or Z100:AC125. If you have assigned a range name to the range of cells you want to test, you can use that name as the argument of these functions. Also like SUM, MAX ignores cells in the argument range that are blank or contain text.

For example, cell D8 in Figure 6-7 contains the formula

    =MAX(B4:B13)

to determine the amount of the largest donation made by an employee: $87.

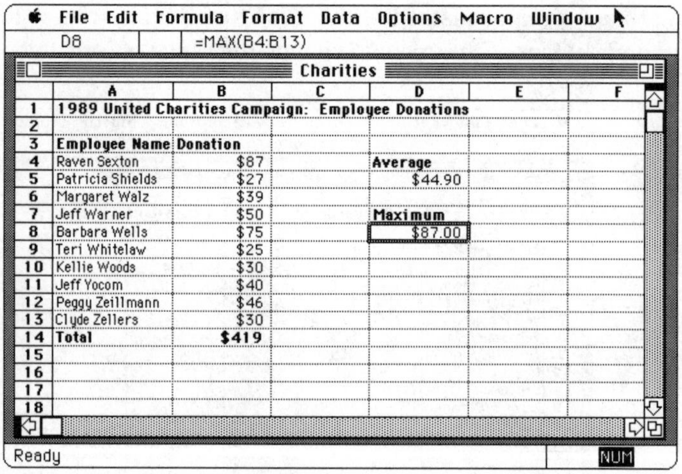

FIGURE 6-7. *You can use the MAX function to find the largest donation.*

The MIN function

The Microsoft Excel MIN function computes the smallest value in a range of cells. The form of this function is

=MIN(*numbers*)

Like the MAX function, the argument of MIN is usually a range, like A1:A10 or Z100:AC125. If you have assigned a range name to the range of cells you want to test, you can use that name as the argument of this function. Also like MAX, MIN ignores cells in the argument range that are blank or contain text.

For example, cell D11 in Figure 6-8 contains the formula

=MIN(B4:B13)

to determine the amount of the smallest donation made by an employee: $25.

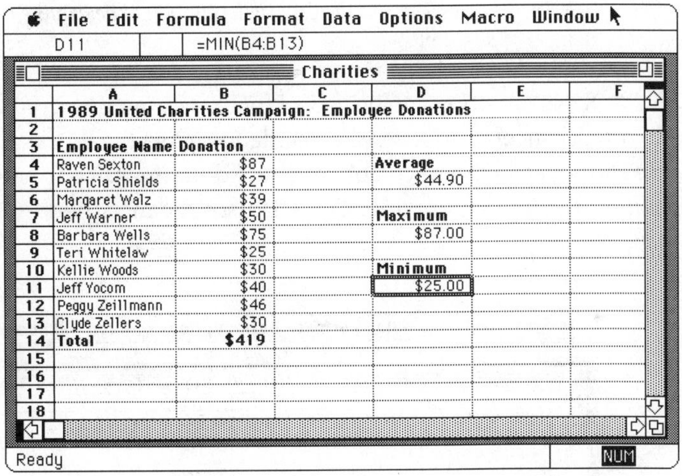

	A	B	C	D	E	F
1	**1989 United Charities Campaign: Employee Donations**					
2						
3	**Employee Name**	**Donation**				
4	Raven Sexton	$87		**Average**		
5	Patricia Shields	$27		$44.90		
6	Margaret Walz	$39				
7	Jeff Warner	$50		**Maximum**		
8	Barbara Wells	$75		$87.00		
9	Teri Whitelaw	$25				
10	Kellie Woods	$30		**Minimum**		
11	Jeff Yocom	$40		$25.00		
12	Peggy Zeillmann	$46				
13	Clyde Zellers	$30				
14	**Total**	**$419**				
15						
16						
17						
18						

FIGURE 6-8. *You can use the MIN function to find the smallest donation.*

The COUNT function

The COUNT function tells you how many cells in a given range contain numbers. For example, cell D14 in Figure 6-9 on the next page contains the formula

=COUNT(B4:B13)

which returns the value 10, the number of cells in the range that contain numbers. Like AVERAGE and SUM, COUNT ignores blank cells and cells that contain text. If cell B4 were blank and cell B5 contained a text entry, the function would return the value 8.

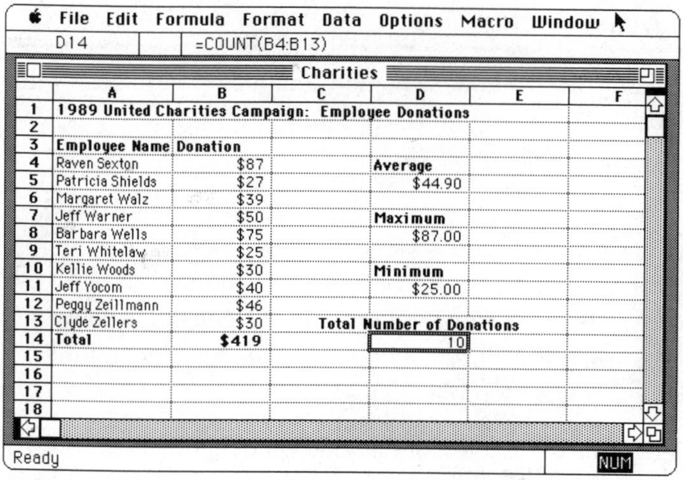

FIGURE 6-9. *You can use the COUNT function to determine the number of donations.*

The COUNT function can be useful for extracting information about a range of cells in a worksheet. Suppose you decide to revise the worksheet in Figure 6-9 to include employees who have not yet made donations. Your new worksheet might look something like Figure 6-10. Cell D14 uses the modified COUNT function

=COUNT(B4:B17)

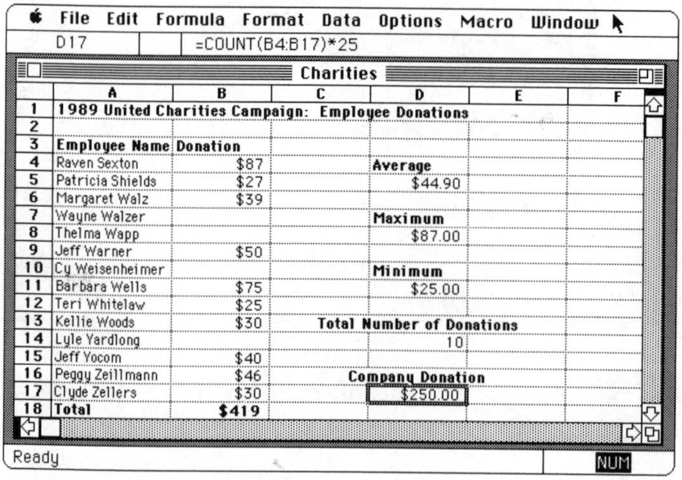

FIGURE 6-10. *You have used the COUNT function to calculate the company's donation.*

to determine the number of employees who have made a donation. As you can see, this formula still returns the number 10, because only 10 of the 14 cells in the range B4:B17 contain numbers. Now, suppose your company has agreed to give $25 for every donation received from an employee. You can enter this formula in cell D17

=COUNT(B4:B17)*25

to tell Microsoft Excel to count the number of donations and multiply that number by 25.

The COUNTA function

The COUNTA function is similar to the Microsoft Excel COUNT function. While the COUNT function counts only the cells with numbers in an argument, the COUNTA function tells you how many cells in a given range contain values of any type—text, numbers, error, or logical values. In other words, COUNTA returns the number of nonblank entries in a range or list of values.

The form of the COUNTA function is

=COUNTA(*value1,value2,...*)

where the *value1*, *value2*, and other arguments can be range references, range names, cell references, or constants. You can include up to 14 arguments in the COUNTA function (the maximum number of arguments for all functions), and you can mix different argument types. For example,

=COUNTA(A1:C3,D5,E4)

is a legitimate form of this function.

Calculating variance and standard deviation: VAR and STDEV

The next two statistical functions, VAR and STDEV, are used to compute the variance and standard deviation of the numbers in a range. Variance and standard deviation are both statistics that measure the dispersion of a group of numbers. (Because the standard deviation is the square root of the variance, we have grouped the discussions of these functions together.)

Let's use the worksheet in Figure 6-11 on the next page to demonstrate these functions. This worksheet includes sample aptitude-test scores for 60 students. Cell F6 contains the formula

=AVERAGE(A4:D18)

which returns the average of the test scores: 83.60. Cells F7 and F8 use the VAR and STDEV functions to calculate the variance and the standard deviation for this sample group of test scores with the formulas

=VAR(A4:D18)

and

=STDEV(A4:D18)

These functions return the values 0.34 percent and 5.79 percent, respectively.

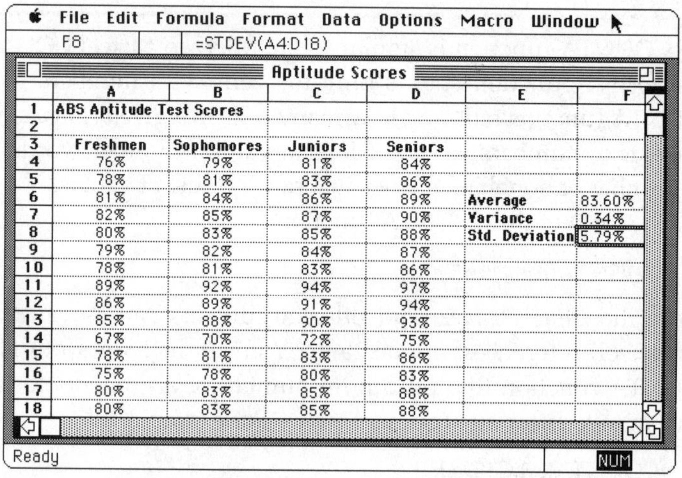

File	**Edit**	**Formula**	**Format**	**Data**	**Options**	**Macro**	**Window**

F8		=STDEV(A4:D18)

Aptitude Scores

	A	B	C	D	E	F
1	ABS Aptitude Test Scores					
2						
3	Freshmen	Sophomores	Juniors	Seniors		
4	76%	79%	81%	84%		
5	78%	81%	83%	86%		
6	81%	84%	86%	89%	Average	83.60%
7	82%	85%	87%	90%	Variance	0.34%
8	80%	83%	85%	88%	Std. Deviation	5.79%
9	79%	82%	84%	87%		
10	78%	81%	83%	86%		
11	89%	92%	94%	97%		
12	86%	89%	91%	94%		
13	85%	88%	90%	93%		
14	67%	70%	72%	75%		
15	78%	81%	83%	86%		
16	75%	78%	80%	83%		
17	80%	83%	85%	88%		
18	80%	83%	85%	88%		

Ready   NUM

FIGURE 6-11. *We used the VAR and STDEV functions to measure the dispersion of sample aptitude-test scores.*

EXCEL

Standard deviation and variance

Variance and standard deviation tell us something specific about a population. As a rule, about 68 percent of a normally distributed population should fall within one standard deviation of the mean, and about 95 percent of the population should fall within two standard deviations of the mean. A large standard deviation indicates that the population is widely dispersed. A small standard deviation indicates that the population is tightly packed. Assuming that the test scores in our example are normally distributed, we can deduce that about 68 percent of the students scored between 77.81 (83.60 minus 5.79) and 89.39 (83.60 plus 5.79).

Sample statistics versus population statistics

Two terms become important when discussing variance and standard deviation: sample and population. Before you begin to calculate the variance and standard deviations of the test scores in Figure 6-11, you must consider whether these scores represent the total population or a representative sample of that population. In other words, did 60 students actually take the test, or did you select a sample of 60 from the hundreds who actually took the test? Different rules apply to the statistical measurement of samples and populations.

The STDEVP function

The Microsoft Excel STDEVP complements the STDEV function. As you may know, the STDEV function assumes that the values you are working with represent only a sample of your total test population. On the other hand, the STDEVP function lets you treat the set of values you are analyzing as a total population, rather than as a sample of a population. This function takes the form

=STDEVP(*numbers1,numbers2,...*)

You can use one or more range references or range names, as well as cell references or constant values, as the argument for the STDEVP function.

The VARP function

The Microsoft Excel VARP function complements the VAR function in the same way that STDEVP complements STDEV. When you use the VAR function, Excel assumes that the values you are working with represent only a sample of your total test population. The VARP function lets you treat the set of values you are analyzing as a total population, rather than as a sample of a population. This function takes the form

=VARP(*numbers1,numbers2,...*)

Again, the *numbers1*, *numbers2*, and other arguments can be one or more range references, range names, cell references, or constants.

Functions for analyzing trends

In addition to a basic set of statistical functions—SUM, AVERAGE, MAX, MIN, COUNT, COUNTA, STDEV, VAR, STDEVP, and VARP—Microsoft Excel offers four more advanced functions—LINEST, TREND, LOGEST, and GROWTH—that allow you to analyze the trend in a data series. These powerful and complex functions are unique to Microsoft Excel. No other spreadsheet that we know of offers a set of functions like these.

The LINEST, TREND, LOGEST, and GROWTH functions are array functions; that is, the results of these functions are arrays. If you are not clear about what array formulas are, how they are entered in the worksheet, and how their results are presented, you should read the section on arrays in Chapter 8, "Other Worksheet Topics," before you read this section.

One of the most important uses of functions that analyze trends is creating data series that can be plotted on graphs.

The LINEST function

The LINEST function computes the slope and y-axis intercept of the regression line that describes a set of numbers. The form of this function is

=LINEST(*Y-array,X-array*)

The easiest way to understand this function is to consider an example. Look at the worksheet shown in Figure 6-12. The cells in column B of this worksheet contain a year's worth of monthly sales figures for a small business. Now, suppose you want to compute the slope and y-axis intercept of the regression line that best describes these sales figures. In other words, you want to describe the trend of the data. To do this, you drag through the range E4:F4, then type the function

=LINEST(B3:B14,A3:A14)

and press the Command and Enter keys at the same time to lock it in. (Pressing Command-Enter identifies this formula as an array formula, rather than a normal formula. We discuss this difference in more detail in Chapter 8, "Other Worksheet Topics.") Figure 6-12 shows the result. The value in cell E4, 367.63986, is the slope of the regression line. The value in cell F4, 10998.0909, is the y-axis intercept of the line.

If you omit the *X-array* argument from the LINEST function, Excel assumes that the *X-array* values are 1, 2, 3, 4, and so on. If, as in the example, the values in this array are in fact 1, 2, 3, 4, and so on, you can omit this argument without affecting the result of the function. In other words, you could have reduced the function in cell F4 to

=LINEST(B3:B14)

This is all well and good, but you may be wondering how this function can be used practically. Let's look at an example. Suppose the sales figures in Figure 6-12 are for 1989 and you now want to know the sales you can expect for March 1990, which would be the 15th month in the series. Because the position of any point on a line is determined by the equation

y=mx+b

where *m* is the slope of the line and *b* is the y-axis intercept, you can use the formula

=(E4∗15)+F4

to compute the predicted sales for March: 16512.6888. This same result could be computed using the complex array formula

=SUM(LINEST(B3:B14)∗{15,1})

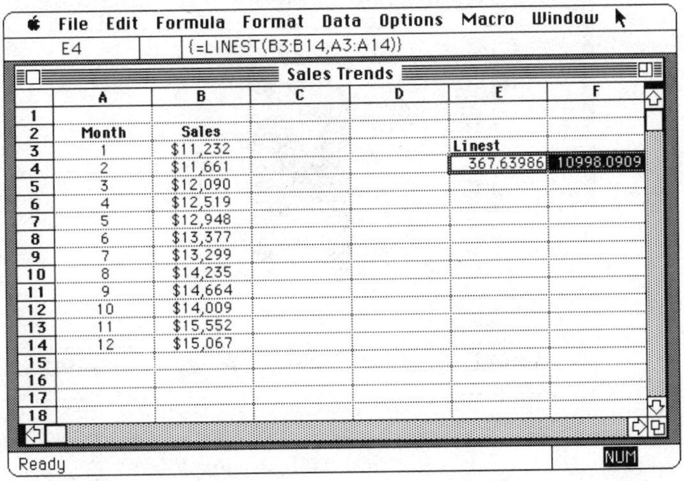

FIGURE 6-12. *You have used the LINEST function to compute the slope and y-axis intercept of a regression line.*

The TREND function

The TREND function is closely related to the LINEST function. The difference is that LINEST computes the value of the y-axis intercept and the slope of the regression line, while TREND returns the actual predicted values for the points on the line. The TREND function can therefore be used to create a data series that can be plotted as a line on a graph. The form of the TREND function is

=TREND(*Y-array,X-array,x-array*)

where *Y-array* and *X-array* are the *Y* and *X* values of the items in the data set. The *x-array* argument is optional. We discuss it in a moment.

Let's look at an example of the TREND function at work. Suppose you want to know the values of each point on the regression line that describes the data set from the previous example. To create these values, select the range C3:C14 and type the formula

=TREND(B3:B14,A3:A14)

then press the Command and Enter keys simultaneously. The result is shown in Figure 6-13. The numbers in the cells in the range C3:C14 are the *Y* values for each of the points on the regression line.

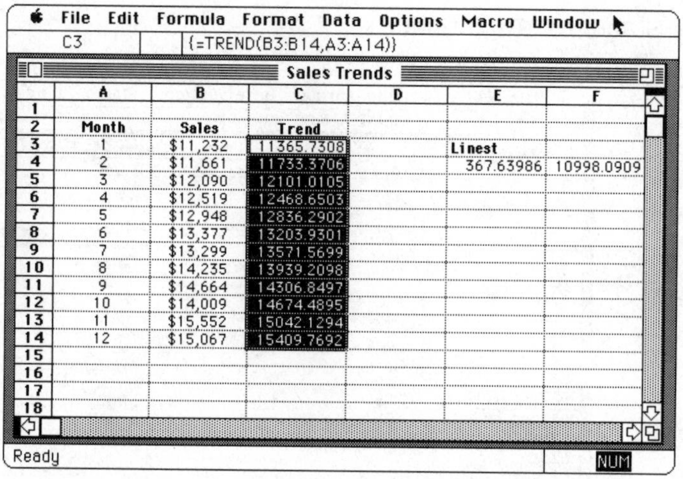

	A	B	C	D	E	F
1						
2	Month	Sales	Trend			
3	1	$11,232	11365.7308		Linest	
4	2	$11,661	11733.3706		367.63986	10998.0909
5	3	$12,090	12101.0105			
6	4	$12,519	12468.6503			
7	5	$12,948	12836.2902			
8	6	$13,377	13203.9301			
9	7	$13,299	13571.5699			
10	8	$14,235	13939.2098			
11	9	$14,664	14306.8497			
12	10	$14,009	14674.4895			
13	11	$15,552	15042.1294			
14	12	$15,067	15409.7692			
15						
16						
17						
18						

FIGURE 6-13. *You have used the TREND function to create a data series that can be plotted as a line on a graph.*

As with LINEST, if you omit the *X-array* argument from the TREND function, Excel assumes that the *X-array* values are 1, 2, 3, 4, and so on. In other words, because the *x-array* argument is also optional, you could have reduced the function in cell C3 to

=TREND(B3:B14)

When you're examining a data trend over time, you'll often be able to omit the *X-array* argument without affecting the result of the function.

Like LINEST, TREND can be used to predict the future. In this example, you can use the TREND function to predict the sales figures for months 13, 14, and 15. To do this, drag through the range C16:C18. Next, enter the formula

=TREND(B3:B14,A3:A14,A16:A18)

then press the Command and Enter keys to lock in the formula. The result is shown in Figure 6-14. The numbers in cells C16, C17, and C18 are the predicted sales values for the 13th, 14th, and 15th months in the series.

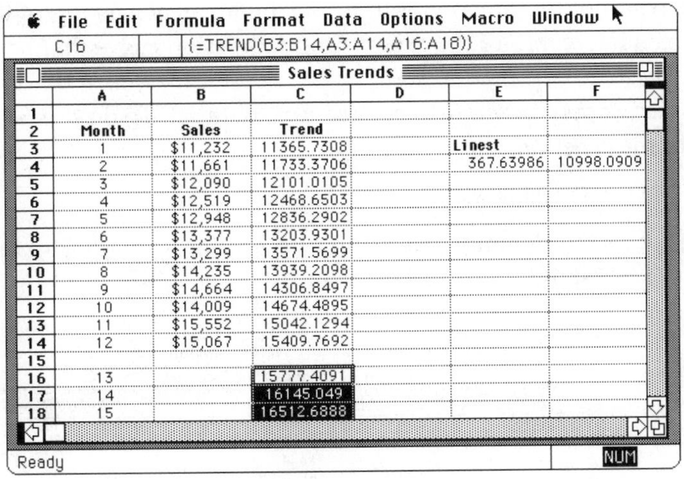

	A	B	C	D	E	F
1						
2	Month	Sales	Trend			
3	1	$11,232	11365.7308		Linest	
4	2	$11,661	11733.3706		367.63986	10998.0909
5	3	$12,090	12101.0105			
6	4	$12,519	12468.6503			
7	5	$12,948	12836.2902			
8	6	$13,377	13203.9301			
9	7	$13,299	13571.5699			
10	8	$14,235	13939.2098			
11	9	$14,664	14306.8497			
12	10	$14,009	14674.4895			
13	11	$15,552	15042.1294			
14	12	$15,067	15409.7692			
15						
16	13		15777.4091			
17	14		16145.049			
18	15		16512.6888			

FIGURE 6-14. *You have used TREND to predict the sales figures for months 13, 14, and 15.*

Notice that this last example includes an *x-array* argument, which causes Excel to display values that help you anticipate future trends. If you include this argument in the function, then the result of the function is an array the same size and shape as *x-array*. In other words, because *x-array* is a vertical array with three elements, the result of the function is a vertical function with three elements (in cells C16, C17, and C18). If it helps, you can think of the *x-array* argument as being a "prediction array." If you include this argument in the function, Excel returns the predicted *Y* values for each of the values in the array. If you don't include this argument, Excel does not make any predictions; instead, it returns the *Y* values of the points in the "known" portion of the regression line. This is what occurred in the example in Figure 6-13.

The LOGEST function

As you might guess from its name, the LOGEST function is similar to the LINEST function. However, unlike LINEST, which returns the slope and y-axis intercept of the regression line that describes a data series, LOGEST returns the constants *m* (the "slope") and *b* (the "y-axis intercept") of the curve that describes the data. The difference between these two functions is very subtle, but it is important that you understand it: LINEST defines a regression line; LOGEST defines an exponential regression curve. The form of LOGEST is

=LOGEST(*Y-array*,*X-array*)

The result of the function is a horizontal array consisting of the "slope" and the "y-axis intercept" of the exponential regression curve that best fits the values in *Y-array*.

Let's apply LOGEST to your sample data set. To do this, select cells E8:F8 and enter the function

=LOGEST(B3:B14,A3:A14)

then press the Command and Enter keys at the same time to lock in the function. Figure 6-15 shows the result.

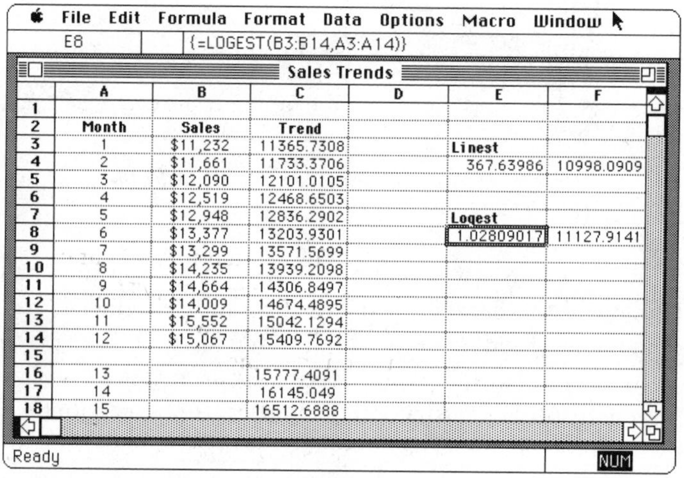

File Edit Formula Format Data Options Macro Window

E8 {=LOGEST(B3:B14,A3:A14)}

Sales Trends

	A	B	C	D	E	F
1						
2	Month	Sales	Trend			
3	1	$11,232	11365.7308		Linest	
4	2	$11,661	11733.3706		367.63986	10998.0909
5	3	$12,090	12101.0105			
6	4	$12,519	12468.6503			
7	5	$12,948	12836.2902		Logest	
8	6	$13,377	13203.9301		1.02809017	11127.9141
9	7	$13,299	13571.5699			
10	8	$14,235	13939.2098			
11	9	$14,664	14306.8497			
12	10	$14,009	14674.4895			
13	11	$15,552	15042.1294			
14	12	$15,067	15409.7692			
15						
16	13		15777.4091			
17	14		16145.049			
18	15		16512.6888			

Ready NUM

FIGURE 6-15. *You have used the LOGEST function to define an exponential regression curve.*

To understand these results, it is important that you know that the formula for the curve is

y=b*mx

The value in cell E8, 1.02809017, is the constant *m* for the regression curve that describes the data. The value in cell F8, 11127.9141, is the constant *b*.

Just as with LINEST, you can use the results of the LOGEST function to predict the future. For example, suppose you want to predict the sales volume for the 15th month in the series. Because the value in E8 is the *m* constant and the value in F8 is the *b* constant, the formula

=F8*(E8^15)

computes the predicted sales for the 15th month: 16860.9434.

As with LINEST, if you omit the *X-array* argument from the LOGEST function, Excel assumes that the *X-array* values are 1, 2, 3, 4, and so on. If, as in the example, the values in this array in fact are 1, 2, 3, 4, and so on, you can omit this argument without affecting the result of the function. In other words, the function in cell F8 could also have been entered as:

=LOGEST(B3:B17)

When you're examining a data trend over time, you'll often be able to omit this argument without affecting the result of the function.

The GROWTH function

The GROWTH function is the last of the trend functions. As you might expect, GROWTH is similar to TREND. In fact, GROWTH is to LOGEST what TREND is to LINEST. Just as TREND returns the *Y* values of the points on the regression line that describes a data series, so GROWTH returns the *Y* values of the points on the regression curve that describes the data. The form of this function is

=GROWTH(*Y-array,X-array,x-array*)

As you can see, the form of GROWTH is identical to that of TREND. In fact, all of the rules that apply to TREND also apply to GROWTH.

Let's work through an example with GROWTH, using the same sales-trend worksheet. To begin, drag through the range D3:D14. In cell D3, type the formula

=GROWTH(B3:B14,A3:A14)

then press the Command and Enter keys together. You can see the result in Figure 6-16 on the next page. The numbers in the cells in the range D3:D14 are the *Y* values for each of the points on the regression curve that describes the data in column B.

If you omit the *X-array* argument from the GROWTH function, Excel assumes that the *X-array* values are 1, 2, 3, 4, and so on. In other words, because the *x-array* argument is also optional, you could have reduced the function in cell D3 to

=GROWTH(B3:B14)

When you're examining a data trend over time, you'll often be able to omit the *X-array* argument without affecting the result of the function.

Like TREND, GROWTH can be used to predict the future. For example, let's use GROWTH to predict the sales figures for months 13, 14, and 15. To do this, first drag through the range D16:D18. Next, enter the formula

=GROWTH(B3:B14,A3:A14,A16:A18)

then press the Command and Enter keys to lock in the formula. The result is shown in Figure 6-17. The numbers in cells D16, D17, and D18 are the predicted sales values for the 13th, 14th, and 15th months in the series.

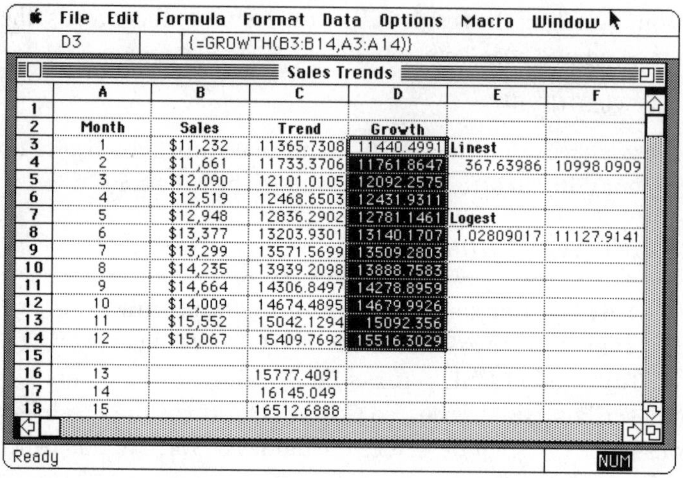

	A	B	C	D	E	F
1						
2	Month	Sales	Trend	Growth		
3	1	$11,232	11365.7308	11440.4991	Linest	
4	2	$11,661	11733.3706	11761.8647	367.63986	10998.0909
5	3	$12,090	12101.0105	12092.2575		
6	4	$12,519	12468.6503	12431.9311		
7	5	$12,948	12836.2902	12781.1461	Logest	
8	6	$13,377	13203.9301	13140.1707	1.02809017	11127.9141
9	7	$13,299	13571.5699	13509.2803		
10	8	$14,235	13939.2098	13888.7583		
11	9	$14,664	14306.8497	14278.8959		
12	10	$14,009	14674.4895	14679.9926		
13	11	$15,552	15042.1294	15092.356		
14	12	$15,067	15409.7692	15516.3029		
15						
16	13		15777.4091			
17	14		16145.049			
18	15		16512.6888			

FIGURE 6-16. *You have used the GROWTH function to create a data series that can be plotted as a curve on a graph.*

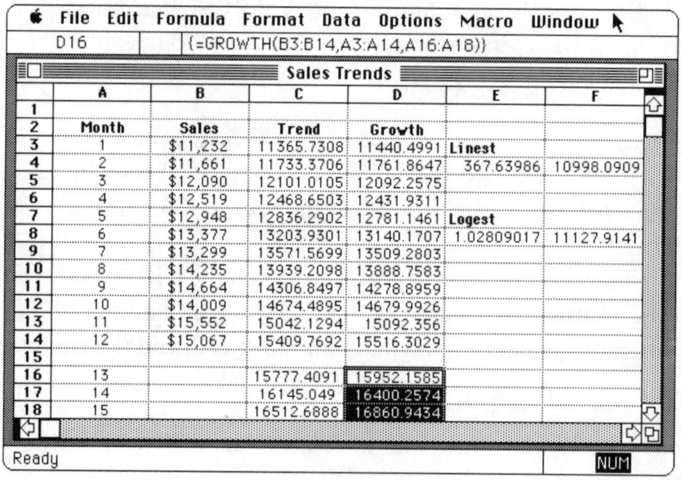

	A	B	C	D	E	F
1						
2	Month	Sales	Trend	Growth		
3	1	$11,232	11365.7308	11440.4991	Linest	
4	2	$11,661	11733.3706	11761.8647	367.63986	10998.0909
5	3	$12,090	12101.0105	12092.2575		
6	4	$12,519	12468.6503	12431.9311		
7	5	$12,948	12836.2902	12781.1461	Logest	
8	6	$13,377	13203.9301	13140.1707	1.02809017	11127.9141
9	7	$13,299	13571.5699	13509.2803		
10	8	$14,235	13939.2098	13888.7583		
11	9	$14,664	14306.8497	14278.8959		
12	10	$14,009	14674.4895	14679.9926		
13	11	$15,552	15042.1294	15092.356		
14	12	$15,067	15409.7692	15516.3029		
15						
16	13		15777.4091	15952.1585		
17	14		16145.049	16400.2574		
18	15		16512.6888	16860.9434		

FIGURE 6-17. *You have used GROWTH to predict the sales figures for months 13, 14, and 15.*

Mathematical functions

The Microsoft Excel mathematical functions allow you to perform specialized mathematical calculations quickly and easily. You'll probably use mathematical functions almost as often as statistical functions. Excel's mathematical functions are ABS, SIGN, ROUND, INT, RAND, SQRT, MOD, PI, FACT, PRODUCT, and TRUNC. (We've put the logarithmic functions LOG10, LN, and EXP in a separate section, which we discuss later in this chapter.)

The ABS function

The ABS function simply returns the absolute value of a number or formula. The form of this function is

=ABS(*number*)

where *number* is a number or a reference to a cell that contains a value.
For example, if cell A1 contains the value –75, the formula

=ABS(A1)

returns 75. If the value referred to by the argument is positive, ABS has no effect. For example, if cell A1 contains the value 75, the function

=ABS(A1)

returns 75.

The SIGN function

You can use the SIGN function to determine whether an argument results in a negative, positive, or zero value. The form of this function is

=SIGN(*number*)

The *number* argument can be a number or a reference to a cell that contains a number. If *number* is greater than 0, the SIGN function returns the value 1. If *number* is negative (less than 0), the function returns the value –1. If *number* is 0, the function returns 0.
For example, suppose cells A1 through A3 contain the numbers 10, –20, and –5. The formula

=SIGN(SUM(A1:A3))

tells Excel to add the numbers 10, –20, and –5 (resulting in the value –15) and to determine whether the resulting value is positive or negative. Because the SUM argument results in a negative value, Excel returns the value –1.

The ROUND function

The ROUND function allows you to eliminate unwanted decimal places from numbers. ROUND rounds the number referred to by its argument to however many decimal places you specify. The form of the ROUND function is

=ROUND(*number, decimal places*)

The *decimal places* argument can be any positive or negative integer. Specifying a negative *decimal places* argument causes rounding to the left of the decimal. Excel rounds just as you would expect it to: Digits less than 5 are rounded down and digits greater than or equal to 5 are rounded up. The table on the next page shows several examples of the ROUND function at work.

EXCEL

Rounding versus formatting

Don't confuse the ROUND function with fixed formats like 0 and 0.00, which are available when you choose Number... from the Format menu. When you use the Number... command to round the contents of a cell to a specified number of decimal places, you change only the way the number in that cell is displayed. You do not actually change the value in that cell. In performing calculations, Excel always uses the underlying value, not the displayed value.

For example, suppose cell A1 contains the number 123.456. If you use the 0.00 format to round this number to two decimal places, the value 123.46 appears in cell A1. However, Excel still uses the underlying value 123.456 in its calculations. If you use the formula

=A1+.001

to add .001 to the value in cell A1, the result is 123.457.

When you use the ROUND function, however, you are actually changing the value itself. For example, if cell A1 contains the value 123.456, the function

=ROUND(A1,2)

returns the value 123.46. Adding .001 to this value returns 123.461. Notice that ROUND has changed the value itself, and not just the way it is displayed.

If you enter...	Excel displays...
=ROUND(123.4567,3)	123.457
=ROUND(123.4567,0)	123
=ROUND(123.4567,2)	123.46
=ROUND(123.4567,−1)	120
=ROUND(123.4567,1)	123.5
=ROUND(123.4567,−2)	100

The INT function

Although both the INT and ROUND functions can be used to get rid of unwanted decimals, the two functions work differently. The INT function does not "round up" or "round down" to the nearest whole number. It simply truncates everything to the right of the decimal, resulting in an integer with no decimal places. The form of the INT function is

=INT(*number*)

For example, the function

=INT(100.01)

returns the value 100, as does the function

=INT(100.99999999)

even though the number 100.99999999 is essentially equal to 101.

The RAND function

The RAND function generates a random number between 0 and 1. The form of the function is

=RAND()

The RAND function is one of the few Microsoft Excel functions that doesn't take an argument. Although RAND has no arguments, you must enter the parentheses after the function name.

Suppose you want to enter a series of random numbers in cells A1 through C18 of your worksheet. Begin by entering the RAND function in cell A1. Now, drag across cells A1:C18 and choose the Fill Right and the Fill Down commands from the Edit menu. Excel copies the RAND function into each of the cells, assigning a different value to each cell, as shown in Figure 6-18 on the next page.

The result of RAND changes each time you recalculate your worksheet. If you are using automatic relcalculation, this means that the value of the RAND function changes each time you make a worksheet entry.

You can also enter the RAND function into a range as an array function. First, select the range you want to use, such as A1:C18, type *=RAND()*, and then press Command-Enter. Your worksheet range contains random numbers and you'll notice that the formula bar indicates that Excel has put braces around the formula =RAND(). The result, however, is the same as the Fill procedure we described in a previous paragraph.

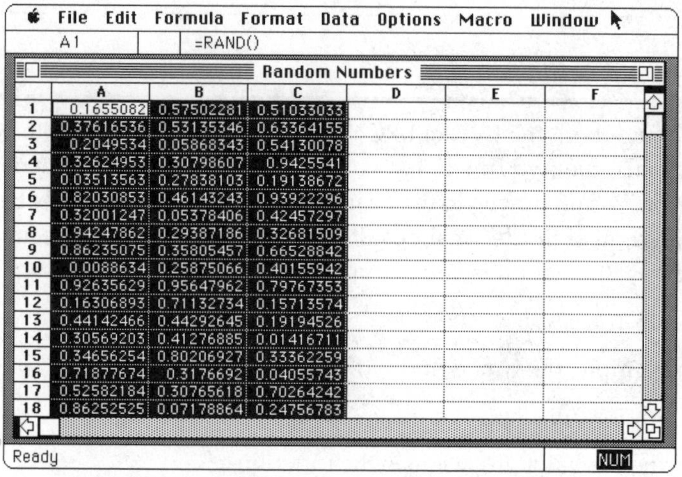

⌘	File	Edit	Formula	Format	Data	Options	Macro	Window	▶

A1		=RAND()				

Random Numbers

	A	B	C	D	E	F
1	0.1655082	0.57502281	0.51033033			
2	0.37616536	0.53135346	0.63364155			
3	0.2049534	0.05868343	0.54130078			
4	0.32624953	0.30798607	0.9425541			
5	0.03513563	0.27838103	0.19138672			
6	0.82030853	0.46143243	0.93922296			
7	0.32001247	0.05378406	0.42457297			
8	0.94247862	0.29387186	0.32681509			
9	0.86235075	0.35805457	0.66528842			
10	0.0088634	0.25875066	0.40155942			
11	0.92635629	0.95647962	0.79767353			
12	0.16306893	0.71132734	0.15713574			
13	0.44142466	0.44292645	0.19194526			
14	0.30569203	0.41276885	0.01416711			
15	0.34656254	0.80206927	0.33362259			
16	0.71877674	0.3176692	0.04055743			
17	0.52582184	0.30765618	0.70264242			
18	0.86252525	0.07178864	0.24756783			

Ready   NUM

FIGURE 6-18. *You have used the RAND function to enter a series of random numbers in a cell range.*

EXCEL *tip*

Using Paste Special… with RAND

The Paste Special… command lets you lock in a series of random numbers so you can re-create a set of calculations later. For example, to lock in the values in cells A1:C18 in the example in Figure 6-18, drag across the range and choose the Copy command from the Edit menu. Next, choose Paste Special… from the Edit menu. Select the Values option from the Paste Special dialog box, and make sure the Operation option is set to None. When you click OK, Excel overwrites the formulas in cells A1:C18 with the displayed values. Because the entries in the range A1:C18 are now numbers and not formulas, their values do not change when the worksheet is recalculated.

The SQRT function

The SQRT function can be used to compute the square root of a number. The form of the function is

=SQRT(*number*)

where *number* is a value or a reference to a cell that contains a value. The result of the function is the square root of *number*. For example, the function

=SQRT(4)

returns the value 2.

The MOD function

The MOD function computes the remainder from a division operation. The form of the function is

=MOD(*dividend, divisor*)

The result of the function is the remainder that results from dividing *dividend* by *divisor*. For example, the function

=MOD(9,4)

returns 1, the remainder that results from dividing 9 by 4. Similarly, the function

=MOD(11,3)

returns 2.

If the dividend is smaller than the divisor, the result of the function equals the dividend. For example, the function

=MOD(5,11)

returns 5. If the dividend is exactly divisible by the divisor, then the result of the function is 0.

The PI function

The PI function returns the value of the constant π, displayed with nine decimal places: 3.141592654. The form of the function is

=PI()

As with RAND, although PI has no arguments, you must enter the parentheses after the function name.

You'll probably use PI in conjunction with another formula or function. For example, to calculate the area of a circle, you would multiply PI by the square of the circle's radius. The formula

=PI()*(5^2)

computes the area of a circle with a radius of 5. The result of this formula is 78.5398163.

The FACT function

The FACT function calculates the factorial value of any number. The factorial of a number is the product of all the positive integers from 1 to the specified number. For example, 4 factorial (expressed 4!) is equivalent to 1×2×3×4, which results in the value 24.

The form of the FACT function is

=FACT(*number*)

The *number* argument must be a positive integer. For example, the formula

=FACT(1)

results in the value 1, but

=FACT(–1)

results in the #NUM! error value. If *number* is not an integer, FACT truncates it. To calculate the factorial value of 10 (10!), use the formula

=FACT(10)

This formula returns the factorial value 3628800.

The PRODUCT function

You can use the PRODUCT function to multiply a group of values. Excel can multiply as many as 14 values with the PRODUCT function, which takes the form

=PRODUCT(*number1,number2,...*)

For example, suppose cells A1, A2, and A3 contain the numbers 5, 10, and 15, respectively. To multiply these values, you can use the formula

=PRODUCT(A1:A3)

Excel returns the value 750.

Notice that the PRODUCT function can accept a range reference or a list of cell references as its argument. As with the SUM function, you can mix argument types in the PRODUCT function.

The TRUNC function

Excel's TRUNC function is similar to the ROUND and INT functions. Although ROUND, INT, and TRUNC can all be used to eliminate unwanted decimals, the three functions work differently. The ROUND function "rounds up" or "rounds down" to the nearest whole number, while INT "rounds down" to the nearest whole number. The TRUNC function simply truncates everything to the right of the decimal, resulting in an integer with no decimal places.

The form of the TRUNC function is

=TRUNC(*number*)

For example, the function

=TRUNC(10.88878)

results in the value 10.

The primary difference between the INT and TRUNC functions is in the treatment of negative values. For example, if you use the value –99.99999999 as your *number* argument in an INT function, Excel returns the value –100. However, the TRUNC function

=TRUNC(–99.99999999)

simply eliminates the decimal portion of the *number* argument and returns the value –99.

Logarithmic functions

Microsoft Excel offers four logarithmic functions: LOG, LOG10, LN, and EXP. If you are an engineer or a scientist, you will probably find these functions valuable. If you are in business, you might not use these functions very often.

The LOG function

Excel's new LOG function returns the logarithm of a positive number to the specified base. The form of the function is

=LOG(*number,base*)

If you don't include the *base* argument, Excel assumes that the *base* is 10. For example, the function

=LOG(5,12)

returns the value 0.64768546, while the function

    =LOG(5)

returns the value 0.69897.

The LOG10 function

The LOG10 function returns the base 10 logarithm for the number or cell reference in the argument. The form of the function is

    =LOG10(*number*)

The *number* argument must be a positive value or a reference to a cell that contains a positive value. If the *number* argument is negative, the function returns the #NUM! error message.

    For example, the function

    =LOG10(100)

returns the value 2.

The LN function

The LN function returns the natural (base e) logarithm of the number referred to by its argument. The form of the function is

    =LN(*number*)

For example, the formula

    =LN(2)

returns the value .069314718055995.

The EXP function

The EXP function computes the value of the constant e (which is equal to 2.7182818), raised to the power specified by the function's argument. For example,

    =EXP(2)

equals 7.3890561, or 2.7182818 times 2.7182818. The EXP function is the inverse of the LN function. For example, if cell A1 contains the formula

    =LN(8)

then, because EXP is the inverse of the LN function, the formula

    =EXP(A1)

returns the result 8.

Trigonometric functions

Microsoft Excel includes several functions that compute common trigonometric values like sine, cosine, tangent, arcsine, arccosine, and arctangent.

The SIN function

The SIN function returns the sine of an angle. This function takes the form

=SIN(*angle in radians*)

For example, the formula

=SIN(1.5)

returns the value 0.99749499.

The COS function

The COS function, the complement of SIN, calculates the cosine of an angle. Like SIN, this function takes the form

=COS(*angle in radians*)

For example, the function

=COS(1.5)

returns the value 0.07073772.

E X C E L *Tip*

Expressing angles in radians

Microsoft Excel measures angles in radians rather than degrees. Radians measure the size of an angle based on the constant π (approximately 3.14). You can convert radians to degrees with the formula

angle in degrees=angle in radians$*(180/\pi)$

For example:

1.57 radians=1.57$*(180/\pi)\cong$90 degrees
3.14 radians=3.14$*(180/\pi)\cong$180 degrees
6.28 radians=6.28$*(180/\pi)\cong$360 degrees

The TAN function

You can use the TAN function to compute the tangent of an angle. The TAN function has the form

=TAN(*angle in radians*)

The formula

=TAN(1.5)

returns the tangent of an angle of 1.5 radians: 14.1014199.

The ASIN and ACOS functions

The ASIN and ACOS functions compute the arcsine and arccosine of a value. These functions return a value that represents the radian measure of an angle. The forms of these functions are

=ASIN(*sine of angle*)

and

=ACOS(*cosine of angle*)

You can remember the purpose of these functions with the phrase "the angle whose." For example, the function

=ASIN(0)

returns the value 0; that is, the radian measure of "the angle whose" sine is 0. The function

=ACOS(0)

returns the value 1.57079633; that is, the radian measure of "the angle whose" cosine is 0.

The argument for the ACOS and ASIN functions must be less than or equal to 1 and greater than or equal to –1. Any value outside this range results in a #NUM! or #DIV/0! error value. The ASIN function always returns a value between –1.57 and 1.57 radians (90 degrees). The ACOS function always returns a value between 0 and 3.14 radians (180 degrees).

The ATAN and ATAN2 functions

The ATAN function computes the arctangent of a tangent value. Its form is

=ATAN(*tangent of angle*)

The ATAN function always returns a value between –1.57 and 1.57 radians (90 degrees). For example, the function

=ATAN(2)

returns the measure, in radians, of the angle whose tangent is 2: 1.10714872.

The ATAN2 function returns the four-quadrant arctangent of the tangent described in the argument. The ATAN2 function requires two arguments and has the form

=ATAN2(*x-number,y-number*)

where *x-number* and *y-number* are the x-axis and y-axis coordinates of a point. The result of this function is the measure of the angle determined by the point. The result of ATAN2 always falls between –3.1416 and 3.1416. Either *x-number* or *y-number* can be 0; however, if both values are 0, the function returns the #DIV/0! error value.

Financial functions

Microsoft Excel includes 13 functions that allow you to perform common business calculations, such as *net present value* and *future value*, without building long and complex formulas. These functions are PV, NPV, FV, PMT, IPMT, PPMT, NPER, RATE, IRR, MIRR, SLN, DDB, and SYD. If you plan to use Microsoft Excel in your business, you will almost certainly use Excel's financial functions. (For the purposes of the following discussion, we round the numbers in the financial examples to two decimal places. Excel displays the results of its financial functions as negative numbers with six decimal places.)

The PV function

Excel's PV function computes the present value (the value today) of a series of equal periodic payments or of a lump-sum payment. (A stream of constant payments is often called an ordinary annuity.) The PV function has the form

=PV(*rate,number of periods,payment,future value,type*)

where *rate* is the discount rate, *number of periods* is the term of the investment, and *payment* is the periodic payment. The *future value* and *type* arguments are optional. You can use the *future value* argument in place of *payment* when you want to compute the present value of a lump-sum payment. The *type* argument tells Excel whether the payments are received at the beginning or at the end of each period.

Suppose you are presented with an investment opportunity that returns $1000 a year over the next five years. To receive this annuity, you have to invest $3000. Are you willing to pay $3000 today to earn $5000 over the next five years? To decide whether this investment is acceptable, you need to determine the present value of the stream of $1000 payments you will receive.

We assume that you can also invest your money in a money-market account at 10 percent, so we'll use 10 percent as the discount rate, or hurdle rate, of the investment.

To determine the present value of this investment, you can use the formula

=PV(10%,5,1000)

E X C E L *Tip*

The concept of present value

Present value is one of the most common methods for measuring the attractiveness of an investment. Simply put, the present value of an investment is the amount of money you are willing to pay to buy the investment. The present value is determined by discounting the inflows of the investment back to the present time. If the present value of the inflows is greater than the cost of the investment, the investment is a good one.

You may be wondering why we bother to compute present value. To see why present value is such a useful concept, consider this example: Suppose someone offered to give you $1000 one year from today in exchange for $1000 today. Would you bite? We expect you would not. If you took your $1000 and invested it in a money-market account, it would earn at least 5 percent in a year. In other words, at the end of the year, you'd have $1050 if you invested your money in the bank. Would you rather have $1050 or $1000 one year from now? Obviously, you'd rather have $1050. The investment you have been offered is a bad one because it does not pay you a return. You wouldn't choose it because you have an alternative investment that will pay a return.

Another way to look at this problem is to say that the present value of $1000, one year from today, is less than $1000. To compute the present

This function returns the value –3,790.7868, meaning that you should be willing to spend $3,790.79 now to receive $5000 over the next five years. Because your investment is only $3000, you decide that this is an acceptable investment.

The future value argument

Now, suppose that you are offered $5000 at the end of five years, rather than $1000 for each of the next five years. Is the investment still as attractive? To find out, you could use the formula

=PV(10%,5,,5000)

This formula returns the present value –3104.6066. This means that, at a hurdle rate of 10 percent, you should be willing to invest $3104.61 to receive $5000 in five years.

value, you must use an appropriate interest rate to discount the amount you will receive in one year, $1000, back to the present time.

The present value of an investment depends upon three factors: the interest or discount rate, the term of the investment, and the amount of the payment. In this example, the term is one year and the amount is $1000, but we need to choose a discount rate.

Because you know that you can earn 5 percent per year if you place your money in a money-market account, you might decide that the investment is not worthwhile unless it will earn more than 5 percent. Because this interest rate is a sort of "hurdle" over which an investment must leap before it becomes attractive to you, it is often called the *hurdle rate*.

Next, you use the formula

$1000/(1+.05)

to compute the present value of the investment: $952.38. (It is this calculation that Excel's PV and NPV functions perform automatically. In this simple example the formula is trivial; in real-world calculations, the formula can become unmanageable.) Because the present value of the investment ($952.38) is less than its cost ($1000), you should pass it by.

Although the proposal is not as attractive under these terms, it is still acceptable, because your investment is only $3000. (Don't forget your argument delimiters when you use the optional *future value* argument. If you skip an argument in the middle of a formula, you must enter an extra comma as a place marker for that argument.) For example, the formula

    =PV(10%,5,,5000)

did not include an argument for *payment*. If you had not included the extra comma between *number of periods* (5) and *future value* (5000), Excel would have assumed that the number 5000 was a payment. As a result, Excel would have returned the present value of five $5000 payments: $18,953.934!

The type argument

The *type* argument is a nice feature not offered by most other spreadsheet programs. It lets you determine whether payments are to be made at the beginning or end of the period. A *type* argument of 1 means the payment occurs at the beginning of each period. A *type* argument of 0 means the payment occurs at the end of each period. If you do not enter a value for *type*, Excel uses the default value of 0.

The NPV function

Net present value is another common formula to determine the profitability of an investment. In general, any investment that yields a net present value greater than 0 is considered profitable.

Although NPV is similar to PV, there are a couple of important differences. First, while PV calculates the present value of a constant stream of inflows, NPV allows the streams of inflows to be uneven. In addition, NPV considers the cost of the investment, not just the inflows. The form of the NPV function is

    =NPV(*rate,investment,inflow 1,inflow 2,...,inflow n*)

where *rate* is the discount rate, *investment* is the cost of the investment, and *inflow 1*, *inflow 2*, and so on are the cash inflows.

For example, suppose you are considering a $15,000 investment that returns $5000 the first year, $7500 the second year, and $8200 the third year. Assuming a hurdle rate of 10 percent, you can use the formula

    =NPV(10%,–15000,5000,7500,8200)

to calculate the net present value of this investment: $1,731.44. Because the result of this formula is greater than 0, you decide that the investment is acceptable.

E X C E L

The timing of payments

As we have noted, the NPV function assumes that all payments occur at the end of each period. In many cases, however, your investment is likely to occur at the beginning of the first period. In other words, your initial investment probably will occur today, while the return on your investment probably will begin one year from now. To account for this difference, you could pull your initial investment out of the NPV function and put it at the end of the formula, as in

=NPV(*rate,inflow 1,inflow 2,...,inflow n*)–*investment*

For example, suppose you are considering a $15,000 investment that returns $5000 one year from today, $7500 two years from today, and $8200 three years from today. Assuming a hurdle rate of 10 percent, you can use the formula

=NPV(10%,5000,7500,8200)–15000

to calculate the net present value: $1,904.58.

The *inflow* arguments in NPV can be either positive or negative. Microsoft Excel assumes that a negative value is a payment made (an investment or production cost, for example) and a positive value is a payment received (such as rental income or sales revenues).

Notice that there is no *type* argument for NPV. Microsoft Excel assumes that all payments are evenly distributed and that they occur at the end of each period. This means that Excel assumes the first cash flow—the initial investment—actually occurs one time period from today.

The FV function

The FV function computes the future value of an investment. The investment can occur as a lump sum or as a stream of payments. Future value is essentially the opposite of present value. This function calculates the value at some future date of a constant stream of payments made over a period of time.

Like the other financial functions we have discussed, the three primary arguments for the FV function are rate, number of periods, and payment. You can also include arguments for present value and type. The FV function takes the form

=FV(*rate,number of periods,payment,present value,type*)

where *rate* is the interest rate, *number of periods* is the term of the investment, and *payment* is the periodic investment. The *present value* and *type* arguments are optional. You can use the *present value* argument instead of *payment* when you want to compute the future value of a lump-sum investment. The *type* argument tells Excel whether the payments are received at the beginning or end of each period.

For example, suppose you are thinking about starting an IRA account. You plan to deposit $2000 at the beginning of each year, and you expect the average rate of return on the IRA to be 11 percent per year for the foreseeable future. Assuming you are now 30 years old, how much money will your account have accumulated by the time you are 65? You can use the formula

=FV(11%,35,–2000,,1)

to learn that your IRA will have accumulated $758,328.81 at the end of 35 years.

Now, assume that you started an IRA account three years ago and have already accumulated $7500 in your account. You can use the formula

=FV(11%,35,–2000,–7500,1)

to learn that your IRA will have accumulated $1,047,640.19 at the end of 35 years.

The *type* argument—which indicates whether payments occur at the beginning (1) or end (0) of the period—is particularly important in financial calculations that span a large number of years. For example, if you had used the default value of 0 for the *type* argument in the formula above, Excel would have returned the value $972,490.49—a difference of more than $75,000!

The PMT function

The PMT function computes the periodic payment that is required to amortize a loan across a specified number of periods. The form of this function is

=PMT(*rate,number of periods,present value,future value,type*)

where *rate* is the interest rate, *number of periods* is the term of the loan, and *present value* is the principal amount that you plan to borrow.

For example, suppose you want to take out a 25-year mortgage for $100,000. Assuming an interest rate of 11 percent, what will your monthly payments be?

You start by dividing the 11 percent interest rate by 12 to arrive at a monthly rate of 0.92 percent. Next, you convert the number of periods into months by multiplying 25 by 12 (300). Now, you can plug the monthly *rate, number of periods,* and loan amount (*present value*) into the PMT formula

=PMT(0.92%,300,100000)

to compute the monthly mortgage payment: $983.

The IPMT function

The IPMT function computes the interest component of a loan payment when the loan is repaid over a specified time period with constant periodic payments and a constant interest rate. The IPMT function has the form

=IPMT (*rate,period,number of periods,present value,future value,type*)

where *rate* is the interest rate, *period* is the period for which you want to compute the interest payment, *number of periods* is the term of the loan, and *present value* is the value today of the amount borrowed. The *future value* argument is the amount you want to reach in the future. When computing IPMT on a loan payment, future value is 0. The *type* argument indicates whether the payments are made at the beginning or end of each period. The *future value* and *type* arguments are optional. If you omit them, Microsoft Excel assumes they are 0. The *period* argument must always be an integer between 1 and the number specified by *number of periods*.

Suppose you have borrowed $100,000 for 25 years at an 11 percent interest rate. The formula

=IPMT((11/12)%,1,300,100000)

tells you that the interest component of the payment due for the first month is –$916.67.

The formula

=IPMT((11/12)%,300,300,100000)

tells you that the interest component of the final payment on the same loan is –$8.90.

The PPMT function

The PPMT function is similar to the IPMT function. However, PPMT computes the component of a loan payment applied to the principal when the loan is repaid over a specified time period, with constant periodic payments and a constant interest rate. If you compute both IPMT and PPMT for the same period, you could add the results to obtain the total payment.

The PPMT function has the form

=PPMT(*rate,period,number of periods,present value,future value,type*)

where *rate* is the interest rate, *period* is the period for the payment you want to compute and must be an integer between 1 and the number specified by the number of periods argument, *number of periods* is the term of the loan, and *present value* is the value today or the amount borrowed. The *future value* argument is the amount you want to reach in the future. When computing PPMT on a loan payment, this argument should be 0. The *type* argument tells Excel whether the payments are made at the beginning or at the end of each period. The *future value* and *type* arguments are optional. If you omit them, Microsoft Excel assumes they are 0.

Using the previous example, suppose you borrow $100,000 for 25 years at 11 percent interest. The formula

    =PPMT((11/12)%,1,300,100000)

tells you that for the first month of the loan, the component of the payment applied to the principal is $63.45. The formula

    =PPMT((11/12)%,300,300,100000)

tells you that the principal component of the final payment of the same loan is $971.21.

The NPER function

The NPER function computes the number of periods required to amortize a loan, given a specified periodic payment. The form of this function is

    =NPER(*rate,payment,present value*)

where *rate* is the interest rate, *payment* is the periodic payment, and *present value* is the principal amount that you plan to borrow.

Let's turn our example around a bit to see how the NPER function works. Suppose you can afford mortgage payments of $1200 per month and you want to know how long it will take you to pay off the $100,000 loan. The formula

    =NPER(0.92%,–1200,100000)

tells you that your mortgage payments will extend over 158.91 months.

If the *payment* argument is too small to amortize the loan at the indicated rate of interest, the function will return an error message. The monthly payment must always be at least equal to the *period* interest rate times the principal amount. Otherwise the loan will never be amortized. For example, the function

    =NPER(0.92%,–750,100000)

results in the #NUM! error value. In this case, the monthly payment must be more than $920, or $100,000 times 0.92 percent.

E X C E L *tip*

Consistency counts

Keep in mind that the *rate* and *number of periods* arguments in financial functions must refer to the same period. For example, if you are using an annual interest rate and want to calculate monthly payments, you must convert the annual rate into a monthly rate before you use the PMT function. To do this, simply divide the interest rate by 12 to arrive at a monthly interest rate. For example, a 10 percent annual interest rate divided by 12 months equals 0.83 percent.

Functions for calculating the rate of return: RATE, IRR, and MIRR

The RATE, IRR, and MIRR functions are used to compute the rates of return on investments. The RATE function computes the rate of return on an investment that generates constant periodic payments. The IRR function computes the internal rate of return on investments that have fluctuating payments. The MIRR function computes the modified internal rate of return.

The RATE function

The RATE function lets you determine the rate of return of an investment that generates a series of equal periodic payments or a lump-sum payment. The RATE function has the form

=RATE(*number of periods,payment,present value,future value,type,guess*)

where *number of periods* is the term of the loan or investment, *payment* is the periodic payment, and *present value* is the principal amount that you plan to borrow or invest.

The *future value* and *type* arguments are optional. You can use the *future value* argument in place of *payment* when you want to compute the rate of a lump-sum payment. The *type* argument tells Microsoft Excel whether the payments occur at the beginning or at the end of each period. The *guess* argument, which is also optional, simply gives Excel a starting place for calculating the rate. If you omit the *future value* or *type* arguments, Excel assumes that they are 0. If you omit the *guess* argument, Excel assumes that it is 0.1.

For example, suppose you are considering an investment that will pay you five $1000 payments. The investment costs $3000. To determine the actual annual rate of return on your investment, you can use the formula

=RATE(5,1000,–3000)

This function returns 0.1985771, the rate of return on this investment.

The RATE function uses an iterative process to compute the rate of return. The function begins by computing the net present value of the investment at the *guess* rate. If that first net present value is greater than 0, the function selects a higher rate and repeats the net present value calculation. If the first net present value is less than 0, a lower rate is selected for the second iteration. The RATE function continues this process until it arrives at the correct rate of return, or until it has gone through 20 iterations.

Most of the time you'll be able to omit the *guess* argument. If you omit this argument, Excel begins with a *guess* of 0.1. However, if you receive the #NUM! error value when you enter the RATE function, Excel is probably trying to tell you that it could not calculate the rate within 20 iterations. If this occurs, try entering a different guess rate to give Excel a running start at the calculation. A rate between 10 percent and 100 percent usually does the trick.

The IRR function

The IRR function is closely related to the RATE function. The IRR function computes the internal rate of return on an investment that generates uneven periodic cash flows. The difference between RATE and IRR is similar to the difference between the PV and NPV functions. Like NPV, IRR accounts for investment costs and irregular payments. The form of the IRR function is

=IRR(*values,guess*)

Let's look at an example of IRR. Suppose you agree to pay $120,000 to buy a condominium. Over the next five years, you expect to receive $25,000, $27,000, $35,000, $38,000, and $40,000 in net rental income.

Notice that IRR allows only one argument for *values*. To enter your investment and rental income information into this formula, you need to set up a simple worksheet like the one in Figure 6-19. Cell B10 contains the formula

=IRR(B1:B6)

which results in the value 10.63 percent. (To show this value as a percentage, you need to format the cell to display 10.63%.) If the hurdle rate is 10 percent, then this condominium purchase is considered a good investment.

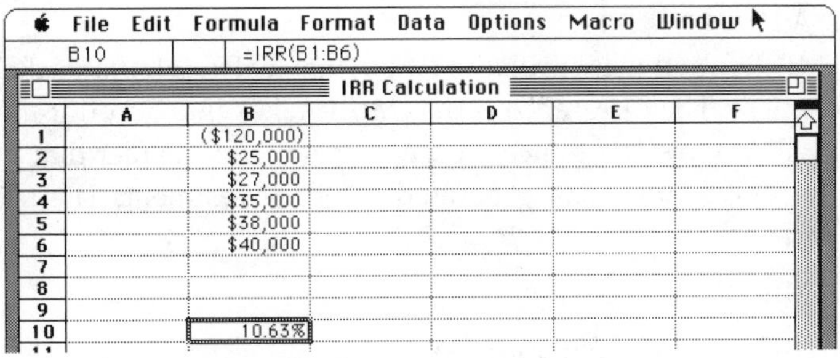

File Edit Formula Format Data Options Macro Window ▶

| B10 | =IRR(B1:B6) |

IRR Calculation

	A	B	C	D	E	F
1		($120,000)				
2		$25,000				
3		$27,000				
4		$35,000				
5		$38,000				
6		$40,000				
7						
8						
9						
10		10.63%				

FIGURE 6-19. *You have used IRR to compute the internal rate of return on an investment.*

As with RATE, the *guess* argument is optional. If you receive a #NUM! error value when you enter this formula, you can include a *guess* argument in the function to help nudge Excel toward the right answer.

EXCEL *Tip*

The concept of internal rate of return

Internal rate of return is commonly used as a financial measurement. Like net present value, it is used to compare one investment opportunity with another.

The internal rate of return of an investment is the rate that causes the net present value of the investment to equal 0. To put it another way, the internal rate of return is the rate that causes the present value of the inflows from an investment to equal exactly the cost of the investment.

Internal rate of return and net present value are really very closely related. Remember, we said that an attractive investment is one whose net present value, discounted at the appropriate hurdle rate, yields a net present value greater than 0. Turn that equation around, and you can see that the discount rate required to generate a net present value of 0 must be greater than the hurdle rate. In other words, an attractive investment is one in which the discount rate required to yield a net present value of 0— that is, the internal rate of return—is greater than the hurdle rate.

The MIRR function

The MIRR function is similar to IRR in that it also calculates the rate of return of an investment. The difference is that MIRR takes into account the cost of the money you will borrow to finance the investment, and the fact that you will almost certainly reinvest the cash generated by the investment. The MIRR function takes the form

=MIRR(*values,safe,risky*)

The *safe* argument is the rate at which you will borrow the money you need to make the investment. The *risky* argument is the rate at which you will reinvest the cash flow.

To continue with the previous example, you can use the formula

=MIRR(B1:B6,10%,12%)

to calculate a modified internal rate of return of 11.17 percent, assuming a *safe* rate of 10 percent and a *risky* rate of 12 percent.

Functions for calculating depreciation: SLN, DDB, and SYD

The SLN, DDB, and SYD functions are used to compute depreciation rates. The SLN function is used for straight-line depreciation, the DDB function is used for double-declining-balance depreciation, and the SYD function is used for sum-of-the-years'-digits depreciation.

The SLN function

The Microsoft Excel new SLN function lets you determine the straight-line depreciation for an asset for a single period. The straight-line depreciation method assumes that depreciation is uniform throughout the useful life of the asset. The cost or basis of the asset, less its estimated salvage value, is deducted in equal amounts over the life of the asset. The SLN function has the form

=SLN(*cost,salvage,life*)

where *cost* is the initial cost of the asset, *salvage* is the asset's value when it is fully depreciated, and *life* is the length of time the asset will be in service.

For example, suppose that you want to depreciate a machine that costs $8000 new, has a serviceable life of 10 years, and has a salvage value of $500. The formula

=SLN(8000,500,10)

tells you that the straight-line depreciation is $750 each year.

E X C E L *tip*

A word of caution

If you switch from one depreciation method to another during the life of the asset, be sure to adjust your *cost* and *life* arguments to compensate for this change. For example, suppose you're calculating the annual depreciation for a $10,000 machine with a 10-year useful life. During the first 5 years, you use the declining-balance depreciation method; then you decide to switch to the straight-line method to depreciate the asset for the remaining 5 years. You must subtract any prior years' depreciation from the *cost* argument before you calculate the remaining years' depreciation, and you must reduce the life of the asset from 10 to 5 years.

The DDB function

The DDB function computes an asset's depreciation with the double-declining-balance method, which returns depreciation at an accelerated rate—more in the early periods and less later. Under this method, depreciation is computed as a percentage of the net book value of the asset (the cost of the asset, less any depreciation from prior years). Although the salvage value is not subtracted from the cost of the asset, an asset cannot be depreciated below its salvage value.

Because the double-declining depreciation method produces a different depreciation expense for each period during the life of the asset, the DDB function requires an argument to indicate which period's depreciation expense you are computing. The first three arguments are the same as the three arguments for SLN. Thus, the DDB function has the form

=DDB(*cost,salvage,life,period*)

where *cost* is the initial cost of the asset, *salvage* is the asset's value when it is fully depreciated, *life* is the length of time the asset will be in service, and *period* is a specific portion of the asset's life. All DDB arguments must be positive numbers. You must use the same time units for *life* and *period*; that is, if you express *life* in months, you must also express *period* in months.

For example, suppose you want to depreciate a machine that cost $5000 new, has a serviceable life of five years, and a salvage value of $100. The formula

=DDB(5000,100,1825,1)

tells you that the double-declining-balance depreciation for the first day is $5.48. The formula

=DDB(5000,100,60,1)

tells you that the double-declining-balance depreciation for the first month is $166.67. The formula

=DDB(5000,100,5,5)

tells you that the double-declining-balance depreciation for the fifth year is $259.20.

The SYD function

The SYD function computes an asset's depreciation for a specific time period using the sum-of-the-years'-digits method. Under the sum-of-the-years'-digits method, depreciation is calculated on the cost of the item, less its salvage value. Like the double-declining-balance method, sum-of-the-years'-digits is an accelerated depreciation method. The SYD function has the form

=SYD(*cost,salvage,life,period*)

where *cost* is the initial cost of the asset, *salvage* is the asset's value when it is fully depreciated, *life* is the length of time the asset will be in service, and *period* is a specific portion of the asset's life.

For example, suppose you want to depreciate a machine that cost $15,000, has a serviceable life of three years, and a salvage value of $1,250. The formula

=SYD(15000,1250,3,1)

tells you that the sum-of-the-years'-digits depreciation for the first year is $6,875.00. The formula

=SYD(15000,1250,3,3)

tells you that the sum-of-the-years'-digits depreciation for the third year is $2,291.67.

Text functions

Four of the Microsoft Excel text functions, VALUE, TEXT, DOLLAR, and FIXED, can be used to convert numeric text entries into numbers and number entries into text strings. The VALUE function converts a text string into a number. The TEXT, DOLLAR, and FIXED functions convert numbers into formatted text strings. Three other functions—REPT, LEN, and MID—allow you to manipulate the text strings themselves. The remaining text functions allow you to work with label entries in your worksheet and can be particularly helpful when you need to edit long lists of database entries for consistency.

The VALUE function

If you have entered numbers in your worksheet in text format, you can use the VALUE function to convert that text into a numeric value. The VALUE function has the form

=VALUE("*text*")

The *text* argument can be a literal string, in quotation marks, or it can be a reference to a cell that contains text. The text string to be converted can be in any recognized format, including user-created custom formats. (See Chapter 3, "Formatting the Worksheet," for more information on Excel's format commands and symbols.)

For example, the function

=VALUE("40205")

returns the value 40205. If cell A10 contains the text entry ="*40205*", the function

=VALUE(A10)

also returns the value 40205.

The VALUE function can also be used to convert text entries in the form of dates into serial date values. For example, the function

=VALUE("1/1/85")

returns the serial date value 29586.

Keep in mind that Microsoft Excel automatically converts numeric text into numbers as necessary when you perform calculations. This means that you don't have to use VALUE before using a number entered as text in a formula. Chapter 2, "Worksheet Basics," contains more information on Excel's treatment of text and values.

The TEXT function

The TEXT function converts a number into a text string with a specified format. This function has the form

=TEXT(*number,format*)

The *number* argument in the TEXT function can be a number, a formula, or a cell reference. The *format* argument tells Excel how you want the resulting string to be displayed. You can use any of Excel's formatting symbols ($, #, 0, and so on), except the asterisk, in *format* to specify the format you desire. For example, the function

    =TEXT(98/4,"0.00")

returns the text string *24.50* and the function

    =TEXT(98/4,"$0.00")

returns the text string *$24.50*. You can't use the General format as a *format* argument. Strangely, the *number* argument of the TEXT function can also be a string in date form. For example, the function

    =TEXT("1/1/85","mmmm d, yyyy")

returns the text string *January 1, 1985*.

The DOLLAR function

The DOLLAR function is similar to the TEXT function in that it converts a number into a string. The difference is that DOLLAR automatically formats the resulting string as currency with the number of decimal places you specify. The DOLLAR function has the form

    =DOLLAR(*number,number of digits*)

For example, the formula

    =DOLLAR(45.899,2)

returns the text string *$45.90*, and the function

    =DOLLAR(45.899,0)

returns the text string *$46*. Notice that Excel automatically rounds the number, as it does when you choose Number... from the Format menu and select the $#,##0.00 or $#,##0 format.

If you do not include a *number of digits* argument for the DOLLAR function, Excel automatically uses two decimal places. If you use a negative number for the *number of digits* argument, Excel rounds to the left of the decimal point.

The FIXED function

The FIXED function rounds a number to the specified number of decimal places and displays the result as text. For example, if you enter the formula

    =FIXED(98.786,2)

Excel returns the text string *98.79*.

If you don't include a *number of digits* argument for the FIXED function, Excel automatically uses two decimal places. If you use a negative number for *number of digits*, Excel rounds to the left of the decimal point. For example, the function

=FIXED(98.786,–1)

returns the text string *100*.

The REPT function

The REPT function allows you to create a string that is made up of one character, or a few characters, repeated a specified number of times. The form of REPT is

=REPT("*text*",*repeat number*)

The *text* argument specifies the text string that you want to be repeated. This argument must be enclosed in quotation marks. The *repeat number* argument tells Excel how many times you want the text string to be repeated. The *repeat number* argument can be any integer from 0 to 255. If you enter a value of 0 for the *repeat number* argument, Excel leaves the cell blank.

For example, suppose you want to create a row of asterisks across 10 columns of a worksheet. Assume that each column is 15 characters wide. With the REPT function, you can click the row header, then press the Return key to skip over to the column in which you want the border row to begin, and enter the function

=REPT("*",150)

The result is a string of 150 asterisks. Like other strings, the asterisks overlap the ten 15-character wide columns.

The *text* argument can be more than one character long. For example, the function

=REPT("*–",75)

results in a row of asterisks and dashes 150 characters long. Keep in mind that the *repeat number* argument does not specify the total number of characters you want to create, but the number of times you want the *text* argument to be repeated. If the text string is two characters long, the length of the resulting label is twice the *repeat number* argument.

The LEN function

The LEN function returns the number of characters in an entry. The argument of LEN can be a literal number, a literal string in quotes, or a reference to a cell. For example, the function

=LEN("Test")

returns 4. If cell A1 contains the label *Test*, then the function

=LEN(A1)

also returns 4. Similarly, the function

=LEN(104)

returns the value 3, as does the function

=LEN(A1)

if cell A1 contains the number 104.

Now, suppose cell A10 contains the formula

=A1+A2+A3+A4+A5+A6+A7+A8

and the result of this formula is the value 25. The function

=LEN(A10)

returns the value 2, the length of the result of the formula.

The cell referred to by the argument of the LEN function can be a cell that contains another string function. For example, if cell A1 contains the REPT function

=REPT("*–",75)

described above, the formula

=LEN(A1)

returns the value 150. Notice that the LEN function returns the length of the displayed text or value, not the length of the underlying formula.

The MID function

You can use the MID function to extract a series of characters (a substring) from a text string. The form of the function is

=MID(*text,starting position,number of characters*)

where *text* is the string from which you want to extract the substring, *starting position* is the place in the string where the substring begins, and *number of characters* is the number of characters you want to extract. The *text* argument can be a literal string, enclosed in quotation marks, but it will usually be a reference to a cell that contains text.

For example, the simple worksheet in Figure 6-20 contains a series of names of varying lengths. Suppose you want to print these names on labels, but you only have room for 14 characters across each label. You can create a formula like this

=MID(A1,1,14)

to extract the first 14 characters of each name. This formula, entered in cell D1, tells Excel to extract the first 14 characters from the string in cell A1. After entering this formula, you could then highlight cells D1:D10 and use the Fill Down command to copy this formula into cells D2 through D10.

Notice that the names in Figure 6-20 that are less than 14 characters long are not altered by this formula. If the length of the string specified by the *text* argument is equal to or less than the *number of characters* argument, Excel extracts the entire string.

⬥	File	Edit	Formula	Format	Data	Options	Macro	Window	▶

D1	=MID(A1,1,14)

MID Test

	A	B	C	D	E	F
1	Patricia A. Flynn			Patricia A. Fl		
2	Laura Heuser			Laura Heuser		
3	Lori Houston			Lori Houston		
4	Lori Junkins			Lori Junkins		
5	J. Timothy Landgrave			J. Timothy Lan		
6	Kathleen Fitzgerald Lane			Kathleen Fitzg		
7	Becky Ledford			Becky Ledford		
8	Tracy Milliner			Tracy Milliner		
9	Joe Pierce			Joe Pierce		
10	Jonathan Pyles			Jonathan Pyles		

FIGURE 6-20. *You can use MID to extract a series of characters from a text string.*

The CHAR and CODE functions

Every computer uses numeric codes to represent characters. Personal computers use a code system called ASCII (American Standard Code for Information Interchange). In the ASCII system, a three-digit code represents each number, letter, and symbol you can produce on a computer.

The CHAR function returns the character that corresponds to the ASCII code number you specify. The CODE function, on the other hand, returns the ASCII code for the character you specify. The forms of these two functions are

=CHAR(*number*)

=CODE(*text*)

If you type a literal character as your *text* argument, don't forget to place the *text* characters in quotation marks. Otherwise, you'll get the #NAME? error value. If *text* is more than one character long, Excel returns the ASCII code representing the first character in the string.

For example, the function

=CHAR(83)

returns the letter *S*, while the function

=CODE("S")

returns the ASCII code 83. Similarly, if cell A1 contains the letter *S*, the formula

=CODE(A1)

also results in the ASCII code 83.

The CLEAN function

The CLEAN function eliminates all nonprintable characters from a string. This function takes the form

=CLEAN(*text*)

For example, if you have imported data from another program, some entries may contain nonprintable characters, such as tab markers and other unrecognized codes. You can use the CLEAN function to remove these nonprintable characters from your text.

The TRIM function

Often leading and trailing blank characters can prevent you from correctly sorting entries in your worksheet or database. In addition, if you use string functions to manipulate labels in your worksheet, these extra spaces can prevent your formulas from working correctly. The TRIM function, which removes all spaces in text except for one space between words, has the form

=TRIM(*text*)

For example, if cell A1 of your worksheet contains the label *This   cell   contains   lots of blanks*, the function

=TRIM(A1)

returns *This cell contains lots of blanks*.

The EXACT function

The EXACT function lets you determine whether two strings match exactly. Unlike using an equal sign (=) to compare two strings, EXACT lets you determine whether two labels contain the same uppercase and lowercase letters, as well as the same characters. The EXACT function takes the form

=EXACT(*text1,text2*)

If *text1* and *text2* are identical, including capitalization, EXACT returns TRUE. If *text1* and *text2* are not identical, EXACT returns FALSE. In other words, EXACT is a conditional-testing function that operates on strings.

For example, if cell A5 of your worksheet contains the label *Totals* and cell A6 contains the label *totals*, the function

=EXACT(A5,A6)

returns a FALSE value. However, if both cells contain the label *Totals* with a capital *T*, the EXACT function returns a TRUE value.

If you want to compare two strings in which differences in capitalization don't matter, use the equal sign instead of EXACT.

The FIND and SEARCH functions

The FIND and SEARCH functions let you locate the position of a substring within a string. Both functions return the number of the character where Microsoft Excel first finds the text. (In counting characters, Excel includes all blank spaces and punctuation marks.)

These two functions work the same way, except that FIND is capitalization-sensitive and SEARCH lets you use wildcards. These functions have the following form:

=FIND(*find text,within text,start at num*)

=SEARCH(*find text,within text,start at num*)

The *find text* argument identifies the text sought and the *within text* argument indicates where Microsoft Excel should look for it. You can use either literal text enclosed in double quotation marks or a cell reference for either of these arguments. The optional *start at num* argument specifies the character position in *within text* where you want to begin your search. This argument can be helpful when there is more than one occurrence of *find text* in *within text*. If you omit *start at num*, Excel reports the first match located.

You get the #VALUE! error value if *find text* isn't contained in *within text*, if *start at num* isn't greater than 0, or if *start at num* is greater than the number of characters in *within text* or greater than the position of the last occurrence of *find text*.

For example, to locate the letter *p* in the string "A Night at the Opera", use the formula

=FIND("p","A Night at the Opera")

This formula returns 17, because the *p* is the 17th character in the string.

If you're not sure of the character sequence you're searching for, you can use the SEARCH function and include wildcards in your *find text* string. To search for a single character occupying a specific position, use a question mark character (?); to search for a sequence of characters occupying a specific position, use an asterisk (*).

For example, suppose you've used the names *Smith* and *Smyth* in your worksheet. To ensure that either name is found when you check the contents of cell A1, use the formula

    =SEARCH("Sm?th",A1)

Then, if cell A1 contains the name *John Smith* or *John Smyth*, the SEARCH function returns the value 6—the starting point (including blank space) for the string *"Sm?th"*. If you're not sure of the number of characters, use the asterisk (*) wildcard character. For example, to find the position of the name *Allan* or *Alan* in cell A1, use the formula

    =SEARCH("A*an",A1)

The LEFT and RIGHT functions

The LEFT function returns the leftmost series of characters from a string argument, while the RIGHT function returns the rightmost series of characters from a string argument. These functions take the form

    =LEFT(*text,number of characters*)

    =RIGHT(*text,number of characters*)

The *number of characters* argument indicates the number of characters you want to extract from the *text* argument. Keep in mind that these functions count blank spaces in your *text* argument as characters. If you do not want the blank characters to be included in the extracted label, use the TRIM or CLEAN function to omit any unwanted blanks from the *text* argument before you use the RIGHT or LEFT function.

The *number of characters* argument must be greater than or equal to 0. If you omit *number of characters*, it is assumed to be 1. If *number of characters* is longer than *text*, the function returns the entire *text* argument.

For example, suppose you have entered the label *This is a test* in cell A1 of your worksheet. You can use the formula

    =RIGHT(A1,4)

to return the label *test*, or use the formula

    =LEFT(A1,4)

to return the label *This*.

The UPPER, LOWER, and PROPER functions

The UPPER and LOWER functions convert a text string to either all uppercase or all lowercase letters. The PROPER function lets you capitalize the first letter in each word of a text string. It also capitalizes other letters in the string that follow any character except a letter. Excel converts all remaining letters of the text string to lowercase. These functions take the form

    =UPPER(*text*)

    =LOWER(*text*)

    =PROPER(*text*)

For example, suppose you have entered a series of names in your worksheet, and you want to ensure that all of these entries appear in capital letters. Cell A1 might contain the label *john Johnson*. You could use the formula

    =UPPER(A1)

to return *JOHN JOHNSON*. Similarly, the formulas

    =LOWER(A1)

    =PROPER(A1)

return the labels *john johnson* and *John Johnson*, respectively.

The REPLACE function

The REPLACE function replaces one string of characters in a label with another string of characters. The REPLACE function takes the form

    =REPLACE(*old text,start num,number of characters,new text*)

The *old text* argument is the text string in which you want to replace some characters. The next two arguments, *start num* and *number of characters*, indicate which characters you want to replace. (The first character in the text is number *1*, the second character is *2*, and so on.) The *new text* argument is the text string that you want to insert. The *old text* and *new text* arguments must be literal strings surrounded by quotation marks, or formulas or references that result in strings. If *new text* would make the label too long (Excel limits cell entries to 255 characters), REPLACE returns the #N/A! error value.

For example, suppose cell A1 contains the label *Andy Davidson.* You want to replace the first through fourth characters from this label with the string *"Andrew".* To do this, you can use the function

    =REPLACE(A1,1,4,"Andrew")

to return *Andrew Davidson.*

The SUBSTITUTE function

The SUBSTITUTE function substitutes new text for old text, as REPLACE does; however, you don't need to tell Excel the start number and the number of characters to replace. Instead, you include the exact text you want to replace.

The SUBSTITUTE function takes the form

    =SUBSTITUTE(*text,old text,new text,instance number*)

The *instance number* argument is optional and tells Excel to replace only the specified occurrence of *old text.* If you don't include an *instance number* argument, Excel changes all *old text* to *new text.*

For example, suppose cell A4 in your worksheet contains the label *candy,* and you want to change it to *dandy.* To do this, you can use the SUBSTITUTE function in the formula

    =SUBSTITUTE(A4,"c","d")

Logical functions

The Microsoft Excel logical functions include IF, the special operators AND, OR, and NOT, and the specialized functions ISERROR, ISNA, TRUE, FALSE, ISBLANK, ISERR, ISLOGICAL, ISTEXT, ISNONTEXT, ISNUMBER, and ISREF.

Conditional tests

The IF function allows you to set up conditional tests in the cells of your worksheets and instruct Excel to return a given value based on the results of that test. If the condition is true, the function returns one value; otherwise, the function returns a different value.

A conditional test is an equation that compares two numbers, functions, formulas, or labels. For example, each of the following formulas is a conditional test.

=A1>A2

=5–3>5*2

=AVERAGE(B1:B6)=SUM(6,7,8)

=C2="Female"

=COUNT(A1:A10)=COUNT(B1:B10)

=LEN(A1)<10

Logical operators

Every conditional test must include at least one logical operator. Logical operators define the test relationship between elements of the conditional test. For example, in the conditional test A1>A2, the greater-than symbol (>) is the logical operator used to compare the test values stored in cells A1 and A2. Excel offers these six simple logical operators:

Operator	Definition	Operator	Definition
=	Equal	>=	Greater than or equal to
>	Greater than	<=	Less than or equal to
<	Less than	<>	Not equal to

If you think about it for a moment, you'll see that every conditional test must be either true or false. For example, the conditional test

Z1=10

is true if the value in Z1 equals 10 and false if Z1 contains any other value. In fact, if you were to enter this conditional test in a cell as a formula, that cell would display the message TRUE if cell Z1 contained the value 10 and FALSE if Z1 contained anything else.

The IF function

Of course, Excel's conditional tests would be of little value if you could use them only to check your math homework. This is where the IF function comes in. The form of the IF function is

=IF(*conditional test,true value,false value*)

This function can be read: If the conditional test is true, then the function returns *true value*; otherwise, the function returns *false value*.

For example, the function

=IF(A1=5,100,200)

returns the value 100 if A1 equals 5, and 200 if A1 contains any other value. Similarly, the function

=IF(Z100<22,5,10)

returns 5 if the value in cell Z100 is less than 22; otherwise, it returns 10.

You can also use functions as the arguments within an IF function. For example, the function

=IF(SUM(A1:A10)>0,SUM(A1:A10),0)

returns the result of SUM(A1:A10) if SUM(A1:A10) is greater than 0; otherwise, the function returns 0.

Assuming that the range A1:A10 has been assigned the range name *Student*, the result of the formula

=IF(AVERAGE(Student)>80,"PASS","FAIL")

is identical to that of

=IF(AVERAGE(A1:A10)>80,"PASS","FAIL")

Using text in IF

As you saw in the two previous examples, you can also use text as the *true value* and *false value* arguments in IF functions. For example, the worksheet in Figure 6-21 lists semester test scores for a group of students.

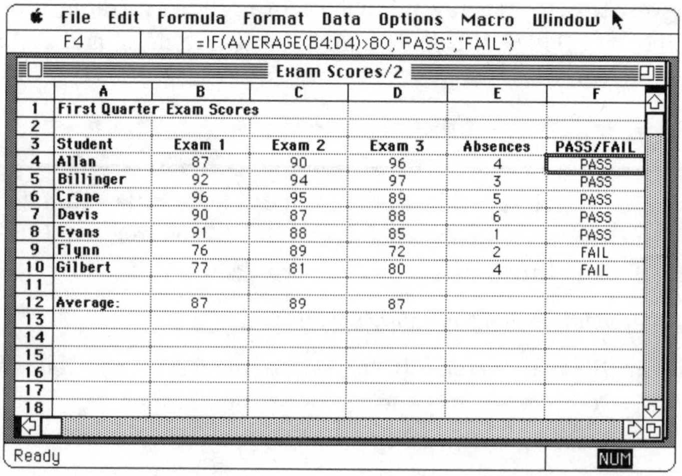

	A	B	C	D	E	F
1	First Quarter Exam Scores					
2						
3	Student	Exam 1	Exam 2	Exam 3	Absences	PASS/FAIL
4	Allan	87	90	96	4	PASS
5	Billinger	92	94	97	3	PASS
6	Crane	96	95	89	5	PASS
7	Davis	90	87	88	6	PASS
8	Evans	91	88	85	1	PASS
9	Flynn	76	89	72	2	FAIL
10	Gilbert	77	81	80	4	FAIL
11						
12	Average:	87	89	87		

FIGURE 6-21. *You can use the IF function to determine pass/fail status.*

The function

=IF(AVERAGE(B4:D4)>80,"PASS","FAIL")

entered in cell F4 tells Microsoft Excel to average the test scores contained in the range B4:D4. If AVERAGE(B4:D4) is greater than 80, the function returns the *true value* PASS, and if AVERAGE(B4:D4) is less than or equal to 80, the function instead returns the *false value* FAIL.

You can take advantage of Fxcel's ability to use text in IF to return a blank, instead of a 0, as the result of a false IF function. For example, the function

=IF(SUM(A1:A10)>0,SUM(A1:A10),"")

returns a blank if the conditional test is false.

You can also use text in the *conditional test* argument of an IF function. For example, the function

=IF(A1="Test",100,200)

returns the value 100 if cell A1 contains the text entry *Test* and 200 if that cell contains any other entry. The match between the two text entries must be exact in all respects, including capitalization. If cell A1 contains any of the text entries *test*, *TEST*, or *TEst*, the conditional test is false. It is important that you always enclose text strings in quotation marks when you use them in the IF function (and in any other function, for that matter). If you do not enclose the text strings in quotation marks, Excel assumes that the text strings are range names.

The TRUE and FALSE functions

The TRUE and FALSE functions offer alternative ways to represent the logical conditions TRUE and FALSE. Neither of these functions accepts arguments. They take the form

=TRUE()

=FALSE()

For example, suppose cell B5 contains a logical test formula. If you enter the formula

=IF(B5=FALSE(),"Warning!","OK")

in another cell, the new formula returns *Warning!* if the result of the logical formula in B5 is FALSE or the cell is blank; if the result of B5 is TRUE, the formula returns *OK*.

The ISBLANK function

You can use the ISBLANK function to determine whether a referenced cell is blank. The ISBLANK function follows the form

=ISBLANK(*reference*)

where *reference* is a cell reference. If *reference* refers to a blank cell, the function returns the value TRUE; otherwise, it returns FALSE.

The ISERR function

The ISERR function is a specialized logical function that tests an argument to determine whether it is an error value. The ISERR function results in a TRUE value if its argument is any error value except #N/A; otherwise, the ISERR function returns FALSE. This function is similar to the ISERROR and ISNA functions. As we explain later in this chapter, the ISNA function tests only for #N/A error values, while the ISERROR function tests for all error values, including #N/A. The ISERR function takes the form

=ISERR(*value*)

Although *value* can be a number or a formula, it is usually a cell reference.

The ISLOGICAL function

The ISLOGICAL function determines whether an argument is a logical value. This function returns a TRUE value if the specified argument is either TRUE or FALSE, and it returns a FALSE value if the specified argument contains any other type of value.

The ISLOGICAL function takes the form

=ISLOGICAL(*value*)

The ISTEXT and ISNONTEXT functions

The ISTEXT and ISNONTEXT functions let you determine whether an argument is text. These two functions take the form

=ISTEXT(*value*)

=ISNONTEXT(*value*)

For example, suppose cell A1 contains the label *test*. You want to determine whether the *value* argument in cell A1 is text. If you use the formula

=ISTEXT(A1)

Excel returns a TRUE value. You can also test the same cell using the formula

=ISNONTEXT(A1)

in which case Excel returns a FALSE value.

The ISNUMBER function

You can use the ISNUMBER function to determine whether a value is a number. The ISNUMBER function takes the form

=ISNUMBER(*value*)

For example, suppose you want to know if the value in cell A5 is a number. The formula

=ISNUMBER(A5)

returns TRUE if the value is a number; otherwise, it returns FALSE.

Complex operators: The AND, OR, and NOT functions

Excel offers three additional functions that let you develop much more sophisticated conditional tests: AND, OR, and NOT. These functions work in conjunction with the simple logical operators =, >, <, >=, <=, and <>. Basically, AND, OR, and NOT serve as complex operators to let you develop compound conditions. The AND and OR operators can take up to 14 logical arguments each, in the forms

=AND(*logical 1,logical 2,...*)

and

=OR(*logical 1,logical 2,...*)

while NOT takes only one argument in the form

=NOT(*logical*)

As you might imagine, AND, OR, and NOT give you a great deal of flexibility in creating conditional tests. To illustrate the power of these functions, let's expand the formula we developed in Figure 6-21. Suppose you want Excel to return the text string *PASS* only if the student has an average test score greater than 80 *and* fewer than 5 unexcused absences. You can accomplish this with the formula

=IF(AND(AVERAGE(B4:D4)>80,E4<5),"PASS","FAIL")

Although the OR function takes the same arguments as AND, the results are radically different. For example, if you enter the formula

=IF(OR(AVERAGE(B4:D4)>80,E4<5),"PASS","FAIL")

you are instructing Excel to return the text string *PASS* if the student's average test score is greater than 80 or if he or she has fewer than 5 absences. In other words, OR returns the *true value* argument if any one of the conditional tests is true, while AND returns the *true value* argument only if all the conditional tests are true.

The NOT function, on the other hand, is used to negate a condition. This concept is a little difficult to grasp at first, because NOT instructs Microsoft Excel to return the *true value* if the argument is false and the *false value* if the argument is true. The NOT function might be better described as the UNLESS function. For example, the formula

=IF(NOT(A1=2),"Go","NoGo")

tells Excel to return the text string *Go* unless cell A1 contains the value 2. This formula could also be stated as

=IF(A1=2,"NoGo","Go")

which can be read: *If A1 equals 2, return the text string* NoGo; *otherwise, return the text string* Go.

Nested IF functions

We've explored various ways to use complex operators like AND, OR, and NOT to build multiple arguments into your conditional functions. However, there are times when a logical problem cannot be resolved even with these methods. Fortunately, Excel lets you build extremely sophisticated conditional tests by nesting IF functions. By nesting one IF function within another, you can create a hierarchy of conditional tests for complex logical problems. For example, the formula

=IF(A1=100,"Always",IF(AND(A1<100,A1>=80),"Usually",
    IF(AND(A1<80,A1>60),"Sometimes","Who cares?")))

uses three separate IF functions. The formula can be read: *If the value in cell A1 equals 100, return the text string* Always; *otherwise, if the value in cell A1 falls in the range from 80 up to 100, return the text string* Usually; *otherwise, if the value in cell A1 falls between 60 and 80, return the text string* Sometimes; *and, finally, if none of these conditions is true, return the text string* Who cares? If the first condition is false, Microsoft Excel evaluates the second condition. In turn, if the second condition is false, Microsoft Excel evaluates the third condition.

You can string together as many as seven nested IF functions, as long as you do not exceed the 255-character limit of single-cell entries.

Trapping errors: The ISERROR and ISNA functions

If a formula in your worksheet refers to a cell that returns an error, that formula also returns an error. For example, if cell A1 returns an error, the formula

=A1/10

also returns an error. The same thing happens if the formula refers to a cell that returns an #N/A message.

The ISERROR and ISNA functions are two specialized logical functions that let you test the value of an argument or cell to determine whether it contains either an error value or the value #N/A. The ISERROR function tests for error values, while ISNA tests for #N/A values. These functions allow you to "trap" errors and #N/A values, preventing them from filtering through the worksheet. These functions take the form

=ISERROR(*value*)

and

=ISNA(*value*)

Although *value* can be a number or a formula, it is usually a cell reference.

Typically, ISERROR and ISNA are used as conditional tests in IF functions. For example, the function

=IF(ISERROR(A1/A2),0,A1/A2)

tests the formula A1/A2. If A1/A2 returns an error (as it will if A2 is blank or contains the value 0), then the ISERROR function is true and the IF function returns the value 0. If A1/A2 does not return an error, then the IF function returns the result of A1/A2. Similarly, the function

=IF(ISNA(A1),0,A1*10)

tests the value in cell A1. If that value is #N/A, then the IF function returns a 0. Otherwise, the IF function returns the product of A1 times 10.

The ISREF function

The ISREF function works much like ISERROR and ISNA. Instead of testing the contents of a cell for an error or #N/A value, however, ISREF tests to see what kind of entry the cell contains. Like ISERROR and ISNA, ISREF takes the form

=ISREF(*value*)

The ISREF function returns the logical value TRUE if the *value* argument is a cell reference. If the argument is any other kind of entry, the function returns the value FALSE.

You probably won't use ISREF at all unless you become heavily involved in macro programming. We haven't come up with any practical way to use this function outside of a macro.

Other uses for conditional functions

Keep in mind that any of the conditional functions we've described can be used as stand-alone formulas in your worksheet. Although you will usually use functions like AND, OR, NOT, ISERROR, ISNA, and ISREF within an IF function, you can also use simple formulas like

=AND(A1>A2,A2<A3)

to perform simple conditional tests. This formula returns the value TRUE if the value in cell A1 is greater than the value in A2 and the value in A2 is less than the value in A3. For example, you might use a simple formula like this one to assign TRUE and FALSE values to a range of database cells, then use the TRUE and FALSE conditions as selection criteria for printing a specialized report. We talk more about using conditional arguments as criteria in the database chapters.

When you begin working with macros, you will also see that the IF function is an invaluable tool for instructing Microsoft Excel to take different actions depending upon various conditions in your worksheet. Chapter 19, "User-Defined Functions," offers detailed instructions for using logical functions in worksheet macros.

Lookup functions

Like most other spreadsheet programs, Microsoft Excel offers several functions that make it possible to "look up" information that has been stored in a list or a table. These functions are CHOOSE, MATCH, VLOOKUP, HLOOKUP, LOOKUP, and INDEX.

The CHOOSE function

The CHOOSE function lets you store a list of values, labels, or cell references in a cell and retrieve items from that list using an index number. The CHOOSE function has the form

=CHOOSE(*index,value 1,value 2,...*)

where *index* is the number of the item that you want to look up and *value 1, value 2,* and so on are the elements of the list. The index value must always be positive and cannot exceed the number of elements in the list. The result of a CHOOSE function is the element of the list that occupies the position indicated by the index value. For example, the function

=CHOOSE(2,6,1,8,9,3)

returns the value 1, because 1 is the second item in the list. Similarly, the function

=CHOOSE(5,6,1,8,9,3)

returns the value 3, the fifth item in the list.

The arguments of the CHOOSE function can also be cell references. If you use a cell reference for the index value, Excel selects an item from the list according to the value stored in that cell. For example, suppose cell A11 contains the formula

=CHOOSE(A10,0.15,0.22,0.21,0.21,0.21)

If cell A10 contains the value 5, the CHOOSE function in cell A11 returns the value 0.21. If cell A10 contains the value 1, the function returns the value 0.15.

Similarly, if cell C1 contains the value 0.15 and C2 the value 0.22, and C3, C4, and C5 each contain the value 0.21, then the function

=CHOOSE(A10,C1,C2,C3,C4,C5)

returns the result 0.15 if cell A10 contains the value 1, and 0.21 if cell A10 contains the value 3, 4, or 5.

Don't make the mistake of thinking that the list of values can be a range. For example, you might be tempted to create a function like

=CHOOSE(A10,C1:C5)

to take the place of the longer function in the previous example. If you did, however, all you would get back would be a #VALUE! error value.

The elements in the list can also be text strings. For example, the function

=CHOOSE(3,"First","Second","Third")

tells Excel to select the third item from the list, so the program returns the text string *Third*.

If you use an index value less than 1 or greater than the number of values in the list, Microsoft Excel returns the #VALUE! error value. For example, if cell A10 contains the value 15, the function

=CHOOSE(A10,C1,C2,C3,C4,C5)

returns the #VALUE! error value.

A CHOOSE application

Although most Microsoft Excel users ignore CHOOSE, the function can be very useful. For example, the function

=CHOOSE(A10,0.29,0.18,0.09,0.06)

could be used in a depreciation calculation. The four *value* arguments in this function are the allowable first-year cost-recovery percentages for each of the four non-real property classes of assets under the Accelerated Cost Recovery System (ACRS). (The classes are 3-year, 5-year, 10-year, and 15-year public-utility property.) The entry in cell A10 is a number that represents the type of asset for which you are computing depreciation. If the assets are in the 3-year class, you enter 1 in cell A10, and the function returns 0.29, the correct first-year ACRS rate for a 3-year asset. This result can then be applied to the cost of the asset to compute first-year depreciation.

As you can see, in this example the CHOOSE function allows you to store all of the appropriate rates for first-year cost recovery in a single cell, and you can then retrieve the rate you want to use with an index value. Many other similar problems can be solved easily with CHOOSE.

The MATCH function

The MATCH function is closely related to the CHOOSE function. However, where CHOOSE returns the item that occupies the position in a list specified by the *index* argument, MATCH returns the position of the item in the list that most closely matches a lookup value. The form of this function is

=MATCH(*lookup value,lookup range,type*)

where *lookup value* is the value or string that you want to look up and *lookup range* is the range that contains the values to be compared with *lookup value*. (The Microsoft Excel manual uses the term *compare vector* to describe *lookup range*.) As you probably expect, the *lookup value* argument can be a value or a cell reference. The *lookup range* argument must be a reference to a range or a range name.

For example, consider the worksheet in Figure 6-22. If you enter the function

=MATCH(10,CA1:D1)

in cell E1, the result is 1, because the value in the first position of the *lookup range* argument contains a value that matches the *lookup value* argument. Similarly, the function

=MATCH(20,A1:D1)

returns the value 2, because the value in the second position of the *lookup range* matches the value of the *lookup value*.

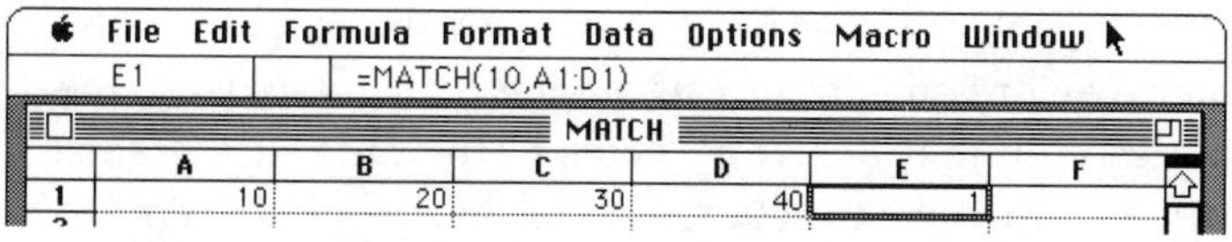

FIGURE 6-22. *You can use the MATCH function to locate the position of a value in a list.*

The *type* argument defines the rules for the search. This argument, which is optional, must be a literal value. It cannot be a cell reference. If the *type* argument is 1, or if it is omitted altogether, then the MATCH function looks for the largest value in the range that is less than or equal to the *lookup value*. For example, the function

=MATCH(19,A1:D1,1)

returns the value 1, because 10, the first item in the range, is the largest value in the range that is less than or equal to the *lookup value*: 19.

If there are no items in the range that are less than or equal to the *lookup value*, then the function returns the error value #N/A. For example, the function

=MATCH(9,A1:D1,1)

returns the error value #N/A because the *lookup value*, 9, is less than the smallest item in the range.

If *type* is 0, then the MATCH function looks for exact matches between the *lookup value* and the values in the range. For example, the function

=MATCH(20,A1:D1,0)

returns 2, because the second item in the list, 20, is equal to the *lookup value*. If there are no items in the range that exactly match the *lookup value*, then the function returns the error value #N/A.

If *type* is 1 or 0, the elements in the *lookup range* must be in ascending order if the function is to work properly. For example, if you rearrange the items in the range A1:D1 to look like Figure 6-23, then the function

=MATCH(20,A1:D1,1)

returns the value 1, instead of the value you probably expected: 4.

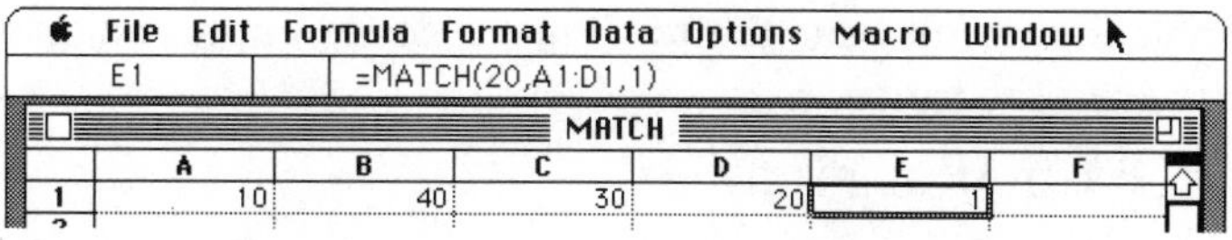

FIGURE 6-23. *The MATCH function will not work properly with a type argument of 1 or 0 if the lookup range is not in ascending order.*

If *type* is –1, then MATCH looks for the smallest value in the range that is greater than or equal to the *lookup value*. When *type* is –1, the items in the list must be in descending order. If no items in the range are greater than or equal to the *lookup value*, then the function returns the error value #N/A.

The *lookup value* and the items in the range can also be text strings. For example, suppose cells A1:D1 contain the text entries shown in Figure 6-24. The function

=MATCH("Twenty",A1:D1,0)

returns the value 2. Whenever you use MATCH to locate text strings, you will probably want to specify a *type* of 0 (an exact match). (The function will still work when you use a *type* argument other than 0.)

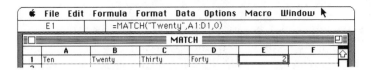

FIGURE 6-24. *You can use MATCH to locate the position of a text string.*

The LOOKUP function

The LOOKUP function has two forms. In both forms, it is similar to the VLOOKUP and HLOOKUP functions. The second form is also identical to the LOOKUP function in Microsoft Multiplan.

The first form
The first form of LOOKUP is

=LOOKUP(*lookup value,lookup range,result range*)

where *lookup value* is the value that you want to look up in the table, *lookup range* is the range that contains the compare values, and *result range* is the range that contains the possible results. (The Microsoft Excel manual uses the terms *lookup vector* and *result vector* to describe *lookup range* and *result range*.)

Like HLOOKUP and VLOOKUP, LOOKUP works by searching the *lookup range* for the largest compare value that is not greater than the *lookup value*. It then selects the matching result from the *result range*. For example, consider the worksheet in Figure 6-25. The function

=LOOKUP(3,B3:B7,E3:E7)

compares the *lookup value*, 3, with the values in the *lookup range*, B3:B7. After determining that the entry in cell B5, the third cell of the *lookup range*, is the largest entry in the range that is not greater than the *lookup value*, the function then looks to the third cell of the *result range*, E5, for the result of the function: 300.

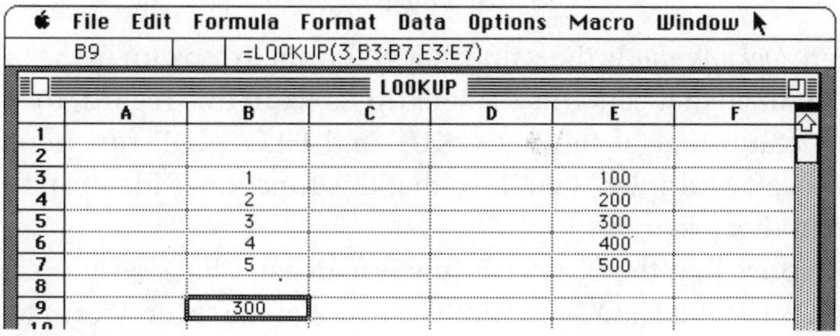

FIGURE 6-25. *You can use the LOOKUP function to retrieve information from a cell range.*

Although the *lookup range* and *result range* will often be parallel in the worksheet, they don't have to be. All that is required is for the *result range* to have exactly the same number of elements as the *lookup range*. For example, look at Figure 6-26. In this worksheet, the function

=LOOKUP(3,A1:A5,D6:D10)

returns 300, the entry in cell D8. To understand how this works, notice that both the lookup range, A1:A5, and the result range, D6:D10, have five elements. The lookup value, 3, matches the entry in the third cell of the lookup range. The result of the function is therefore the entry in the third cell of the result range: 300.

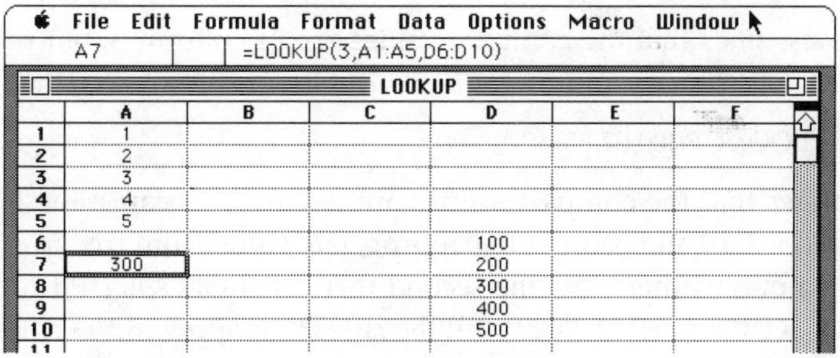

FIGURE 6-26. *You can use the LOOKUP function to retrieve information from a non-parallel cell range.*

In every other way, the first form of LOOKUP is identical to VLOOKUP and HLOOKUP. All of the rules that apply to VLOOKUP and HLOOKUP also apply to LOOKUP. (We cover the VLOOKUP and HLOOKUP functions after the discussion of the LOOKUP function.)

The second form

The second form of LOOKUP is

=LOOKUP(*lookup value,lookup range*)

where *lookup value* is the value that you want to look up in the table and *lookup range* is the range that contains the lookup table. In this regard, the form of LOOKUP is identical to that of the VLOOKUP and HLOOKUP functions. If you have used Microsoft Multiplan, you'll see that this function is identical to the LOOKUP function in that program.

Notice that the LOOKUP function doesn't have an *index number* argument as VLOOKUP and HLOOKUP do. The result of the second form of LOOKUP is always taken from the last row or the last column of the lookup range.

The other difference between LOOKUP and VLOOKUP and HLOOKUP is that LOOKUP can be used to read from either a horizontal or a vertical table. LOOKUP uses the dimensions of the table to figure out where the compare values are. If the table is taller than it is wide, or is square, the function assumes that the compare values are in the leftmost column of the table. If the table is wider than it is tall, the function views the table as a horizontal table and assumes that the compare values are in the first row of the table.

For example, the function

=LOOKUP(100,B2:D5)

assumes that the compare values are located in column B and returns the appropriate value from column D. The function

=LOOKUP(100,B2:E5)

also assumes that the compare values are in column B, but returns a value from column E, the last column in the table. On the other hand, the function

=LOOKUP(100,B2:F5)

assumes that the compare values are in row 2 (because the table range is wider than it is tall) and returns the appropriate value from row 5.

In every other way, the second form of the LOOKUP function is identical to VLOOKUP and HLOOKUP. All the rules that apply to VLOOKUP and HLOOKUP also apply to LOOKUP.

For the most part, you will find VLOOKUP and HLOOKUP preferable to LOOKUP, because they are more predictable and controllable. The LOOKUP function will probably only be important to you if you import Microsoft Multiplan models into Microsoft Excel.

The VLOOKUP and HLOOKUP functions

The VLOOKUP and HLOOKUP functions are nearly identical functions that allow you to look up information stored in a table. The forms of both these lookup functions are

=VLOOKUP(*lookup value,lookup range,index number*)

and

=HLOOKUP(*lookup value,lookup range,index number*)

where the *lookup value* is the value that you want to look up in the table, *lookup range* is the range that contains the lookup table, and *index number* determines the column or row of the table from which the result of the function will be selected. (The Microsoft Excel manual uses the term *table array* to describe *lookup range*.)

Lookup tables

Both of these functions require that a lookup table exist in the worksheet. This table is defined by the *lookup range* argument of the functions.

The VLOOKUP and HLOOKUP functions work by comparing the *lookup value* argument to a list of compare values in the lookup table. The only difference between VLOOKUP and HLOOKUP is the type of table that each function uses. The VLOOKUP function works with vertical tables, while HLOOKUP works with horizontal tables. In every other way the functions are identical. When we say that a table is vertical or horizontal, what we are really doing is telling Excel where the compare values are located. If the compare values are located in the leftmost column of the table, then the table is vertical. If the compare values are in the first row of the table, then the table is horizonal. The VLOOKUP function always looks for the compare values in the leftmost column of the table range, and HLOOKUP always looks for the compare values in the top row of the table range. (We occasionally use the term *compare range* to denote the row or column that contains the compare values.)

The compare values in a lookup table can be numbers or text entries. However, the compare values must be arranged in ascending order if the table is to function properly. In addition, no compare value can be repeated in a table.

Figure 6-27 shows a simple vertical lookup table. In this table, column A contains the compare values. Notice that the values in this column are arranged in ascending numeric order. This is critical to the proper functioning of the table. Columns B and C in Figure 6-27 and rows 3 and 4 in Figure 6-28 on the next page (the horizontal lookup table) contain the information you want to look up. Notice that this information is not arranged in any special order.

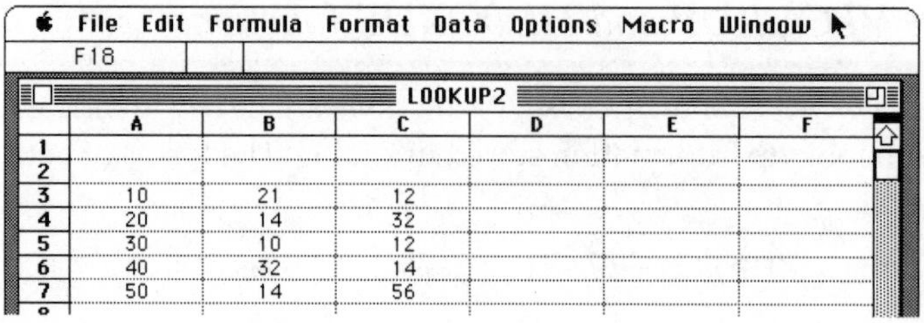

FIGURE 6-27. *This is a simple vertical lookup table.*

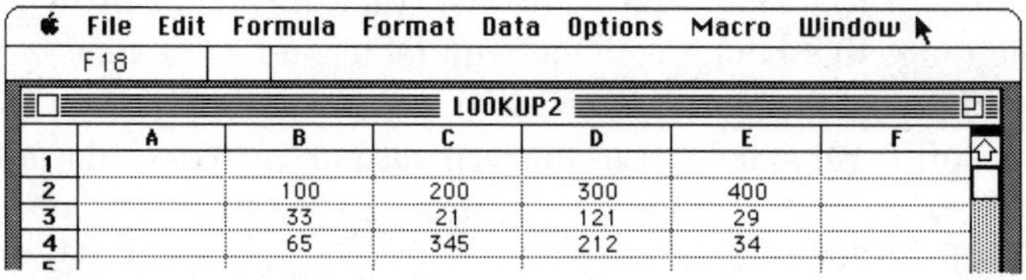

FIGURE 6-28. *This is a simple horizontal lookup table.*

The index number

The *index number* argument (sometimes called the *offset*) tells the lookup function which column or row of the table to look in for the function's result. The first row or column in the table has an index number of 1.

The *index number* argument must be greater than or equal to 1 and must never be greater than the number of rows or columns in the table; that is, if a vertical table is three columns wide, the offset cannot be greater than 3. Any offset value that does not comply with these rules causes the function to return an error message.

Going back to our examples, column B in Figure 6-27 has an index number of 2 and column C has an index number of 3. In Figure 6-28, row 3 has an index number of 2 and row 4 has an index number of 3.

The VLOOKUP function

Let's look at how these functions work. To access the table in Figure 6-29, you use the VLOOKUP function. For example, the function

=VLOOKUP(8,B2:E6,3)

in cell B8 returns the value 21. The function works by first locating the table range and then the column containing the compare values—in this case, column B. Next, the function scans the compare values in column B to find the largest compare value that is less than or equal to the lookup value in the function. In the example, because 8, the third compare value, is equal to 8, the lookup value, and the fourth compare value, 11, is greater than 8, the function knows that its result is somewhere in row 4.

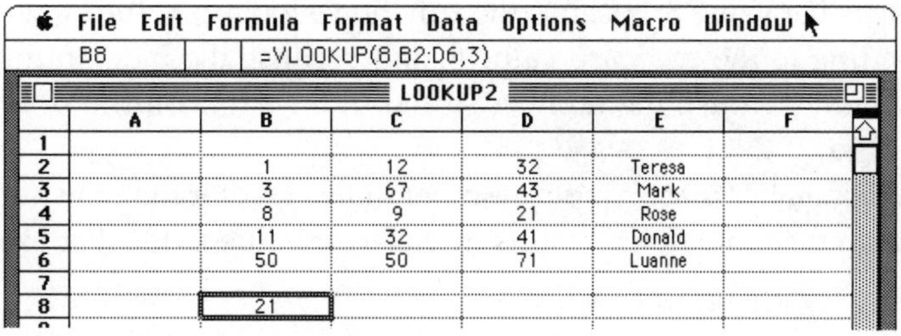

FIGURE 6-29. *You can use the VLOOKUP function to retrieve information from a table.*

Next, the function uses the index number to determine which column in the lookup table should be probed for the data. In this case, the index number is 3, so column D contains the desired data (remember that the column that contains the compare values has an index number of 1). The function therefore returns the number from row 4, column D: 21.

The lookup value in a lookup function can be a value or a cell reference. The table range can be indicated by cell references or a range name. For example, if you assign the name *Table* to the range B2:E6 in Figure 6-29 and enter the number 8 in cell A1, the function

=VLOOKUP(A1,Table,3)

returns a result identical to that of the previous example.

Remember that the lookup functions look for the greatest compare value that is less than or equal to the lookup value, and not for an exact match between the compare value and the lookup value. This means that the function

=VLOOKUP(9,B2:E6,3)

also returns the value 21. Similarly, the function

=VLOOKUP(51,B2:E6,3)

returns the value 71, because 50, the compare value that corresponds with 71, is the largest compare value in the table that is less than 51, the lookup value.

If all of the compare values in the first row or column of the table range are greater than the lookup value, the function returns the value #N/A. If, on the other hand, all of the compare values are less than the lookup value, the function returns the data value that corresponds to the last (largest) compare value in the table.

If the index number in a lookup function is 1, the result of the function is one of the compare values. For example, the function

=VLOOKUP(8,B2:E6,1)

returns the value 8, because the function's lookup value, 8, selects the row corresponding to the compare value 8, and because the index number of 1 causes the function to return the number stored in the first column of the table in the indicated row.

Remember that an index number that is greater than the number of columns or rows in the table range results in the error value #REF!. For example, the function

=VLOOKUP(8,B2:E6,5)

does not work with the table in Figure 6-29, which is only four columns wide. Using index numbers that are larger than the number of columns or rows in the table range is one of the most frequent causes of errors when working with lookup tables. Always be sure your index number and your table range agree.

You can also use the lookup functions to look up text from a lookup table. For example, the function

=VLOOKUP(8,B2:E12,4)

returns the text string *Rose*.

Not only can the data items in a table be text strings, but the compare values can be strings as well. Figure 6-30 shows a vertical lookup table that uses text as compare values. For example, the function

=VLOOKUP("Doug",B3:C7,2)

returns the value 46000. As with most other functions, if you use a text string as the lookup value in your lookup table, the text string must be enclosed in double quotation marks.

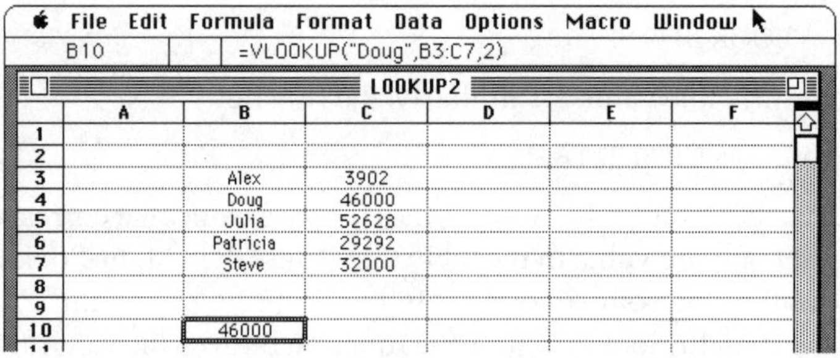

FIGURE 6-30. *You can use VLOOKUP with string compare values.*

Unfortunately, the usefulness of text compare values is limited in Microsoft Excel. For one thing, the program requires that the compare values be arranged in alphabetic order if the table is to work properly. In addition, Excel uses the same "greatest value that is not greater than the lookup value" method that it uses with numeric values for selecting the correct compare value, rather than an absolute match method. This means that the function

=VLOOKUP("Russell",B3:C7,2)

returns the value 29292, the number that corresponds to the compare value *Patricia*, which is the "greatest" compare value that is "less than" the lookup value *Russell*. Although this method is consistent, it does not yield the result you might expect. Other programs return an error message if there is no exact match between a text lookup value and a compare value.

You can even combine numbers, text entries, and logical entries in the compare range, although it is unlikely that you will find a worksheet that requires a mixed compare range. If you do this, however, the elements in the range still must be arranged in ascending order, according to Excel's sorting rules: numbers first, then text, then logical entries.

Tables that don't work

You may recall that we said that the compare values in a table must be in ascending order if the table is to work properly. Let's look at a couple of examples of tables that fail to work correctly. The vertical lookup table in Figure 6-31 does not work properly because the compare values in column B are not in ascending order. For instance, the function

=VLOOKUP(4,B3:C7,2)

returns the value 100, instead of 500, the number you might expect. This occurs because the VLOOKUP function searches the compare value list only until it comes

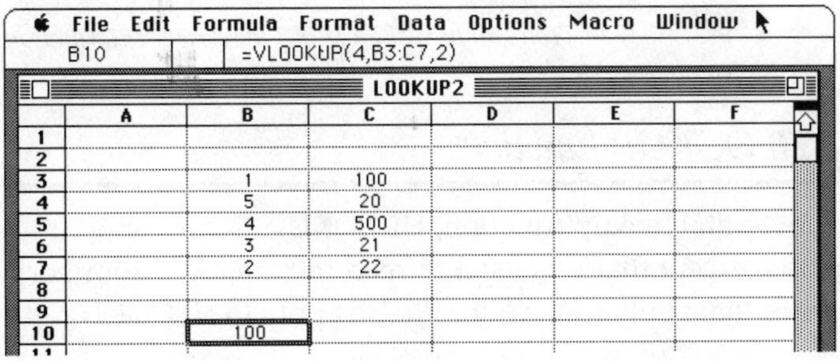

FIGURE 6-31. *The VLOOKUP function does not work properly unless the compare values are in ascending order.*

to a number that is greater than the lookup value. When it finds a compare value that is greater than the lookup value—in this case, when it comes to 5—it stops the search, backs up to the previous compare value, and then searches across the table. Any compare values below the first value that is greater than the lookup value are ignored.

A VLOOKUP application

One of the nicest features of lookup functions is that they let you build various rate tables directly into your worksheet. For example, the range A4:C18 in Figure 6-32 contains a lookup table of sales levels and commission rates. The function in cell C2

=((C1–VLOOKUP(C1,A4:C18,1))*VLOOKUP(C1,A4:C18,2))+VLOOKUP(C1,A4:C18,3)

computes the commission on the sales figure in cell C1. Notice that this function looks up data from all three columns of the table.

	A	B	C	D	E	F
1	Sales this month:		$17,500.00			
2	Commission:		$4,025.00			
3						
4	$0.00	0%	$0.00			
5	$2,390.00	11%	$262.90			
6	$3,540.00	12%	$424.80			
7	$4,580.00	14%	$641.20			
8	$6,760.00	15%	$1,014.00			
9	$8,850.00	16%	$1,416.00			
10	$11,240.00	18%	$2,023.20			
11	$13,430.00	20%	$2,686.00			
12	$15,610.00	23%	$3,590.30			
13	$18,940.00	26%	$4,924.40			
14	$24,460.00	30%	$7,338.00			
15	$29,970.00	34%	$10,189.80			
16	$35,490.00	38%	$13,486.20			
17	$43,190.00	42%	$18,139.80			
18	$57,550.00	48%	$27,624.00			

FIGURE 6-32. *You can use VLOOKUP to retrieve information from a commission table.*

The HLOOKUP function

The horizontal lookup function, HLOOKUP, is very similar to the vertical lookup function, except that it is used to read information from horizontal tables. All of the rules that apply to VLOOKUP also apply to HLOOKUP.

Let's examine an example of HLOOKUP at work. The worksheet in Figure 6-33 shows a horizontal lookup table. The function

=HLOOKUP(6,B3:E10,3)

returns the value 101 from this table, because 6, the lookup value, equals 6, the compare value in column C, and because 3, the index number, tells the function to look in the third row of the table for the correct item.

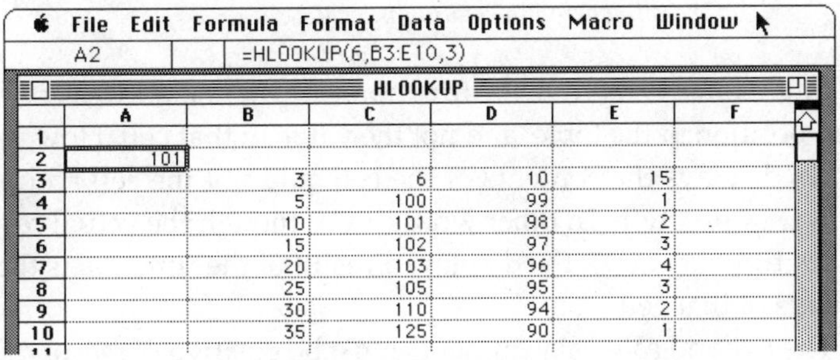

	A	**B**	**C**	**D**	**E**	**F**
1						
2	101					
3		3	6	10	15	
4		5	100	99	1	
5		10	101	98	2	
6		15	102	97	3	
7		20	103	96	4	
8		25	105	95	3	
9		30	110	94	2	
10		35	125	90	1	

A2 =HLOOKUP(6,B3:E10,3)

HLOOKUP

❡ File Edit Formula Format Data Options Macro Window ▶

FIGURE 6-33. *You can use the HLOOKUP function to retrieve information from a table.*

The INDEX function

Like CHOOSE and LOOKUP, INDEX is a lookup function. Its form is

=INDEX(*index range,row,column,area*)

where *index range* is the range that contains the index table and *row* and *column* describe the row and column coordinates within the table of the particular cell being referenced. The *area* argument comes into play only when the index area contains more than one range. (We discuss this in more detail in a few paragraphs.)

Like the lookup functions, the INDEX function requires that you create a table, called an index table. An index table is a rectangular range that includes at least four cells (although most index tables are much larger). The cells in the table can contain numbers, text, or formulas.

Figure 6-34 on the next page shows an example of an index table. The function in cell A1

=INDEX(C3:E6,A2,A3)

uses the row coordinate in cell A2 and the column coordinate in cell A3 to extract a value from the table. In the example, because cell A2 contains the number 3 and cell A3 contains the number 2, the function returns the address of the cell in the third row and the second column of the table: D5.

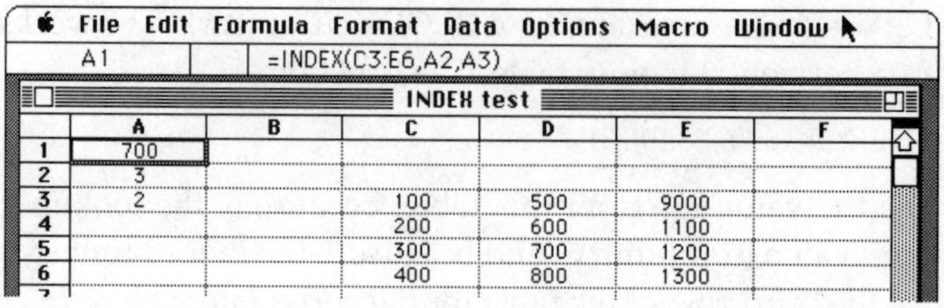

🍎	File	Edit	Formula	Format	Data	Options	Macro	Window ▶

| A1 | | =INDEX(C3:E6,A2,A3) | | | |

INDEX test

	A	B	C	D	E	F
1	700					
2	3					
3	2		100	500	9000	
4			200	600	1100	
5			300	700	1200	
6			400	800	1300	

FIGURE 6-34. *You can use the INDEX function to retrieve the address of the cell where information is located.*

Interestingly, the INDEX function returns the address of the cell at the indicated position in the table, and not the value in that cell. However, Microsoft Excel always displays the contents of the cell, and not the cell address, as the result of the INDEX function. In other words, even though the actual result of the previous INDEX function is D5, the displayed result of the function is the number 700—the contents of that cell.

The *row* and *column* arguments must be positive. If *row* or *column* is less than or equal to 0, the function returns the #VALUE! error value.

However, because INDEX actually returns the cell reference of the indicated position in the table, a *row* or *column* argument of 0 returns a reference to the entire column or row indicated. For example, in Figure 6-34, while the function

=INDEX(C3:E6,0,2)

returns the #VALUE! result, the function

=SUM(INDEX(C3:E6,0,2))

sums the values contained in the second column, D, and returns the result 2600.

If the *row* argument is greater than the number of rows in the table, or if the *column* argument is greater than the number of columns in the table, the function returns the #REF! error value.

If the index table is only one row deep or one column wide, you can use only one index to select a value. For example, the function

=INDEX(C3:C6,2)

returns the value 200 from the table in Figure 6-34. Similarly, the function

=INDEX(C3:E3,2)

returns the value 500. Notice that INDEX is very similar to CHOOSE when it is used with a one-dimensional table.

The area argument

The *area* argument is only important when the index range contains several areas. If the index range does contain several areas, then you must use the *area* argument to tell the INDEX function which area you want it to use. For example, in the function

=INDEX((A1:C5,D6:F10),1,1,2)

the index range is made up of two areas: A1:C5 and D6:F10. The *area* argument, 2, tells INDEX to work on the second of these areas.

The *area* argument must always be a positive integer. If *area* is less than 1, the function returns the #REF! error value.

An INDEX application

It just so happens that the forms of a Microsoft Excel INDEX table and the ACRS (Accelerated Cost Recovery System) real property depreciation table are identical. Under ACRS, the amount of depreciation you can claim on real property is based on two factors: the month in which the asset was originally placed in service, and the year in the life of the asset for which you are making the computation. The index table in Figure 6-35 duplicates part of the ACRS Table for Real Property.

In this table, the numbers in row 5 represent the month an asset was placed in service. The numbers in column A represent the years in the life of the asset.

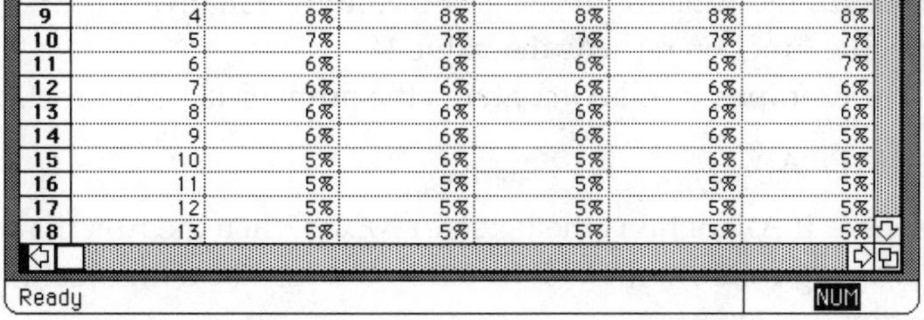

	A	B	C	D	E	F
1	Month Placed in Service:		5		Depreciation:	$7,000
2	Asset Cost		$100,000			
3	Year in Life:		3			
4						
5		1	2	3	4	5
6	1	12%	11%	10%	9%	8%
7	2	10%	10%	11%	11%	11%
8	3	9%	9%	9%	9%	10%
9	4	8%	8%	8%	8%	8%
10	5	7%	7%	7%	7%	7%
11	6	6%	6%	6%	6%	7%
12	7	6%	6%	6%	6%	6%
13	8	6%	6%	6%	6%	6%
14	9	6%	6%	6%	6%	5%
15	10	5%	6%	5%	6%	5%
16	11	5%	5%	5%	5%	5%
17	12	5%	5%	5%	5%	5%
18	13	5%	5%	5%	5%	5%

FIGURE 6-35. *You can use an index table to calculate property depreciation schedules.*

If you enter in cell C1 the number of the month the asset was placed in service, in cell C2 the net cost of the asset, and in cell C3 the current year in the asset's life, you can use the formula

=C2*INDEX(B6:F18,C1,C3)

to compute the current year's depreciation for the asset. If, for example, cell C1 contains the number 5 and cell C3 contains the number 3, the INDEX function returns the value 0.07, the number in the fifth row and the third column of the index table. The result of the INDEX function, then, is $7,000, which is 7 percent of $100,000.

Like LOOKUP, INDEX has two forms. We look at the second form of INDEX in Chapter 8, "Other Worksheet Topics," when we discuss array functions.

Other functions

In addition to all of the functions you have learned about so far, there are a handful of others that don't fit in any particular group. We cover the miscellaneous functions that don't fit logically into a specific category—TYPE, AREAS, ROW, COLUMN, and NA, CELL, INDIRECT, N, T—in this section.

The TYPE function

You can use the TYPE function to determine whether a cell contains text, numbers, a logical value, or an error value. The TYPE function takes the form

=TYPE(*cell reference*)

The result of the TYPE function depends upon the type of entry in the referenced cell. If the cell contains a number, the function returns the value 1. If the cell contains text, the function returns the value 2. If the cell contains a logical value (TRUE or FALSE), the function returns the value 4. Finally, if the cell contains an error value, the function returns the value 16.

For example, if cell A1 contains the number 100, the function

=TYPE(A1)

returns 1. If A1 contains the text entry *Excel*, then the function returns 2.

The argument of a TYPE function can also be a literal entry. For example, the function

=TYPE("Test")

returns the value 2. However, it is unlikely that you will use this form of the function; after all, you can tell by inspection that *Test* is a text entry.

The AREAS function

The AREAS function can be used to determine the number of areas in a range. An area is a single cell or a rectangular block of cells. The AREAS function has the form

=AREAS(*range reference,range reference,....,range reference*)

The result of the function is the number of areas referred to by the argument. For example, the function

=AREAS(A1,B1:C5,A1:D10,Z100:Z101)

returns the number 4, because the argument refers to four areas.

Although this function has limited applications, there is one clever way in which it can be used. Suppose you have assigned the name *Test* to the range A1:C5,D6,E7:G10. The function

=AREAS(Test)

returns the number 3, the number of areas in the range *Test*.

The ROW and COLUMN functions

Although the names of the ROW and COLUMN functions are nearly the same as the names of the two array functions ROWS and COLUMNS, which we discuss in Chapter 8, "Other Worksheet Topics," they are really quite different. The form of these functions is

=ROW(*cell reference*)

and

=COLUMN(*cell reference*)

The result of these functions is the row number or column number of the cell referred to by the function's argument. For example, the function

=ROW(H5)

returns the result 5. Similarly, the function

=COLUMN(H5)

returns the result 8.

If the argument is omitted, then the result is the row or column number of the cell that contains the function. For example, if you enter the function

=ROW()

in cell C10, the result is the value 10.

If the argument of the ROW or COLUMN function is a range, the result of the function is the row or column number of the first row or column in the range. For example, the function

=ROW(A1:A10)

returns the result {1}.

The NA function

The NA function is an infrequently used placeholder function. Unlike most functions, NA takes no arguments. The form of the function is simply

=NA()

When you enter the NA function in a cell, that cell, and all formulas that refer to that cell, returns the result #N/A. Some functions return the NA function as a type of error value.

Suppose several formulas in your worksheet depend on the value in a cell, but you are not yet certain of the value that the cell should contain. Rather than entering a guess, you can enter the NA function in the cell as a placeholder. Until you replace the NA function with the correct value, any formula in the worksheet that refers to the cell that contains the NA function displays the result #N/A.

The CELL function

You can use the CELL function to obtain information about the formatting, location, or contents of a cell. Usually, you will use the CELL function to learn about a single cell. But if you use it for a selected range of cells, Microsoft Excel furnishes information about the upper-left cell in the selection.

The CELL function takes the form

=CELL(*"type of info"*,*reference*)

The result of the CELL function depends upon the type of entry in the referenced cell. The table in Figure 6-36 shows the nine available *type of info* arguments and the information that each argument returns. The CELL function requires that you specify one of these arguments enclosed in quotation marks.

If you use "format" as the *type of info* argument, Microsoft Excel returns a code indicating the cell's format. The table in Figure 6-37 lists the codes that correspond to Excel's formats.

Type of information	Returns
"width"	The width of the specified cell, rounded to the nearest whole number
"row"	The row number of the current cell; same as ROW(*reference*)
"col"	The column number (column A = 1) of the specified cell; same COLUMN(*reference*)
"protect"	The protection status of the specified cell; 0 means the cell is not locked; 1 means the cell is locked
"address"	The absolute address of the specified cell
"contents"	The contents of the specified cell (returns the result of a formula, rather than the formula itself)
"format"	The format of the specified cell, represented as a code; Figure 6-37 explains the resulting format codes
"prefix"	The label prefix of the specified cell containing the label; in Excel, CELL returns a single quote if the cell has been formatted with left or general alignment, a double quote if the cell has been formatted with right alignment, a caret if the cell has been formatted with center alignment, and a backslash if the cell has been formatted with fill alignment
"type"	The type of entry in the specified cell; CELL returns *b* if the cell is blank, *l* if the cell contains a text constant, and *v* if the cell contains anything else

FIGURE 6-36. *Here are the nine* type of info *arguments for the CELL function, together with the information each returns.*

Format	Code	Format	Code
General	G	m/d/yy or m/d/yy h:mm	D4
0 or #,##0	F0	d-mmm-yy	D1
0.00 or #,##0.00	F2	d-mmm	D2
$#,##0 ;($#,##0)	C0	mmm-yy	D3
$#,##0.00 ;($#,##0.00)	C2	h:mm AM/PM	D7
0%	P0	h:mm:ss AM/PM	D6
0.00%	P2	h:mm	D9
0.00E+00	S2	h:mm:ss	D8

FIGURE 6-37. *These codes correspond to Excel's formats.*

For example, suppose you have applied the $#,##0.00; ($#,##0.00) format to cell
A1. The formula

    =CELL("format",A1)

returns C2.

The INDIRECT function

You can use the INDIRECT function to determine the contents of a cell from its
reference. The INDIRECT function takes the form

    =INDIRECT(*reference,type of ref*)

where *reference* is a cell containing a text constant, or the text result of a formula.
The *type of ref* argument is a logical value that indicates the type of reference you
are using. If *type of ref* is TRUE (or 1), Excel interprets *reference* as the A1 format; if
type of ref is FALSE (or 0), Excel interprets *reference* as the R1C1 format. If your entry
for *reference* is not valid, INDIRECT returns the #REF! error value.

For example, suppose cell A1 contains the text *B3* and cell B3 contains the value
2.888. The formula

    =INDIRECT(A1)

returns the value 2.888. But if cell A1 contains *R3C2* (the R1C1-style reference for
cell B3), the formula

    =INDIRECT(A1,0)

still returns the value 2.888. Or, if your worksheet is in the R1C1 mode

    =INDIRECT(R1C1,0)

also returns the value 2.888.

The N and T functions

The N and T functions are translation aids. The N function translates values into
numbers, while the T function translates values into text. When you enter an argument that doesn't generate the correct type of data, Excel translates it. Although
you generally don't need to use these two functions in formulas, Microsoft Excel
includes them to be compatible with other spreadsheet programs.

These translation functions follow the form

    =N(*value*)

and

    =T(*value*)

If you enter a number as the *value* argument, the N function returns that number. If you enter a reference to a cell containing a date, the N function returns the date's serial number. If the value you enter is TRUE, Excel returns 1. If you enter a FALSE value, cell references, or anything else, Excel returns 0.

Other functions

Microsoft Excel offers three other groups of functions that we have not discussed in this chapter: date and time functions, array functions, and database statistical functions.

Date and time functions allow you to enter date and time values in the worksheet. Before you can use these functions, you need to understand more about how Excel keeps time. We cover date and time functions in Chapter 7, "Date and Time."

Array functions operate on arrays. Because you have to understand arrays to use these functions, we cover them in the section on arrays in Chapter 8, "Other Worksheet Topics."

Database statistical functions allow you to compute statistics about the contents of a Microsoft Excel database. Before you can use these functions, you need to understand more about database management in Excel. We explain the program's 11 database statistical functions in Chapter 15, "Working with a Database."

In addition to all of these built-in functions, Excel allows you to create your own functions. You will learn how to do this in the section on building macro functions in Chapter 19, "User-Defined Functions."

Conclusion

In this rather long chapter, we have explained most of the Microsoft Excel functions. As you can now see, functions are among Excel's most useful tools. You'll want to keep these tools in mind as you construct your worksheets.

7

Date and Time

*L*ike most other advanced spreadsheet programs, Microsoft Excel allows you to enter date values and time values in the cells of your worksheet. You can use these values to "date stamp" worksheets or to perform date and time arithmetic. In this chapter, we show you how to enter dates and times into the Excel worksheet.

If you have ever tried to create a production schedule or a monthly billing system by counting the days on your desk calendar, you'll be excited about Excel's date and time capabilities. For example, the Series... command on the Data menu lets you enter a long series of row or column headers in your worksheet in date format. Instead of spending your time entering dozens of individual dates, you can enter a month's or even a year's worth of dates in seconds. Or you can go beyond simply entering dates in the spreadsheet and take advantage of Excel's convenient date and time functions to perform calculations quickly and accurately. If you're using your worksheet to calculate your company's monthly payroll, for example, you might use the HOUR function to determine the number of hours worked each day and the WEEKDAY function to determine whether employees should be paid at the standard rate (for Monday through Friday) or at the overtime rate (for Saturday and Sunday). We look at each of these topics in the following pages, but first, let's see how Excel defines date and time values.

How Excel remembers dates and times

The basic unit of time in Microsoft Excel is a day. In Excel, all dates are represented by an integer that represents the number of days that have elapsed between Excel's base date, January 1, 1904, and the specified date. For example, the date January 2, 1904, is represented by the integer 1. Similarly, the date January 1, 1989, is represented by the integer 31047, because 31047 days elapsed between January 1, 1989, and the base date (January 1, 1904).

Just as dates are represented by an elapsed number of days, in Excel all times are remembered as a fraction that represents the portion of a day that has elapsed between the specified time and the beginning of the day—12:00 A.M. (midnight). For example, the time 12:00 P.M. (noon) is represented by the value .5, because the difference between midnight and noon is exactly half a day. Similarly, the time 3:00 A.M. is represented by the value .125, because the difference between midnight and 3:00 A.M. is exactly $3/24$ (or $1/8$) of a day.

If dates are represented by integers, and times are represented by fractions, then it only makes sense that date/time combinations are represented by combinations of integers and fractions. For example, the time/date combination 10:11 A.M., June 1, 1989, is represented in Excel by the number 31198.4243.

You may find it confusing at first to think of dates and times in terms of serial values, but this technique makes sense if you think about it for a moment. By assigning serial values to days, hours, minutes, and even seconds, Excel lets you perform sophisticated date and time arithmetic. You can manipulate dates and times in your worksheet formulas just as you do other types of values.

The 1904 Date System option

In Chapter 2, "Worksheet Basics," at the end of our discussion of the Calculation… command on the Options menu, we mentioned Excel's 1904 Date System option. This option lets you change Excel's base date to January 1, 1900. You can use this option to change the Microsoft Excel base date to match the base date system used by many other spreadsheets, such as Microsoft Excel for IBM PCs and compatibles. To do this, simply turn off the 1904 Date System option in the Calculation dialog box. The display of all date functions in the worksheet will change. However, literal date values will remain the same as they were under the previous Date System. When you deactivate the 1904 Date System option, any serial dates you enter in your Excel 2.2 worksheets match corresponding serial dates from other spreadsheets. If you ever need to transfer information into Microsoft Excel 2.2 from a spreadsheet created in another program, this option ensures that the serial date values in the two programs are uniform. We use the 1904 date system in this book.

Functions and formats

Because the serial values Microsoft Excel uses to represent dates and times don't look anything like the representation of dates and times most of us are familiar with, they are difficult to interpret. Fortunately, Excel includes two sets of tools that make it easy to work with dates: date functions and time functions.

Entering a date or time into an Excel worksheet is a two-step process. First, you use a date or time function to enter the date or time into a cell; this entry results in the serial value of the specified date or time. Then, you use a date or time format to display that date or time in a recognizable form.

The DATE function

The basic date function in Microsoft Excel is DATE, which allows you to enter a date into a cell of the worksheet. The form of this function is

=DATE(*yy,mm,dd*)

where *yy* is the year portion of the date, *mm* is the month portion, and *dd* is the day portion. The result of DATE is always a value that represents the number of days that have elapsed between the indicated date and the base date.

For example, suppose you want to enter the date December 25, 1989, into the worksheet. The function

=DATE(89,12,25)

does the trick. The result of this function is the serial value 31405 (32867 if the 1904 Date System option is off).

If you have a problem with DATE, it is probably because you forgot the order of the year, month, and days arguments of the date. Just remember that the arguments are in descending order of magnitude: years first, then months, then days.

If you use an "illegal" argument in DATE, Excel does its best to interpret the function. For example, Excel assumes that the function

=DATE(89,11,31)

refers to December 1, 1989. When it evaluates the "illegal" days argument in this function (illegal because November, the 11th month, has only 30 days), Microsoft Excel simply carries the extra day over into the next month. Similarly, Excel assumes that the function

=DATE(89,12,32)

refers to January 1, 1990. When Excel evaluates this function, it carries the extra day over into the next month. Because December is the last month in the year, this carryover changes not only the month but also the year of the resulting date. In fact, the date January 1, 1990, can also be represented by the functions DATE(89,13,1) and, of course, DATE(90,1,1).

If you want to refer to a date that falls after December 31, 1999, you should use a three-digit years argument. For example, the function

=DATE(101,12,25)

represents the date December 25, 2001.

The largest date that Excel can display is December 31, 2078, which is represented by the number 63918. If you try to enter a DATE function that defines a date after this maximum date, the function returns the result #NUM!.

Formatting dates

Once you have used DATE to enter a date in the worksheet, you can use Excel's date formats to present that date in a recognizable form. Microsoft Excel offers four date formats: m/d/yy, d-mmm-yy, d-mmm, and mmm-yy. These formats appear when you scroll through the list in the Number dialog box. Here is the result of the function DATE(89,12,25)—serial value 31405—under each of these formats:

If you use...	Excel displays...
m/d/yy	12/25/89
d-mmm-yy	25-Dec-89
d-mmm	25-Dec
mmm-yy	Dec-89

To assign a date format to a cell, just click that cell, choose the Number... command from the Format menu, select the date format you want to use, and then press Enter or click OK.

An easier way

Now that you understand how Excel actually remembers dates and are familiar with the two-step method for entering dates into the worksheet, let's look at an easier way to create date entries. You will recall from Chapter 3, "Formatting the Worksheet," that you can both enter a number in a cell and format that number in one step. To do this, you simply type the number "in format." For example, selecting a cell and typing

$1,234.56

both enters the value 1234.56 into the cell and assigns that value the format $#,##0.00 ;($#,##0.00). You can use the same technique to enter dates into an Excel worksheet. For example, to enter the date December 25, 1989, into a cell, you can click that cell and type

12/25/89

When you press Enter, Excel enters the serial value 31405 into that cell but displays the m/d/yy format. If you reformat the cell with the general format, you'll see the serial value, 31405, in the formula bar.

E X C E L

Use the VALUE function to determine a date's serial value

When you type a date value in your worksheet instead of using the DATE function, you won't see the underlying serial value for that date. Using Excel's VALUE function, however, you can easily determine the serial value. For example, if cell A1 of your worksheet contains the date entry 5/1/89, you can use the formula

=VALUE

to determine that the serial value for this entry is 31167.

Using dates in mathematics

Once you have entered a date into a worksheet, you can use it in formulas and functions much as you would any other value. For example, suppose you want to figure out the date that is 200 days after December 25, 1989. If cell A1 contains the function

=DATE(89,12,25)

you can use the formula

=A1+200

to compute the serial value of the date 200 days after December 25, 1989: 31605. Once the formula is in place, you can use one of Excel's date formats to display the result in an understandable form. For example, if you assign the d-mmm-yy format to the cell that contains this function, the cell displays the date *13-Jul-90*.

Now, suppose you want to know how many days will elapse between December 25, 1989, and May 13, 1991. You can use the function

=DATE(91,5,13)–DATE(89,12,25)

to compute the answer: 504 days. Now, suppose you want to know how many weeks will elapse between those two dates. The function

=(DATE(91,5,13)–DATE(89,12,25))/7

gives the answer: 72 weeks.

Creating date series

There will be times in your work with Excel when you'll want to create an evenly spaced series of dates in a row or column of a spreadsheet. Although there are several ways you can create such a series, Microsoft Excel offers a special tool that makes the job easy: the Series... command from the Data menu. This command allows you to build a series of dates that are days, weeks, months, or years apart.

Let's look at an example of the Series... command. Suppose you want to create a series of dates in cells A1 to A17 in a worksheet. The series begins with May 1, 1989, and the dates in the series are exactly one month apart. To create this series, you first enter the function

=DATE(89,5,1)

in cell A1. Next, you select the range A1:A17 and choose Series... from the Data menu. Figure 7-1 shows the Series dialog box. From this box, select Date to create a date series. (The Columns option is already selected because the highlighted range is a column.) Finally, you select Month to specify the interval and press Enter or click OK.

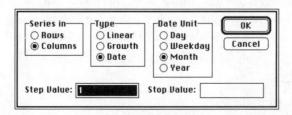

FIGURE 7-1. *This is the Series dialog box.*

Figure 7-2 shows the result of this command. Notice that each of the cells in the range A1:A17 contains a serial date value. If you now choose the Number... command from the Format menu and select the m/d/yy format, you will see that these date values are all exactly one month apart. Figure 7-3 shows the worksheet after these cells have been formatted.

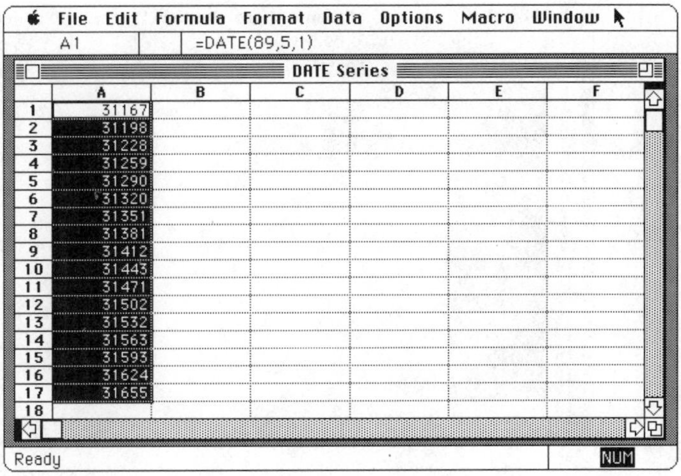

FIGURE 7-2. *You have used the DATE function and the Series...
command to create a series of dates one month apart.*

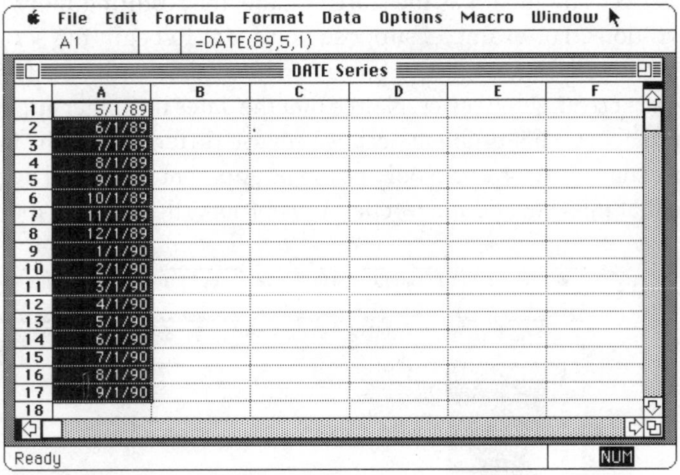

FIGURE 7-3. *You have used the Number... command to format the date
series in understandable form.*

You can begin a monthly date series with any date. For example, suppose you enter the function

=DATE(89,5,12)

in cell A1, then create the series. Figure 7-4 on the next page shows the result. Notice that all of the dates in the series are still exactly one month apart.

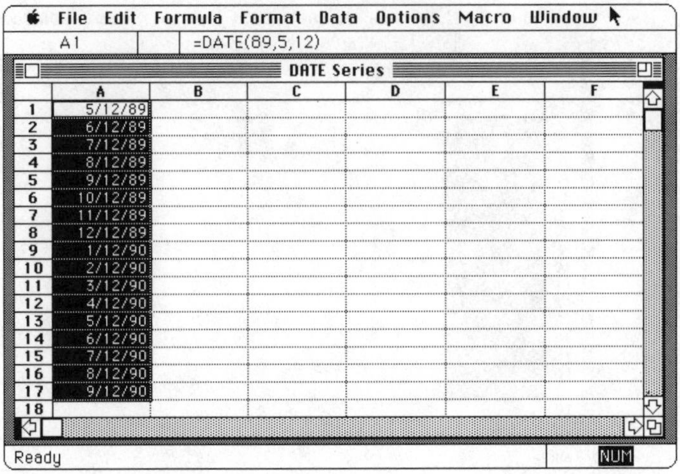

FIGURE 7-4. *This figure shows another series of dates one month apart.*

There is, however, one exception to this rule. If you use a date that falls after the 28th of any month as the starting date, the resulting monthly series has a few aberrations. For example, suppose you want to begin the series not with May 1, 1989, but with May 31, 1989. Figure 7-5 shows the result of entering this date in cell A1, then creating the series. Notice that the dates no longer appear to be exactly one month apart. This problem occurs because different months have different numbers of days. The problem only becomes apparent when you begin the series with a date that falls beyond the last day in February, the shortest month of the year.

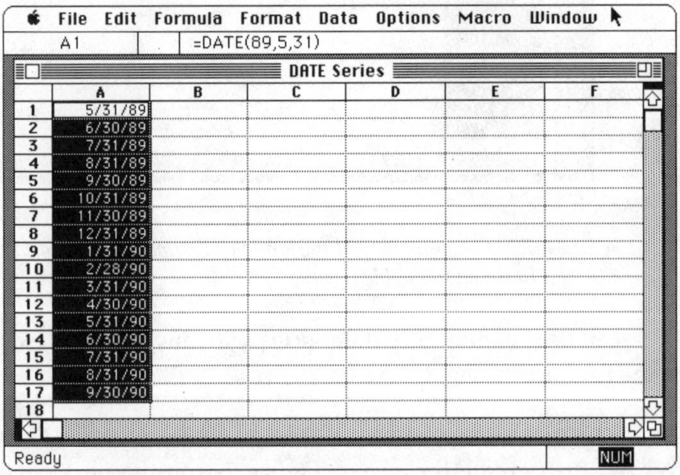

FIGURE 7-5. *This figure shows the result of trying to create a monthly series starting with a date that falls after the 28th of any month.*

The other choices in the Date Unit box of the Series dialog box allow you to specify different intervals for your date series. The Day option builds a series of dates that are all one day apart. The Weekday option creates a series of dates using the five working days of the week. (This is a useful option among worksheet programs to distinguish between weekday and weekend dates.) The Year option builds an annual date series.

The ability the Series... command gives you to create custom date series (especially monthly series) is one of the nicest features of the program. As far as we know, Microsoft Excel is the only worksheet program to offer this feature.

The TIME function

Making time entries is a similar process to making date entries. First, you use a function to enter the appropriate time into a cell, then you use one of Excel's four time formats to make the result understandable.

The primary time function is TIME. The form of this function is

=TIME(*hh,mm,ss*)

where *hh* is the hours argument of the time, *mm* is the minutes argument, and *ss* is the seconds argument. The result of the function is a decimal fraction that represents how much of the day has elapsed between midnight and the specified time.

The *ss* argument is optional and can be omitted. If you do leave it out, however, you still need to include a comma after the *mm* argument, as in

=TIME(*hh,mm,*)

Let's look at a couple of examples of the TIME function. Suppose you want to enter the time 10:15 A.M. into a cell. To do this, you click the cell and enter the function

=TIME(10,15,)

The result of this function is the decimal fraction 0.42708333.

The TIME function uses the 24-hour, or military, time convention. On the 24-hour clock, 3 A.M. is 3 o'clock, 2 P.M. is 14 o'clock, and 11 P.M. is 23 o'clock. This means that the time 2:15 P.M. is represented by the function

=TIME(14,15,)

and the time 11:55 P.M. is represented by the function

=TIME(23,55,)

For times between 12:00 A.M. midnight and 1 A.M., the *hh* argument is always 0. For example, the time 12:01 A.M. is represented by the function

=TIME(0,1,)

As with the DATE function, you may have some trouble recalling the order of the arguments in the TIME function. If you just remember that the arguments occur in descending order of magnitude—first hours, then minutes, then seconds—you shouldn't have any problem.

Also like DATE, TIME accepts and attempts to interpret "illegal" arguments. For example, Excel assumes that the function

=TIME(12,60,)

refers to the time 1:00 P.M. When it encounters the argument 60, Excel simply carries the extra minute over into the next hour because the maximum value for the *mm* argument is 59. To Excel, this function is equivalent to the function

=TIME(13,0,)

Formatting times

Excel offers four built-in formats that you can use to display times in a desired form. These four formats, which are available when you choose Number... from the Format menu, are h:mm AM/PM, h:mm:ss AM/PM, h:mm, and h:mm:ss. There is also a format that combines both date and time: m/d/yy h:mm. Here is the result of the function TIME(13,52,32)—serial value 0.57814815—under each of these formats (notice that the first two formats display the time in traditional 12-hour clock form, while the last two use the 24-hour convention):

If you use...	Excel displays...
h:mm AM/PM	1:52 PM
h:mm:ss AM/PM	1:52:32 PM
h:mm	13:52
h:mm:ss	13:52:32

To assign a time format to a cell, you simply click that cell, choose Number... from the Format menu, select the time format you want to use, then press Enter or click OK.

An easier way

As you have probably guessed, you can bypass the standard two-step method of entering time. To do this, you click the cell into which you want to make the entry and type the time in one of the following forms:

hh:mm:ss

hh:mm

hh:mm:ss AM/PM

hh:mm AM/PM

For example, suppose you want to enter the time 2:15 P.M. in a cell. Instead of using the two-step method, you can click the cell and type either 2:15 P.M. or 14:15. Either way, Excel assigns a time format to that value. (Remember that if you don't include the AM/PM notation in the time, Excel interprets the time using the 24-hour clock convention.)

Using times in mathematics

Like date values, time values can be used in formulas and functions. However, the results of time math are not as easy to understand as the results of date math.

For example, suppose you want to know how much time elapsed between 2:45 P.M. and 10:22 A.M. You can do this using the formula

=TIME(14,45,)−TIME(10,22,)

Unfortunately, the result of the formula, .18263889, is not at all easy to interpret. This number represents the fraction of a day that has elapsed between the two times in question. If you want to get a more meaningful answer, you can change the function to

=(TIME(14,45,)−TIME(10,22,))*24

The result of this function, 4.38333333, is the number of hours that have elapsed between the two times. Although this number is still not in a form you are used to using, it is at least understandable.

Now, suppose you want to figure out the time that is 2 hours, 23 minutes, and 17 seconds after 12:35:23 P.M. The formula

=TIME(12,35,23)+TIME(2,23,17)

returns the correct answer: .62407407. In this formula, you used the function TIME(2,23,17) not as an absolute time (2:23:17A.M.), but as an interval of time (2 hours, 23 minutes, and 17 seconds). This is perfectly acceptable to Excel.

Combining date and time formats

In addition to the built-in formats that let you display dates and times, Microsoft Excel offers a combined format—m/d/yy h:mm—that lets you display the date and time in one cell. For example, if a cell in your worksheet contains the serial value 32261.125 and you apply the m/d/yy h:mm format to that entry, you'll see the date and time displayed as *4/29/92 3:00*. When you're entering both date and time "in format," you can type either *4/29/92 15:00* or *3:00 PM 4/29/92*. However, you'll have to widen the column in which the entry is displayed. If you enter such a long entry into a 10-character wide cell, you'll see seven # symbols in the cell.

The NOW function

The NOW function can be used to enter the current date and time into a cell. The form of this function is simply

    =NOW()

Notice that NOW does not take an argument. The result of the function is a date/time value that includes both an integer (the date) and a fraction (the time). For example, if today is June 11, 1989, and the time is 4:05 P.M., the function

    =NOW()

returns the value 31208.67013889 (32670.67014 if the 1904 Date System is off).

Microsoft Excel offers a date format that is intended especially for use with the NOW function: m/d/yy h:mm. This format displays both the date and time portions of the NOW result. For example, if you assign the m/d/yy h:mm format to the cell that contains the NOW function above, the result is displayed as

    6/11/89 16:05

There is one problem with this format: It is too wide to be displayed entirely in a standard-width column. If you want to see the complete date/time display, you must increase the width of the column that contains the cell that has been assigned this format to approximately 12 characters.

The NOW function draws its value from the Macintosh system clock. If, for some reason, the system clock is wrong, you can correct it by choosing the Control Panel command from the Apple menu and adjusting the system clock. If the problem persists, you might want to have the battery checked in your Macintosh.

The value of the NOW function is updated each time you recalculate the worksheet (either by making an entry, by choosing Calculate Now from the Options menu, or by pressing Command-=). If you should notice that the value of a cell that contains the NOW function is not up to date, you can correct the problem by recalculating the worksheet.

Creating your own date and time formats

In addition to the four standard date formats and four standard time formats, Microsoft Excel allows you to create custom date and time formats. The general technique for creating your own date and time formats is the same as the technique for creating custom formats that we explained in Chapter 3, "Formatting the Worksheet."

There are several formatting symbols you can use to create special date and time formats. These symbols are shown in Figure 7-6. (We used 1:01:01 A.M. on January 1, 1990, as an example.)

Symbol	Displays
d	Day number without leading 0 (1)
dd	Day number with leading 0 (01)
ddd	Day of week abbreviation (Mon)
dddd	Day of week name (Monday)
m	Month number without leading 0 (1)
mm	Month number with leading 0 (01)
mmm	Month name abbreviation (Jan)
mmmm	Complete month name (January)
yy	Last two digits of year (90)
yyyy	Entire year number (1990)
h	Hour without leading 0 (1)
hh	Hour with leading 0 (01)
m	Minute without leading 0 (1)
mm	Minute with leading 0 (01)
s	Second without leading 0 (1)
ss	Second with leading 0 (01)
AM/PM	Time in AM/PM notation (1:01:01 AM)
am/pm	Time in am/pm notation (1:01:01 am)
A/P	Time in A/P notation (1:01:01 A)
a/p	Time in a/p notation (1:01:01 a)

FIGURE 7-6. *Use these formats to create custom dates and times in Excel.*

There are a couple of things to keep in mind about these symbols. First, when you use the symbol *m* immediately after an *h*, Microsoft Excel interprets *m* as meaning minutes. Otherwise, the program assumes that *m* means months. Second, if you include one of the symbols *AM/PM, am/pm, A/P,* or *a/p* in a time format, Excel displays the time in conventional 12-hour clock form. If you leave out these symbols, Excel displays the time in 24-hour form.

So that you can see how versatile this capability is, let's look at a few examples. Suppose you want to create a format that displays a date in the fullest possible form; that is, the date December 25, 1989, would be displayed as *December 25, 1989*. To do this, you can click the cell containing the entry that you want to format, choose Number... from the Format menu, and type

mmmm d, yyyy

When you press Enter, the new format is stored in the list of formats, and the date in the selected cell is displayed in full.

Similarly, suppose you want to create a format that spells out the day of the week of a date, in addition to displaying the date itself. The format

dddd, mmmm d, yyyy

does the trick. If the cell is wide enough, this format causes the result of the function DATE(89,6,11) to be displayed in the form

Sunday, June 11, 1989

These techniques can also be used to display only a portion of a date or time. For example, the format *mmmm* causes the date December 25, 1989, to be displayed as just the word *December*. Similarly, the format *s* displays the result of the function TIME(14,15,16) as 16.

Custom date and time formats, like other formats, are saved only with the worksheet in which they are created. As we discussed in Chapter 3, "Formatting the Worksheet," you can create a worksheet with each of your custom formats applied to a cell. Then, whenever you want to apply these custom formats, you can copy them to your active worksheet. This copy-and-paste procedure saves you a great deal of time because you don't need to open the Number dialog box for each custom format you want to apply.

Secondary functions

In addition to the primary date and time functions DATE, TIME, and NOW, Microsoft Excel offers a set of less important, secondary date functions. This group includes the functions WEEKDAY, YEAR, MONTH, DAY, HOUR, MINUTE, and SECOND.

The WEEKDAY function

The WEEKDAY function can be used to determine the day of the week of a particular date. As far as we know, this function is unique to Microsoft Excel. The form of this function is

=WEEKDAY(*date*)

The result of the function is a number from 1 to 7 that matches the day of the week of the date. For example, if the date is a Sunday, then the function returns the number 1. If the date is a Monday, the function returns the number 2.

By itself, this function is not very useful. However, when it is used in conjunction with a lookup table, WEEKDAY can be a valuable tool. Figure 7-7 shows a simple vertical lookup table that could be used with WEEKDAY. Notice that the comparison values in this table are the same as the possible results of WEEKDAY: 1, 2, 3, and so on, up to 7. The second column contains the names of the days of the week: Sunday, Monday, and so on.

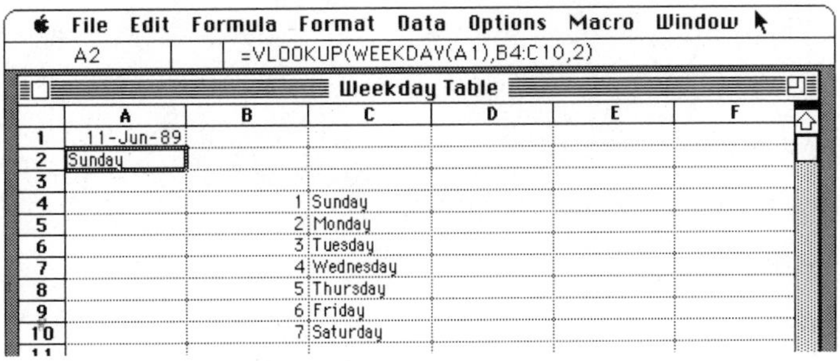

FIGURE 7-7. *We used the WEEKDAY function to retrieve the day of the week for a specific date from a lookup table.*

Cell A1 in this worksheet contains the function

=DATE(89,6,11)

We have assigned the d-mmm-yy format to this function so that it is displayed in the form *11-Jun-89*. Now, suppose you want to know the day of the week of this date. The function

=VLOOKUP(WEEKDAY(A1),B4:C10,2)

entered in cell A2 returns the correct day from the table: Sunday.

The YEAR, MONTH, and DAY functions

The YEAR, MONTH, and DAY functions can be used to determine the value of the year, month, and day components of a serial date/time number. The forms of these functions are nearly identical:

=YEAR(*date*)

=MONTH(*date*)

and

=DAY(*date*)

The *date* argument can be a literal serial date value (like 21677), a date function, or a reference to a cell that contains either a date function or a serial date value.

The result of these functions is the value of the specified term of the *date* argument. For example, suppose cell A1 contains the function

=DATE(89,12,25)

The function

=YEAR(A1)

returns the value 1989. Likewise, the function

=MONTH(A1)

returns the value 12, and the function

=DAY(A1)

returns the value 25.

You may wonder about the value of these functions, because you can easily determine the year, month, and day portions of a date just by looking at the DATE function or the formatted date. Although you may find some clever uses for these functions, your instincts are correct: You probably will not use these functions very often.

The HOUR, MINUTE, and SECOND functions

Just as the YEAR, MONTH, and DAY functions can be used to determine the year, month, and day components of a serial date/time number, the HOUR, MINUTE, and SECOND functions can be used to determine the hour, minute, and second components of a serial date/time number. The forms of these functions are very similar:

=HOUR(*time*)

=MINUTE(*time*)

and

=SECOND(*time*)

The result of these functions is the value of the specified term of the *time* argument. For example, if cell B1 contains the function

=TIME(12,15,35)

then the function

=HOUR(B1)

returns the value 12, the function

=MINUTE(B1)

returns the value 15, and the function

=SECOND(B1)

returns the value 35.

Like the functions YEAR, MONTH, and DAY, you probably won't use these functions very often.

The DATEVALUE and TIMEVALUE functions

The DATEVALUE function translates a date into a serial number. It is similar to the DATE function, except that you must enter a *"date text"* argument. The form of this function is

=DATEVALUE(*"date text"*)

where *"date text"* represents any date between January 1, 1904, and December 31, 2078; it can be written in any of Excel's built-in date formats. For example, the formula

=DATEVALUE("1/1/89")

returns the serial number 31047. If you enter *"date text"* without a year, Excel uses the current year from your computer's internal clock.

Similarly, the TIMEVALUE function translates a time into a decimal value. It is similar to the TIME function, except that you must enter a *"time text"* argument. The form of this function is

=TIMEVALUE(*"time text"*)

where *"time text"* represents a time in any of the Microsoft Excel built-in time formats. For example, if you enter

=TIMEVALUE("3:32 PM")

the function returns the decimal value 0.64722222.

Conclusion

You may find it confusing at first to think of dates and times in terms of serial values, but if you think about it for a moment, you'll discover that there is a definite method to Excel's "madness." By assigning serial values to days, hours, minutes, and even seconds, Microsoft Excel allows you to perform sophisticated date and time arithmetic. In other words, you can manipulate dates and times in your worksheet formulas just like any other type of worksheet value.

Microsoft Excel offers the most flexible date and time capabilities we've seen in any spreadsheet program. The ability to specify weekdays in a date series or function is a unique luxury. If you have used other spreadsheet programs, you know that most programs have to perform a tedious series of calculations to distinguish between weekday and weekend dates. Similarly, the ability to create your own date and time formats is a convenience that you probably won't appreciate until you need it to create that one special report.

8

Other Worksheet Topics

*I*n earlier chapters, we covered most of the important features and capabilities of the Microsoft Excel program. A few advanced topics still remain, however, such as arrays, data tables, the Formula menu's Find… and Replace… commands, and worksheet links. We cover these topics in this chapter, as well as methods for auditing and protecting a worksheet. In a number of the sample worksheets in this chapter, we've altered the widths of some columns. You may want to make the same changes as you go along, so that your screen looks like our figures.

Arrays

In Microsoft Excel, an array is simply a group of two or more values that can be used like a single value in formulas and functions. Microsoft Excel is the only spreadsheet program we know of that has the ability to work with arrays.

The most important thing to understand about arrays is that you don't need to know anything about them to use Excel. For the most part, you can do little with an array that you cannot do nearly as well with a traditional formula and the Copy, Paste, Fill Down, and Fill Right commands.

However, some of Excel's most exciting features require the use of arrays. You've already seen in Chapter 6, "Built-in Functions," the functions TREND and GROWTH, which return arrays. Arrays are also used in linking one worksheet to another and have important applications in user-defined functions. For these reasons, you'll probably want to take the time to become familiar with arrays.

Before we proceed, we need to define a few terms. An *array formula* takes much the same form as a standard worksheet formula, except that it acts on two or more sets of values, called *array arguments,* to return either a single result or multiple results. An *array range* is a block of cells that share a common array formula. An *array constant* is a specially organized list of constant values that you can use as arguments in your array formulas.

Using arrays

Perhaps the easiest way to learn about arrays is to look at a few examples. Usually, the formulas you enter in your worksheet produce a single result. For example, suppose cells A1 and A2 of your worksheet contain the values 10 and 15. To determine the sum of these two values, you can enter the simple formula

=A1+A2

which results in a single value, 25, that occupies a single cell in the worksheet.

Now, suppose you've entered several groups of values in rows 1 and 2 of your worksheet, as shown in Figure 8-1. Typically, to total the values in each of these columns, you would create five separate formulas, as we've done in cells A3:E3. The formula in cell A3 calculates the total of the values in cells A1 and A2, the formula in cell B3 calculates the total of the values in cells B1 and B2, and so on.

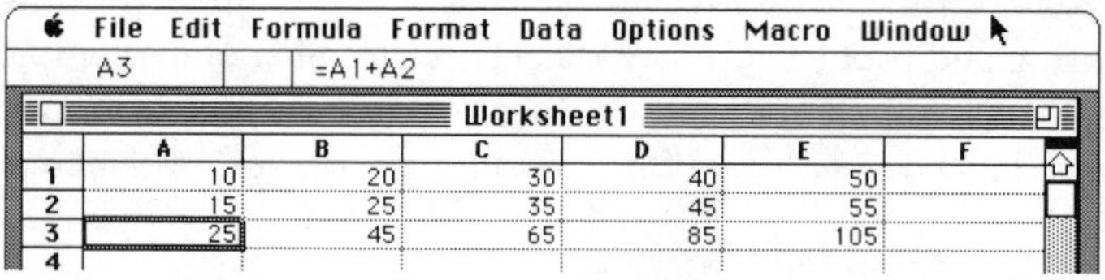
File Edit Formula Format Data Options Macro Window
A3
=A1+A2
Worksheet1
A B C D E F
1 10 20 30 40 50
2 15 25 35 45 55
3 25 45 65 85 105
4

FIGURE 8-1. *We used five formulas to calculate the totals of the values in columns A through E.*

But here's an alternative. Using arrays, you can calculate the sum of each column of values in Figure 8-1 with a single formula. The first step is to select the array range that will contain the results of the formula. In this case, begin by selecting cells A3:E3 and typing the formula

=A1:E1+A2:E2

Next, lock in the formula by pressing Command-Enter. Figure 8-2 shows the results.

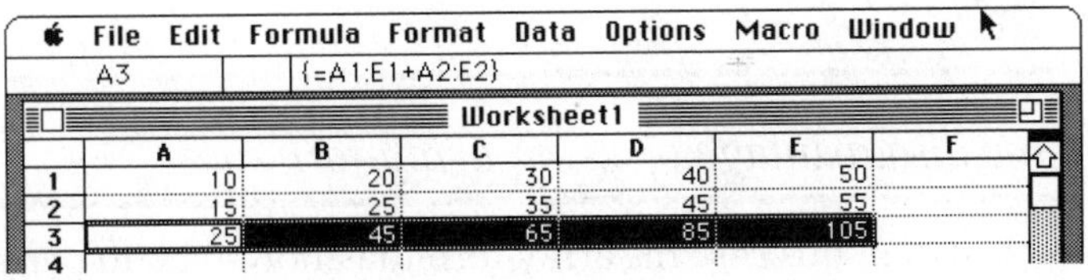

FIGURE 8-2. *You have used a single array formula to total the values in each column.*

As you can see, a single array formula computes the sum of each group of values: A1:A2, B1:B2, C1:C2, D1:D2, and E1:E2. Cells A3:E3 serve as the array range in this simple example, and the array formula

{=A1:E1+A2:E2}

is stored in each cell of the array range. You must press Command-Enter to lock in an array formula. When you do this, Excel places a set of braces around the formula to indicate that it is an array formula. Don't type the braces yourself. If you do, Excel will interpret your entry as a label. In this example, the array arguments are the range references A1:E1 and A2:E2.

The array formula in Figure 8-2 occupies a horizontal array range. Let's look at a similar example that uses a vertical array range. Suppose you have a worksheet that contains the even numbers between 10 and 22 in cells A1:A7 and the odd numbers between 11 and 23 in cells B1:B7. You want to compute the sums of the products of each pair of values in this worksheet; that is, the sum of A1*B1, plus A2*B2, plus A3*B3, and so on. To compute this with an array formula, you first click cell D1 or any blank cell, then type

=SUM(A1:A7*B1:B7)

and press Command-Enter. Figure 8-3 shows the result.

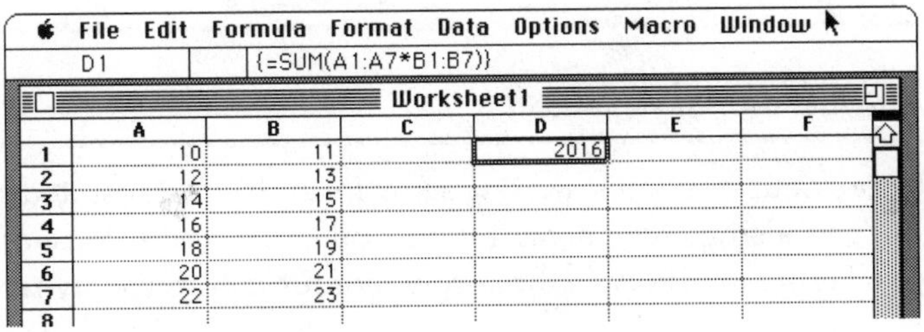

FIGURE 8-3. *You have used an array formula in cell D1 to compute the sum of the products of the pairs of values in columns A and B.*

EXCEL

One disadvantage of using array formulas

Although in this case the array formula allows you to perform your computation very efficiently, there is a way to arrive at this same result without using arrays. Instead of using an array formula, you could enter the formula

    =A1*B1

in cell C1, then use the Fill Down command to copy that formula into cells C2 through C7. Then, you could enter the formula

    =SUM(C1:C7)

in cell D1. Here is the result:

	File	**Edit**	**Formula**	**Format**	**Data**	**Options**	**Macro**	**Window**	

| D1 | | | =SUM(C1:C7) | | | | | |

Worksheet1

	A	B	C	D	E	F
1	10	11	110	2016		
2	12	13	156			
3	14	15	210			
4	16	17	272			
5	18	19	342			
6	20	21	420			
7	22	23	506			

Although this method is a bit less efficient, it has one advantage over the method that uses the array formula: It leaves an audit trail that is easier to follow than the array formula. The importance of this kind of trail increases with the complexity of your worksheet, but audit trails are handy even in simple worksheets.

Two-dimensional arrays

In the previous examples, we saw array formulas that resulted in a vertical, a horizontal, and a single-cell array range. You can also create two-dimensional array ranges. Figure 8-4 shows a three-row-by-four-column array range.

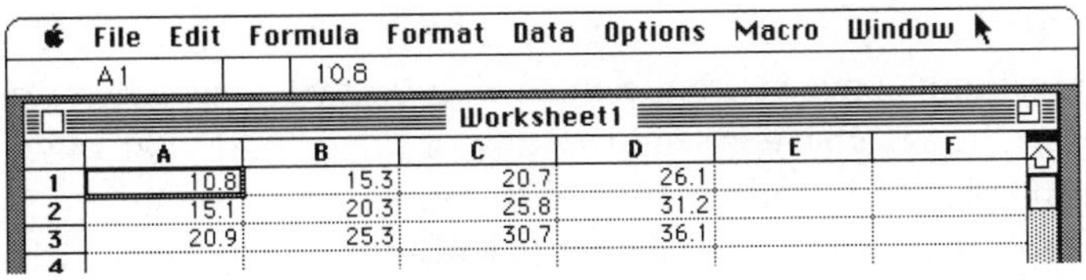

FIGURE 8-4. *This figure shows a two-dimensional array range.*

For example, if you want to create an array formula to compute the integer value of each number in the range A1:D3, you first select a three-row-by-four-column range, like A5:D7. Next, enter the formula

=INT(A1:D3)

in cell A5, then press Command-Enter. Figure 8-5 shows the result. As you can see, each cell in the range A5:D7 displays the integer value of the corresponding cell in the range A1:D3. In fact, Excel has entered the array formula

{=INT(A1:D3)}

in each cell in the range A5:D7.

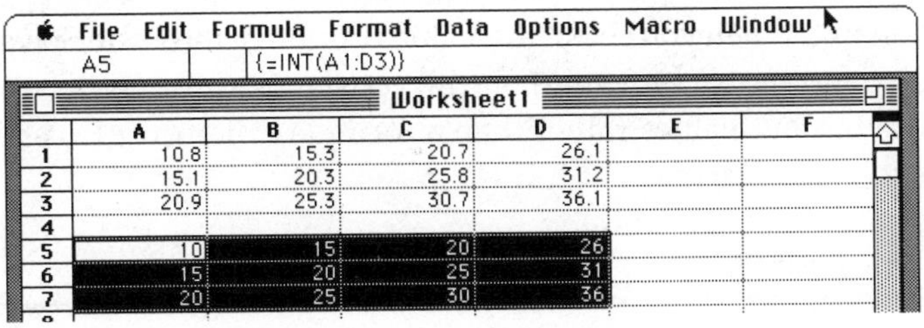

FIGURE 8-5. *You have computed integer values of numbers in a two-dimensional array.*

Array formula rules

As you saw in the examples above, array formulas can return either single or multiple values. Either way, you enter array formulas by first selecting the cell or range that will contain your result(s).

Selecting ranges

If the formula will produce multiple results, you select a range the same size and shape as the range(s) on which you're performing your calculations. In the preceding example, we selected a three-row-by-four-column array range to hold our array formula.

Editing array formulas and ranges

Interestingly, once you have entered an array formula in a range, you cannot cut, clear, edit, or otherwise modify any of the cells in that range individually; your editing procedures must address the entire array range.

To edit an array formula in Microsoft Excel 2.2, you only have to select a single cell and activate the formula bar. When you do this, Excel removes the braces that designate the formula as an array formula, allowing you to alter it. When you press Command-Enter, Excel replaces the braces around the formula, enters it, and adjusts the results in the worksheet.

To move or clear the contents of an array range, you must first select all the cells in a range and then choose the Clear... command from the Edit menu.

Although you can't cut, clear, or edit part of an array, you can assign different formats to individual cells. You can also copy a single cell from an array range and paste it in another area of your worksheet. Excel adjusts any relative references in the pasted array formula just as it does when you copy and paste any standard worksheet formula.

As with any other formula, you can convert the results of an array formula into a series of constant values by selecting the array range, choosing the Copy command, and, without changing your selection, choosing the Paste Special... command. When you select the Values option in the Paste Special dialog box, Excel overwrites the array formulas with constant values. Because the range now contains constant values rather than a formula, Microsoft Excel no longer treats the selection as an array.

Array constants

Array constants are to arrays what literal values are to cell references. As with array formulas, the best way to understand array constants is to look at an example.

Suppose you want to compute the integer value of the three numbers 123.456, 1.234, and 12345.678, but you don't want to enter the values into the worksheet. Microsoft Excel allows you to perform the computation by selecting the range A1:C1 (or any other horizontal three-cell range), typing the function

    =INT({123.456,1.234,12345.678})

and pressing Command-Enter to lock the formula in place. Notice that the argument of the INT function is made up of the three numbers enclosed in braces. The inner braces, which you must type yourself, indicate that these numbers are an array constant. By way of a reminder, the outer braces that Excel inserts when you press Command-Enter identify an array formula. If you were to type the outer braces yourself, Excel would read your formula as a label.

Figure 8-6 shows the results of this formula. Each cell in the range contains the array formula

{=INT({123.456,1.234,12345.678})}

However, the value displayed in each cell is the result of the INT function for the element of the array that corresponds to the position of the cell in the range. For example, cell B1, the second cell in the range, displays the result of INT for the value 1.234, the second element in the range.

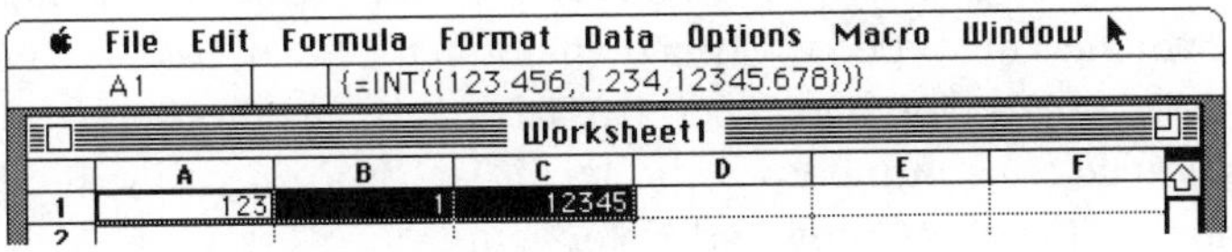

FIGURE 8-6. *Using array constants in a formula causes only the results of the formula to be displayed in the selected range.*

Excel also allows you to create vertical array constants. In a vertical array constant, the elements in the array are separated by semicolons, instead of commas. For example, the array constant

{123.456;1.234;12345.678}

is a three-row vertical array. Not surprisingly, you must enter formulas that refer to vertical array constants in vertical ranges. For example, if you want to compute the integer values of the three numbers in this vertical array constant, you can select the range A1:A3, type the formula

=INT({123.456;1.234;12345.678})

and press Command-Enter. Figure 8-7 shows the results.

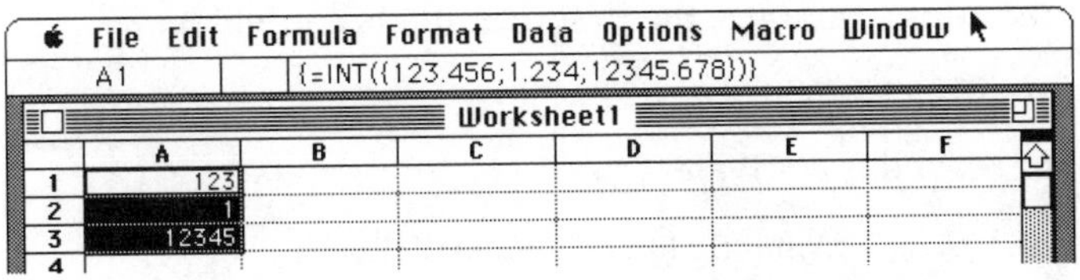

FIGURE 8-7. *These are the results when you use a vertical array constant.*

Just as you can create two-dimensional variable arrays, you can also create two-dimensional array constants. In a two-dimensional array constant, commas are used to separate the elements of each row of the constant, and semicolons are used to separate the rows that make up the constant.

A problem with array constants

Because one of the primary applications for spreadsheet programs like Microsoft Excel is helping you to perform "what if" analyses that are easy to follow, it's not the best idea to build your formulas in such a way that they are difficult to keep track of.

Array constants have the same problem as other constants. Like all formulas that use constant values, array formulas that use array constants violate Excel's rule about being able to vary the assumptions on which an analysis is based. It is harder to change a formula that is based on an array constant. For example, suppose you had mistyped the first element in the array constant used in the previous example; that is, you had typed 123.567. To change this entry to 123.456, you would double click the number on the formula bar. You could then edit the formula, being sure to press Command-Enter again.

Array expansion

When you use arrays as arguments in a formula, all your arrays should be the same dimension. If the dimensions of your array arguments or array ranges don't match, Excel often expands the arguments as required to complete its calculations. For example, suppose you want to multiply all the values in cells A1:B5 of your worksheet by 10. You can accomplish this with a simple array formula like

> {=A1:B5*10}

or, if you're using array constants, you can use a formula like

> {={1,2;3,4;5,6;7,8;9,10}*10}

Notice that these two formulas are not balanced—there are ten values on the left side of the multiplication operator and only one value on the right. Fortunately, Excel can expand the second argument to match the size and shape of the first. In the preceding examples, the first formula is equivalent to

> {=A1:B5*{10,10;10,10;10,10;10,10;10,10}}

and the second is equivalent to

> {={1,2;3,4;5,6;7,8;9,10}*{10,10;10,10;10,10;10,10;10,10}}

As you can see, single-value arguments are repeated as needed to balance the dimensions of the other arguments in your array formula. If you use a one-row or one-column array argument, Excel repeats that row or column of values as needed to match the dimensions of the other arguments. For example, the formula

> {={1,2,3;4,5,6}*{7,8,9}}

is equivalent to

{={1,2,3;4,5,6}*{7,8,9;7,8,9}}

and results in an array range like this:

7	16	27
28	40	54

When you are working with two or more sets of multivalue arrays, each set of arguments must have the same number of rows as the argument with the greatest number of rows and the same number of columns as the argument with the greatest number of columns. It is important to note that Microsoft Excel doesn't expand an array when you use cell references as your array arguments. For example, in the formula

{=A1:A6*B1:B3}

you might expect Excel to repeat the argument B1:B3 to match the size and shape of the argument A1:A6, like this

{={A1;A2;A3;A4;A5;A6}*{B1;B2;B3;B1;B2;B3}}

Instead, the formula above results in an array that looks like the one in Figure 8-8:

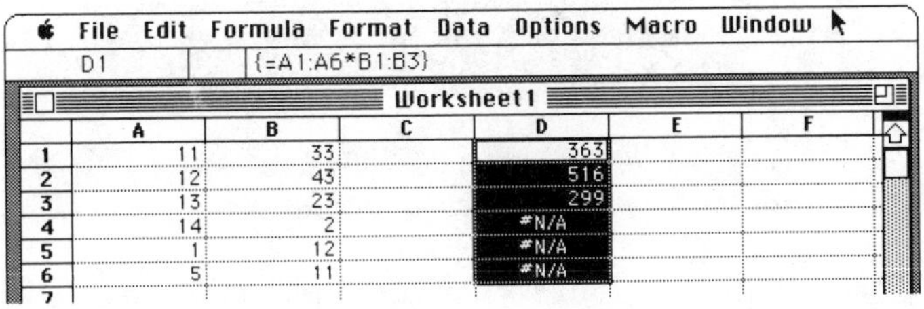

FIGURE 8-8. *Excel does not repeat the argument B1:B3 to match the size and shape of the argument A1:A6.*

Whether you're using array constants or cell references, if you select an array range that is larger than the array arguments, Excel attempts to expand the array formula to fill the selection. For example, in the worksheet shown in Figure 8-2, we used two one-row-by-five-column array arguments and a corresponding one-row-by-five-column array range. If we had selected cells A3:E7 rather than A3:E3 as the array range, the worksheet would look like the one in Figure 8-9 on the next page. In effect, the formula in range A3:E7 produces a five-by-five array by repeating one row, A3:E3, five times.

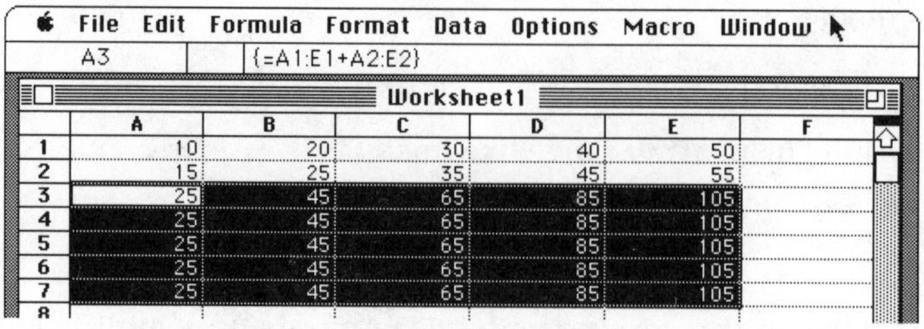

FIGURE 8-9. *If the array range is larger than the array arguments, Excel repeats the array formula to fill the selection.*

When you select an array range smaller than the argument range, Excel simply fills the available rows and columns. For example, in the sample worksheet in Figure 8-5, if we had selected the range A5:B6 rather than A5:D7 to enter the INT function, the worksheet would look like the one in Figure 8-10.

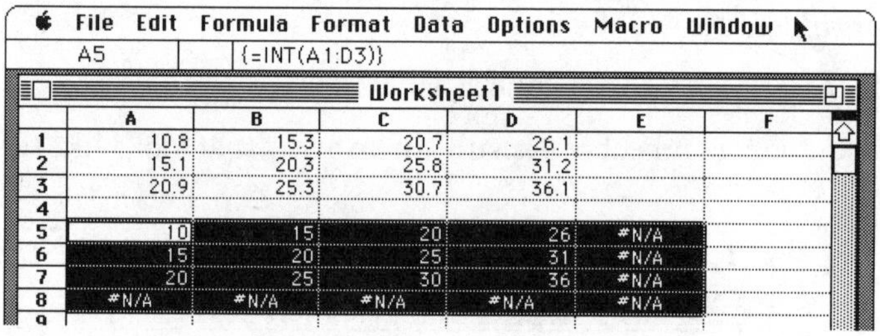

FIGURE 8-10. *If the array range is smaller than the argument range, Excel fills only the available rows and columns.*

Finally, if the array range is not a multiple of the same dimensions as the array arguments, Excel returns #N/A error values. For example, in the worksheet shown in Figure 8-5, if you select the range A5:E8, rather than A5:D7, to enter the INT function, the worksheet looks like the one in Figure 8-11. Notice that #N/A error values appear in row 8 and in column E, because the array argument, A1:D3, is only three rows deep and four columns long.

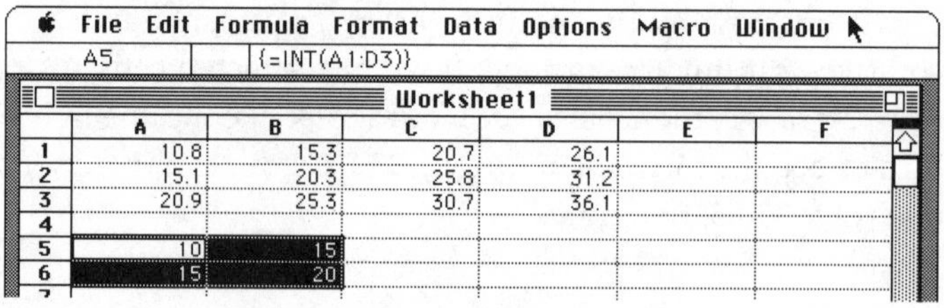

FIGURE 8-11. *If the array range is not a multiple of the same dimension as the array arguments, Excel returns #N/A error values.*

Array functions

As you have already seen, you can use arrays as the arguments of functions in Microsoft Excel. Although most of Excel's functions can accept array arguments, a few, such as ROWS, COLUMNS, TRANSPOSE, INDEX form two (recall that INDEX form one was discussed in Chapter 6, "Built-in Functions"), MDETERM, MMULT, and MINVERSE, require arrays as arguments. Be sure you select a block of cells that is the correct size before you enter these functions. We cover these functions in this section.

The ROWS function

The ROWS function returns the number of rows in an array. The form of the ROWS function is

   =ROWS(*array*)

The *array* argument can be a literal array (for example, {1;2;3;4;5}), or it can be a range defined by cell coordinates or by a range name. The result of the function is the number of rows in the array. For example, the result of the function

   =ROWS({100,200,300;1000,2000,3000})

is 2, because the literal array argument contains two "rows." Similarly, the function

   =ROWS(A1:A10)

returns 10, because there are ten rows in the range A1:A10.

The COLUMNS function

The COLUMNS function is identical to the ROWS function, except that COLUMNS returns the number of columns in the array argument. For example, the function

   =COLUMNS(A1:C10)

returns 3, because there are three columns in the range A1:C10. Likewise, the result of the function

   =COLUMNS({100,200,300;1000,2000,3000})

is 3, because this literal array contains three "columns." Similarly, the function

   =COLUMNS(A1:C1)

returns the value 3.

The ROWS and COLUMNS functions are analogous to the COUNT function. However, unlike COUNT, which returns the number of cells in a range that contain numeric values, ROWS and COLUMNS return the absolute number of rows or columns in the range. Because of this difference, these functions can be used in combination to determine the ratio between the cells in a range that contain numeric values and the total number of cells in the range.

For example, in Chapter 6, "Built-in Functions," you used the COUNT function to determine the number of employees who had contributed to the United Charities Fund. You could combine the COUNT and ROW functions to determine the percentage of employees that made a contribution, using the formula

=COUNT(##:##)/ROWS(##:##)

where ##:## is the range of cells that contain the donations.

The TRANSPOSE function

The TRANSPOSE function can be used to exchange the rows and columns of a range or an array. The form of this function is

=TRANSPOSE(*array*)

If the array is vertical, the resulting array is horizontal. If the array is horizontal, the resulting array is vertical. For example, the result of the function

=TRANSPOSE({5,4,3,2,1})

is the array {5;4;3;2;1}, and the result of the function

=TRANSPOSE({1;2;3;4;5})

is the array {1,2,3,4,5}.

Let's look at a more practical example. Suppose you want to transpose the entries in cells A1:D1 in the worksheet shown in Figure 8-12 so that they fill cells B3:B6. To do this, you select the range B3:B6, type the function

=TRANSPOSE(A1:D1)

and press Command-Enter. The result is shown in Figure 8-13.

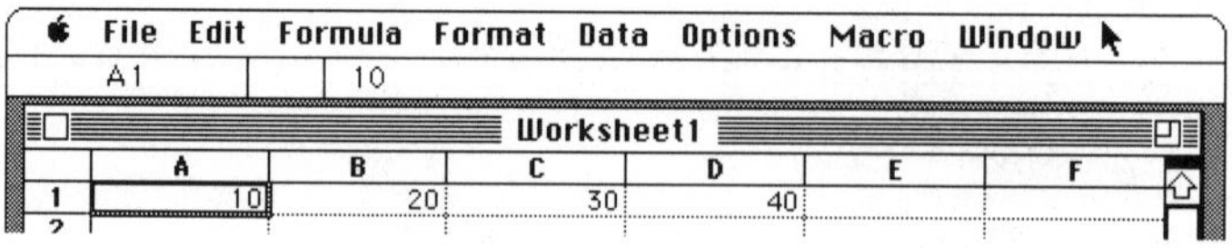

FIGURE 8-12. *This is a horizontal array.*

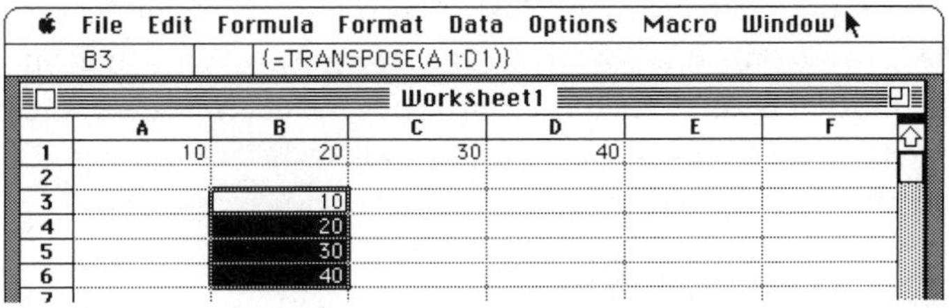

FIGURE 8-13. *You have used the TRANSPOSE function to convert the horizontal array into a vertical array.*

Notice that Excel has transposed the entries from the horizontal array A1:D1 into the vertical array B3:B6. Each cell in this range contains the array formula

{=TRANSPOSE(A1:D1)}

The INDEX function (form two)

The second form of the INDEX function is used only with arrays. It has the form

=INDEX(*array,row,column*)

The result of the INDEX function's second form returns the array-range value located at the intersection of the *row* and *column* arguments.

For example, in Figure 8-14 the function

=INDEX({10,20,30;40,50,60},1,2)

returns the value 20, because 20 is the item in the second column of the first row of the array. Similarly, the function

=INDEX({10,20,30;0,50,60},2,3)

returns the value 60, because 60 is the item in the third column of the second row of the array.

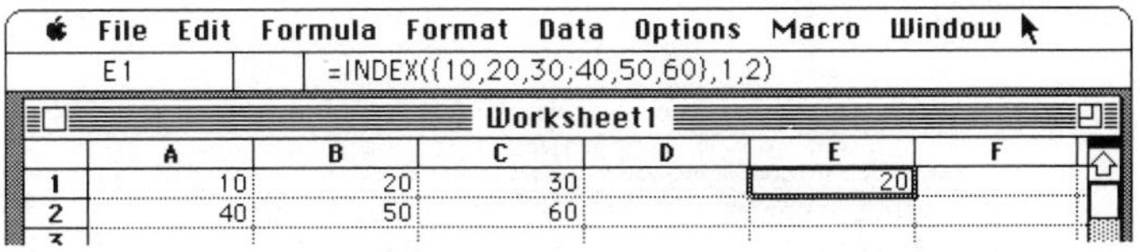

FIGURE 8-14. *This INDEX function returns the value located at the intersection of row 1 and column B (the second column).*

As with the first form of INDEX, you need to supply the *column* argument only if the array is only one row deep or the *row* argument if it is only one column wide. Also like that form of the function, the *row* and *column* arguments must be positive integers. In addition, if *row* or *column* exceeds the number of rows or columns in the array, the function returns the #REF! error message.

The MDETERM function

The MDETERM function returns a single value, the determinant of an array. The determinant, which is computed by mathematically combining the elements of the array, is used for solving systems of equations with multiple variables. For example, suppose you want to compute the determinant of the two-by-two array in A1:B2. You could do this with the formula

=(A1*B2)–(A2*B1)

For larger arrays, the formula for the determinant is considerably more complex. For example, to compute the determinant of the three-by-three array in cells A1:B3, you could enter the formula

=A1*(B2*C3–B3*C2)+A2*(B3*C1–B1*C3)+A3*(B1*C2–B2*C1)

Fortunately, Excel's new MDETERM function offers a far easier and faster alternative to entering these long, tedious formulas. The form of this function is

=MDETERM(*array*)

where *array* must contain an equal number of columns and rows and each element of *array* is a numeric value. If *array* contains one or more blank cells or one or more text entries, the MDETERM function returns the #VALUE! error message.

Suppose your worksheet contains the array shown in Figure 8-15. To calculate the determinant of this array, you enter the function

=MDETERM(A1:C3)

which returns the result 6000.

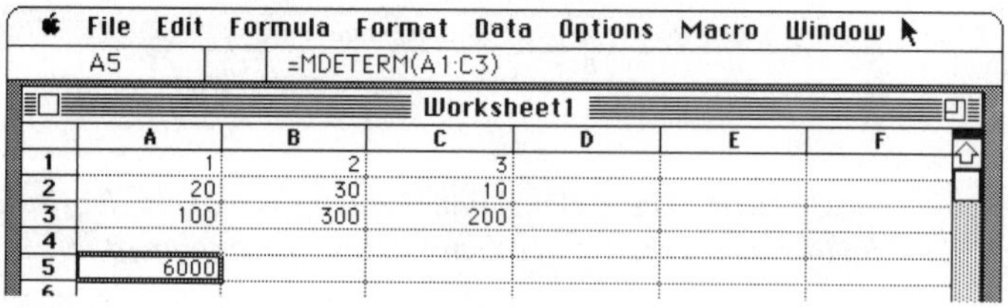

	A	B	C	D	E	F
1	1	2	3			
2	20	30	10			
3	100	300	200			
4						
5	6000					
6						

A5 =MDETERM(A1:C3)

FIGURE 8-15. *You have used the MDETERM function to compute the determinant of this three-by-three array.*

The *array* argument of the MDETERM function can be a reference to a range in the worksheet, a range name, or an array constant. Regardless of how you state the *array* argument, be sure the array contains the same number of columns and rows.

The MMULT function

The MMULT function returns the matrix product of two arrays. The form of this function is

=MMULT(*array1*,*array2*)

where the number of columns in *array1* is equal to the number of rows in *array2*. The result of the MMULT function is always an array that contains the same number of rows as *array1* and the same number of columns as *array2*. For example, suppose you want to compute the matrix product of the array in cells A1:B3 (*array1*) and cells D1:E2 (*array2*). First, select a block of cells two columns wide and three rows deep with no empty cells in the block. Then, type the function

=MMULT(A1:B3,D1:E2)

and press Command-Enter. Excel computes the product of the two arrays by multiplying each element in a row of the first array (A1:B3) by each element in a column of the second array (D1:E2) and summing those products. The diagram below shows how Excel performs these calculations:

(A1*D1)+(B1*D2)	(A1*E1)+(B1*E2)
(A2*D1)+(B2*D2)	(A2*E1)+(B2*E2)
(A3*D1)+(B3*D2)	(A3*E1)+(B3*E2)

Of course, you don't actually see these formulas in your worksheet. Instead, you see an array of the numeric results.

As in the MDETERM function, the arguments for the MMULT function can be range references, range names, or array constants. Each element of *array1* and *array2* must be a numeric value. If either array contains one or more blank cells or one or more text entries, the MMULT function returns the #VALUE! error value.

The MINVERSE function

The MINVERSE function returns the inverse of an array or matrix. The form of this function is

=MINVERSE(*array*)

As in the MDETERM function, the *array* argument for the MINVERSE function must contain an equal number of rows and columns, and each element of *array* must be a numeric value. The MINVERSE function accepts a range reference, a range name, or an array constant as its *array* argument.

Because the result of the MINVERSE function is an array, you must select a block of cells that is the same size as the *array* argument before you enter the function. For example, suppose you want to compute the inverse of the array shown in Figure 8-15. First, select a block of cells three columns wide and three rows deep, such as cells E1:G3. Then, type the function

=MINVERSE(A1:C3)

and press Command-Enter. Figure 8-16 shows the result. (In this figure, we've widened columns F and G and added one more decimal place to the values contained there.)

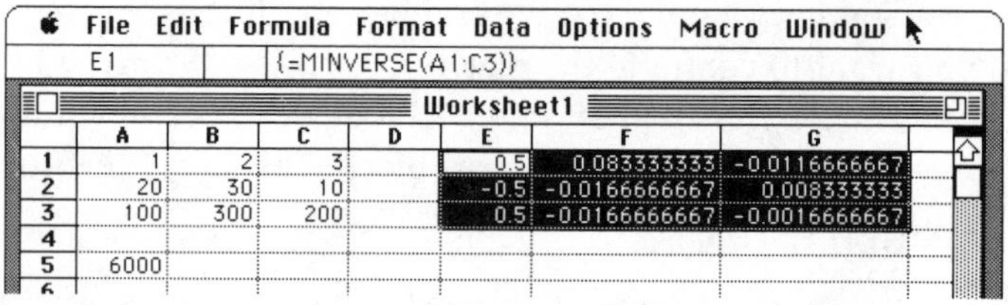

FIGURE 8-16. *Cells E1:G3 contain the inverse of the array in cells A1:C3.*

When you compute the matrix product of an array and its inverse, the result is the *identity matrix*. The identity matrix is an array containing all zero values, except the values along the upper-left to lower-right diagonal of that array. These diagonal values are all 1.

Data tables

One of the most important benefits of spreadsheet software is that it allows you to perform "what if" analysis quickly and easily. When you perform "what if" analysis, you change the values of certain key variables in a formula or a worksheet and measure the effect of the change on the "bottom line."

You're probably used to performing "what if" analysis manually. For example, suppose you are considering buying a house that will require you to take out a 30-year, $100,000 mortgage. You need to know what your monthly payments on that loan will be. Obviously, the size of the monthly payment is affected directly by the rate of interest that the bank charges on the mortgage.

To solve this problem manually, you might create a simple table like the one shown in Figure 8-17. Column A of this table lists several different interest rates that you think you might have to pay for your mortgage. Column B shows the monthly payments that result from each of the interest rates. (You have probably used a loan amortization table or a financial calculator to compute the monthly payments.) By scanning the table, you get a feeling for the effect of varying interest rates on your monthly payments.

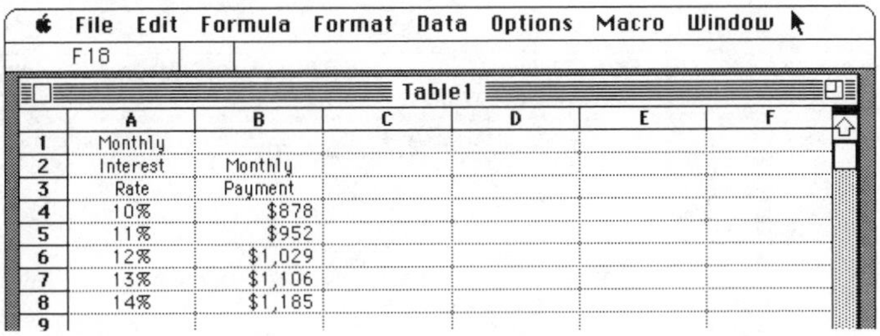

	A	B	C	D	E	F
1	Monthly					
2	Interest	Monthly				
3	Rate	Payment				
4	10%	$878				
5	11%	$952				
6	12%	$1,029				
7	13%	$1,106				
8	14%	$1,185				
9						

FIGURE 8-17. *This table shows the monthly payments on a 30-year, $100,000 loan at varying interest rates.*

Microsoft Excel includes a command on the Data menu that allows you to build this kind of table in the Excel worksheet. The Table... command is very powerful, because it automatically performs a series of calculations for you, given a formula and a series of variables. This command is the perfect tool for quickly computing the monthly payment required to amortize a 30-year, $100,000 mortgage at several rates of interest.

The Table... command lets you build two types of data tables: one-variable tables and two-variable tables. (These two types are also called one-input and two-input tables.) We'll look at one-variable tables first and then consider two-variable tables.

One-variable tables

Let's build a data table that computes the monthly payment on the sample mortgage at six different interest rates: 10, 11, 12, 13, 14, and 15 percent. To build the table, first enter the various interest rates you want to test in cells B3:B8 of your worksheet. We'll call this range the *input range*, because it contains the inputs we want to test. Next, enter the function

=PMT(A2/12,360,100000,,)

in cell C2. We'll call this function the *table formula*. In this formula, *A2/12* is the monthly interest rate, *360* is the term of the loan in months, and *100000* is the loan principal. Notice that this function refers to cell A2, which is currently blank. (Also, we omitted two optional arguments: *future value* and *type*. We discussed this function and the practice of using commas to indicate an omitted argument in Chapter 6, "Built-in Functions".) As you can see in Figure 8-18, because A2 is blank (Excel assigns a value of 0 to blank cells for division operations), the function returns a spurious result: the payment required to amortize the loan at an interest rate of 0 percent. You'll see in a moment why this function refers to cell A2.

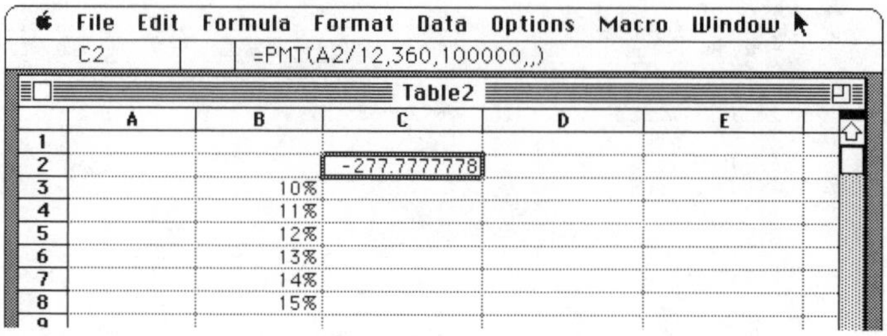

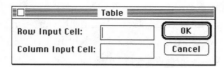

FIGURE 8-18. *This worksheet contains the interest rates and the PMT function.*

Next, you define the data-table range by selecting it. In Microsoft Excel, the data-table range is always the smallest rectangular range that includes the table formula and all of the values in the input range. In this case, you need to select the range B2:C8.

Now, you are ready to choose Table... from the Data menu. When you choose this command, Excel displays the dialog box shown in Figure 8-19. Notice that there are two fields in the box: Row Input Cell and Column Input Cell. Both fields are used to define the location of what we call the *input cell*. The input cell is a cell that is referred to, at least indirectly, by the table formula. Do you recall that the table formula (in cell C2) referred to the blank cell A2? In this example, A2 is the input cell.

FIGURE 8-19. *This is the Table dialog box.*

For the table to work properly, you must enter the input cell reference in the correct field in the dialog box. If the values in the input range are arranged in a column, then the input cell reference should be entered in the Column Input Cell field. If the input values are arranged in a row, then the input cell reference should be entered in the Row Input Cell field. Because the input values in this example are arranged in a column, you enter the input cell reference in the Column Input Cell field. To do this, click the Column Input Cell field, and either type the absolute reference of the input cell, *$A$2*, or click that cell.

By the way, notice the black stripes in the title bar of the Table dialog box. These stripes indicate that the dialog box can be moved around on the screen, so that you can point to cells easily. To move the box, simply drag the title bar.

Finally, press Enter or click OK to activate the table. When you do this, Excel takes a moment to compute the table, then enters the six results of the table formula (one result for each input value) into the range C3:C8, as shown in Figure 8-20.

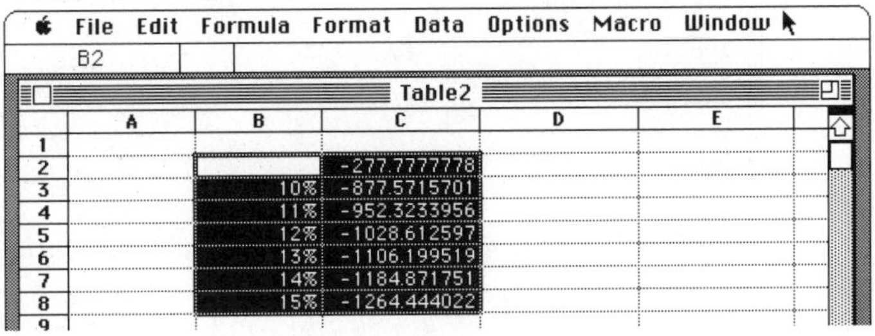

FIGURE 8-20. *You have used the Table… command to compute monthly loan payments.*

Let's consider what happens when Excel computes the data table. When you press Enter or click OK, Excel automatically enters the array formula

{=TABLE(,A2)}

into each cell in the range C3:C8 (the results range). These formulas compute the value of the table formula at each of the interest rates in column B. For example, the formula in cell C5 computes the value of the table formula at a rate of 12 percent per year.

Once the table has been built, you can change any of the variables in the list or the table formula to create a different set of results. For example, suppose you decide to borrow only $85,000 to buy your house. If you change the formula in cell C2 to

=PMT(A2/12,360,85000,,)

the values in the table also change, as shown in Figure 8-21 on the next page.

You can also copy the results to a different part of the worksheet. You might want to do this to save the table's current results before you make a change to the table formula or to the variables. For example, suppose you decide to copy the results of the sample table in Figure 8-21 from the range C3:C8 to the range E11:E16.

To do this, select the range C3:C8, choose the Copy command from the Edit menu, click cell E11, and choose the Paste command. Figure 8-22 shows the result. Interestingly, the numbers in cells E11:E16 are not array formulas but are numeric values. For example, cell E11 contains the value –745.93583457547. Apparently, Excel changes the results of the table from a set of array formulas to their numeric values when you copy the results from the table range.

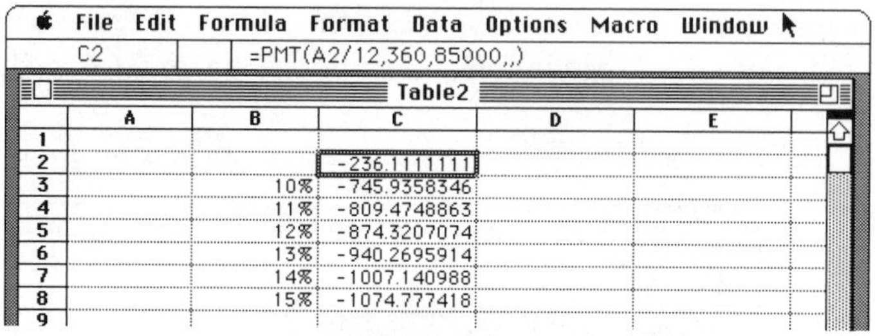

FIGURE 8-21. *This figure computes monthly loan payments with a new loan amount.*

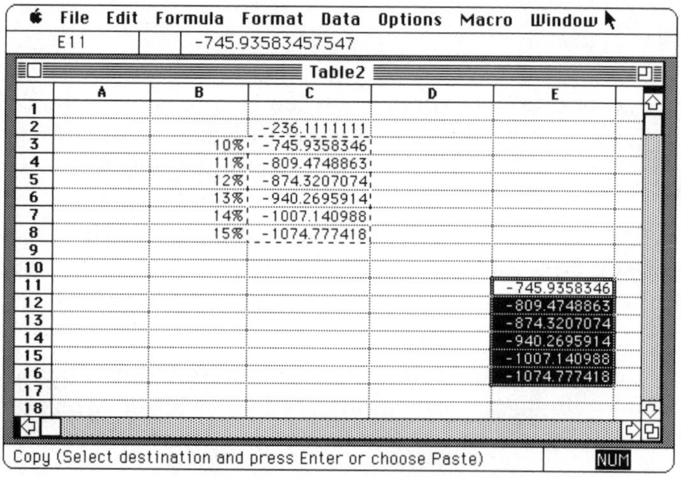

FIGURE 8-22. *Copying the results range to another range transfers the numeric values, not the formulas.*

Horizontal tables

In Excel, you can also create horizontal data tables. For example, Figure 8-23 shows a horizontal version of the simple one-equation vertical data table for the $100,000 loan. In the new table, the input values are in cells B3:G3. The formula

=PMT(A2/12,360,100000,,)

is in cell A4. Notice that this table formula also refers to cell A2, which is the input cell for the table.

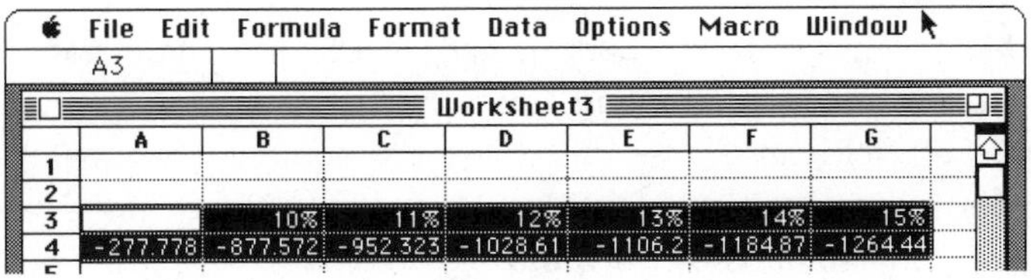

FIGURE 8-23. *This figure shows a horizontal version of the table in Figure 8-20.*

To construct this table, you first select the range A3:G4 (the smallest rectangular range that includes all of the input values and the table formula), then you choose the Table... command. Because in this table the input values are stored in a row, this time you must enter the input cell reference, $A$2, in the Row Input Cell field. When you press Enter or click OK to lock in this entry, Excel computes the table shown in Figure 8-23.

As before, Excel has entered a series of TABLE formulas in the results range of the table. This time, however, the formulas are

{=TABLE(A2,)}

Notice that in this formula the reference to the input cell is before the comma. Whenever you enter the input cell reference in the Row Input Cell field, the reference comes before the comma in the TABLE formula. When you enter the input cell reference in the Column Input Cell field, the reference to the input cell follows the comma in the TABLE formula.

Tables with two formulas

You can include as many formulas as you want in a one-variable data table. The second formula is entered in the cell immediately to the right of the cell that contains the first ("main") formula when the input range is a column. Other formulas are entered in the same row to the right of the second formula.

For example, let's expand the first example table in Figure 8-20 to include two formulas. Suppose you are thinking about buying a house that will require you to take out a $90,000 mortgage instead. You want to know what your monthly payments will be on that mortgage at each of the interest rates in the input range, and you want to be able to compare these payments easily with those for the $100,000 mortgage.

The first step in creating this new table is to enter the formula

=PMT(A2/12,360,90000,,)

in cell D2. Notice that, like the first formula, this table formula also refers to cell A2, the input cell.

Next, select the new table range, B2:D8. After you have done this, you can choose the Table... command, enter the input cell reference, $A$2, in the Column Input Cell field, and press Enter. After a moment, Excel enters the results for the new formula in the range D3:D8, as shown in Figure 8-24. As before, each cell in the range D3:D8 contains the formula

{=TABLE(,A2)}

These formulas compute the result of the formula in cell D2 at each of the interest rates in the input range. For example, the formula in cell D4 computes the result of the formula in cell D2 at the rate in cell B4: 11 percent.

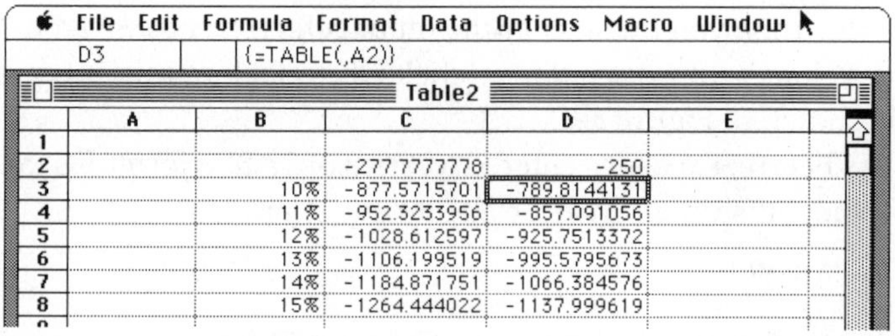

	File	Edit	Formula	Format	Data	Options	Macro	Window
D3			{=TABLE(,A2)}					

Table2

	A	B	C	D	E
1					
2			-277.7777778	-250	
3		10%	-877.5715701	-789.8144131	
4		11%	-952.3233956	-857.091056	
5		12%	-1028.612597	-925.7513372	
6		13%	-1106.199519	-995.5795673	
7		14%	-1184.871751	-1066.384576	
8		15%	-1264.444022	-1137.999619	

FIGURE 8-24. *We computed the monthly payments on two loan amounts at varying interest rates.*

Indirect references to the input cell

In the three examples presented so far, the data-table formulas have referred directly to the input cell. However, you can also create data tables that have formulas that refer indirectly to the input cell.

For example, consider the worksheet in Figure 8-25. The formula for the data table in this worksheet

=B4

is in cell C6. This formula is a simple reference to cell B4, which contains the formula

=PMT(B2/12,B3,B1)

This formula computes the monthly payments on the mortgage described by the entries in cells B1, B2, and B3.

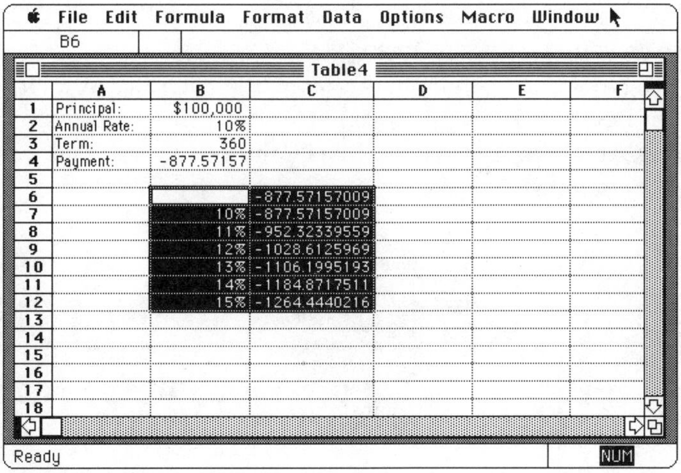

FIGURE 8-25. *In this data table, the formula in cell C6 refers to cell B4, which contains a formula that refers to the input cell, B2.*

To compute this table, you first select the table range, B6:C12, then choose the Table… command. Next, you specify the input cell. In this example, B2 is the input cell. Because the input values in this table are stored in a column, you should enter the input cell reference into the Column Input Cell field. When you press Enter or click OK to lock in the input cell reference, Excel computes the table.

Notice that, although the table formula in C6 in Figure 8-25 does not refer directly to the input cell, B2, there is an indirect link between them: The formula in cell C6 refers to cell B4, and the formula in cell B4 in turn refers to cell B2. As long as there is at least this kind of indirect link between the table formula and the input cell, the table works properly.

Also notice that the input cell in this table contains an entry. This is no problem for Microsoft Excel. In fact, in most cases the input cell of your data tables will contain entries.

Two-variable tables

All of the data tables we have considered so far have been alike in one important way: In each case, we computed the results of a formula as we varied a single variable, the interest rate. However, Microsoft Excel also allows you to create data tables that compute the results of a formula as two variables change.

Continuing with the previous scenario, suppose you want to build a data table that computes the monthly payment on a $100,000 mortgage, but this time you want to vary not only the interest rate, but also the term of the mortgage. You want to know what effect a term of 30, 25, 20, or 15 years (360, 300, 240, or 180 months) will have on your monthly payment.

The first step in creating this table is to enter the six interest rates you want to test in the range B4:B9. Next, you enter the different terms you want to test in the range C3:F3. Your screen looks like Figure 8-26. Notice that we've entered the term in months, not years.

	A	B	C	D	E	F
1						
2						
3			180	240	300	360
4		10%				
5		11%				
6		12%				
7		13%				
8		14%				
9		15%				
10						

FIGURE 8-26. *This is a two-variable table, after you have entered the interest rate values and the term values.*

Note: For convenience, we have positioned all of the example data tables in the upper-left corner of the worksheet. However, there are no restrictions on the position of a data table. You can create a data table in any part of the worksheet.

Now, you're ready to create the table formula. Because this is a two-variable table, the formula must be put in the cell at the intersection of the row and column that contain the two sets of input values—cell B3 in this example. The formula for this table is

=PMT(A1/12,B1,100000)

Notice that this formula, shown in Figure 8-27, refers to two blank cells, A1 and B1. In just a moment, you will define those cells as the input cells for the table. Because both of these cells are blank, the table formula returns the #DIV/0! error message. This is a spurious result that does not affect the performance of the table.

Next, you must select the table range. Just as with the one-variable table, the table range for a two-variable table is the smallest rectangular range that includes all of the input values and the table formula. In this example, the table range is therefore B3:F9.

After you have selected this range, you are ready to use the Table... command and define the input cells. Because this is a two-variable data table, you must define two input cells: one for the input values stored in column B, and one for the input values stored in row 3. As you can see in Figure 8-28, the reference for the first input cell, $A$1, should be entered in the Column Input Cell field, and the reference for the second input cell, $B$1, should be entered in the Row Input Cell field, either by typing in each cell reference or by clicking the pertinent cell.

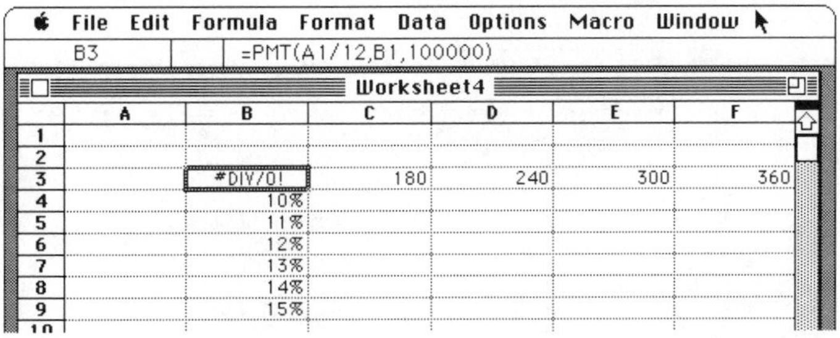

FIGURE 8-27. *The table formula has been entered in cell B3.*

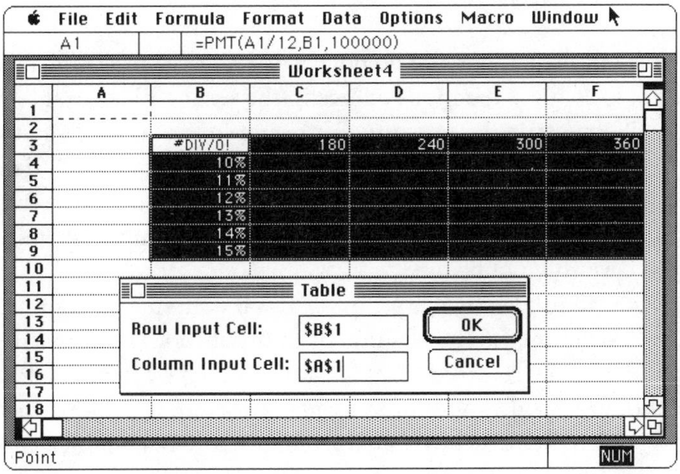

FIGURE 8-28. *You have entered the input cells for a two-variable table in the Table dialog box.*

After the input cells have been entered, press Enter or click OK to compute the table. The result is shown in Figure 8-29 on the next page. As in the previous examples, Excel has entered a TABLE formula in each of the cells in the results range, C4:F9. Because this table has two sets of variables, the TABLE formulas include the two references

{=TABLE(B1,A1)}

The numbers in the results range are the monthly payments required to amortize the mortgage at each combination of interest rates and terms. For example, the number in cell D7, –1171.5757, is the payment required to amortize a $100,000 mortgage over 240 months at an annual interest rate of 13 percent.

⚹ File Edit Formula Format Data Options Macro Window ▸

D7	{=TABLE(B1,A1)}

▤◻	Worksheet4	⊡▣

	A	B	C	D	E	F
1						
2						
3			#DIV/0!	180.0000	240.0000	300.0000	360.0000
4			10%	-1074.6051	-965.0216	-908.7007	-877.5716
5			11%	-1136.5969	-1032.1884	-980.1131	-952.3234
6			12%	-1200.1681	-1101.0861	-1053.2241	-1028.6126
7			13%	-1265.2422	-1171.5757	-1127.8353	-1106.1995
8			14%	-1331.7414	-1243.5208	-1203.7610	-1184.8718
9			15%	-1399.5871	-1316.7896	-1280.8306	-1264.4440
10							

FIGURE 8-29. *We computed the monthly payments on varying loan amounts at varying interest rates.*

It is important that you do not reverse the input cells in a two-variable table. If you do, Excel uses the input values in the wrong place in the table formula, creating a set of meaningless results. For example, if you reversed the input cells in this example, entering the reference $A$1 in the Row Input Cell field and the reference $B$1 in the Column Input Cell field, Excel would use the numbers in the range C3:F3 as interest rates and the numbers in the range B4:B9 as terms. The results would certainly not be what you wanted.

We have used cells A1, A2, and B1 as the input cells in our examples, but there are no restrictions on the position of an input cell. The only rule about an input cell is that it must be referred to, at least indirectly, by the table formula.

Although you can include as many formulas as you want in a one-variable table, you can include only one formula in a two-variable table.

One further note about tables: The calculation of tables in Microsoft Excel slows the calculation of a worksheet. Every time you change a value, name, or formula, Excel recalculates all formulas that depend on the changed value, name, or formula. You can turn off calculation of tables by changing the default setting in the Calculation dialog box. When the Calculation dialog box is open, simply activate the Automatic Except Tables option. When you do this, Excel can calculate your worksheets more quickly. (We discuss the features of the Calculation dialog box in Chapters 2, 4, 7, and 13.)

Linking worksheets

In Microsoft Excel, you can have many different worksheets active at the same time. Each active worksheet occupies its own window on the desktop. What is really exciting about Excel is that it allows you to create links between different worksheets, so that the formulas in one worksheet can be *dependent* on the values in another *supporting* worksheet. You'll find a number of advantages to linking worksheets. First, you can break large, complex worksheet models into more manageable portions. For example, instead of placing all your company's budget data in one model, you might create several departmental budgets. Then, you can create a master budget worksheet to draw relevant data from the individual department models. Linked worksheets also give you the flexibility to extract any number of reports and analyses from a group of supporting worksheets.

In addition to creating more manageable and flexible models, linked worksheets can save recalculation time and memory. You can keep only the data you need open in your workspace at any given time. As long as you use simple dependent formulas, Excel can read the relevant data from disk to ensure that your linked references are always up to date.

Creating links

Creating a formula that links two worksheets is almost as easy as creating any other formula. The only difference between a formula that refers to a cell in another worksheet and a regular formula is that you must include the name of the remote worksheet, followed by an exclamation mark, in a *dependent formula* that links the two worksheets.

For example, consider the two worksheets shown in Figure 8-30 on the next page. Suppose you want to link cell A1 in the worksheet named *LinkTest1* to cell A10 in the worksheet named *LinkTest2*. To enter the formula in cell A1 of *LinkTest1*, you select the cell, type an equal sign, then activate the *LinkTest2* worksheet and select cell A10. However, there is an alternate way to paste the linked reference in *LinkTest1*. You can paste the reference by first activating the cell and worksheet you want to refer to—cell A10 of *LinkTest2*—choosing the Copy command, and then activating the dependent worksheet and choosing the Paste Link command from the Edit menu. Figure 8-31 on the next page shows the screen as it looks with this formula in place. Notice that cell A1 in *LinkTest1* has assumed the value of cell A10 in *LinkTest2*.

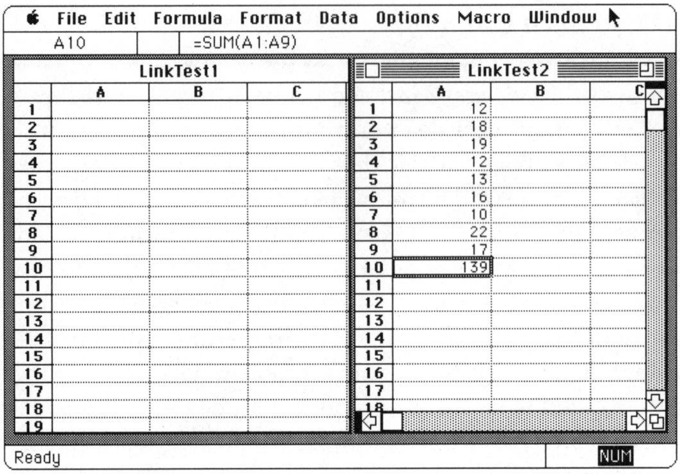

FIGURE 8-30. *Two worksheets before linking.*

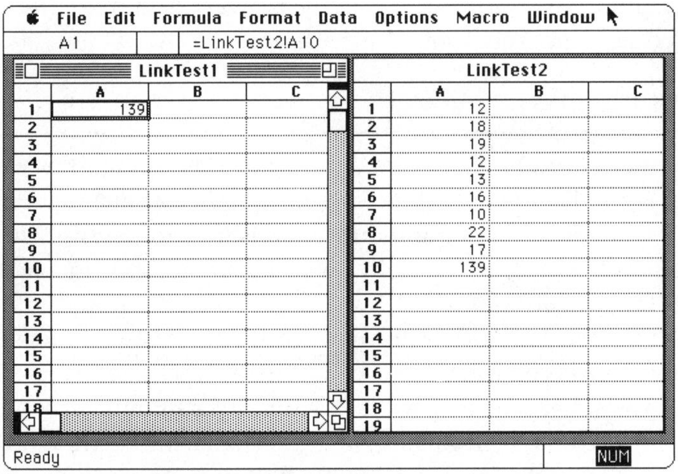

FIGURE 8-31. *The same worksheets after linking.*

The Paste Link command allows you to create simple dependent formulas such as linked array references. (We discuss the difference between simple and complex dependent formulas shortly.) For example, you can use Paste Link to create a linked array formula that refers to cells A1:A9 in *LinkTest2*. To do this, select cells A1:A9 in *LinkTest2*, choose the Copy command, activate *LinkTest1*, select the cell you want to use as the first cell in your linked array formula, and choose

Paste Link. Excel automatically selects an array range the same size and shape as the copy range and enters the dependent formula

{=LinkTest2!$A$1:$A$9}

in each cell of the range.

Excel also lets you type dependent formulas directly into a worksheet. Using the example from Figure 8-30, you can click cell A1 in *LinkTest1* and type the dependent formula

=LinkTest2!A10

The result is the same as that shown in Figure 8-31.

Names serve the same purpose as cell references in dependent formulas. For example, if cell A10 in *LinkTest2* is named *Test*, then the formula

=LinkTest2!Test

is identical to

=LinkTest2!A10

You can also create formulas that refer to entire ranges in the supporting worksheet. For example, suppose you want to enter a formula in cell A2 of *LinkTest1* that averages the values in cells A1:A9 in *LinkTest2*. To do this, you enter the formula

=AVERAGE(LinkTest2!A1:A9)

in cell A2 of *LinkTest1* to get the result 15.4444444.

You can also use the pasting technique to build simple dependent formulas, as we showed you earlier in our discussion about creating links. For example, suppose you want to enter the formula

=LinkTest2!A10

in cell A1 of *LinkTest1*. You can do this by clicking cell A1 in *LinkTest1*, typing an equal sign, clicking somewhere in the window of *LinkTest2*, and then clicking cell A10. When you press Enter to confirm the entry, Excel enters the formula

=LinkTest2!$A$10

in cell A1 of *LinkTest1*. Notice that the reference to cell A10 in *LinkTest2* is absolute. When you use pasting to build dependent formulas, Excel always assumes that you want the reference to be absolute.

Linking several worksheets

Microsoft Excel also lets you build formulas that link several worksheets at once. For example, suppose you have created three worksheets: *Worksheet1*, *Worksheet2*, and *Worksheet3*. You want to build a formula in cell A1 of *Worksheet1* that totals the values in cell A1 of *Worksheet2* and cell A1 of *Worksheet3*. You can do this by entering the dependent formula

    =Worksheet2!A1+Worksheet3!A1

into cell A1 of *Worksheet1*.

Saving linked worksheets

You probably remember from Chapter 1, "Introducing Microsoft Excel," that you should use the Save As... command from the File menu to give your worksheets descriptive names when you save them. For example, suppose you are modeling your company's 1989 budget in a worksheet called *Worksheet1*.

Now, suppose that another active worksheet, called *Actual*, contains links to your budget worksheet and is therefore dependent on the budget worksheet for some of its information. These links identify the budget worksheet as *Worksheet1*. When you are ready to end your session, you use the Save As... command to save *Worksheet1* as *Budget89*. If you use Save As... while *Actual* is still active, all of the references to *Worksheet1* in the *Actual* worksheet change to *Budget89*. For example, if *Actual* contains a reference like

    =Worksheet1!A1

it changes to

    =Budget89!A1

If, on the other hand, you save and close *Actual* before you save and rename *Worksheet1*, Excel displays the warning *Save with references to unsaved documents?* If you click OK, Excel saves *Actual*. However, if you then use Save As... to save *Worksheet1* as *Budget89*, Excel doesn't update the references to *Worksheet1* in *Actual*. The dependent formulas in *Actual* continue to assume that the budget worksheet is named *Worksheet1*.

When you then reopen *Actual*, Excel asks you if you want to *Update references to unopened documents?* If you click OK, Excel is unable to find the worksheet *Worksheet1* and displays the dialog box shown in Figure 8-32. Normally, when you see this dialog box you select the file or insert the disk that contains the file Excel is searching for in the disk drive. However, because *Worksheet1* doesn't exist any more (it's now called *Budget89*), Excel will never be able to update any references to that worksheet.

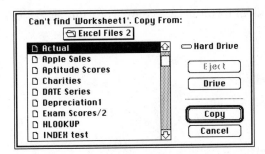

FIGURE 8-32. *This is the Can't Find dialog box.*

For this reason, whenever you create a set of linked worksheets, always save the supporting worksheet or worksheets first and the dependent worksheets last. If you see the *Save with references...* message, you should click Cancel and save the supporting worksheets before you save the dependent ones.

Calculating dependent formulas

When you open a worksheet that depends on other worksheets, or when you create a formula that refers to another worksheet, Excel attempts to evaluate all of the dependent formulas in the opened worksheet. The program first checks to see whether the worksheets to which the dependent formulas refer are open. If the supporting worksheets are open, Excel reads the correct values from those worksheets and calculates the dependent formulas. If the supporting worksheets are closed, however, things are a bit trickier.

Two kinds of dependent formulas

Excel recognizes two kinds of dependent formulas: simple dependent formulas and complex dependent formulas.

Simple dependent formulas include only absolute references to cells or ranges of cells in another worksheet, by name or by address, or named constant values. For example, the formulas

=Worksheet2!$A$1

and

{=Worksheet2!$A$1:$A$10}

are simple dependent formulas. The formula

=Worksheet2!Test

is a simple dependent formula if the name *Test* describes a single cell (such as $A$1), a range (such as $A$1:$A$10), or a constant (such as 100).

All other dependent formulas are complex formulas. For example, the following formulas

=Worksheet2!A1

=Worksheet2!A1+1

=SUM(Worksheet2!A1:A10)

and

=Worksheet2!A1+Worksheet3!A1

are all complex dependent formulas. If *Test* describes a formula like A1–A2, then

=Worksheet2!Test

is also a complex dependent formula.

The distinction between simple and complex dependent formulas becomes important when you open a dependent worksheet without opening its supporting worksheets, or when you create a dependent formula that refers to a closed worksheet. Excel can only evaluate simple dependent formulas that refer to closed worksheets. Excel cannot evaluate complex formulas that refer to closed worksheets because those formulas would have to be recalculated to return a meaningful value, and the worksheet must be open for a recalculation to occur.

If you create a formula that includes a simple reference to a closed worksheet, Excel attempts to evaluate that formula automatically. If the supporting worksheet to which the dependent formula refers is on an active disk, Microsoft Excel immediately reads the appropriate value from that worksheet. If the worksheet to which the dependent formula refers is not in an active folder on your hard drive or on an active disk, Excel prompts you to find the worksheet or to insert the disk that contains that worksheet.

For example, suppose you enter the formula

=Worksheet2!$A$1

in cell A1 of *Worksheet1*. If *Worksheet2* is closed, but in the active folder, Excel immediately reads the value from cell A1 of *Worksheet2* and displays that value in cell A1 of *Worksheet1*.

If *Worksheet2* is not in the active folder, Excel displays a dialog box like the one already shown in Figure 8-32. From this dialog box, you can tell Excel to look in a different folder or disk drive for the file *Worksheet2*.

If you have made an error, you can use the Cancel button to cancel the search for *Worksheet2*. If you choose this option, the formula displays a zero in the cell that contains the formula with the external reference.

Alternatively, you can use the Copy option in the Can't Find dialog box to copy values from any of the files already on the active disk. To use this option, click the name of the file you want to read from, then click Copy. Excel copies the corresponding values from the selected file and uses these as temporary values in the dependent worksheet.

If, on the other hand, you create a formula that contains a complex reference to a closed worksheet, Microsoft Excel cannot evaluate the formula until you open the worksheet to which the formula refers. The formula instead returns the #REF! error message.

Opening a dependent worksheet

When you save a worksheet that contains external references, Excel remembers the last values of those references. When you open a worksheet that contains external references, Excel at first assigns the external references their old values. This is true for both simple and complex external values.

Remember, however, that the supporting cells may not have the same value when you open a dependent worksheet that they had when you closed the worksheet. If you have opened and used the supporting worksheet since you last used the dependent worksheet, it is likely that the values of some of the cells in the supporting worksheet, to which the formulas in the dependent worksheet refer, have changed.

Fortunately, as soon as a worksheet that contains external references is opened, Excel displays the alert box shown in Figure 8-33. This alert box allows you to instruct Excel to read from the closed worksheets on the disk the current values of the cells to which the formulas refer.

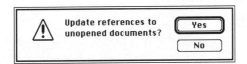

FIGURE 8-33. *This is the Update Reference alert box.*

If you click No, Excel opens the dependent worksheet without updating any references to the supporting worksheets. All of the simple external references in the worksheet retain their last-saved values. The values of all the complex references in the worksheet change from the last saved value to the #REF! error message.

If you click OK, Excel first attempts to find the supporting worksheets on the current disk drive. If Excel finds them there, it reads the values from the supporting files and updates the simple external references in the dependent worksheet.

Excel does not open the supporting worksheets. It merely reads the appropriate values from those worksheets.

As already mentioned, if Excel cannot find one or more of the supporting files on the current disk drive, it displays a dialog box like the one shown in Figure 8-32. From this dialog box, you can choose to cancel the update process, change folders, change the active disk drive, or copy an existing file to create the file Excel is looking for.

Updating complex references

As you have seen, Excel cannot evaluate complex dependent formulas that refer to closed worksheets. If you create a complex formula with a reference to a closed worksheet, or if you open a worksheet that contains a complex formula with a reference to a closed worksheet, the formula returns the #REF! error message.

Until you actually open the worksheet to which the complex reference refers, Excel cannot evaluate the dependent formula. When you open the supporting worksheet and calculate the dependent worksheet, Microsoft Excel reads the values that it needs from the supporting worksheet and properly evaluates the complex formula.

For example, suppose you have created a linked pair of worksheets, *Worksheet1* and *Worksheet2*. Cell A1 in *Worksheet1* contains the complex dependent formula

    =SUM(Worksheet2!A1:A10)

If you open *Worksheet1* while *Worksheet2* is closed, Excel cannot evaluate the complex dependent formula and cell A1 returns the #REF! error message. If you then open *Worksheet2*, Excel reads the values from the range A1:A10 in *Worksheet2* and evaluates the formula correctly.

The Links... command

The File menu's Links... command is a convenient way to open all of the worksheets on which another worksheet depends with one command. In many ways, this command is like the Open... command. The main difference between the two is that Open... presents a list of all the files on the disk in the current drive, while Links... limits the list to those files that support the active worksheet.

For example, suppose you are building a worksheet, *Worksheet3*, that depends on two other worksheets, *Worksheet1* and *Worksheet2*. *Worksheet1* and *Worksheet2* are currently closed, but you want to open them so that the complex dependent formulas in *Worksheet3* can be calculated. To open these worksheets, you can choose the Links... command. When you choose Links..., Excel displays the dialog box shown in Figure 8-34. Notice that the file list includes only the two files that support *Worksheet3*.

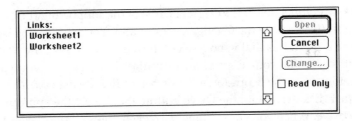

FIGURE 8-34. *This is the Links dialog box.*

You are now ready to open *Worksheet1* and *Worksheet2*. Although you could open both of the supporting worksheets individually, it is more efficient to open both of them at once. To do this, you drag across both names while holding down the Shift key. If you now click Open, Excel opens both of the worksheets on which *Worksheet3* depends.

If the supporting file you want to open is not in the disk drive, Excel displays a dialog box warning you that Links can't find the file. Once you supply the files and choose the Links... command again, clicking Open instructs Excel to open the supporting files. Clicking Cancel cancels the Links... command.

Although you will usually open all of the supporting worksheets at once, you can open them one at a time. To do this, you simply double click the name of *Worksheet1*. After a moment, *Worksheet1* opens onto the desktop. Now, you could repeat the Links... command to open *Worksheet2*. If you use the command immediately after *Worksheet1* is opened, however, you will not get the result you expected. Because *Worksheet1* is now the active worksheet, when you choose the Links... command, Microsoft Excel displays a list of any worksheets that support *Worksheet1* instead of those that support *Worksheet3*.

Because you want the list to show the worksheets that support *Worksheet3*, you need to activate that worksheet after you open *Worksheet1* and before you repeat the Links... command. (If *Worksheet1* is large, you may need to shrink it a bit before you can click *Worksheet3*.) Then, once *Worksheet3* is active, you can repeat the Links... command, select *Worksheet2* from the list of supporting worksheets, and click Open.

Of course, you don't have to use the Links... command. Supporting worksheets can be opened with the Open... command, and their links to the dependent worksheet are still maintained.

Redirecting Links

If you've changed the name of a supporting worksheet or moved it to another directory, you need to redirect your linked references to let Microsoft Excel know where to find the supporting data for your dependent formulas. To redirect your worksheet links, select the original name of the supporting file or files in the Links list box, then choose the Change… command. You see a dialog box like the one in Figure 8-35. In this dialog box, select the name of the new file or renamed file you want to use for your dependent formulas. If necessary, you can choose a new directory from the drop-down list on top of the file list box. You also can activate another disk drive with the Drive button, then select the appropriate file from the new drive. When you click Change, Excel changes all references to the supporting worksheet to use the new file name.

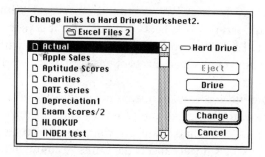

FIGURE 8-35. *When you use the Change button to redirect your worksheet links, you see a dialog box like this one.*

Copying, cutting, and pasting in linked worksheets

Just as you can use absolute or relative references to cells within a single worksheet in Excel, you can also use absolute or relative references to cells in other worksheets. Absolute and relative references to cells in supporting worksheets respond to the Copy, Cut, and Paste commands in much the same way as absolute and relative references to cells in the same worksheet.

For example, suppose you have created the formula

    =Worksheet2!Z1

in cell A1 of *Worksheet1*, and you have used the Copy and Paste commands to copy this formula into cell B1. The formula in cell B1 is

    =Worksheet2!AA1

Notice that the original formula changed when it was copied to cell B1 because the reference to cell Z1 in *Worksheet2* is relative. If, on the other hand, the formula in cell A1 in *Worksheet1* contained an absolute reference to cell Z1 in *Worksheet2*, as in

    =Worksheet2!$Z$1

the result of copying and pasting the formula in cell B1 would remain

=Worksheet2!$Z$1

Wherever you copied this formula, it would always refer to cell Z1 in *Worksheet2*.

Copying and pasting between worksheets

As you learned in Chapter 4, "Editing the Worksheet," Excel allows you to copy entries from one worksheet to another. In addition, you can also copy dependent formulas from one worksheet to another.

When you copy from one worksheet to another a dependent formula that includes a relative reference to yet another worksheet, that reference is adjusted to reflect the new position of the formula. For example, suppose cell A1 in *Worksheet1* contains the formula

=Worksheet2!A1

If you copy and paste that formula from cell A1 in *Worksheet1* into cell B5 in *Worksheet3*, the result is the formula

=Worksheet2!B5

As you can see, the formula is adjusted to take into account its new relative position.

If, on the other hand, you copy a formula that contains an absolute reference to another worksheet, that formula is not adjusted. For example, suppose cell A1 in *Worksheet1* contains the formula

=Worksheet2!$A$1

If you copy and paste that formula into cell B5 in *Worksheet3*, the resulting formula remains

=Worksheet2!$A$1

If you copy a dependent formula into the worksheet to which the formula refers, it continues to be a dependent formula. For example, if you copy the formula

=Worksheet2!A3

from cell A1 of *Worksheet1* into cell A1 of *Worksheet2*, the result is the formula

=Worksheet2!A3

Notice that this formula still includes a reference to the worksheet name *Worksheet2*, even though it now exists in the same worksheet.

Cutting and pasting between worksheets

Just as you can copy and paste a dependent formula from one worksheet to another, you can also cut a dependent formula and paste it into another worksheet. Cutting and pasting dependent formulas is no different from cutting and pasting regular formulas. The main thing to keep in mind is that Excel does not adjust the references in a dependent formula when you cut it from one worksheet and paste it into another.

For example, suppose cell A1 in *Worksheet1* contains the formula

    =Worksheet2!A1

If you cut that formula and paste it into cell B5 of *Worksheet3*, the result is still the formula

    =Worksheet2!A1

As you can see, Excel did not adjust the reference to cell A1 in *Worksheet2* when this formula was cut.

Cutting and pasting cells that are referred to by dependent formulas

In Chapter 4, "Editing the Worksheet," you learned that when you cut and paste cells, Excel adjusts any references to those cells in the formulas of the worksheet. Unfortunately, this isn't true for formulas in other worksheets that refer to the cut-and-pasted cells with explicit cell references. When you cut and paste a cell that is referred to by a formula in another worksheet, that formula is not adjusted to reflect the change unless the cell is a named cell.

For example, suppose you have created the formula

    =Worksheet2!A10

in cell A1 in *Worksheet1*. If you use the Cut and Paste commands to move the entry in cell A10 of *Worksheet2* to cell B10 of *Worksheet2*, the formula in cell A1 of *Worksheet1* remains

    =Worksheet2!A10

Because cell A10 in *Worksheet2* is blank after the cut-and-paste operation, the formula in cell A1 of *Worksheet1* returns the result 0.

You can overcome this problem by using a name in the dependent formula. For example, suppose you name cell A10 in *Worksheet2 Test*, then enter the formula

    =Worksheet2!Test

in cell A1 of *Worksheet1*. Now, if you use Cut and Paste to move the entry in cell A10 of *Worksheet2* to cell B10 of *Worksheet2*, Excel automatically moves the name *Test* to cell B10 as well, and the link is preserved.

Using array formulas to link worksheets

You can also use array formulas to link several cells in one worksheet to several cells in another worksheet. For example, suppose you want to link cells A1:A10 in *WorksheetA* to cells B1:B10 in *WorksheetB*. You would first select the empty range A1:A10 in *WorksheetA*, then type the formula

=WorksheetB!$B$1:$B$10

Because you want this formula to be an array formula, press Command-Enter to lock it in. Figure 8-36 shows the screen at this point. Notice that every cell in the range A1:A10 in *WorksheetA* is linked to the corresponding cell in the range B1:B10 in *WorksheetB*. In fact, each cell in the range A1:A10 contains the array formula

{=WorksheetB!$B$1:$B$10}

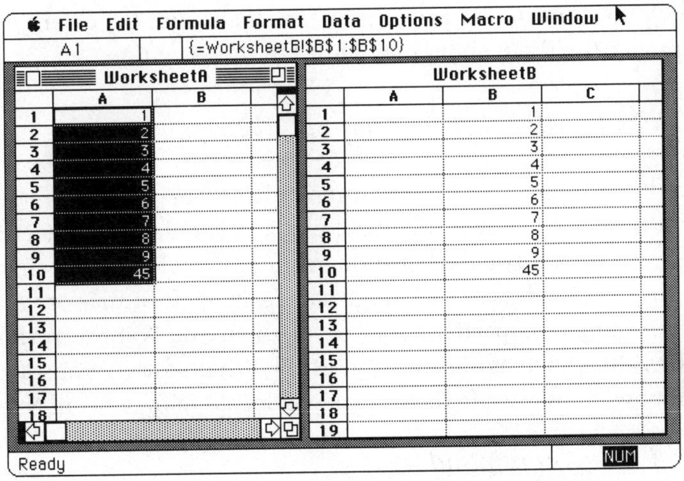

FIGURE 8-36. *You have used an array formula to link worksheets.*

Essentially, the most efficient way to create array formulas as a method to link worksheets is to use the Paste Link command as described in the "Creating links" section of this chapter.

Severing links between worksheets

If you want to cut the links between worksheets, you can use the Paste Special... command from the Edit menu to change all the external references in your dependent formula to constant values. (Of course, you won't be able to update the references, because all ties to the supporting worksheets will be removed.)

First, select the linked cell or cells and then choose, in turn, the Copy and Paste Special... commands from the Edit menu with the cells still selected. When the Paste Special dialog box appears, select the Values option and click OK. Excel then pastes the values of the linked cells over the formula linking the formula to the other worksheet.

Next, as a precaution, you can use the Find... command, which we discuss shortly, from the Formula menu to look for any dependent formulas you may have missed. Simply enter the exclamation point required in all dependent formulas in the Find What field, then select the Formulas option. When you click OK, Excel searches your worksheet for any references to supporting worksheets.

When a cell contains both an external reference and a formula, you can preserve the formula and also change the external reference to a constant value. To do this, select the cell; then, in the formula bar, select the portion of the cell that contains the external reference. Now, choose the Calculate Now command from the Options menu and press Enter. Excel changes the external reference to a constant value without changing the rest of the formula.

Locating and replacing strings

Imagine that you have built a large worksheet and you now need to find every formula in that worksheet that contains a particular character string or value. The Find... command on the Formula menu lets you locate any string of characters, including cell references and range names, in the formulas or values in a worksheet. This command is particularly useful when you want to find linked formulas or error values such as #NAME? or #REF!. What's more, you can use the Replace... command to overwrite the strings you locate with new entries.

The Find... command

To locate a character string, begin by selecting the range you want to search. If you want to look through the entire worksheet, select a single cell. Microsoft Excel begins its search from that cell, travels through the worksheet, and ends back in the selected cell. If you want to search only a portion of the worksheet, select the appropriate range.

When you choose the Find... command, Excel displays the dialog box shown in Figure 8-37. The first step in using this command is to specify the Find What string; that is, the group of characters you want Excel to search for. The string can include any letter, number, punctuation mark, or special character. You enter the string by typing it.

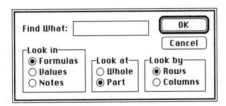

FIGURE 8-37. *This is the Find dialog box.*

Once you have specified the Find What string, you press Enter or click OK to begin the search. When you do this, Excel begins to search for an occurrence of the Find What string in the worksheet. If you select a range before you choose the Find... command, Excel searches for the Find What string in the cells of that range only. The search is governed by the settings in the Look By, Look In, and Look At boxes, which we cover next.

The Look By setting

The Look By setting instructs Excel to search by row or by column. When you select the Rows option, Excel begins looking through the worksheet row by row, starting with the currently selected cell. If it finds an occurrence of the Find What string, it highlights the cell that contains the occurrence and stops searching. If Excel does not find an occurrence before it reaches the last cell in the active portion of the worksheet, Excel goes back to cell A1 and continues to search through the worksheet until it either finds an occurrence or until it returns to the cell that was selected when the search began.

The Columns option works in almost the same way, except that it searches through the worksheet column by column, beginning with the selected cell.

The Look In setting

The Look In setting tells Excel whether you want to search the formulas, the values, or the notes in the worksheet for the Find What string. If you select Formulas, Excel searches for the string in the formulas contained in the worksheet's cells. If you select Values, Excel searches for the string in the displayed results of the entries in the worksheet. If you select Notes, Excel searches the text attached to the worksheet's cells, which you entered through the Info window.

The distinction between the first two Look In settings can be confusing. To understand the difference between the Formulas and Values options, you need to remember that the underlying contents of a cell and the displayed value of that cell are often two different things. For example, if a cell contains a formula (like =A1+B2), then the displayed value of the cell is usually the result of that formula—a number like 100 or a character string, if the formula involves text.

If a cell contains a pure number—like 100—then the displayed value of the cell may or may not agree with the cell's underlying contents. If the cell has been assigned the General format, then the displayed value of the cell and the cell's contents usually agree. If the cell contains a number that has been assigned another format, however, the contents of the cell and its displayed value are different. The contents and the displayed value of a cell that contains a text entry are almost always the same.

For example, consider the simple worksheet in Figure 8-38. Cells B2 and B3 in this worksheet both contain the number 1000. The entry in cell B2 has the General format, while the entry in cell B3 has been assigned the $#,##0 format. Cell C2 in this worksheet has been assigned the name *Test*. Cell C4 contains the formula

=Test+C3

which returns the value 1000. Cell E5 contains the text entry *Test*.

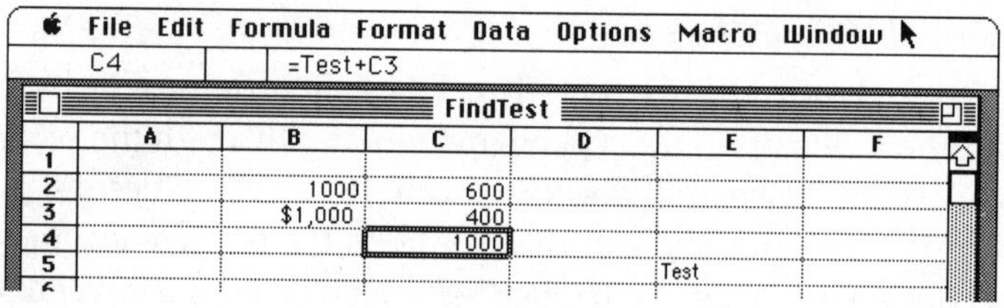

FIGURE 8-38. *We used this worksheet to experiment with the Find…* *command.*

Now, suppose you select cell A1, choose the Find… command, and type *1000* to specify the Find What string. If you select Values as the Look In setting, Excel first finds the occurrence of the string 1000 in cell B2. If you press Command-H, Excel next finds the occurrence of the string in the displayed value of cell C4.

Notice that Excel ignored the entry in cell B3 when we searched for the string 1000 with the Look In Values option. This cell was skipped because its displayed value, $1,000, does not precisely match the Find What string, 1000. Because we are searching values and not formulas, Excel ignores the fact that the underlying content of the cell is the number 1000.

Now, suppose that you once again select cell A1 and repeat the search, this time with the Formulas option selected. As before, Excel first finds the occurrence of the Find What string in cell B2. If you press Command-H, Excel highlights cell B3, which contains the value $1,000. Because you are now searching the formulas, and not the displayed values, of the cells, Excel ignores the format that has been assigned to this cell and matches the Find What string to the underlying contents of the cell.

If you press Command-H again, Excel once again highlights cell B2. Because this time you are searching the formulas and not the displayed values of the cells, the value in cell C4 is ignored by the search. Although this cell displays the value 1000, it actually contains the formula =Test+C3, which does not match the Find What string.

Let's look at one more example. If you specify *test* as the Find What string and accept the default selection (the Look In Formulas option), Microsoft Excel first finds the occurrence of *test* in the formula =Test+C3 and highlights the cell that contains that formula, cell C4. Note, however, that this search is not case-sensitive, so if you press Command-H, Excel highlights cell E5, which contains the entry *Test*. If you repeat the search, but this time select the Look In Values option, Excel finds only the occurrence of the string *test* in the text entry *Test* in cell E5.

The Look At setting

The Look At setting tells Excel whether to find only whole-word occurrences of the string or any occurrence of the string, even when it is a part of another string. For example, suppose a worksheet contains only two entries: the number 998 and the number 99. If you specify *99* as the Find What string and select Whole as the Look At option, Microsoft Excel finds only the entry 99. If you select the Part option, however, Excel finds both the entry 99—which matches the Find What string exactly—and the entry 998—which contains a string that matches the Find What string.

The Part option finds more occurrences of the string than the Whole option. The Whole option should be used on those occasions when you want to narrow the search to precise matches between the Find What string and the contents/displays of the cells in the worksheet.

E X C E L *tip*

Finding your way home

Once you choose the Find… command, there is no direct way to return to the cell from which you began the search. However, with a little advance planning, you should be able to find your way back. If you note the location of your starting point before you use the command, you can choose the Goto… command from the Formula menu to jump back to the starting cell when the search is completed. Alternatively, you could note the contents of the starting cell before you use the command and then use the Find… command to return to it after the search is completed.

Wildcard characters

You can use wildcard characters to widen the scope of your searches. Excel's Find... command accepts the two wildcard characters * and ?. Wildcards can be very helpful when you are searching for a group of similar, but not identical, entries, or when you are searching for an entry that you don't quite remember.

The ? character takes the place of any single character in the Find What string. For example, the Find What string *100?* matches the values 1000, 1001, 1002, 1003, and so on up to 1009. (It also matches entries like 100a, 100B, and so on.)

The * character takes the place of one or more characters in a Find What string. For example, the string *1** matches the entries 10, 15, 100, 1111, 10001, 123456789, 123 Maple Street, and 1-800-223-8720.

The * wildcard character need not be used only at the end of a Find What string. For example, you could use the string **s* to find all entries in the worksheet that end with the letter *s*. Or, you could use the string **es** to find each cell that contains the string sequence *es* anywhere in its formula or value.

Repeating the search

Once you have found the first occurrence of the Find What string, you can press Command-H to instruct Excel to search for the next occurrence. If there is another occurrence, Excel highlights that cell. If there is not, the highlight remains on the cell that contains the first occurrence of the string.

If the worksheet contains several occurrences of the string, then you can jump from occurrence to occurrence by repeatedly pressing Command-H. If you press Command-H while the highlight is on the last occurrence of the string, the highlight jumps back to the first occurrence. If you want to jump backward from occurrence to occurrence, you can press Shift-Command-H.

The Replace... command

The Replace... command allows you to locate and replace a specified character string with a new string. When you select the Replace... command from the Formula menu, you see a dialog box like the one in Figure 8-39. Simply type the character string you want to search for in the Replace field and type the string you want to substitute in the With field.

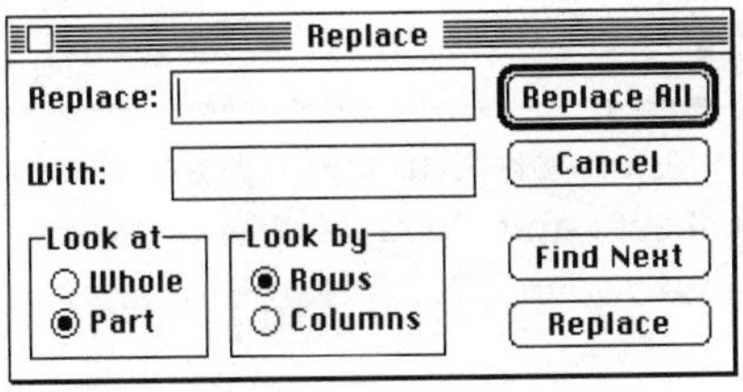

FIGURE 8-39. *You can use the Replace... command to replace a specified string with a new string.*

For example, suppose you want to replace one occurrence of the name *Joan Smith* with *John Smith* in a document. Type *Joan Smith* in the Replace field and *John Smith* in the With field. Click the Find Next button to move from one occurrence of the Replace string to the next without changing the contents of the current cell. When you locate an occurrence you want to change, use the Replace button to substitute the Replace string with the contents of the With field. After replacing the character string in the current cell, Excel automatically moves to the next occurrence.

If you want to replace every occurrence of the Replace string with the contents of the With field, choose the Replace All button. Instead of pausing at each occurrence to allow you to change or skip the current cell, Excel seeks out all the cells that contain the Replace string and changes them automatically.

You can also use wildcard characters (? and *) in the Replace field to broaden your search. For example, suppose you want to change all occurrences of the names *Joan Smith* and *John Smith* to *John Smythe*. Begin by typing *Jo*n Smith* in the Replace field and *John Smythe* in the With field, then click the Replace All button. Excel changes all instances of both *John Smith* and *Joan Smith* to *John Smythe*. Remember not to enter a wildcard character in the With field. If you do, Excel uses a literal ? or * as it replaces each occurrence of your Replace text.

The Look At and Look By settings allow you to direct your search even more precisely. If you select the Whole option in the Look At portion of the dialog box, Excel matches the character you want to find with the entire formula or value in the cell. The Part option, chosen by default, tells Excel to match the characters you want to find with any part of the formula or value in the cell. The Rows option in the Look By portion of the dialog box, chosen by default, tells Excel to search horizontally through columns. The Columns option tells Excel to search vertically through columns.

Worksheet auditing and documentation

Microsoft Excel offers a number of powerful and flexible commands that help you audit and debug your worksheets and document your work. In this section, we look at cell notes, the Info window, and the Select Special... command.

Cell notes

Excel's notes feature lets you attach notes to cells to document your work, explain calculations and assumptions, or provide reminders. Simply select the cell you want to work with, then select Note... from the Formula menu. You'll see a dialog box like the one in Figure 8-40. Notice that the reference to the active cell appears in the Cell field at the top of the window. Type your entry in the Note field and click Add or OK to attach the note to the active cell. When you click OK, Excel closes the window and returns to the worksheet. When you click Add, the window remains open so that you can edit or add additional notes.

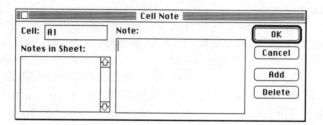

FIGURE 8-40. *You have used the Note... command to attach a note to a cell.*

Although you can attach only one note to a cell, you can make your note text as long as you like. As you make entries in the Note field, Excel automatically wraps text from one line to the next. Don't use the Return key to insert line breaks, or you'll lock in the note and close the dialog box. If you want to begin a new paragraph of Note text, press Command-Return.

Although creating extremely long notes seems to contradict the idea behind the notes feature, you can use the Up and Down arrow keys (and the Home and End keys on extended keyboards) to move through long notes.

After you add a note to a cell, the cell reference and the first few characters of that note appear in the Notes In Sheet list box on the left side of the window. To edit a note, you can select it from the list box, activate the Note field, and then make your changes.

However, Excel doesn't allow you to use the cut-and-paste techniques from the Edit menu. You can use the Delete button to delete the selected note. (You can also use the Notes option in the Clear dialog box to remove notes from a cell or from a range of cells.)

While the Note window is active, you can also select other cells, to edit their notes or add new notes. First, activate the Cell field and type a reference, or use the mouse or arrow key to select a cell. (If the window blocks your view of the cell you want to select, you can move it by dragging the title bar.) After selecting the cell you want, reactivate the Note field by clicking the box. Then, edit the contents of this field just as you would edit an entry in the formula bar.

While working in the worksheet window, you can review, edit, or delete your notes by double clicking the cell you want to work with. The Note window reappears and the note for the active cell is displayed.

In addition to using the OK button, you can close the Note window by clicking the Cancel button or by clicking the close box on the title bar. Cancel does not undo any additions or deletions you've already locked in. It simply cancels any new entries in the Note field and removes the Note window from your screen.

You can print your notes by choosing the Notes option in the Print dialog box, described in Chapter 9, or by printing the contents of the Info window.

The Info window

The Info window offers a great way to monitor the status of the cells in your worksheet. Using this special window, you can quickly see all the "vital statistics" on the active cell. To open an Info window, select a cell and choose the Show Info command from the Window menu. Figure 8-41 shows a sample Info window.

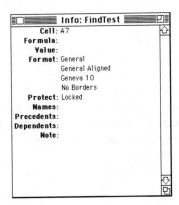

FIGURE 8-41. *You can use the Info window to monitor the status of your cells.*

Notice that the contents of the application menu bar change when the Info window is active. The Edit, Formula, Format, Data, and Options menus disappear and a new menu called Info takes their place. Initially, you see only three pieces of information in the Info window: the cell reference, the underlying formula in the cell, and any note attached to the cell. However, you can use the commands on the Info menu to display more information. The Info menu offers nine display options: Cell, Formula, Value, Format, Protection, Names, Precedents (a list of cells the active cell refers to), Dependents (a list of cells that refer to the active cell), and Note. All the commands on the Info menu are toggle commands. A check mark appears beside those currently selected. (We selected all nine display options in Figure 8-41.) To deselect a display option, simply choose that option again.

To toggle between the active worksheet and the Info window, use the Show Document and Show Info commands on the Window menu. Alternatively, if you want to keep the Info window in view as you work in your worksheet, resize and reposition the worksheet and Info windows so that they don't overlap. (To quickly arrange the windows on your screen, choose the Arrange All command from the Window menu.)

To print the contents of the Info window, select the cell or range for which you want to print information (the entire worksheet, if you like), then activate the Info window and choose the Print command. (For more information about printing, see Chapter 9, "Printing the Worksheet.")

The Select Special... command

Select Special... is a powerful debugging and auditing tool which lets you quickly find cells that meet certain specifications. For example, suppose you find an error in a formula and want to trace all the cells that support the formula, to locate your mistake. You can use the Precedents option in the Select Special dialog box to locate all the direct and indirect precedents.

When you choose the Select Special... command from the Formula menu, you see a dialog box like the one in Figure 8-42 on the next page. The options in the Select Special dialog box allow you to specify certain selection criteria. When you select one of these options and then click OK, Excel highlights the cell or cells that match the criteria you select. If you select a range of cells before opening the Select Special dialog box, Excel searches only the selected range. If only a single cell is active, Excel searches the entire worksheet.

Several of the Select Special options, such as Notes, Precedents, and Dependents, may result in multiple discontinuous ranges. To navigate through these selections, you use the Return and Tab keys to move down or to the right one cell at a time. Shift-Return and Shift-Tab let you move up or to the left one cell at a time.

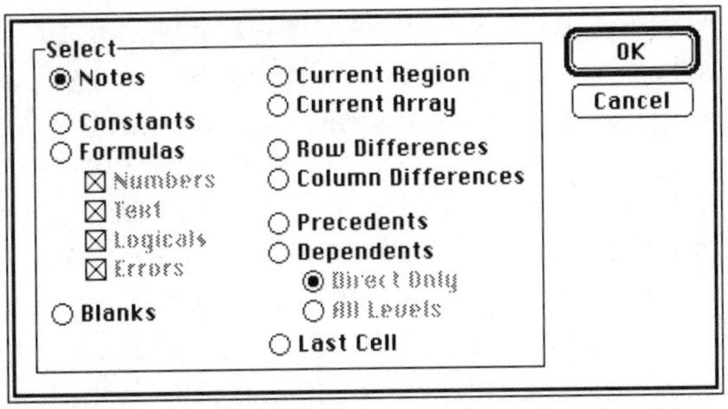

FIGURE 8-42. *The Select Special dialog box is a handy auditing and debugging tool.*

The Constants, Formulas, and Blanks options locate cells that contain specified types of entries. When you select either the Constants or the Formulas option, Microsoft Excel activates the Numbers, Text, Logicals, and Errors options as well. Use these options to narrow your selection criteria.

The Current Region option is handy when you're working in a large, complex worksheet and need to select blocks of cells. (A region, as you may recall, is defined as a continuous rectangular block of cells bounded by blank rows, blank columns, or worksheet borders.) When you select Current Region, your search is limited to the area of the worksheet.

If the selected cell is part of an array range, you can use the Current Array option to select all the cells in the array.

The Row Differences and Column Differences options let you spot potential inconsistencies by comparing the entries in a range of cells. The first step in using these debugging tools is always to select the range of cells you want to compare. The position of the active cell in your selection determines which cell or cells Excel uses to make its comparisons. When searching for row differences, Excel compares the cells in the selection to the cells in the same column as the active cell. When searching for column differences, Excel compares the cells in the selection to the cells in the same row as the active cell.

For example, suppose you have selected the range B10:G20 and cell B10 is the active cell. If you use the Row Differences option, Excel compares the entries in cells C10:G10 to the entry in cell B10. The entries in cells C11:G11 are compared to cell B11, and so forth. If you select the Column Differences option, Excel compares the entries in cells B11:B20 to the entry in cell B10. The entries in cells C11:C20 are compared to cell C10, and so forth.

Among other things, Excel looks for differences in your cell and range references and selects those cells that don't conform to the comparison cell. Suppose cell B10 is your comparison cell and contains the formula

=SUM(B1:B9)

This formula refers to the range of cells that begins nine rows above and ends one row above the formula cell. If you select cells B10:G10 and select the Row Differences option, Excel scans through cells C10:G10 to check for any formulas that don't fit this pattern. For example, cells C10 and D10 should, presumably, contain the formulas

=SUM(C1:C9)

and

=SUM(D1:D9)

If any of the formulas in row 10 don't match this pattern, the Select Special… command flags those cells. If they all match, you get a *No cells found* message.

Of course, you can use the Row Differences and Column Differences options to check that all your cells in the selected range contain the same types of entries.

E X C E L *Tip*

Using the Select Special… command with the Show Info command

You can also use Select Special… in conjunction with the Info window to select a range of cells and move through that range to review the relevant data in each cell in the selection. For example, suppose you want to quickly scan all the notes you've entered in a specific range of your worksheet. First, select the range you're interested in (or a single cell, for the entire worksheet), then choose the Show Info command and, if necessary, select the Notes command from the Info menu. Arrange the worksheet and Info windows so that they don't overlap—that way, you can see the selected cells and the Info window at the same time. Next, choose the Select Special… command, select the Notes option, and click OK. Excel highlights all the cells in the selected range that have notes attached to them. Now, you can use the Enter and Tab key combinations previously described to browse through the annotated cells and view their notes in the Info window.

For example, if your comparison cell contains a SUM function, Microsoft Excel flags any cells that contain a function, formula, or value other than SUM. If the comparison cell contains a constant text or numeric value, Excel flags any cells in the selected range that don't exactly match the comparison value.

The Precedents and Dependents options are perhaps the most powerful options in the Select Special dialog box. They let you trace calculations by locating all the cells that feed into a formula or that depend on the formula in the selected cell. To use these options, begin by selecting the cell whose dependents or precedents you want to trace. Then, choose the Select Special... command and select the Precedents or Dependents option. When you select either of these options, Excel activates the Direct Only and All Levels options. Use these options to set the parameters of your search: Direct Only finds only those cells that are directly dependent on or that directly refer to the active cell; All Levels locates direct precedents and dependents plus those cells that are indirectly linked to the active cell.

Protecting a worksheet

In certain situations, you may want other people to be able to use your worksheet models without being able to edit them. Like most other advanced electronic spreadsheet programs, Microsoft Excel gives you the ability to protect the contents of your worksheets from accidental or unauthorized changes. In Excel, protection is controlled by two commands: Cell Protection... from the Format menu and Protect Document... from the Options menu. The Cell Protection... command controls the protection of individual cells and ranges in the worksheet, while the Protect Document... command controls the protection of the entire worksheet.

The Cell Protection... command

Excel has two different protection attributes—Locked and Hidden—that you can assign to any cell in the worksheet. Both of these attributes are controlled by the Cell Protection... command. When you use this command, you see the dialog box shown in Figure 8-43.

FIGURE 8-43. *This is the Cell Protection dialog box.*

When a cell is locked and the worksheet protected, you cannot edit the contents of the cell or replace them with a different entry. If the locked cell is blank, you cannot make an entry into that cell. If you try to make a change to a locked cell, Excel returns the error message *Locked cells can't be changed*.

When you assign the Hidden attribute to a cell that contains a formula, you cannot see the formula in the formula bar when you click that cell, but you can see the result of the formula in the worksheet.

You can use the Cell Protection… command to assign the Locked attribute, Hidden attribute, or both, to any cell or range in the worksheet, or to remove those attributes from any cell. To lock and/or hide a cell or range, you select that cell or range, choose the Cell Protection… command, and then click the box next to the attribute you want to assign or remove.

Unless you use the Cell Protection… command to change their attributes, every cell in the worksheet is locked, but not hidden. However, even though all of the cells in a newly created worksheet are locked, Excel does not prevent you from making changes to the worksheet. For example, if you create a new worksheet, select cell A1, and choose the Cell Protection… command, Excel displays the dialog box previously shown in Figure 8-43. As you can see, cell A1 in this new worksheet is locked. However, if you click OK, then type *100* and press Enter, Excel accepts the entry without a hitch.

Here's why this happens. Even though every cell in a newly created worksheet is locked, the worksheet as a whole is unprotected. Because the worksheet as a whole is unprotected, you can make changes to locked cells. In order for cell protection to take effect, you must choose the Protect Document… command from the Options menu to protect the entire worksheet. Protecting the worksheet activates the Locked and Hidden attributes that have been assigned to the cells of the worksheet. You can think of the Protect Document… command as a master switch that controls the protection status of all the cells in a worksheet.

The Protect Document… command

Because every cell in a new worksheet is automatically locked, all you have to do to protect the worksheet from accidental changes is use the Protect Document… command. When you choose this command, Excel displays the dialog box shown in Figure 8-44 on the next page. This dialog box lets you protect the worksheet and gives you the option of specifying a password that prevents someone else from removing this protection.

If you click OK without typing a password, you activate the protection attributes of all the cells in the worksheet. If you have not used the Format menu's Cell Protection… command to change the protection status of any cells, clicking

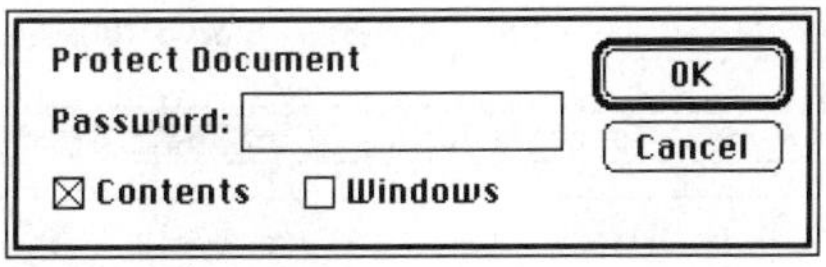

FIGURE 8-44. *This is the Protect Document dialog box.*

OK locks every cell in the worksheet. However, anyone may unlock the worksheet by choosing the Unprotect Document... command.

If you type a password before you click OK, you can make it almost impossible for anyone who doesn't know the password to unprotect the worksheet. The password can be up to 255 characters long and can contain any character. However, you'll usually want the password to be short and to contain characters that are easy to remember.

A word of caution: Entering a password in the Protect Document dialog box protects your document from being altered, not from being opened. A password in the Protect Document dialog box is not the same as a password in the Save As Options dialog box, which prevents unauthorized opening of the document.

You can protect the worksheet window itself by choosing the Windows option from the Protect Document dialog box. This option prevents moving, resizing, or hiding the document's windows. If you want Excel to protect the worksheet but not the windows, select only the Contents check box.

Most of the time, you won't want every cell in a worksheet to be locked. Although you may want to protect every cell that contains an important formula, you'll usually want to leave a few cells unlocked so that you can change variables or enter new information into the worksheet. For this reason, you'll usually use the Cell Protection... command to unlock a few cells just before you use the Protect Document... command.

In addition to activating the protection attributes of all the cells in the worksheet, protecting the worksheet also disables many of Excel's commands, including all of the commands on the Format menu and all of the commands on the Edit menu except Copy. This is because the Protect Document... command makes it impossible to clear any cell in the worksheet, to delete rows or columns, to assign or remove range names, or to change the format or protection attribute of any cell.

Unless you use the Info window to monitor the status of the cells in your worksheet, Excel does not give you any on-screen indication of the protection status of a cell. However, there is a way to distinguish locked cells from unlocked cells. If you use the Display... command from the Options menu to deactivate gridlines in the worksheet, Excel continues to display a horizontal gridline below every unlocked cell in the worksheet. In Figure 8-45, only cells B5 through E12 are unlocked. Although gridlines have been turned off, Excel displays a gridline beneath these cells.

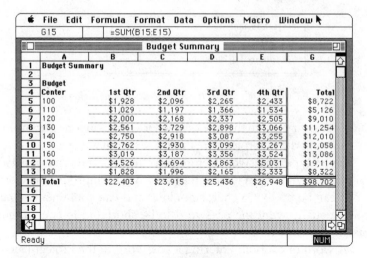

FIGURE 8-45. *Even though gridlines have been deactivated with the Display… command, they continue to be displayed below unlocked cells.*

Unprotecting the worksheet

If you pull down the Options menu when a worksheet is protected, you'll see that the Protect Document… command has changed to the Unprotect Document… command. If you choose this command, Excel deactivates the protection attributes of all of the cells in the worksheet and reactivates all of Excel's menu commands.

If you supplied a password when you protected the worksheet, Excel does not unprotect the worksheet until you type that password. If you type the wrong password, Excel displays the message *Incorrect password* and does not unprotect the worksheet. The password you type must match the worksheet's protection password in every detail, including capitalization. For example, if the worksheet's password is *aaaa*, you must type *aaaa*; *AAAA* won't work. So be sure to keep a record of your passwords.

Also, if you're merely protecting your worksheet from your own mistakes, you should protect your worksheet without a password. This makes it very easy to unprotect your worksheet. You simply select the Unprotect Document… command from the Options menu. Excel bypasses the dialog box and unprotects your document.

Conclusion

In this chapter, you've seen some of the special tools that make Microsoft Excel such a powerful and flexible spreadsheet program. Sophisticated worksheet capabilities, like data tables and document links, let you perform complex calculations quickly and easily. Worksheet protection can keep your worksheets safe from your mistaken entries and the mistakes of others. Microsoft Excel's sophisticated auditing and debugging aids prove very useful to you when you work with complex worksheets.

Array formulas, while they are extremely helpful, can also be a dangerous tool if your work is not well documented. As we mentioned earlier, if you use arrays to combine data in one or more ranges of cells simultaneously, you will not have an accounting trail by which to retrace your steps. In many cases, you may be safer with the old-fashioned copy-and-paste techniques described in Chapter 4, "Editing the Worksheet."

In Chapter 9, "Printing the Worksheet," we move on to the last worksheet topic: printing. Here you'll learn to use the File- and Options-menu commands to create a finished report from your worksheet documents.

9

Printing the Worksheet

After creating, formatting, and editing a document, you're ready to print it. However, if you're like most worksheet program users, you'll want to print at least one draft of your document before you complete all your editing and formatting changes. Fortunately, the default Print and Page Setup settings of Microsoft Excel are generally adequate for printing quick drafts and simple worksheets. After you have installed and selected a printer, you simply choose the Print command from the File menu and click OK in the Print dialog box.

Of course, with a program as powerful as Microsoft Excel, it's no surprise that printing can also be a very complex issue. Microsoft Excel lets you specify a number of settings that apply directly to printing, such as the number of copies you want to create, the section of a document you want to print, and the method of feeding the paper into the printer. In addition, you can automatically add certain elements to a document that enhance the printed pages, such as page numbers, headers, and footers.

In this chapter, we explore the various settings that can affect printing and show you how to number pages and create headers and footers. Then we show you how to use the page preview feature to see how the printed document will look— without actually printing. Let's begin, however, with a look at the procedures you follow to install and select a printer.

Installing a printer

In order to use a printer, you must first install the appropriate driver or printer resource file on your Startup disk. This is simply a matter of copying the driver file to your System Folder. Then, after you start up your Macintosh, you must use the Chooser desk accessory to select that printer driver.

If you are using an Apple ImageWriter or LaserWriter, you will find the driver files for these printers on the disks that came with them. To install a driver in your hard disk's System Folder, place the disk containing the driver in your disk drive and double click the icon for the disk containing the printer drivers so that you can view the disk's contents. Next, click the icon that represents the printer you want to use and drag that driver file to the System Folder. You must be sure that the driver is in your System Folder; otherwise, the Chooser won't recognize your printer.

If you are using a LaserWriter, you need to copy two files to your System Folder: the LaserWriter printer driver file and the file labeled *Laser Prep*. Finally, if you plan to use more than one printer, be sure to copy all appropriate driver files.

Selecting a printer

The first time you use any printer, you need to use the Chooser desk accessory on the ( ) menu to select that printer. You can select a printer from the Finder or while in Microsoft Excel.

When you choose the Chooser desk accessory, you see a dialog box like the one in Figure 9-1. The contents of the dialog box vary, depending on the number and type of printer drivers you have installed. The dialog box in Figure 9-1 shows that drivers for both the LaserWriter and the ImageWriter are installed in the System Folder. The design of the icons may also vary, depending on which version of a printer driver you're using.

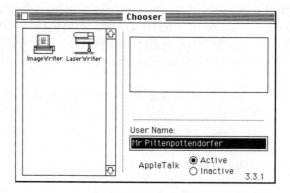

FIGURE 9-1. *Use the Chooser dialog box to select a printer.*

Selecting an ImageWriter

If you plan to use an ImageWriter printer, begin by clicking the ImageWriter icon on the left side of the Chooser dialog box. You'll then see an alert box with the message *Be sure to select Page Setup and confirm the settings so that the application can format documents correctly for the ImageWriter.* When you click Continue in this box or press Enter, you see an additional set of icons on the right side of the dialog box, as shown in Figure 9-2. These icons represent your printer port (the printer icon) and your communications or modem port (the telephone icon).

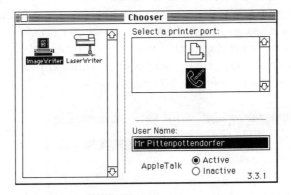

FIGURE 9-2. *When you choose the ImageWriter printer icon, Excel asks which port you plan to use.*

Click the icon that represents the port you want to use. Generally, you attach an ImageWriter to the printer port. If you are using the printer port for something else—another printer, for example—you might want to attach the ImageWriter to the communications port. Be careful! Do not select the communications port if you have attached an external hard disk to that port. This might cause your hard disk to be erased! After selecting the port, close the Chooser dialog box to record your selection.

You can select the printer port icon only if you are not actively using Apple-Talk. If you select the printer port while the AppleTalk setting is active, you see another alert box with the message *ImageWriter cannot be used on the Printer port while AppleTalk is active. Do you want to make AppleTalk inactive? Access to current network services has to be re-established.* If you click OK in this alert box, you see the message *Please make sure that the AppleTalk Network is disconnected.* If you click Continue in this second alert box (or press Enter), Excel automatically changes the AppleTalk setting to Inactive. If you don't want to disconnect from AppleTalk, click Cancel when you see the alert message. Excel leaves the AppleTalk setting at Active and does not select the printer port, leaving the modem port selected.

Selecting a LaserWriter

If you plan to use a LaserWriter, first click the Active option in the lower-right portion of the dialog box to indicate that you are connected to the AppleTalk network.
When you do this, you see the message *Please make sure that you are connected to an
AppleTalk network.* Click Continue in this alert box, then click the LaserWriter icon.
If you click the LaserWriter icon while the Inactive AppleTalk option is selected,
you see the alert message, *LaserWriter requires AppleTalk. Please make sure that you are
connected to an AppleTalk network.* When you click OK in response to this alert message, the Active option is selected automatically.

Having activated AppleTalk, click the LaserWriter icon in the Chooser dialog
box. You see the message *Be sure to choose Page Setup and confirm the settings so that
the application can format documents correctly for the LaserWriter.* When you click
Continue in this alert box, one or more printer names appear on the right side of
the dialog box as shown in Figure 9-3.

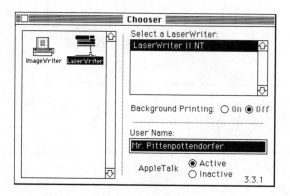

FIGURE 9-3. *When you choose the LaserWriter printer icon,*
you see a list of available printers.

Only the names of those printers connected to your Macintosh appear. (If you
don't see any names, check your printer cable to make sure the connection is
secure.) Click the name of the printer you want to use. Then, type your name or initials in the User Name field. This field appears primarily for users who are sharing
a printer on an AppleTalk network. When more than one Macintosh is connected
to the same printer, the Macintosh presents a status box that identifies the user
who is currently printing. (By the way, you need to type your name only once. The
Macintosh remembers the text you type in the User Name field. You can, however,
change the name in this field at any time.) After completing these steps, close the
Chooser dialog box to lock in your selections.

If you use only one printer, you probably won't have to choose the Chooser desk accessory again. If you want to switch to another printer, however, you need to select the printer and AppleTalk settings you want to use.

Selecting other printers

It is not within the scope of this book to discuss all the possible hardware configurations for printing from the Macintosh. Your *Macintosh System Software User's Guide* and your printer manual give you information on installing other printers.

Preparing the worksheet for printing

Microsoft Excel makes it easy to produce a polished, professional-quality report from your worksheet. In this section, we show you how to use the Page Setup... command to define the layout of your printed page. Then, you learn how to control awkward page breaks, print a partial worksheet, and define print titles with the printing commands from the Options menu. Finally, we talk about the Microsoft Excel Print... command and preview capabilities.

We walk through the printing process with the Apple ImageWriter and LaserWriter printers because they are the most common printers for the Macintosh.

Setting up the page

When you get ready to print your document, you need to decide what size paper to use, how big you want your margins to be, and whether you want headers and footers. As you get used to Excel's printing options, you might decide that you like printing your worksheets without gridlines or row and column headings.

The Page Setup... command on the File menu allows you to control the layout of your printed worksheets. When you choose this command, depending upon whether your Macintosh is connected to an ImageWriter or a LaserWriter, Excel displays a dialog box that lists all of your page-layout options.

You use the top half of the Page Setup dialog box to tell Excel what type of paper you are using, how you want the worksheet to be oriented on the paper, and whether you want the worksheet reduced. The remaining options allow you to create a header across the top of the page and a footer across the bottom, change the page margins, and indicate whether row and column headers and gridlines should appear on your printed worksheet. Let's consider each of these options in more detail. First, we look at the settings that are common to the Page Setup... dialog boxes for both printers. Then, we discuss the settings that differ.

The Header and Footer settings

The Page Setup… command allows you to insert headers and footers in your printed worksheets. A header is a single line of text printed ½ inch from the top; a footer is a single line of text printed ½ inch from the bottom of each page of a worksheet.

If you look at the Page Setup dialog boxes in Figures 9-4 and 9-5, you can see that Excel automatically creates both a header and a footer for your worksheets. The default header, &f, instructs Microsoft Excel to print the name of the document at the top of each page. The default footer, Page &p, tells Microsoft Excel to

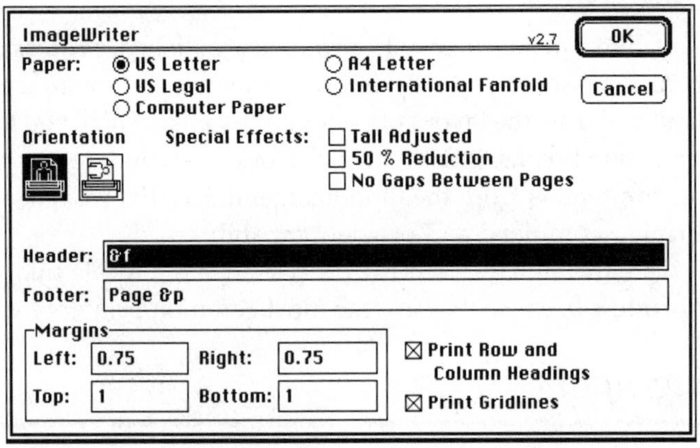

FIGURE 9-4. *This is the Page Setup dialog box for the ImageWriter.*

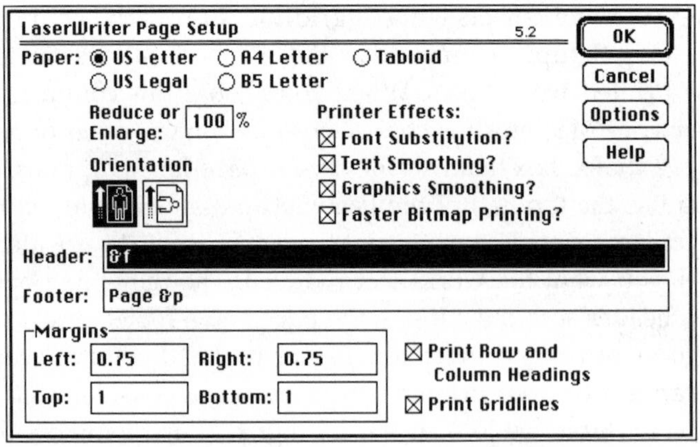

FIGURE 9-5. *This is the Page Setup dialog box for the LaserWriter.*

print the word *Page*, followed by the page number, at the bottom of each page. Excel automatically centers your headers and footers unless you instruct it to do otherwise.

The symbols &f and &p are just 2 of the 16 special codes that you can use in headers and footers. Here is a list of the Microsoft Excel header and footer codes and what they mean:

If you use...	Excel...
&l	Left-aligns characters
&c	Centers characters
&r	Right-aligns characters
&p	Includes a page number in the header or footer
&d	Includes the current date in the header or footer in mm/dd/yy format
&t	Includes the current time in the header or footer in hh:mm AM/PM format
&f	Includes the document name in the header or footer
&&	Includes a single ampersand (&) in the header or footer
&b	Prints the subsequent portion of the header or footer in bold type
&i	Prints the subsequent portion of the header or footer in italic type
&s	Prints the subsequent portion of the header or footer in strikeout style
&u	Prints the subsequent portion of the header or footer in underline style
&o	Prints the subsequent portion of the header or footer in outline style
&h	Prints the subsequent portion of the header or footer in shadow style
&"*font name*"	Prints the subsequent portion of the header or footer in the specified font; specify *font name* in quotation marks
&*num*	Prints the subsequent portion of the header or footer in the specified font size

You can use Excel's header and footer symbols alone, or you can mix and match them with regular text and with other symbols. For example, the default header is the symbol &f, while the standard footer mixes the text *Page* with the symbol &p. If you change the header to

&l&f

Excel prints the document name, aligned at the left margin of the printed page. If you change this header to

&b&l&f

Microsoft Excel prints the document name in bold type, starting at the left margin.

The bold (&b) and italic (&i) options apply to each individual portion of the header. For example, the header

&l&i&d&c&b&f&r&i&t

tells Excel to print the date left-aligned in italic, followed by the file name centered in bold and the time right-aligned in italic. For example, suppose you are working with a document called *Worksheet1*. When the settings in the dialog box are selected as shown in Figure 9-6, Excel prints the header

7/10/89   **Worksheet1**   *9:08 AM*

Notice that only the center portion of the header appears in bold, while the right- and left-aligned portions appear in italic. Microsoft Excel allows you to format each of these three portions separately, to emphasize key information in your headers and footers.

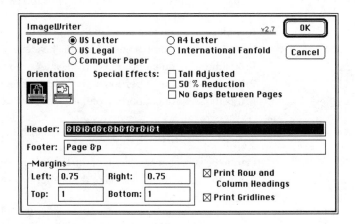

FIGURE 9-6. *These are the sample settings for page headers and footers.*

As you can see in Figure 9-6, when you choose Page Setup... from the File menu, Excel automatically highlights the Page Header box. If you want to delete the existing header, all you do is press Delete. After you have erased the existing header, you can type a new header, or you can leave the header field blank if you do not want a heading to appear.

If you want to use the existing header as the basis for a new one, you can edit the header just as you would edit a formula in the formula bar. For example, if you want to change &f, Excel's standard header, to &l&f, you can point to the space before the & in the existing header, click an insertion point, and type *&l*.

You create a new footer in exactly the same way you create a header. The only difference is that you begin creating a footer by clicking in the footer field instead of in the header field.

Note: Do not press the Enter or Return key to lock your entries in the header and footer fields, unless you have already filled in the other Page Setup options. When you press Enter or Return, Microsoft Excel assumes you have completed your entries in the dialog box and returns you to the worksheet. Excel automatically locks in your header and footer text when you click another option in the Page Setup dialog box.

The Margins settings

The Page Setup dialog box also gives you control over the left, right, top, and bottom margins of your printed worksheets. In Excel, as in most Macintosh software, margins are expressed in inches. As shown in Figure 9-6, the default settings are

Margin	In inches	Margin	In inches
Left	0.75	Right	0.75
Top	1	Bottom	1

You'll probably find that these default settings are acceptable for most of your printing requirements. However, you can easily change any setting by editing it just as you edit entries in the formula bar.

The Print Row And Column Headings option

The Page Setup dialog box includes a Print Row And Column Headings option that tells Excel whether you want to include in your printed worksheets the row numbers and column letters that appear on the screen. Figure 9-7 on the next page shows the sample worksheet printed with the Print Row And Column Headings option selected.

Typically, you will want to print your rough drafts with the Print Row And Column Headings option active. The row and column headings make it easy to identify the location of any entry in the worksheet. However, when you print the final version of the worksheet, you'll probably want to turn this option off so that the row and column headings don't clutter the worksheet.

Check Register 1/89

Checking Account Register: January 1989						
						Previous Balance
						$1,631.78
	Check					
Date	Number	Amount	To	Description	Cleared	Balance
1/1/89	101	($141.56)	Finance Company	Car loan	x	$1,490.22
1/1/89	102	($123.65)	Long Plumbing	unclog drain	x	$1,366.57
1/1/89	103	($12.33)	Drug store	allergy medici	x	$1,354.24
1/4/89	104	($623.65)	House payment		x	$730.59
1/5/89	105	($80.91)	Clothes		x	$649.68
1/7/89	106	($63.35)	Book club		x	$586.33
1/9/89	107	$0.00	VOID		x	$586.33
1/10/89		$809.42	Deposit			$1,395.75
1/13/89	108	($123.65)	Record store		x	$1,272.10
1/15/89		$12.98	Deposit			$1,285.08
1/18/89	109	($63.65)	Patty's stuff		x	$1,221.43
1/18/89	110	($345.00)	Dr. Feelgood			$876.43
1/18/89	111	($76.32)	Dinner with Clara		x	$800.11
1/18/89	112	($65.87)	Karen's birthday		x	$734.24
1/19/89	113	($435.00)	Property taxes		x	$299.24
1/20/89	114	($23.87)	Groceries		x	$275.37
1/20/89	115	($65.32)	Phone bill		x	$210.05
1/20/89	116	($73.56)	LG&E		x	$136.49
1/20/89	117	($63.87)	Film and Developing		x	$72.62
1/20/89	118	($12.21)	Water bill		x	$60.41
1/25/89		$49.99	Refund			$110.40
1/25/89	119	($23.65)	Cleaners		x	$86.75
1/25/89	120	($32.00)	Tara	lunch loan	x	$54.75
1/25/89	121	($12.45)	Liquor store		x	$42.30
1/25/89	122	($10.00)	cash		x	$32.30
1/28/89		$430.80	Deposit			$463.10
1/28/89	123	($2.56)	Sarah's toy		x	$460.54
1/28/89	124	($23.30)	Clinic		x	$437.24
1/28/89	125	($15.98)	Book club			$421.26
1/30/89	126	($121.00)	Car repairs	brakes	x	$300.26
1/30/89	127	($65.90)	Clothes	accessories	x	$234.36
1/30/89	128	($34.56)	Sushi bar		x	$199.80
1/31/89	129	($23.98)	Dylan		x	$175.82
1/31/89	130	($12.08)	Hardware Store		x	$163.74

Page 1

FIGURE 9-7. *This is the sample worksheet printed with the Print Row And Column Headings option of the Page Setup... command turned off.*

The Print Gridlines option

The Print Gridlines option controls the printing of gridlines. When this option is active, Microsoft Excel includes in your printed worksheets the gridlines that you see on the screen. When the option is not selected, Excel prints the worksheet without gridlines.

Even if you use the Display... command from the Options menu to turn off the gridlines on the screen, the status of the Print Gridlines option in the Page Setup dialog box still matters. Although you cannot actually see the gridlines on the screen, unless you deactivate Print Gridlines in the Page Setup dialog box, you get gridlines in your printed worksheets.

As with the Print Row And Column Headings option, you will probably want to have Print Gridlines active when you are printing drafts and inactive when you are printing final versions of your worksheets. Gridlines, like those in Figure 9-7 above, help you identify the location of an entry quickly, but tend to clutter the printed page.

The ImageWriter options

While many of the same Page Setup options appear in the Page Setup dialog box for both the ImageWriter and LaserWriter, other options are different. The specific ImageWriter options follow.

The Paper setting

The Paper setting tells Excel the size of the sheets of paper on which you are printing. The following table shows each of the five options on the ImageWriter. Simply click the one that matches the paper you will be using.

Option	Size
US Letter	8½ by 11 inches
US Legal	8½ by 14 inches
Computer Paper	15 by 11 inches
A4 Letter	210 by 297 millimeters
International Fanfold	8¼ by 12 inches

The Orientation setting

The Orientation setting allows you to tell Excel whether you want your worksheet to be printed vertically or horizontally. When you select the vertical icon, Excel prints your worksheet in the normal way, with each line running horizontally across the paper. Figure 9-8 (top) on the next page shows a sample page printed in the vertical mode. Vertical is the default setting, and you will probably use it most of the time.

When you select the horizontal icon, Excel prints the worksheet so that each line runs vertically from the top of the paper to the bottom. Instead of printing a complete line each time it makes a pass across the page, the ImageWriter prints a tiny cross-section of every line with each pass. Figure 9-8 (bottom) on the next page shows a page printed in the horizontal mode.

The horizontal option is useful for printing pages that are wider than they are high on 8½- by 11-inch paper. For example, if you want to print a schedule that is 15 columns wide but only 8 rows deep, you could use the horizontal option to print the whole schedule on one sheet of paper.

The main problem with the horizontal option is that it produces characters that are not quite as crisp as the characters produced when you use the vertical option. For most applications, this reduced quality won't be too much of a limitation. In cases where your worksheet has to look perfect, however, the horizontal option might not be acceptable.

Checking Account Register: January 1989

Previous Balance
$1,631.78

Date	Check Number	Amount	To	Description	Cleared	Balance
1/1/89	101	($141.56)	Finance Company	Car loan	x	$1,490.22
1/1/89	102	($123.65)	Long Plumbing	unclog drain	x	$1,366.57
1/1/89	103	($12.33)	Drug store	allergy medici	x	$1,354.24
1/4/89	104	($623.65)	House payment		x	$730.59
1/5/89	105	($80.91)	Clothes		x	$649.68
1/7/89	106	($63.35)	Book club		x	$586.33
1/9/89	107	$0.00	VOID		x	$586.33
1/10/89		$809.42	Deposit			$1,395.75
1/13/89	108	($123.65)	Record store		x	$1,272.10
1/15/89		$12.98	Deposit			$1,285.08
1/18/89	109	($63.65)	Patty's stuff		x	$1,221.43
1/18/89	110	($345.00)	Dr. Feelgood			$876.43
1/18/89	111	($76.32)	Dinner with Clara			$800.11
1/18/89	112	($65.87)	Karen's birthday		x	$734.24
1/19/89	113	($435.00)	Property taxes		x	$299.24
1/20/89	114	($23.87)	Groceries		x	$275.37
1/20/89	115	($65.32)	Phone bill		x	$210.05
1/20/89	116	($73.56)	LG&E		x	$136.49
1/20/89	117	($63.87)	Film and Developing		x	$72.62
1/20/89	118	($12.21)	Water bill		x	$60.41
1/25/89		$49.99	Refund			$110.40
1/25/89	119	($23.65)	Cleaners		x	$86.75
1/25/89	120	($32.00)	Tara	lunch loan	x	$54.75
1/25/89	121	($12.45)	Liquor store		x	$42.30
1/25/89	122	($10.00)	cash		x	$32.30
1/28/89		$430.80	Deposit			$463.10
1/28/89	123	($2.56)	Sarah's toy		x	$460.54
1/28/89	124	($23.30)	Clinic			$437.24
1/28/89	125	($15.98)	Book club			$421.26
1/30/89	126	($121.00)	Car repairs	brakes	x	$300.26
1/30/89	127	($65.90)	Clothes	accessories	x	$234.36
1/30/89	128	($34.56)	Sushi bar			$199.80
1/31/89	129	($23.98)	Dylan		x	$175.82
1/31/89	130	($12.08)	Hardware Store		x	$163.74

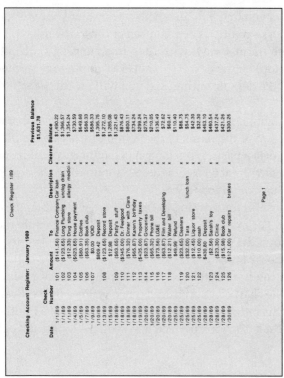

FIGURE 9-8. (Top) *This sample printout shows the vertical mode; other settings are Computer Paper, no row and column headings, and no gridlines.   (Bottom) This sample printout shows the horizontal mode; other options are US Letter, no row and column headings, and no gridlines.*

The Special Effects options

Microsoft Excel offers three options designed to give you even more control over how your worksheets are printed.

The Tall Adjusted option You'll use the Tall Adjusted option only when you print from chart files. The Tall Adjusted setting tells Microsoft Excel to make adjustments so that the chart fills the page. We discuss this feature in Chapter 13, "Other Chart Topics."

The 50% Reduction option The 50% Reduction option lets you reduce the printed size of your worksheet by 50 percent. This option allows you to squeeze much more information on each page. For example, you can normally print about 12 standard-width columns and about 60 rows from the worksheet on 15- by 11-inch computer paper. If you use the 50% Reduction option, however, you can squeeze twice as many columns and twice as many rows on each page.

Figure 9-9 shows the sample worksheet printed with the 50% Reduction option active. As you can see, reduction makes the characters quite small. Unless you have problems reading small characters, however, you may find that the benefits of having more information on each page sometimes outweigh the inconvenience caused by the smaller characters.

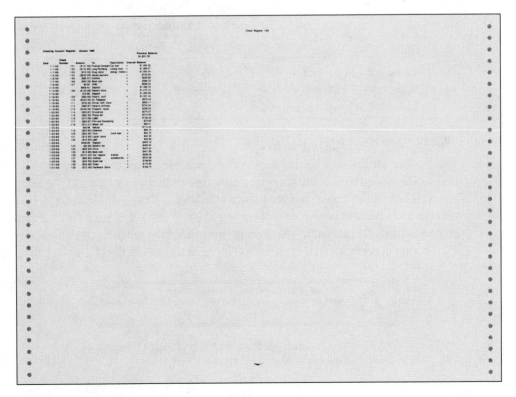

FIGURE 9-9. *This sample worksheet was printed using the 50% Reduction option of the Page Setup...* command.

The No Gaps Between Pages option   The No Gaps Between Pages option controls the page breaks in your worksheet. As a default, Microsoft Excel leaves a small space above and below each page break for the perforations in fanfold paper. If you select the No Gaps Between Pages option, Excel prints right through the perforations.

It might surprise you to learn that we prefer to use the No Gaps Between Pages option. When you ask Microsoft Excel to include breaks between pages, the breaks frequently fall in awkward places. When you select No Gaps Between Pages, Excel prints your spreadsheet in a continuous stream, eliminating unwanted gaps in the worksheet.

The LaserWriter options

The following discussion focuses on the Page Setup options that are specific to the LaserWriter.

The Paper setting
The LaserWriter Paper setting also tells Excel the size of the sheets of paper on which you are printing. Because the LaserWriter can only work with cut-sheet paper, it offers fewer paper options than the ImageWriter. The following table shows each of the five options. Click the one that matches the paper you are using.

Option	Size	Option	Size
US Letter	8½ by 11 inches	B5 Letter	182 by 257 millimeters
US Legal	8½ by 14 inches	Tabloid	11 by 17 inches
A4 Letter	210 by 297 millimeters		

The Reduce Or Enlarge setting
The Reduce Or Enlarge setting lets you print a reduced or enlarged worksheet. Unlike the ImageWriter, which offers only one reduction option (50 percent), the LaserWriter allows you to reduce your worksheet in 1 percent increments from 99 percent to 25 percent (one-fourth the normal size), or to enlarge it in 1 percent increments from 101 percent to 400 percent (four times the normal size). If you choose a reduction percentage that is either too large or too small, Excel displays the alert

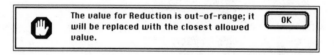

FIGURE 9-10. *Excel displays this alert box if you want to enlarge or reduce your document beyond the allowable range.*

box shown in Figure 9-10. Within the allowable range, though, you have tremendous flexibility in determining how much information appears on each page of your worksheet. Figure 9-11 shows this flexibility. If you want to include a lot of information on each page, you can choose a reduction factor of 30 or 40 percent. With a setting in this range, each character in your worksheet is printed very small, and Excel can squeeze a large number of characters onto each page. If you want to print large characters, or if you want to print only a small amount of information on each page, you can select an enlargement factor instead.

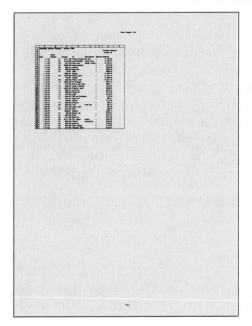

	A	B	C
		Check Register 1/89	
1	Checking Account Register:		January 19
2			
3			
4		Check	
5	Date	Number	Amount
6	1/1/89	101	($141.56)
7	1/1/89	102	($123.65)
8	1/1/89	103	($12.33)
9	1/4/89	104	($623.65)
10	1/5/89	105	($80.91)
11	1/7/89	106	($63.35)
12	1/9/89	107	$0.00
13	1/10/89		$809.42
14	1/13/89	108	($123.65)
15	1/15/89		$12.98
16	1/18/89	109	($63.65)
17	1/18/89	110	($345.00)
18	1/18/89	111	($76.32)
19	1/18/89	112	($65.87)
20	1/19/89	113	($435.00)
21	1/20/89	114	($23.87)
22	1/20/89	115	($65.32)
23	1/20/89	116	($73.56)
		Page 1	

FIGURE 9-11. *This worksheet was printed first with a reduction factor of 40 percent, then with an enlargement factor of 200 percent.*

You can also use the Standard Font... command from the Options menu to increase or decrease the size of the characters in your printed worksheets. You may recall, however, that when you use the Standard Font... command, you change the size of the characters on the screen as well as in the printed worksheet. In addition, you can use the Font... command to change the size of characters in individual cells of your worksheet. With the Page Setup... command's Reduce Or Enlarge setting, you change the size of the characters only for printing.

The Orientation setting

The Orientation setting tells Microsoft Excel whether you want your worksheet printed vertically or horizontally. With the LaserWriter, as with the ImageWriter, Excel uses vertical and horizontal icons. The vertical option lets you print your worksheet in the normal way, with the text running horizontally across the paper. The horizontal option lets you print your worksheet so that each line runs vertically from the top of the paper to the bottom. (A more complete discussion of the vertical and horizontal Orientation settings appeared earlier in this chapter, when we discussed these icons in relation to the ImageWriter.)

The Printer Effects options

The Apple LaserWriter offers four printer effects options: Font Substitution, Text Smoothing, Graphics Smoothing, and Faster Bitmap Printing.

The Font Substitution option If you are using a font other than one that is supplied with your printer, but one that is a standard Macintosh font, you can use the Font Substitution option to control the way the LaserWriter interprets the characters you send to it for printing. If Font Substitution is selected, the LaserWriter substitutes one of its own fonts for the font you are using in the worksheet. The following table shows which LaserWriter font is used to print each Macintosh font:

If you use...	LaserWriter substitutes...
New York	Times
Geneva	Helvetica
Monaco	Courier

If Font Substitution is not selected, the LaserWriter uses its graphics capabilities to duplicate—as well as it can—the font you are using in the worksheet.

Neither choice is optimum: Font substitution is slow and often results in text that contains gaps. Font duplication is even slower. If you are printing your worksheets with a LaserWriter, we suggest that you use one of the three main Laser-Writer fonts for the characters in the worksheet. You'll find instructions in the LaserWriter manual for installing these fonts in your System File.

The Text and Graphics Smoothing options When you're using a font size that isn't installed in your System File, the Smoothing option rounds the rough edges in characters that have curves, such as *p*, *r*, and *s*. Because everything the LaserWriter prints is formed from an arrangement of small opaque squares, the Smoothing option ensures that your text loses some of its jagged look.

As you may have noticed, curved lines in your charts and other graphics often look slightly jagged on the screen. The Smoothing option also tells the LaserWriter to cheat a little in order to make curved lines in graphics more attractive.

The Faster Bitmap Printing option If you have installed some unusual fonts in your System File, such as Cairo or San Francisco, and you use them in your worksheets, the LaserWriter must approximate the shape of any characters you might want to use in those fonts by drawing the characters pixel by pixel. The Faster Bitmap Printing option tells the LaserWriter to "speed up" the process by which it imitates characters it doesn't have in its own font library.

Other options

The Page Setup dialog box for the LaserWriter includes a button labeled Options. When you click this button, Microsoft Excel makes four additional options available, as shown in Figure 9-12. In most instances, each time you click an option, the canine drawing on the left side of the dialog box changes to show you how that option affects your printed document.

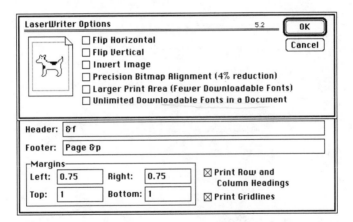

FIGURE 9-12. *When you click the Options button in the Page Setup dialog box, you access these additional printing options.*

The Flip Horizontal option The Flip Horizontal option tells your LaserWriter to print a "mirror image" of your document pages. When you choose this option, the lines of text in your document run from right to left across the page, instead of left to right, and each letter is printed backward. For example, Figure 9-13 shows some normal text, while Figure 9-14 shows this same text printed with the Flip Horizontal option selected. If you were to hold the text in Figure 9-14 up to a mirror, its reflected image would look like normal text.

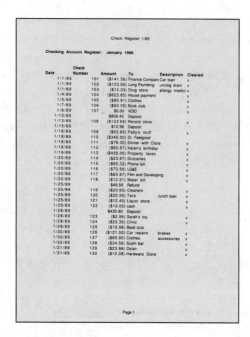

FIGURE 9-13. *This text was printed without using special printing options.*

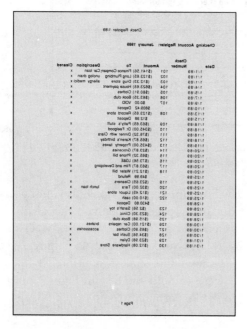

FIGURE 9-14. *This text was printed using the Flip Horizontal option in the Page Setup Options dialog box.*

The Flip Vertical option The Flip Vertical option causes the LaserWriter to print an upside-down mirror image of your document pages. For example, Figure 9-15 shows the text from Figure 9-13 printed with the Flip Vertical option selected. (We turned off the Flip Horizontal option before printing.)

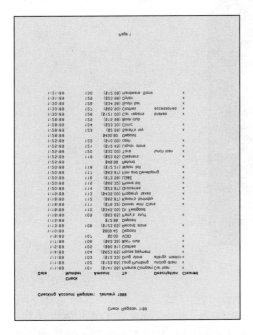

FIGURE 9-15. *This text was printed using the Flip Vertical option in the Page Setup Options dialog box.*

The Invert Image option Selecting Invert Image causes your LaserWriter to print white text on a black background instead of the normal black text on a white background. For example, Figure 9-16 shows the text from Figure 9-14 printed with the Invert Image option selected. Notice that the black background does not extend to the edge of the page since this is the LaserWriter's "no print" zone.

The Precision Bitmap Alignment option The Precision Bitmap Alignment option reduces text and graphics by 4 percent and, in some cases, gives a slightly cleaner appearance. It also can speed up the printing of graphics and bitmapped fonts. You'll find that selecting Precision Bitmap Alignment does not always result in a noticeable improvement in your printed text and graphics. However, if you want to enhance the appearance of printed graphics and bitmapped fonts, you should try this option.

The Larger Print Area option The LaserWriter cannot print all the way to the edge of the paper; normally it stops printing ⅜ inch from the edge. If you have text

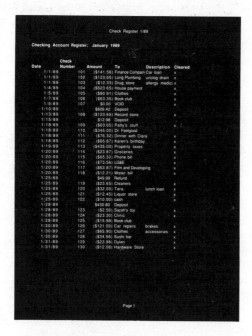

FIGURE 9-16. *We used the Invert Image option to create white text on a black background.*

or graphics that extend into this "no-print" zone, they do not appear in the printed document. When you select the Larger Print Area (Fewer Downloadable Fonts) option, the unprintable area is reduced to approximately ¼ inch. This gives you a larger area on the page in which to print. Increasing the size of the print area consumes some of the LaserWriter's memory, allowing for fewer downloadable fonts. Because different fonts require different amounts of memory, it's impossible to specify exactly how many fonts can be downloaded with this option selected.

Unlimited Downloadable Fonts In A Document As the name implies, the Unlimited Downloadable Fonts In A Document option allows you to use any number of downloadable fonts in a document. The LaserWriter downloads one set of fonts, creates a partial page image, clears its memory, then downloads another set of fonts and repeats the procedure. As you might guess, this process of switching downloadable fonts in and out of memory can make for slower printing.

The Options-menu printing commands

In addition to the File menu's Page Setup... command, three commands on the Options menu affect the way your worksheet is printed: Set Print Area, Set Print Titles, and Set Page Break.

The Set Print Area command

Normally when you choose the Print... command, Excel prints the contents of the entire active area. In other words, if your worksheet occupies 75 rows and 16 columns, Excel assumes that you want to print the contents of cells A1:P75 when you choose the Print... command.

The Set Print Area command lets you print selected sections of your worksheet. To define a print area, simply drag through the cells you want to print and choose Set Print Area from the Options menu. Then, when you use the Print... command, only the selected area is printed. Your selection should be a single rectangular range. Excel cannot skip rows or columns when printing the worksheet. If you choose the Set Print Area command while you have an active multiple selection, Excel prints each selection in the order in which it was selected.

Excel defines the print area you select as a range named *Print_Area*. You can edit or delete the range name by using the Define Name... command from the Formula menu. If you delete the range *Print_Area*, Excel again prints your entire worksheet when you use the Print... command.

The Set Print Titles command

When you print a large worksheet, Excel breaks it into page-sized sections, based on the current Page Setup options. The width of your columns and the font size you select also affect the number of rows and columns Excel can fit on each page. Although Excel's automatic page-break capability is a big help, it can lead to a problem. Most of the time, the column and row labels that identify the contents of your worksheet are located in only the top few rows and leftmost columns of your worksheet. For example, in the worksheet shown in Figure 9-17, the row labels (division and product names) are in column A, and the column labels (*1/1/88*, *2/1/88*, and so on) are in rows 3 and 4, and so on.

When Excel breaks this large worksheet into sections, these labels are not printed on all of the pages. For example, notice that in Figure 9-17 only the first page, which includes the upper-left corner of the worksheet, has both row labels and column labels. Page 2 has row labels but no column labels, and page 3 has column labels but no row labels. Page 4 doesn't have any labels, which makes it next to impossible to figure out what the numbers on that page mean.

Fortunately, the Set Print Titles command on the Options menu lets you print the contents of one or more rows and/or one or more columns on every page of your worksheet. Let's use an example to demonstrate how this command works. Suppose you want to print the contents of rows 3 and 4 and column A on all four pages of the printed version of the sample worksheet in Figure 9-17. To do this, drag through the headers for rows 3 and 4, then hold down the Command key while you click the header for column A. Figure 9-18 shows the result. Now, select the Set Print Titles command from the Options menu.

	A	B	C	D	E	F	G	H	I	J	K	L	M
1	MONTHLY SALES: 1/1/88 THROUGH 4/1/89												
2													
3	Division/												
4	Product	1/1/88	2/1/88	3/1/88	4/1/88	5/1/88	6/1/88	7/1/88	8/1/88	9/1/88	10/1/88	11/1/88	12/1/88
5													
6	Division 1												
7	Widgets	$6,584	$643	$6,690	$5,818	$8,432	$6,760	$2,075	$1,653	$4,951	$7,242	$8,067	$6,702
8	Wombats	$2,373	$4,349	$120	$5,927	$5,342	$1,274	$1,218	$1,352	$6,950	$4,595	$9,981	$7,700
9	Woofers	$101	$9,534	$7,657	$1,580	$4,968	$9,698	$3,022	$128	$6,741	$1,237	$1,862	$8,304
10	Whatzits	$6,320	$9,852	$2,267	$7,566	$300	$9,188	$6,843	$678	$3,310	$1,589	$7,123	$6,450
11	Total	$15,378	$24,378	$16,734	$20,891	$19,042	$26,920	$13,158	$3,811	$21,952	$14,663	$27,033	$29,156
12													
13													
14	Division 2												
15	Widgets	$8,862	$2,858	$385	$7,004	$1,143	$3,343	$8,777	$8,304	$2,727	$2,102	$2,792	$9,183
16	Wombats	$4,807	$5,487	$3,650	$4,663	$6,870	$3,973	$2,372	$2,883	$5,643	$6,861	$2,000	$4,538
17	Woofers	$166	$8,045	$4,644	$1,231	$8,589	$4,213	$3,427	$1,233	$3,281	$6,749	$3,334	$2,930
18	Whatzits	$53	$5,813	$356	$6,261	$8,528	$3,315	$1,136	$9,129	$1,809	$8,353	$619	$4,300
19	Total	$13,888	$22,203	$9,035	$19,159	$25,130	$14,844	$15,714	$21,549	$13,460	$24,065	$8,745	$20,951
20													
21													
22	Division 3												
23	Widgets	$1,935	$6,934	$773	$6,131	$5,681	$7,951	$3,130	$2,709	$9,478	$3,963	$4,654	$1,611
24	Wombats	$7,006	$6,973	$9,183	$7,207	$4,093	$4,076	$4,834	$8,575	$6,333	$3,714	$4,164	$6,172
25	Woofers	$432	$3,965	$6,597	$7,538	$7,878	$3,107	$9,082	$3,390	$3,442	$6,072	$8,922	$9,280
26	Whatzits	$3,221	$4,187	$2,903	$811	$7,717	$3,347	$778	$2,535	$9,923	$6,057	$3	$3,576
27	Total	$12,594	$22,059	$19,456	$21,687	$25,369	$18,481	$17,824	$17,209	$29,176	$19,806	$17,743	$20,639
28													
29													
30	Division 4												
31	Widgets	$714	$439	$4,049	$8,318	$6,538	$3,686	$4,309	$2,816	$7,266	$4,195	$4,638	$9,843
32	Wombats	$5,805	$577	$7,598	$7,948	$1,997	$3,625	$915	$373	$493	$534	$7,408	$1,625
33	Woofers	$8,632	$6,326	$8,227	$4,294	$808	$3,399	$4,115	$8,931	$6,066	$3,841	$8,914	$6,095
34	Whatzits	$1,620	$6,536	$10	$3,888	$1,241	$9,864	$7,059	$3,734	$9,895	$767	$4,209	$9,837
35	Total	$16,771	$13,878	$19,884	$24,448	$10,584	$20,574	$16,398	$15,854	$23,720	$9,337	$25,169	$27,400
36													
37													
38	Division 5												
39	Widgets	$4,424	$5,388	$4,512	$4,669	$7,347	$5,826	$3,618	$1,318	$1,318	$6,192	$1,813	$5,371
40	Wombats	$2,982	$5,624	$9,411	$6,974	$5,635	$4,050	$8,590	$994	$7,720	$4,561	$6,018	$4,297
41	Woofers	$2,282	$3,928	$4,910	$6,184	$1,851	$7,997	$5,503	$4,327	$1,713	$8,744	$2,486	$7,744
42	Whatzits	$5,439	$606	$8,232	$6,572	$8,659	$172	$8,359	$3,324	$1,552	$1,116	$3,456	$2,087
43	Total	$15,127	$15,546	$27,065	$24,399	$23,492	$18,045	$26,070	$9,963	$12,303	$20,613	$13,773	$19,499
44													
45													
46	Division 6												
47	Widgets	$848	$2,975	$8,993	$6,678	$2,688	$3,622	$7,728	$6,744	$5,561	$8,829	$3,320	$3,731
48	Wombats	$6,668	$9,392	$821	$8,121	$8,878	$2,072	$3,400	$5,764	$9,091	$2,094	$9,359	$7,622

	A	B	C	D	E	F	G	H	I	J	K	L	M
49	Woofers	$1,817	$8,831	$7,288	$162	$4,898	$4,929	$5,402	$306	$3,021	$6,910	$1,612	$8,367
50	Whatzits	$911	$7,806	$1,927	$33	$5,548	$6,838	$183	$9,328	$6,625	$6,296	$9,024	$1,943
51	Total	$10,244	$29,004	$19,029	$14,994	$22,012	$17,461	$16,713	$22,142	$24,318	$26,129	$23,315	$21,663
52													
53													
54	Division 7												
55	Widgets	$730	$7,528	$5,655	$2,215	$3,579	$3,450	$5,905	$5,651	$5,224	$154	$9,506	$6,931
56	Wombats	$4,065	$3,102	$768	$1,964	$3,548	$3,791	$5,609	$3,544	$9,776	$5,149	$6,786	$1,284
57	Woofers	$1,622	$2,734	$5,704	$7,542	$9,508	$7,440	$7,956	$2,169	$445	$163	$6,025	$1,704
58	Whatzits	$5,283	$8,672	$2,680	$622	$6,801	$9,137	$5,031	$3,972	$9,663	$4,871	$4,208	$7,610
59	Total	$11,700	$22,036	$14,807	$12,343	$23,436	$23,818	$24,501	$15,336	$25,108	$10,337	$26,525	$17,529
60													
61													
62	Division 8												
63	Widgets	$1,008	$4,142	$8,784	$6,673	$1,655	$5,103	$5,750	$2,475	$717	$8,625	$7,026	$3,076
64	Wombats	$3,336	$8,020	$3,465	$141	$4,127	$3,056	$1,919	$4,429	$4,414	$1,571	$7,113	$1,630
65	Woofers	$2,587	$88	$6,652	$3,580	$8,623	$3,268	$2,938	$9,424	$4,245	$537	$3,200	$9,392
66	Whatzits	$351	$9,425	$3,079	$3,262	$5,413	$586	$2,049	$6,336	$5,313	$3,761	$8,790	$3,863
67	Total	$7,282	$21,675	$21,980	$13,656	$19,818	$12,013	$12,656	$22,664	$14,689	$14,494	$26,129	$17,961
68													
69													
70	Division 9												
71	Widgets	$6,747	$9,319	$6,758	$8,142	$5,562	$7,241	$677	$3,295	$544	$3,297	$9,063	$2,842
72	Wombats	$9,608	$3,598	$3,014	$115	$7,584	$5,726	$2,999	$4,266	$1,520	$9,224	$9,759	$7,230
73	Woofers	$9,669	$2,937	$1,673	$6,730	$3,105	$5,099	$7,582	$9,496	$9,676	$403	$1,502	$8,805
74	Whatzits	$2,930	$4,501	$1,726	$1,816	$6,190	$1,421	$6,621	$6,721	$3,529	$3,481	$7,348	$6,470
75	Total	$28,954	$20,355	$13,171	$16,803	$22,441	$19,487	$17,879	$23,778	$15,269	$16,405	$27,672	$25,347
76													
77													
78	Division 10												
79	Widgets	$6,804	$1,198	$3,581	$7,406	$9,974	$6,388	$1,768	$7,865	$665	$176	$3,084	$2,504
80	Wombats	$3,235	$8,654	$4,975	$7,269	$9,167	$601	$6,738	$894	$9,947	$5,977	$4,796	$968
81	Woofers	$2,051	$4,095	$4,426	$8,406	$4,191	$8,423	$8,562	$674	$1,790	$4,917	$3,014	$450
82	Whatzits	$8,949	$9,102	$9,462	$7,621	$2,244	$13	$7,159	$5,063	$3,542	$5,426	$8,088	$3,387
83	Total	$21,039	$23,049	$22,444	$30,702	$25,576	$15,425	$24,227	$14,496	$15,944	$16,496	$18,982	$7,309
84													
85													
86	Combined Sales: All Divisions												
87	Widgets	$38,656	$41,424	$50,180	$63,054	$52,599	$53,370	$43,737	$42,830	$38,471	$44,775	$53,963	$51,794
88	Wombats	$49,885	$55,776	$43,005	$50,329	$57,241	$32,244	$38,594	$33,074	$61,887	$44,280	$67,384	$43,066
89	Woofers	$29,359	$50,483	$57,778	$47,247	$54,419	$57,573	$57,589	$40,078	$40,420	$41,573	$40,871	$63,071
90	Whatzits	$35,077	$66,500	$32,642	$38,452	$52,641	$43,881	$45,220	$50,820	$55,161	$41,717	$52,868	$49,523
91	Total 2	$152,977	$214,183	$183,605	$199,082	$216,900	$187,068	$185,140	$166,802	$195,939	$172,345	$215,086	$207,454

FIGURE 9-17. *This sample printout shows Excel's default placement of row and column labels.*

	N	O	P	Q	R
1					
2					
3					
4	1/1/89	2/1/89	3/1/89	4/1/89	Total
5					
6					
7	$3,436	$1,635	$7,418	$38	$78,144
8	$9,420	$541	$8,861	$7,064	$77,067
9	$9,600	$9,460	$619	$9,000	$83,511
10	$1,586	$4,900	$4,781	$4,787	$77,540
11	$24,042	$16,536	$21,679	$20,889	$316,262
12					
13					
14					
15	$7,062	$2,912	$9,063	$329	$76,846
16	$3,906	$5,260	$3,930	$8,609	$75,452
17	$2,195	$4,662	$2,241	$5,779	$62,719
18	$757	$5,180	$458	$3,345	$59,414
19	$13,920	$18,014	$15,692	$18,062	$274,431
20					
21					
22					
23	$9,937	$4,041	$2,800	$3,486	$75,214
24	$2,017	$1,919	$7,627	$4,076	$87,969
25	$5,925	$2,207	$3,827	$9,937	$91,601
26	$5,366	$7,160	$5,620	$7,134	$70,338
27	$23,245	$15,327	$19,874	$24,633	$325,122
28					
29					
30					
31	$4,952	$5,752	$6,655	$7,108	$81,278
32	$3,409	$4,921	$5,907	$9,658	$62,793
33	$7,012	$4,947	$3,729	$7,229	$92,565
34	$5,428	$4,806	$9,513	$6,735	$85,142
35	$20,801	$20,426	$25,804	$30,730	$321,778
36					
37					
38					
39	$6,481	$2,558	$2,444	$6,380	$69,659
40	$7,723	$5,353	$8,222	$4,432	$92,586
41	$4,899	$5,039	$7,074	$8,064	$82,745
42	$2,659	$5,601	$8,384	$4,990	$71,208
43	$21,762	$18,551	$26,124	$23,866	$316,198
44					
45					
46					
47	$2,236	$1,850	$1,867	$5,825	$73,515
48	$3,793	$278	$498	$8,944	$86,795

	N	O	P	Q	R
49	$4,645	$8,077	$5,897	$6,234	$80,396
50	$6,771	$2,200	$5,785	$4,055	$75,273
51	$17,445	$12,405	$14,047	$25,058	$315,979
52					
53					
54					
55	$4,070	$9,256	$769	$1,487	$72,110
56	$7,513	$3,719	$8,544	$693	$69,855
57	$9,229	$1,410	$2,713	$8,094	$74,458
58	$5,065	$5,006	$6,856	$5,552	$91,029
59	$25,877	$19,391	$18,882	$15,826	$307,452
60					
61					
62					
63	$5,258	$405	$3,176	$7,187	$71,060
64	$7,976	$9,564	$9,263	$4,015	$74,039
65	$4,614	$8,203	$1,913	$2,783	$72,047
66	$3,180	$8,091	$3,593	$2,904	$69,996
67	$21,028	$26,263	$17,945	$16,889	$287,142
68					
69					
70					
71	$6,562	$5,163	$3,689	$400	$79,301
72	$5,297	$754	$6,958	$784	$78,436
73	$223	$9,150	$7,578	$301	$83,929
74	$622	$5,077	$6,465	$2,300	$67,218
75	$12,704	$20,144	$24,690	$3,785	$308,884
76					
77					
78					
79	$2,186	$81	$7,793	$2,243	$63,716
80	$5,552	$6,032	$2,636	$1,096	$78,537
81	$2,767	$4,932	$4,715	$9,264	$72,677
82	$8,311	$6,221	$1,537	$7,113	$93,238
83	$18,816	$17,266	$16,681	$19,716	$308,168
84					
85					
86					
87	$52,180	$33,653	$45,674	$34,483	$740,843
88	$56,606	$38,341	$62,446	$49,371	$783,529
89	$51,109	$58,087	$40,306	$66,685	$796,648
90	$39,745	$54,242	$52,992	$48,915	$760,396
91	$199,640	$184,323	$201,418	$199,454	$3,081,416

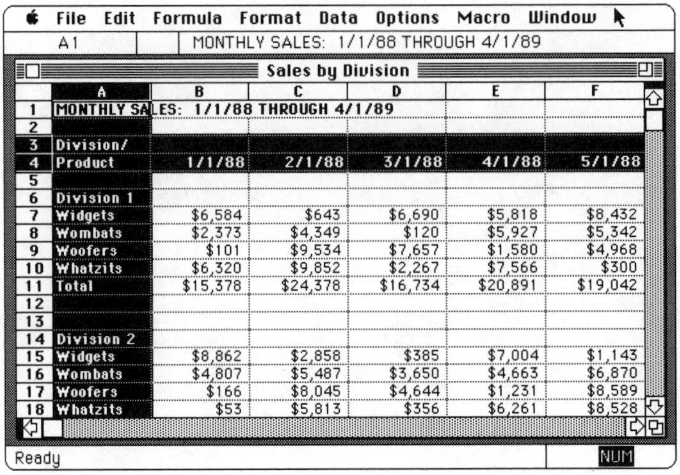

FIGURE 9-18. *You have selected the row and column labels and used the Set Print Titles command to print labels on each page of a worksheet.*

You must select an entire row or column for your print-titles range. Excel does not accept partial rows or columns. Although you can select multiple columns and rows for your print-titles area, the rows and columns you select must be adjacent to each other. In other words, you can include rows 1 and 2 and columns C and D in your print-titles range, but you cannot use rows 1 and 3 or columns A and C. If you attempt to select nonadjacent rows or columns, Excel presents an alert box with the message *Print title is not valid.*

Like the print area, the rows and columns you select for print titles are stored as a named range, this time with the name *Print_Titles*. You can edit or delete the print-titles range through the Define Name dialog box.

When you use Set Print Titles, you must specify a print range that does not overlap the print-titles area; otherwise, you get two sets of row and column titles in your printed worksheet. The effects can be quite confusing, as you can see in Figure 9-19. In this sample worksheet, Excel has printed the contents of rows 3 and 4 and column A once in response to your Set Print Titles command and a second time in response to your print-area specifications.

Remember, the default print area includes the entire active worksheet. Unless you exclude the print-title cells from the print area, Excel assumes that they are to be printed twice. The printout in Figure 9-20 shows the same worksheet, with a print area of B5:R91.

	A	A	B	C	D	E	F	G	H	I	J	K
3	Division/	Division/										
4	Product	Product	1/1/88	2/1/88	3/1/88	4/1/88	5/1/88	6/1/88	7/1/88	8/1/88	9/1/88	10/1/88
1	MONTHLY SA	MONTHLY SALES: 1/1/88 THROUGH 4/1/89										
2												
3	Division/	Division/										
4	Product	Product	1/1/88	2/1/88	3/1/88	4/1/88	5/1/88	6/1/88	7/1/88	8/1/88	9/1/88	10/1/88
5												
6	Division 1	Division 1										
7	Widgets	Widgets	$6,584	$643	$6,690	$5,818	$8,432	$6,760	$2,075	$1,653	$4,951	$7,242
8	Wombats	Wombats	$2,373	$4,349	$120	$5,927	$5,342	$1,274	$1,218	$1,352	$6,950	$4,595
9	Woofers	Woofers	$101	$9,534	$7,657	$1,580	$4,968	$9,698	$3,022	$128	$6,741	$1,237
10	Whatzits	Whatzits	$6,320	$9,852	$2,267	$7,566	$300	$9,188	$6,843	$678	$3,310	$1,589
11	Total	Total	$15,378	$24,378	$16,734	$20,891	$19,042	$26,920	$13,158	$3,811	$21,952	$14,663
12												
13												
14	Division 2	Division 2										
15	Widgets	Widgets	$8,862	$2,858	$385	$7,004	$1,143	$3,343	$8,777	$8,304	$2,727	$2,102
16	Wombats	Wombats	$4,807	$5,487	$3,650	$4,663	$6,870	$3,973	$2,372	$2,883	$5,643	$6,661
17	Woofers	Woofers	$166	$8,045	$4,644	$1,231	$8,589	$4,213	$3,427	$1,233	$3,281	$6,749
18	Whatzits	Whatzits	$53	$5,813	$356	$6,261	$8,528	$3,315	$1,138	$9,129	$1,809	$8,353
19	Total	Total	$13,888	$22,203	$9,035	$19,159	$25,130	$14,844	$15,714	$21,549	$13,460	$24,065
20												
21												
22	Division 3	Division 3										
23	Widgets	Widgets	$1,935	$6,934	$773	$6,131	$5,681	$7,951	$3,130	$2,709	$9,478	$3,963
24	Wombats	Wombats	$7,006	$6,973	$9,183	$7,207	$4,093	$4,076	$4,834	$8,575	$6,333	$3,714
25	Woofers	Woofers	$432	$3,965	$6,597	$7,538	$7,878	$3,107	$9,082	$3,390	$3,442	$6,072
26	Whatzits	Whatzits	$3,221	$4,187	$2,903	$811	$7,717	$3,347	$778	$2,535	$9,923	$6,057
27	Total	Total	$12,594	$22,059	$19,456	$21,687	$25,369	$18,481	$17,824	$17,209	$29,176	$19,806
28												
29												
30	Division 4	Division 4										
31	Widgets	Widgets	$714	$439	$4,049	$8,318	$6,538	$3,686	$4,309	$2,616	$7,266	$4,195
32	Wombats	Wombats	$5,805	$577	$7,598	$7,948	$1,997	$3,625	$915	$373	$493	$534
33	Woofers	Woofers	$8,632	$6,326	$8,227	$4,294	$808	$3,399	$4,115	$6,931	$6,066	$3,841
34	Whatzits	Whatzits	$1,620	$6,536	$10	$3,888	$1,241	$9,864	$7,059	$3,734	$9,895	$767
35	Total	Total	$16,771	$13,876	$19,884	$24,448	$10,584	$20,574	$16,398	$15,854	$23,720	$9,337
36												
37												
38	Division 5	Division 5										
39	Widgets	Widgets	$4,424	$5,388	$4,512	$4,669	$7,347	$5,826	$3,618	$1,318	$1,318	$6,192
40	Wombats	Wombats	$2,982	$5,624	$9,411	$6,974	$5,635	$4,050	$8,590	$994	$7,720	$4,561
41	Woofers	Woofers	$2,282	$3,928	$4,910	$6,184	$1,851	$7,997	$5,503	$4,327	$1,713	$8,744
42	Whatzits	Whatzits	$5,439	$606	$8,232	$6,572	$8,659	$172	$8,359	$3,324	$1,552	$1,116
43	Total	Total	$15,127	$15,546	$27,065	$24,399	$23,492	$18,045	$26,070	$9,963	$12,303	$20,613
44												
45												
46	Division 6	Division 6										

	A	A	B	C	D	E	F	G	H	I	J	K
3	Division/	Division/										
4	Product	Product	1/1/88	2/1/88	3/1/88	4/1/88	5/1/88	6/1/88	7/1/88	8/1/88	9/1/88	10/1/88
47	Widgets	Widgets	$848	$2,975	$8,993	$6,678	$2,688	$3,622	$7,728	$6,744	$5,581	$8,829
48	Wombats	Wombats	$6,668	$9,392	$821	$8,121	$6,878	$2,072	$3,400	$5,764	$9,091	$2,094
49	Woofers	Woofers	$1,817	$8,831	$7,288	$162	$4,898	$4,929	$5,402	$306	$3,021	$8,910
50	Whatzits	Whatzits	$911	$7,806	$1,927	$33	$5,548	$6,838	$183	$9,328	$6,625	$6,296
51	Total	Total	$10,244	$29,004	$19,029	$14,994	$22,012	$17,461	$16,713	$22,142	$24,318	$26,129
52												
53												
54	Division 7	Division 7										
55	Widgets	Widgets	$730	$7,528	$5,655	$2,215	$3,579	$3,450	$5,905	$5,651	$5,224	$154
56	Wombats	Wombats	$4,065	$3,102	$768	$1,964	$3,548	$3,791	$5,609	$3,544	$9,776	$5,149
57	Woofers	Woofers	$1,622	$2,734	$5,704	$7,542	$9,508	$7,440	$7,956	$2,169	$445	$163
58	Whatzits	Whatzits	$5,283	$8,672	$2,680	$622	$6,801	$9,137	$5,031	$3,972	$9,663	$4,871
59	Total	Total	$11,700	$22,036	$14,807	$12,343	$23,436	$23,818	$24,501	$15,336	$25,108	$10,337
60												
61												
62	Division 8	Division 8										
63	Widgets	Widgets	$1,008	$4,142	$8,784	$6,673	$1,655	$5,103	$5,750	$2,475	$717	$8,625
64	Wombats	Wombats	$3,336	$8,020	$3,465	$141	$4,127	$3,056	$1,919	$4,429	$4,414	$1,571
65	Woofers	Woofers	$2,587	$88	$6,652	$3,580	$8,623	$3,268	$2,938	$9,424	$4,245	$537
66	Whatzits	Whatzits	$351	$9,425	$3,079	$3,262	$5,413	$586	$2,049	$6,336	$5,313	$3,761
67	Total	Total	$7,282	$21,675	$21,980	$13,656	$19,818	$12,013	$12,656	$22,664	$14,689	$14,494
68												
69												
70	Division 9	Division 9										
71	Widgets	Widgets	$6,747	$9,319	$6,758	$8,142	$5,562	$7,241	$677	$3,295	$544	$3,297
72	Wombats	Wombats	$9,608	$3,598	$3,014	$115	$7,584	$5,726	$2,999	$4,266	$1,520	$9,224
73	Woofers	Woofers	$9,669	$2,937	$1,673	$6,730	$3,105	$5,099	$7,582	$9,496	$9,676	$403
74	Whatzits	Whatzits	$2,930	$4,501	$1,726	$1,816	$6,190	$1,421	$6,621	$6,721	$3,529	$3,481
75	Total	Total	$28,954	$20,355	$13,171	$16,803	$22,441	$19,487	$17,879	$23,778	$15,269	$16,405
76												
77												
78	Division 10	Division 10										
79	Widgets	Widgets	$6,804	$1,196	$3,581	$7,406	$9,974	$6,388	$1,768	$7,865	$665	$176
80	Wombats	Wombats	$3,235	$8,654	$4,975	$7,269	$601	$6,738	$894	$9,947	$5,977	
81	Woofers	Woofers	$2,051	$4,095	$4,426	$8,406	$4,191	$8,423	$8,562	$674	$1,790	$4,917
82	Whatzits	Whatzits	$8,949	$9,102	$9,462	$7,621	$2,244	$13	$7,159	$5,063	$3,542	$5,426
83	Total	Total	$21,039	$23,049	$22,444	$30,702	$25,576	$15,425	$24,227	$14,496	$15,944	$16,496
84												
85												
86	Combined Sal	Combined Sales: All Divisions										
87	Widgets	Widgets	$38,656	$41,424	$50,180	$63,054	$52,599	$53,370	$43,737	$42,830	$38,471	$44,775
88	Wombats	Wombats	$49,885	$55,776	$43,005	$50,329	$57,241	$32,244	$38,594	$33,074	$61,887	$44,280
89	Woofers	Woofers	$29,359	$50,483	$57,778	$47,247	$54,419	$57,573	$57,589	$40,078	$40,420	$41,573
90	Whatzits	Whatzits	$35,077	$66,500	$32,642	$38,452	$52,641	$43,881	$45,220	$50,820	$55,161	$41,717
91	Total	Total	$152,977	$214,183	$183,605	$199,082	$216,900	$187,068	$185,140	$166,802	$195,939	$172,345

FIGURE 9-19. *Two pages of this sample worksheet show the effect of selecting overlapping print and print-titles ranges (using left and right margins of 1 inch and top and bottom margins of 0.75 inch).*

Sales by Division — Page 1

	A	B	C	D	E	F	G	H	I	J	K	L	M
3	Division/												
4	Product	1/1/88	2/1/88	3/1/88	4/1/88	5/1/88	6/1/88	7/1/88	8/1/88	9/1/88	10/1/88	11/1/88	12/1/88
5													
6	Division 1												
7	Widgets	$6,584	$643	$6,690	$5,818	$8,432	$6,760	$2,075	$1,653	$4,951	$7,242	$8,067	$6,702
8	Wombats	$2,373	$4,349	$120	$5,927	$5,342	$1,274	$1,218	$1,352	$6,950	$4,595	$9,981	$7,700
9	Woofers	$101	$9,534	$7,657	$1,580	$4,968	$9,698	$3,022	$128	$6,741	$1,237	$1,862	$8,304
10	Whatzits	$6,320	$9,852	$2,267	$7,566	$300	$9,188	$6,843	$678	$3,310	$1,589	$7,123	$6,450
11	Total	$15,378	$24,378	$16,734	$20,891	$19,042	$26,920	$13,158	$3,811	$21,952	$14,663	$27,033	$29,156
12													
13													
14	Division 2												
15	Widgets	$8,862	$2,858	$385	$7,004	$1,143	$3,343	$8,777	$8,304	$2,727	$2,102	$2,792	$9,183
16	Wombats	$4,807	$5,487	$3,650	$4,663	$6,870	$3,973	$2,372	$2,883	$5,643	$6,861	$2,000	$4,538
17	Woofers	$166	$8,045	$4,644	$1,231	$8,589	$4,213	$3,427	$1,233	$3,281	$6,749	$3,334	$2,930
18	Whatzits	$53	$5,813	$356	$6,261	$8,528	$3,315	$1,138	$9,129	$1,809	$8,353	$619	$4,300
19	Total	$13,888	$22,203	$9,035	$19,159	$25,130	$14,844	$15,714	$21,549	$13,460	$24,065	$8,745	$20,951
20													
21													
22	Division 3												
23	Widgets	$1,935	$6,934	$773	$6,131	$5,681	$7,951	$3,130	$2,709	$9,478	$3,963	$4,654	$1,611
24	Wombats	$7,006	$6,973	$9,183	$7,207	$4,093	$4,076	$4,834	$8,575	$6,333	$3,714	$4,164	$6,172
25	Woofers	$432	$3,965	$6,597	$7,538	$7,878	$3,107	$9,082	$3,390	$3,442	$6,072	$8,922	$9,280
26	Whatzits	$3,221	$4,187	$2,903	$811	$7,717	$3,347	$778	$2,535	$9,923	$6,057	$3	$3,576
27	Total	$12,594	$22,059	$19,456	$21,687	$25,369	$18,481	$17,824	$17,209	$29,176	$19,806	$17,743	$20,639
28													
29													
30	Division 4												
31	Widgets	$714	$439	$4,049	$8,318	$6,538	$3,686	$4,309	$2,816	$7,266	$4,195	$4,638	$9,843
32	Wombats	$5,805	$577	$7,598	$7,948	$1,997	$3,625	$915	$373	$493	$534	$7,408	$1,625
33	Woofers	$8,632	$6,326	$8,227	$4,294	$808	$3,399	$4,115	$8,931	$6,066	$3,841	$8,914	$6,095
34	Whatzits	$1,620	$6,536	$10	$3,888	$1,241	$9,864	$7,059	$3,734	$9,895	$767	$4,209	$9,837
35	Total	$16,771	$13,878	$19,884	$24,448	$10,584	$20,574	$16,398	$15,854	$23,720	$9,337	$25,169	$27,400
36													
37													
38	Division 5												
39	Widgets	$4,424	$5,388	$4,512	$4,669	$7,347	$5,826	$3,618	$1,318	$1,316	$6,192	$1,813	$5,371
40	Wombats	$2,982	$5,624	$9,411	$6,974	$5,635	$4,050	$8,590	$994	$7,720	$4,561	$6,018	$4,297
41	Woofers	$2,282	$3,928	$4,910	$6,184	$1,851	$7,997	$5,503	$4,327	$1,713	$8,744	$2,486	$7,744
42	Whatzits	$5,439	$606	$8,232	$6,572	$6,659	$172	$8,359	$3,324	$1,552	$1,116	$3,456	$2,087
43	Total	$15,127	$15,546	$27,065	$24,399	$23,492	$18,045	$26,070	$9,963	$12,303	$20,613	$13,773	$19,499
44													
45													
46	Division 6												
47	Widgets	$848	$2,975	$8,993	$6,678	$2,688	$3,622	$7,728	$6,744	$5,581	$8,829	$3,320	$3,731
48	Wombats	$6,668	$9,392	$821	$8,121	$8,878	$2,072	$3,400	$5,764	$9,091	$2,094	$9,359	$7,622
49	Woofers	$1,817	$8,831	$7,288	$162	$4,898	$4,929	$5,402	$306	$3,021	$8,910	$1,612	$8,367
50	Whatzits	$911	$7,806	$1,927	$33	$5,548	$6,838	$183	$9,328	$6,625	$6,296	$9,024	$1,943

Sales by Division — Page 2

	A	B	C	D	E	F	G	H	I	J	K	L	M
3	Division/												
4	Product	1/1/88	2/1/88	3/1/88	4/1/88	5/1/88	6/1/88	7/1/88	8/1/88	9/1/88	10/1/88	11/1/88	12/1/88
51	Total	$10,244	$29,004	$19,029	$14,994	$22,012	$17,461	$16,713	$22,142	$24,318	$26,129	$23,315	$21,663
52													
53													
54	Division 7												
55	Widgets	$730	$7,528	$5,655	$2,215	$3,579	$3,450	$5,905	$5,651	$5,224	$154	$9,506	$6,931
56	Wombats	$4,065	$3,102	$768	$1,964	$3,548	$3,791	$5,609	$3,544	$9,776	$5,149	$6,786	$1,284
57	Woofers	$1,622	$2,734	$5,704	$7,542	$9,508	$7,440	$7,956	$2,169	$445	$163	$6,025	$1,704
58	Whatzits	$5,283	$8,672	$2,680	$622	$6,801	$9,137	$5,031	$3,972	$9,663	$4,871	$4,208	$7,610
59	Total	$11,700	$22,036	$14,807	$12,343	$23,436	$23,818	$24,501	$15,336	$25,108	$10,337	$26,525	$17,529
60													
61													
62	Division 8												
63	Widgets	$1,008	$4,142	$8,764	$6,673	$1,655	$5,103	$5,750	$2,475	$717	$8,625	$7,026	$3,076
64	Wombats	$3,336	$8,020	$3,465	$141	$4,127	$3,056	$1,919	$4,429	$4,414	$1,571	$7,113	$1,630
65	Woofers	$2,587	$88	$6,652	$3,580	$8,623	$3,268	$2,938	$9,424	$4,245	$537	$3,200	$9,392
66	Whatzits	$351	$9,425	$3,079	$3,262	$5,413	$586	$2,049	$6,336	$5,313	$3,761	$8,790	$3,863
67	Total	$7,282	$21,675	$21,980	$13,656	$19,818	$12,013	$12,656	$22,664	$14,689	$14,494	$26,129	$17,961
68													
69													
70	Division 9												
71	Widgets	$6,747	$9,319	$6,758	$8,142	$5,562	$7,241	$677	$3,295	$544	$3,297	$9,063	$2,842
72	Wombats	$9,608	$3,598	$3,014	$115	$7,584	$5,726	$2,999	$4,266	$1,520	$9,224	$9,759	$7,230
73	Woofers	$9,669	$2,937	$1,673	$6,730	$3,105	$5,099	$7,582	$9,496	$9,676	$403	$1,502	$8,805
74	Whatzits	$2,930	$4,501	$1,726	$1,816	$6,190	$1,421	$6,621	$6,721	$3,529	$3,481	$7,348	$6,470
75	Total	$28,954	$20,355	$13,171	$16,803	$22,441	$19,487	$17,879	$23,778	$15,269	$16,405	$27,672	$25,347
76													
77													
78	Division 10												
79	Widgets	$6,804	$1,198	$3,581	$7,406	$9,974	$6,388	$1,768	$7,865	$665	$176	$3,084	$2,504
80	Wombats	$3,235	$8,654	$4,975	$7,269	$9,167	$601	$6,738	$894	$9,947	$5,977	$4,796	$968
81	Woofers	$2,051	$4,095	$4,426	$8,406	$4,191	$8,423	$8,562	$674	$1,790	$4,917	$3,014	$450
82	Whatzits	$8,949	$9,102	$9,462	$7,621	$2,244	$13	$7,159	$5,063	$3,542	$5,426	$8,088	$3,387
83	Total	$21,039	$23,049	$22,444	$30,702	$25,576	$15,425	$24,227	$14,496	$15,944	$16,496	$18,982	$7,309
84													
85													
86	Combined Sales: All Divisions												
87	Widgets	$38,656	$41,424	$50,180	$63,054	$52,599	$53,370	$43,737	$42,830	$38,471	$44,775	$53,963	$51,794
88	Wombats	$49,885	$55,776	$43,005	$50,329	$57,241	$32,244	$38,594	$33,074	$61,887	$44,280	$67,384	$43,066
89	Woofers	$29,359	$50,483	$57,778	$47,247	$54,419	$57,573	$57,589	$40,078	$40,420	$41,573	$40,871	$63,071
90	Whatzits	$35,077	$66,500	$32,642	$38,452	$52,641	$43,881	$45,220	$50,820	$55,161	$41,717	$52,868	$49,523
91	Total	$152,977	$214,183	$183,605	$199,082	$216,900	$187,068	$185,140	$166,802	$195,939	$172,345	$215,086	$207,454

FIGURE 9-20. *Here, the sample worksheet has row and column labels on each page.*

The print area in this example includes all the cells below and to the right of the print-titles range. This means that the cells in rows 1 and 2 are not included in the printed worksheet. Fortunately, these rows contain only the title used to identify the document. You can easily place this information in the page header in the Page Setup dialog box. As you develop your worksheet, however, you should keep this restriction in mind: If you plan to use print titles, make sure that you do not place important information above or to the left of the rows and columns in your print-titles range.

In the example in Figure 9-20, the print-titles range and the print area occupy adjacent rows and columns, but this need not be the case. The print-area/print-titles combination is also helpful when you want to print only selected parts of your worksheet. For example, suppose you want to print only cells N87:R91 of the *Sales by Division* worksheet. Of course, the labels in rows 3 and 4 and column A are not included in the print area, so they do not appear on the printed worksheet if they have not yet been defined. To get around this problem, drag through the headers for rows 3 and 4, then hold down the Command key and click the header

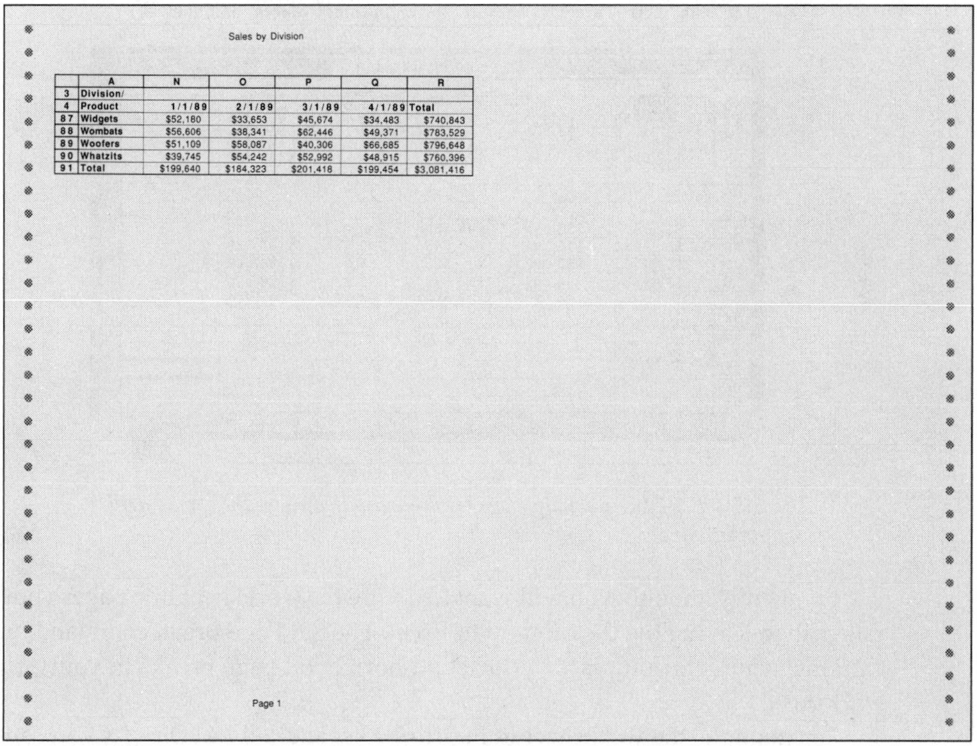

Sales by Division

	A	N	O	P	Q	R
3	Division/					
4	Product	1/1/89	2/1/89	3/1/89	4/1/89	Total
87	Widgets	$52,180	$33,653	$45,674	$34,483	$740,843
88	Wombats	$56,606	$38,341	$62,446	$49,371	$783,529
89	Woofers	$51,109	$58,087	$40,306	$66,685	$796,648
90	Whatzits	$39,745	$54,242	$52,992	$48,915	$760,396
91	Total	$199,640	$184,323	$201,418	$199,454	$3,081,416

Page 1

FIGURE 9-21. *You have used nonadjacent print and print-titles ranges to print only a selected part of the worksheet.*

for column A. Again, your worksheet looks like Figure 9-18. Now, choose the Set Print Titles command. Next, drag through cells N87:R91 and choose the Set Print Area command. The resulting printed worksheet looks like Figure 9-21.

Notice that only the row labels in columns N through R appear in the printed worksheet, even though your print-titles range included the entire two rows. Similarly, only the labels in cells A87:A91 appear, even though all of column A was included in the print-titles range. Microsoft Excel automatically matches the labels in the print-titles area with the corresponding columns and rows in the print area so that the titles and data are correctly aligned.

The Set Page Breaks command

As you know, when you print a worksheet that is too large to fit on a single sheet of paper, Microsoft Excel automatically breaks that worksheet into page-sized sections based upon the current options in the Page Setup dialog box. As you can see in Figure 9-22, Excel's automatic page breaks are indicated on the screen by dashed gridlines.

	N	O	P	Q	R	S
80	$5,552	$6,032	$2,636	$1,096	$78,537	
81	$2,767	$4,932	$4,715	$9,264	$72,677	
82	$8,311	$6,221	$1,537	$7,113	$93,238	
83	$18,816	$17,266	$16,681	$19,716	$308,168	
84						
85						
86						
87	$52,180	$33,653	$45,674	$34,483	$740,843	
88	$56,606	$38,341	$62,446	$49,371	$783,529	
89	$51,109	$58,087	$40,306	$66,685	$796,648	
90	$39,745	$54,242	$52,992	$48,915	$760,396	
91	$199,640	$184,323	$201,418	$199,454	$3,081,416	
92						
93						
94						
95						
96						
97						

FIGURE 9-22. *Automatic page breaks are indicated on the screen with dashed lines.*

Frequently, though, you will want to divide the worksheet into pages yourself, rather than leaving the decision up to Excel. The Set Page Break command on the Options menu lets you place vertical and horizontal page breaks in your printed worksheet.

For example, the worksheet in Figure 9-23 spans cells A1:O35. As you can see, Excel's automatic page breaks make this worksheet a little awkward to read. Only one column of data appears on page 3 of the worksheet. To distribute the data in

	A	B	C	D	E	F	G
1	1988 Product Summary						
2							
3		January	February	March	April	May	June
4	Product1	$4,426	$4,869	$5,355	$5,891	$6,480	$7,128
5	Product2	$8,406	$9,247	$10,171	$11,188	$12,307	$13,538
6	Product3	$4,191	$4,610	$5,071	$5,578	$6,136	$6,750
7	Product4	$8,423	$9,265	$10,192	$11,211	$12,332	$13,565
8	Product5	$8,562	$9,418	$10,360	$11,396	$12,536	$13,789
9	Product6	$674	$741	$816	$897	$987	$1,085
10	Product7	$1,790	$1,969	$2,166	$2,382	$2,621	$2,883
11	Product8	$4,917	$5,409	$5,950	$6,545	$7,199	$7,919
12	Product9	$3,014	$3,315	$3,647	$4,012	$4,413	$4,854
13	Product10	$450	$495	$545	$599	$659	$725
14	Product11	$2,767	$3,044	$3,348	$3,683	$4,051	$4,456
15	Product12	$4,932	$5,425	$5,968	$6,564	$7,221	$7,943
16	Product13	$4,715	$5,187	$5,705	$6,276	$6,903	$7,594
17	Product14	$9,264	$10,190	$11,209	$12,330	$13,563	$14,920
18	Product15	$8,949	$9,844	$10,828	$11,911	$13,102	$14,412
19	Product16	$9,102	$10,012	$11,013	$12,115	$13,326	$14,659
20	Product17	$9,462	$10,408	$11,449	$12,594	$13,853	$15,239
21	Product18	$7,621	$8,383	$9,221	$10,144	$11,158	$12,274
22	Product19	$2,244	$2,468	$2,715	$2,987	$3,285	$3,614
23	Product20	$13	$14	$16	$17	$19	$21
24	Product21	$7,159	$7,875	$8,662	$9,529	$10,481	$11,530
25	Product22	$5,063	$5,569	$6,126	$6,739	$7,413	$8,154
26	Product23	$3,542	$3,896	$4,286	$4,714	$5,186	$5,704
27	Product24	$5,426	$5,969	$6,565	$7,222	$7,944	$8,739
28	Product25	$8,088	$8,897	$9,786	$10,765	$11,842	$13,026
29	Product26	$3,387	$3,726	$4,098	$4,508	$4,959	$5,455
30	Product27	$8,311	$9,142	$10,056	$11,062	$12,168	$13,385
31	Product28	$6,221	$6,843	$7,527	$8,280	$9,108	$10,019
32	Product29	$1,537	$1,691	$1,860	$2,046	$2,250	$2,475
33	Product30	$7,113	$7,824	$8,607	$9,467	$10,414	$11,456
34							
35	Total	$159,769	$175,746	$193,320	$212,653	$233,918	$257,310

	A	H	I	J	K	L	M
1	1988 Product						
2							
3		July	August	September	October	November	December
4	Product1	$7,841	$8,625	$9,488	$10,436	$11,480	$12,628
5	Product2	$14,892	$16,381	$18,019	$19,821	$21,803	$23,983
6	Product3	$7,425	$8,167	$8,984	$9,882	$10,870	$11,957
7	Product4	$14,922	$16,414	$18,055	$19,861	$21,847	$24,032
8	Product5	$15,168	$16,685	$18,353	$20,189	$22,208	$24,428
9	Product6	$1,194	$1,313	$1,445	$1,589	$1,748	$1,923
10	Product7	$3,171	$3,488	$3,837	$4,221	$4,643	$5,107
11	Product8	$8,711	$9,582	$10,540	$11,594	$12,753	$14,029
12	Product9	$5,339	$5,873	$6,461	$7,107	$7,818	$8,599
13	Product10	$797	$877	$965	$1,061	$1,167	$1,284
14	Product11	$4,902	$5,392	$5,931	$6,524	$7,177	$7,895
15	Product12	$8,737	$9,611	$10,572	$11,629	$12,792	$14,072
16	Product13	$8,353	$9,188	$10,107	$11,118	$12,229	$13,452
17	Product14	$16,412	$18,053	$19,858	$21,844	$24,028	$26,431
18	Product15	$15,854	$17,439	$19,183	$21,101	$23,211	$25,533
19	Product16	$16,125	$17,737	$19,511	$21,462	$23,608	$25,969
20	Product17	$16,763	$18,439	$20,283	$22,311	$24,542	$26,996
21	Product18	$13,501	$14,851	$16,336	$17,970	$19,767	$21,744
22	Product19	$3,975	$4,373	$4,810	$5,291	$5,820	$6,402
23	Product20	$23	$25	$28	$31	$34	$37
24	Product21	$12,683	$13,951	$15,346	$16,881	$18,569	$20,425
25	Product22	$8,969	$9,866	$10,853	$11,938	$13,132	$14,445
26	Product23	$6,275	$6,902	$7,593	$8,352	$9,187	$10,106
27	Product24	$9,612	$10,574	$11,631	$12,794	$14,074	$15,481
28	Product25	$14,328	$15,761	$17,337	$19,071	$20,978	$23,076
29	Product26	$6,000	$6,600	$7,260	$7,986	$8,785	$9,664
30	Product27	$14,723	$16,196	$17,815	$19,597	$21,557	$23,712
31	Product28	$11,021	$12,123	$13,335	$14,669	$16,136	$17,749
32	Product29	$2,723	$2,995	$3,295	$3,624	$3,987	$4,385
33	Product30	$12,601	$13,861	$15,247	$16,772	$18,449	$20,294
34							
35	Total	$283,041	$311,345	$342,479	$376,727	$414,400	$455,840

FIGURE 9-23. *This sample worksheet shows Excel's default page breaks.* (continued)

FIGURE 9-23. *continued*

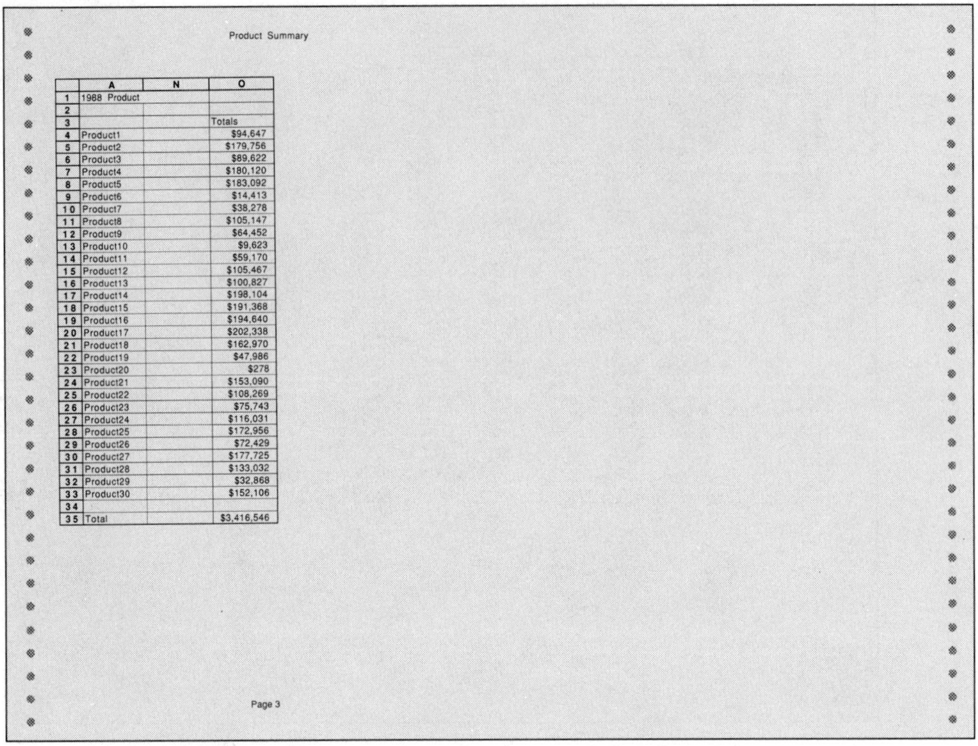

Product Summary

	A	N	O
1	1988 Product		
2			
3			Totals
4	Product1		$94,647
5	Product2		$179,756
6	Product3		$89,622
7	Product4		$180,120
8	Product5		$183,092
9	Product6		$14,413
10	Product7		$38,278
11	Product8		$105,147
12	Product9		$64,452
13	Product10		$9,623
14	Product11		$59,170
15	Product12		$105,467
16	Product13		$100,827
17	Product14		$198,104
18	Product15		$191,368
19	Product16		$194,640
20	Product17		$202,338
21	Product18		$162,970
22	Product19		$47,986
23	Product20		$278
24	Product21		$153,090
25	Product22		$108,269
26	Product23		$75,743
27	Product24		$116,031
28	Product25		$172,956
29	Product26		$72,429
30	Product27		$177,725
31	Product28		$133,032
32	Product29		$32,868
33	Product30		$152,106
34			
35	Total		$3,416,546

Page 3

this three-page worksheet a bit more evenly, you can select cell G1 of the worksheet and choose Set Page Break from the Options menu, then select cell L1 and choose Set Page Break again. The Set Page Break command tells Excel to insert a forced page break above and to the left of the selected cell. Because all the worksheet rows fit on each page, you can force a page break at row 1 to keep all the rows together. As you can see in Figure 9-24, forced page breaks are indicated on the screen by dark dashed lines. When you force a page break, Excel adjusts the subsequent automatic page breaks in the document, so that the worksheet prints as shown in Figure 9-25.

To remove forced page breaks, select the cell below or to the right of the dark dashed line and choose Remove Page Break, which has replaced Set Page Break on the Options menu. You cannot remove Excel's automatic page breaks.

If you want to force a horizontal page break without affecting the vertical breaks in your document, click the header of the row with which you want to begin a new page, then choose the Set Page Break command. Excel inserts the horizontal page break just above the row you have selected.

If you want to force a vertical page break without affecting the horizontal pagination, click the header of the column with which you want to begin the new page and choose the Set Page Break command. Excel inserts the page break to the left of the column you select.

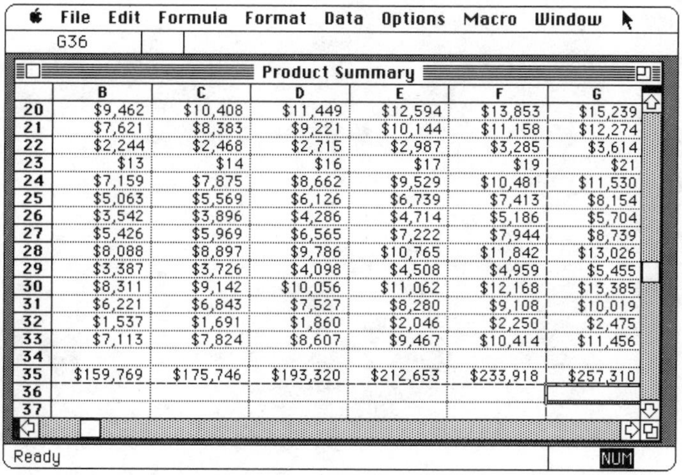

	B	C	D	E	F	G
20	$9,462	$10,408	$11,449	$12,594	$13,853	$15,239
21	$7,621	$8,383	$9,221	$10,144	$11,158	$12,274
22	$2,244	$2,468	$2,715	$2,987	$3,285	$3,614
23	$13	$14	$16	$17	$19	$21
24	$7,159	$7,875	$8,662	$9,529	$10,481	$11,530
25	$5,063	$5,569	$6,126	$6,739	$7,413	$8,154
26	$3,542	$3,896	$4,286	$4,714	$5,186	$5,704
27	$5,426	$5,969	$6,565	$7,222	$7,944	$8,739
28	$8,088	$8,897	$9,786	$10,765	$11,842	$13,026
29	$3,387	$3,726	$4,098	$4,508	$4,959	$5,455
30	$8,311	$9,142	$10,056	$11,062	$12,168	$13,385
31	$6,221	$6,843	$7,527	$8,280	$9,108	$10,019
32	$1,537	$1,691	$1,860	$2,046	$2,250	$2,475
33	$7,113	$7,824	$8,607	$9,467	$10,414	$11,456
34						
35	$159,769	$175,746	$193,320	$212,653	$233,918	$257,310
36						
37						

FIGURE 9-24. *Forced page breaks are indicated on the screen with dark dashed lines.*

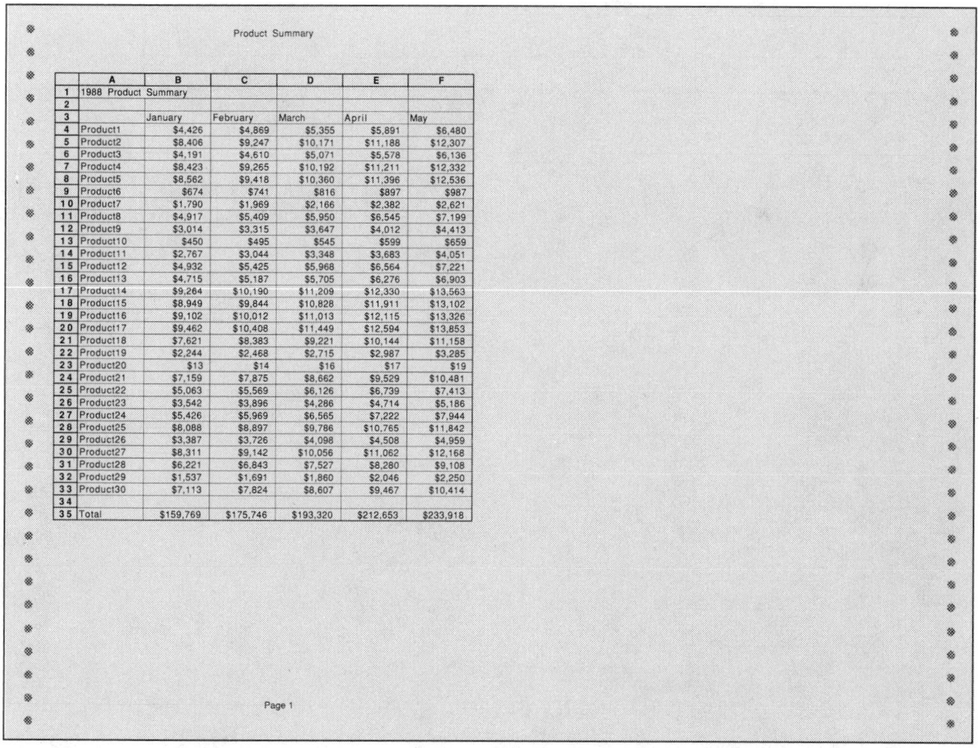

FIGURE 9-25. *This is the sample worksheet after forcing new page breaks to create a balanced worksheet.*

(continued)

FIGURE 9-25. *continued*

Product Summary

	A	G	H	I	J	K
1	1988 Product					
2						
3		June	July	August	September	October
4	Product1	$7,128	$7,841	$8,625	$9,486	$10,436
5	Product2	$13,538	$14,892	$16,381	$18,019	$19,821
6	Product3	$6,750	$7,425	$8,167	$8,984	$9,882
7	Product4	$13,565	$14,922	$16,414	$18,055	$19,861
8	Product5	$13,789	$15,168	$16,685	$18,353	$20,189
9	Product6	$1,085	$1,194	$1,313	$1,445	$1,589
10	Product7	$2,883	$3,171	$3,488	$3,837	$4,221
11	Product8	$7,919	$8,711	$9,582	$10,540	$11,594
12	Product9	$4,854	$5,339	$5,873	$6,461	$7,107
13	Product10	$725	$797	$877	$965	$1,061
14	Product11	$4,456	$4,902	$5,392	$5,931	$6,524
15	Product12	$7,943	$8,737	$9,611	$10,572	$11,629
16	Product13	$7,594	$8,353	$9,188	$10,107	$11,118
17	Product14	$14,920	$16,412	$18,053	$19,858	$21,844
18	Product15	$14,412	$15,854	$17,439	$19,183	$21,101
19	Product16	$14,659	$16,125	$17,737	$19,511	$21,462
20	Product17	$15,239	$16,763	$18,439	$20,283	$22,311
21	Product18	$12,274	$13,501	$14,851	$16,336	$17,970
22	Product19	$3,614	$3,975	$4,373	$4,810	$5,291
23	Product20	$21	$23	$25	$28	$31
24	Product21	$11,530	$12,683	$13,951	$15,346	$16,881
25	Product22	$8,154	$8,969	$9,866	$10,853	$11,938
26	Product23	$5,704	$6,275	$6,902	$7,593	$8,352
27	Product24	$8,739	$9,612	$10,574	$11,631	$12,794
28	Product25	$13,026	$14,328	$15,761	$17,337	$19,071
29	Product26	$5,455	$6,000	$6,600	$7,260	$7,986
30	Product27	$13,385	$14,723	$16,196	$17,815	$19,597
31	Product28	$10,019	$11,021	$12,123	$13,335	$14,669
32	Product29	$2,475	$2,723	$2,995	$3,295	$3,624
33	Product30	$11,456	$12,601	$13,861	$15,247	$16,772
34						
35	Total	$257,310	$283,041	$311,345	$342,479	$376,727

Product Summary

	A	L	M	N	O
1	1988 Product				
2					
3		November	December		Totals
4	Product1	$11,480	$12,628		$94,647
5	Product2	$21,803	$23,983		$179,756
6	Product3	$10,870	$11,957		$89,622
7	Product4	$21,847	$24,032		$180,120
8	Product5	$22,208	$24,428		$183,092
9	Product6	$1,748	$1,923		$14,413
10	Product7	$4,643	$5,107		$38,278
11	Product8	$12,753	$14,029		$105,147
12	Product9	$7,818	$8,599		$64,452
13	Product10	$1,167	$1,284		$9,623
14	Product11	$7,177	$7,895		$59,170
15	Product12	$12,792	$14,072		$105,467
16	Product13	$12,229	$13,452		$100,827
17	Product14	$24,028	$26,431		$196,104
18	Product15	$23,211	$25,533		$191,368
19	Product16	$23,608	$25,969		$194,640
20	Product17	$24,542	$26,996		$202,338
21	Product18	$19,767	$21,744		$162,970
22	Product19	$5,820	$6,402		$47,986
23	Product20	$34	$37		$278
24	Product21	$18,569	$20,425		$153,090
25	Product22	$13,132	$14,445		$108,269
26	Product23	$9,187	$10,106		$75,743
27	Product24	$14,074	$15,481		$116,031
28	Product25	$20,978	$23,076		$172,956
29	Product26	$8,785	$9,664		$72,429
30	Product27	$21,557	$23,712		$177,725
31	Product28	$16,136	$17,749		$133,032
32	Product29	$3,987	$4,385		$32,868
33	Product30	$18,449	$20,294		$152,106
34					
35	Total	$414,400	$455,840		$3,416,546

Printing a worksheet

Once you have selected the print area, defined your page layout, and adjusted any other relevant options, you are ready to select the Print… command from the File menu. When you choose this command, depending on whether your Macintosh is connected to an ImageWriter or a LaserWriter, Microsoft Excel presents one of the dialog boxes shown in Figures 9-26 and 9-27.

Some features are common to both the ImageWriter and the LaserWriter Print dialog boxes: Copies, the page-range settings, Print Using Color, Page Preview, and Print Sheet/Notes/Both. We discuss these common features first.

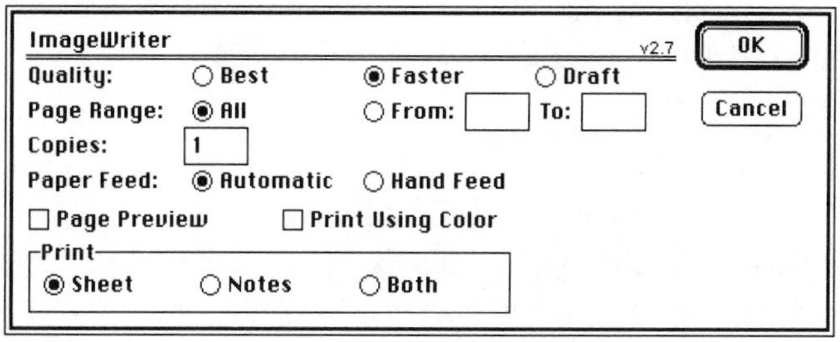

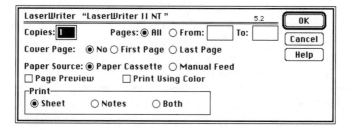

FIGURE 9-26. *This is the Print dialog box for an ImageWriter.*

FIGURE 9-27. *This is the Print dialog box for a LaserWriter.*

The Copies setting

Use the Copies setting to specify how many copies of the document you want to print. The default setting is 1. If you want Excel to print the document more than once, type the number of copies that you want into the Copies field. When Excel prints multiple copies of a document, it prints all the pages of the first copy, then all the pages of the second copy, and so forth. There is no practical limit to the number of copies of a document that Excel can print.

The Page-Range settings

The ImageWriter Page-Range setting and the LaserWriter Pages setting allow you to specify which pages of a document you want Excel to print. The default setting, All, instructs Excel to print every page of the defined print area. If you want to print only part of a document, click the From button and type the number of the first page you want to print in the From field. Now, click the To field and type the number of the last page you want to print.

If you leave the From field blank and enter a number in the To field, Excel prints from page 1 to the end of the page specified in To. If you enter a number in the From field and leave the To field blank, Excel begins printing with the specified From page and prints through to the end of the document (or to the end of the selected print area).

The Print Using Color option

If you have a printer with color capabilities, you can use Excel's Print Using Color option. Turning on this option tells Excel to use the colors options you set with the Font..., Standard Font..., and Format... commands when it prints the worksheet. Excel always prints in black and white unless this option is selected.

If you have formatted a cell or a range in your worksheet to be printed in a color that your printer can't print, the printer substitutes a specific color that it can reproduce. To find out what color is substituted, consult your printer manual. If you are printing a worksheet that has been formatted for color on a black-and-white printer, the worksheet appears in black and white.

The Page Preview option

If you want to take a look at the page breaks and format of your document before you begin printing, simply click the Page Preview option in the Print dialog box. Microsoft Excel shows you a picture of the printed page on the screen, reflecting all of the Page Setup and Print options you have selected. For example, Figure 9-28 shows a preview of the first page of the printed worksheet in Figure 9-17.

If you want to see the next page as you're previewing a worksheet, click the Next button at the top of the screen. (You can't click Next on the last preview page because Excel dims the button.) Similarly, to see the previous page, click the Previous button, which is dimmed when Excel displays the first page of your document. To return to your worksheet, click Cancel.

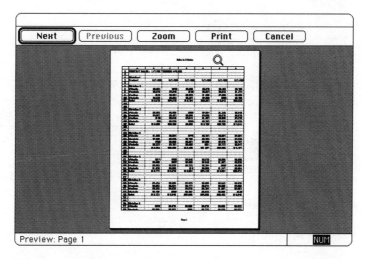

FIGURE 9-28. *This is a preview of the first page of the budget worksheet.*

Zooming in on selected areas

Although you can get a general idea of the page layout from this preview, the image is too small to read clearly. Fortunately, Microsoft Excel provides two methods for getting a closer look.

If you're using a mouse, Excel turns your pointer into a magnifying glass while the Page Preview option is in effect, so you can zoom in on the selected portion of the page to take a closer look. For example, to be sure your page header is formatted correctly, place the magnifying glass pointer at the top of the page and click. Your screen then looks like Figure 9-29. If you want to see another area of the worksheet, use the scroll bars at the edge of the window. You can return to the full-page preview by clicking again, then using the mouse to move the magnifier to a new location.

The Zoom button provides an alternative to the mouse pointer, allowing you to magnify your worksheet to see the page full size. All you need to do is click the Zoom button at the top of the preview screen. You can then use the scroll bars to move the range of cells you want to see into view. Click Zoom again to return to the preview size.

Printing the document from the preview screen

After you've previewed your document and decided to print it, you don't need to leave the preview window to choose the Print... command. You can tell Excel to print a document by clicking Print at the top of the Page Preview window. If you need to make changes or don't want to print, click Cancel.

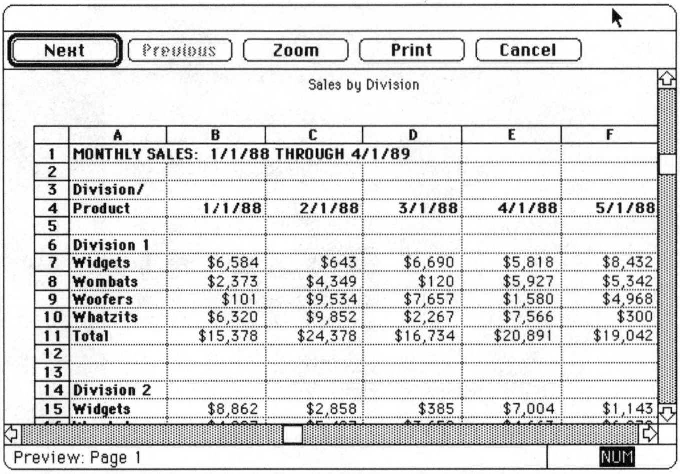

	A	B	C	D	E	F
1	MONTHLY SALES: 1/1/88 THROUGH 4/1/89					
2						
3	Division/					
4	Product	1/1/88	2/1/88	3/1/88	4/1/88	5/1/88
5						
6	Division 1					
7	Widgets	$6,584	$643	$6,690	$5,818	$8,432
8	Wombats	$2,373	$4,349	$120	$5,927	$5,342
9	Woofers	$101	$9,534	$7,657	$1,580	$4,968
10	Whatzits	$6,320	$9,852	$2,267	$7,566	$300
11	Total	$15,378	$24,378	$16,734	$20,891	$19,042
12						
13						
14	Division 2					
15	Widgets	$8,862	$2,858	$385	$7,004	$1,143

FIGURE 9-29. *You have magnified an area of the preview screen to verify header formatting.*

The Print Sheet/Notes/Both option

With the Print Sheet/Notes/Both option, you can print cell notes (which we discussed in Chapter 8, "Other Worksheet Topics") either by themselves or with the entire worksheet. This option is very useful when you want to display explanatory text you've added to the cells in your worksheet.

The default option for this option is Sheet, which explains why the Print... command usually prints only the active worksheet. The Both option, of course, prints both the worksheet and the cell notes. This option prints the worksheet first, then prints the notes. Of course, the Notes option prints only the notes and comes in handy when you decide to print the notes after you've already printed the worksheet. If the Print Row And Columns Headings option is selected in the Page Setup dialog box, the cell reference of each note is printed before each note.

Suppose that you are printing a worksheet whose information gains more significance with a little explanation. Instead of writing a memo to accompany the worksheet or explaining the worksheet in person, you can annotate the worksheet with notes attached to specific cells. To print the notes with the worksheet, you click the Both button in the Print dialog box. Excel first prints your worksheet and then, on a separate page, the notes.

The ImageWriter print options

The print dialog boxes for the ImageWriter and the LaserWriter share several options. However, some are specific to each printer. The following options are specific to the ImageWriter.

The Quality setting
The Quality setting determines how "crisply" your ImageWriter prints a document. The Faster option tells Excel to print the characters as they appear on the screen. The Best option produces darker, more defined print. The Draft option produces low-quality print, and ignores any fonts you have used. The speed at which your ImageWriter prints depends on the print quality you select: When you select Best, Excel prints slowly; when you select Draft, the program prints quickly.

The Paper Feed setting
The Paper Feed setting determines whether your ImageWriter pauses at the end of each page that it prints. If you are printing on individual "cut sheets" of paper, you should click the Hand Feed option, so you can insert a new sheet after Microsoft Excel prints each page. If you are using fanfold paper, you should leave this setting at Continuous.

Printing with an ImageWriter

Once you are satisfied with your print options, you can begin printing. If you decide that you don't want to print the document after all, click Cancel to remove the dialog box and cancel the printing process. Otherwise, click the OK button in the upper-right corner of the ImageWriter's Print dialog box (remember to turn Page Preview off first). Excel displays a status box like the one shown in Figure 9-30, letting you know its progress until the entire document (or the specified number of pages) has been printed.

To cancel the printing process, simply press the Command and period (.) keys simultaneously. Excel stops sending information to the printer and closes the dialog box. If you are in the middle of a page, it may take a moment for printing to

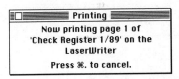

FIGURE 9-30. *This is the printing status box.*

stop. The printer continues printing until it has printed all of the information already transmitted to it by Excel.

The LaserWriter print options

Notice that the LaserWriter Print dialog box has no Quality options. Because the LaserWriter is a laser printer rather than an impact printer, it produces consistently high-quality output by printing at 300 dots per inch.

The Paper Source setting

The Paper Source setting includes the Paper Cassette and Manual Feed options. Click Paper Cassette if you want the LaserWriter to feed the paper automatically. Use the Manual Feed option if you are using envelopes or some other special paper that must be "hand fed" into the LaserWriter.

The Cover Page setting

The Cover Page setting is handy for dating a document or identifying the beginning of a document when a number of people share a printer. When you select either the First Page option or the Last Page option, Excel prints a sheet with the following information: the user's name (from the User Name field in the Chooser dialog box), the name of the application from which the document was printed, the document name, the date and time the document was printed, and the name of the printer.

Printing with a LaserWriter

When you click OK to begin printing, you'll see the two status boxes shown in Figure 9-31. The status box in the center of the screen is identical to the one described for the ImageWriter, while the status box at the top of the screen gives you the name of the document currently being printed and tells you the status of the printing assignment. If a paper jam or some other problem occurs, a diagnostic message also appears in this status box. If you are on a network, you may have to wait for another printing job to be completed.

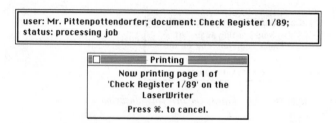

FIGURE 9-31. *This is the LaserWriter printing status box.*

Printing from the Finder

As you already know, when you choose the Print… command from within Microsoft Excel, only the active document is printed. If you need to print several documents, you may be able to save some time by printing them from the Finder. Here, you can select several documents to print one after the other by dragging across all the files you want to work with or by pressing the Shift key and clicking each document icon in turn. Once you have selected all the files you want to print, choose the Print… command from the Finder's File menu.

Excel's Print dialog box appears only once when you use this technique. Excel prints one copy of each document, using the same Print dialog box options for each. The documents print in the order in which they appear on the desktop—from left to right and top to bottom.

Background printing with MultiFinder

If you share a LaserWriter on a network with several other users, you may want to take advantage of MultiFinder's ability to print documents "in the background" while you work in Microsoft Excel. In order to take advantage of background printing with MultiFinder, you may need the files named *PrintMonitor* and *Backgrounder* in your System Folder. If you need it, you will find a copy of *PrintMonitor* on the disk that came with your Macintosh.

To use MultiFinder, you must choose the Set Startup… command from the Special menu while you are in the Finder. Then, in the Set Startup dialog box, click the MultiFinder button and then click OK. Now, restart your computer. When you do this, MultiFinder is active, as indicated by the icon that appears at the far-right edge of the menu bar. When you open your Excel document, this icon changes to a small version of the Microsoft Excel icon.

After starting your computer with MultiFinder, open the Chooser dialog box to make sure that the On option for Background Printing is selected. When you're ready to print, just choose the Print… command and specify your Print dialog box options as you normally do. When you click OK, the PrintMonitor program takes over, spools your file to your System Folder, and sends it to the printer. While the file is being printed, you can continue to work in Excel, although the program is considerably slower while background printing is underway.

Conclusion

As you've seen, Microsoft Excel enables you to produce professional-quality printed worksheets on an Apple printer. In fact, once you've set up your printer, you will probably need to work with only two commands from the File menu: the Page Setup… and Print… commands. Unless you're using more than one printer, the Chooser command is a one-time-only choice.

If you are planning to do a lot of printing, we recommend that you invest in an ImageWriter or a LaserWriter. These printers let you take full advantage of the many font and size selections available with the Macintosh. If you are using a non-Apple printer, you're likely to spend a lot of time learning how to work with printing and formatting restrictions.

In this chapter, we've concentrated only on printing worksheets. When we discuss Excel's sophisticated charting capabilities in Section Three, we show you a few more tricks and techniques that enable you to produce high-quality printed charts as well.

SECTION THREE

CHARTS

10

Basic Charting Techniques

*T*he well-worn phrase "A picture is worth a thousand words" holds true for numbers as well. Often, you can summarize pages of complex worksheet data in one or two easily understandable charts. Microsoft Excel can produce an impressive variety of charts from the data in your worksheets. Excel's sophisticated charting capabilities give you the power to create and enhance effective, presentation-quality charts quickly and easily.

Microsoft Excel offers six main types of chart: column charts, area charts, bar charts, line charts, pie charts, and scatter diagrams. Each of these major chart types has several formats. For example, if you are creating a column chart, you can choose between stacked, overlapped, or clustered columns. In addition, Excel offers five combination formats that allow you to display two charts at once. You can also create your own formats and combine different chart types by creating overlay charts. All of these chart types, combined with a number of powerful formatting options, let you tailor a virtually endless variety of charts.

Creating charts

The easiest way to learn about the Microsoft Excel chart environment is to experiment with the many options available to you. We use the simple worksheet in Figure 10-1 to create a basic column chart, then we build on this basic chart throughout the remainder of this section. If you'd like to follow along with the examples, begin by creating this sample worksheet.

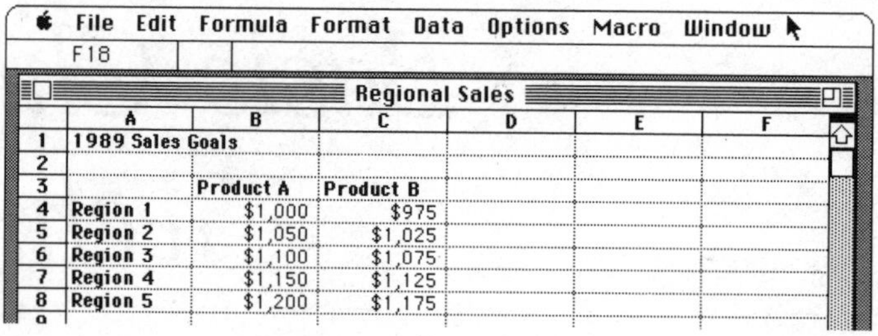

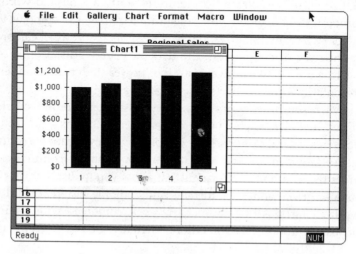

File Edit Formula Format Data Options Macro Window
F18
Regional Sales
A B C D E F
1 1989 Sales Goals
2
3 Product A Product B
4 Region 1 $1,000 $975
5 Region 2 $1,050 $1,025
6 Region 3 $1,100 $1,075
7 Region 4 $1,150 $1,125
8 Region 5 $1,200 $1,175

FIGURE 10-1. *This worksheet is the basis for the examples throughout this chapter.*

To chart the product sales in column B of the worksheet, begin by selecting the range B4:B8. Now, select New... from the File menu and double click the Chart option in the New dialog box. It's that easy! Your screen looks like the one shown in Figure 10-2.

File Edit Gallery Chart Format Macro Window
Chart1
E F
$1,200
$1,000
$800
$600
$400
$200
$0
1 2 3 4 5
16
17
18
19
Ready
NUM

FIGURE 10-2. *You have used the New... command's Chart option to chart the sales from column B.*

As you can see, Excel has built a simple column chart from the data in the *Regional Sales* worksheet. Each of the five columns (also called markers) that you see in the chart in Figure 10-2 represents a data point. As you've probably figured out, each data point corresponds to one of the values in cells B4:B8 in Figure 10-1. The first column corresponds to cell B4, the second column corresponds to cell B5, and so on.

You may wonder why Microsoft Excel created a column chart when you chose the New... command. It's because the default type of chart in Excel is a column chart. Every chart you create in Excel appears as a column chart unless you choose another format. You can use the Gallery menu commands and the Main Chart... command from the Format menu to change the chart from column to area, line, pie, or one of Excel's other types. We show you how to do that in Chapter 11, "Plotting More Than One Series."

The area defined by the two chart axes is called the *plot area*. The bottom axis is called the *category axis*, and the axis on the left is called the *value axis*. You probably know these as the x and y axes. In math, the x axis is always horizontal and the y axis is always vertical, as shown in our sample column chart. In Microsoft Excel, however, the orientation of the axes may be reversed.

Notice that the values along the value (in this case, y) axis range from $0 to $1,200. Excel automatically sets the upper and lower limits of the value axis according to the chart type and range of values being plotted. You can use the Axes... command from the Chart menu to set your own limits. We show you how to do this later in this chapter.

Notice also that the points on the category (in this case, x) axis are numbered from 1 to 5. Because you have not specified any labels for these points, Excel has simply numbered them consecutively. In a few pages, we show you how to replace these numbers with meaningful labels.

A tour of the chart window

Before we jump into any major enhancements of this basic chart, let's take a brief tour of the chart window and introduce a few new terms. After discussing the Microsoft Excel basic formatting options, we look at how chart data is organized and show you how to add a data series to the chart we just created.

The column chart in Figure 10-2 is displayed in a chart window. At the top of the window, as usual, is the title bar. And as with worksheet windows, you can move the chart window around the screen by dragging the title bar.

As you can see, Microsoft Excel has named this first chart *Chart1*. Subsequent charts will be named *Chart2*, *Chart3*, and so on. Of course, you can assign the chart any name you like when you save it.

Notice that the chart window Excel created is a partial-screen window. If you wish, you can drag the size box in the bottom-right corner of the window to change its size. If you want the chart window to fill the screen temporarily, you can double click the title bar (or click the zoom box once). When you do this, Excel expands the window, as shown in Figure 10-3. As you can see, the size of the chart depends upon the size of the chart window. When you expand the window, Excel automatically expands the chart to fill the available space. (We use this technique throughout the chapter to make the chart figures more readable.) To restore the window to its original size, double click the title bar again (or click the zoom box).

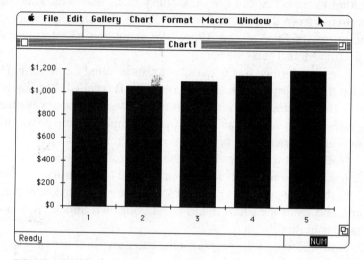

FIGURE 10-3. *You have expanded the chart window to full-screen size by double clicking its title bar.*

Notice also that no scroll bars or split bars appear in the chart window. When you think about it, this makes sense. Because the entire chart is visible within the window no matter what the window's size, there is no need to scroll around. Similarly, if you take a look at the Window menu, you'll also see that no New Window command appears in the chart environment. Again, this is because you can view the entire chart in one chart window.

The menu bar

Now that you're working with a chart, you've probably noticed that the menu bar at the top of the screen has changed (the active chart window is in front of all the other windows). Although some of the choices on this menu—like Apple, File,

Edit, Format, Macro, and Window—are familiar to you from your experience in the worksheet environment, you'll discover that many of the chart commands work differently from the worksheet commands we've discussed so far.

The other menus on the menu bar—Gallery and Chart—may be new to you. As we hinted earlier, you select the chart type and format you want to use from the Gallery menu. If you want to tailor your own chart, rather than using one of Excel's standard formats, you can choose the Chart menu commands to control the use of axes and gridlines, legends, text, and arrows.

Saving charts

If you've used other integrated spreadsheet programs, you may be accustomed to thinking of a chart as a specialized extension of a worksheet. In programs like Symphony and Lotus 1-2-3, for example, charts are a part of the worksheet file. They are stored with the worksheet and cannot be edited independently of the worksheet file. In Microsoft Excel, however, each chart is a file unto itself. You create new charts from the File menu, not from the Window menu. You must save each chart—and reopen it—as a separate file. Your charts are not saved automatically when you save the worksheet from which they are created.

There are several advantages to Excel's method of storing chart files. First, in Excel it is simple to combine data from several worksheets into one chart file. You can also copy data and formats from one chart to another, without opening the worksheet files that they depend upon. We talk more about file management and links in the section of this chapter entitled "Linking Text to the Worksheet."

Enhancing charts

Now that you know how easy it is to create a chart, let's look at how the basic chart we have just created can be enhanced. In this part of the chapter, we show you how to format the axis labels on your chart, create and format chart titles and data-point labels, and use the many pattern options available in the Microsoft Excel chart environment.

Chart objects

Excel divides a chart into *classes*. A class is a major component of the chart, such as the chart area, the plot area, the legend, a data series, or an axis. Each class can be divided into individual objects, such as a particular data-point marker or label, an individual text block, and so forth.

Before you can perform many editing and formatting actions in a chart window, you must select the chart object you want to work with. To select a chart object with the mouse, simply point and click. To select the entire chart or plot area, use the Select Chart and Select Plot Area commands from the Chart menu.

If you prefer to use the keyboard, you can press the arrow keys to move around the chart window. To move among classes of objects, use the Up and Down arrow keys. As you repeatedly press the Up arrow key, Excel moves through the various chart classes in this order:

Chart area
Plot area
Legend
Value axis
Category axis
Text
Arrows
Gridlines
Data-point labels
First data series
Second and subsequent data series
Drop lines
Hi-Lo lines

(Don't worry if some of these terms are unfamiliar; we explain them as we go along.) When you have selected the correct class, you can use the Left and Right arrow keys to move among objects in that class. For example, to select the second data-point marker in our chart, press the Up arrow key four times to move to the desired class (the first data series), then press the Right arrow key once to move to the second data-point marker.

Regardless of the selection method you use, Excel places a set of black or white squares on the object or class that is currently selected. An item marked with white squares is *attached* and cannot be moved or sized with the mouse or the keyboard. However, you might be able to format or realign it using commands. An item surrounded by black squares is *unattached* text and can be repositioned and resized with the mouse. We discuss attached and unattached text in greater detail in the section entitled "Adding your own text."

As you move among classes and among objects, the reference area at the left side of the formula bar tells you what type of item is selected. For example, if you select the value axis, you see the notation *Axis 1*. If you select the first column in the sample chart, as shown in Figure 10-4, you see the notation *S1P1* (series 1, point 1), which indicates that you've selected the first data point in the first (and only, in this case) data series.

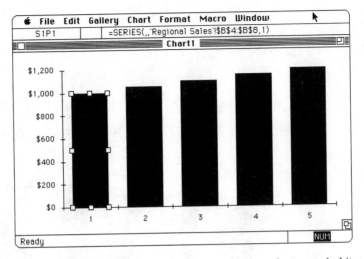

FIGURE 10-4. *When you select the first data-point marker, a set of white squares indicates your selection and the notation S1P1 appears in the reference area of the formula bar.*

Automatic chart text

In the first chart you created, you selected only the worksheet cells that contained the values you wanted to plot. By including a few adjacent cells in the selected range, however, you can add category-axis labels and a title to the chart.

To see how this works, go back to the *Regional Sales* worksheet window and select the range A3:B8. Now, choose New... from the File menu and double click the Chart option in the New dialog box. Figure 10-5 on the next page shows the resulting chart.

In most ways, this new chart is identical to the first one you created. But notice that Excel uses the text label *Product A* from cell B3 as a chart title. In addition, Excel uses the label as a series name, to identify the data series in cells B4:B8. The importance of the series name becomes evident as you learn more about how Microsoft Excel builds charts.

Also, notice that Excel uses the text entries in cells A4:A8 as labels for the data points along the category axis. These labels are called *tick-mark labels* or *category labels*, because they identify the various categories of information in the chart.

When you create a chart, Microsoft Excel looks for a series name and category labels in the top row and left column of the worksheet range you select. If the first row and first column in the range you select do not contain labels—as in the first example—Excel assumes that you do not want to use a series name or category labels in the chart. In that case, no series name appears in the chart, and the tick marks on the category axis are numbered, not labeled.

Notice also that the new chart is slightly smaller than the first one. As you add titles, legends, and other objects to the chart, Excel automatically adjusts the size of the plot area to make room for your additions. In other words, the more enhancements you add to the chart area, the less room there is for the chart itself.

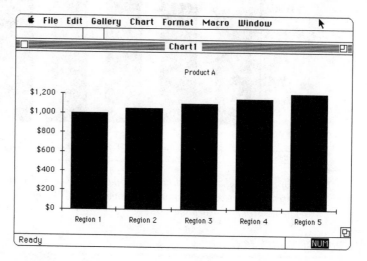

FIGURE 10-5. *This figure shows a chart with category-axis labels and a title produced by including cells containing labels in the range selected in the worksheet.*

Editing titles

For the chart in Figure 10-5, you included the label *Product A* in your selection from the worksheet. When you did this, Excel used *Product A* as the title of the chart—not a particularly descriptive name. However, Excel makes the process of editing very easy for you. You can edit the contents of the chart formula bar in the same way you edit the contents of the worksheet formula bar—with one important difference: You must press Command-Return to make a line break. (Pressing Return or Enter enters the text in the formula bar into the chart.) With this in mind, you should have no problem creating descriptive titles of one and two lines.

To expand the title in Figure 10-5, first click the chart title to select it. As you can see in Figure 10-6, Excel places white squares around the title *Product A* to indicate that you are editing the chart title. In addition, the chart title appears in the formula bar.

The white squares indicate that you cannot move the selection around in the chart window; in other words, the chart title is attached text. As we mentioned earlier, Excel places black squares around those elements that you can manually reposition on the screen.

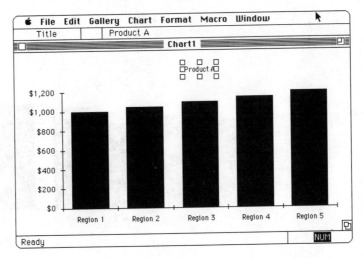

FIGURE 10-6. *When you select the chart title for editing, Excel activates the title and surrounds it with white squares.*

Now, click in front of the title in the formula bar, type *Regional Sales:*, and then press Command-Return to move the name *Product A* to the second line in the formula bar. Figure 10-7 shows the screen at this point. Finally, press Return or Enter to lock in your new title. When you lock in the title, Excel centers the two lines of text over the plot area and adjusts the chart's size to allow room for the added title line. The chart now looks like Figure 10-8 on the next page.

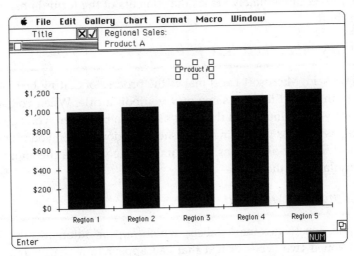

FIGURE 10-7. *You have edited the chart title in the formula bar.*

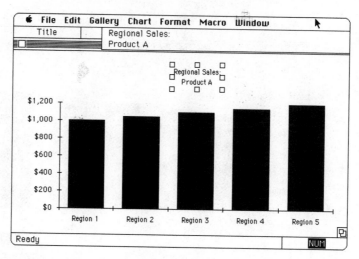

FIGURE 10-8. *This is the edited chart title.*

You can cut, copy, and paste entries in the chart formula bar, just as you do in a worksheet window. If you want to completely overwrite the existing title, simply select all the title text in the formula bar and begin typing. The original entry is replaced with your new entry. To delete a title altogether, select the text in the formula bar and press the Delete key. (If you change your mind and want to restore the contents of the formula bar before the deletion is locked in, click the Cancel box to the left of the formula bar.) When you press Return or Enter to lock in your deletion, Excel immediately erases the contents of the formula bar and the title from the chart.

Editing other chart text

As we said, Microsoft Excel makes the process of editing text very easy. You can edit other chart text the same way you edit a title. When you select a chart text block, you see the text in the chart's formula bar. Then, you can delete, cut, copy, and paste just as you do in a worksheet window. When you press Return or Enter to lock in your alterations, Excel immediately enters the altered contents of the formula bar in the chart.

Adding your own text

In addition to tick-mark labels, which appear automatically, we have already mentioned two types of text that can appear in a chart window: attached and unattached. Attached text is linked to a specific chart object—a data point, data series, or axis, for example. (You can also attach a title to the chart itself, independent of the file name you use when you save the chart.) If you move a chart object, the attached text moves with it. Unattached text is freestanding text that you can position anywhere on the chart. For example, you can use unattached text to create a subtitle for your chart or to add a comment line.

Let's start with attached text. To add attached text to a chart, you must first choose the Attach Text... command from the Chart menu. When you choose this command, you see a dialog box like the one in Figure 10-9. If no chart object is selected when you choose the Attach Text... command, the Chart Title option is your default selection. However, you can speed up the process by selecting the object to which you want to attach text before choosing the command. When you do this, Excel chooses the appropriate dialog-box settings for you. For example, if you want to attach a label to the second column in a chart, select that data-point marker, then choose the Attach Text... command. Excel selects the Series And Data Point option in the dialog box and enters the values 1 and 2 in the Series Number and Point Number fields. Press Enter or click OK to accept these settings.

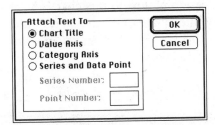

FIGURE 10-9. *You have used the Attach Text dialog box to add text to a chart.*

Adding a new title

You can easily add a new title to a chart that doesn't have a title. Simply choose the Attach Text... command from the Chart menu and double click the Chart Title option. Microsoft Excel displays the word *Title* surrounded by white squares, to indicate the position of the title on the chart. The formula bar also displays *Title* as the default chart title. To replace the generic text *Title*, type the text you want into the formula bar.

For example, if you are working with the chart in Figure 10-2 and you don't want to return to the *Regional Sales* worksheet to reselect the range that includes the name *Product A*, you can easily add the name *Product A* as a chart title. First, choose the Attach Text... command and double click the Chart Title option. When you see the word *Title* surrounded by white squares at the top of the chart and the word *Title* in the formula bar, type *Product A*, then press Enter. *Product A* immediately replaces *Title* in the formula bar and appears at the top of your chart surrounded by white squares.

Adding axis titles

Now that the chart title is in place, let's assign titles to the category and value axes. Because no titles exist as yet for these axes, you must now choose the Chart menu's Attach Text... command to add these new titles to the chart. Select the Category Axis option in the Attach Text dialog box and click the OK button (or simply double click the option). Excel displays an X, surrounded by a set of white squares, below the category axis. You'll also see an X in the formula bar, indicating that you are assigning a title to this chart's X, or category, axis. Type the category-axis label *Regions* in the formula bar, then press Return or Enter to lock in your title.

To add a title to the value axis, choose the Attach Text... command again and double click the Value Axis option. Excel automatically places a Y in the formula bar to indicate that you are assigning text to this chart's Y, or value, axis. Also, notice the Y, surrounded by white squares, near the chart's value axis. Replace this generic title by typing *Goals* in the formula bar and pressing Return or Enter. Figure 10-10 shows the chart at this point.

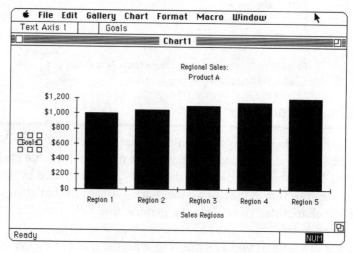

FIGURE 10-10. *This is the sample chart after you have labeled the category axis and the value axis.*

Adding series or data-point labels

Now, let's attach descriptive labels to the data points in the chart. Suppose you want to include at the top of each column the total sales goals for each region in the chart. To do this, first choose Attach Text... from the Chart menu. Then, click the Series And Data Point option in the Attach Text dialog box. When you do this, Excel changes the display of the Series Number and Point Number options to black type, to indicate that these options are now active.

Now, click the Point Number field and type *1*. (Because the chart has only one series so far, leave the Series Number field blank.) Press the Enter key or click OK to return to the chart window.

Excel immediately enters $1,000 in the formula bar and above the first column in the chart. If you'll look back at the worksheet in Figure 10-1, you'll see that $1,000 is the value in cell B4—the cell on which the first column of the chart is based. For every data point in the chart, Microsoft Excel sets up a link between the values in the appropriate cells in the worksheet and the chart. If the value in B4 changes, Excel automatically changes the label to reflect the new value.

Now that you have defined the data-point label for the first column, you can repeat the same procedure to define data-point labels for data points 2, 3, and 4. (We leave the fifth data point alone for now.) To define these other labels, you choose the Attach Text... command and select the Series And Data Point option, then select the Point Number field and type the appropriate data-point number (2 for the second column, 3 for the third, and so on). Figure 10-11 on the next page shows the chart with these data-point labels in place. As you can see, Excel uses the values from cells B5, B6, and B7—the other cells on which the chart is based—as the labels for the second, third, and fourth columns in the chart.

To add the data-point labels quickly, select the column in the chart you want to label and choose the Attach Text... command. When the Attach Text dialog box appears, you can see that the Series And Data Point option is selected and the Point Number field contains the number that corresponds to the column you selected in your chart. When you press Enter or click OK to accept the settings in the dialog box, Excel adds the label to your chart.

You can also create your own series and data-point labels. To see how, let's create a data-point label for the fifth column. Choose the Attach Text... command, select the Series And Data-Point option, type *5* in the Point Number field, and press Enter. When Excel displays the value for this data point in the formula bar, place the insertion point just in front of the number, type *Most promising goal:*, and press Command-Return to break the label into two lines. Otherwise, the label is too long for the chart. Press Return or Enter to lock in your entry. Figure 10-12 on the next page shows the result.

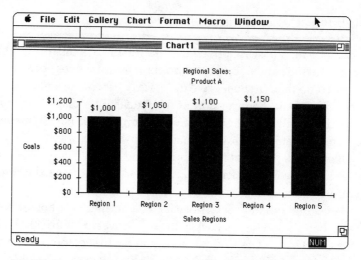

FIGURE 10-11. *You have added a custom data-point label to the chart.*

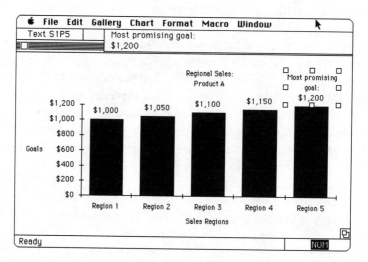

FIGURE 10-12. *This chart has a custom data-point label for the fifth column.*

Keep in mind that Microsoft Excel does not update the value for a data-point label after it has been edited. If the value in cell B8 changes, you have to adjust the label manually.

Adding unattached text

To add unattached or floating text to your chart, you need only type the text in the formula bar. Press Command-Return to begin a new line of text and press Enter to lock in your entry.

Before you begin typing, be sure that you have not selected any chart objects. If no chart object is selected, there are no black or white squares in the chart window, and no text appears in the formula bar. If a chart object is selected, particularly a data point or a text block, you may inadvertently destroy information in your chart when you create the unattached text. To make sure no chart object is selected, click a blank area of the chart window.

Let's add a subtitle to the chart in Figure 10-12. First, make sure that none of the chart objects on your screen is selected, then type *Product A sales goals reflect an average 10% increase over last year's sales* on the first line of the formula bar, and press Enter or click the enter box. The text is automatically placed in the center of the chart, below the title line and partially obscured by the third, fourth, and fifth columns, as shown in Figure 10-13.

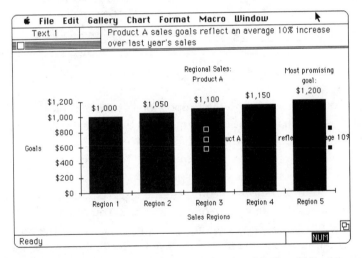

FIGURE 10-13. *The unattached subtitle is displayed in the middle of the chart, surrounded by black squares.*

You can see a border of black squares around the subtitle, indicating that you can reposition the text on your screen. To do this, simply point anywhere inside the border of squares and drag. To properly position the subtitle, drag it toward the bottom of the chart window, so that it is centered under the category-axis label, as shown in Figure 10-14. Notice that Excel displays a solid black line around the text area as you drag it in the chart window.

The Move command on the Format menu provides an alternate method for repositioning the subtitle. Choose the Move command and a solid border appears around the selected text. Use the arrow keys to reposition this border, and press Return or Enter. The text appears where you placed the border.

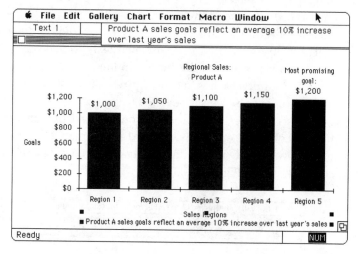

FIGURE 10-14. *This is the repositioned subtitle.*

You can also change the proportions of the text block by dragging the black squares or by using the Size command on the Format menu in conjunction with the arrow keys. To change the height or width of the block with the mouse, drag one of the black squares at the sides of the block. To change the height and width simultaneously, drag one of the corner squares.

For example, suppose you want the text block to appear in a narrower, multiline format rather than as a long, single line. You can achieve this effect by selecting the text block, then clicking the square marker at the top-right corner of the selection, and dragging up and to the left. Figure 10-15 shows the results. (For readability, we also repositioned the text block in a blank area of the window.)

To resize the unattached block with the keyboard, first select the text block, then choose the Size command from the Format menu. Now, use the arrow keys to make your changes. The Up and Down arrow keys let you increase and decrease the height of the block. To increase and decrease the width of the block, use the Left and Right arrow keys. You can use the Control key in combination with any of the arrow keys to "fine tune" the size of the text block. When the text block reaches the desired proportions, press Enter to lock in your changes.

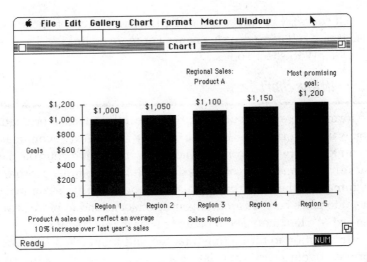

FIGURE 10-15. *The unattached text block has been resized and repositioned.*

Linking text to the worksheet

In Chapter 8, "Other Worksheet Topics," you learned how to link worksheets. When you're creating a chart from values in a worksheet, changing the worksheet automatically changes the values in the chart. You can also link any text—attached or unattached—to a cell in the worksheet so that any changes you make to the text in the worksheet are automatically made in the chart as well.

To link text to a cell in a worksheet, you must build a formula in the chart that contains an external reference to either a cell or value name or a single cell in the worksheet. For example, suppose you want to use the contents of cell A1 in the worksheet in Figure 10-1 as attached text for the title of the chart you've been creating. To link the title of the chart to cell A1 of the worksheet, choose the Attach Text... command from the Chart menu and double click the Chart Title option. (The title drops the *Regional Sales:* prefix you added earlier.) Next, type an equal sign (=) to replace the text in the formula bar. Now, activate the worksheet and select cell A1 to paste the external reference in the formula bar. When you press Enter, your chart reappears and its title reads *1989 Sales Goals.* The formula bar contains the linked reference

=Regional Sales!$A$1

You can also link unattached text to a worksheet. To do this, first be sure no text is selected on your screen. Then, type an equal sign in the formula bar, activate the source worksheet, and select the cell that contains the label you want to use. Finally, press Enter to lock in your linked text formula.

Of course, you can type a cell reference instead of clicking the cell. You can also type a cell name or value name. For more on linking documents, see Chapter 8, "Other Worksheet Topics."

Formatting chart text

To format the text in your chart, first select the attached or unattached text block you want to work with. Then, use the Font... and Text... commands on the Format menu to specify your formats. The Font... command controls the font, size, style, background, and color of the text. The Text... command primarily controls the alignment of the text. You can also use the Patterns... command on the Format menu to place borders around your text blocks and to place area patterns behind the text. We talk more about patterns later in this chapter.

In addition to formatting attached and unattached text, you can control the format of your chart's axis labels and legend text. We show you how to format category and values axis labels later in this chapter. We take a look at legends when we discuss multiseries charts in the next chapter.

The Font... command

The default font in a new chart is regular 10-point Geneva. To assign a new font to the entire chart (including all attached and unattached text, as well as the axis labels and the legend, if one exists), choose the Select Chart command from the Chart Menu or use the arrow keys to select the entire chart area before you choose the Font... command.

When you choose Font... from the Format menu, you see a dialog box like the one in Figure 10-16. Many of the options in this dialog box should look familiar to you by now—you used a version of them in Chapter 3, "Formatting the Worksheet," to format your worksheet text.

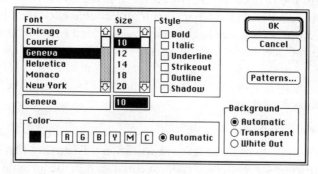

FIGURE 10-16. *We used the Font dialog box to change the font, style, size, color, and background of the chart text.*

As you might expect, you use the Font, Size, and Style options to specify the typeface and format you want to use for the selected text. The Background options let you control the appearance of the area behind the text. If you use the default setting, Automatic, Excel selects a pattern for you. If you select Transparent, the area behind the text is "see-through," so that any objects behind the text are visible— that is, the text appears as if it were simply typed on top of the chart. If you select White Out, on the other hand, Excel blocks out an area behind your text. The blocked-out area obscures any chart objects behind it, making your text stand out clearly from the chart. (By the way, when you select White Out, the area that is blocked out around your text doesn't necessarily appear in white. It appears in the color or pattern you've selected for your background.) The effects of the Background options become more evident when you use the Patterns options to format the text block and the rest of the chart. We return to these options later in this chapter when we talk about the Patterns... command.

You can use the Color options in the Font dialog box to change the color of selected chart text for emphasis. Be sure to choose a color for your text that contrasts sufficiently with any background colors you may choose. (To change the background color of the text area or underlying areas of the chart, you can use the Patterns... command, which we discuss later in this chapter.)

Now, let's look at the effects of using some of the Font dialog box options. As we hinted earlier, all you need to do to change the default font for your chart is to select the entire chart, then choose a new font, size, and style. For example, Figure 10-17 on the next page shows the results of selecting the chart area, choosing Font..., and selecting the Times and 12-point options.

Let's change the format of the chart title and the axis titles. Start by selecting the chart title. Choose the Font... command and select the New York, 14-point, and Bold options. Next, select the value-axis label, choose the Font... command, and select the Bold option. Now, select the category-axis label and choose Repeat Font from the Edit menu to apply the same Font specifications to that title. Finally, select the comment line at the bottom of the screen, choose the Font... command again, and select the Italic option. Figure 10-18 on the next page shows the results.

When you select a data-point label before choosing the Font... command, one additional option appears in the dialog box: Apply To All. Select this option if you want your font selections to apply to all the data-point labels in the chart. If you don't select the Apply To All option, only the selected data-point label is formatted with the options you select.

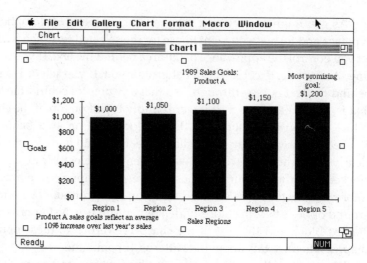

FIGURE 10-17. *The font for the entire chart has been changed from the default to 12-point Times.*

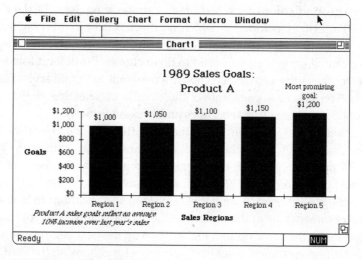

FIGURE 10-18. *The chart title, axis titles, and comment line have been formatted to add emphasis.*

The Font dialog box contains two more options: the Patterns... option and the Text... option. You can use these buttons to access the Patterns and Text dialog boxes just as you would by choosing the Patterns... and Text... commands from the Format menu. All three dialog boxes (Font, Patterns, and Text) are linked by buttons. When you open one of the dialog boxes, you see buttons for access to the other two.

The Text... command

The Text... command lets you control the alignment of your chart text and the use of Excel's vertical-text and automatic-sizing features, as well as several other options. When you choose this command, you see the Text dialog box shown in Figure 10-19.

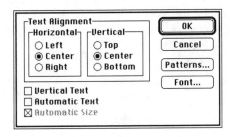

FIGURE 10-19. *This is the Text dialog box.*

Unless you specify otherwise, Excel assumes that you want all the text in your chart window displayed horizontally. However, you can use the Vertical Text option in the lower portion of the dialog box to indicate that you want the text to run vertically, instead. About the only time you'll use the Vertical Text option is to change the display of your value-axis title so that it occupies less room in the chart area. For example, Figure 10-20 shows the results of applying the Vertical Text option to the value-axis title in the sample chart. As you can see, the characters in the

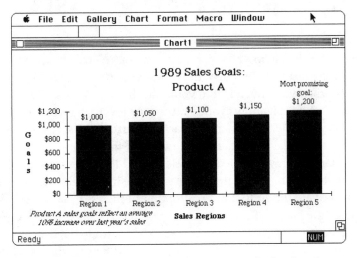

FIGURE 10-20. *We used the Vertical Text option to display the value-axis title vertically.*

word *Goals* now appear one above the other, rather than side by side. As a result, the value-axis title is only one character wide, rather than five characters wide. Although this format is less attractive than the standard horizontal format, it does leave more room to display the chart's plot area.

The Horizontal and Vertical options at the top of the Text dialog box let you specify how you want your chart text to be aligned. The Vertical options go into effect only if you have selected the Vertical Text option in the lower portion of the dialog box. Figure 10-21 shows the effects of the various Text Alignment options on your vertical and horizontal text.

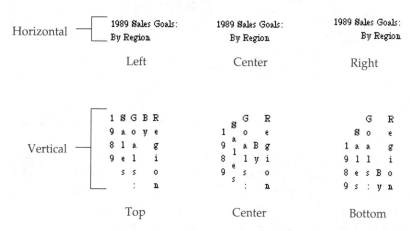

FIGURE 10-21. *The Text Alignment options let you display chart text six ways.*

The Automatic Text option As we mentioned earlier, when you select cells containing labels in your worksheet as you're creating a chart, Excel uses those labels as chart text. Similarly, the values you use to plot data are used as data-point labels when you attach text to your data-point markers. If you edit text, the Automatic Text option allows you to return the text to the worksheet labels or values.

For example, in the sample chart in Figure 10-5, Excel automatically created the chart title *Product A* because you included the label in cell B3 in your worksheet selection. Later, you edited this title to read *1989 Sales Goals: Product A*. If you now decide to restore the original title, you can simply select the title text on the chart, then activate the Automatic Text option in the Text dialog box. Excel changes the edited title back to *Product A*. (After you use Automatic Text to revert to the original title, you can't reverse the process and return to the text you entered manually. You have to re-edit the title. However, any formats you've added from the Font dialog box remain.)

The Automatic Size option The Automatic Size option applies only to unattached text. Although this is the default option, Microsoft Excel deselects Automatic Size whenever you manually resize a text block. After you manually resize an unattached text block, you can use this option to revert to automatic sizing. When the Automatic Size option is in effect, the text block fits exactly around the text. The advantage of the Automatic Size option is that Excel adjusts the size of the text block as needed whenever you edit the text or use the Font... or Text... commands to change the display characteristics of that text.

Sizing text blocks in the chart window becomes particularly important when you're using borders, because the size of the block determines the size of the border that appears around the text. (We show you how to create borders when we discuss the Patterns... command.)

The Show Value and Show Key options The last two options in the Text dialog box, Show Value and Show Key, appear only when you select a data-point label before choosing the Text... command. The Show Value option works in conjunction with the Automatic Text option to determine the default text for your data-point labels. When Show Value is in effect, Excel labels your data-point markers by extracting the corresponding values from the worksheet. If you deselect this option, Excel uses the series name instead; if your chart contains only one data series, Excel labels the data-point marker with the category name when you deselect Show Value. Finally, if your data series doesn't contain a series name at all, Excel places the numbers 1,2,3, and so forth, over each data-point marker.

The Show Key option tells Excel to display a small square next to the data-point label that reflects the pattern or color you've applied to the corresponding data-point marker. This option can be a handy alternative to a chart legend when you're short on space.

The Main Chart... command

The Main Chart... command on the Format menu lets you change your chart type and format. If you choose the Main Chart... command while your window displays a column chart, you see a dialog box like the one in Figure 10-22 on the next page. The dialog box contains two major sections: Type and Format. Initially, the selected option in the Type section reflects the type of chart you're working with. For example, when you choose the Main Chart... command from within our sample chart window, you'll see the Column option selected. (We look at the other Type options in Chapter 12.)

As you can see, some of the options in the Format section of the dialog box appear dimmed, indicating that they are not available. The type of chart you're working with determines which of the Format Options are available at any given time.

Here, we cover two of the Format options that apply to column charts: % Cluster Spacing and Vary by Categories. In Chapter 11, we look at additional Format options.

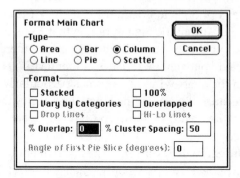

FIGURE 10-22. *This is the Format Main Chart dialog box.*

The % Cluster Spacing setting

The % Cluster Spacing setting lets you control the spacing between the columns (or clusters of columns) in your chart. If you are working with only one data series, the amount of space determined by the cluster-spacing percentage appears between columns. If you are working with two or more data series, the space appears between each group of columns. In the next chapter we show how this option applies to multiseries charts.

The default cluster spacing, 50%, means that the distance between columns in the chart is half the width of one column. The cluster spacing is expressed as a percentage, because the width of the column depends on the number of columns in the chart. Microsoft Excel automatically adjusts the size of the columns to create an equal distribution across the chart. By expressing cluster spacing as a percentage of the column width, Excel can also adjust the distance between columns as you add or remove data points. However, if you are working with a chart that contains only a few data points, you may want to increase the cluster spacing so that the columns do not appear extremely wide and bulky. Figure 10-23 shows the chart with a % Cluster Spacing of 25. This new setting results in less spaces between columns, because the columns are wider.

The Vary By Categories option

When you create a chart with only one data series, Excel automatically makes all of the columns black, as we've seen in the figures presented so far. If you want to use a different pattern for each data point, select the Vary By Categories option in the Format Main Chart dialog box. Your chart is redrawn to look like Figure 10-24. Notice that each column in the chart now has a different pattern.

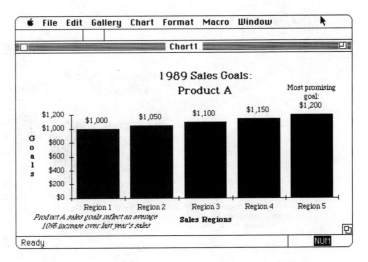

FIGURE 10-23. *The space between columns is narrower, because we changed the % Cluster Spacing setting to 25.*

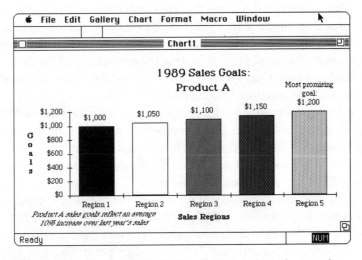

FIGURE 10-24. *You have used the Vary By Categories option to assign a different pattern to each column.*

Using arrows for emphasis

One of Excel's interesting Chart menu commands is Add Arrow. When you choose this command, Excel places a black arrow on the screen, as shown in Figure 10-25 on the next page. You use this arrow to draw attention to a key element in your chart.

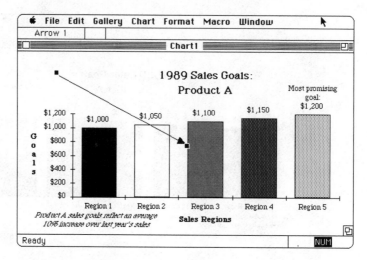

FIGURE 10-25. *This is the arrow that appears when you choose the Chart menu's Add Arrow command.*

Notice the black squares that appear at either end of the arrow in Figure 10-25. By dragging these squares, you can change the length or angle of the arrow. If you drag the square at the point of the arrow, the square at the other end remains anchored. This makes it easy to drag the arrowhead to the desired point. Once the arrowhead is in place, you can use the opposite square to pivot the arrow to the desired angle and drag it to the desired length.

As you change the length and angle of the arrow, you might find that the shaft looks jagged or broken. To overcome this problem, simply reposition one of the black squares until the line straightens out again. You may have to do a little fine-tuning to get the effect you want. To move the entire arrow, click the shaft and drag the arrow to the desired position.

For example, suppose you want to point out that the *Region 3* goal on the chart in Figure 10-25 represents the goal that exceeds the average 10% increase over last year's goal. You can create an unattached comment, then use the arrow in the chart area to connect the comment line to the data point. To create the unattached comment, click an empty area of the chart, type *20% increase*, and press Enter. Use the Font... command on the Format menu to display the comment in 9-point bold New York. Finally, drag this text block until it appears above the first two columns.

Now, let's position the arrow so that it connects the comment and the column. Begin by clicking the arrow to select it. A pair of black squares indicates your selection. Now, drag the black square near the end of the arrow until it appears just under the *e* in the word *increase*. Finally, point to the shaft of the arrow and drag until the arrowhead points to the data-point label *$1,100*. If the shaft of the arrow looks jagged, then adjust the angle a bit. Figure 10-26 shows the result.

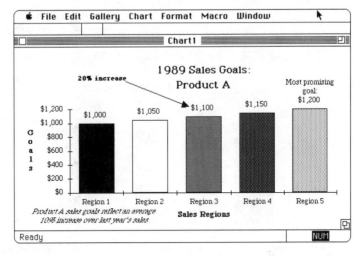

FIGURE 10-26. *You have emphasized a column with a comment and an arrow.*

Formatting the axes

Microsoft Excel gives you a great deal of control over the format and contents of your chart's category and value axes. You can use the Axes... command on the Chart menu to determine which axis appears—value, category, or neither. When you choose to display one axis or both axes, you can use the Scale... command on the Format menu to maintain precise control over the axis content and format. Let's look at the Axes... and Scale... commands in detail.

The Axes... command

The Axes... command on the Chart menu lets you control the display of the category and value axes. When you choose the Axes... command, Excel displays the dialog box shown in Figure 10-27.

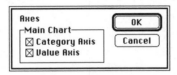

FIGURE 10-27. *This is the Axes dialog box.*

Notice that the Axis options are already selected for both axes. If you click these options to cancel their selection, Excel removes both sets of axis lines and tick-mark labels, as shown in Figure 10-28.

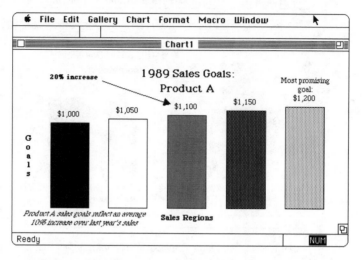

FIGURE 10-28. *Canceling the Axis options removes the axis lines and tick-mark labels.*

The Scale... command

The Scale... command on the Format menu gives you several more formatting options. The options available to you depend upon which axis you select before you choose the command. For all chart types except the scatter chart, the Scale dialog box differs for the category axis and the value axis. When you are formatting the axes of a scatter chart, both dialog boxes look like the Value Axis Scale dialog box.

Formatting the category axis If you select the category axis and then choose Scale... from the Format menu, you'll see a dialog box like the one in Figure 10-29.

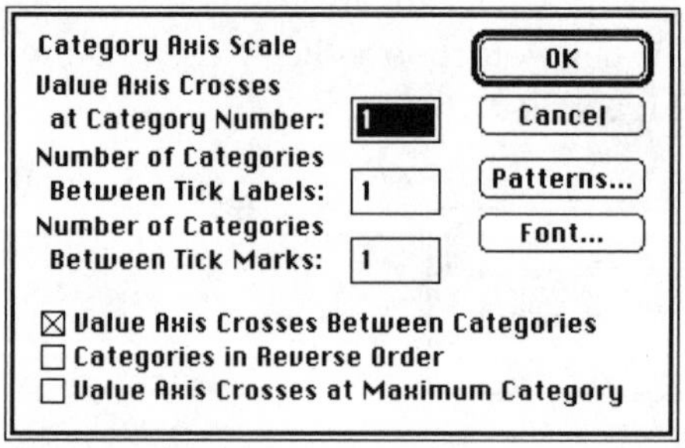

FIGURE 10-29. *This is the Category Axis Scale dialog box.*

The first option in the Scale dialog box, Value Axis Crosses At Category Number, lets you determine where the value axis intersects the category axis. The default value—and the one you use most often—is 1, meaning that the value axis is placed in front of the first data-point marker or cluster, as it has been in the sample charts thus far. If you change the value to 3, Excel places the value axis in front of the third data-point marker or cluster, as shown in Figure 10-30. Notice that the value labels overlap the second column. To overcome this problem, you need to change the tick-mark label position in the Value Axis dialog box. We show you that option in a moment.

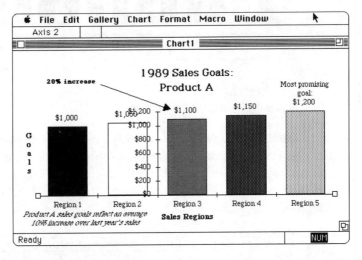

FIGURE 10-30. *This figure shows the effect of changing the Value Axis Crosses At Category Number setting to 3.*

The next option in the Category Axis dialog box, Number Of Categories Between Tick Labels, lets you control the number of category labels that appear on the chart. The default value for this option is 1, which means that every tick mark at the bottom of the chart is accompanied by a tick-mark label. Normally, this is the value you want to use.

However, if there is a large number of data points on the chart, or if the category-axis tick-mark labels are too long to fit across the chart, Excel might break the tick-mark labels into two lines. For example, notice that the tick-mark labels in Figure 10-31 on the next page have been broken into two lines because the labels are long. As a result, the labels for some months are formatted inconsistently.

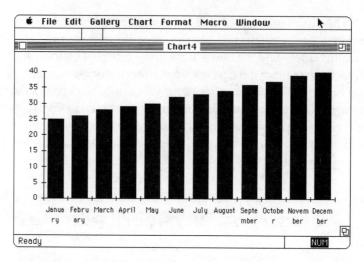

FIGURE 10-31. *Long tick-mark labels have been broken into two lines,*
resulting in inconsistent presentation.

To get around this problem, you can enter 2 in the Number Of Categories field.
Excel then uses every other tick-mark label, as shown in Figure 10-32. Excel accepts
any whole number between 1 and 127 for the Number Of Categories option. However, keep in mind that too many gaps between tick-mark labels make your chart
difficult to read.

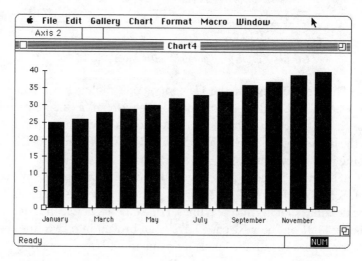

FIGURE 10-32. *Eliminating every other tick-mark label keeps the chart's*
presentation clear and consistent.

The third option in the Category Axis Scale dialog box, Number Of Categories Between Tick Marks, controls the number of data points (or clusters, if you're working with a multiseries column or bar chart) that appear between tick marks. Microsoft Excel accepts any whole number between 1 and 127 for this option. The default value is 1, which means that one data point or cluster is displayed between each pair of tick marks. Normally, you want to use this value.

Just as you can tell Excel to omit some of the tick-mark labels, you can omit some of the tick marks. To do this, enter a number that indicates the tick marks you want to omit in the Number Of Categories Between Tick Marks field. For example, to omit every other tick mark, enter 2 in the Number Of Categories Between Tick Marks field. Excel then eliminates every other tick mark along the axis.

The fourth option in the Category Axis dialog box is Value Axis Crosses Between Categories. This is the default, as indicated by its preset selection. If you deselect this option, the *Regional Sales* chart looks as shown in Figure 10-33. Notice that the value axis and its labels now fall in the middle of the first column rather than to its left, and that half of the sixth column seems to have been erased. For this reason, you want to make sure that the Value Axis Crosses Between Categories option is selected for column and bar charts. However, this option works well with line charts, telling Excel that you want the first data point for each series to appear next to the value axis and the last data point to appear flush with the last category on the category axis.

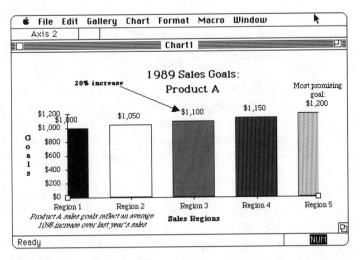

FIGURE 10-33. *This figure shows the effect of deselecting Value Axis Crosses Between Categories.*

The Value Axis Crosses At Maximum Category option tells Excel to move the value axis from the left to the right edge of the chart. For example, Figure 10-34 shows the sample chart after selecting this option. Notice the position of the value axis. You may want to use this option when you create overlay charts that use different scales.

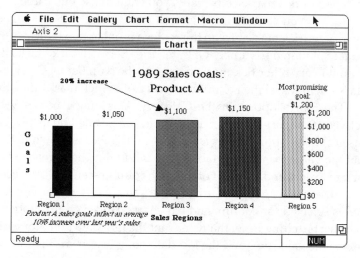

FIGURE 10-34. *This figure shows the effect of selecting Value Axis Crosses At Maximum Category.*

You can reverse the order in which the categories are displayed by clicking the Categories In Reverse Order option. If you select this option with the sample chart, column 5 appears first, column 4 second, and so on. The value axis automatically moves to the right side of the chart. However, you can select the Value Axis Crosses At Maximum Category option to move the value axis back to the left side of the chart. Figure 10-35 shows the result of selecting this option. The reversal procedure only affects the categories, not the added text or the titles. If the column representing Region 3 had moved, we would have had to reposition the arrow pointing to it.

The Category Axis Scale dialog box includes both a Patterns... and a Font... button. When you press either of these buttons, Excel carries out all the changes you made in the Scale dialog box and opens either the Patterns or the Font dialog box. From these dialog boxes you can make further changes in the display of the category axis in your chart. (We discuss the Patterns... command later in this chapter. We discussed the Font... command earlier.)

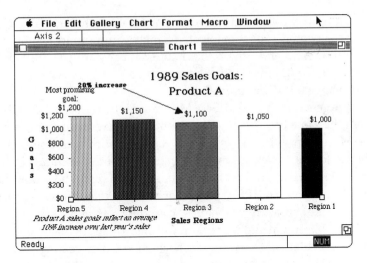

FIGURE 10-35. *Reversing the categories affects only the categories, not additional text or titles.*

Formatting the value axis If you select the value axis before you choose the Scale… command, you will see a dialog box like the one in Figure 10-36. The Minimum and Maximum fields contain the lowest and highest values of the plotted series. Microsoft Excel automatically determines the scales along the value axis according to these values. In the sample chart, the low and high values are $0 and $1,200, respectively. Excel automatically creates an equal distribution to fill in the values between.

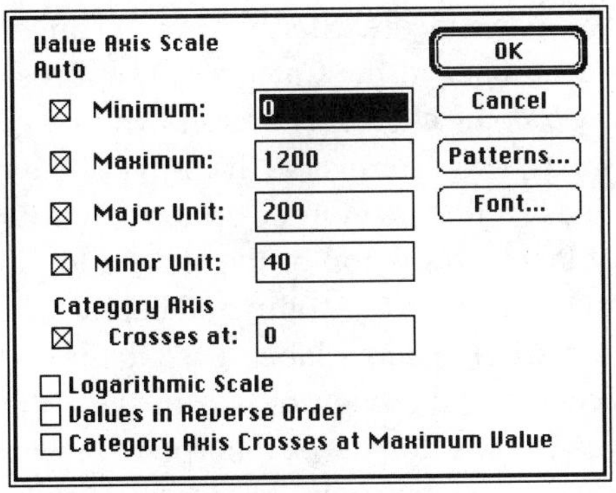

FIGURE 10-36. *This is the Value Axis Scale dialog box.*

Of course, you can always override Excel's automatic scaling factor by typing your own values. For example, to change Minimum to 4, simply double click the Minimum field and type 4. Excel automatically adjusts the Maximum value, the Major Unit and Minor Unit options, and the Category Axis Crosses At value when you change the Minimum value.

We generally prefer to use a Minimum setting of 0, so that all of the charts start from the same base point. Often, you'll find Excel exaggerates data trends when the Minimum setting is as high as the minimum data point. Of course, you can choose to use some intermediate value as your Minimum setting. You can also override the default Maximum value. Keep in mind, however, that it is very easy to misrepresent statistics, particularly when they are being expressed in chart form. Make sure your axis values accurately reflect the trends being presented.

The Minimum and Maximum settings are particularly important if you need to compare data in two or more charts. If you are creating several charts to compare various trends, you might decide to change the Minimum and Maximum values so that all of your charts use the same scales.

Notice that when you change the values of any of the options in the Value Axis Scale dialog box, the Xs in the boxes to the left of those options disappear. If you want to go back to the original scale, all you have to do is click the boxes.

If you change the Minimum or Maximum value, you should generally let Excel adjust the Major Unit, Minor Unit, and Category Axis Crosses At settings automatically. If you do enter your own numbers, keep in mind that Excel might change your Maximum setting slightly so that it can create an equal distribution of numbers between the high and low values.

In the sample chart, the category axis currently crosses at 0, which is the setting we suggest. As we mentioned earlier, you can change the position of the category axis by typing a number in the Category Axis Crosses At field. If you select this option and type *600*, the chart looks as shown in Figure 10-37.

As with the category axis, you can reverse the order of the values on the value axis by selecting the Values In Reverse Order option. Microsoft Excel automatically moves the category labels to the top of the chart and places the data-point labels you created with the Attach Text... command below the columns, as shown in Figure 10-38. You can move the category labels back to the bottom of the chart by selecting the axis, then choosing the High option in the Patterns... dialog box; however, you can't change the position of the data-point labels.

All of the charts you've seen so far in this chapter have used arithmetic scales. Arithmetic scales are divided into segments of equal size and value. In Microsoft Excel, you can change the value-axis scale from an arithmetic scale to a logarithmic scale. Logarithmic scaling means that the value-axis scale is divided into tiers.

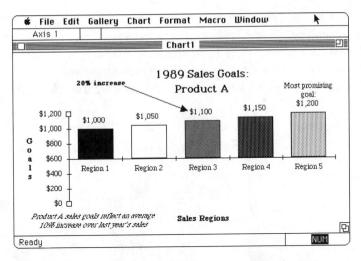

FIGURE 10-37. *This figure shows the effect of changing the Category Axis Crosses At setting to 600.*

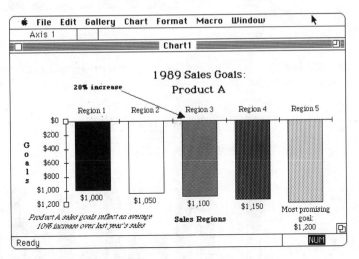

FIGURE 10-38. *This figure shows the effect of selecting the Values In Reverse Order option.*

Each tier represents a power of 10, so that the value axis displays the numbers 10, 100, 1000, and so on. If your chart contains values less than 10, Excel uses the number 1 as its Minimum value.

You'll seldom use this scaling technique unless you are charting scientific or engineering data. However, you might want to consider using a log scale if the values in your chart are widely distributed. For example, Figure 10-39 shows a chart with data-point values ranging between 7 and 1000. Notice that some of the data-point markers disappear altogether in this chart. Because the scale is so large, the smaller values are overpowered by the larger ones. Now, look at the chart in Figure 10-40, which plots the same data on a logarithmic scale.

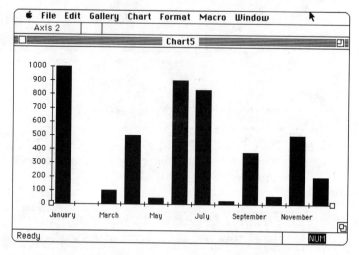

FIGURE 10-39. *You have plotted values between 1 and 1000 on an arithmetic scale.*

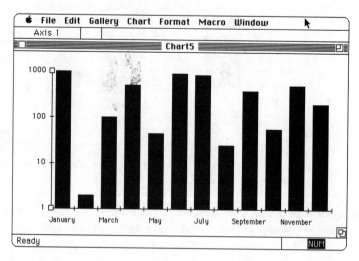

FIGURE 10-40. *You have plotted values between 1 and 1000 on a logarithmic scale.*

The scale used in Figure 10-40 is called a *semilogarithmic scale*, because only one of the axes is displayed in logarithmic form. You can also display both axes in logarithmic format.

The Value Axis Scale dialog box includes both a Patterns... and a Font... button. When you press either of these buttons, Excel carries out all the changes you made in the Scale dialog box and opens either the Patterns or the Font dialog box. From these dialog boxes, you can make further changes in the display of the value axis in your chart. (We discuss the Patterns... command later in this chapter. We discussed the Font... command earlier.)

Formatting gridlines

The Gridlines... command on the Chart menu lets you add horizontal and vertical gridlines to your charts. When you choose the Gridlines... command, Excel displays the dialog box shown in Figure 10-41.

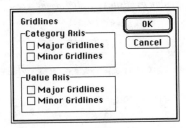

FIGURE 10-41. *This is the Gridlines dialog box.*

The Major Gridlines and Minor Gridlines options let you decide whether Excel displays gridlines parallel to the category axis and/or gridlines parallel to the value axis. If you select Major Gridlines for both axes, Excel displays only those gridlines corresponding to the tick-mark labels. For example, Figure 10-42 on the next page shows how the sample chart looks if you select Major Gridlines for both axes. If you select Minor Gridlines, Excel displays the intermediate gridlines as well. For example, Figure 10-43 on the next page shows the chart with both Major Gridlines and Minor Gridlines selected for both axes. If you select Minor Gridlines without selecting Major Gridlines, Microsoft Excel includes both major and minor gridlines in the chart.

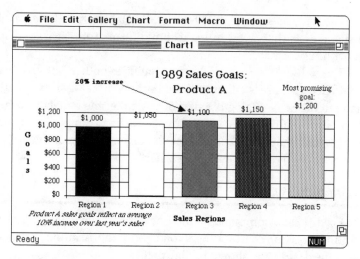

FIGURE 10-42. *You have used the Major Gridlines option of the Gridlines… command to display gridlines parallel to the axes.*

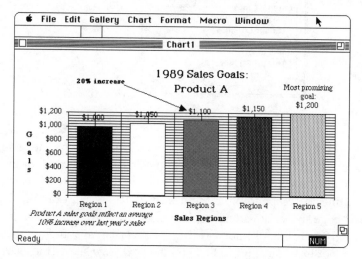

FIGURE 10-43. *You have added minor gridlines by selecting the Minor Gridlines option.*

The Patterns… command

The Patterns… command on the Format menu allows you to change the patterns and borders Excel uses to display chart objects. To use this command, you must first select the item you want to format, then choose Patterns… from the Format menu. The contents of the Patterns dialog box vary according to the type of chart and the chart object you're working with, so you need to select a chart area or object before you choose the Patterns... command. You can use the following three methods to select chart objects: Choose the Select Chart and Select Plot Area commands from the Chart menu; use the arrow keys; or double click the specific chart area you want to enhance. The Patterns dialog box is also accessible from the Font, Text, Scale, and Legend dialog boxes. Double clicking a chart area selects the area and brings up the Patterns dialog box at the same time.

Formatting the chart area

In the sample charts you've seen so far, the background pattern is plain and no border appears around the chart area. Excel's default area pattern and default border setting are both Invisible when the entire chart is selected. Suppose you want to change the background to a shaded pattern and add a shadow border around the entire chart. Double click a blank area in the chart to bring up the Patterns dialog box shown in Figure 10-44. To change the default settings from the Patterns dialog box, click the options you want to use. For example, if you select the fourth pattern from the 16 Area Patterns options in the Patterns dialog box, Excel places a light screen behind the chart. (You can also choose a color option, but we can't display color in our figures.) After specifying the Area Pattern option, select the solid Style option (the leftmost option) from the Border section of the dialog box. When you do this, Excel automatically selects the first Border Weight option (the lightest

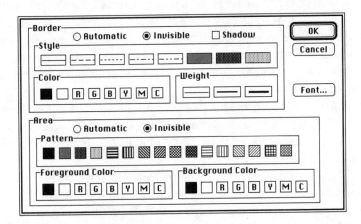

FIGURE 10-44. *Excel displays the Patterns dialog box when you double click the chart area..*

weight). Now, click the Shadow check box above the Border Style patterns and click OK. Figure 10-45 shows the results of these selections. (Notice that we've returned the columns to their default black color. In black, they contrast better with the different backgrounds we display in subsequent examples.)

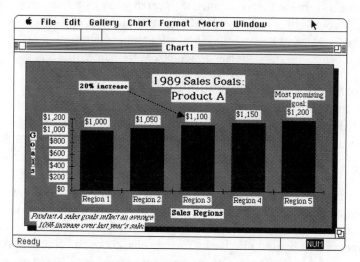

FIGURE 10-45. *The Patterns... command can be used to add a pattern and shadowed border to the chart area.*

If you select a border pattern that contrasts with the area pattern, selecting a heavier border weight makes a noticeable difference. Striped and crosshatched border patterns often create confusion and clutter, and even the heavy Border Weight setting is often too narrow to make the pattern obvious. As a result, the border looks somewhat uneven. We recommend that you use solid borders for most of your charts.

The default Invisible options turn off all background patterns to allow whatever is behind them to show through. For example, if you add unattached text to your chart, you can see the text if you haven't formatted the background of your chart area.

The Automatic options come in handy when you need to distinguish data points or series from one another. If a data point or series is selected, Automatic picks a pattern that distinguishes each data point or series from the other ones.

The Patterns dialog box for the chart area, shown in Figure 10-44, includes a Font... button that allows you to move from the Patterns dialog box to the Font dialog box. When you click the Font... button, Excel enters all the changes you have made in the Patterns dialog box and opens the Font dialog box.

Formatting the plot area

To separate the plot area from the rest of the chart, you can use a thin border and a gray screen pattern so that the plot area stands out from the chart as a whole. To create this format, first select the plot area by choosing the Select Plot Area command from the Chart menu, then choose the Patterns... command from the Format menu. In the Patterns dialog box for the plot area (shown in Figure 10-46),

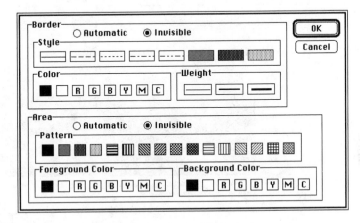

FIGURE 10-46. *This is the Patterns dialog box for the plot area.*

EXCEL

Combining chart-area and plot-area patterns

The effect of the chart-area pattern depends upon the plot-area pattern you have defined. If you are using the Invisible Background Pattern option in the plot area, the pattern you select for the chart area fills the plot area as well. If you are using any other Background Pattern option in the plot area, however, Microsoft Excel fills only the chart area outside the plot area when you define a chart pattern.

If you want to add a pattern only to the part of the chart outside of the plot area, select the solid white Background Color option for the plot area, then select the chart pattern you want to use. Although the white color in the plot area looks just like the Invisible pattern, it keeps the chart pattern out of the plot area. Keep in mind that to Excel an invisible pattern and a white pattern are not the same thing.

select the first Border Style option (a plain line). Notice that when you select this option, Microsoft Excel selects the black Border Color and the first Border Weight option. Now, select the fourth Area Pattern option. Notice that when you choose this option, Excel selects the black Foreground Color and the white Background Color. When you click OK or press Enter, your chart looks the one in Figure 10-47.

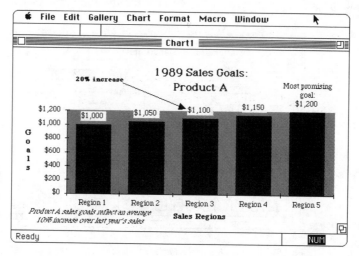

FIGURE 10-47. *The plot area is now set apart from the rest of the chart.*

Formatting the axes

You can then use the Patterns… command to format the axis lines and tick marks.

If you select one of the chart axes and then choose the Patterns… command, Excel displays the dialog box shown in Figure 10-48. You can use the Axis Style and Axis Weight options to change the pattern and the weight of the selected axis. The default (or Automatic) axis style—the preferred style—is solid black. Typically, you won't change this setting. The Axis Weight option allows you to increase the weight of the axis line.

The Tick Mark Type option lets you set the type of major and minor tick marks you want to use in your chart. The default Major tick-mark setting is Cross, which means that the tick marks cross the axis. If you don't want major tick marks to appear at all, you can select Invisible. The Inside and Outside options allow you to position the tick marks inside or outside of the axis.

The default Minor tick-mark setting is Invisible. To add minor tick marks to your chart, select one of the other options: Inside, Outside, or Cross.

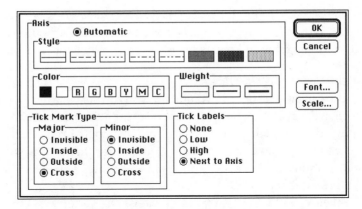

FIGURE 10-48. *This Patterns dialog box appears when one of the axes has been selected.*

At the bottom of the Axis Patterns dialog box is the Tick Labels position setting. If you look back at Figure 10-30, you will recall that we changed the Value Axis Crosses At Category Number option in the Scale dialog box to move the value axis in front of the third column. The resulting chart was difficult to read because the tick-mark labels along the value axis overlapped the second column. To get around this problem, you can use the Low or High options in the Tick Labels position box to move the value labels to the low or high end of the axis. For example, if you select the Low option, your chart looks like Figure 10-49.

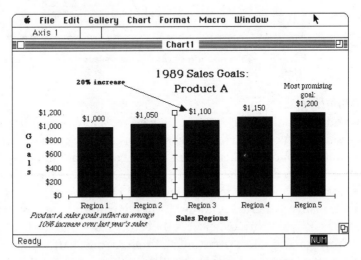

FIGURE 10-49. *You have moved the value labels to one side by selecting Low as the Tick Labels position setting.*

The Axis Patterns dialog box includes two buttons: a Font... button and a Scale... button. Pressing either of these buttons carries out your changes in the Patterns dialog box and opens the Font or Scale dialog box.

Formatting the gridlines

If you are using gridlines in your chart, you can also use the Patterns... command to format the gridlines. Simply click one of the gridlines and choose the Patterns... command. If you click a major gridline, Microsoft Excel applies the pattern settings you specify to all of the major gridlines for that axis. If you select one of the minor gridlines, Excel applies the pattern settings you select to all of the minor gridlines for that axis.

When you select a gridline and choose the Patterns... command, Excel displays the dialog box shown in Figure 10-50. You can use the Line Style, Line Weight, and Line Color options to define the gridline pattern you want to use. The default (or Automatic) Line Color option—and the preferred option—is solid black. Although you can change this setting, the results are usually not very desirable. The default Line Weight setting is the lightest of the three options. Once again, the default is the best option to use in most cases.

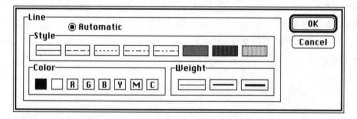

FIGURE 10-50. *This Patterns dialog box appears when a gridline is selected.*

Formatting arrows

There is even a special Patterns dialog box, shown in Figure 10-51, for arrows. You'll see this box if you select a chart arrow and choose the Patterns... command. Most of the options in this Patterns dialog box are familiar. The Arrow Shaft Style option lets you define the pattern Excel uses to display the arrow. We suggest that you leave the option set to the default: solid black (or Automatic). If you do select an alternative pattern, try to use a simple pattern that contrasts with the other patterns in your chart. Otherwise, the arrow fades into the background.

You can also select from among three Arrow Shaft Weight options. The thinnest shaft weight is the default. You'll usually want to use this option. If the arrow falls across an area with a dark pattern, however, you might want to use a heavier shaft weight.

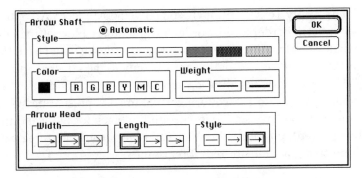

FIGURE 10-51. *This Patterns dialog box appears when an arrow has been selected.*

Finally, Excel offers you three different options for the width, length, and style of the arrowhead. You can select any combination of width, length, and style, although the straight head style cancels out your width and length selections. Once you have selected the arrow formats you want to use, click OK to lock in the change.

Formatting data points and series

If you choose the Patterns... command with either of the remaining chart items, data points and series, selected, you'll see a dialog box that looks like the one for the plot area, as shown in Figure 10-46. The Data Point And Series Patterns dialog box operates in the same fashion as all the other Patterns dialog boxes. However, this dialog box has two extra options: Apply To All and Invert If Negative. Figure 10-52 shows this Patterns dialog box.

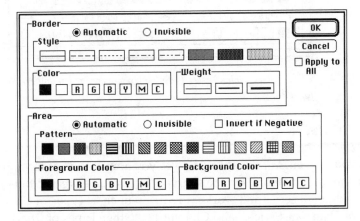

FIGURE 10-52. *This is the Data Point And Series Patterns dialog box.*

The Apply To All option If you click the Apply To All option, Excel uses the Area Pattern, Border Style, Border Weight, and Color settings that you define in the dialog box for all of the data points and series in your chart. If this option is not selected, the setting you define applies only to the selected data point.

The Invert If Negative option When you activate the Invert If Negative option, you reverse the pattern for columns representing negative values. For example, if you have set the foreground to black (or blue) and the background to white (or red), positive columns have a black (or blue) foreground and negative columns have a white (or red) foreground.

Formatting text

The text Patterns dialog box is the same as the chart-area Patterns dialog box that was shown in Figure 10-44. However, as you can see in Figure 10-53, the text dialog box has one additional option: a Text… button. This option allows you to choose the Text… command from the Patterns dialog box. Clicking the Text… button carries out all the changes you have made in the Patterns dialog box and opens the Text dialog box so that you can position the text in the selected area of your chart.

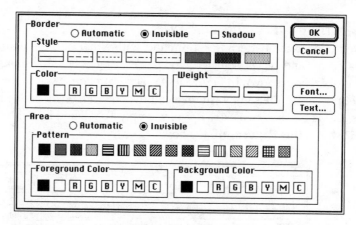

FIGURE 10-53. *This Patterns dialog box appears when you are formatting text.*

Conclusion

As you've seen, Microsoft Excel gives you a multitude of formatting options that you can use to tailor even the simple charts you've created thus far. However, as you add data series and work with different chart types in Chapter 11, "Plotting More Than One Series," and Chapter 12, "Other Types of Charts," you'll see that you've only scratched the surface.

11

Plotting More Than One Series

So far, we have been working with only one data series. In this chapter, we show you how to create and format charts that have more than one data series.

Adding a data series to a chart

To add a data series to the chart you created in Chapter 10, "Basic Charting Techniques," you must return to the worksheet window and select the cells that contain the second data series you want to plot. We use cells C3:C8 in the worksheet shown in Figure 11-1 on the next page. After selecting the cells, choose Copy from the Edit menu. Now, move back to the chart window and choose Paste from the chart Edit menu. Your chart looks like Figure 11-2, also on the next page.

The sales goals for *Product B* are now included in your chart. Notice that Microsoft Excel automatically groups each of the values in cells C4:C8 into the appropriate category—Region 1, Region 2, and so on. Each data series in your chart should contain an equal number of data points. Otherwise, Excel cannot correctly group the data points in the various series into categories.

In addition, although it's not apparent on the chart, the name *Product B* from cell C3 has become the series name for the new set of data points. The importance of this name becomes clear in a few pages.

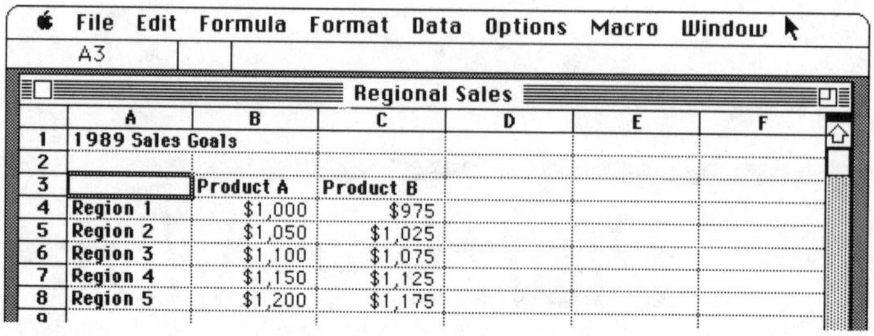

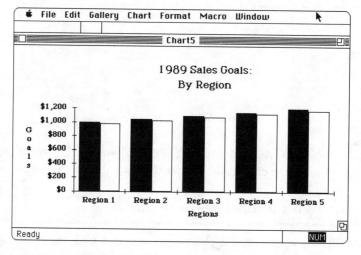

FIGURE 11-1. *This worksheet is used throughout Chapter 11 to demonstrate how to plot more than one series on a chart.*

FIGURE 11-2. *The sample chart now includes a second data series.*

Creating a multiple-series chart

Of course, you can also create this chart from scratch. To do this, activate the worksheet and select the range A3:C8, then choose New... from the File menu, select Chart, and click OK. Figure 11-3 shows the result. (We've enlarged the chart in the figure for ease of viewing.) Although this chart lacks the text and formatting enhancements you added to the chart in Chapter 10, it is identical in every other way.

Notice that the chart in Figure 11-3 does not have a title, even though you included the entry *Product A* in cell B3 in the selection. Interestingly, Excel uses the series name as the chart title if the chart is created with only one data series. In charts with two or more data series, like this one, Excel does not provide a default title. When you choose the Attach Text… command from the Chart menu, Excel displays in the formula bar and centered at the top of the chart only the word *Title*.

Once the chart has been created, you can use any of the techniques we have explained so far to enhance it. Figure 11-4 shows the chart with a few enhancements, including a title and data-point labels for the second series.

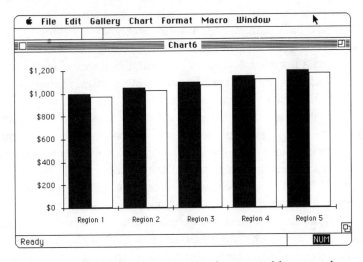

FIGURE 11-3. *This is the same two-series chart, created from scratch.*

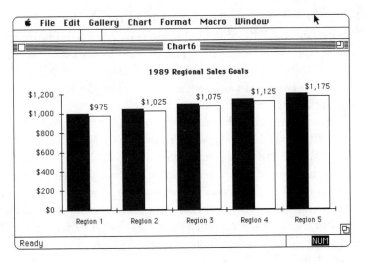

FIGURE 11-4. *We enhanced this two-series chart.*

To create the data-point labels for the second series, we used the Attach Text...
command, clicked the Series And Data Point option, then typed 2 in the Series
Number field. For each data point in the series, we typed the data-point number in
the Point Number field.

How Excel distinguishes data series from categories

When you select the range A3:C8, choose the New... command, and select the
Chart option, Microsoft Excel keeps track of which cells fall into which data series,
and which data points fall into which category, by referring to the shape of the
range you selected and the kinds of entries contained in each cell of the selection. If
you select a horizontal range of cells (that is, a range that is wider than it is tall),
Excel plots the values by row. If you select a vertical range (one that is taller than it
is wide), Excel plots the values by column.

Perhaps this rule will be easier to remember if you keep in mind that Excel
always assumes that you want fewer data series than data points. Thus, if your
selection has more rows than columns, each column becomes a data series. Each
row, in turn, becomes a category. Because the selected range in the worksheet in
Figure 11-1 contains more rows than columns, Excel organizes the values in each
column into a data series. Each row becomes a category.

If your selection has more columns than rows, however, each row becomes a
data series and each column becomes a category. If your selection contains an
equal number of rows and columns, Excel treats it like a vertical range. Each row
becomes a data series and each column becomes a category.

Overriding Excel's default organization

Suppose you want to use the values in cells A3:D10 in Figure 11-5 to create a chart
that plots the categories Exam 1, Exam 2, and Exam 3. As you know, Excel typically
organizes the chart by rows, plotting the categories as Allan, Billinger, and so on.
To override Excel's default organization, you can use the Paste Special... command to plot the values by columns.

Begin by dragging through the range A3:D10 and then choose Copy from the
Edit menu. Next, choose New... from the File Menu and double click the Chart
option. Excel displays an empty chart window. Now, choose Paste Special... from
the chart Edit menu. You'll see a dialog box like the one in Figure 11-6.

As you can see, Microsoft Excel assumes that you want to organize the chart
data by columns using the labels in row 3 as series names and the labels in column
A as category names. If you click the Rows option, however, Excel changes the bottom two options to Series Names In First Column and Categories In First Row.

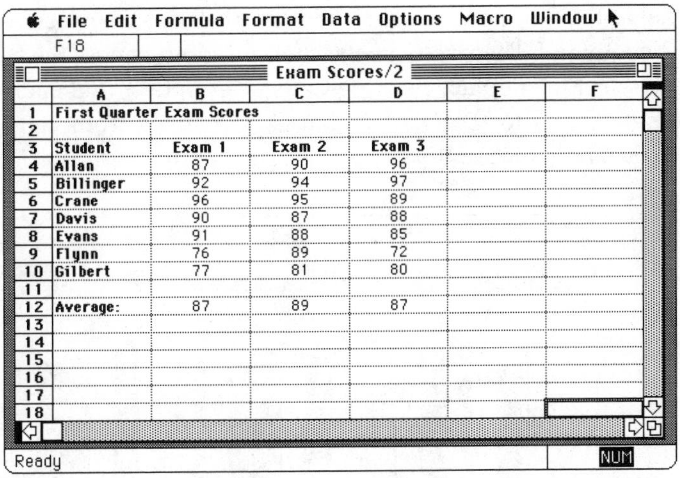

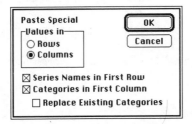

FIGURE 11-5. *You want to plot this horizontal worksheet by columns instead of by rows.*

Paste Special
┌Values in─┐
○ Rows
◉ Columns

☒ Series Names in First Row
☒ Categories in First Column
☐ Replace Existing Categories

OK

Cancel

FIGURE 11-6. *This is the Paste Special dialog box.*

Assuming that you want to accept these settings, click OK in the Paste Special dialog box to create a chart like the one in Figure 11-7 on the next page. Excel then uses the labels in row 3 as category names and the labels in column A as series names.

The Paste Special dialog box also offers a Replace Existing Categories option. Select this option if you want to use the categories in the current copy range as your data-series names, thus overwriting any existing series names. Before the categories are replaced, Excel asks you to confirm your decision by presenting an alert box that says *Existing categories will be permanently deleted.*

For example, suppose you've created a chart that uses the default category labels *1, 2, 3,* and *4* below the category axis. Figure 11-8 on the next page shows a generic chart that plots four values. Now, suppose you decide to add a new data series to this chart. Cells A1:A4 of your worksheet contain the labels *1st Qtr., 2nd Qtr., 3rd Qtr.,* and *4th Qtr.* Cells B1:B4 contain four numeric values. To add the labels as well as the four new values to your chart, select the range A1:B4 and choose the Copy command. Then, activate the chart window, choose the Paste Special... command, select the Replace Existing Categories option, and click OK. Excel adds the new data series to the chart and uses the labels from cells A1:A4 as the new category labels. Figure 11-9 shows the effect of the Paste Special... command.

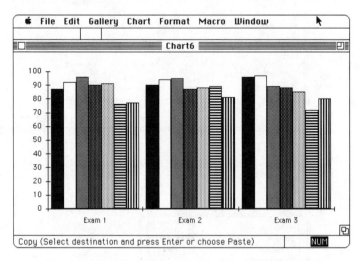

FIGURE 11-7. *This column chart was created from the horizontal worksheet using the Paste Special... command.*

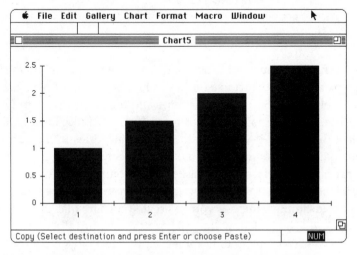

FIGURE 11-8. *This is a relatively nondescript chart that displays four numeric values.*

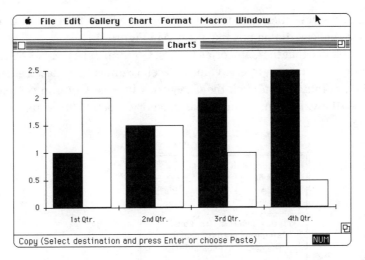

FIGURE 11-9. *You have enhanced the chart with new labels and four additional values.*

Overriding Excel's choice of labels

As we mentioned earlier, if Excel does not find labels in the first row or first column of your copy area, the program assumes that you do not want to use category labels or series names in your chart. However, there are times when you might want to use numeric labels in your chart.

For example, suppose you want to use the names in column A of Figure 11-10 as category labels. Begin by selecting cells A3:B13 and choosing the Copy command.

	A	B	C	D	E	F
1	Monthly Expense Summary					
2						
3	Budget Code	Total Expenditures				
4	101	$1,145.08				
5	102	$1,234.87				
6	103	$2,456.67				
7	104	$2,765.12				
8	105	$3,456.54				
9	106	$3,124.37				
10	107	$1,234.58				
11	108	$5,432.12				
12	109	$4,362.75				
13	110	$6,751.53				
14						
15						
16						
17						
18						

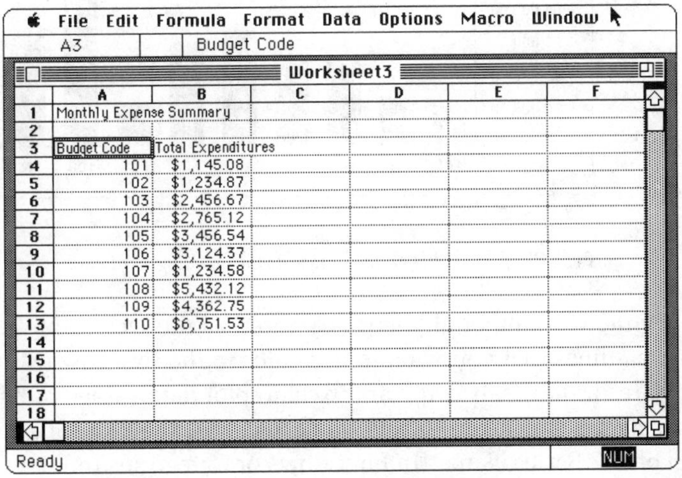

FIGURE 11-10. *This horizontal worksheet shows numeric values as labels.*

Create a new chart window and choose the Paste Special... command. You see a Paste Special dialog box like the one in Figure 11-11.

Notice that the Categories In First Column option is not selected. Because column A contains numeric values, Excel assumes that these cells are to be used as data points. If you click the Categories In First Column option, however, Excel uses the values in column A as category labels. The resulting chart appears in Figure 11-12.

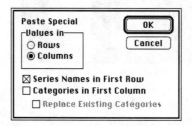

FIGURE 11-11. *This is the Paste Special dialog box.*

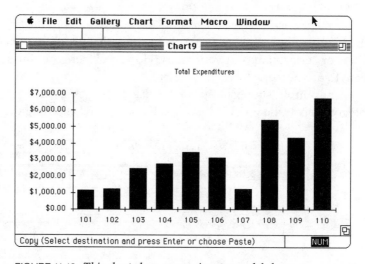

FIGURE 11-12. *This chart shows numeric category labels.*

By the way, although dates are stored as numeric values in your worksheet, Excel assumes that you want to use dates in the first row or first column of your copy area as labels. If you want Excel to plot date values rather than use them as series names or category labels, you can choose the Paste Special... command and turn off the Series Names In First Rows or Categories In First Column option.

Charting discontinuous ranges

With Microsoft Excel 2.2, you can select two or more discontinuous areas in a worksheet, then instruct the program to chart all of the data at once. (In earlier versions of the program, you could chart multiple ranges only by cutting and pasting the individual data series into a chart window.) This new capability is handy when you want to create a chart from data that does not appear in adjacent columns or rows of your worksheet.

For example, suppose you want to plot the test scores in columns B, C, and E of the worksheet shown in Figure 11-13. You could create your chart by plotting the first two columns of test scores, then copying and pasting the third set of test scores into the chart. A much easier way, however, is to select all the test scores as a discontinuous range, then create the chart. To do this, you begin by selecting the first area you want to plot, A3:C10, as shown in Figure 11-14 on the next page. Notice that the first selected area includes some of the category labels in column A as well as some of the test scores in columns B and C.

```
 ₡   File   Edit   Formula   Format   Data   Options   Macro   Window  ▶
      A1                    First Quarter Exam Scores
┌────────────────────── Exam Scores/2 ──────────────────────┐
│         A          B          C          D         E         F      │
│  1  First Quarter Exam Scores                                        │
│  2                                                                   │
│  3  Student     Exam 1     Exam 2     Absences   Exam 3   PASS/FAIL  │
│  4  Allan         87         90          4         96       PASS     │
│  5  Billinger     92         94          3         97       PASS     │
│  6  Crane         96         95          5         89       PASS     │
│  7  Davis         90         87          6         88       PASS     │
│  8  Evans         91         88          1         85       PASS     │
│  9  Flynn         76         89          2         72       FAIL     │
│ 10  Gilbert       77         81          4         80       FAIL     │
│ 11                                                                   │
│ 12  Average:      87         89                    87                │
│ 13                                                                   │
│ 14                                                                   │
│ 15                                                                   │
│ 16                                                                   │
│ 17                                                                   │
│ 18                                                                   │
│ Ready                                                      NUM       │
└─────────────────────────────────────────────────────────────────────┘
```

FIGURE 11-13. *You can plot the test scores from this worksheet in a column chart.*

After you select the first area you want to plot, hold down the Command key while you select additional areas to plot. For this example, hold down the Command key and select the range E3:E7. The result is the discontinuous selection shown in Figure 11-15 on the next page.

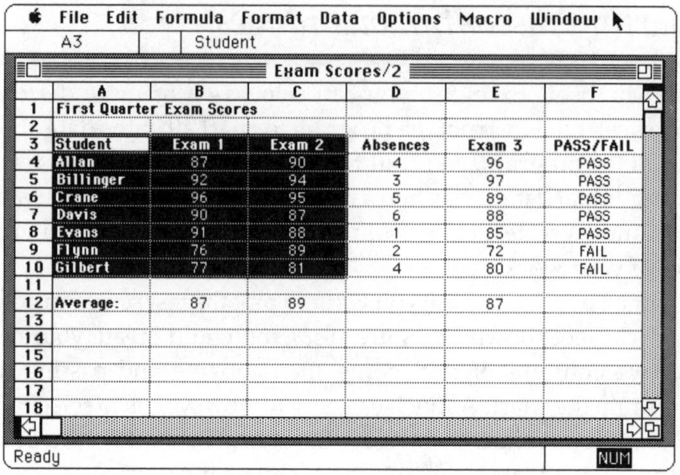

FIGURE 11-14. *To plot the test scores, begin by selecting the data in columns A through C.*

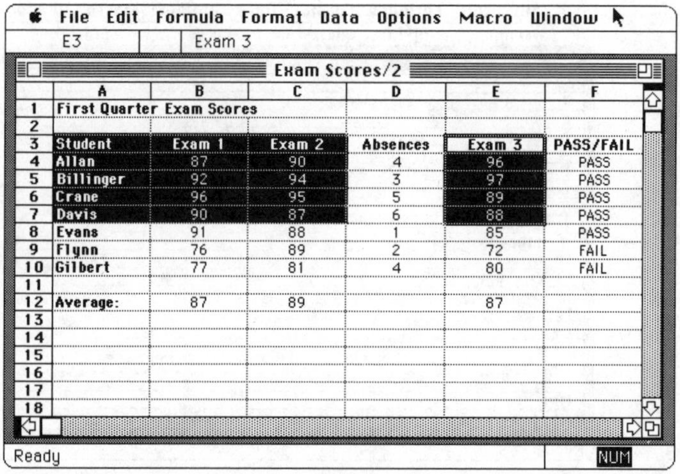

FIGURE 11-15. *You can create a chart from this discontinuous selection.*

Once you have selected all the areas you want to plot, choose New... from the File menu and create a new chart. Excel then plots a chart that looks like the one in Figure 11-16. (We have added a legend to the chart in this example.)

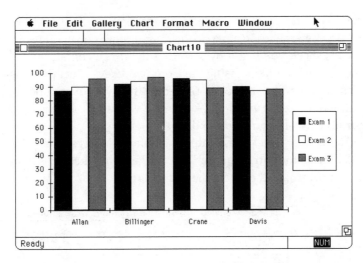

FIGURE 11-16. *This chart was created from the discontinuous selection shown in Figure 11-15.*

Overriding Excel's default organization of series and categories

As we've shown, Excel's ability to plot multiple selections in a worksheet can make it easier and faster to create a chart. This feature offers another significant benefit. By selecting multiple ranges, you can override the automatic assignment of categories and series. As we explained earlier, when Excel creates a chart, it assumes that there should be fewer data series than data points in that chart. Thus, if you select a vertical range (with more rows than columns), Excel treats each column as a data series and each row as a category. Similarly, if you select a horizontal range (one that contains more columns than rows), Excel treats each column as a category and each row as a data series.

For example, suppose you want to create a graph from a worksheet like the one in Figure 11-17 on the next page. You want to create a separate data series for each year's sales and use the regions (South and West) as your categories. If you simply select cells A2:C5, choose New... from the File menu, then select Chart and click OK, the results look like Figure 11-18, also on the next page. (Again, we've added a legend to this chart.) Because the selection A2:C5 contains more rows than columns, Excel assumes that each region's sales should be a separate series and that each year should be a category.

You can reverse Excel's default organization of data series and categories by selecting two ranges instead of one range before you create your chart. In the sample worksheet, you begin by selecting the range containing your category labels (A2:C2). Then, while pressing the Command key, select the range containing your series names and data points (A3:C5). When you open a new chart window, the result looks like Figure 11-19. (Again, we've added a legend to the chart to make it clear how Excel organized the data.)

Notice that Excel has created the data series from the entries in each row instead of from the entries in each column, and the categories (South and West) from the first row instead of from the first column.

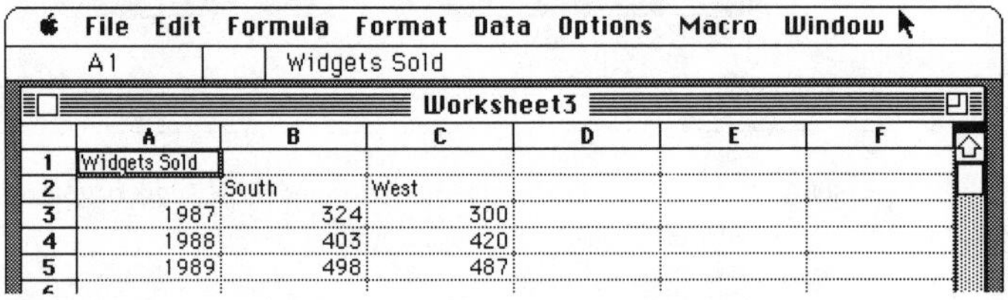

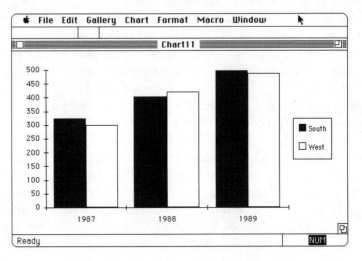

FIGURE 11-17. *This worksheet shows widget sales by year and by region.*

FIGURE 11-18. *The selection A2:C5 from the worksheet in Figure 11-17 looks like this after choosing New... and selecting Chart.*

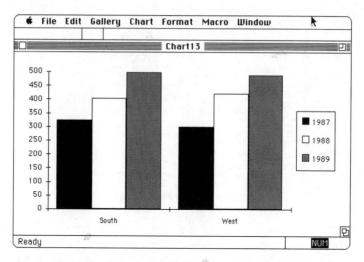

FIGURE 11-19. *The chart created from the two-part selection, A2:C2 and A3:C5, in the worksheet shown in Figure 11-17 looks like this.*

Deleting a data series from a chart

To eliminate a data series from a chart, simply select the series by clicking one of the data-point markers in the series or by using the arrow keys. Then, press the Delete key and press Enter, or click the enter box in the formula bar.

Once you've eliminated a data series from a chart, you cannot use the Undo command to replace it. If you want to add the series back to your chart, you must use the Copy and Paste commands, just as if you were creating a new data series.

Enhancing multiple-series charts

In Chapter 10, "Basic Charting Techniques," we explained many of the Microsoft Excel chart-formatting options. There are some options, however, that apply only to charts with more than one data series. In addition, there are a few options that behave a bit differently when you add more than one series to the chart. We cover those options in the following sections.

The Main Chart... command

As you already know, the Main Chart... command on the Format menu lets you control the way your chart is displayed. When you choose the Main Chart... command, you see a dialog box like the one in Figure 11-20 on the next page.

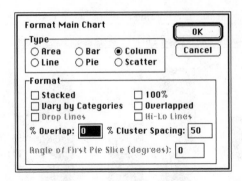

FIGURE 11-20. *This is the Format Main Chart dialog box.*

You have already seen how the Vary By Categories and the % Cluster Spacing options work. The remaining options—100%, Stacked, and Overlapped—apply only to charts that contain two or more data series. We consider those options in this section, too. Then, we discuss the Drop Lines and Hi-Lo Lines options. (We discuss the Type options in the next chapter.)

The options in the Main Chart dialog box are available or unavailable, depending upon which chart type you have selected. For example, in Figure 11-20, Column is the chart type selected by default when you choose the Main Chart... command. You notice that three of the Main Chart dialog box options are unavailable in the Column chart environment. However, if you select the Line chart type, Excel activates the Drop Lines and Hi-Lo Lines options, and dims the Overlapped, % Overlap, and % Cluster Spacing options. In a similar fashion, Excel makes available only the options that apply to the chart type you select.

The Vary By Categories option

As you saw in the previous chapter, when you create a chart with only one data series and select the Vary By Categories option, Excel displays each column in a different pattern. In a chart with more than one data series, Excel automatically displays each data series in a different pattern. Thus, selecting Vary By Categories in a chart with more than one data series has no effect on the chart.

The % Cluster Spacing option

The % Cluster Spacing option lets you control the spacing between the columns (or clusters of columns) in your chart. The default cluster spacing, 50%, means that the distance between each column in the chart is half the width of one column.

If you are working with only one data series, the amount of space determined by the cluster spacing percentage appears between each column. If you are working with two or more data series, the spaces appear between each group of columns. For example, Figure 11-21 shows the chart that appeared in Figure 11-4 after the % Cluster Spacing setting has been changed to 100%.

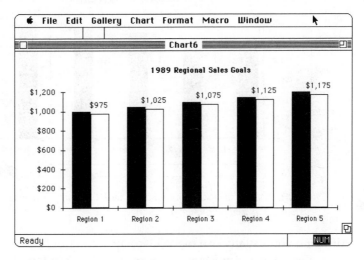

FIGURE 11-21. *This is the column chart from Figure 11-4 with the % Cluster Spacing setting changed from 50% to 100%.*

The Overlapped option

The Overlapped option lets you control how the columns in each cluster are positioned relative to one another. Overlapping is controlled by two settings in the Main Chart dialog box: Overlapped and % Overlap. The default for Overlapped is unselected and the default setting for % Overlap is 0%, which means that the columns in each cluster do not overlap, but appear side by side. All of the charts you have created thus far have had 0% overlap.

If you select the Overlapped option, type 25 in the % Overlap field, with cluster spacing of 50%, and click OK, your chart looks like Figure 11-22 on the next page. Notice that each column overlaps the column to its left by one quarter of the column width. You can use any percentage from 0 to 100 to overlap the columns in a chart.

The Overlapped format works best when there is a noticeable difference in the heights of the columns within each cluster. If all of the columns in a cluster are about the same height, using Overlapped simply makes the column that is plotted last look wider than the other columns. Also, as you can see in Figure 11-22, your data-point labels might overlap the columns slightly when you use the Overlapped option.

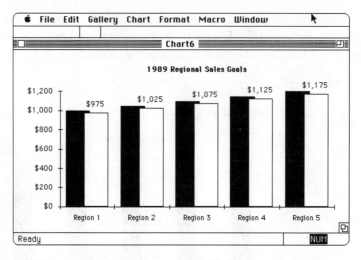

FIGURE 11-22. *This is the column chart with Overlapped selected,
25% overlap, and 50% cluster spacing.*

Although you usually use the % Overlap setting only when the Overlapped
option is selected, you can enter a percentage other than 0 in the % Overlap field
when the Overlapped option is not selected. When you do this, Excel separates the
columns in each cluster by the amount of space indicated by the percentage. For
example, if you choose the Main Chart... command, deselect the Overlapped option, enter 25 in the % Overlap field, and click OK, your chart changes to look like
Figure 11-23. Notice that the columns in each cluster are now separated by 25 percent of a column width.

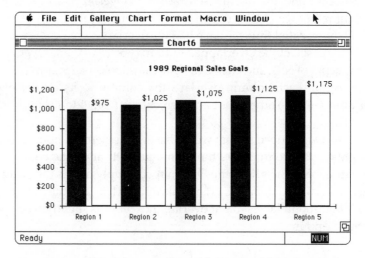

FIGURE 11-23. *This is the same chart with Overlapped deselected,
25% overlap, and 50% cluster spacing.*

The Stacked option

The Stacked option allows you to convert clustered columns into sets of stacked columns. For example, if you choose the Main Chart... command and select the Stacked option, the chart in Figure 11-23 changes to look like Figure 11-24.

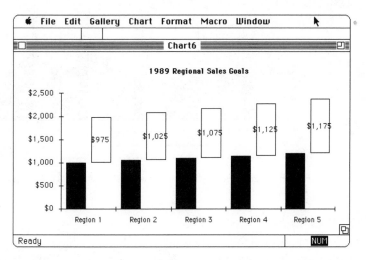

FIGURE 11-24. *This is a two-series chart with the Stacked option selected.*

Notice that although the second column in each cluster in this chart begins where the first column ends, the columns in each cluster are still side by side instead of being stacked one above the next. This type of chart is called a step chart. If you want to convert the chart to a true stacked column chart, you must select the Overlapped option and enter *100* in the % Overlap field. Unless you do this, the columns in the chart do not align properly. Figure 11-25 on the next page shows the chart with 100% overlap.

Notice that Excel adjusts the scale along the value axis to accommodate the new format, reflecting the sum of the two series. If you select the Stacked option, make sure your value-axis Minimum and Maximum settings are set to Auto or contain values large enough to accommodate the stacked chart format. Otherwise, Excel cannot adjust the value scale and truncates the columns.

If you do find that some of your columns are truncated, click the value axis, then choose Scale... from the Format menu. Enter values large enough to accommodate your stacked columns in the Minimum and Maximum fields.

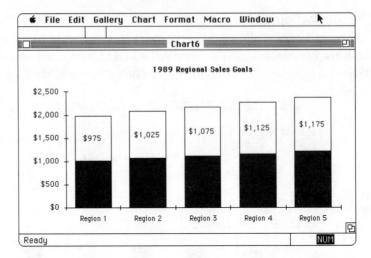

FIGURE 11-25. *This is a stacked chart with Overlapped selected and 100% overlap.*

The 100% option

The 100% option, which is only effective when you have selected the Stacked option, changes the value-axis scale in the chart from actual values to a percentage scale. If you select the 100% option, your chart looks like Figure 11-26.

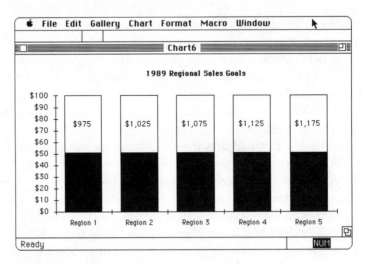

FIGURE 11-26. *This is a 100%, stacked, two-series chart.*

Notice that the value axis now has a minimum value of 0 and a maximum value of 100. Each of the data-point markers reflects the relative value of that data point on a 100% scale. What you have created, in effect, is a series of pie charts in column format. Each of your data-point values is converted into a proportional "slice" of the column.

The Drop Lines option

When you are working with an area or line chart, which we discuss in Chapter 12, "Other Types of Charts," the Drop Lines option is available. When selected, this option draws a line from the highest value in each category to the category axis. As you can see in Figure 11-27, this feature allows you to maintain the connection between a data point and its position relative to the category axis.

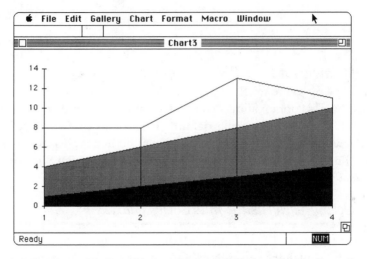

FIGURE 11-27. *The Drop Lines option is available for an area or line chart.*

The Hi-Lo Lines option

When you are working with a line chart, the Hi-Lo Lines option is available. When applied, this option drops lines from the highest value in the category to the lowest value in the category. This feature enables you to track the rise and fall of comparable data over time. Figure 11-28 on the next page shows a line chart with the Hi-Lo Lines option selected.

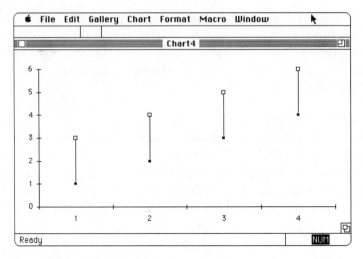

FIGURE 11-28. *We have used the Hi-Lo Lines option in this line chart.*

The Angle Of First Pie Slice option

The last option in the Format Main Chart dialog box is the Angle Of First Pie Slice option. This option allows you to determine the angle of the first pie slice in a pie chart. If you accept Excel's default choice, your first pie slice begins with its left edge vertical. All other angles are measured in degrees clockwise from this vertical line. As you might expect, the Angle Of First Pie Slice option appears only when you are working with a pie chart.

Selecting patterns for multiseries charts

You can use the Format menu's Patterns... command to change the pattern Excel uses to display the columns or stacked portions of columns in a multiseries chart. When you use Patterns... in a multiseries chart, the command applies to all of the columns in a series, instead of just to individual columns.

To use patterns in a multiseries chart, you must first select the data series you want to format by clicking any of the markers in that series. Excel places squares in some of the markers in that series to indicate your selection. When you choose the Patterns... command from the Format menu, Excel displays the familiar dialog box shown in Figure 11-29. (As we mentioned in Chapter 10, "Basic Charting Techniques," if you double click one of the markers in the series, you select the series and choose the Patterns... command at the same time.)

As you know, the default Area Pattern setting is Automatic. In a multiseries chart, when Automatic is selected, Excel assigns the first pattern option (black) to the first series in the chart, white to the second series, the second pattern option to the third series, the third pattern option to the fourth series, and so on.

Of course, you can alter this default by selecting one of the series in the chart, choosing the Patterns... command, and clicking one of the 16 pattern options. For example, Figure 11-30 shows the result of selecting the first series in the sample chart, choosing Patterns..., and selecting a diagonal area pattern. (We gave this chart a non-stacked, non-overlapped format for clarity.) Notice that the new pattern is assigned to every column in the selected series.

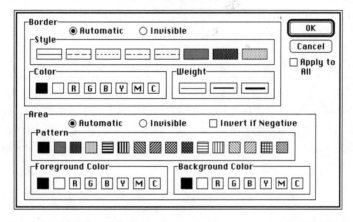

FIGURE 11-29. *This is the Patterns dialog box.*

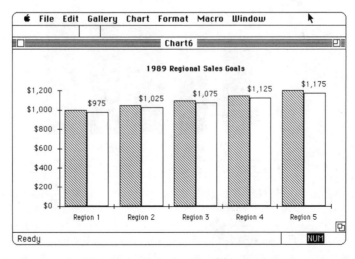

FIGURE 11-30. *The pattern of the first data series has been changed.*

As before, if you select the Invisible option, Excel displays only the column border. This means that if you use overlapping columns in your chart, the overlapped column is visible through the overlapping column. To avoid this problem, select a white pattern for the overlapping column.

Because we discussed the Patterns dialog boxes at length in Chapter 10, "Basic Charting Techniques," we won't discuss all the Patterns options here. However, the last option in the Patterns dialog box, Apply To All, is worth mentioning. If you click the Apply To All box, Excel uses the Area Pattern, Border Style, and Border Weight options that you define in the dialog box for all of the data series in the chart. If this option is not selected, the settings you define apply only to the selected data series.

Using legends

Legends are special labels that identify the data series in charts. You can use legends in single-series or multiseries charts. For most chart types, however, you find that legends add little information to single-series charts, unless you have assigned a different pattern to each category. For example, the chart in Figure 11-31 contains a legend for a single data series.

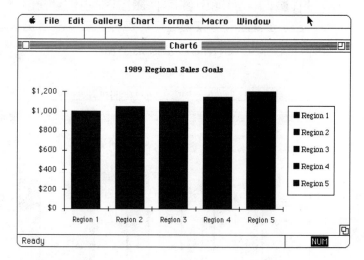

FIGURE 11-31. *Assigning a legend to a single-series chart is not very useful.*

Notice that Microsoft Excel simply repeats in the legend the labels that already appear below the category axis. Pie charts, which we discuss in the next section, and column charts that use different patterns rather than category labels to distinguish categories, are probably the only types of charts that need legends for single data series.

If your chart includes more than one data series, you will probably want to add a legend to help the reader distinguish between each series. To add a legend to the chart in Figure 11-30, simply choose Add Legend from the Chart menu. As you can see in the chart in Figure 11-32, the series names *Product A* and *Product B* now appear in the legend.

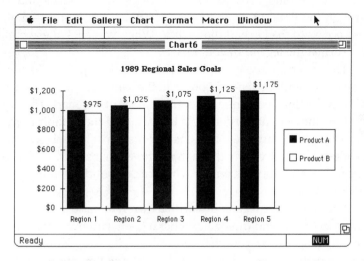

FIGURE 11-32. *You have added a legend to identify the series.*

Moving the legend

Microsoft Excel automatically centers the legend along the right side of the chart area and adjusts the size of the plot area to accommodate the addition. If you want to reposition the legend on the screen, you must first click the legend and then choose Legend... from the Format menu. Microsoft Excel displays the dialog box shown in Figure 11-33, offering four options: Bottom, Corner, Top, and Vertical. Vertical is the default.

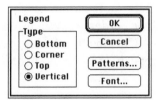

FIGURE 11-33. *This is the Legend dialog box.*

If you select Corner, Excel moves the legend to the upper-right corner of the chart. If you select Top, Excel changes the legend to a horizontal format and centers it under the chart title. If you select Bottom, Excel moves the legend to one line at the bottom of the chart, where it is less conspicuous and takes up less room. As a result, Excel has more room to display the contents of the plot area. You cannot drag the legend box.

Formatting legend patterns and text

The Legend dialog box provides access to the Patterns and Font dialog boxes through the Patterns... and Font... buttons, just as those dialog boxes provide easy access to the Legend dialog box. When you click these buttons, you can further format the legend in your chart.

The Patterns... command lets you control the pattern Excel uses to display the legend area and the legend border in the same ways we discussed in Chapter 10, "Basic Charting Techniques," for other areas of the chart. The default Area Pattern is white, the default Border Style is black, and the default Border Weight is light. The white Area Pattern setting ensures that any chart objects that might be under the legend are not visible through it. The white background also means that your legend box still appears with a white background, even if you use a background pattern in the chart area.

You can fill the legend box with a different pattern by clicking the Patterns... button in the Legend dialog box, clicking any pattern in the Area Pattern box, and then clicking OK. If you change the legend's area pattern, you must be sure to select a pattern that differs from the patterns you are using for the series in the chart. Otherwise, the key box for that series fades into the background as you can see in Figure 11-34, where we've deliberately formatted one of the series with the same area pattern as the legend box.

You can use the Invisible option to get rid of the area pattern altogether. If you set the area pattern to Invisible, any area pattern that you assign to the chart also appears in the legend box. In addition, any chart options that might be under the legend show through.

As with the plot and chart areas, you can also change the pattern and weight of the border box that appears around the legend. If you don't want a border, you can select the Border Weight setting's Invisible option to remove it.

You can add a black drop-shadow border to your legend by clicking the Shadow option in the Border Style box. (Clicking the Shadow option also activates the Automatic button.) The shadow appears in black, no matter what border pattern you select.

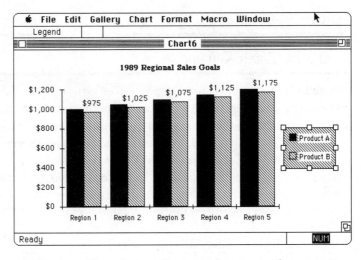

FIGURE 11-34. *The series keys disappear when you use the same pattern for the legend area as for a data series.*

You can use the Font... command to change the way the text appears in the legend box. To use this command, click the Font... button in the Legend dialog box. The Font dialog box, shown in Figure 11-35, allows you to set the font, size, color, style, and background of the legend text. For example, if you think the legend box takes up too much room on your chart, but you still want to display it, you can reduce the size of the legend text. When you do this, Excel reduces the size of the legend box, as well.

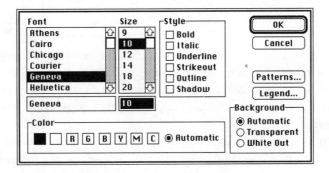

FIGURE 11-35. *This is the Font dialog box.*

EXCEL *tip*

Using the Show Key option

If you're tight on space, use the Show Key option in the Text dialog box instead of a chart legend. First, select one of the data-point markers on the chart. Then, choose the Attach Text... command from the Chart menu. In the Attach Text dialog box, Excel indicates the current series number and data-point number, so simply click OK. At this point, you see a value just above the data-point marker that you selected. Now, choose the Text... command from the Format menu. In the Text dialog box, activate the Show Key option, then deactivate the Show Value option.

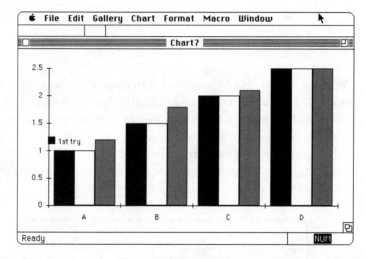

By deactivating the Show Value option, you tell Microsoft Excel to replace the value that formerly appeared as your data-point marker with the series name. When you click OK, you see a small pattern box or marker symbol above your selected data point. Next to this box or symbol, you see the series name.

In a multiseries chart, you can keep your markers and labels from crowding into one another by placing each one over a different category.

More about legends

Deleting a legend is just as easy as adding one. Add Legend is a toggle command, so as soon as you choose it from the Chart menu, its name changes to Delete Legend. To delete a legend you have created, choose the Delete Legend command.

When you delete the legend, Excel automatically expands the size of the plot area again, to use the space that was occupied by the legend.

Of course, Microsoft Excel automatically changes the legend keys whenever you alter the patterns assigned to series in the chart or their corresponding labels in the worksheet.

Excel does not allow you to edit the contents of the legend box. To alter the legend text, you must either edit the cells that contain the category labels or change the SERIES function used to create the chart. We talk more about the SERIES function in Chapter 13, "Other Chart Topics."

If your chart does not include series names (that is, if you did not include cells containing labels in the columns or rows that make up your data series), Microsoft Excel does not display any text in the legend box. Only the data-point marker keys appear.

Browsing through the chart gallery

There are a number of ways to format the charts you create in Microsoft Excel. You've already seen all the hard ways. Now that you've gone the scenic route to learn how charts are created and formatted in Excel, let's take a quick look at the shortcuts you can use to format your charts.

The easiest way to format your charts in Excel is to select the chart type and format you want from the Gallery menu. When you pull down this menu, you notice that the current chart format, Column..., is marked in this list with a check mark. When you select a chart type, Excel displays a "gallery" of common formats for that chart. For example, Figure 11-36 shows the gallery that appears if you choose the Column... option from the Gallery menu. Notice that this gallery offers eight common column chart formats.

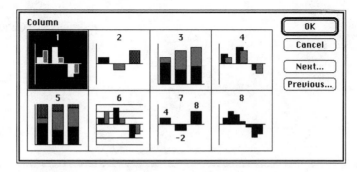

FIGURE 11-36. *This is the column chart gallery.*

To select a format, simply double click the picture of the chart you want. Excel automatically selects all of the appropriate axis, main chart, and pattern options for you. For example, if you select the fifth column chart option, Excel converts your chart into a stacked, overlapped column chart in 100% format.

It's important to understand that the Gallery menu simply offers a shortcut to formatting the chart manually. For example, you can also create a 100% stacked column chart by using the settings listed in Figure 11-37.

Menu	Command	Option
Format	Main Chart...	Column
Chart	Axes...	Category Axis
		Value Axis
Format	Patterns...	Area Pattern: Automatic
		Border Pattern: Automatic
		Border Weight: Light
		Apply To All: Unactivated
	Main Chart...	Stacked
		100%
		Overlapped
		% Overlap: 100
		% Cluster Spacing: 50
Select category axis		
Format	Scale...	Value Axis Crosses At Category Number: 1
		Number of Categories Between Tick Labels: 1
		Number of Categories Between Tick Marks: 1
		Value Axis Crosses Between Categories
Select value axis		
Format	Scale...	Minimum: 0
		Maximum: 100
		Major Unit: 10
		Minor Unit: 2
		Category Axis Crosses At: 0

FIGURE 11-37. *These settings are required to duplicate the fifth option from the column chart gallery.*

It is much easier to use the Gallery-menu command to format a chart than it is to issue all of these commands separately. However, it's best to use the Gallery menu to select a chart type and format when you first create a chart. If you format a chart manually and then use the Gallery menu to change the format, you lose much of your special formatting.

Even if none of the Gallery options exactly meets your needs, you can still benefit by using the Gallery-menu commands. Simply choose the format that is closest to the one you want, and then use the formatting commands we discussed earlier to tailor the chart.

For further browsing, you might click the Next... or Previous... button to see the other types of available charts: Area, Bar, Line, Pie, Scatter, and Combination. For example, if you're looking at the Column chart gallery and you press Next..., you see the Line chart gallery. If you're looking at the Column chart gallery and you press Previous..., you see the Bar chart gallery.

Using the Gallery menu to change the type of a chart

In addition to using the Gallery menu to change the format of a chart, you can also use this option to change the type of the chart completely. For example, suppose you are working with the chart shown in Figure 11-32. If you choose Line... from the Gallery menu, you see the gallery shown in Figure 11-38. If you select the first option from this gallery, your chart looks like Figure 11-39 on the next page.

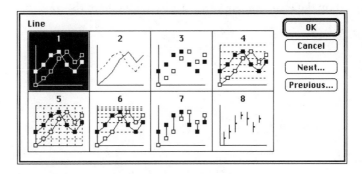

FIGURE 11-38. *This is the Line chart gallery.*

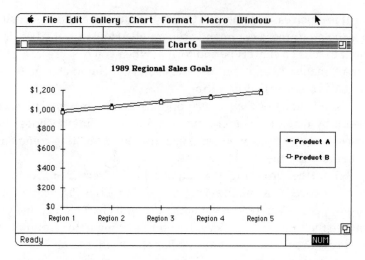

FIGURE 11-39. *You have converted the two-series column chart to a line chart.*

Conclusion

In the next chapter, we explain the special formats associated with each gallery option as we discuss the various chart types available in Microsoft Excel. We also offer a few tips on the best charts for various types of data and show you how to expand on the basic formats and styles available in the gallery.

12

Other Types of Charts

So far, we've looked mainly at column charts. Of course, Microsoft Excel can create many other types of charts, including area charts, bar charts, line charts, pie charts, scatter diagrams, and combination charts. In this chapter, we consider each of these chart types in turn.

Changing the type of a chart

The default chart type in Microsoft Excel is the column chart. This means that every chart you create appears as a column chart unless you tell Excel you prefer another chart format. You can change the default chart type from column to any of Excel's other chart types. We show you how to do that in this chapter.

Of course, even if you leave the default as it is, you are not limited to working only with column charts. As we hinted in Chapter 11, "Plotting More Than One Series," you can use the Gallery-menu commands or the Main Chart... command to change the chart type. In the following discussion, we also show you how these commands work.

The Main Chart... command

When you choose the Main Chart... command from the Format menu, Microsoft
Excel presents a list of chart types and formats. Figure 12-1 shows the Format Main
Chart dialog box. When you select a chart from the list, Excel converts the current
chart into the selected type.

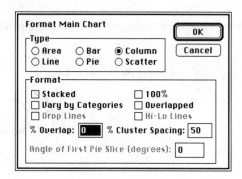

FIGURE 12-1. *The Format Main Chart dialog box appears
when you choose Main Chart... from the Format menu.*

To convert the column chart in Figure 12-2 into a bar chart, select Bar from the
Type list and click OK. Your chart is redrawn to look like Figure 12-3.

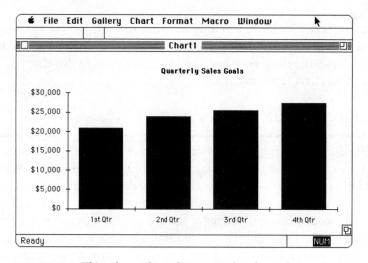

FIGURE 12-2. *This column chart plots quarterly sales goals.*

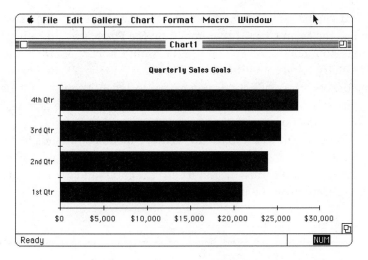

FIGURE 12-3. *The quarterly sales goals column chart is converted into a bar chart.*

Microsoft Excel activates different formatting options in the lower half of the Format Main Chart dialog box, depending upon the chart type you select in the upper portion of the dialog box or the type of chart you're working with before you open the dialog box. For example, if you choose the Main Chart... command from the Format menu while you're working with a line chart, the Stacked, Vary By Categories, Drop Lines, 100%, and Hi-Lo Lines options are available. The Overlapped, % Overlap, % Cluster Spacing, and Angle Of First Pie Slice options appear dimmed, indicating that they don't apply to a line chart.

The Gallery menu

You can also use the Gallery menu to change the type of an existing chart. All you have to do is pull down the Gallery menu, choose a chart type, then select the chart format that you want to use. For example, to change the column chart in Figure 12-2 to a bar chart, you would have chosen Bar... from the Gallery menu, then selected one of the bar-chart gallery options. As you learned in the previous chapter, the charts you see in each gallery carry their own preset formats. When you choose a chart type and format from the Gallery menu, Excel may override some of the formatting changes you have made to your chart so that it conforms to the chosen type and format. For example, if you choose the Format menu's Scale... command to change the position of your value or category axis, Excel may move the axis again to fit the chart type and format that you select.

If you have already made changes to the format of your chart, you might want to use the Main Chart... command on the Format menu rather than the Gallery-menu commands. When you use the Main Chart... command to change the type of a chart, Excel converts the current chart into the selected type, without disturbing the other format options you have selected. (Of course, any formats that are not applicable for the chart type you select are ignored. For example, your axis settings have no effect on pie charts.)

Generally, it's best to use the Gallery-menu commands to choose a chart type and format as soon as you create a new chart. If you've already done some custom tailoring, however, use the Main Chart... command to make sure your formatting changes are preserved.

EXCEL *Tip*

Category- and value-axis titles

If you have created titles for your column chart's value and category axes and then you decide to convert your chart to a bar chart, you'll probably want to change the Orientation and Alignment settings for those titles. For example, in this chart, the value-axis titles have been assigned the Vertical Text option from the Format Text dialog box:

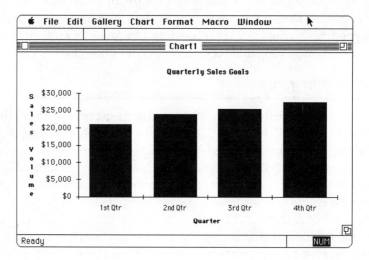

Changing the default

Every chart you create in Microsoft Excel automatically appears in the Preferred format. Excel's default Preferred chart style is a simple column chart—the first chart format in the dialog box that appears when you choose Column... from the Gallery menu.

If you use another type of chart more often than the column type, you can change the Preferred chart type. To change the default chart type, select the format you prefer, then choose the Set Preferred command from the Gallery menu. Any new charts you create automatically appear in the new Preferred format, which has every characteristic of the chart that is active when you choose the

If you convert this column chart to a bar chart, Excel retains the orientation settings for the axis titles, as you can see here:

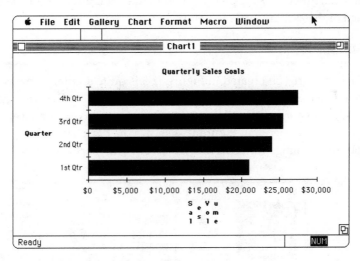

When you switch to the bar-chart format from the column-chart format, you'll want to deselect the Vertical Text option for the value-axis title, select the Vertical Text option for the category-axis title, and adjust Alignment settings.

Set Preferred command. Even such small details as line thickness, position of tick marks, and text formats are included in the new Preferred format.

Usually, you set the Preferred format to match one of the basic options in the Microsoft Excel chart gallery. If none of Excel's chart formats meet your needs, you can tailor your own Preferred format. For example, Figure 12-3 shows a bar chart with a chart title formatted to appear in 10-point bold Geneva. You can use these settings as your Preferred format simply by choosing the Set Preferred command from the Gallery menu. Then, whenever you create a new chart, Excel automatically applies the format you see in Figure 12-3 to that chart.

Of course, you can always return to the default Preferred format by choosing Column… from the Gallery menu and double clicking the first column-chart option. Then, you can choose Set Preferred from the Gallery menu to reestablish the default Preferred format.

The available chart types

As we've already mentioned, Microsoft Excel has six major chart types: area, bar, column, line, pie, and scatter. In addition, you can create combination charts using the Chart menu's Add Overlay command. In the rest of this chapter, we look at each of these chart types in detail.

Bar charts

The bar chart you created in Figure 12-3 is quite similar to the column charts you have been using until now, except that the data series are organized vertically rather than horizontally. Notice that the category axis is now vertical and the value axis is now horizontal. Figure 12-4 shows the bar-chart gallery. You can use these options to change the basic format of your bar charts.

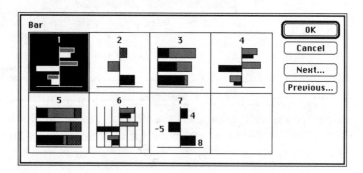

FIGURE 12-4. *This dialog box shows the gallery of bar charts.*

If none of these formats are exactly right, you can use the Chart- and Format-menu commands to tailor the chart to your own needs. You can add titles, legends, attached text, unattached text, and many other enhancements to your bar chart, in exactly the same ways that you enhanced the column charts in Chapter 10, "Basic Charting Techniques." About the only things you need to keep in mind as you format your bar chart are that the category axis is now vertical and the value axis is now horizontal.

Column and bar charts are well suited to illustrating data trends over a period of time. The specific format you use for these charts depends upon the type of trend you are plotting. For example, stacked bar charts work best when you need to illustrate the relationship between two or more data series across time. The length of the stacked bar gives the reader an idea of the general trend, while the stacked sections illustrate the relative contribution of each item to the whole. Clustered bar charts, on the other hand, make it easy to compare the relative value of a set of data points over time.

Line charts

Line charts are also excellent tools for illustrating trends. Generally, line charts are preferable for plotting continuous data, where subtle variations are important. Bar and column charts are more useful for plotting discrete data, where the emphasis falls on comparative analysis of two or more sets of values.

To convert the column chart in Figure 12-2 into a line chart, choose Line... from the Gallery menu and select one of the options shown in Figure 12-5. Figure 12-6 on the next page shows the chart that results if you select the fifth option. (Of course, you can also create this chart by selecting the Line option from the Type section of the Format Main Chart dialog box, then using the options provided by the Format section of the dialog box.)

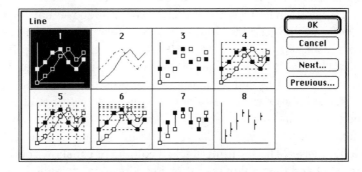

FIGURE 12-5. *This dialog box shows the gallery of line charts.*

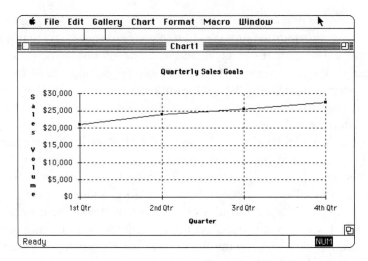

FIGURE 12-6. *The quarterly sales goals chart has been changed to line-chart format.*

As you can see, Microsoft Excel plots the data series in this line-chart as a line and uses symbols to mark each data point. Because you selected the fifth option in the line-chart gallery, this new chart also includes major category-axis and value-axis gridlines.

Formatting the line chart

You can enhance a line chart in almost every way you can enhance bar and column charts. There are a few differences, however, worth covering in more detail.

The Stacked and 100% options   The first option in the Format portion of the Main Chart dialog box is Stacked. (This option applies only to multiseries charts because it determines the order in which the data points are stacked.) If you select the Stacked option, Excel creates a "stacked" line chart. For example, compare the two line charts in Figures 12-7 and 12-8. (We've added actual 1988 quarterly sales to the 1989 sales projections.) Figure 12-7 is a standard line chart, while Figure 12-8 shows a stacked line chart. In the stacked line chart, the top line represents the sum of 1988 and 1989 sales. The bottom line represents 1988 sales only. The distance between the top line and the bottom line represents 1989 sales.

Stacked line charts are a rather odd format so you should use them with care. When you create stacked bar and column charts, the reader can easily see that the values are additive; that is, the values in the second data series are added to the first data series. The resulting stacked column or bar shows both the value of each data point and the total of the parts. Readers are accustomed to interpreting each data series in a line chart as a separate entity, however, and may not realize that the values are additive.

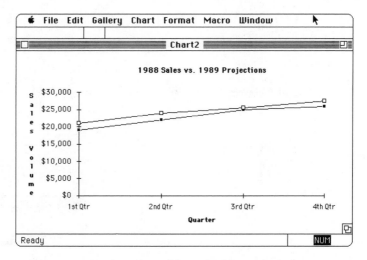

FIGURE 12-7. *This chart shows the standard line-chart format.*

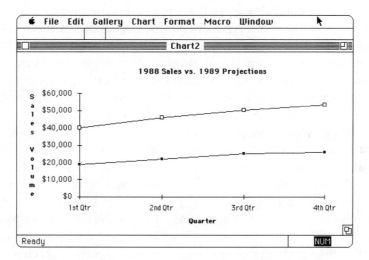

FIGURE 12-8. *The same data are expressed here as a stacked line chart.*

Stacked line charts can become even more confusing when you select the 100% option. As with column and bar charts, the 100% option converts the value axis in a line chart from an absolute scale to a percentage scale. If you select this option when working with a line chart, the result looks like Figure 12-9 on the next page. In this chart, the top line represents 100% of the combined 1988 and 1989 sales. The bottom line represents 1988 sales as a percentage of the combined sales.

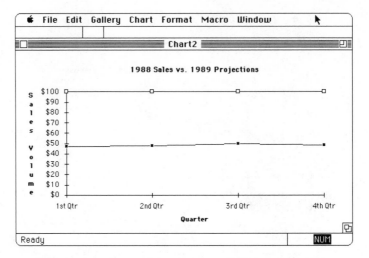

FIGURE 12-9. *The chart has been changed to 100% stacked format.*

You will probably agree that this chart is difficult to understand. One of the major problems with it is that the numbers along the value axis still look like dollar values. Because the numbers in the worksheet that are the basis for this chart are formatted as currency, Excel automatically assigns the currency format to the value labels. Even though the chart now reflects percentages, Excel retains the currency format. The only way around this problem is to change the format of the cells in the worksheet from which the chart is created.

If you want to use the Stacked or 100% options, you should probably use an area chart rather than a line chart so that the additive values are more clearly illustrated. We show you how to create an area chart later in this chapter. If you do use the Stacked or 100% options in a line chart, make sure the chart is clearly labeled.

The Hi-Lo Lines option If you use your Excel worksheet to track stock-market trends, you'll be happy to know that Excel also offers a hi-lo format for line charts. Hi-lo charts use vertical lines to connect the data points in each category rather than horizontal lines to connect the data points in each series. For example, the worksheet in Figure 12-10 tracks daily stock prices for Soft Wares, Inc. To plot the daily high and low stock prices for this company, select cells A3:C8 and create a new chart window. Then, choose Line… from the Gallery menu and double click the seventh line-chart option. As you can see in Figure 12-11, the marker patterns that appear for each data series make it easy to find the high and low values at a glance. You can also add the stock's opening and closing prices.

	A	B	C	D	E	F
1	Weekly Stock Prices: Soft Wares, Inc.					
2						
3	Date	High	Low	Open	Close	
4	5/1/89	58	54	56	58	
5	5/2/89	57	52	55	56	
6	5/3/89	56	53	54	55	
7	5/4/89	55	49	52	53	
8	5/5/89	54	50	51	53	

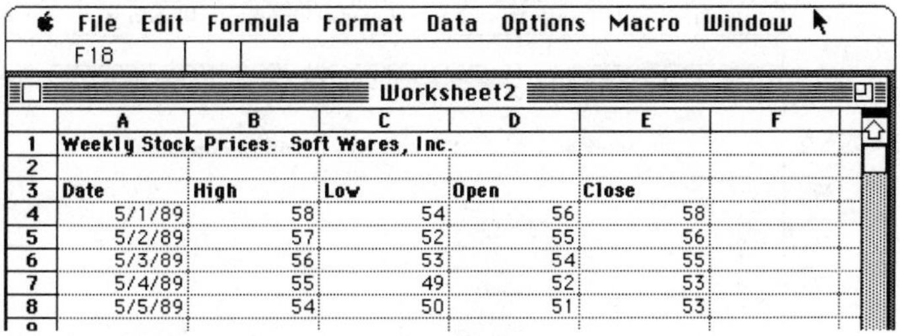

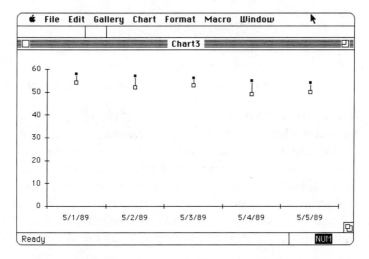

FIGURE 12-10. *This worksheet shows daily stock prices.*

FIGURE 12-11. *This line chart uses the Hi-Lo Lines option to emphasize high and low stock prices.*

The Drop Lines option The Drop Lines option in the Format Main Chart dialog box tells Excel to draw a vertical line from the highest data point in each category down to the category axis. Drop lines are useful in helping identify which data points in a multiseries line chart align with one another. They are especially helpful when the lines in a line chart crisscross each other. For example, the Drop Lines option was used to create the chart in Figure 12-12 on the next page. You can also use the Drop Lines option in a hi-lo chart to extend all the way down to the category axis the vertical lines that connect the data points.

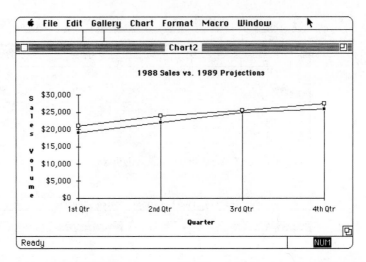

FIGURE 12-12. *This line chart uses the Drop Lines option for emphasis.*

Selecting patterns and colors for a line chart

Just as Excel allows you to change the area pattern, border style, border weight, and color used in column and bar charts, it also allows you to change the line style, line weight, line color, and marker-symbol styles used for each line and the foreground and background colors in a line chart. To do this, click the line you want to format and choose Patterns… from the Format menu. When you choose this command, Excel displays a dialog box like the one in Figure 12-13. As you can see, the default Line Style, Color, and Weight settings are Automatic. The default Line

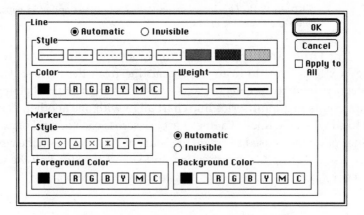

FIGURE 12-13. *This Patterns dialog box appears if you choose Patterns… while working with a line chart.*

Weight setting is the lightest of the three weight options. The default Line Color is black. The default Line Style setting usually displays all of the lines in the chart in solid black with a different type of data marker for each series. If you decide to eliminate the data-point markers from the chart, however, the Automatic setting tells Excel to use a different line pattern or color for each line in the chart.

In general, you're better off staying with the lightest of the three Line Weight settings. If you use the heavier settings, you find that the lines clutter the plot area considerably, especially if the chart displays three or more data series.

You might have occasion to set Line Style to Invisible. When you do this, Excel does not connect the points in the selected data series with a line. Instead, the program displays only the markers that identify the data points. To suppress the display of lines for all of your data series, choose Apply To All after you select the Invisible option.

The default Marker Style option is Automatic. When Marker Style is set to Automatic and you're viewing your chart on a monochrome monitor, Excel assigns a small black square marker to the first data series in the chart. Additional data series are marked with the symbols in the Marker Style box as follows: Excel assigns the first symbol to the second data series, the second symbol to the third data series, and so on. To change the marker symbol, click the symbol you want to use. If you're viewing a line chart on a color monitor, Excel uses the same marker symbol for each data series but assigns a different color to each series—red for the markers in the first series, green for the second data series, and so forth. After plotting the first eight data series with the same marker but different colors, Excel assigns a new marker symbol to the ninth data series and recycles the color assignments, beginning again with red.

To change the marker symbol for the currently selected data series, choose the symbol or color you want to use in the Patterns dialog box. If you do not want any markers to appear, select the Invisible option. To suppress the display of the markers for all the data series in the chart, choose Apply To All after you select Invisible. When you choose not to display marker symbols, Microsoft Excel displays each line in your chart in a different pattern or color to help distinguish between line patterns or colors and between marker patterns, particularly if you're using a thin line weight.

Area charts

Area charts, sometimes referred to as surface charts, are similar to stacked line charts. Area charts allow you to illustrate subtle trends in an easy-to-interpret format—and they don't force you to trace dozens of lines as they crisscross the screen. In addition, the area between each line is filled in so that the reader can easily compare the relative values of each data point in the chart. Area charts are generally used only when you are charting more than one data series. If you are charting only one data series, you are probably better off using a line chart.

To create an area chart, choose Area... from the Gallery menu, then select one of the area-chart options shown in Figure 12-14. Figure 12-15 shows the result of selecting the first area-chart option and applying it to the chart in Figure 12-8.

The area chart in Figure 12-15 looks a lot like the stacked line chart in Figure 12-8. Excel simply shades the areas between each line to emphasize the relationship. As we mentioned in the description of stacked line charts, the area format is a much better way to show the relative proportions of two or more data series, because it is easier for the reader to interpret.

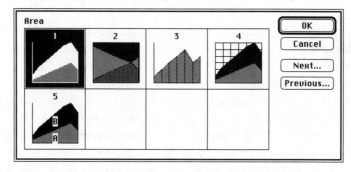

FIGURE 12-14. *This dialog box shows the gallery of area charts.*

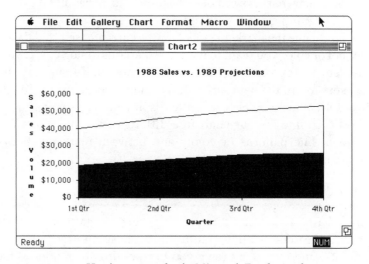

FIGURE 12-15. *Here's an example of a Microsoft Excel area chart.*

Formatting an area chart

If you choose the Main Chart… command from the Format menu while you are working with an area chart, you see that you have only three Format Main Chart options: Stacked, 100%, and Drop Lines.

The default setting for all area charts is Stacked. You can turn off the Stacked option if you want, but the results are typically not very meaningful because some of the data markers are hidden.

As with line, bar, and column charts, the 100% option changes the value axis from an absolute scale to a percentage scale.

You can use the Drop Lines option to help distinguish between the categories of your chart. When you select Drop Lines, Excel changes the area patterns to make the drop lines visible.

Selecting patterns and colors for an area chart

You can use the Format menu's Patterns… command to change the area patterns and colors, the border style and colors, and the border weight for each of the data series in the chart. The Patterns dialog box for an area chart works just like the one you used earlier for column and bar charts. For example, suppose you want to change the pattern of a data series. First, select that series, then choose the Patterns… command from the Format menu. In the Patterns dialog box, select the area pattern you want, then click OK or press Enter. You can also use the Patterns dialog box to remove the thin lines that appear between the different series of an area chart. Simply select the Invisible Border option and choose Apply To All.

Pie charts

The fifth choice on the Gallery menu is the Pie… command. Pie charts make it easy to illustrate the relationship between components of a total. To change a chart to the pie format, choose Pie… from the Gallery menu, then select one of the pie-chart options shown in Figure 12-16 on the next page.

One major difference between pie charts and the other chart types we have discussed is that pie charts can chart only a single data series at a time. You cannot use a pie chart to compare the values in two or more data series.

Also notice that if you choose the sixth pie-chart format, Excel automatically assigns data-point labels to your chart, reflecting the proportion of each slice of the pie. Because pie charts plot only one data series at a time, each data point in your pie chart becomes a category. If you use the Add Legend command from the Chart menu to create a legend for your pie chart, Excel uses the category names in the legend box. For example, Figure 12-17 on the next page shows a simple pie chart with data-point labels and a legend.

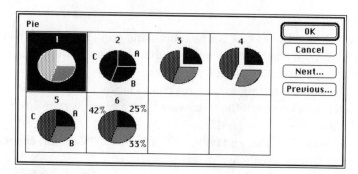

FIGURE 12-16. *This dialog box shows the gallery of pie-chart options.*

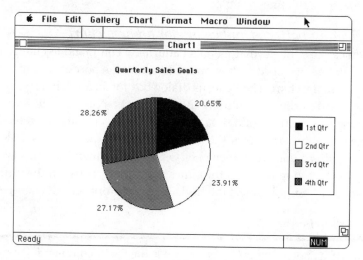

FIGURE 12-17. *This pie chart has data-point labels and a legend.*

As we have said, you can chart only one data series at a time in a pie chart. If you try to use the Gallery menu or Main Chart... command to convert a multi-series chart into a pie chart, Excel uses only the first data series. Your other data series reappear if you change the chart type again, but they remain in limbo while you are using the pie-chart format.

As you might expect, some of the options available for other types of charts are not available when you are working with pie charts. For example, because pie charts have no axes, you cannot use the Chart menu's Axes... command or the Format menu's Scale... command. However, other Chart- and Format-menu commands do work with pie charts.

Formatting a pie chart

If you choose the Main Chart... command from the Format menu while working with a pie chart, the Format Main Chart dialog box has only two options available: Vary By Categories and Angle Of First Pie Slice.

The Vary By Categories option is selected as the default option, which means that Microsoft Excel automatically assigns a different pattern to each slice in the pie. You can use the Angle Of First Pie Slice option to rotate your pie charts. For example, to create the chart in Figure 12-18, you can type *90* in the Angle Of First Pie Slice field to move the first marker in the chart to the lower-right quadrant.

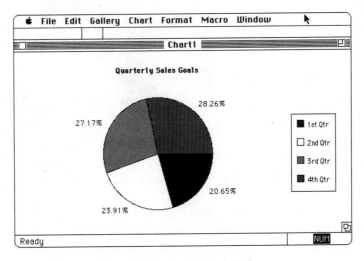

FIGURE 12-18. *The pie chart has been rotated 90 degrees.*

The default setting for this option is 0, which means that the line that forms the left edge of the first slice in the pie points straight up. You can use any whole number up to 360 to change the position of the first slice of the pie.

Selecting patterns and colors for a pie chart

You can also use the Patterns... command to assign specific patterns and colors to individual slices of the pie. The Patterns dialog box that appears when you choose this command for a pie chart is identical to the one discussed for column, bar, and area charts. As with those types of charts, this command allows you to change the area patterns and colors, the border style and color, and the border weight of each section of the pie.

Exploding sections of a pie chart

You can create "exploded" pie charts by clicking the slice you want to explode and dragging it away from the main chart. For example, Figure 12-19 shows the pie chart from Figure 12-18 with the first slice exploded.

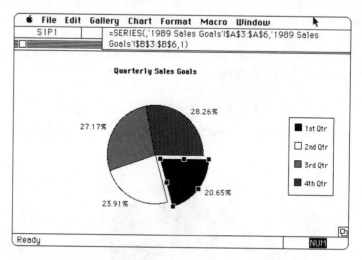

FIGURE 12-19. *This pie chart has one slice exploded for emphasis.*

When you create an exploded pie chart, you won't want to drag the slice far. As you can see in Figure 12-19, Excel reduces the overall size of the pie chart when you explode a slice. You will probably find that an exploded slice stands out well even if you drag it only a very small distance from the rest of the pie slices. If you need to, you can move the legend to the side of the chart to give the pie more room.

Excel does not allow you to drag a pie slice in any direction other than straight out from the center of the pie. You can, however, "slide" the slice across the pie by dragging it toward the pie's center. In fact, you can even drag it to the other side of the chart, but the resulting chart is very small.

To put exploded slices back in place, you can either drag them individually, or you can choose Pie… from the Gallery menu again and select any option that does not offer exploded slices. When you use this command, Excel puts the pieces back together for you.

Scatter diagrams

Scatter diagrams are used to illustrate the relationship between two characteristics of a population. For example, you have probably seen scatter diagrams that illustrate the relationship between items like age and income, height and weight, or net income and stock prices of a company. In Microsoft Excel, scatter diagrams are very much like line charts, with one important difference: The categories in a scatter diagram are more than just labels; they are coordinates that help to determine the locations of the data points in the chart. This means that in a scatter diagram, it is possible to have two or more data points in the same series that share the same category, whereas in a line chart, it is impossible for two or more data points in the same series to share a category.

Creating a scatter diagram in Microsoft Excel is different from creating line, bar, column, or area charts. To create a scatter diagram, the cells you select for your category axis must contain values. In effect, every scatter diagram has two value axes.

For example, the worksheet in Figure 12-20 lists the annual income and education levels of several individuals. To compare income and education levels in a scatter diagram, you select cells A5:B16 and choose the Copy command. Then, choose New... from the File menu and double click the Chart option. Excel displays an empty chart window. Next, choose Paste Special... from the Edit menu.

	A	B	C	D	E	F
	File Edit Formula Format Data Options Macro Window					
	F18					
	Worksheet3					
1	Income vs. Education					
2						
3	Education	Annual				
4	Level	Income				
5	12	$12,104				
6	10	$11,270				
7	11	$11,437				
8	15	$17,205				
9	14	$14,138				
10	16	$17,373				
11	14	$14,839				
12	11	$12,187				
13	12	$13,464				
14	16	$16,972				
15	19	$21,173				
16	9	$8,903				
17						
18						
	Ready					NUM

FIGURE 12-20. *The scatter-diagram examples will be created from this Income versus Education worksheet.*

When you choose Paste Special..., Excel assumes that you do not want to use category names in the chart, because both columns in the worksheet contain values. You may remember from our discussion of the Paste Special... command in Chapter 11, "Plotting More Than One Series," that Excel looks for labels in the first row and first column of the selected area of your worksheet. If it finds no labels, the program assumes that you want to use all of the selected cells as data-point values. In order to create a scatter diagram, you must click the Categories In First Column option to let Excel know that the values in column A of your worksheet are to be used as category-axis values.

Of course, after you choose the Paste Special... command, Excel displays the new chart in the default format. To change this chart into a scatter diagram, choose Scatter... from the Gallery menu and select one of the options shown in Figure 12-21. (When the dialog box appears, the second chart format is highlighted.) Selecting the first chart format creates the chart in Figure 12-22. As you can see, this chart shows a positive correlation between education and annual income.

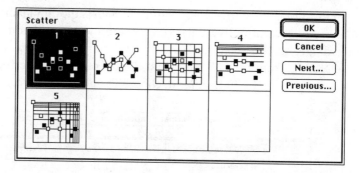

FIGURE 12-21. *This dialog box shows the gallery of scatter-diagram options.*

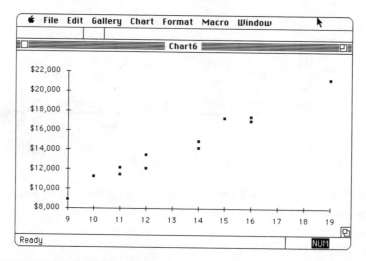

FIGURE 12-22. *The data in the Income versus Education worksheet produces this scatter diagram.*

Most of the time, you want to use the first or third scatter-diagram options. If you use the second option, you generally find that the lines connecting your data points create confusion rather than lending clarity. This is especially true when you are charting two or more data series.

The logarithmic options—the fourth and fifth formats—are typically used only for scientific and engineering data. The fourth format uses a semilogarithmic scale, meaning only one axis is logarithmic. The fifth format uses a log-log scale; that is, both axes are logarithmic.

Formatting a scatter diagram

Microsoft Excel offers fewer formatting options for scatter diagrams than for other chart types. In fact, when you choose Main Chart... from the Format menu while working with a scatter diagram, you find only one option in the Format Main Chart dialog box: the Vary By Categories option. If you are working with a single-series scatter diagram, you can use the Vary By Categories option to assign a different marker to each data-point symbol in the chart.

You can use the Patterns... command to change the line styles, line weights, line colors, marker colors, and marker styles in your scatter diagram. Be sure to select the Apply To All option if you want all the markers and lines in the scatter diagram to be displayed in the same style and color. This command works exactly the same way with scatter diagrams as it does with line charts.

Of course, you can add attached and unattached text to scatter diagrams, change the font, style, and size of the text, and control the display and format of your axes, just as you can with a line chart.

Combination charts

Choose Combination... from the Gallery menu when you want to add an overlay chart to an existing chart. Microsoft Excel offers five different types of combination charts, as shown in Figure 12-23 on the next page. Each of these types of charts really includes two charts: a *main* chart and an *overlay* chart.

To create a combination chart, first select the range of cells that you want to chart, then use the New... command to create a new chart. After you have created the new chart, choose Combination... from the Gallery menu and select one of the five combination-chart options.

For example, the chart in Figure 12-24 on the next page contains quarterly sales statistics for two products for 1988, as well as sales totals for the year. Suppose you want to chart the quarterly statistics as a column chart and the totals as an overlaid line chart. To do this, choose Combination... from the Gallery menu and select the second combination-chart option. Figure 12-25 shows the result.

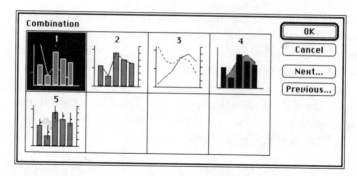

FIGURE 12-23. *This dialog box shows the gallery of combination-chart options.*

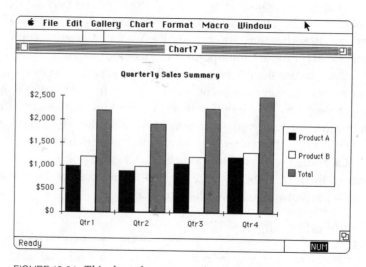

FIGURE 12-24. *This chart shows quarterly sales statistics.*

When you create a combination chart, Excel automatically divides the data series evenly between the main chart and the overlay chart. For example, if your chart has four data series, the first two appear in the main chart and the second two appear in the overlay chart. If your chart has an odd number of data series, the main chart contains one more data series than the overlay chart. As you can see in Figure 12-25, Excel includes the first two data series in the main chart and the last data series in the overlay chart. In other words, Excel draws the first two ranges as

columns and the last range as an overlaid line. (You can tell Excel how many data
series you want to appear in the overlay chart by using the First Series In Overlay
Chart field in the dialog box that appears when you choose Overlay... from the
Format menu. We show you how to do this soon.)

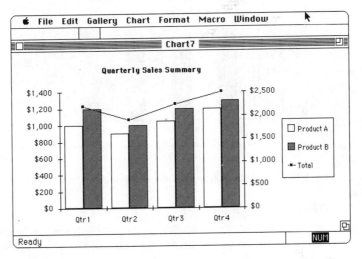

FIGURE 12-25. *The same sales chart has been plotted as a combination
chart.*

As you can see in Figure 12-25, Excel includes two value axes in the sample
chart. The value axis on the right is for the totals in the overlay chart. The second,
third, and fifth options in the combination-chart gallery cause Excel to include two
value axes. Having two value axes is particularly useful when you are plotting
data series with widely disparate scales. For example, if you had used a single
value axis to plot the quarterly sales and annual totals in Figure 12-25, the quarterly
sales figures would have seemed quite small in comparison to the totals in the
third data series.

Not only can you add a second value axis to an overlay chart, you can also add
a second category axis, for a total of four axes. To do this, choose the Axes... command from the Chart menu, then select the Category Axis option in the Overlay
box. When you click OK or press Enter, Excel displays a chart like the one shown in
Figure 12-26 on the next page.

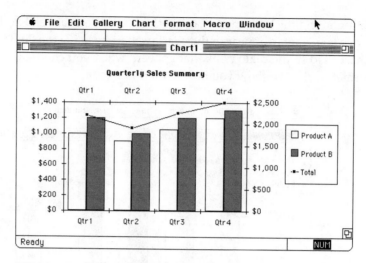

FIGURE 12-26. *This combination chart contains four axes.*

Formatting the overlay chart

After you select the combination you want, you can use the Overlay... command on the Format menu to tailor the overlay chart to your needs. When you choose this command, Microsoft Excel displays the dialog box shown in Figure 12-27. Notice that this dialog box is nearly identical to the Format Main Chart dialog boxes you see when working with Excel's other chart types. In fact, the main difference between the Format Main Chart dialog box and the Format Overlay Chart dialog box is that the latter includes a First Series In Overlay Chart option. This option lets you control the distribution of data series between the main and overlay charts. For example, you can type 2 in the Format Overlay Chart dialog box to display the *Product B* and *Total* data series in the overlay chart, leaving the *Product A* data series in the main chart.

When you enter a number in the First Series In Overlay Chart box, Microsoft Excel deselects the Automatic Series Distribution option at the bottom of the dialog box. To return to Excel's default series-distribution scheme, simply select the Automatic Series Distribution option again.

Suppose you want to plot data series 1 and 3 on your main chart and data series 2 and 4 on your overlay chart. You can control which data series appears in which chart by changing the number assigned to the data series. We explain this technique in the next chapter, when we discuss the SERIES function.

All of the other options in the Format Overlay Chart dialog box have the same effect on the overlay chart that the corresponding options in the Format Main Chart dialog box have on the main chart.

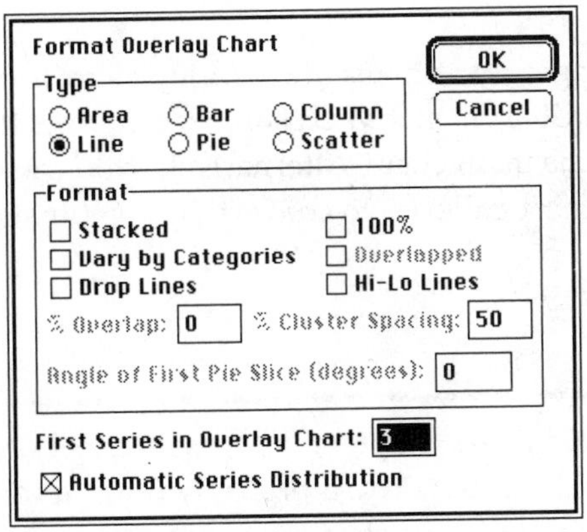

```
┌─────────────────────────────────────────────┐
│ Format Overlay Chart          ┌──────────┐   │
│ ┌Type──────────────────────┐  │   OK     │   │
│ │ ○ Area   ○ Bar   ○ Column │  └──────────┘   │
│ │ ● Line   ○ Pie   ○ Scatter│  ┌──────────┐   │
│ └───────────────────────────┘  │  Cancel  │   │
│ ┌Format────────────────────────────────────┐ │
│ │ ☐ Stacked          ☐ 100%                │ │
│ │ ☐ Vary by Categories  ☐ Overlapped       │ │
│ │ ☐ Drop Lines       ☐ Hi-Lo Lines         │ │
│ │ % Overlap: [0]   % Cluster Spacing: [50] │ │
│ │ Angle of First Pie Slice (degrees): [0]  │ │
│ └───────────────────────────────────────────┘ │
│ First Series in Overlay Chart: [3]            │
│ ☒ Automatic Series Distribution               │
└─────────────────────────────────────────────┘
```

FIGURE 12-27. *This dialog box appears when you choose Overlay... from the Format menu.*

Creating your own combination charts

You can also create your own combination charts from an existing chart by choosing Add Overlay from the Chart menu. When you choose this command, Microsoft Excel divides the data series in the chart evenly between the main chart and the overlay chart. For example, if your chart has four data series, the first two appear in the main chart and the second two appear in the overlay chart.

After you have created the combination chart, you can change the type of either the main chart or the overlay chart. To change the type of the overlay chart, select one of the data series in the overlay chart, then choose Overlay from the Format menu. In the dialog box, select the type of chart you want to use, then click OK or press Enter. Microsoft Excel displays all the data series in the overlay chart in the format you specify. Similarly, to change the type of chart used for the main chart, select a data series in the main chart, then choose Main Chart... from the Format menu. In the Format Main Chart dialog box, select the chart type, and click OK or press Enter.

After you create a combination chart and select your chart types, you probably need to use the Main Chart... and Overlay... commands to format the result. If you want to use independent axes for the main and overlay charts, choose the Axes command from the Chart menu and select the appropriate options from the Overlay portion of the dialog box. To format the overlay-chart axes, select the axis you want to work with, then choose the Scale... command from the Format menu. At this point, you can use the techniques we described in Chapter 10, "Basic Charting Techniques," to format the selected axis.

Deleting overlay charts

If you decide you no longer want to use the overlay chart format, simply choose Delete Overlay from the Chart menu. Microsoft Excel merges the data series in the overlay chart back into the main chart. Alternatively, you can choose a new chart format from one of the chart galleries to convert the combination chart to another chart type.

Conclusion

As you've seen in the last three chapters, Microsoft Excel offers an impressive variety of chart styles and formats. You'll probably find that the many formats in the chart galleries meet most of your charting needs. However, when you need to create that special chart, with its own unique formats, it's nice to know that you have the power to control virtually every aspect of the chart's appearance.

In the next chapter, we first show you how to use the SERIES function to gain even more control over your chart's appearance and content. Then, we briefly discuss how to print your finished charts on the Apple ImageWriter and Laser-Writer printers.

13

Other Chart Topics

*I*n the first three chapters of this section, we showed you how to create and format charts in Microsoft Excel. In this chapter, we take a look behind the scenes to see how Excel plots your worksheet data. We also show you how to use the Edit-menu commands with charts, and how to print the charts you create.

The SERIES function

As you have worked through the examples in the last three chapters, you may have noticed the long formula that appeared in the formula bar whenever you selected a marker on your chart. This formula is a SERIES function, which tells Microsoft Excel how to interpret your worksheet data. The SERIES function takes the form

=SERIES(*"series name",categories reference,values reference,plot order number*)

The *series name* argument is the name of the data series being charted. The *categories reference* argument indicates where your category labels are located in the worksheet. The *values reference* argument indicates where the data-point values are located in the worksheet. The *plot order number* argument determines the order in which your data series appear on the chart.

Whenever you create a chart in Microsoft Excel, one SERIES formula is created for each data series in that chart. Let's use the chart in Figure 13-1 to illustrate the mechanics of the SERIES function. This chart was drawn from cells A3:D7 of the worksheet in Figure 13-2. As you can see in the formula bar, the SERIES function for the first data series in Figure 13-1 is

=SERIES(Worksheet1!$B$3,Worksheet1!$A$4:$A$7,Worksheet1!$B$4:$B$7,1)

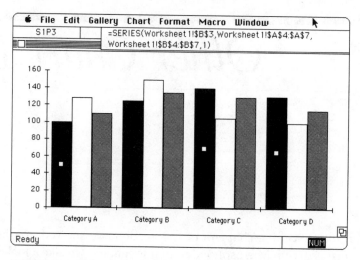

FIGURE 13-1. *This sample chart shows the SERIES function in the formula bar.*

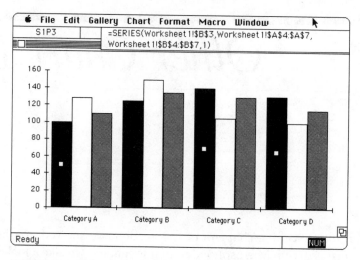

FIGURE 13-2. *The sample chart in Figure 13-1 was plotted from this worksheet.*

The *series name* argument in this formula is *Worksheet1*. Although Microsoft Excel draws the series name from the worksheet, the *series name* argument also can appear as a text string, enclosed in quotation marks, when the worksheet has been saved and named.

The *categories reference* and *values reference* arguments are *Worksheet1!$A$4:$A$7* and *Worksheet1!$B$4:$B$7*. These arguments tell Excel where to look in the worksheet named *Worksheet1* for the category labels and data-point values. You may remember from our discussion of linked worksheets in Chapter 8, "Other Worksheet Topics," that Excel always uses the worksheet name, followed by an exclamation point, to indicate a reference to an external worksheet. We call this name an *external reference*. Also, notice that Excel automatically uses absolute cell references in its external references.

The *plot order number* argument tells Excel the order in which it should plot the data series in the chart. The plot order number in the example SERIES function, 1, tells Excel to plot this data series before any of the others in this chart. As you will soon see, you can change the order in which your data series are plotted simply by changing the *plot order number* argument at the end of the formula.

The *series name* and *categories reference* arguments won't always appear in the SERIES function. Excel uses these arguments only if you select cells in your worksheet that contain category and series labels. For example, if you select cells B4:B7 in Figure 13-2, Excel creates a single-series chart like the one in Figure 13-3.

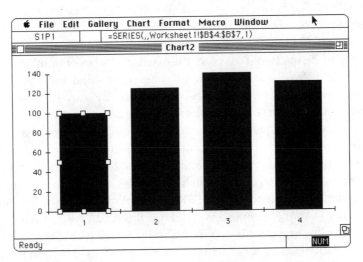

FIGURE 13-3. *This column chart contains only one data series with no series name or category labels.*

The SERIES function for this single-series chart is

=SERIES(,,Worksheet 1!$B$4:$B$7,1)

The first two arguments—*series name* and *categories reference*—are missing from this formula. Notice that Excel automatically assigns the plot order number 1 to this data series, even though no other data series exist at this point. If you were to paste another data series into this chart, Excel would automatically assign that data series the plot order number 2.

Editing the SERIES function

In general, the SERIES function works very much like the worksheet functions you learned about in Chapter 6, "Built-in Functions." If you want to edit a SERIES function, you must first select the series by clicking any of its markers to make the function appear in the formula bar, as shown in Figure 13-1. Then, you can edit the SERIES function to change the contents of the chart window, using the same techniques you would use to edit a worksheet function.

Changing the plot order

As we've said, you can change the order in which data series are charted simply by changing the *plot order number* argument at the end of the formula. When you do this, Excel automatically adjusts the plot order number of the other data series in the chart. For example, the chart shown in Figure 13-1 contains three data series. Suppose you want the first data series to be plotted last. First, select that data series by clicking one of its markers. Then, drag across the number *1* at the end of the SERIES function. To replace the existing plot order number, type *3* and click the enter box. Excel moves the first data series behind the other two. Series 2 then becomes series 1, and series 3 becomes series 2. Figure 13-4 shows the result of this move. As you can see, Excel plots the three data series in the order you request.

As you know, when you use the Combination… command from the Gallery menu or the Add Overlay command from the Chart menu, Excel automatically distributes your data series evenly between the main chart and the overlay chart. However, you can control which data series appears in which chart by changing the plot order numbers of the SERIES functions that make up your chart.

For example, suppose you choose the Add Overlay command to create an overlay line graph for the column chart you created in Figure 13-1. Excel automatically includes data series 3 in the overlay chart, as shown in Figure 13-5.

Suppose you want only the first data series to appear in the overlay chart, instead of the third series. You might try to achieve this effect by choosing the Add Overlay command from the Chart menu, then choosing the Overlay… command from the Format menu and entering *1* in the First Series In Overlay Chart field. If you do this, however, all three data series appear as lines in the overlay chart and the main chart is empty. To get around this problem, you need to change the series number of the first data series. First, select the data series you want to include in the overlay chart—in this case, series 1. Change its plot order number to 3, as we just described, and then click the enter box. Excel automatically changes the data series 2 to 1, 3 to 2, and so on, for you. The resulting chart looks like Figure 13-6 on the next page.

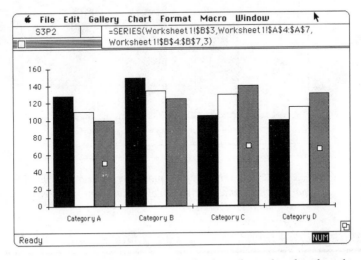

FIGURE 13-4. *The plot order number has been changed to alter the order in which data series are presented.*

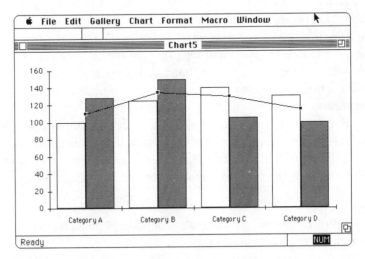

FIGURE 13-5. *Two of the series have been plotted in the main chart and one in the overlay chart.*

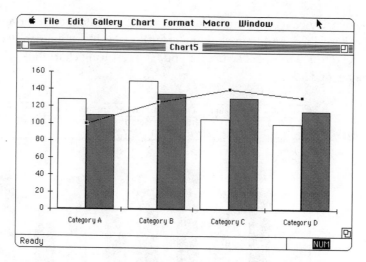

FIGURE 13-6. *By changing the plot order number in a SERIES function,*
you can change the distribution of the data series between the main
chart and the overlay chart.

Adding series names and category labels

If your worksheet does not include suitable series names or category labels, you
can enter your own labels in the SERIES function. For example, suppose you want
to add a series name to the chart in Figure 13-3. Click in front of the first comma in
the series formula and type *"New Series 1"*, then press Enter. If you compare the
SERIES function for the data series in Figure 13-3 to the function for the same data
series in Figure 13-7, you will see that they are identical, except for the addition of
the series name. Also, notice that Excel used the series name you provided to
create a title for the chart in Figure 13-7. In a multiseries chart, Excel also includes
the series name in the chart legend.

Suppose you want to change the rather cryptic default category labels—1, 2, 3,
and 4—in the chart in Figure 13-7. To add more meaningful category labels, you
can edit the SERIES function to include a *categories reference* argument that refers to
the location of labels in your worksheet. For example, to edit the SERIES function

=SERIES("New Series 1",,Worksheet1!$B$4:$B$7,1)

in Figure 13-7, you can place an insertion point between the first and second
commas in the formula and type

Worksheet1!$A$4:$A$7

If your worksheet does not contain appropriate category labels, you can use a text-
string array to create your own labels, by placing the insertion point between the
first and second commas and typing, for example,

{"First Quarter","Second Quarter","Third Quarter","Fourth Quarter"}

You must enclose the entire array in braces, enclose each text string in double quotation marks, and use a comma to separate each text string from the next. The results of these two techniques are identical (if you use the same category names in the array as those in the worksheet, of course). Your chart looks like Figure 13-8, which shows the sample chart after the quarter labels have been added.

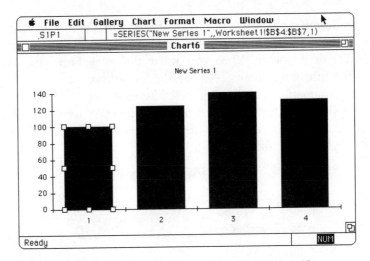

FIGURE 13-7. *The SERIES function has been edited to provide a series name.*

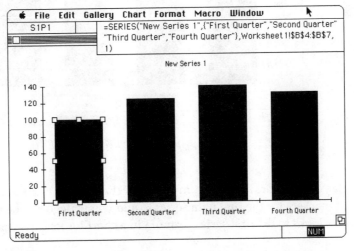

FIGURE 13-8. *The SERIES function has been edited to provide category labels.*

Pasting references into the SERIES function

Another way to add category labels to your chart is to paste the cell references into the SERIES function. For example, to create the single-series chart in Figure 13-3, you selected cells B4:B7. To add the labels in cells A4:A7 as category labels to the chart, begin by selecting a column in the data series. Excel displays the formula

=SERIES(,,Worksheet1!$B$4:$B$7,1)

in the formula bar. Click the space after the first comma in the SERIES function. Now, move back to the worksheet window by choosing the worksheet name from the Windows menu. When you are in the worksheet, you will notice that the SERIES function remains active in the formula bar. Select cells A4:A7. Microsoft Excel automatically pastes the cell references in the formula bar and uses the selected cells as its *categories reference* argument. When you press Enter, Excel converts the labels in cells A4:A7 into category labels, as shown in Figure 13-9. The SERIES function now reads

=SERIES(,Worksheet1!$A$4:$A$7,Worksheet1!$B$4:$B$7,1)

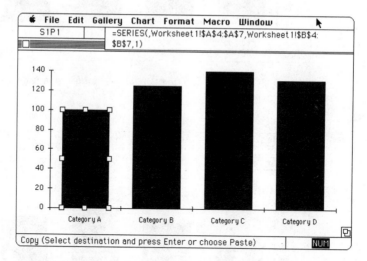

FIGURE 13-9. *You can paste cell references into the SERIES function to create category labels.*

If you are working with a multiseries chart, you must select one of the data-point markers for the first data series to add your category labels. Microsoft Excel always looks to the first series formula in a chart for its category labels.

Using the SERIES function with discontinuous data

Suppose you want to plot the values in cells D4:D7 of Figure 13-2 quickly, using the labels in cells A4:A7 as category labels. If you select cells A4:A7, press the Command key, select D4:D7, then choose New…, Excel displays a chart like the one you see in Figure 13-10.

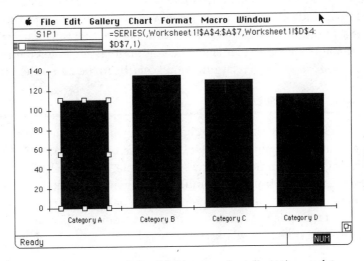

FIGURE 13-10. *Microsoft Excel 2.2 lets you chart discontinuous data.*

Building a SERIES function from scratch

The easiest way to add a data series to your chart is to copy the cells you want to plot into a chart window. However, you can also build a data series from scratch. For example, you could have created the data series in the chart in Figure 13-9 by typing its SERIES function into an empty chart window.

To open an empty chart window, select a blank cell in your worksheet. (If you select a cell or range that contains data, Excel attempts to plot that data when you open the new chart file.) Then, choose New… from the File menu and select the Chart option. Excel displays the blank chart window. In the formula bar, type

=SERIES(,Worksheet1!A4:A7,Worksheet1!D4:D7,1)

The resulting chart looks exactly like the one in Figure 13-10. If you like, you can type a series name in front of the first comma, to use in your chart title or legend.

You can also create a SERIES formula that is not dependent upon a worksheet. For example, to create the chart shown in Figure 13-10, you could type this SERIES formula in a new chart document:

=SERIES(,{"Category A","Category B","Category C","Category D"},{110,135,130,115},1)

The *values reference* argument is actually the only required argument in this function. The *series name* and *categories reference* arguments are optional. If you decide not to include these arguments, however, you must enter the commas that separate the arguments from the rest of the formula. The *plot order number* argument is also optional. As long as you enter the comma that separates the plot order number from the *values reference* argument, Excel fills in the plot order number for you.

Deleting data series

To delete a data series from a chart, start by bringing the SERIES function for that series into the formula bar by clicking one of the markers in the series. Without clicking the formula bar, press the Delete key. Excel immediately erases the SERIES function from the formula bar. When you click the enter box, the SERIES function is deleted, and Excel removes the data series from the chart.

If you decide not to remove the series from the chart after all, click the cancel box instead of the enter box.

Copying information between chart files

Microsoft Excel allows you to copy the contents or format of one chart file into another chart file. Copying chart information is much like copying information between cells.

For example, suppose you want to copy the chart in one chart window into another chart window. Begin by choosing the Select Chart command from the Chart menu, and then choose Copy from the Edit menu. When you choose this command, Excel places a marquee around the chart area, just as it does when you are copying worksheet cells. Now, activate the chart window into which you want to paste the information, or use the New... command to create a new chart window, then choose Paste Special... from the Edit menu. Excel displays the Paste Special dialog box shown in Figure 13-11.

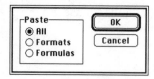

FIGURE 13-11. *This is the Paste Special dialog box.*

If you select All, Excel duplicates the contents and formats of the copied chart in the new chart window. If the chart window into which you are pasting already contains data, Excel adds the copied data series to any existing data series. The chart into which you're copying maintains its formatting. If the chart window is empty, Excel simply creates a replica of the existing chart.

If you select Formats from the Paste Special dialog box, Excel applies any special formats you have assigned to the copied chart to the new chart. This can be a convenient method of assigning consistent formats to a series of charts if you do not want to change the Preferred format. (We discussed this format in Chapter 12, "Other Types of Charts.")

Finally, if you select Formulas, Excel adds the SERIES function(s) from the copied chart to the selected chart window. If you are pasting information into a new chart window, the data series you have copied appears in the current Preferred format. If you have used Excel's chart commands to change the destination chart's type or format, Excel displays the copied data series in the assigned format for that chart.

Copying SERIES functions

You can also copy an individual SERIES function from one chart to another. For example, suppose you want to copy the data series in Figure 13-9 into another chart window. Further suppose that you created this data series from scratch, and you don't want to retype the long formula. Instead, you can simply click one of the markers for the data series you want to copy, drag through the entire formula in the formula bar, and choose Copy from the Edit menu. Then, click the enter box to leave the formula bar, and click in another chart window or choose the New... command to create a new chart window. Now, click an empty area of the second chart window to ensure that no data points are selected, and click the formula bar to activate it. Once the formula bar is active, choose Paste from the Edit menu, and click the enter box. Microsoft Excel immediately displays the copied data series in the chart window.

Of course, you can copy any part of a SERIES function. Suppose you have created a set of special category labels, like the ones in Figure 13-8. If you want to use these labels in another chart, simply click one of the markers for the data series, and drag through the *categories reference* argument. For this example, select

{"First Quarter","Second Quarter","Third Quarter","Fourth Quarter"}

Then, choose the Copy command and click the enter box to leave the formula bar. Now, move to the chart window into which you want to paste the category labels. If this window contains more than one series, click one of the markers for the first series to put its SERIES function into the formula bar. (Excel always applies the category labels for the first data series to the entire chart.) Place the insertion point between the first and second commas, choose Paste from the Edit menu, and click the enter box. Excel displays the pasted labels below the category axis.

To copy the *categories reference* argument into a SERIES function you are creating from scratch, click the formula bar and type

=SERIES(,

and choose Paste from the Edit menu. After Excel pastes the category labels into your SERIES formula, type another comma, then enter the *values reference* argument, a third comma, and the *plot order number* argument. Finally, type the closing parenthesis and click the enter box or press Enter.

The Clear... command

You can use the Clear... command on the Edit menu to erase the contents of a chart window, the formats assigned to that window, or both. To delete all of the data series in your chart without affecting the chart's format settings, begin by choosing the Chart menu's Select Chart command, then choose Clear... from the Edit menu. Microsoft Excel displays the dialog box shown in Figure 13-12.

If you select All from this dialog box, Excel erases all of your series formulas as well as any special formats you have assigned to the chart. The chart window is then completely empty; even the chart axes have disappeared. Any new data series you create for this window appear in the Preferred format.

As you might expect, if you select Formulas from the Clear dialog box, Excel erases all of the data series from the chart, but not the formats you have assigned to the chart window.

Finally, if you select Formats from the Clear dialog box, Excel leaves your series formulas unchanged, but changes the chart formats back to the Preferred format. If you have selected part of the formula in the formula bar, the Clear... command clears only the selected part.

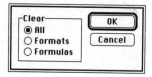

FIGURE 13-12. *This is the Clear dialog box.*

The Calculation... command

If you are working with a complex chart or if you have several charts on the Microsoft Excel desktop at once, you may notice that worksheet calculation time increases considerably. This is because Excel must redraw each of the visible charts every time it recalculates your worksheet.

If you do not want to wait for Excel to redraw your charts every time you change an entry, you can save time by choosing Calculation... from the Options menu in the worksheet window and selecting Manual from the Calculation dialog box. This setting instructs Excel not to recalculate your worksheet—or the linked chart file—until you choose Calculate Now from the Options menu. (Excel also includes a Calculate Now command on the Chart menu, so you don't have to switch back to the worksheet window each time you want Excel to update your chart.)

Building charts from two or more worksheets

There might be occasions when you want to combine data from two or more separate worksheet files to create a single chart. For example, the worksheet in Figure 13-13 contains 1988 summary budget statistics. The worksheet in Figure 13-14 on the next page contains a similar set of data for 1989.

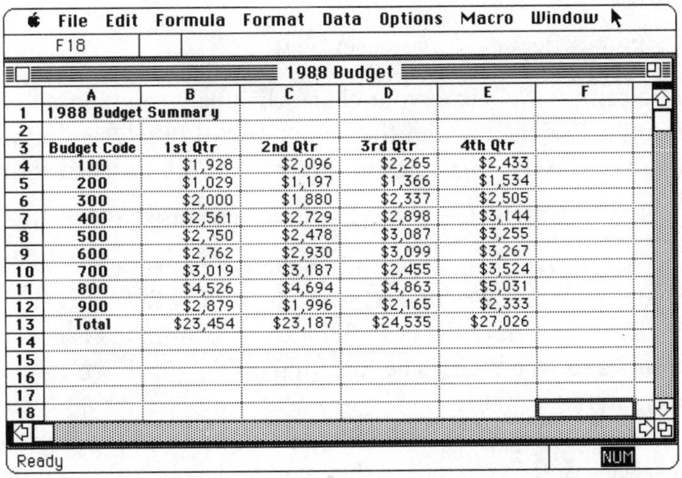

ú File Edit Formula Format Data Options Macro Window ▶						
F18						

1988 Budget

	A	B	C	D	E	F
1	1988 Budget Summary					
2						
3	Budget Code	1st Qtr	2nd Qtr	3rd Qtr	4th Qtr	
4	100	$1,928	$2,096	$2,265	$2,433	
5	200	$1,029	$1,197	$1,366	$1,534	
6	300	$2,000	$1,880	$2,337	$2,505	
7	400	$2,561	$2,729	$2,898	$3,144	
8	500	$2,750	$2,478	$3,087	$3,255	
9	600	$2,762	$2,930	$3,099	$3,267	
10	700	$3,019	$3,187	$2,455	$3,524	
11	800	$4,526	$4,694	$4,863	$5,031	
12	900	$2,879	$1,996	$2,165	$2,333	
13	Total	$23,454	$23,187	$24,535	$27,026	
14						
15						
16						
17						
18						

Ready   NUM

FIGURE 13-13. *This worksheet contains the 1988 Budget Summary worksheet.*

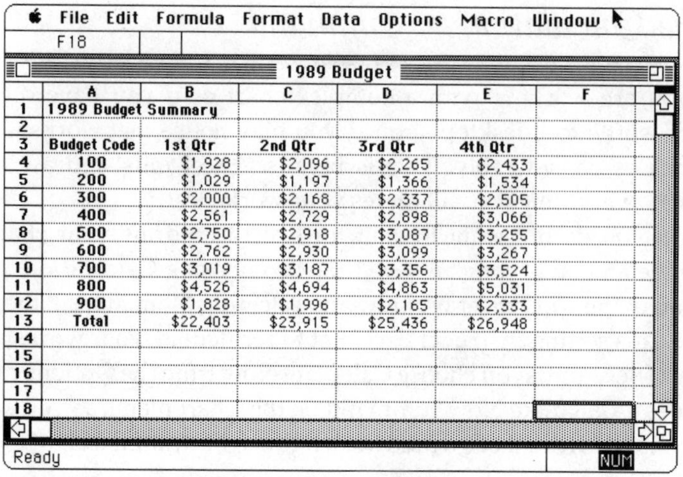

FIGURE 13-14. *This worksheet contains the 1989 Budget Summary worksheet.*

Suppose you want to compare the 1988 and 1989 budget totals in a single chart. Begin by opening both worksheet files, then select cells B13:E13 in the 1988 Budget worksheet. Next, use the New... command to plot this data in a chart window. Microsoft Excel creates a single-series chart. The SERIES function for this data series is

=SERIES(,,'1988 Budget'!$B$13:$E$13,1)

To add category labels to your chart, click between the first and second commas in the SERIES function and then move back to the 1988 Budget worksheet. Drag through cells B3:E3, then click the enter box. Your finished formula is

=SERIES(,'1988 Budget'!$B$3:$E$3,'1988 Budget'!$B$13:$E$13,1)

Excel uses the labels in cells B3:E3 as category labels.

Now, select the 1989 Budget worksheet, drag through cells B13:E13, and choose Copy. Then, return to the chart window and use the Paste command to add this data series to your chart. The resulting chart, which we've named Budget Chart, appears in Figure 13-15.

Even though you did not include a set of category cells in your second data series, Microsoft Excel applies the category labels from your first data series to all subsequent data series. As long as the second data series contains the same number of cells as the first, both sets of data points are evenly distributed along the category axis.

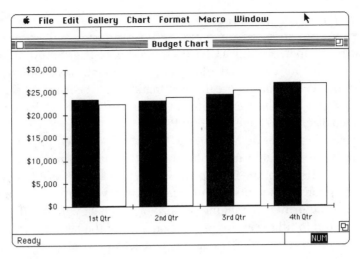

FIGURE 13-15. *This two-series column chart draws data from two worksheets.*

Protecting charts

If you've created a chart and don't want anyone else who views it to be able to change the chart's data series or formats, you can use the Protect Document... command on the Chart menu to lock the chart. Figure 13-16 shows the Protect Document dialog box. This command works the same way as the Protect Document... command on the worksheet Options menu, explained in Chapter 8, "Other Worksheet Topics." Also, as we discussed in Chapter 1, "Introducing Microsoft Excel," you can use the Password option in the Options section of the Save As dialog box to prevent others from opening the chart file without the correct password.

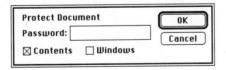

FIGURE 13-16. *This is the Protect Document dialog box.*

Printing charts

You should already be familiar with the basic techniques for printing Microsoft Excel documents, discussed in Chapter 9, "Printing." For the most part, printing charts is the same as printing worksheets. There are a just a few minor differences you need to know about when you print your charts. In this section, we explain those differences.

The Page Setup... command

The first step in printing a Chart is to choose the Page Setup... command from the
File menu. This command allows you to define the layout of the page you will be
printing. When you choose this command, you'll see that Excel presents three size
options for the chart environment at the bottom of the Page Setup dialog box:
Screen Size, Fit To Page, and Full Page.

Fit To Page, the default setting, tells Microsoft Excel to print the screen as large
as possible without losing the height:width ratio shown on the screen. If you select
the Screen Size option, Excel prints your chart exactly as it is shown on the screen.
This option gives you some manual flexibility, because you can resize the chart
before you print by changing the size of the chart window. The Full Page option
tells Excel to fill the entire page, regardless of the height:width ratio of the chart.
When you use the Full Page option, you get a very tall chart, compared to the way
it looks on the screen.

The Print... command

When you choose the Print... command in the Microsoft Excel chart environment,
you see a dialog box like the one you see when you choose the Print... command in
the worksheet environment. The only difference between them is that in the chart
environment, the Print dialog box doesn't contain options for printing the worksheet and notes.

Of course, the Pages option does not apply when you're in the chart environment, because all your charts are one page long. However, you can use the Copies
field to indicate the number of charts you want to print.

If you want to see what your chart will look like before you print it, select the
Page Preview option from the Print dialog box. As in the worksheet environment,
Excel displays the chart as it appears on the printed page. Your pointer is shaped
like a magnifying glass so that you can select parts of the chart to get a full-scale
view of the finished product.

Conclusion

Over the course of the last four chapters, we've covered the chart environment of
Microsoft Excel in detail. In the next section, we move on to a third component
of the Microsoft Excel program: the database.

SECTION FOUR

DATABASES

Excel Database Management

*S*o far, you have seen how you can use Microsoft Excel as an electronic worksheet and as a graphics program. As you probably know, Excel is also a database
manager. In this chapter, we show you how to use Excel to manage simple
databases. We begin by discussing the structure of a database. Then, we show you
how to create, define, and format a database. Next, we show you how to add,
delete, and move records and fields, then we look at calculated fields. We end the
chapter with a discussion of data forms—special dialog boxes through which you
can enter and edit database records.

What is a database?

A database is a structured collection of information. By structured, we mean
arranged in some convenient, logical, consistent order. Because the information in
a database is structured, it is easy to locate and retrieve individual pieces of
information quickly.

The information in a database can be anything from telephone numbers and names to part numbers and prices. You probably use simple databases every day, perhaps without even realizing that they are databases. For example, a dictionary is a database of words and their definitions. Another commonly used database is the telephone book.

A telephone book contains thousands of listings, each of which generally includes four pieces of information: a last name, a first name, a street address, and a telephone number. If you think about it for a moment, you'll see that the information in a telephone book is arranged in a rough tabular form. Each listing occupies one line, or row, in the book, and each piece of information (last name, first name, and so on) occupies a single "column." Microsoft Excel databases use this same row-and-column structure. In database terminology, each of the listings in the telephone book is called a *record*. The individual pieces of information within a listing are called *fields*.

The usefulness of a database depends on how well organized its information is and on how easily the information can be reorganized, if necessary. For example, the alphabetical order of the listings in a telephone book is the key to its usefulness. Because the listings are arranged in alphabetical order based on the last-name entry of each listing, you can easily find the name (and the phone number) of any person you want to call.

However, the usefulness of a telephone book is limited. Because a telephone book is printed, the order of the information in it is fixed. In addition, it is nearly impossible to locate all the listings for people who live on a certain street (like Main Street) or who have the same first name. Furthermore, computing statistics for groups of the listings in a telephone book (such as the number of people named *Williams*) must be done manually and is very difficult.

Unlike the printed telephone book, Microsoft Excel stores information electronically. For this reason, the data in an Excel database is dynamic and can be easily manipulated. For example, if you enter the listings (records) from a telephone book into an Excel database, you can sort the records in that database into ascending or descending order based on any of the pieces of information (fields) in the listings. You can also locate, extract, or delete any information in the database that shares a common characteristic—for example, all the records for people who live on Elm Street, or all the records for people named *Jones*.

As you might expect, Excel can do more than just sort a database and locate information in that database. It can also print hard-copy reports of the information in your database. It can even perform statistical calculations on the fields of those records that meet certain criteria.

The structure of a database

Figure 14-1 shows a sample Excel database that contains ten records, each of which has six fields. The most important thing to notice about Figure 14-1 is that this database is really nothing more than a rectangular range of worksheet cells. Within this range, each row contains a single record, and each column is a separate field. For example, row 2 contains the record for T. S. Monk, and column D contains the Date of Birth field.

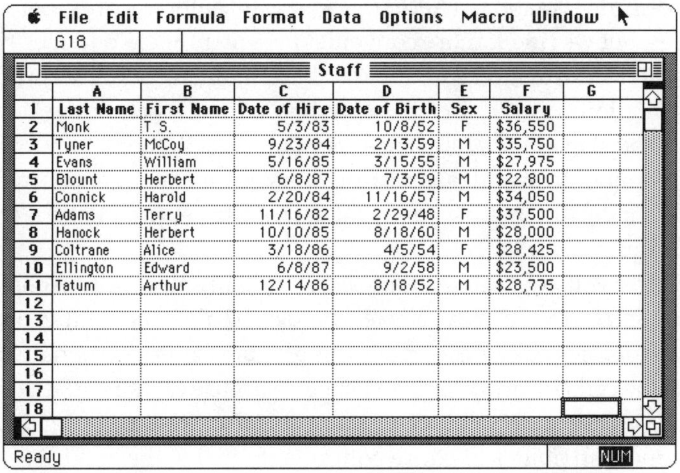

	A	B	C	D	E	F	G
1	Last Name	First Name	Date of Hire	Date of Birth	Sex	Salary	
2	Monk	T. S.	5/3/83	10/8/52	F	$36,550	
3	Tyner	McCoy	9/23/84	2/13/59	M	$35,750	
4	Evans	William	5/16/85	3/15/55	M	$27,975	
5	Blount	Herbert	6/8/87	7/3/59	M	$22,800	
6	Connick	Harold	2/20/84	11/16/57	M	$34,050	
7	Adams	Terry	11/16/82	2/29/48	F	$37,500	
8	Hanock	Herbert	10/10/85	8/18/60	M	$28,000	
9	Coltrane	Alice	3/18/86	4/5/54	F	$28,425	
10	Ellington	Edward	6/8/87	9/2/58	M	$23,500	
11	Tatum	Arthur	12/14/86	8/18/52	M	$28,775	
12							
13							
14							
15							
16							
17							
18							

FIGURE 14-1. *A database is simply a specially organized group of worksheet cells.*

Notice that the top row of this database contains field names. These names, which must always be entered in the top row of the database, identify the information stored in each field. For example, the entries in the First Name field are all first names, the entries in the Sex field are abbreviations for male or female, and so forth. You see later that these field names are the key to the use of selection criteria.

Creating a database

Creating a Microsoft Excel database is as easy as creating a worksheet. For example, suppose you want to create the database shown in Figure 14-1. To do this, begin by entering the field names *Last Name, First Name, Date of Hire, Date of Birth, Sex,* and *Salary* into any six adjacent cells on a single row of a worksheet. These field names are simple text entries. They can go in any row as long as it's the top row of the database. For this example we've entered them in row 1.

You'll usually want to keep the field names in your databases fairly short so that they are easy to remember and use. However, like all text entries in Excel, they can be up to 255 characters long and can contain any character (including spaces) that you can type from the Macintosh keyboard. Although field names are usually simple labels, they can also be the results of text-producing functions. You should not use numbers (unless you enclose them in quotation marks) or value-producing formulas or functions as field names. If you do, Excel's database commands (Find, Extract..., Delete, and so on) do not work properly.

After you have specified the field names for a database, you are ready to begin entering information. (Actually, you can enter records before you enter field names, but we find it more convenient to enter the field names first.) Although you can enter information into the database in any order, you probably want to start with the leftmost field of the row immediately below the field names. You can make the same kinds of entries in a database that you can make in a worksheet: text, numbers, formulas, and functions. To make an entry in a database, simply select the cell into which you want to make the entry and type the entry just as you would in the worksheet.

After you've created a database, you'll usually want to change the format and alignment of the cells in selected fields and alter the widths of certain fields. You can format and align the entries in a database in the same way you format and align the cells in any other worksheet. Because all the entries in each field of most databases are of a similar type, you typically want to assign the same formats and alignment attributes to entire columns (fields) of the database. For example, in the sample database, we applied the m/d/yy format to all the date entries in the Date of Hire and Date of Birth fields and the $#,##0 ;($#,##0) format to the Salary fields.

Defining the database

Although you may recognize the worksheet in Figure 14-1 as a database, Microsoft Excel does not know that it is a database until you use the Set Database command from the Data menu to tell it so. To define a block of cells as a database, you first select the entire rectangle that contains the database (including the field names). In this case, you select the range A1:F11. Once this range is selected, you need only choose the Set Database command to define the range as a database.

Surprisingly, the Set Database command does nothing more than assign the range name *Database* to the selected block of cells. You can do the same thing by selecting the block of cells, choosing the Define Name... command from the Formula menu, typing the name *Database*, and pressing Return. However, you'll find the Set Database method much faster and easier in almost every case.

When you choose a database command, Excel looks for the name *Database* in order to know which area of the worksheet to work with. For this reason, each worksheet can have only one database. (You can have any number of databases set up in a worksheet, but only the one you're currently working with can be actively defined with the name *Database*.) To switch between databases, you must redefine the database range.

Changing records and fields

After you create a database, you might find that you need to add, delete, or move one or more of its records or fields. Because records are worksheet rows and fields are worksheet columns, the process of adding, deleting, and moving records and fields is the same process as that of adding and deleting rows and columns of the worksheet.

Adding records and fields

To add a record to the end of a database, enter each field of the new record in the first blank row below the final record. Then, select the entire range that contains the database and choose Set Database from the Data menu to expand the database range to include this new record. Whenever you add one or more new records to the end of a database, you must use the Set Database or Define Name... command to redefine the range so that it includes the new records. If you omit this step, Excel does not include the new record in the database.

To avoid this problem, you can add new records in the middle of the database rather than at the end. To add a record in the middle of a database, click the heading of the row where you want to add the record, then choose the Insert... command from the Edit menu. When you choose this command, Excel adds a blank row to the database above the selected row and pushes the existing rows down one row. Because the database range is a named range, Excel expands the range automatically when you add a new record in the middle of the database.

Alternatively, if you want to keep your database records in the order in which you entered them, you can include an extra blank row at the bottom of the database so that you can select that row whenever you want to add a new record. For example, if your database records currently occupy cells A1 through G50, you can define the database range as A1:G51. Then, whenever you want to add a new record, you can select the last row of the database, which is blank, and use the Insert... command. As in the example above, Excel adds a blank row to the database above the selected row and pushes the existing "dummy record" down one row.

You can also add new fields to existing Excel databases. To add a new field at the right edge of a database, select the cell in the field-names row (the first row of the database range) immediately to the right of the last existing field name, and type the new field name. Then, make entries in the new field for the existing records in the database. Because the new field is outside the original database range, you use the Set Database or Define Name... command to include the new field in the database range.

Of course, you can also add a new field within an existing database range. To do this, click the heading of the column where you want to add the new field. Once this column is selected, choose the Insert... command. When you do this, Excel inserts a blank column into the worksheet to the left of the selected column and pushes the existing columns one column to the right. The new field, then, is automatically included in the existing database range.

Deleting records and fields

Because the records and fields of a database are rows and columns of a worksheet, you can delete records and fields from a database in the same way you delete rows and columns from a worksheet. To delete a record, select the row that contains the record by clicking its heading. When you choose the Delete... command from the Edit menu, Excel removes that record from the database. Additionally, Excel shifts all rows below the removed record up one row to fill in the "empty" space and contracts the database range to reflect the deletion.

Deleting a field is just as simple. To delete a field from a database, select the column that contains the field by clicking its heading, then choose the Delete... command. Excel removes that column from the database and automatically contracts the database range to reflect the deletion of a field, whether the field is at the end or in the middle of a database range.

Reordering records and fields

You can reorder records and fields within an Excel database by moving the rows and columns of the worksheet. To move a field to a new location within the database range, first insert a new column at the destination of the move. Then, click the heading of the column you want to move, choose the Cut command from the Edit menu, click the heading of the newly inserted column, and choose Paste. To move a record within the database range, insert a new row at the destination of the move, click the heading of the row that you want to move, and choose Cut. Then, click the heading of the newly inserted row and choose Paste. Excel automatically adjusts the database range to reflect the movement of records and fields.

Calculated fields

Most of the entries you make into the fields of an Excel database are text, numbers, and dates. However, you can also make formula and function entries. Fields whose entries are the result of formulas or functions are called *calculated fields*.

The database shown in Figure 14-2 contains an example of a calculated field. This database is identical to the one in Figure 14-1, except for the addition of the Age field. To add this field to the database, you enter the text *Age* into cell G1 and expand the database range by selecting cells A1:G11 and choosing Set Database from the Data menu. Next, enter the formula

=YEAR(NOW())–YEAR(D2)–IF(MONTH(NOW())<MONTH(D2),1,
    IF(MONTH(NOW())=MONTH(D2),IF(DAY(NOW())<=DAY(D2),1)))

into cell G2. This formula tells Microsoft Excel to subtract the year in cell D2 (the Date of Birth entry for the first record) from the current year (the result of the NOW function), subtracting 1 from the result if the current month and day are not exactly the same as those in D2. To calculate the Age field for the remaining records, use the Copy and Paste commands or the Fill Down command to copy this formula to the range G3:G11.

	File Edit Formula Format Data Options Macro Window						
	G2		=YEAR(NOW())-YEAR(D2)-IF(MONTH(NOW())<MONTH(D2), 1,IF(MONTH(NOW())=MONTH(D2),IF(DAY(NOW())<=DAY(D2) ,1)))					

	A						
	Last Name	**First Name**	**Date of Hire**	**Date of Birth**	**Sex**	**Salary**	**Age**
1	Last Name	First Name	Date of Hire	Date of Birth	Sex	Salary	Age
2	Monk	T.S.	5/3/83	10/8/52	F	$36,550	36
3	Tyner	McCoy	9/23/84	2/13/59	M	$35,750	30
4	Evans	William	5/16/85	3/15/55	M	$27,975	34
5	Blount	Herbert	6/8/87	7/3/59	M	$22,800	29
6	Connick	Harold	2/20/84	11/16/57	M	$34,050	31
7	Adams	Terry	11/16/82	2/29/48	F	$37,500	41
8	Hanock	Herbert	10/10/85	8/18/60	M	$28,000	28
9	Coltrane	Alice	3/18/86	4/5/54	F	$28,425	35
10	Ellington	Edward	6/8/87	9/2/58	M	$23,500	30
11	Tatum	Arthur	12/14/86	8/18/52	M	$28,775	36
12							

FIGURE 14-2. *You have added the calculated field Age to the employee database.*

As you can see, the entries in calculated fields result from individual formulas in the cells of that field. (Because the Age values derive from the NOW function, your Age values may be different from those in Figure 14-2. Also, because the NOW function returns the date from your system's clock, your Age value will change with time. Don't be surprised if, for the rest of this chapter and the examples in Chapter 15, your Age values and those in the figures do not match.)

Whenever you add a new record to a database, you can copy and paste the formula into the new record so that Excel can calculate a value for it. If you're entering a group of records, you can save time by entering all the records first, selecting the cells where the calculated field is to appear, then using the Copy and Paste commands or Fill Down to enter the formula into the calculated field of every new record in one step.

Data forms

As you've learned, a database is a listing of information in the cells of an Excel worksheet. In many cases, you'll find it convenient to view a database as a list of records. However, Excel also allows you to view the contents of a database through a simple one-page form. Using data forms, you can add records to a database, delete records from a database, and edit existing records. You can even specify criteria in the data-form window and use those criteria to help you locate database records. (We talk more about that in Chapter 15, "Working with a Database.")

The primary advantage of data forms is that they allow you to view all the fields of a record at once. When you view a database in a worksheet window, only a few fields are visible at a time and you see several records at once on the screen. (The number of fields that are visible depends upon the width of the columns and the size of your screen.) Data forms let you view one complete record at a time.

Let's take a look at Excel's default data form. Then, we'll show you how to put forms to work.

Creating a data form

Before you can create a data form, you must use the Set Database command on the Data menu to define a database range in your worksheet. Be careful to include the cells that contain the database's field names in the database range—Excel uses these labels to identify each of the fields in your data form. After you define your database range, choose the Form... command from the Data menu. Excel tailors a data form for your database and displays it in a special dialog box.

For example, to create a data form for the database shown in Figure 14-2, select the range A1:G11 and choose the Set Database command from the Data menu to define the database range. Next, choose the Form... command from the Data menu to create a data form like the one in Figure 14-3.

As you can see in Figure 14-3, at the top of the data form Excel displays the name of the worksheet that contains the database on which the data form is based. Immediately under this title bar are all the field names from the first row of the database. If you've already entered some records into your database, you see the field entries for your first record to the right of the field names. At the top-right

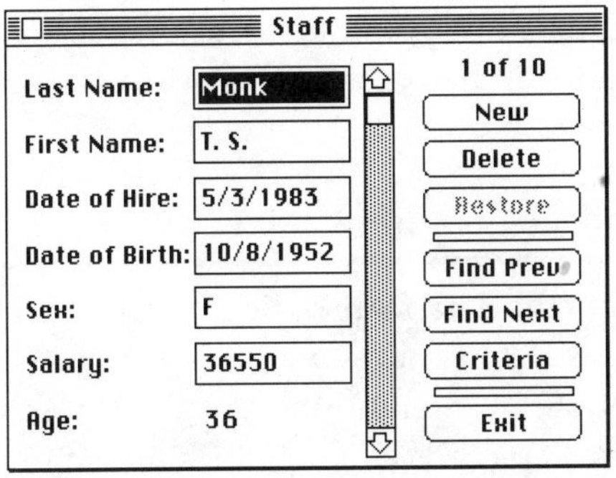

FIGURE 14-3. *The Form dialog box contains the first record from the database.*

corner of the dialog box is a notation in the form "x *of* y" that tells you which record is currently displayed and how many records are included in the database range. For example, the *1 of 10* that appears in the dialog box in Figure 14-3 indicates that the first record of 10 total records is being displayed. If you haven't yet entered any records, the entry boxes to the right of the field names are blank, and you see the notation *New Record* at the top-right corner of the dialog box. Down the right side of the data form are several command buttons that allow you to work with the database records. We discuss these buttons in the next section, when we talk about selecting records, and in Chapter 15, "Working with a Database."

Fields whose entries are displayed in boxes—in this example, the Last Name, First Name, Date of Hire, Date of Birth, Sex, and Salary fields—are called *editable fields* and can, as their name implies, be edited. Fields whose entries do not appear in boxes—Age, in this example—are called *calculated fields*. Calculated fields display the result of a function or formula and cannot be edited. (We show you how to define calculated fields in a form in a few pages.) If you've used the Cell Protection… and Protect Document… commands to lock and protect any of the cells in the database, your data form may contain protected fields. Excel displays the contents of a locked field on the data form, but locked fields don't appear inside boxes, indicating that you can't edit them.

To close a data-form dialog box, you can click the Exit button at the bottom-right corner of the dialog box, or click the close box in the upper-left corner of the dialog box. The data form disappears from view. If you want to reopen the form, choose the Form… command from the Data menu again.

If you need to peek at the worksheet while you're working in the data form, you can move the form aside by dragging the title bar. However, you can only view the worksheet. You can't scroll through the database or edit cells. You must scroll through each record in the Form dialog box.

Nor does Microsoft Excel allow you to activate another window or choose any commands while the data-form dialog box is open. If you want to choose a command or activate a window, you must first close the form.

Navigation techniques

The scroll bar in the center of the data-form dialog box allows you to scroll through the records in your database. You can move backward or forward through the database one record at a time by clicking the up or down scroll arrow. You can move through the database 10 records at a time by clicking in the gray area of the scroll bar above or below the scroll box. You can also drag the scroll box to the approximate position of a record. For example, if your database contains 10 records and you drag the scroll box to the middle of the scroll bar, the fifth record appears in the form. As you drag the scroll box up or down, the number of the record you are currently on changes. When you reach the record you want to view, simply release the mouse button. If you drag the scroll box to the bottom of the scroll bar, Excel displays a set of empty entry fields, ready for a new database record.

You can also use the arrow keys to move through the database. To move from one record to the next record or the previous record, press the Up arrow key or the Down arrow key. To move to the first record in the database, press Command-Up arrow; to move to the end of the database—for example, to enter a new record— press Command-Down arrow. To move through the database 10 records at a time, press Page Up or Page Down (on Apple's extended keyboard).

There are also two techniques you can use to move from field to field in a data form. With the mouse, you can move to a new field simply by clicking that field. If you prefer to use the keyboard, you can use Tab or Enter to move forward to the next field.

Editing records

To edit a record in a data form, simply bring that record into view, move to the field that contains the entry you want to change, then edit the information in that field using the usual Excel editing techniques.

For example, suppose you want to edit the record for employee Blount to reflect a raise in salary from $22,800 to $26,400. To begin, you have to bring this record (number 4) into view in the form, as shown in Figure 14-4. To display the record, press the Down arrow key three times or drag or click the scroll bar. When the record is in view, select the Salary field by pressing the Tab key or clicking the field. Then, type *26400* and press Enter to lock in your change. Figure 14-5 shows the result.

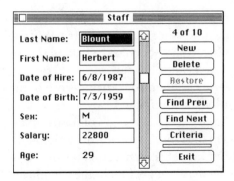

FIGURE 14-4. *You can use data forms to edit records.*

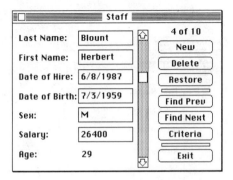

FIGURE 14-5. *You have changed the entry in the Salary field to 26400.*

As soon as you make a change to a record, the Restore button on the right side of the data-form window becomes available. If you make a change to an existing record and then discover a mistake before you move to another record, you can click Restore to return the record to its original condition.

Remember, you can edit only those fields that are displayed in boxes. You cannot edit calculated or protected fields. In fact, you can't even move to a calculated or protected field in a data form.

Adding records

It's easy to add a record to a database using the data form. First, select the New option or drag the scroll box to the bottom of the scroll bar. Microsoft Excel displays a blank record at the end of the database and the words *New Record* appear at the upper-right corner of the data form. You can now add a new record by entering the information for that record into the fields of the form. If you make an error while you're entering a record using a data form, you can edit the field entries in the data form just as you would edit an existing entry. When you're finished, lock in the new record by moving to another record, clicking the New or Exit button, or pressing Enter. Microsoft Excel adds the new record to the database.

For example, suppose you want to add a new record to the example database. To begin, use the New button, the Command-Down arrow key combination, or the scroll box to move to the blank record at the end of the database. Then, add the new record by making entries in the fields of the form. Figure 14-6 shows a new record in the form and on the worksheet. When you enter the record, Microsoft Excel adds it to the end of the database range, fills in the calculated Age field, and formats the numeric entries in columns C, D, and F. (We moved the form dialog box to the upper-right corner of the screen so that you can see the added record for Malcolm Rebennack.)

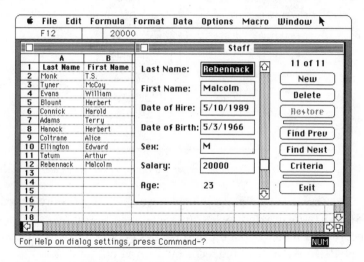

FIGURE 14-6. *We added a new record for Malcolm Rebennack.*

When you use the data form to add new records to your database, Microsoft Excel adds those new records to the bottom of the database and extends the database range to include your additions. In addition, if the last record in the database includes calculated fields, Excel "copies" the formulas from those fields into the new record. Always be sure that plenty of extra room for new records is available below the database range. If Excel can't find room to expand the database, you see the alert message *Can't extend database* when you try to create a new record.

Deleting records

To delete a record using a data form, simply bring that record into view in the data form and click the Delete button. Excel presents an alert box that says *Displayed record is deleted permanently*. If you click OK in the alert box, the record is deleted from both the data form and the worksheet. Any records below that record in the worksheet are shifted upward to fill in the resulting gap. If you choose Cancel, the record is not deleted.

Defining criteria and selecting records

You can also use a data form to define selection conditions (called *criteria*) and to find records in the database based on the criteria you've defined. This capability comes in handy when you need to move from one record to another that contains a particular entry. We explain criteria and show how you can define and use criteria in data forms in Chapter 15, "Working with a Database."

Custom data forms

The data forms you've seen thus far can help to speed your database entry and editing tremendously. However, these simple default forms represent only the beginning of Excel's forms capabilities. You can also develop your own custom form dialog boxes to prompt you for input and to display information in any format and arrangement you choose. We show you how to create custom forms in Chapter 20, "Customizing Excel."

Conclusion

In this first chapter of the database section of *Excel in Business*, we have explored the fundamentals of Microsoft Excel databases. We began by discussing the structure of an Excel database; then we showed you how to create and define a database in a Microsoft Excel worksheet. Next, we showed you how to "customize" a database by formatting, aligning, and widening fields, and adding, deleting, and moving records and fields. We ended the chapter with a discussion of calculated fields and data forms.

In the next chapter of this section, we show you how to use criteria to locate and use information in a Microsoft Excel database. In that chapter, we cover three commands—Find, Extract..., and Delete—as well as seven special database statistical functions. In the final chapter of this section, we deal with sorting the records in a database.

15

Working
with a Database

So far, we've been concerned with how Microsoft Excel stores information in a database. Of course, Excel can do much more than just store your data. Once you have created a database range, you can locate and manipulate the information stored in that range. The tools you can use to work with the information include both database commands and special database functions.

Microsoft Excel features four commands that operate on the records in a database, all located on the Data menu: Find, Extract..., Delete, and Sort.... The Find command instructs Excel to locate, one at a time, those records in the database that match the criteria in the criteria range. The Extract... command lets you copy the entries from those records that match the criteria to another location in the worksheet. The Delete command allows you to delete from the worksheet all the records that match the criteria. We discuss the Sort... command in Chapter 16, "Sorting the Database."

Microsoft Excel also offers 11 special database statistical functions: DSUM, DAVERAGE, DCOUNT, DCOUNTA, DMAX, DMIN, DPRODUCT, DSTDEV, DSTDEVP, DVAR, and DVARP. These functions calculate statistics about the records that match the criteria you have defined.

All of these functions and commands are based on the use of selection criteria. Before you can use the commands and functions, you must know how to specify those criteria within an Excel worksheet.

Selection criteria

Selection criteria are the "tests" that Microsoft Excel uses to determine which database records it should act upon when you choose a database command. For example, you might use a criterion such as "all the people who live on Main Street" to extract information from a telephone-book database. Like the records in an Excel database, selection criteria are simply entries in an Excel worksheet. In addition, as with Excel databases, selection criteria must be stored in a specially defined range of cells. This group of cells is known as the *criteria range*.

Cells A15:G16 in Figure 15-1 contain a sample criteria range that could be used to select records from the employee database you created in Chapter 14, "Excel Database Management." As you can see, the structure of a criteria range is much like that of a database range. The first row of a criteria range must contain one or more of the field names from the database with which the criteria range is associated. The first row of the criteria range in Figure 15-1, for example, contains all of the field names from the database. The entries that you make in the row or rows immediately below these field names will be the criteria themselves. You might want to think of each row as a *criteria record*.

	A	B	C	D	E	F	G	H
	Last Name	First Name	Date of Hire	Date of Birth	Sex	Salary	Age	
1	Last Name	First Name	Date of Hire	Date of Birth	Sex	Salary	Age	
2	Monk	T.S.	5/3/83	10/8/52	F	$36,550	36	
3	Tyner	McCoy	9/23/84	2/13/59	M	$35,750	30	
4	Evans	William	5/16/85	3/15/55	M	$27,975	34	
5	Blount	Herbert	6/8/87	7/3/59	M	$22,800	29	
6	Connick	Harold	2/20/84	11/16/57	M	$34,050	31	
7	Adams	Terry	11/16/82	2/29/48	F	$37,500	41	
8	Hanock	Herbert	10/10/85	8/18/60	M	$28,000	28	
9	Coltrane	Alice	3/18/86	4/5/54	F	$28,425	35	
10	Ellington	Edward	6/8/87	9/2/58	M	$23,500	30	
11	Tatum	Arthur	12/14/86	8/18/52	M	$28,775	36	
12	Rebennack	Malcolm	5/10/89	5/3/66	M	$20,000	23	
13								
14								
15	Last Name	First Name	Date of Hire	Date of Birth	Sex	Salary	Age	
16							23	
17								
18								

FIGURE 15-1. *Cells A15:G16 contain the criteria range.*

The field names in the criteria range must be identical to the corresponding field names in the database. If a field name in the criteria range does not exactly match a field name in the database (except for capitalization differences), Excel cannot use the criteria you enter into that field.

A criteria range can be as small as two cells: one that contains a field name and one immediately below it that contains a single criterion. A large criteria range might include 30 or more fields and 10 or more criteria. In most cases, your criteria range will be somewhere between these two extremes—usually five or so columns and approximately two or three rows.

Creating and defining a criteria range is a three-step process. First, you enter one or more field names across one row of an Excel worksheet. Second, you select the cells that contain the field names and the cells below the names (in which you will enter the criteria), and you choose Set Criteria from the Data menu. This command assigns the range name *Criteria* to the selected cells and thereby tells Excel that those cells are the criteria range. Each worksheet can have only one range of cells with the name *Criteria*. Finally, you enter selection criteria into the cells below the field names.

To construct the criteria range in Figure 15-1, you first select cells A1:G1 (the cells of the database range that contain the field names) and choose the Copy command. You then click cell A15 and choose the Paste command to place a copy of those entries in cells A15:G15. (You could construct this criteria range by typing the field names directly into cells A15:G15 instead of copying them from cells A1:G1. By copying the field names rather than typing them, however, you eliminate the risk of misspelling one or more of the names.) Next, you select cells A15:G16 and choose the Set Criteria command to define that block of cells as the criteria range.

Although the example criteria range includes every field name from the database, your criteria ranges don't have to include every field name. In fact, you need include the name of only one field in the criteria range—the field you want to use to select records. For example, if you want to select records only on the basis of entries in the Age field, the criteria range can include only the name of that one field. If you want to make selections based on the entries in more than one field, you must include all those field names in your criteria range. In general, we recommend that you include the names of all the fields from your database in a criteria range, to make it easy to specify criteria for any field without having to reuse the Set Criteria command every time you make a new entry in the criteria range.

The next step is to enter the selection criteria into the cells in row 16. Excel database criteria can be divided into two broad categories: *comparison criteria* and *computed criteria*. Comparison criteria compare the entries in one field to a numeric or text value—for example, is the entry in the Salary field greater than $30,000?

Computed criteria are more complex, because they use the values in two or more fields—for example, is Salary divided by Age greater than 1,000?—or they use Excel functions to act upon field entries. Because of the relative complexity of computed criteria, let's explore comparison criteria first.

Comparison criteria

Comparison criteria compare the entries in a field of an Excel database to text, numbers, or the results of formulas. The comparison can be an equality (=) or one of five relational operators (>, <, >=, <=, or <>).

In Figure 15-1, the criteria range encompasses cells A15:G16. The top row of the criteria range contains the field names of the database to which the criteria relate. The entries below the field names tell Excel which entries to look for in each field when it selects records from the database.

To continue with this example, enter the number 23 below the field name Age in your criteria range. When you use one of the criterion-dependent commands or functions, this comparison criterion causes Excel to work with only those records that contain the number 23 in the Age field. (As we pointed out in Chapter 14, "Excel Database Management," the Age values in your database may be different from those in our figures because of the dynamic NOW function in the Age formula.)

The number 23 below the field name Age in the criteria range of Figure 15-1 is an example of an exact-match number criterion. When you use one of Excel's criterion-dependent commands or functions, this entry tells Excel to use only those records that have exactly the value 23 in their Age field.

Instead of just entering the value that you want Excel to match, you can preface that value with an equal sign. For example, you could enter

=23

in cell G16 and achieve the same result as if you had entered only the number 23.

You can also use the >, <, >=, <=, and <> signs in numeric comparison criteria. For example, if you enter the criterion

>35

into cell C16, Excel operates on only those records with an Age entry that is greater than 35. Similarly, you can enter

<=65

if you want Microsoft Excel to select only those records with an Age entry that is less than or equal to 65.

Text criteria

You can also use comparison criteria in text fields. For example, suppose you want Excel to find each record in the database shown in Figure 15-1 that has a Sex entry of *M*. To do this, you can enter the single letter *M* into cell E16 (the cell immediately below the Sex-field name in the criteria range).

When you enter a simple number into a cell of the criteria range, Excel matches only those records that have that exact number in the specified field. However, when you use a simple text entry as a criterion, Excel finds each record that has an entry in the specified field that *begins* with the text string you have specified. For example, the criterion *M* matches not only records that have the entry *M* in the Sex field, but all records that have Sex entries that begin with *M*, such as *Male, Man,* and *Mailman,* or any other Sex entry that begins with the letter *M*, either upper- or lowercase.

Similarly, suppose you want to find all of the records that have a Last Name entry that begins with *E*. To do this, you can erase the current contents of the criteria range and enter the letter *E* in cell A16. This criterion finds each record with a Last Name entry that begins with *E*. In this case, the criterion finds two records: record number 4, which contains the Last Name entry *Evans,* and record number 10, which contains the Last Name entry *Ellington.*

If you want to make the criterion more selective, you can replace the single letter *E* in cell A16 with the letters *Ev*. This criterion finds each record that has a Last Name entry that begins with the letters *Ev*. In this case, this criterion selects only one record: record number 4, which has the Last Name entry *Evans.*

You can also use the >, <, >=, <=, and <> signs in a text criterion. The operators act upon the "value" of the text entry, where *A* is less than *B*, *B* is less than *C*, and so on. Upper- and lowercase forms of the same letter are equal (meaning that *z* and *Z* have the same value). For example, you could enter

<N

in cell A16 of the example criteria range to match all records whose Last Name field begins with a letter before *N* (the first half of the alphabet). Or you could enter

<>M

in cell E16 to match all records whose Sex field does not start with an *M* (or *m*).

Exact-match criteria If you wish, you can force Excel to find only those records with an entry that exactly matches your criterion in the specified text field. To do this, you have to enter the criterion in the form

="=*text*"

where *text* is the string you want to match. You should always use this alternate
form when you want Excel to match a text criterion exactly. For example, if you
enter the criterion

="=White"

in cell A16 (under the Last Name field name), Excel selects only those records that
have a Last Name entry of *White*—not all of the other records that have a Last
Name entry like *Whiteman, Whitelaw,* and so on. (In the example database, this criterion would not select any records.)

Wildcards Excel allows you to use the wildcard characters ? and * as a part of
any text criterion. The question mark (?) takes the place of any single character. For
example, you can use the criterion

="=Sm?th"

to match the names *Smith* or *Smyth*. You can also use multiple question marks
within the same criterion. For example, the entry

="=H??t"

matches the names *Hart, Hurt, Heit,* and so forth.

The asterisk (*) is Excel's second wildcard character. Unlike the question
mark, which substitutes for only one character, the asterisk can replace a large
number of characters. For example, the exact-match criterion

="=S*n"

matches, among others, the names *Stevenson, Svenson,* and *Smithson*. You can also
use the * wildcard at the beginning of an exact-match text criterion. When you do
this, Excel matches every entry that ends with the letters that follow the *. For
example, the criterion

="=*th"

matches the names *North, Smith, Roth,* and any other name that ends with *th*.

You can use the * wildcard at the end of an exact-match text criterion to make
Excel select all entries that begin with the specified text but end with any characters. For example, the criterion

="=St*"

matches the names *Stevenson, Stack,* and any other names that begin with the letters
St. However, you can accomplish the same thing with the simple text criterion

St

which also matches any entries that begin with the letters *St*.

You can use wildcards in text criteria that are not exact-match criteria. However, the results you get may not be what you expect. For example, the criterion

Sm?th

matches the names *Smith* and *Smyth*, but it also matches *Smythe*, *Smithson*, and *Smithsonian*. Similarly, the criterion

*th

matches not only the names *Smith* and *Roth*, but also the name *Smithson*.

To find an actual asterisk or question mark in a data field, you must precede the character in the criteria range with a tilde (~). For example, ~? matches any entry beginning with a question mark.

Combining criteria

In many cases, you will want Excel to find records that meet several different criteria or that meet at least one of several criteria. For example, you might want to find every record in a database that has a Salary-field value greater than 30,000 and a Date of Hire before January 1, 1986. Or you might want to find every record that has a Salary-field value less than 30,000 and a Date of Hire after December 31, 1985. In these cases, you have to make entries into more than one cell below the criteria field names.

Logical AND

When you make two or more entries on the same row of a criteria range, Excel selects only those records that meet both (or all) of those criteria. This condition is called a *logical AND*. For example, suppose you want to find only the males who are over 30 years of age from the database shown in Figure 15-2 on the next page. To do this, you enter *>30* in cell G16, and enter *M* (or *="=M"* if you want an exact match) in cell E16. Because both of these criteria are on the same line of the criteria range (which you have defined as cells A15:G16), Excel works with only those records that meet both criteria—in this case, the records for *Evans*, *Connick*, and *Tatum* (records 4, 6, and 11)—when you use a criteria-dependent command or function.

You'll sometimes want to match records that have an entry that falls between two values in a particular field. In this case, you need to combine two criteria that relate to the same field into a logical AND form. For example, suppose you want Excel to select those records from the database shown in Figure 15-2 that have an Age entry between 30 and 36, inclusive. To do this, you need to specify two criteria that relate to the Age field: >=30 and <=36. Because both of these criteria relate to the Age field but there is only one cell you can put them in, you must add another Age column to the criteria range to accommodate the extra Age entry. To do this, click cell H15 and type *Age*, or copy that entry from cell G1 or G15. Next, type *>=30* in cell G16 and *<=36* in cell H16 (or vice versa). Finally, include column H in the criteria range by selecting cells A15:H16 and choosing Set Criteria from the Data menu. When you finish, your criteria range and database look like the ones in Figure 15-3.

	A	B	C	D	E	F	G	H
1	Last Name	First Name	Date of Hire	Date of Birth	Sex	Salary	Age	
2	Monk	T.S.	5/3/83	10/8/52	F	$36,550	36	
3	Tyner	McCoy	9/23/84	2/13/59	M	$35,750	30	
4	Evans	William	5/16/85	3/15/55	M	$27,975	34	
5	Blount	Herbert	6/8/87	7/3/59	M	$22,800	29	
6	Connick	Harold	2/20/84	11/16/57	M	$34,050	31	
7	Adams	Terry	11/16/82	2/29/48	F	$37,500	41	
8	Hanock	Herbert	10/10/85	8/18/60	M	$28,000	28	
9	Coltrane	Alice	3/18/86	4/5/54	F	$28,425	35	
10	Ellington	Edward	6/8/87	9/2/58	M	$23,500	30	
11	Tatum	Arthur	12/14/86	8/18/52	M	$28,775	36	
12	Rebennack	Malcolm	5/10/89	5/3/66	M	$20,000	23	
13								
14								
15	Last Name	First Name	Date of Hire	Date of Birth	Sex	Salary	Age	
16					M		>30	
17								
18								

FIGURE 15-2. *You have combined two criteria with a logical AND to find only the males who are over 30 years of age.*

	A	B	C	D	E	F	G	H
1	Last Name	First Name	Date of Hire	Date of Birth	Sex	Salary	Age	
2	Monk	T.S.	5/3/83	10/8/52	F	$36,550	36	
3	Tyner	McCoy	9/23/84	2/13/59	M	$35,750	30	
4	Evans	William	5/16/85	3/15/55	M	$27,975	34	
5	Blount	Herbert	6/8/87	7/3/59	M	$22,800	29	
6	Connick	Harold	2/20/84	11/16/57	M	$34,050	31	
7	Adams	Terry	11/16/82	2/29/48	F	$37,500	41	
8	Hanock	Herbert	10/10/85	8/18/60	M	$28,000	28	
9	Coltrane	Alice	3/18/86	4/5/54	F	$28,425	35	
10	Ellington	Edward	6/8/87	9/2/58	M	$23,500	30	
11	Tatum	Arthur	12/14/86	8/18/52	M	$28,775	36	
12	Rebennack	Malcolm	5/10/89	5/3/66	M	$20,000	23	
13								
14								
15	Last Name	First Name	Date of Hire	Date of Birth	Sex	Salary	Age	Age
16							>=30	<=36
17								
18								

FIGURE 15-3. *You have added an additional Age entry to the criteria range in order to find those records whose Age fields fall between two criteria.*

Because these two entries are both on the same row of the criteria range and both are beneath an Age field name (although in different cells), Excel combines them with a logical AND and therefore finds only those records with an Age entry that is both greater than or equal to 30 and less than or equal to 36. At the time of writing, Excel works with all the records except those in rows 5, 7, 8, and 12 when you use any criteria-dependent command or function.

Logical OR

In some cases, you'll want Excel to find records that meet either of two (or more) criteria. This condition is called a *logical OR*. Whenever you make entries into more than one row below the criteria field names and then include those rows in the criteria range, Microsoft Excel finds records that match the specified criteria in any one or more of the rows.

For example, suppose you want to select from the employee database all records with an Age entry that is less than or equal to 35, as well as all records with an Age entry that is greater than or equal to 40. To do this, you enter <=35 in cell G16 and >=40 in cell G17, as shown in Figure 15-4. (You could also enter >=40 in cell G16 and <=35 in cell G17.) After you make these entries, you must expand the criteria range to include row 17. When entries are on two separate rows of the worksheet and both rows are within the criteria range, Excel matches any record that meets either condition. In this example, Excel selects all but two of the records. It does not select record 2, *Monk*, and record 11, *Tatum*.

	File	Edit	Formula	Format	Data	Options	Macro	Window
G17		>=40						

Staff

	A	B	C	D	E	F	G	H
1	Last Name	First Name	Date of Hire	Date of Birth	Sex	Salary	Age	
2	Monk	T.S.	5/3/83	10/8/52	F	$36,550	36	
3	Tyner	McCoy	9/23/84	2/13/59	M	$35,750	30	
4	Evans	William	5/16/85	3/15/55	M	$27,975	34	
5	Blount	Herbert	6/8/87	7/3/59	M	$22,800	29	
6	Connick	Harold	2/20/84	11/16/57	M	$34,050	31	
7	Adams	Terry	11/16/82	2/29/48	F	$37,500	41	
8	Hanock	Herbert	10/10/85	8/18/60	M	$28,000	28	
9	Coltrane	Alice	3/18/86	4/5/54	F	$28,425	35	
10	Ellington	Edward	6/8/87	9/2/58	M	$23,500	30	
11	Tatum	Arthur	12/14/86	8/18/52	M	$28,775	36	
12	Rebennack	Malcolm	5/10/89	5/3/66	M	$20,000	23	
13								
14								
15	Last Name	First Name	Date of Hire	Date of Birth	Sex	Salary	Age	
16							<=35	
17							>=40	
18								

Ready   NUM

FIGURE 15-4. *You have combined two criteria with a logical OR to find those records with Age entries that are 35 or less or 40 or more.*

Combining logical AND and OR You can also combine logical ANDs and ORs by making more than one entry in one or more rows of a multiple-row criteria range. For example, suppose you want to select the females older than 40 or the males older than 36 from the employee database. To do this, you have to create the criteria range shown in Figure 15-5.

É	File	Edit	Formula	Format	Data	Options	Macro	Window	↖

G17		>36	

Staff

	A	B	C	D	E	F	G	H
1	Last Name	First Name	Date of Hire	Date of Birth	Sex	Salary	Age	
2	Monk	T.S.	5/3/83	10/8/52	F	$36,550	36	
3	Tyner	McCoy	9/23/84	2/13/59	M	$35,750	30	
4	Evans	William	5/16/85	3/15/55	M	$27,975	34	
5	Blount	Herbert	6/8/87	7/3/59	M	$22,800	29	
6	Connick	Harold	2/20/84	11/16/57	M	$34,050	31	
7	Adams	Terry	11/16/82	2/29/48	F	$37,500	41	
8	Hanock	Herbert	10/10/85	8/18/60	M	$28,000	28	
9	Coltrane	Alice	3/18/86	4/5/54	F	$28,425	35	
10	Ellington	Edward	6/8/87	9/2/58	M	$23,500	30	
11	Tatum	Arthur	12/14/86	8/18/52	M	$28,775	36	
12	Rebennack	Malcolm	5/10/89	5/3/66	M	$20,000	23	
13								
14								
15	Last Name	First Name	Date of Hire	Date of Birth	Sex	Salary	Age	
16					F		>40	
17					M		>36	
18								

Ready   NUM

FIGURE 15-5. *You can combine logical ANDs and ORs to find females aged more than 40 or males aged more than 36.*

In this criteria range, the entries in row 16 tell Excel to find only those females whose age is greater than 40, and the entries in row 17 tell Excel to find only those males whose age is greater than 36. Because the logical AND pairs are on separate rows of the criteria range, Excel combines them with a logical OR. As a result, Excel selects each record that meets both of the criteria on either line; that is, each record that has an Age entry over 36 AND a Sex entry of *M*, OR any record that has an Age entry over 40 AND a Sex entry of *F*.

Avoiding blank rows

In each of the previous examples, we left some blank cells in each row of the criteria range. When Microsoft Excel encounters a blank cell underneath any field name in a criteria range, it selects any entry in that field. For example, the criterion shown in Figure 15-6 can be interpreted like this: *Select all records that have any entry in the Last Name, First Name, Date of Hire, Date of Birth, Salary, or Age field and that have an M in the Sex field.*

	A	B	C	D	E	F	G	H
	Last Name	**First Name**	**Date of Hire**	**Date of Birth**	**Sex**	**Salary**	**Age**	
2	Monk	T.S.	5/3/83	10/8/52	F	$36,550	36	
3	Tyner	McCoy	9/23/84	2/13/59	M	$35,750	30	
4	Evans	William	5/16/85	3/15/55	M	$27,975	34	
5	Blount	Herbert	6/8/87	7/3/59	M	$22,800	29	
6	Connick	Harold	2/20/84	11/16/57	M	$34,050	31	
7	Adams	Terry	11/16/82	2/29/48	F	$37,500	41	
8	Hanock	Herbert	10/10/85	8/18/60	M	$28,000	28	
9	Coltrane	Alice	3/18/86	4/5/54	F	$28,425	35	
10	Ellington	Edward	6/8/87	9/2/58	M	$23,500	30	
11	Tatum	Arthur	12/14/86	8/18/52	M	$28,775	36	
12	Rebennack	Malcolm	5/10/89	5/3/66	M	$20,000	23	
13								
14								
15	**Last Name**	**First Name**	**Date of Hire**	**Date of Birth**	**Sex**	**Salary**	**Age**	
16					=M			
17								
18								

FIGURE 15-6. *The blank cells in the criteria range match any entry in that field.*

As long as at least one of the cells in each row of a criteria range contains an entry, blank cells do no harm. If you include a completely blank row in the criteria range, however, Excel matches every record in the database, instead of the subset of records you intended. To understand why, suppose you have made the entry

="=M"

into cell E16, as shown in Figure 15-6, intending to select only the males from the database in cells A1:G12. Instead of specifying cells A15:G16 as the criteria range, however, you specify cells A15:G17. Because a totally blank row causes Microsoft Excel to select any entry in any field, and a multirow criteria range causes Excel to select those records that meet the criteria in any row, this criteria range tells Excel to select all records that have the text *M* in the Sex field, as well as all records that have any entry in any field. As a result, Excel selects every record in the database. This mistake can be particularly disastrous when you use the Delete command from the Data menu, which deletes from the database all records that match the selection criteria.

Formulas and functions in comparison criteria

Most of your comparison criteria compare the entries in a field of a database to a simple text or number entry. However, these criteria can also compare the entries in a field to the result of a formula or function.

For example, suppose you want to locate in the sample database the records for all employees who were hired on May 3, 1983. To do this, you enter the criterion

=DATE(83,5,3)

in cell C16, as shown in Figure 15-7. This criterion causes Excel to select each record with a Date of Hire entry equal to 28977 (the serial date equivalent of May 3, 1983). Next, make sure your criteria range includes only rows 15 and 16.

	File	Edit	Formula	Format	Data	Options	Macro	Window	
	C16		=DATE(83,5,3)						

Staff

	A	B	C	D	E	F	G	H
1	Last Name	First Name	Date of Hire	Date of Birth	Sex	Salary	Age	
2	Monk	T.S.	5/3/83	10/8/52	F	$36,550	36	
3	Tyner	McCoy	9/23/84	2/13/59	M	$35,750	30	
4	Evans	William	5/16/85	3/15/55	M	$27,975	34	
5	Blount	Herbert	6/8/87	7/3/59	M	$22,800	29	
6	Connick	Harold	2/20/84	11/16/57	M	$34,050	31	
7	Adams	Terry	11/16/82	2/29/48	F	$37,500	41	
8	Hanock	Herbert	10/10/85	8/18/60	M	$28,000	28	
9	Coltrane	Alice	3/18/86	4/5/54	F	$28,425	35	
10	Ellington	Edward	6/8/87	9/2/58	M	$23,500	30	
11	Tatum	Arthur	12/14/86	8/18/52	M	$28,775	36	
12	Rebennack	Malcolm	5/10/89	5/3/66	M	$20,000	23	
13								
14								
15	Last Name	First Name	Date of Hire	Date of Birth	Sex	Salary	Age	
16			28977					
17								
18								

Ready   NUM

FIGURE 15-7. *You have used the DATE function in your comparison criterion.*

Cell references in comparison criteria

In some cases, you might want Excel to work with records that have an entry in a certain field that matches the contents of a cell located outside the database and the criteria range. For example, suppose you want Excel to work with the records from the employee database that have an Age entry equal to the number in cell H18. To do this, you enter =H18 into cell G16 and then make sure that your criteria range includes only rows 15 and 16. Now, when you use a criteria-dependent command or function, Excel checks the current value in cell H18, then acts upon any records with Age entries equal to that value. In our example, if cell H18 contains the number 29, Excel selects only the record in row 5.

Comparison criteria that are determined by cells outside of the database range can also be in the form of formulas. For example, you can enter the criteria

=H17*H18

into cell G16 to find those records with Age entries that are equal to the product of the numbers in these two cells. You can also use the formula

=H18+5

in that cell to select records that have Age entries that are equal to the number in cell H18 plus 5.

Computed criteria

Suppose you want to select from a database every record with an Age entry that is less than the value in cell H18. Further suppose that cell H18 contains the value 40. You might attempt to do this by entering the criterion

<H18

in cell G16 of the criteria range. Unfortunately, this would not work. Instead of selecting the records that have an Age entry less than the number in cell H18, Excel would select those records that have the text entry <H18 in the Age field. Whenever you begin comparison criteria with the symbols >, <, >=, <=, or <>, Microsoft Excel does not treat the entry like a formula as you intended. Instead, Excel treats it like a text entry.

To instruct Excel to find the records with Age entries less than the value in cell H18, you have to use a computed criterion. To create a computed criterion for this example, enter the formula

=G2<$H$18

in cell H16, then select the range A15:H16 and choose the Set Criteria command from the Data menu to expand the criteria range to include this cell. Figure 15-8 on the next page shows the worksheet at this point.

There are several things to note about this simple computed criterion. First, you've placed the computed criterion in a cell below a blank cell. (Recall that a comparison criterion is always entered below a cell that contains a field name.) You must enter a computed criterion below a blank cell or below a cell that contains a label other than a field name. If you place a computed criterion below a cell that contains a field name, the criterion does not work as you intended it to. For the sake of convenience, you will usually want to enter the computed criterion in the same row as your other criteria.

If you want to put a label above the computed criterion, you'll probably want it to be a description of the purpose of the criterion. For example, you might want to enter the label *Age Test* into cell G15, the cell above G16.

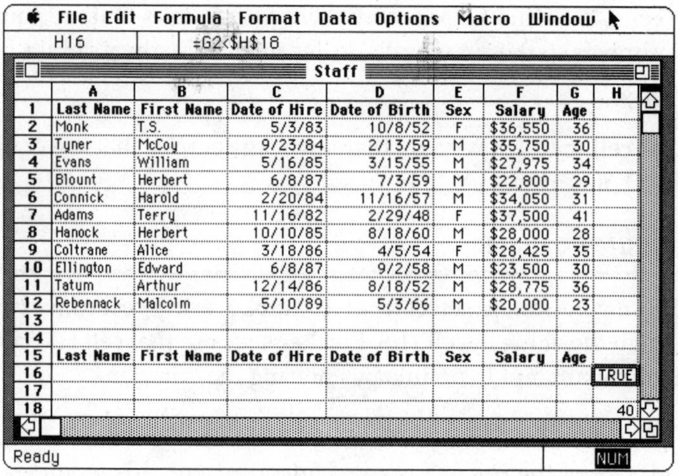

	A	B	C	D	E	F	G	H
1	Last Name	First Name	Date of Hire	Date of Birth	Sex	Salary	Age	
2	Monk	T.S.	5/3/83	10/8/52	F	$36,550	36	
3	Tyner	McCoy	9/23/84	2/13/59	M	$35,750	30	
4	Evans	William	5/16/85	3/15/55	M	$27,975	34	
5	Blount	Herbert	6/8/87	7/3/59	M	$22,800	29	
6	Connick	Harold	2/20/84	11/16/57	M	$34,050	31	
7	Adams	Terry	11/16/82	2/29/48	F	$37,500	41	
8	Hanock	Herbert	10/10/85	8/18/60	M	$28,000	28	
9	Coltrane	Alice	3/18/86	4/5/54	F	$28,425	35	
10	Ellington	Edward	6/8/87	9/2/58	M	$23,500	30	
11	Tatum	Arthur	12/14/86	8/18/52	M	$28,775	36	
12	Rebennack	Malcolm	5/10/89	5/3/66	M	$20,000	23	
13								
14								
15	Last Name	First Name	Date of Hire	Date of Birth	Sex	Salary	Age	
16								TRUE
17								
18								40

FIGURE 15-8. *You can use a computed criterion to select those records with an Age entry less than the value in cell H18.*

The second thing to notice is that the computed criterion includes a reference to cell G2, which is the first cell in the database under the Age field name. This reference tells Excel that the criterion applies to the Age field. Every computed criterion must include a reference, like this one, to the cell immediately below one field name in the database. It is this reference that tells Excel to which field the criterion applies. In the example database, any computed criteria that apply to the Age field must refer to cell G2. Similarly, any criteria that applied to the Salary field would have to refer to cell F2.

Computed criteria generally must refer to the cells in the second row of the database; they cannot refer to the fields of a database by name. For example, the criterion

=Age<$H$18

causes Excel to return the #NAME? error message, instead of selecting records from the desired Age field.

As you can see in Figure 15-8, Excel displays TRUE as the result of the computed criterion in cell H16. This criterion refers directly to the entry in cell G2, so Excel uses the number in that cell when it evaluates the first record in the database against the criterion's formula. Because cell G2 contains the number 36 and because 36 is less than 40, which is the value in cell H18, the criterion is true for that record and Excel displays the constant TRUE. If the entry in cell G2 were 60 or if the entry in cell H18 were 20, Excel would display the result FALSE in cell H16.

The result of any computed criterion generally is either TRUE or FALSE. However, the result that Excel displays in the criteria range has absolutely no meaning, other than telling you whether Excel will select the first record in the database. When Excel evaluates a computed criterion, it calculates the criterion's function or formula once for every record in the database, using the entries in the referenced fields of the current record. If the result of the evaluation is TRUE, Excel selects the record. If the result is FALSE or zero, or is a text or error value, Excel doesn't select the record. In our example, Excel selects the records in all rows except row 7.

The third thing to notice is that the reference to cell H18 in this formula is an absolute reference. Whenever you create a computed criterion that refers to a cell outside of the database range, you must make the reference to that cell absolute (or at least mixed, with the row reference absolute). Unless the reference is "fixed" in terms of the rows, Excel moves down one cell each time it "tests" a new record.

Let's consider another example of a computed criterion. Suppose you want to act on those records in the employee database whose Salary entry divided by the Age entry produces a value greater than 1000. To do this, you enter the formula

=F2/G2>1000

into any blank cell that is below a blank cell. Notice that this criterion refers to more than one cell in the database. Another property of a computed criterion is that it allows you to compare the contents of one field to the contents of another field in the same record. Whenever you create a criterion that applies to more than one field in a database, the criterion must refer to the first cell under the field names of each of those fields. In this case, the criterion applies to the Age and Salary fields, so it must refer both to cells G2 and F2.

Using functions in computed criteria

You use computed criteria to test the result of a function on the entries in a database field. For example, suppose you want Excel to find only those records from the database with a Last Name entry that is five characters long. To do this, you can enter the function

=LEN(A2)=5

in cell H16 (or any other blank cell that has another blank cell above it) and define the criteria range to include that cell. This criterion causes Excel to select only records with a Name entry that is five characters long. In this case, Excel selects only the records in rows 3, 4, 7, and 11.

Logical ANDs and ORs in computed criteria

Functions in computed criteria also provide an alternative way to create logical ANDs and ORs, all within a single cell. For example, the function

   =AND(F2>30000,F2<40000)

matches every record that has a Salary entry between $30,000 and $40,000. This is equivalent to entering >30000 and <40000 in two cells in the same row, both under the Salary field name. In a similar way, the function

   =OR(F2<20000,F2>60000)

matches every record whose Salary entry is less than $20,000 or greater than $60,000. This is equivalent to entering <20000 and >60000 in two cells in the same column, under the Salary field name.

Comparing entries in different records

You can also use a computed criterion to compare the entry in a field of one record to the entry in a record above it. For example, suppose you want to select every record in the employee database that has an Age entry at least five years greater than the record above it. (This sort of criterion is most useful after you have sorted a database, which we show you how to do in the next chapter.) The criterion

   =G2>G1+5

does the trick. This criterion explicitly compares the entry in cell G2 to the entry in cell G1. However, as with all other computed criteria, Excel evaluates this criterion formula once for every record in the database, comparing each entry in the Age field to the entry immediately above it in that field.

E X C E L *tip*

Using different windows for database and criteria ranges

In this chapter, we have intentionally kept the example database small so that we can display both the database and the criteria range at the same time on the screen, in the same window. When you work with larger databases, it is a good idea to use two windows: one for the database itself and one for the criteria range. That way, you can easily switch back and forth between the database and the criteria range by clicking a window, instead of scrolling to distant parts of the worksheet in a single window.

You can extend this technique to compare an entry in any record to the record that is two, three, four, or more records above it, as long as there are enough blank rows above the database for comparison of the first few records to make sense. In this database, for example, you can use the criterion

=G3>G1

to compare each entry in the Age field to the entry two records above it.

Using selection criteria

Now that you know how selection criteria are structured and how they work, let's take a look at what you can use them for. We begin with a discussion of Excel's three criteria-dependent commands: Find, Extract..., and Delete. These commands, which are located on the Data menu, instruct Microsoft Excel to locate, copy, and erase, respectively, criteria-matching records from a database range.

The Find command

The Find command instructs Excel to select, one at a time, the records in a database that match the criteria in the criteria range. For example, suppose you want Excel to find in the database in Figure 15-9 every record that has the entry *M* in its Sex field. To do this, enter the letter *M* into cell E16, select cells E15:E16, and choose

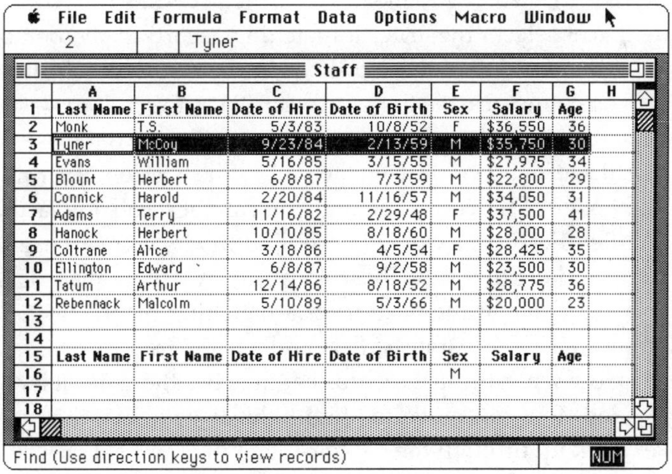

FIGURE 15-9. *You have used the Find command to locate the first record in the database with* M *in its Sex field.*

the Set Criteria command. Now, you are ready to use the Find command. When you choose this command from the Data menu, Excel selects the first record in the database that matches the current criteria. As you can see in Figure 15-9, Excel has selected the record on row 3.

The first record Microsoft Excel finds when you use the Find command depends upon which cell of the worksheet is active when you choose the command. If a cell outside of the database range is active, Excel finds the criteria-matching record that is closest to the top of the database. This was the case in our example, and will often be the case in your work with Excel. If, on the other hand, a cell within the database range is active when you choose the Find command, Excel locates the first criteria-matching record below the record that contains the active cell. If no records in the database meet the stated criteria, Excel beeps and displays the alert message *No match*.

To search the database in reverse order, hold down the Shift key as you choose the Find command. When you choose the Find command, Excel changes the command's name on the Data menu to Exit Find. To choose the Find command again, you first must choose the Exit Find command and then choose the Find command. There are additional ways to exit the Find mode: You can edit the contents of a cell; you can select a cell outside the database range and choose another command; or you can press Command-. (period).

When your database contains criteria-matching records, the scroll boxes change to a striped pattern. These striped boxes indicate that the actions of these tools are restricted. If you move the scroll box while Microsoft Excel is in the Find mode, Excel selects the criteria-matching record in the database that is proportional to the position of the scroll box in the scroll bar. While Excel is in the Find mode, you cannot use the horizontal scroll bar to scroll the last column of the database out of view. When the rightmost column of the database (in this case, the Age field) is the leftmost column on the screen, the horizontal scroll box is all the way at the right edge of the scroll bar, and you cannot scroll any farther.

While Microsoft Excel is in the Find mode, you can use the scroll arrows to move up and down the database, locating only those records that meet the stated criteria. To move to the next criteria-matching record in the database, click the down scroll arrow. Instantly, Excel selects the next record. If you click the down scroll arrow when the last record that matches the criteria is selected, Excel beeps at you and does not move the highlight. If you click the up scroll arrow, Excel moves back up through the database, stopping only at criteria-matching records. By clicking the gray area of the scroll bar above or below the scroll box, you can move to the next criteria-matching record that is at least one screen above or below the current selection.

You can also use the keyboard to move among the criteria-matching records in the database. Use the Up or Down arrow key to move forward or backward one record at a time. Use the Left and Right arrow keys to bring additional columns into view. (As with the horizontal scroll bar, however, you can't scroll past the boundaries of the database range with the Left and Right arrow keys.) If you have an extended keyboard, you can use the Page Up and Page Down keys to move to the next criteria-matching record that is at least one screen above or below the current selection.

Editing in Find mode

While Excel is in the Find mode, you can use the Cut, Copy, and Clear... commands to move, copy, and delete any criteria-matching records. To edit one of these records, first choose the Find command, then use the vertical scroll bar in order to locate the record you want to cut, copy, or clear. When this record is selected, choose the Cut, Copy, or Clear... command from the Edit menu.

If you choose Cut, Excel removes that record from the database the next time you use the Paste command. If you choose Copy, Excel saves the cell references of that record on the Clipboard, but does not remove the record from the database. If you choose Clear..., Excel removes the record from the database immediately.

When you choose any of these commands, as we indicated earlier, Excel leaves the Find mode. For this reason, you have to choose the Find command to locate a record, then use the Cut, Copy, or Clear... command for each of the criteria-matching records that you want to cut, copy, or clear from a database.

The Extract... command

Unlike the Find command, which finds criteria-matching records in their original location within the database, the Extract... command allows you to copy those records with entries that match the current criteria to another location in the worksheet, in one operation. Extracting records is a three-step process. First, you use the Set Criteria command to define a criteria range. Second, you define the area in which you want Excel to place the records it extracts. And third, you choose the Extract... command from the Data menu.

Specifying criteria

Suppose you want Excel to extract from the Last Name and Salary fields in the employee database the entries for those records with a Salary entry between $30,000 and $40,000. To begin, you enter the criterion

    =AND(F2>=30000,F2<=40000)

into cell H16. Then, select cells A15:H16 (or just H15:H16) and use the Set Criteria command to define the criteria range, so your worksheet looks like Figure 15-10.

	File	Edit	Formula	Format	Data	Options	Macro	Window
H16	=AND(F2>=30000,F2<=40000)							

Staff

	A	B	C	D	E	F	G	H
1	Last Name	First Name	Date of Hire	Date of Birth	Sex	Salary	Age	
2	Monk	T.S.	5/3/83	10/8/52	F	$36,550	36	
3	Tyner	McCoy	9/23/84	2/13/59	M	$35,750	30	
4	Evans	William	5/16/85	3/15/55	M	$27,975	34	
5	Blount	Herbert	6/8/87	7/3/59	M	$22,800	29	
6	Connick	Harold	2/20/84	11/16/57	M	$34,050	31	
7	Adams	Terry	11/16/82	2/29/48	F	$37,500	41	
8	Hanock	Herbert	10/10/85	8/18/60	M	$28,000	28	
9	Coltrane	Alice	3/18/86	4/5/54	F	$28,425	35	
10	Ellington	Edward	6/8/87	9/2/58	M	$23,500	30	
11	Tatum	Arthur	12/14/86	8/18/52	M	$28,775	36	
12	Rebennack	Malcolm	5/10/89	5/3/66	M	$20,000	23	
13								
14								
15	Last Name	First Name	Date of Hire	Date of Birth	Sex	Salary	Age	
16								TRUE
17								
18								

Ready   NUM

FIGURE 15-10. *You can use the computed criterion in cell H16 to extract the Last Name and Salary entries for employees with incomes between $30,000 and $40,000.*

Defining the extract range

Now, you can define the area where you want Excel to copy the selected records. We call this area the *extract range*. The first step in defining the extract range is to enter the names of the fields you want Excel to extract into a row of cells in a blank portion of the worksheet. In this example, you want Excel to extract only entries from the Last Name and Salary fields, so you need to include only those two field names at the top of the extract range. Although you could place these field names anywhere in the Excel worksheet, for this example, put them in cells A18 and B18.

Note that the field names in the extract range must be in a single row, as with the field names at the top of the database and criteria ranges. When you choose the Extract… command, Excel places the extracted information into the cells below these names.

You can either copy and paste or type the field names into the top row of the extract range. If you decide to type them, make sure that you enter them exactly as they appear in the database range. If a field name in the extract range does not exactly match a field name in the database (except for capitalization differences, which Excel ignores), Excel does not recognize the field name in the extract range.

You can avoid this sort of problem by using the Copy and Paste commands to copy the field names from the top row of the database into the extract range.

Although you recognize the entries you just made in cells A18 and B18 as field names for the extract range, Microsoft Excel doesn't know where you want it to place the extracted field entries until you tell it. Defining the extract range is a bit different from defining the database and criteria ranges. Instead of selecting the range, then choosing a Data-menu command, you define the extract range by simply selecting it.

You can define the extract range as either just the cells that contain the field names (in this case, cells A18:B18) or as a block of cells headed by those field names (such as the range A18:B50). Your choice affects the number of records Microsoft Excel can extract. If you define only the field-name entries as the extract range, Excel extracts the specified fields of every record in the database that matches the current criteria. If you select a multirow block of cells, however, Excel extracts only as many records as can fit into the selected area. For example, if you select cells A18:B23 as the extract range, Excel extracts a maximum of five records, because there are only five blank rows in the range. If Excel fills up the extract range before it can copy every criteria-matching record from the database, it beeps and displays the message *Extract range is full*.

Extracting information

Once you have specified the criteria, decided which fields you want to extract, and selected the extract range, you are ready to extract the records that match your criteria. You do this by choosing the Extract... command, with the extract range still selected. When you choose this command, Excel presents the dialog box shown in Figure 15-11. This dialog box controls whether Excel extracts the selected fields from all of the records that match the criteria or from only those records in which the extracted fields do not duplicate those of another record.

FIGURE 15-11. *This is the Extract dialog box.*

In most cases, you will want Excel to extract every criteria-matching record to the extract range. To do this, click the OK button or press Return. Excel first erases the contents of every cell in the extract range, then it copies the entries in the selected fields of the records that match the criteria to the cells of the extract range, beginning at the top of the database. Figure 15-12 shows the result of an example extraction.

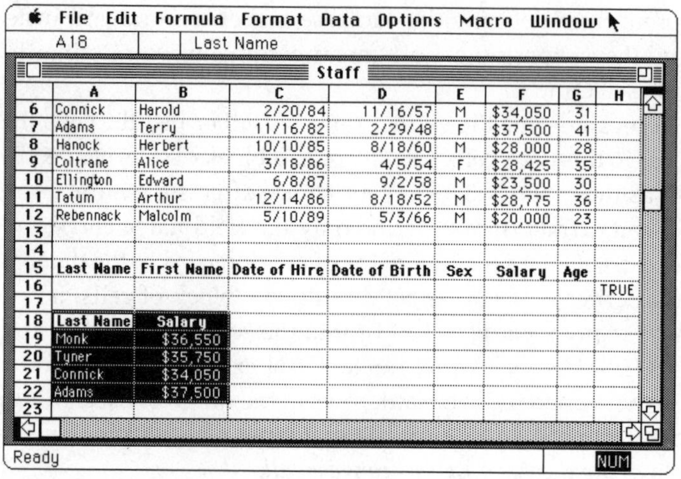

FIGURE 15-12. *Excel extracted the criteria-matching records.*

The Unique Records Only option

Excel can also copy to the extract range only the set of unique entries in the database. Suppose your database contains several duplicate records and you want only one record from each set of duplicates to be extracted. If you click the Unique Records Only option in the Extract dialog box before you click OK or press Return, Excel copies only one record from each set of duplicates to the extract range.

A record does not have to be identical in all fields to a previously extracted record to be omitted from the extract range. Only the entries in the extracted fields need to match the entries of a previously extracted record.

For example, suppose you add a record for Roeland Connick to the sample database. Let's assume that, like Harold Connick, whose record appears in row 6, Roeland Connick earns $34,050. Figure 15-13 shows the result of extracting records without activating the Unique Records Only option.

Figure 15-14 shows the result of performing an extraction on this employee database with the Unique Records Only option selected. As you can see, Excel has excluded the record on row 13 from the extraction, because the entries in the two extracted fields, Last Name and Salary, in this record are identical to the entries in those fields of the record on row 6. Notice that the entries in the nonextracted fields of the excluded record differ from those in the record on row 6. Because the entries in the extracted fields are identical, however, Excel does not extract the record in row 13.

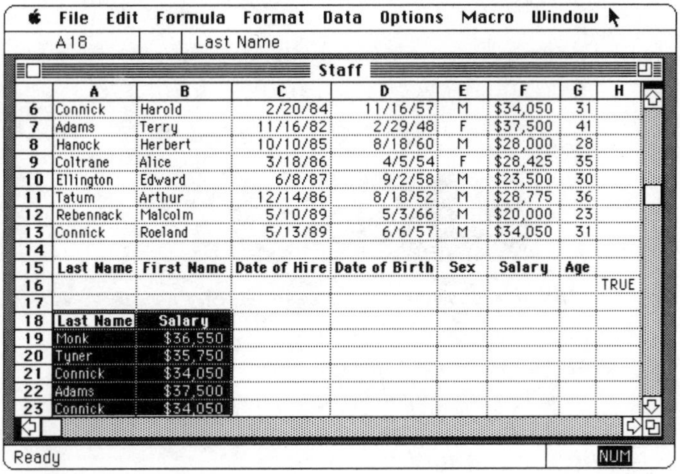

File Edit Formula Format Data Options Macro Window
A18 Last Name
Staff
A B C D E F G H
6 Connick Harold 2/20/84 11/16/57 M $34,050 31
7 Adams Terry 11/16/82 2/29/48 F $37,500 41
8 Hanock Herbert 10/10/85 8/18/60 M $28,000 28
9 Coltrane Alice 3/18/86 4/5/54 F $28,425 35
10 Ellington Edward 6/8/87 9/2/58 M $23,500 30
11 Tatum Arthur 12/14/86 8/18/52 M $28,775 36
12 Rebennack Malcolm 5/10/89 5/3/66 M $20,000 23
13 Connick Roeland 5/13/89 6/6/57 M $34,050 31
14
15 Last Name First Name Date of Hire Date of Birth Sex Salary Age
16 TRUE
17
18 Last Name Salary
19 Monk $36,550
20 Tyner $35,750
21 Connick $34,050
22 Adams $37,500
23 Connick $34,050
Ready NUM

FIGURE 15-13. *This extraction includes records for both Harold Connick and Roeland Connick.*

EXCEL *tip*

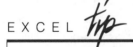

Erasing the extract range

When you use the Extract... command, Excel erases the contents of the extract range before it begins extracting records. This can lead to problems if you have designed a one-row extract range. When you define only the row of field names as the extract range, Excel considers the extract range to extend from that row all the way to the bottom of the worksheet. Excel therefore erases any entries in the cells below the field names, all the way down to the bottom of the worksheet, whenever you choose the Extract... command. Any information that is in those cells is permanently erased.

When you define a multiple-row extract range, however, Excel considers the extract range to be only that block of selected cells. Excel still erases the contents of the entire extract range when you choose the Extract... command. But because the extract range is limited, you do not run the risk of erasing valuable information unintentionally.

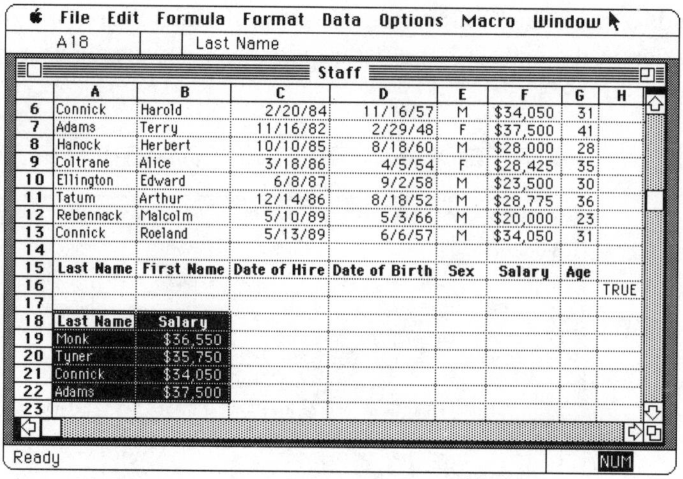

FIGURE 15-14. *Here are the results of the same extraction, but this time with the Unique Records Only option selected.*

The Delete command

The Data menu's Delete command allows you to delete all of the records that match the current criteria. For example, suppose you want to delete from the employee database every record that has the entry *M* in the Sex field. To do this, first enter the criterion *M* into cell E16. Next, define the criteria range by selecting cells E15:E16 and choosing the Set Criteria command.

To delete the records that match this criterion, choose the Delete command (there is no Command-key equivalent for this command). When you choose this command, Excel displays the warning message *Matching records will be deleted permanently*. If you don't want to delete the records that match the current criterion, click the Cancel button to stop the command. If you really do want to delete those records, click OK or press Return. When you do this, Microsoft Excel erases the entries in every field of every criteria-matching record and then shifts the remaining records up into the blank spaces.

Figure 15-15 shows the result of using the Delete command with the example database. As you can see, Excel has removed the records from rows 3, 4, 5, 6, 8, 10, 11, and 12 of the original database and contracted the database so that the remaining records fill rows 2 through 4.

Because the effects of the Delete... command are potentially disastrous, you should use it only with extreme caution. You can't use the Undo command with a Data-menu Delete command. When you delete records, there is no way to get them back, unless you have saved the database on disk before choosing Delete. If

```
 É   File  Edit  Formula  Format  Data  Options  Macro  Window ▶
┌──────────┬──────────────────────────────────────────────────────────┐
│   E15    │         Sex                                                │
├──────────┴──────────────────────────────────────────────────────────┤
│▛▔▔▔▔▔▔▔▔▔▔▔▔▔▔▔▔▔▔▔▔  Staff  ▔▔▔▔▔▔▔▔▔▔▔▔▔▔▔▔▔▔▔▔▔▔▔▔▔▔▔▟│
│     │    A     │    B     │    C     │    D     │ E │   F   │ G │ H │ │
│  1  │Last Name │First Name│Date of Hire│Date of Birth│Sex│Salary│Age│   │
│  2  │Monk      │T.S.      │    5/3/83│  10/8/52 │ F │$36,550│ 36│   │
│  3  │Adams     │Terry     │ 11/16/82 │   2/29/48│ F │$37,500│ 41│   │
│  4  │Coltrane  │Alice     │  3/18/86 │   4/5/54 │ F │$28,425│ 35│   │
│  5  │          │          │          │          │   │       │   │   │
│  6  │          │          │          │          │   │       │   │   │
│  7  │          │          │          │          │   │       │   │   │
│  8  │          │          │          │          │   │       │   │   │
│  9  │          │          │          │          │   │       │   │   │
│ 10  │          │          │          │          │   │       │   │   │
│ 11  │          │          │          │          │   │       │   │   │
│ 12  │          │          │          │          │   │       │   │   │
│ 13  │          │          │          │          │   │       │   │   │
│ 14  │          │          │          │          │   │       │   │   │
│ 15  │Last Name │First Name│Date of Hire│Date of Birth│Sex│Salary│Age│   │
│ 16  │          │          │          │          │ M │       │   │   │
│ 17  │          │          │          │          │   │       │   │   │
│ 18  │          │          │          │          │   │       │   │   │
├──────────────────────────────────────────────────────────────────────┤
│ Ready                                                          │NUM│  │
└──────────────────────────────────────────────────────────────────────┘
```

FIGURE 15-15. *You have used the Delete command to delete all the records in the database with* M *in the Sex field.*

you have saved the database, you can recover the lost information by closing the worksheet (without saving it), then reopening the same worksheet. However, you lose any other changes you have made to the database since you last saved it.

There are two ways to minimize the disastrous effects of unintentionally deleting records from a database. First, as we just said, you can use the Save or Save As… command immediately before you choose the Delete command. That way, you have an exact copy of the database as it existed before the deletion. Alternatively, you can use the Extract… command to make a copy of every field of each record that matches the current criteria just before you choose the Delete command. This technique allows you to view the records that Excel will delete before it deletes them. It also stores a backup copy of the deleted entries within the worksheet. We strongly recommend that you always use Extract… before Delete.

EXCEL

Watch out for blank rows in the criteria range!

As mentioned earlier, using the Delete command when your criteria range contains a totally blank row is a common mistake that you'll want to avoid. A criteria range that contains a blank row matches every record in a database. Therefore, if you choose the Delete command when there is a blank row in the criteria range, Excel erases the entire database.

Using criteria in data forms

You can use criteria to select database records from within a data form dialog box. This dialog box includes three options that let you define and use criteria: Criteria, Find Next, and Find Prev. The Criteria option allows you to define criteria in a data form. The Find Next and Find Prev options let you use those criteria to find matching records—the Find Next option searches down through the database for the next matching record; the Find Prev option searches up through the database for the previous match.

   To define criteria from within a data form, click the Criteria button in the Form dialog box. Microsoft Excel blanks out all fields in the data form to allow you to establish the criteria. As you can see in Figure 15-16, the word *Criteria* appears in the upper-right corner of the form and the Criteria button changes to read *Form*. When you finish entering selection criteria, you can click the Form button to return to the data form.

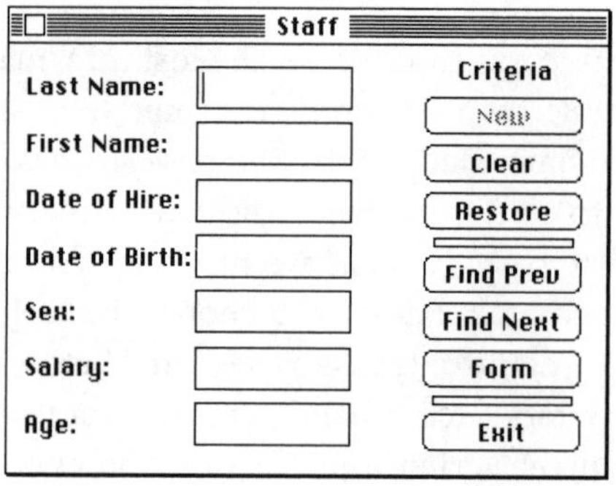

FIGURE 15-16. *You can use the Criteria option to enter selection criteria in a data form dialog box.*

   For example, let's create a criterion that finds the record for the employee Monk in the example database. First, choose the Form... command from the Data menu. When the data form appears, it displays the first record in the database. To define the criterion, click the Criteria button. Excel blanks out the fields in the data form and changes the Criteria option to Form, as shown in Figure 15-16. Now enter the criterion *Monk* in the Last Name field, as shown in Figure 15-17. Finally, click the Find Next button. Excel displays the record for employee Monk in the data form, as shown in Figure 15-18.

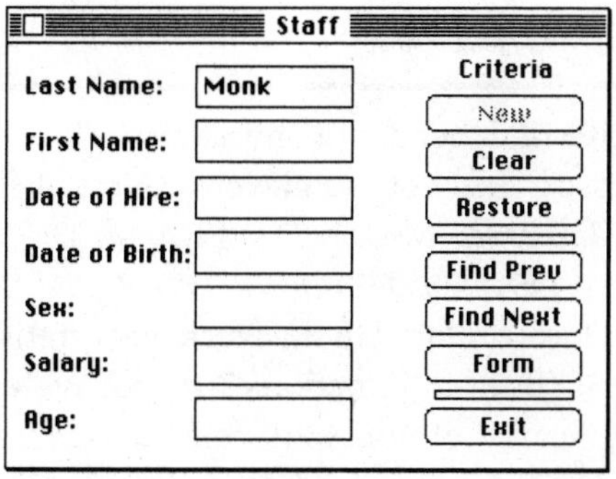

FIGURE 15-17. *To define a criterion, you can simply make an entry in one of the fields of the form.*

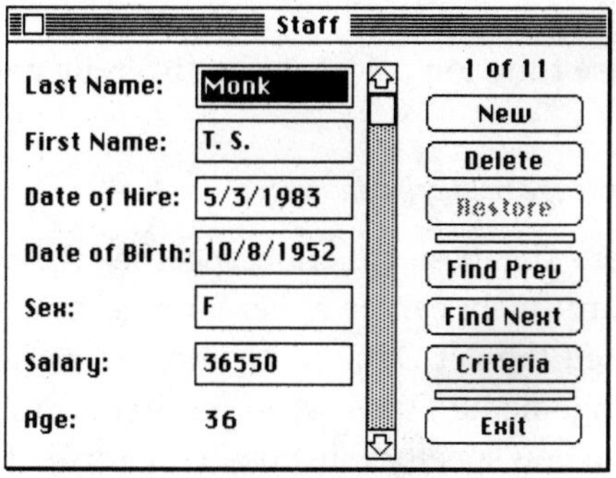

FIGURE 15-18. *You have clicked the Find Next button to display the matching record.*

You can use most of the selection criteria we've discussed in data-form criteria. You can ask Excel to match a series of characters by entering text, numbers, or logical values, and you can compare a quantity by entering =, >=, >, <=, <, or <>. You can also use the wildcard characters ? and * in your selection criteria. Remember, if you're searching for an actual ? or *, you must precede the character with a tilde (~). However, you can't use computed criteria to search in a data form. For example, you can't enter a criterion that compares the values in two or more fields.

If you have several records that share one or more characteristics, you can combine criteria to narrow your search. For example, suppose the example database contained several employees named Monk. To search for a specific record, you would enter *Monk* in the Last Name field and a name in the First Name field, or an *F* or *M* in the Sex field to further restrict the search for employee Monk.

Database statistical functions

In addition to its three criteria-dependent commands—the Find, Extract..., and Delete commands—Microsoft Excel offers eleven statistical functions that operate on the records in a database: DSUM, DAVERAGE, DCOUNT, DCOUNTA, DMAX, DMIN, DPRODUCT, DSTDEV, DSTDEVP, DVAR, and DVARP. These database functions, which are closely related to the worksheet statistical functions you learned about in Chapter 6, "Built-in Functions," respectively calculate the sum, average, count of numbers, count of nonblank cells, maximum value, minimum value, product, standard deviation, standard deviation of a population, variance, and variance of a population of the values in a specified field of the records in a database that match the criteria you have defined. Except for DCOUNT and DCOUNTA, these functions can be used only on fields that contain numeric entries.

Although each database function calculates a different statistic, they all have the form

=DFUNCTION(*database range,field,criteria range*)

The first argument of every database function specifies the *database range* upon which it should act. This argument can be either a range name or the coordinates of a range. If you have used the Set Database command to name your database range, you can use the range name *Database* as the first argument of these functions. In all cases, the range you specify must be in the form of an Excel database.

The second argument of any database function tells Excel which *field* of the database contains the entries it should use to calculate the statistic. This argument can be in one of two forms. First, you can enter the name of the field, enclosed in quotation marks. For example, if you want a function to work on the Salary field of a database, you can enter the second argument as

"Salary"

Except for capitalization differences, the *field* argument must be identical to the field name in the database range. If the name you use in the function is not identical to the name of one of the fields in the database, the function returns the #NAME? error message. Alternatively, you can specify *field* as the position of the field within the database. If you want the function to use the entries in the leftmost column of the database, you can use the field index number 1 as the second argument of the function. If you want the function to use the entries in the second column of the database, you can use the number 2, and so on. When you specify *field* in this manner, you do not need to enclose the number in quotes.

The third argument of any database function identifies the *criteria range* that the function should use to select the records on which it will operate. You can use either a range name or cell coordinates to specify this range. If you have used the Set Criteria command to define your criteria range, you can use the name *Criteria* as the third argument of the database function. The range you specify must be in the form of an Excel criteria range.

Let's use a database function to calculate the average value in the Age field for the females in the example employee database. As a first step, create a criterion in cell E16 that selects only records with the entry *F* in the Sex field. Then, use the Set Criteria command to define cells A15:G16 as the criteria range. Next, make sure that the proper block of cells (in this case, A1:G12) is defined as the database range. Now, enter the function

=DAVERAGE(Database,"Age",Criteria)

into any empty cell of the worksheet outside the database or criteria ranges. In this case, enter the function into cell G18, as shown in Figure 15-19. As soon as you enter this function, Excel calculates its result by summing the entries in the Age field for those records that meet the selection criterion and dividing by the total number of records that meet the criterion. In this case, Excel adds the Age values of the records in rows 2, 7, and 9 (producing a total of 112), then divides by the number of criteria-matching records (3), and returns the value 37.333333333333.

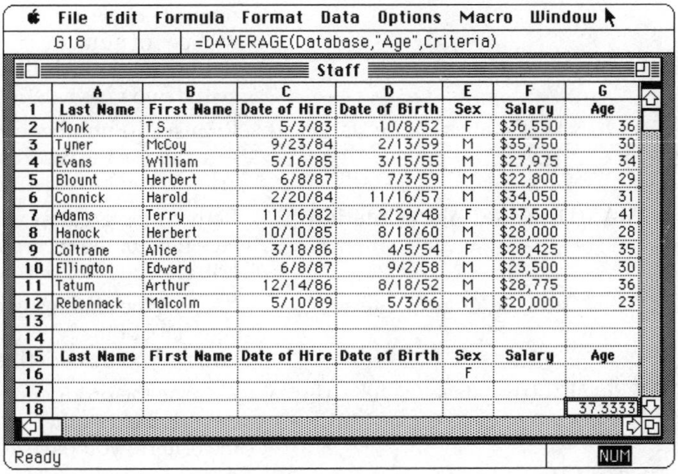

```
 File   Edit   Formula   Format   Data   Options   Macro   Window
      G18               =DAVERAGE(Database,"Age",Criteria)
```

	A	B	C	D	E	F	G
1	Last Name	First Name	Date of Hire	Date of Birth	Sex	Salary	Age
2	Monk	T.S.	5/3/83	10/8/52	F	$36,550	36
3	Tyner	McCoy	9/23/84	2/13/59	M	$35,750	30
4	Evans	William	5/16/85	3/15/55	M	$27,975	34
5	Blount	Herbert	6/8/87	7/3/59	M	$22,800	29
6	Connick	Harold	2/20/84	11/16/57	M	$34,050	31
7	Adams	Terry	11/16/82	2/29/48	F	$37,500	41
8	Hanock	Herbert	10/10/85	8/18/60	M	$28,000	28
9	Coltrane	Alice	3/18/86	4/5/54	F	$28,425	35
10	Ellington	Edward	6/8/87	9/2/58	M	$23,500	30
11	Tatum	Arthur	12/14/86	8/18/52	M	$28,775	36
12	Rebennack	Malcolm	5/10/89	5/3/66	M	$20,000	23
13							
14							
15	Last Name	First Name	Date of Hire	Date of Birth	Sex	Salary	Age
16					F		
17							
18							37.3333

Ready   NUM

FIGURE 15-19. *You have used the DAVERAGE function to calculate the average age of the females in the employee database.*

Once you enter this function, you can use it to calculate the average age of other groups of records just by changing the entries in the criteria range. For example, the function calculates the average age of the males in the database if you replace the *F* in cell E16 with *M*. Or, if you want to calculate the average income of the females in the database, you can replace the second argument, *"Age,"* with the text *"Salary"*.

There are several other ways you can state the function in cell G18. You can replace the second argument, *"Age,"* with a field index number that indicates the position of the Age field within the database, as in

=DAVERAGE(Database,7,Criteria)

You can also replace the range names *Database* and *Criteria* with the coordinates of the database range and the criteria range, as in

=DAVERAGE(A1:G12,3,A15:E16)

The other ten database functions work the same way as DAVERAGE, as follows:

If you use...	Excel does this...
=DSUM(Database,"Salary",Criteria)	Computes the total of the Salary-field values of the records that match the criteria you have defined
=DCOUNT(Database,"Age",Criteria)	Returns the number of nonblank, nontext entries (in other words, the number of numeric entries) in the Age field of the records that match the criteria you have defined
=DCOUNTA(Database,"Age",Criteria)	Returns the number of entries in the Age field of the records that match the criteria you have defined
=DMAX(Database,"Age",Criteria)	Returns the greatest value from the Age field of the records that match the criteria you have defined
=DMIN(Database,"Age",Criteria)	Returns the smallest value from the Age field of the records that match the criteria you have defined
=DPRODUCT(Database,"Age",Criteria)	Returns the product of numbers from the Age field of the records that match the criteria you have defined
=DSTDEV(Database,"Age",Criteria)	Returns the sample standard deviation based on a sample using numbers in the Age field of the records that match the criteria you have defined

(continued)

continued

If you use...	Excel does this...
=DSTDEVP(Database,"Age",Criteria)	Returns the population standard deviation using numbers in the Age field of the records that match the criteria you have defined
=DVAR(Database,"Age",Criteria)	Returns the sample variance based on a sample using numbers in the Age field of the records that match the criteria you have defined
=DVARP(Database,"Age",Criteria)	Returns the variance of a population based on an entire population using numbers in the Age field of the records that match the criteria you have defined

Conclusion

In this chapter, we have explored the ways in which you can use criteria to work with the information in a Microsoft Excel database. We started with a general discussion of criteria, including the structure of criteria ranges, comparison criteria, and computed criteria. After you learned how to specify and use criteria, we showed you how to use the Find, Extract..., and Delete commands to locate, copy, and remove criteria-matching records in a database. Finally, we showed you how to use Excel's 11 database functions to calculate statistics based on the entries in criteria-matching records.

In the final chapter of this section, we present yet another tool for working with the information in a database, the Data menu's Sort... command, which lets you rearrange database records into an order that makes it easier for you to locate specific pieces of information.

16

Sorting the Database

*I*n addition to the three criteria-dependent commands we explored in the previous chapter, Microsoft Excel offers one more Data-menu command that you can use to manipulate the records in a database: the Sort… command. The Sort… command allows you to rearrange the records in a database based on one, two, or three fields at a time. Rearranging your database records makes them easier to locate as you scan through the database.

Although the Sort… command is the key to rearranging the order of the records in a database, the command is not limited to use with Excel databases. Instead, the Sort… command can work on the entries in any rectangular block of cells in a worksheet. Because the most common use of the Sort… command is for databases, however, we focus on that application in this chapter.

Sorting basics

To sort a database, first select the range that contains the database records. The range you select should include all the records and all the fields in the database, but it should not include the field names at the top of the database. After you've selected the database you want to rearrange, choose the Sort… command from the Data menu. Microsoft Excel presents the dialog box shown in Figure 16-1 on the next page. The entries you make in this dialog box tell Excel which fields to use to sort the database.

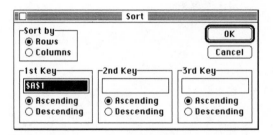

FIGURE 16-1. *This is the Sort dialog box.*

When the Sort dialog box appears, use the 1st Key, 2nd Key, and 3rd Key edit bars to define the fields on which you want to sort and the order of the sort. When you choose the Sort… command, Excel always displays the reference of the cell in the upper-left corner of the selected range in the 1st Key edit bar. To redefine the first sort field, simply enter a reference to any cell in the column that contains the field on which you want to sort. (The selected cell doesn't have to be within the group of cells you're sorting. It can be anywhere in that column.)

After you've specified the sort field, specify the order of the sort. The default order, Ascending, instructs Excel to arrange the records so that the record with the lowest value in the sort field appears at the top of the database, and the one with the highest value appears at the bottom. The Descending option tells Excel to arrange the records so that the one with the highest value in the sort field appears first and the one with the lowest value appears last.

If you want to sort on more than one field, enter a cell reference in the 2nd and 3rd Key edit bars and again select the appropriate sort order. When all the sort fields have been defined, click OK or press Enter. Excel then sorts the database so that the entries in the specified fields are arranged in the specified order.

An example

Let's use the Sort… command to rearrange the records in the database that's shown in Figure 16-2. As you can see, this database includes two fields: Student and GPA (grade point average). Currently, the records appear in random order. To make this information more useful, you'll sort the database so that the record with the highest GPA is at the top of the database, and the record with the lowest GPA is at the bottom.

To sort this database, begin by selecting the range A2:B18, which includes every record in the database. Notice that the sort range does not include the row of field names at the top of the database. If you include this row in the sort range, Excel sorts the field names with the records. The result could be a real mess.

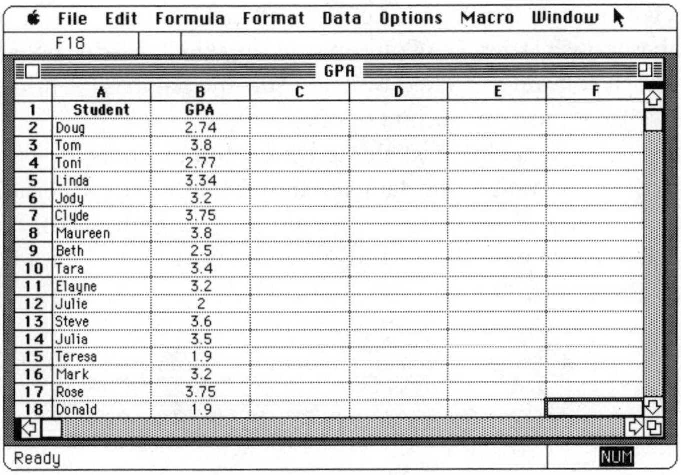

					GPA				

File Edit Formula Format Data Options Macro Window

F18

	A	B	C	D	E	F
1	Student	GPA				
2	Doug	2.74				
3	Tom	3.8				
4	Toni	2.77				
5	Linda	3.34				
6	Jody	3.2				
7	Clyde	3.75				
8	Maureen	3.8				
9	Beth	2.5				
10	Tara	3.4				
11	Elayne	3.2				
12	Julie	2				
13	Steve	3.6				
14	Julia	3.5				
15	Teresa	1.9				
16	Mark	3.2				
17	Rose	3.75				
18	Donald	1.9				

Ready   NUM

FIGURE 16-2. *This database contains two fields: Student and GPA.*

When you have selected from the database the records you want to rearrange, choose the Sort... command from the Data menu. When the Sort dialog box appears, define the Sort fields. For this example, you want Microsoft Excel to sort the data based on the values in the GPA field, which is located in column B of the worksheet. To do this, type the reference of any cell from column B (such as B1) into the 1st Key edit bar.

Having specified the sort field, you should specify the order of the sort. In this case, click Descending so that Excel places the record with the highest GPA at the top of the database.

Once you are satisfied with the sort settings, you are ready to sort the database. Before you do, however, make sure that the Rows setting in the Sort By field is

E X C E L

A sorting shortcut

When you use the Sort... command, Excel always displays the reference of the active worksheet cell in the 1st Key edit bar. You can save yourself the time of typing a cell address into this box if you use the Tab key to activate a cell in the proper column in the selected sort range before you choose the Sort... command. That way, all you have to do is check the sort order, then press Enter to perform the sort.

selected. This option tells Excel to treat each row as a fixed unit and to sort the database row by row. The Columns option, which we discuss shortly, tells Excel to treat each column as a fixed unit and sort the database column by column. You'll rarely, if ever, use this second option.

To sort the database, click the OK button or press Return or Enter. Immediately, Excel rearranges the database into the order you specified in the Sort dialog box. In this case, Excel places the record with the highest GPA at the top of the database, the record with the next-highest GPA next, and so on. Figure 16-3 shows the result of the sort.

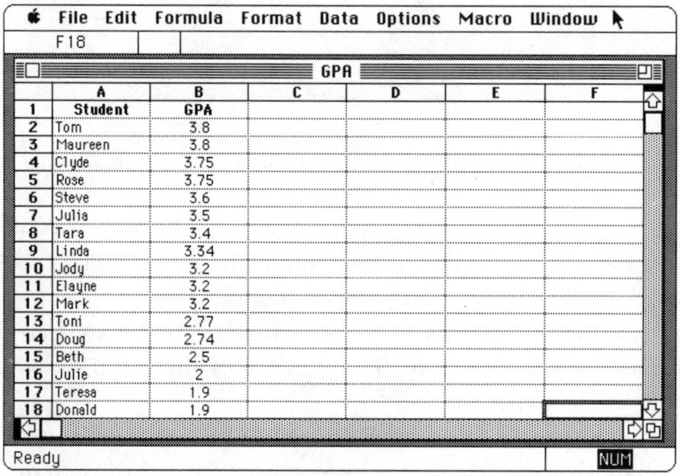

FIGURE 16-3. *This is the example database after sorting.*

Undoing a sort

Once you have sorted an Excel database, it is difficult to get that database back into its original order. The Undo Sort command on the Edit menu returns the records to their previous order, but it works only if you decide to use it before you choose another command or make an entry in your worksheet. The safest way to ensure that you can return a database to its original order is to save it before you sort it. To do this, just use the Save or Save As... command immediately before sorting the database. That way, you can return the database to its pre-sort order by using the Open... command to open the saved database. Unfortunately, this technique is really only useful for restoring a database to its original order immediately after you use the Sort... command. If you make other changes to the database after you sort it, the pre-sort copy does not reflect those changes.

An alternate technique that allows you to restore a database to its original order at any time involves adding to the unsorted database a new field that contains ascending number or text entries. When a database contains such a field, you can restore it to its original order by performing an ascending sort on that field. You can use Excel's Series… command to create such a field quickly.

Sort order

Microsoft Excel sorts the entries in a database field based on the ASCII code of the characters displayed in those entries. If a field contains numbers or number-producing formulas or functions, an Ascending sort puts the smallest numbers at the top of the database and the largest numbers at the bottom. A Descending sort on a numeric field places the largest numbers first and the smallest numbers last.

When Microsoft Excel performs an Ascending sort on the entries in a text field, it arranges those entries in ascending alphabetical order; that is, entries that begin with *A* come first and entries that begin with *Z* come last. For purposes of sorting, Excel does not differentiate between upper- and lowercase letters; that is, *a* is the same as *A*, and *Z* is the same as *z*.

When two entries begin with the same letter, Excel uses the second letter in the word to determine its order. If both the first and second letters are the same, Excel then uses the third letter, and so forth. For example, in an Ascending sort, AAA comes before AAB, which comes before AAC.

Occasionally, text fields contain characters other than letters of the alphabet. Using ASCII codes to determine the sort order, Excel sorts the characters in the following order.

(space)!"#$%&'()*+,-./0123456789:;<=>?@ABCDEFGHIJKLM
NOPQRSTUVWXYZ[\]^_{¦}^~

(The uppercase version of each letter in this list represents both the upper- and lowercase forms of the letter.)

In most cases, the entries in any field of a database are either numbers or text. In some databases, however, one field might contain both number and text entries. If a field contains both text and number entries in an Ascending sort, Excel places all number entries before text entries. If a field contains other entries, such as logical results (TRUE or FALSE) and error messages, Excel performs an Ascending sort in this order:

Numbers
Text
Logical results (FALSE before TRUE)
Error messages (all errors are equal)
Blank cells

Descending sorts arrange the field's entries in the opposite order, except that Microsoft Excel always places any blank cells at the bottom of a database, whether you choose Ascending or Descending sort order.

Multiple-field sorts

In many circumstances, you will sort a database only on a single field, as you did in the previous example. However, when a database contains many fields and some fields contain duplicate entries, you will want to sort on the basis of more than one field. Microsoft Excel lets you sort on as many as three fields at the same time. To explain why you might want to sort a database on more than one field and how to do it, let's work through another example.

The database in Figure 16-4 includes three fields: Product, Size, and Color. The records in this database are randomly arranged. To make this information more meaningful, suppose you want to sort the database on the basis of the entries in the Product field. To do this, you select cells A2:C17, choose Sort…, specify any cell in column A as the sort column, select Ascending Order, then press Enter. Figure 16-5 shows the result of this single-field sort.

As you can see, Excel has rearranged the database in ascending order, based on the entries in the Product field. Because this field contains duplicate entries, the sort has grouped the records according to the entries in that column.

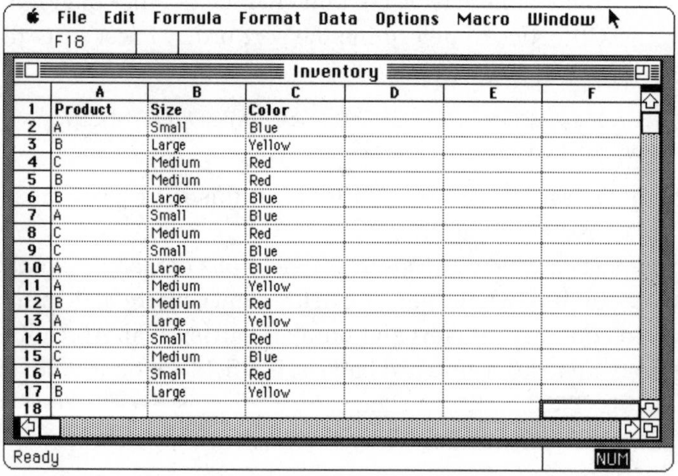

	A	B	C	D	E	F
1	Product	Size	Color			
2	A	Small	Blue			
3	B	Large	Yellow			
4	C	Medium	Red			
5	B	Medium	Red			
6	B	Large	Blue			
7	A	Small	Blue			
8	C	Medium	Red			
9	C	Small	Blue			
10	A	Large	Blue			
11	A	Medium	Yellow			
12	B	Medium	Red			
13	A	Large	Yellow			
14	C	Small	Red			
15	C	Medium	Blue			
16	A	Small	Red			
17	B	Large	Yellow			
18						

FIGURE 16-4. *This is the Inventory database with three fields, arranged in random order.*

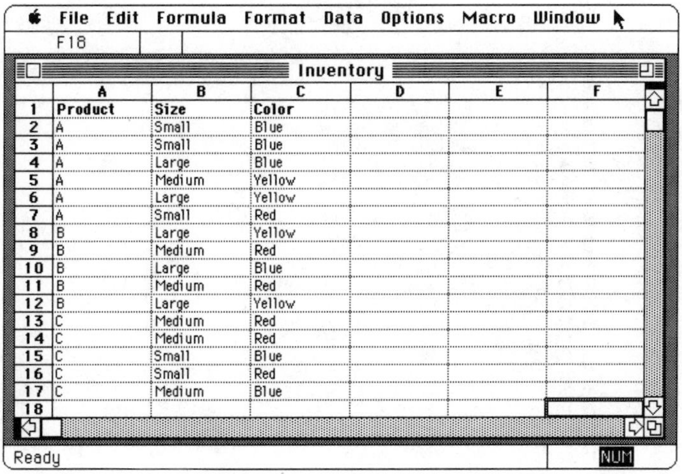

	A	B	C	D	E	F
1	**Product**	**Size**	**Color**			
2	A	Small	Blue			
3	A	Small	Blue			
4	A	Large	Blue			
5	A	Medium	Yellow			
6	A	Large	Yellow			
7	A	Small	Red			
8	B	Large	Yellow			
9	B	Medium	Red			
10	B	Large	Blue			
11	B	Medium	Red			
12	B	Large	Yellow			
13	C	Medium	Red			
14	C	Medium	Red			
15	C	Small	Blue			
16	C	Small	Red			
17	C	Medium	Blue			
18						

FIGURE 16-5. *You have arranged the Inventory database in ascending order by Product.*

Even though the database in Figure 16-5 is better organized than the database in Figure 16-4, the records within each group still appear too randomly arranged. The records within each group are, in fact, in the same relative order as they were in the original database. You can use a secondary sort to add some order to the records within the groups that are produced by a primary sort.

For example, suppose you want to arrange the records in the Inventory database into ascending order based on the entries in the Product field, and arrange the records within each Product group in descending order based on the entries in the Size field. To perform this sort, you first select cells A2:C17 and choose the Sort... Command from the Data menu to display the Sort dialog box. You then type the reference of any cell in column A into the 1st Key edit bar and click Ascending Order. Next, you type the reference of any cell in column B (the Size field) into the 2nd Key edit bar and again click Ascending Order. Once you have entered these settings, click OK or press Return or Enter, to initiate the sort. Figure 16-6 on the next page shows the result of this two-key sort.

As you can see, Excel has grouped all the *Product A* records at the top of the database, followed by the *Product B* records, then the *Product C* records. In this respect, this sort is just like the original one-key sort. A look at column B (the Size field), however, reveals the difference. Instead of being arranged in their original order, the records within each group are now arranged in descending order by size (which is alphabetically ascending). All the Large records come first within each group, then the Medium, then the Small. Excel arranges the records this way, not because it knows that Large is bigger than Medium, which is in turn bigger

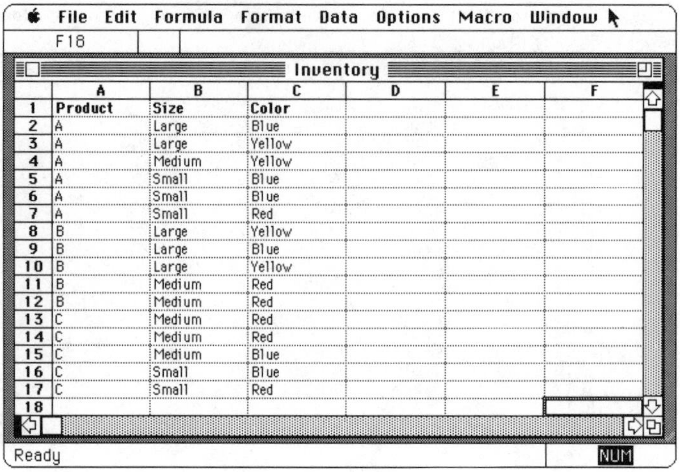

FIGURE 16-6. *You have arranged the Inventory database in ascending order by Product and descending order by Size.*

than Small, but because *L*, the first letter in *Large*, comes before *M*, the first letter in *Medium*, in the alphabet. Similarly, the Medium records come before the Small records because *M* comes before *S* in the alphabet.

Obviously, specifying a secondary sort field adds additional organization to the database. You can use a three-key sort to further organize the data. For example, if you look at the Color field, you will see that the records within each Size-field group appear to be arranged randomly. To organize the records within each secondary-sort group, you can perform a three-field sort.

In this case, let's sort the database so that the records within each secondary sort group are arranged in descending order, based on the entries in the Color field. To perform this sort, again select cells A2:C17, then choose the Sort... Command from the Data menu. Next, type the reference of any cell in column A in the 1st Key edit bar and click Ascending Order. Then, type the reference of any cell in column B in the 2nd Key edit bar and click Ascending Order. Finally, type the reference of any cell in column C in the 3rd Key edit bar, only this time select Descending Order. After you have entered these settings, press Enter to start the sort. Figure 16-7 shows the results of this three-field sort.

As you can see, Excel has arranged the records so that all of the *Product A* entries appear at the top of the database, all of the *Product B* entries next, and all of the *Product C* entries last. Within each Product group, Excel presents the records in descending order by Size (or ascending order alphabetically). Within each Size group, Excel has arranged the records in descending alphabetical order on the basis of the entries in the Color field.

	A	B	C	D	E	F
1	Product	Size	Color			
2	A	Large	Yellow			
3	A	Large	Blue			
4	A	Medium	Yellow			
5	A	Small	Red			
6	A	Small	Blue			
7	A	Small	Blue			
8	B	Large	Yellow			
9	B	Large	Yellow			
10	B	Large	Blue			
11	B	Medium	Red			
12	B	Medium	Red			
13	C	Medium	Red			
14	C	Medium	Red			
15	C	Medium	Blue			
16	C	Small	Red			
17	C	Small	Blue			
18						

FIGURE 16-7. *This time, you have sorted the Inventory database by Product, by Size, and by Color.*

E X C E L

Sorting on more than three fields

Excel allows you to sort a database on only three fields at a time, and in most cases, you will not need to sort a database on more than three fields. However, on those occasions when you want to sort a large database on more than three fields, you can do so by performing successive single- or multiple-field sorts.

When you perform a three-field sort, you specify the sort fields in order of importance. You use the least important field as the 3rd Key and the most important field as the 1st Key. You should follow this same rule when you sort a database on more than three fields.

For example, suppose you want to sort a database on the basis of five fields. To do this, first decide which field is the primary (first) field, which is the second, third, fourth, and fifth. Then, perform a two-key sort of the entire range of the database with the fifth most important field as the 2nd Key and the fourth field as the 1st Key. Next, perform a three-field sort on the rearranged database, with the third field as the 3rd Key, the second as the 2nd Key, and the most important field as the 1st key. You can use this technique to sort a database on any number of fields.

Column sorts

The Sort By option in the Sort dialog box offers you the choice of sorting by rows or columns. You'll usually use the Rows option when you choose the Sort... command. The Rows option tells Microsoft Excel to treat each row of the selected sort range as an unbreakable unit and to sort the database by switching the positions of entire rows.

The Columns option changes the way Excel looks at the sort range by "tilting" it 90 degrees. This option tells Excel to consider the cells in each column in that range to be inseparable. Therefore, Excel sorts the selected range by switching the positions of the columns, not the rows, within that range.

Although the Columns option is not generally used for sorting the fields in a database, it can be useful in some other worksheet applications. For example, suppose you have created the simple financial worksheet shown in Figure 16-8. As you can see, this model consists of five columns of financial information, each of which contains Revenues, Expenses, and Profit entries. Currently, columns B, C, D, E, and F contain the information for 1989, 1988, 1987, 1986, and 1985, respectively. Suppose you want to rearrange this worksheet so that the information for 1985 is in column B, the information for 1986 is in column C, and so on. To rearrange the worksheet in this way, you can perform a column sort.

🍎 File Edit Formula Format Data Options Macro Window ▶					
F18					

Finance

	A	B	C	D	E	F
1						
2		1989	1988	1987	1986	1985
3	Revenues	$123,000	$119,000	$107,000	$102,000	$97,000
4	Expenses	$67,000	$63,000	$52,000	$50,000	$42,000
5						
6	Profit	$56,000	$56,000	$55,000	$52,000	$55,000
7						

FIGURE 16-8. *We want to organize this simple financial worksheet.*

You begin this process by selecting the sort range. In this case, you select cells B2:F6. Then, choose the Sort... command from the Data menu to display the Sort dialog box. Because you want Excel to sort this range on the basis of the entries in row 2 (the year headers), type the reference of any cell in that row (such as cell B2) into the 1st Key edit bar. You want Excel to place 1985's information in column B, and 1989's in column F, so click the Ascending option. Before you sort this range, select the Columns option in the Sort By field. When you click OK or press Enter, Excel sorts the range into the order shown in Figure 16-9.

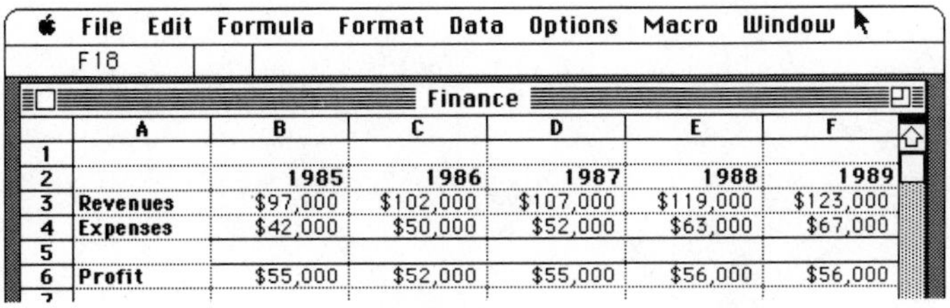

FIGURE 16-9. *You have used the Columns option of the Sort...*
command to reverse the column order of the financial worksheet.

Conclusion

In this chapter, we have shown you how to use the Microsoft Excel Sort... command to sort the records in a database into a more useful order. We began by showing you how to sort a database on the entries in a single field. Then, we showed you how to sort using two and three fields to give even more order to a database. Finally, we showed you how a column sort can be useful in some applications, although not usually in a database.

This chapter concludes our discussion of Excel's database-management feature. In the next section of this book, we look at Excel's exciting macro capabilities.

SECTION FIVE

MACROS

17

Macro Basics

An Excel macro is a series of formulas and statements that instruct Microsoft Excel to take an action or to perform a calculation. Macros are like computer programs that run completely within Excel. You can use macros to automate tedious or frequently repeated tasks. You can also use macros to create user-defined functions that supplement Excel's extensive library of built-in functions.

Excel's macro capabilities are among the most interesting—and the most useful—facets of the program. As you can probably imagine, macros add a great deal of power and flexibility to Excel.

What is a macro?

Microsoft Excel macros can be divided into two groups: command macros and function macros. Command macros carry out sequences of actions for you. For example, you can create a command macro that automatically enters a series of dates across a row of the worksheet, then center those dates in their cells. You can create a command macro that automatically chooses the Page Setup... command from the File menu, defines your print settings, then chooses the Print... command. Or you can create macros that automatically change the Preferred chart format or that create a user-defined format that you use in every worksheet. Command macros can be very simple or extremely complex. They can even be interactive; that is, you can write macros that request information from a user and then act upon that information. We cover command macros here and in the next chapter.

Function macros perform calculations and return values. For example, you can create a function macro that computes the interest paid to date on a loan, or one that computes the weighted average of a range of numbers. We cover function macros in the third chapter of this section.

Macro sheets

In Microsoft Excel, macros are created and stored on macro sheets. In many programs, including Lotus 1-2-3 and Symphony, macros are stored in the cells of the worksheet. Because macros are created and stored independently of your worksheets in Excel, you can create one macro and use that macro with many different worksheets. Storing the macro with its own working name in a separate macro sheet also helps to prevent accidents that might damage the macro. You can even create many different macros on one macro sheet and use that sheet as a library.

Creating a macro sheet

To create an Excel macro, you must first open a macro sheet. To do this, simply choose the New... command from the File menu and double click the Macro Sheet option. After a moment, you'll see a macro sheet like the one in Figure 17-1.

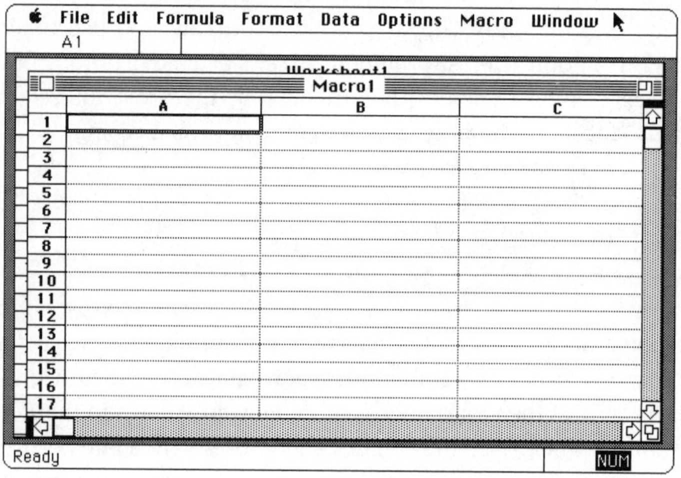

FIGURE 17-1. *This new macro sheet looks very much like a worksheet.*

As you can see, a macro sheet looks very much like a worksheet. The macro sheet is divided into rows and columns, which have numbers and letters just like the rows and columns in a worksheet. The menu bar above the macro sheet is identical to the menu bar above a worksheet. There are a few differences between the commands in the two environments, which we should discuss before going any further.

Macro sheets versus worksheets

One difference that becomes apparent right away is that the columns in the macro sheet appear to be quite a bit wider than those in a worksheet. Actually, the columns in the macro sheet are not wider; the difference is that the Formulas option of the Display... command on the Options menu is selected by default in a macro sheet. This means that you will see the formulas in the cells in the macro sheet instead of the results of those formulas. In a worksheet, the Formulas option is deactivated by default.

Another difference is that instead of being calculated automatically by default, macros are calculated only when they are invoked, and they are always calculated in a strict linear order. In a macro sheet, Excel begins calculating the macro formulas at a definite beginning point (the first cell in the macro), and Excel calculates the formulas in a specific order until it reaches a point of termination (a RETURN or HALT function). The only time Excel deviates from the order of the macro function is when Excel encounters a GOTO function or another macro call (see Chapter 18, "Macro Functions").

An additional difference, as you will see, is that the Define Name... command works a bit differently in macro sheets.

Other than these differences, macro sheets are nearly identical to worksheets. The procedures for making entries, editing entries, copying and moving entries, inserting and deleting rows, and so forth in a macro sheet are all identical to the same procedures in a worksheet. In addition, you use the same commands and techniques to save and open macro files that you use to save and open worksheets and charts.

The Excel macro language

When you choose the Paste Function... command from the Formula menu in a macro sheet, you immediately see the most important difference between your macro sheet and a worksheet: Macro sheets offer many more functions than worksheets. These functions are the building blocks you use to construct your command and function macros. Collectively, these functions make up the Microsoft Excel macro language.

Macro functions fall into three groups. The first group includes functions that exist in both worksheets and macro sheets and have the same purpose in both. These functions return values to the macro, much as worksheet functions such as ABS, NPV, FV, and VLOOKUP return values to the worksheet. You learned about these functions in Chapter 6, "Built-in Functions." As you will see, you can use these functions in your macros in the same way that you use them in the worksheet.

In addition to these functions, macro sheets offer a second class of functions that take the place of the commands on the Excel menus. We call them *command-equivalent functions*, because they are the macro equivalents of Excel's menu commands. They allow you to use Excel commands in your macros.

For example, the CLEAR function is the macro equivalent of the Clear... command on the Edit menu. This function allows you to create macros that erase cells. Similarly, the A1.R1C1 function is the macro equivalent of the R1C1 display option from the Workspace... command on the Options menu, and the ACTIVATE function is the equivalent of selecting a window name from the Window menu.

Many of Excel's command-equivalent functions have two forms: one that causes Excel to present a dialog box and another that performs the requested action without displaying a dialog box. For example, the CLEAR function, which as we've said is the macro equivalent of the Clear... command on the Edit menu, has the two forms

=CLEAR?()

and

=CLEAR(*parts*)

When Excel encounters the first form of this function in a macro, it presents the Clear dialog box, just as if you had chosen the Clear... command from the Edit menu. From this box, you can select the options you want to use. When you click OK or press Enter, Excel performs the action you have specified, then continues with the next function in the macro. If you click Cancel, Excel does not clear any cells, but it does continue with the macro.

The second form of this function allows you to clear the selected range without using the Clear dialog box. In this form, *parts* is a number (1, 2, 3, or 4) that tells Excel whether you want to erase all of the contents of the selected cells, or just the formats, or just the formulas, or just the notes. When Excel encounters this form of the function in a macro, it immediately performs the requested action without presenting the Clear dialog box, then proceeds with the rest of the macro. All command-equivalent functions that have two forms behave in this same way.

The remaining functions are unique to macro sheets. The functions in this group perform a variety of programming tasks. For example, you can use these functions to create loops and branches in your macros. Some of the functions in this group allow you to make entries in cells, select ranges, and perform other similar tasks from within a macro. We call these Microsoft Excel functions *action-equivalent functions*, *informational functions*, and *macro control functions*.

The rules for entering functions in macro sheets are the same as those you have already used for entering functions in worksheets. To enter a function in a macro sheet, simply select a cell and type an equal sign (=). Then, enter the function name followed by an open parenthesis, the function's arguments, and a closing parenthesis. If the function has more than one argument, the arguments must be separated by commas.

Of course, you can also use the Paste Function… command on the macro sheet Formula menu to paste functions into the cells of the macro sheet. You'll find that the macro sheet version of this command works just like the worksheet version.

When you enter a command-equivalent or action-equivalent macro function into a macro sheet, Excel does not immediately calculate that function and take action. Instead, it assigns the value FALSE to that function. Then, when you run the macro that includes the function, Excel calculates the function and performs the function's action. After the function has been correctly calculated, the function returns the value TRUE.

We use functions in this chapter as we show you how to create and use macros. We do not, however, cover each function in detail here. Instead, we cover many of Excel's macro functions in detail in Chapter 18, "Macro Functions."

Creating a simple command macro

Creating a command macro is a three-step process. First, you create a macro sheet or open an existing sheet. Second, you enter the functions that make up the macro, one function per cell, into a single column in the macro sheet. Third, you use the Formula menu's Define Name… command to assign a name to the macro and identify it as a command macro. When you want to use the macro, you choose the Run… command from the Macro menu to invoke the macro. (The process of creating and using function macros is very similar to creating and using command macros. We show you how in Chapter 19, "User-Defined Functions.")

Let's create a simple command macro to illustrate each step. If you have not done so already, begin by opening a new macro sheet. To do this, choose the New… command from the File menu, then double click the Macro Sheet option.

Next, select cell A1 and type the text entry *FIRST*. Although this name is not technically a part of the macro, as you'll see in a moment, it serves two important purposes. (Notice that we've increased the width of column A to accommodate the long entry in cell A2.)

Now, select cell A2 in the new macro sheet and type the formula

=FORMULA("This is my first Excel macro.")

After entering the formula, press Return to lock in the entry and select cell A3. In this cell, enter the function

=RETURN()

Your screen now looks like Figure 17-2.

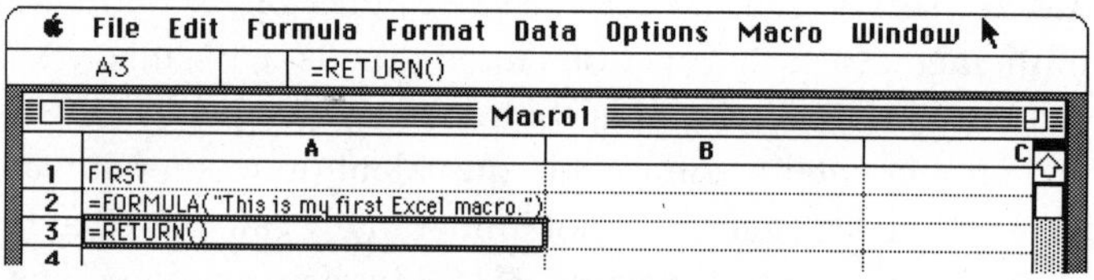

FIGURE 17-2. *You have entered a label and two functions to create a simple command macro.*

The two functions FORMULA and RETURN are from the Microsoft Excel macro language. The FORMULA function allows you to enter text, numbers, or formulas into the cells of the Excel worksheet. In this case, the FORMULA function in cell A2 enters the text

This is my first Excel macro.

into the cell that is selected when you run the macro. The information described by the argument of FORMULA can also be a formula or a value. For example, the function

=FORMULA(100)

enters the number 100 in the selected cell.

As we mentioned previously, the RETURN function signals the end of the macro. All Excel macros must end with a RETURN function or a HALT function. (We talk about HALT in the next chapter.) If you do not include one of these functions at the end of your macro, when the macro is run, Excel displays the alert box shown in Figure 17-3. Although the macro may run correctly without the RETURN function, you are better off including it in all of your macros.

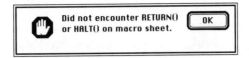

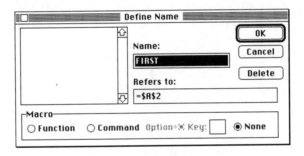

FIGURE 17-3. *This is the alert box that appears when
a macro does not end with the RETURN or HALT function.*

The RETURN function is also used to signal the end of a function macro. When RETURN is used in a function macro, however, it does far more than simply mark the end of the function—it returns a value. We cover the RETURN function in more detail in Chapter 18, "Macro Functions."

After creating a macro, you should give it a name. The name of a macro is just a range name assigned to the first cell in the macro. You name macros in the same way you name cells in the worksheet—by choosing the Define Name... command from the Formula menu.

For example, to name the example macro, select cell A2, then choose Define Name... from the Formula menu. When you do this, Excel displays a dialog box like the one in Figure 17-4.

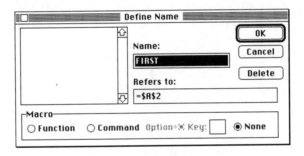

FIGURE 17-4. *This is the Define Name dialog box.*

Notice that Excel has entered the reference of the selected cell, A2, in the Refers To Field in this dialog box, and has entered the text from cell A1, *FIRST*, in the Name field. You may recall from Chapter 2, "Worksheet Basics," that when you use the Define Name... command, Excel always looks for a possible name in the cells above or to the left of the cell you have selected. If it finds a text entry in either of those cells—as it did here—then it suggests that entry as the name for the selected cell.

Before you click OK to accept this name, you should tell Excel that the macro you have created is a command macro. To do this, click the Command button at the bottom of the dialog box. If you forget to select this option, Excel still assigns the name *FIRST* to cell A2, but it does not know that cell A2 is the first cell in a command macro. Consequently, it will be more difficult (but not impossible) to run the macro. As a general rule, you should inform Excel about the type of all of your macros.

When you click the Command option, you'll notice that the Option-Command-Key option becomes available. This option lets you assign an alternate Option-Command-Key name for the macro, so that you can run the macro by pressing Option-Command and the specified key. For now, assign the letter *a* to the Option-Command-Key field. (We come back to this option in a few pages.) You can then click the OK box, or press Enter, to lock in the name of the macro.

As you've just seen, the name in cell A1 is, after all, rather useful. It both serves as a visual reminder of the name of the macro and makes the job of naming the macro much easier. Although you don't have to enter a name for your macros in the macro sheet, you'll find that doing so makes your work in Microsoft Excel a great deal easier.

Now, let's run the macro. To do this, move back to your worksheet window (using the Window menu or choosing the New... command from the File menu to create a worksheet if one is not currently open) and select any empty cell. (We chose cell A1 in the empty worksheet called Worksheet1.) Now, choose Run... from the Macro menu. You'll see a dialog box like the one in Figure 17-5.

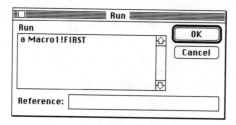

FIGURE 17-5. *This is the Run dialog box.*

The scroll box at the left side of the Run dialog box shows you the names of all of the command macros that reside in open macro sheets. Because you have created only one macro, only one name appears in the list. Notice that the name has three parts. The first part is the Option-Command-Key shortcut letter. (If you have not chosen a shortcut letter, a hyphen appears at the beginning of the name.) The second part is the name of the macro sheet that contains the macro. The third part is the name of the actual macro. As with all external references in Microsoft Excel, the name of the macro sheet and the name of the macro are separated by an exclamation point.

To run the macro, double click the name *aMacro1!FIRST* in the Run dialog box, then watch what happens. When the macro is finished, your screen looks like Figure 17-6. As you can see, Excel has entered in the selected cell, A1, the text string *This is my first Excel macro.*

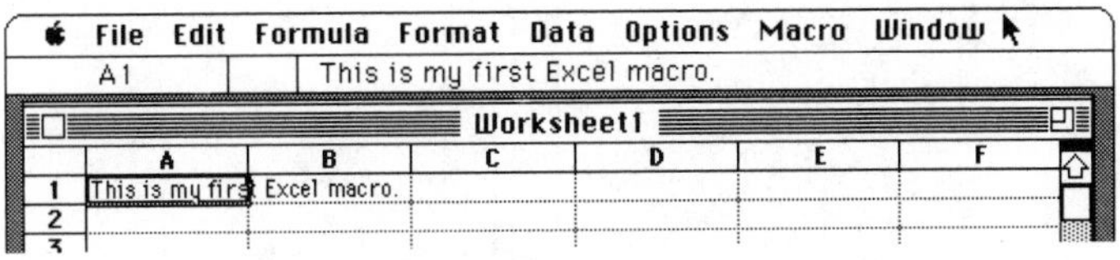

FIGURE 17-6. *The command macro has entered a text string into the active worksheet.*

In effect, this simple command macro is a storehouse for the keystrokes *This is my first Excel macro.* Once you have created this macro, you need never type these keystrokes again. Instead, to enter these characters in a cell, you simply select that cell and run the macro.

Of course, the macro shown in Figure 17-2 is very simple. You probably won't find yourself creating too many macros like this one. Still, it complies with all of the basic rules of macros. It is stored in a macro sheet; it is made up of functions; it has a name, which is simply a range name assigned to its first cell; and it is executed by selecting its name from the list in the Run dialog box. Every command macro you create will follow these same basic rules.

Although this macro seems trivial, macros that are not too much more complex than this one can be extremely useful tools. For example, suppose you are creating a monthly report. You want to enter abbreviations for the names of the months (Jan, Feb, Mar, and so on) into the range B4:M4. Because you create reports like this one fairly often, you decide to write a macro that will perform this task for you automatically. You can use a macro like the one shown in two windows in Figure 17-7 on the next page to create these headers for you. We've used two windows so that you can see the whole macro at once. Let's walk through this macro one line at a time.

The label in cell A1, *HEADER*, serves as the name of the macro. The function in cell A2 is

=SELECT(!B4)

The SELECT function is one of the most commonly used functions in the Microsoft Excel macro language. It is an action-equivalent function; that is, it corresponds to the action of selecting a cell. For example, the result of this function is identical to clicking cell B4.

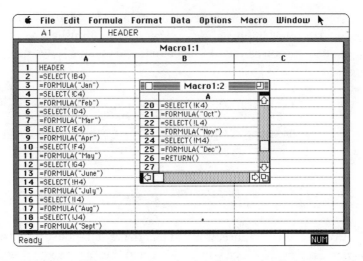

FIGURE 17-7. *This macro creates often-used column headings.*

Notice that the reference to cell B4 is preceded by an exclamation point. This exclamation point marks the reference as an external reference. Since the exclamation point is not preceded by a document name, Microsoft Excel assumes that you are referring to cell B4 on the active worksheet. If you omit the exclamation point, Excel assumes that you are referring to cell B4 on the macro sheet itself.

This is an important concept. If you want the cell references in your macros to apply to the cells in the worksheet that is active when the macro is run, you must make those references external references. If you want the references to apply to cells in the macro sheet, you must not include the exclamation point.

The next line of the function should look familiar. This FORMULA function tells Excel to enter the text *Jan* into the selected cell. Then, the function in cell A4

=SELECT(!C4)

selects cell C4, and the FORMULA function in cell A5 enters the text *Feb* into that cell. The macro continues in this way to cell A26, which marks the end of the macro with a RETURN() function.

Before you can use this macro, of course, you have to give it a name. To do this, select cell A2 and choose the Define Name... command. As before, Excel suggests the text from cell A1, HEADER, as the name for the macro. To name the macro, first click the Command button to define this as a command macro, type *b* in the Option-Command-Key field, and then click OK to accept the suggested name.

Now, you are ready to run the macro. To do this, activate an open worksheet, or open a new one, and choose the Run... command from the Macro menu. When Microsoft Excel presents the list of available macro names, double click the name *bMacro1!HEADER.* When you do this, Excel immediately runs the HEADER macro. Figure 17-8 shows the result. As you can see, Excel has entered the headers *Jan, Feb, Mar,* and so on into row 4.

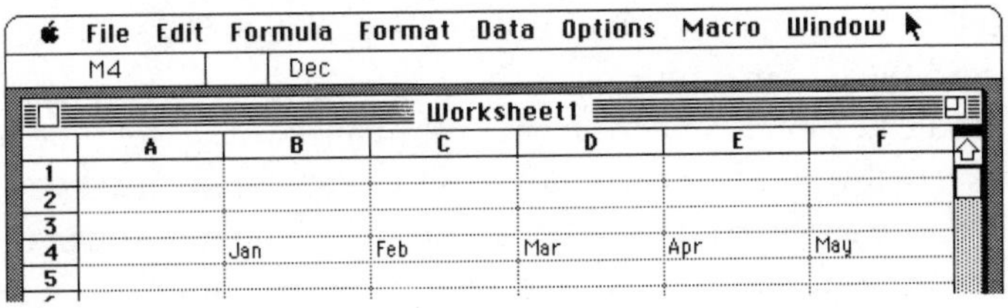

FIGURE 17-8. *This command macro creates a series of column headings.*

A closer look

Now, let's take a closer look at how macros work. When you run a macro, Microsoft Excel begins by calculating whatever formula or function is in the first cell in the macro. After it calculates the formula in that cell, it calculates the function in the next cell in that column, then the next, and the next, and so on. Macro calculation continues in this linear fashion until Excel comes across either a RETURN or HALT function (which stops the macro), a GOTO function (which causes the macro to run another macro), or an error.

Macros can include formulas that return values, functions that take actions, and constant values. If a cell contains a function that takes an action, the macro takes that action when the cell is calculated. If a cell contains a formula that produces a value, Excel calculates the value of the formula, which can then be used by other formulas in the macro. If the cell contains a constant value—a text entry or number—or is blank, Excel simply skips over that cell and proceeds to the next cell. (You see later that you can document your macros by interspersing text among the functions that make up the macro.)

Macro sheet rules

Although the macros you have built so far have been in column A, there is no restriction on where you can put a macro in a macro sheet. You could just as easily have entered your first example macro in cells Z1, Z2, and Z3, or cells AZ100, AZ101, and AZ102. However, convention—and sound practice—calls for macros to be entered only in the first few columns of your macro sheets. If you stick macros in faraway corners of your macro sheets, you'll have a very difficult time figuring out where they are when you need to edit them.

One advantage of the Microsoft Excel version 2.2 sparse matrix memory is that you don't need to worry about using up available memory if you store macros in remote locations in your macro sheets. Version 2.2 of Excel no longer penalizes you for storing macros in unused areas in your macro sheets or for leaving lots of blank spaces between macros. However, as we just stated, scattering macros throughout a macro sheet is an inefficient habit.

You can run any macro from within any worksheet. The only rule to keep in mind is that you can only run macros that are stored on active macro sheets. If you want to use a macro on a closed macro sheet, you must open that sheet before you can run the macro. Simply open the file containing the desired macro, choose Run… from the Macro menu, and double click the macro you want.

The number of macro sheets that can be open at any time is limited only by your Macintosh's memory. As soon as you open a macro sheet, Microsoft Excel adds the names of the macros on that sheet to the list in the Run dialog box. When you close a macro sheet, Excel removes the names of the macros on that sheet from the list. As you have seen, the name of every macro in the Run list includes the name of the sheet on which the macro is stored. This makes it easy to determine the location of a given macro.

Excel assigns the name *Macro1* to the first macro sheet you create in a given work session, the name *Macro2* to the second sheet you create, and so on. Of course, you can always use the Save As… command to save a macro sheet under any name you want.

One macro sheet can hold many macros. To enter a new macro in an existing sheet, you simply select a blank portion of that sheet and enter the macro. As soon as you name a new macro in an existing macro sheet, Excel adds the name of that macro to the Run list.

As you might expect, each macro on a macro sheet must have a different name. Just like in the worksheet, Microsoft Excel allows only one cell in each macro sheet to have a given name. If you attempt to assign to a cell a name that already exists in the macro sheet, Excel removes the name from its old location as it assigns it to the new one.

Another example

Let's look at another simple macro. Suppose you want to write a macro that enters the label *Last revision* into cell A2 of a worksheet and the NOW function into cell B2, then formats the result of the function in cell B2 to be displayed in the m/d/yy date format. The macro that begins in cell A33 in *Macro1* (Figure 17-9) does the trick. Let's walk through this macro step by step.

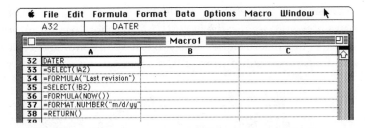

FIGURE 17-9. *This macro enters the revision date of a worksheet.*

To begin, enter the name of the macro, *DATER*, into the cell above the first cell in the macro. Then enter the macro instructions, cell by cell. The first cell in the macro, A33, contains the function

=SELECT(!A2)

which selects cell A2 in the active worksheet. The FORMULA function in cell A34 should be familiar. This function tells Microsoft Excel to enter the text *Last revision* into the selected cell. The function in cell A35

=SELECT(!B2)

selects cell B2 in the active worksheet, and the FORMULA function

=FORMULA(NOW())

in cell A36 enters the result of the function *NOW()* into that cell.

Moving down to the next row, the function in cell A37

=FORMAT.NUMBER("m/d/yy")

is a command-equivalent function that instructs Excel to assign the m/d/yy date format to the selected cell, B2. Finally, the RETURN function in cell A38 tells Excel that this is the end of the macro.

Before you can use this macro, you must name it and identify it as a command macro. To do this, select cell A33 in the macro sheet, choose Define Name... from the Formula menu, click Command, and click OK to accept the default name. (Don't assign an Option-Command-Key letter to this macro, so you can see how Excel displays the name in the Run list box.)

Now, let's run the macro. First open a blank worksheet and select any cell. Then, choose the Run... command from the Macro Menu and double click the name -*Macro1!DATER*. (Notice the hyphen.) Figure 17-10 on the next page shows the result. Excel has entered the text *Last revision* in cell A2 and the current date in cell B2 and has given the date the m/d/yy format.

This simple but useful macro illustrates a couple of important concepts. First, it shows how you can use the FORMULA function to enter information into cells. In addition, this macro shows how you can use a command-equivalent function to choose a menu command from within a macro.

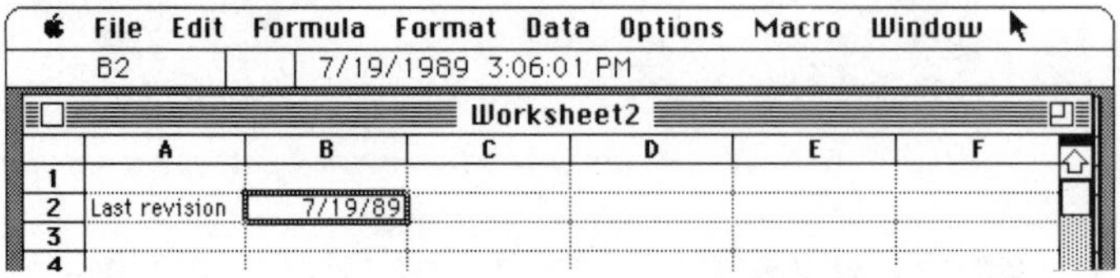

FIGURE 17-10. *This worksheet shows the result of the last-revision macro.*

Interactive macros

Microsoft Excel includes a macro function, INPUT, that causes Excel to stop and display a dialog box that requests information. After the user enters the requested information, the macro continues. If you use the INPUT function in your macros, you can supply information to the macro as it runs. Macros that include the INPUT function are called interactive macros, because INPUT allows the user to interact with the macro. (We cover the INPUT function in more detail in Chapter 18, "Macro Functions.")

Let's modify the *DATER* macro to accept user input. To do this, select cell A38 and enter the function

=SELECT(!A3)

then select cell A39 and enter the function

=FORMULA(INPUT("Enter a note about this version",,"Header"))

Now, enter =*RETURN()* in cell A40, and you're ready to run the macro again.

When you run the macro, Excel enters the text *Last revision* in cell A2 and the current date in cell B2 and formats the date in B2. Then, Excel displays the dialog box shown in Figure 17-11 and waits for the user to enter information.

You can type any number or text entry you want into this box; however, the macro is designed to allow you to enter a note about the current version. Let's assume you enter the note

DFC—Tested changes in growth rate

in response to the prompt. When you click OK, the FORMULA function in cell A39 stores your message in cell A3 of the worksheet as shown in Figure 17-12.

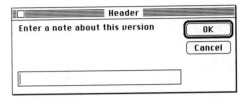

FIGURE 17-11. *This dialog box is displayed when you run the revised* DATER *macro.*

	A	B	C	D	E	F	
	A3		DFC—Tested changes in growth rate				
1							
2	Last revision	7/19/89					
3	DFC—Tested changes in growth rate						

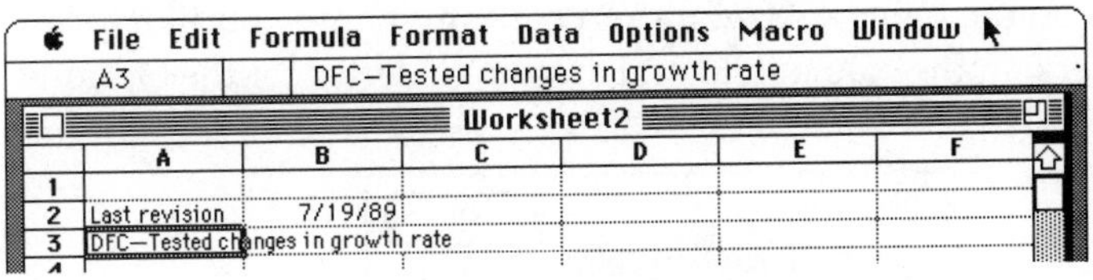

FIGURE 17-12. *This is the result of the revised* DATER *macro.*

You can also use the INPUT function to pass numbers, logical values, and cell references to functions. We have just barely scratched the surface of this function's capabilities with this example. If you decide to become more involved with macro programming, you'll want to spend some time with this powerful function.

Recording macros

Now that you're familiar with the structure and syntax of Microsoft Excel macros, we can show you a shortcut for creating command macros. Rather than typing macros character by character into the cells of a macro sheet, you can instead instruct Excel to create macros by recording the keystrokes you type and the commands you choose.

Once you have recorded a set of commands, you can ask Excel to "play back" the keystrokes and commands. When Excel plays back the recorded macro, it duplicates exactly the actions you performed when you created the macro. As you might expect, this playback capability is very useful for writing scripts that automate long or repetitive processes, such as entering month headers in the worksheet or printing a certain section of the worksheet.

Excel's macro recorder facility has changed slightly since earlier versions of the program. Now, you don't have to define a recorder range before choosing the Start Recorder command. If you have not defined a recorder range, Excel opens a new macro sheet and creates a recorder range for you. The program even assigns a macro name and an Option-Command-Key name to the newly recorded macro.

However, Excel still allows you to create the macro manually or with the Set Recorder and Start Recorder commands, as we show in the section "Using the Relative Record and Absolute Record commands."

To record a command macro, simply choose Record... from the Macro menu (or Record Macro... from the File menu if no worksheets or macro sheets are open). Excel displays a dialog box like the one in Figure 17-13, which asks you to enter a name and an Option-Command key. Excel automatically assigns the name *Record1* to your first macro, *Record2* to your second macro, and so on. Similarily, it assigns the Option-Command key *a* to your first macro, *b* to your second macro, and so on. Of course, you can enter any name you like for the macro (under 256 letters) in the Name field and any single letter for the Option-Command key.

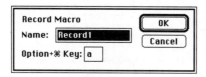

FIGURE 17-13. *You can name your macro in the Macro Recorder dialog box.*

After you enter the information, click OK or press Enter to begin recording your macro. Microsoft Excel opens a new macro sheet to record all the macros you create in one session.

Now, you can perform the actions you want to record. By entering keystrokes and choosing commands, you instruct Excel to record your actions in the macro sheet. (As Excel records your macro, you'll see *Recording* in the status bar.)

Once you have completed all the steps of the macro, choose Stop Recorder from the Macro menu. Microsoft Excel automatically adds an =RETURN() command at the end of the macro.

Be aware that every action you take is recorded as a part of the macro until you choose Stop Recorder. For this reason, you should know exactly what you want to do before you start the macro recorder. It might be a good idea to practice the keystrokes and commands before you start recording. This helps you record the macro in the most efficient manner possible.

For example, let's create the simple date-header macro, using the recorder. To begin, open a new worksheet and choose the Record... command from the Macro menu. When the dialog box shown in Figure 17-13 appears, type the macro title *HEADER* in the Name field, then click OK. (Clicking OK at this point also selects the default Option-Command-Key, *a*.) Now, you are ready to begin recording the macro. To do this, select the range B4:M4 in the worksheet, then type *Jan*, press Tab, type *Feb*, press Tab, type *Mar*, press Tab, and so on through *Dec*. Then press Enter instead of Tab after the last entry. As you type, Excel records your keystrokes.

After you have filled all of the cells in the selected range, choose the Stop Recorder command from the Macro menu. It is very important that you remember to choose this command. When the recorder is on, Excel records every keystroke you type and every command you use. If you leave the recorder on accidentally, Excel records keystrokes you don't want in the macro.

Now, switch back to the macro sheet by selecting it from the Window menu. The macro sheet looks like Figure 17-14. Notice that we have opened two windows on the macro sheet so that you can see the entire macro.

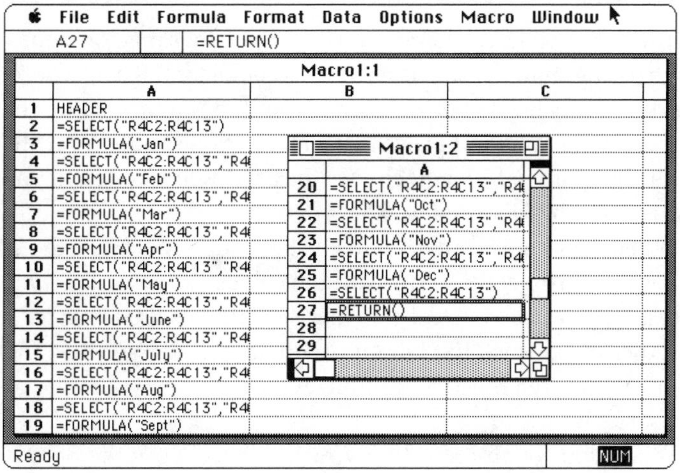

FIGURE 17-14. *This macro sheet shows the effects of the commands and entries we recorded in the worksheet.*

The macro name *HEADER* appears in cell A1. The entries that now appear in cells A2 to A27 are the recorder versions of the keystrokes you typed when you entered the date labels across row 4. For example, the formula in cell A2

=SELECT("R4C2:R4C13")

is the macro equivalent of selecting the range B4:M4. Notice that Excel has recorded this range as an absolute reference in the R1C1 format. This happened because the Absolute Record command on the Macro menu is active by default. (We talk about this command in detail later in this chapter.) The function in cell A3

=FORMULA("Jan")

is the equivalent of typing *Jan* from the keyboard. The function in cell A4

=SELECT("R4C2:R4C13","R4C3")

is the equivalent of selecting the range B4:M4 and making cell C4 the active cell. The macro continues in this way until it reaches cell A27, which contains a RETURN function. When you choose the Stop Recorder command, Excel automatically enters a RETURN function in the last cell of the macro.

Now, reactivate your worksheet. When the new worksheet is ready, choose Run… from the Macro menu and double click the name *Macro1!HEADER* or press Option-Command-*a* to invoke your macro. As soon as you do this, Excel selects the range B4:M4 in the new worksheet and proceeds to enter the labels *Jan*, *Feb*, and so on into the selected cells.

Setting the recorder range and naming your macro

If you want to position your macro in a specific range on your macro sheet or add to an existing macro, all you need to do is select the cell where you want to begin recording and choose Set Recorder from the Macro menu. Then choose the Start Recorder command and proceed as usual. (You should activate the window you'll be working with before you choose the Start Recorder command, or your window selection will be recorded, too.)

When you choose the Set Recorder command from the Macro menu, Excel defines the entire column beneath the cell as the recorder range. If, however, you select a range of cells, Excel sets that selection as the recorder range. It is difficult to predict in advance the length of a macro when you use the recorder. For this reason, we prefer the first option, which allows your macros to be as long as necessary.

When you finish recording your macro, choose the Stop Recorder command from the Macro menu. Now, you'll see on your macro sheet the results of your recording process. Before you use a macro you have recorded in this way, you need to name it. To do this, select the first cell in the macro and choose the Define Name… command from the Formula menu. Type a name in the Name field, click Command, and type a letter in the Option-Command-Key field. Now, click OK or press Return to close the dialog box. After you do this, you can run the macro in two ways: by choosing the Run… command from the Macro menu or by pressing the Option-Command-Key combination you entered in the Define Name dialog box.

Adding to the macro

Now, suppose you want to change this macro so that it not only enters the headers into row 4 but also centers them. To make this change, you need only select the worksheet in which you just used the macro, choose the Start Recorder command from the Macro menu, choose the Alignment… command from the Format menu, select Center, and click OK. When you have done this, choose the Stop Recorder command from the Macro menu to stop recording. Figure 17-15 shows the result of this action on the macro sheet.

Notice that the entry in cell A27 is now

=ALIGNMENT(3)

and that the RETURN function that was in cell A27 is now in cell A28.

Here's what happens when you add to a macro. When you turn on the recorder, Excel first determines if there are any entries in the recorder range. If there aren't any entries, Excel stores the first function in the macro you are creating in the first cell of the recorder range.

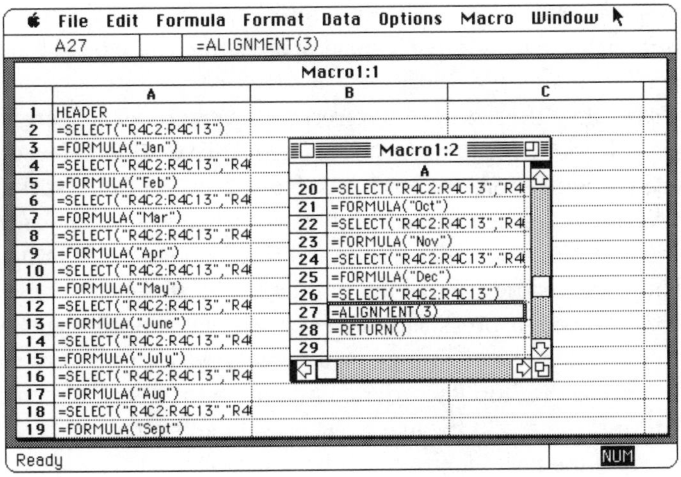

FIGURE 17-15. *The* HEADER *macro now includes the alignment revision.*

If the range *does* contain entries, however, Excel looks to see if the last entry in the recorder range is a RETURN function. If the last entry is a RETURN function, Excel erases that function and stores the first new function it records into that cell. It then continues to record your work until you turn off the recorder, at which point Excel enters a new RETURN function to mark the end of the extended macro. This means that if you start recording again without resetting the recorder range, Excel adds whatever you type to the macro that is already in the recorder range. If you have more than one macro in the recorder range, the new function is stored starting at the position of the last RETURN in the range, which may not be where you intended.

If the last entry in the recorder range is not a RETURN function, Excel enters the first new function that it records in the first blank cell of the recorder range.

In many cases—such as the one we just demonstrated—this "automatic append" capability is very handy. If you don't want Excel to add your new work to the existing macro, however, you must either redefine the recorder range or make an entry in the recorder range below the RETURN function that marks the end of the existing macro.

Using the Relative Record and Absolute Record commands

While each of the macros in the previous examples was being recorded, the Absolute Record option was active. As a result, all of the cell references in the macros were recorded as absolute references in R1C1 format. If you had wanted the references to be relative instead of absolute, you would have used the Relative Record command.

To see the difference, let's re-record the macro we just created, this time using Relative Record instead of Absolute Record. To do this, select cell B2 in *Macro1* and choose the Set Recorder command. Now, create a new worksheet (for example, *Worksheet3*) and select cell B4 in that worksheet. Next, choose the Start Recorder command to turn on the recorder and then choose the Relative Record command to change the recording method to relative. Next, select the range B4:M4, type *Jan*, press Tab, type *Feb*, press Tab, type *Mar*, and so on until you have entered labels in all 12 cells in the selected range. After you type *Dec*, press Enter. When you are finished, choose the Stop Recorder command to turn off the recorder.

Figure 17-16 shows the macro sheet as it looks after you create this macro. Since you started the new macro in cell B2, it appears side by side with the old version. Notice the differences between the two macros. For example, the function in cell A2 is

=SELECT("R4C2:R4C13")

while the parallel entry in cell B2 is

=SELECT("RC:RC[11]")

Similarly, the entry in cell A4 is

=SELECT("R4C2:R4C13","R4C3")

while the entry in cell B4 is

=SELECT(,"RC[1]")

As you can see, the new version of the macro in column B uses only relative references.

Here's the difference between the two macros. The first macro always creates the column headings in the range B4:M4, no matter which cell is active when the macro is run. The second macro, on the other hand, creates the column headings in the row that includes the cell that is active when the macro is run. The headings created by this second version begin in the column that contains the active cell and extend 11 columns to the right of that column. The advantage of this version is that it allows you to enter these headings anywhere in any worksheet.

For example, if you name the macro HEADER 2, select cell C10 in *Worksheet3*, and run the new macro, Excel creates your headings in the range C10:N10. If you ran the *HEADER* macro in *Worksheet3* or any other worksheet, Excel would enter the headings in the range B4:M4.

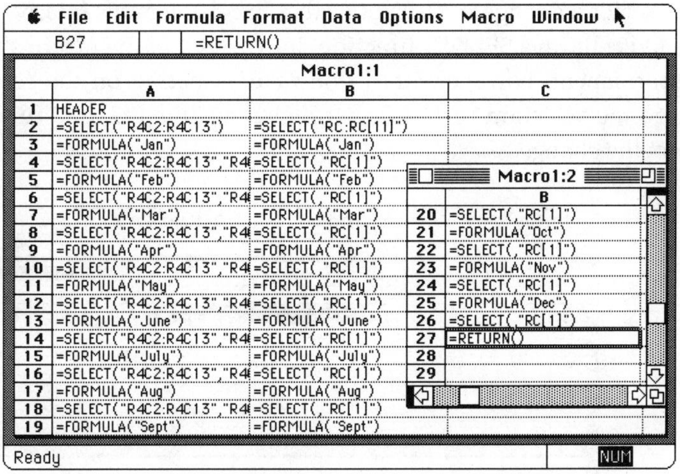

FIGURE 17-16. *The macro in column B was created with Relative Record.*

Obviously, the position of the active cell makes a great deal of difference when you use a macro that was recorded with relative references. Before you run the macro, always select the cell in which you want to start the series. Otherwise, the series is created beginning wherever the active cell happens to be.

You can switch back and forth between Relative Record and Absolute Record at any time—even in the middle of recording a macro. This allows you to make some of the references in a recorded macro absolute and others relative.

Which form is better? Neither is, and both are. Absolute cell references are useful when you want to perform the same action in exactly the same spot in several worksheets, or when you want to perform the same action repeatedly in the same part of one worksheet. Relative cell references are useful when you want the freedom to perform an action anywhere in a worksheet.

More about recording

Excel's macro recorder runs very smoothly. Fortunately, Microsoft Excel does not record an action until you complete it. For example, Excel does not record a cell as being selected until you take some action on it, like choosing a formatting or an editing command. Similarly, Excel does not record a command until you fully complete it. If you click Cancel to abandon the command, Excel does not include the unfinished command in the macro.

For example, look at Figure 17-17. This figure shows a worksheet and a macro sheet on the screen. To begin recording keystrokes in the macro sheet, select cell C1 and choose the Set Recorder command. Now, select the worksheet (the macro sheet remains in view), select cell B1, and choose the Start Recorder command. Next, select the range B1:D1. Notice that Excel enters the relative coordinates of the selected cells, in a SELECT function, into cell C1 in the macro sheet. This record is not permanent, however, until you take an action on the selected cells. If you change the selection to B2:D2, Excel changes the SELECT function in cell C1 to reflect the change.

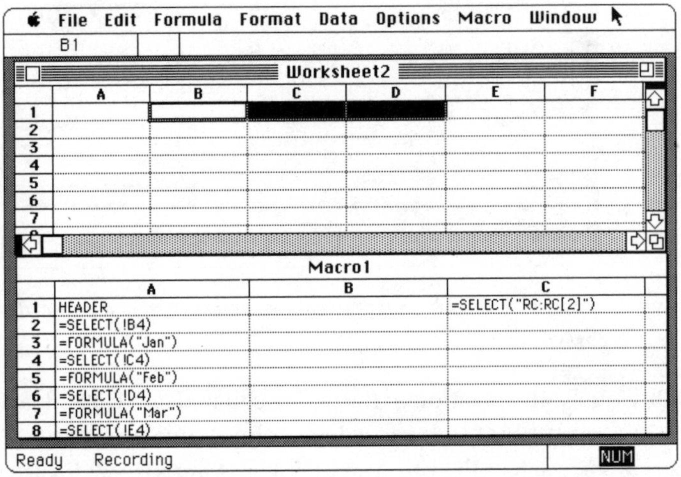

FIGURE 17-17. *A recorded macro is not permanent until the action is completed.*

Once you take an action on the selected range, however, the selection is made permanent. For example, after selecting B2:D2, if you choose the Number... command from the Format menu, select the #,##0 Format, and click OK, Excel makes the SELECT function in cell C1 permanent and adds a new function

=FORMAT.NUMBER("#,##0")

to the macro in cell C2. If you click Cancel instead of OK, however, Excel does not add this new line to the macro and does not make the function in cell A1 in the macro sheet permanent.

You will find this feature of the recorder very helpful. Because Excel waits until you're sure you want to do something before it records your actions, you'll end up with fewer errors in your recorded macros. Even so, realize that Excel records your commands very literally while the recorder is on. When the recorder is on, you should be careful to only choose commands, select cells, and make entries you want recorded. Also remember to turn off the recorder when you are finished recording, or when you need to correct a mistake.

If you choose to use a range instead of a single cell as the recorder range, the recorder range might become full before you are finished recording your macro. If that occurs, Excel displays an alert box with the message *Recorder range is full* and stops recording. If you see this error and you want to continue recording, you must activate the macro sheet and extend the recorder range. If there are blank cells immediately below the current recorder range, you can just extend the record range to include those cells. If there are no blank cells below the recorder range, then you must define a new recorder range in a different part of the macro sheet and use a GOTO function to join the two parts of the macro together.

For example, suppose you defined the recorder range to be A1:A10 in the macro sheet, then filled that range with a macro. When the range becomes full, Excel displays the error message and stops recording. Now, suppose you redefine the recorder range to be cells B1:B10 and continue recording. Before you can use the macro, you must add the function

=GOTO(B1)

to cell A11. This function lets Excel know that the next instruction in this macro is in cell B1. In programming terms, it tells Excel to "branch" to cell B1. We explain the GOTO function in more detail in the next chapter.

Debugging macros

Macros don't always work correctly. Macros can fail because of syntax errors or because of function arguments that don't make sense. For example, the function

=COLUMN.WIDTH(−1)

causes an error, because the argument −1 is not acceptable. Similarly, the function

=GALLERY.PIE(10)

causes an error because its argument is invalid.

One thing is certain: If you create macros, you will create macros that contain errors. Like all programmers, you will spend a good part of your time correcting, or debugging, your macros.

Fortunately, Microsoft Excel makes it relatively easy to debug macros. When Excel encounters an error in a macro, it stops calculating the macro and displays an alert box like the one in Figure 17-18. This alert box tells you that an error has occurred, shows you the location of the error, and gives you three options: Halt, Step, or Continue.

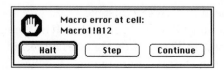

FIGURE 17-18. *This is the Macro Error alert box.*

Most of the time, you'll click Halt to stop the macro, then select the macro sheet and try to discover the source of the error. Because Excel tells you where the error occurred, it is usually fairly easy to find and correct the error.

Clicking Continue causes Excel to ignore the error and continue to the next formula in the macro. Typically, you won't select this option, because an error in one line of a macro often results in errors in other parts of the macro as well. If you select Continue, you are likely to encounter more errors before the macro is finished. Once you have encountered an error, you are usually better off halting the macro and correcting the error before you rerun the macro.

Clicking Step causes Excel to continue processing the macro one step at a time, beginning with the line of the macro after the line that caused the error. As Excel calculates each line of the macro, it stops, displays a dialog box like the one shown in Figure 17-19, and waits for your instructions.

```
▤☐▦▦▦▦▦ Single Step ▦▦▦▦▦
  Cell:  Macro1!A13
                              ┌──────────┐
  Formula:                    │   Step   │
  =FORMULA("June")            └──────────┘
                              ┌──────────┐
                              │   Halt   │
                              └──────────┘
                              ┌──────────┐
                              │ Continue │
                              └──────────┘
```

FIGURE 17-19. *This is the Single Step dialog box.*

The Step mode can help you identify errors in your macros by letting you watch the macro run. Because the macro proceeds step by step, it is easy to locate errors in your macros. However, clicking Step *after* an error has occurred is usually not very helpful, because Excel begins stepping with the cell following the cell that contains the error. You are better off clicking Halt, and then rerunning the macro from the beginning using the Step mode.

There are two ways to invoke the Step mode before an error occurs. You can interrupt a running macro at any time by pressing Command-. (period). When you do this, Excel displays the alert box shown in Figure 17-20. If you want to stop the macro, you can click Halt. If you want the macro to continue, you can click Continue. If you want the macro to continue but to proceed step by step, you can click Step. If you use Command-period to halt a macro just after it has begun, and then click Step, you can step through all but the first few steps of the macro.

FIGURE 17-20. *Pressing Command-period interrupts macro execution.*

Alternatively, you could insert one or more STEP functions with the form

=STEP()

into your macro at the spot(s) where you want to begin to use the Step mode. When the macro encounters a STEP function, Excel presents the dialog box shown in Figure 17-19 and allows you to walk through the statements one at a time. The Single Step dialog box displays the reference of the cell that will be executed next, not the reference of the cell that was just executed. If your macro contains more than one STEP function, you can use the Continue button in the Single Step dialog box to tell Excel to run the macro as usual until it locates another STEP function, whereupon the program enters Step mode again.

A different kind of error

So far, we've only considered errors that make it impossible for Microsoft Excel to compute the macro. There is another type of macro error, however, that can be even more troublesome. This type of error occurs when a macro runs properly, but does not do what you expect it to. This kind of error can occur when you are running a macro for the first time, or if you use a macro in the wrong situation.

Because Excel does not recognize this type of error, it does not stop the macro when such an error occurs. As a result, this type of error can be very destructive. If the macro includes functions like CLEAR or DELETE, your worksheet may be ruined before you know it.

There are a couple of things you can do to avoid this type of error. First, it makes sense to build your macro in stages and test each stage before you add more functions. This allows you to debug the macro one step at a time, which is much easier than debugging the entire macro at once. We also suggest that you use a "dummy" worksheet, whenever possible, to test your macros. You can either use a blank sheet or create a copy of the worksheet in which you plan to run the macro, so that your original worksheet is safe from damage.

The Option-Command-Key option

Earlier in this chapter, we mentioned that Microsoft Excel allows you to assign an Option-Command-Key "name" to a macro. If you do assign this special kind of name to a macro, you can run the macro without using the Run... command. All you have to do is simultaneously press Option, Command, and the key you assigned to the macro. When you do this, Excel immediately runs the macro.

For example, let's give an Option-Command-Key name to the relative reference date-header macro, which begins in cell B2 of *Macro1*. To do this, simply select cell B2 and choose the Define Name... command. When the Define Name dialog box comes into view, type *HEADER2* in the Name Field or select the name if you have already defined it, and click Command. As you've seen, the Option-Command-Key option becomes available when you click Command. To assign an Option-Command-Key name to this macro, select this Field and type the letter *b*. Now, click OK to lock in the name.

Let's see how this new name works. To run the macro, select any cell in a worksheet and press Option, Command, and *b* at the same time. The macro runs immediately, entering the date headers across the row that contains the cell you selected.

Of course, you could still run the macro by choosing the Run... command and selecting its name, *HEADER2*, from the list. The Option-Command-Key name is just an alternative that allows you to run the macro more quickly.

You can assign only single-letter Option-Command-Key names to macros. If you attempt to use two or more letters, Microsoft Excel displays an alert box and does not accept the name. The same thing occurs if you try to use a number or a special symbol as the name.

In addition, Microsoft Excel distinguishes between upper- and lowercase letters in Option-Command-Key names. For example, the name *A* is different from the name *a*. To run macros named with an uppercase letter, you must also press the Shift key. For example, to use the letter *A*, you would have to press Option-Command-Shift and the letter *a*.

If you don't assign an Option-Command-Key name to a macro when you first name it, you can always go back later and add the Option-Command-Key name. All you have to do is choose the Define Name... command and select the name of the macro to which you want to add an Option-Command-Key name. Then simply select the Option-Command-Key field and type the letter you want to assign to the macro. When you are finished, click OK.

Autoexecuting macros

If you want Microsoft Excel to run a macro every time a document is opened or closed, you can identify that macro as an autoexecuting, or autoexec, macro.

To create an autoexec macro that runs whenever a document is opened, begin by activating the document (worksheet or macro sheet) with which you want the macro to be associated. Next, choose Define Name... from the Formula menu. When the Define Name dialog box appears, enter the name *Auto_Open* in the Name Edit field. In the Refers To field, enter the reference of the first cell of the macro you want to run and then click the OK button or press the Enter key. If you want to assign the name *Auto_Open* to a macro that is not located on the currently active document, you can enter an external reference in the Refers To field.

For example, suppose you've created a macro called *HEADER* that begins at cell A2 on the macro sheet named *Macro1*. You want to run this macro every time you open the worksheet named *Budget*. To do this, you activate the *Budget* worksheet and then choose Define Name... from the Formula menu. In the Name field, enter *Auto_Open* and type the external reference *Macro1!$A$2* or *Macro1!HEADER* in the Refers To field. Now, whenever you open the *Budget* worksheet, Excel automatically opens the *Macro1* macro sheet and executes the *HEADER* macro.

If you want to open a document and bypass an autoexec macro, select the Open... command from the File menu, select the file name from the list box, and hold down the Shift key while you click Open or press Enter.

If an autoexec macro opens a macro sheet that has an autoexec macro of its own, Excel won't run the second macro. To run the second macro automatically, include a RUN statement in the first autoexec macro.

To create an autoexec macro that runs automatically whenever a document is closed, you follow the same procedure, except that you enter *Auto_Close* in the Name field of the Define Name dialog box. Microsoft Excel executes the macro when you close the document, provided that its macro sheet is open. To close the document without executing the macro, press the Shift key as you choose the Close command.

Documenting your macros

As you are probably beginning to realize, even relatively simple macros can be difficult to read. After all, you are used to reading English, and Microsoft Excel macros are written in Excel's own special macro language.

However, you can do a lot to make your macros easier to understand. First, you can enter explanatory text in the cells next to a macro in the macro sheet. For example, Figure 17-21 shows the modified *DATER* macro. Notice the text in cells B33:B38. As you can see, this text explains the purpose of each line in the macro.

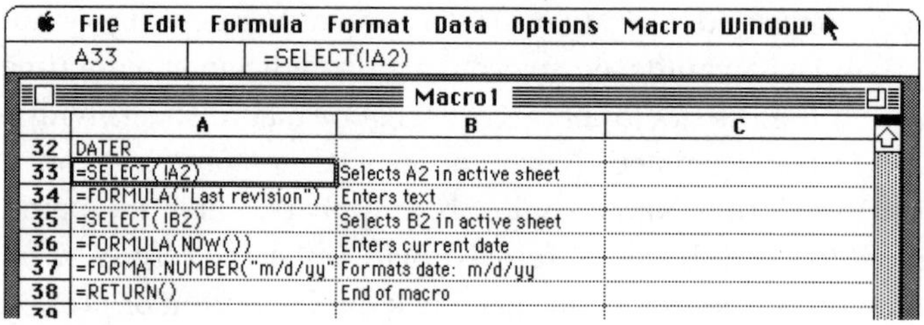

FIGURE 17-21. *This figure shows the* DATER *macro with comments.*

Because Excel ignores any text values it encounters in the process of calculating a macro, you can even include documentation between the functions in your macros. For example, Figure 17-22 shows the same *DATER* macro. This time we've inserted the notes for this macro between the lines of the macro.

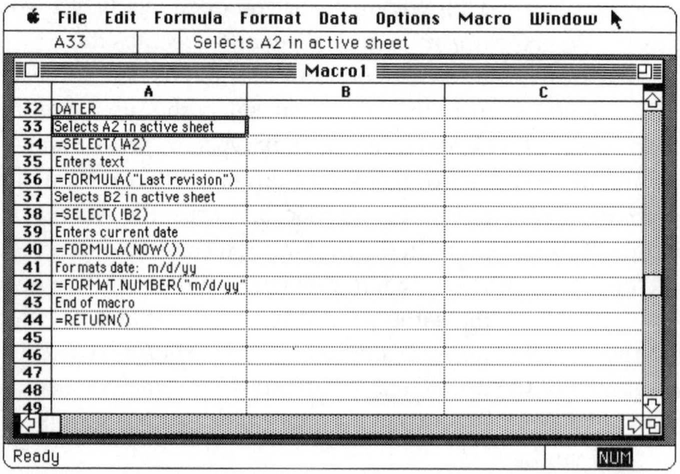

FIGURE 17-22. *This figure shows the* DATER *macro with embedded comments.*

One final method for documenting your macros is to choose the Note... command on the Formula menu. This command allows you to include notes, which might explain how to use a macro sheet or describe what each macro function does. Then, when other users open your macro sheet, they can choose the Show Info command from the Window menu to display the explanatory notes you've added to the cells of your macro sheet.

The way you document your macros is a matter of personal preference. Some people prefer to include the documentation in an adjacent column, while others like to embed the documentation in the macro. It doesn't matter which method you select—as long as you always document your macros. Although it takes a little time to do, including documentation in your macros makes them much easier for you to understand and explain. Documentation is most important for long and complex macros, for macros you will look at only once in a long while, or for macros you must explain to others. We suggest that you document all of your macros.

Another way to "document" your macros is to give them descriptive names. The more descriptive the name, the better. For example, instead of just naming a macro *HEADER*, you could name it *REL MONTHS HEADER*, where *REL* indicates that the macro uses relative references, and *MONTHS HEADER* describes the type of header the macro creates. Because you don't have to type the names of your command macros in order to run them, there is no reason to keep the names of these macros short, although if the name is too long, it is too wide to be completely visible in the Run dialog box.

Using descriptive names for your macros becomes more important as you create more and more macros, and particularly as you create macros that have similar, but not identical, purposes.

Interestingly, you do not have to name macros in Excel. If you choose not to give a macro a name, you can still run it by choosing the Run... command from the Macro menu. If the macro you want to use does not have a name, however, it does not appear in the list of macros in the Run dialog box. To run the macro, you must type its location in the Reference field at the bottom of the Run dialog box. For example, suppose you have created a macro that begins in cell A1 of the *Macro1* macro sheet, and you have not given it a name. To run that macro, you can choose the Run... command, type

Macro1!A1

in the Reference field and click OK or press Enter.

Similarly, if you do not tell Excel that a macro you have created is a command macro, Excel does not include the name of that macro in the Run list. We suggest that you always tell Excel the type of all macros you create.

Subroutines

Excel allows you to run one macro from within another by including the name of the second macro as a function in the first macro. For example, if you include the function

    =TEST()

in a macro, that function immediately activates and runs the macro that begins at *TEST*. When Excel encounters the RETURN function at the end of the second macro, it returns to the cell below the one that contains the calling function and resumes executing the original macro.

This feature of Excel allows you to create subroutines in your macros. A subroutine is a small program that contains instructions that are used over and over in a larger macro. (The Microsoft Excel manual calls subroutines *nested programs*.) Subroutines simplify macros, because they allow you to write a set of frequently used functions once, instead of including those functions everywhere in the macro that they are needed. When you need to use the functions, you can call them as a subroutine.

E X C E L *Tip*

Protecting the macro sheet

After you've finished entering one or more macros into a macro sheet, you'll probably want to protect the macro sheet to prevent any accidental changes or destruction of data. Fortunately, you can apply all the same protection techniques to your macro sheets that are available for worksheets. For example, you can protect the document by entering a password in the Save As Options dialog box.

You can easily lock the cells in the macro sheet by choosing the Cell Protection… command from the Format menu, applying the Locked setting, then using the Protect Document command on the Options menu. You may also want to use the Windows option in the Protect Document dialog box to prevent the user from activating the macro sheet. You can even hide the macro sheet from view by using the Hide command on the Window menu.

If your macro is designed to work with a worksheet template, you may want to apply many of the same protection measures to the template as well. For example, you may want to lock all the cells in the template except for the specific input cells in which you want the user to enter data.

The date-header macro can be simplified considerably by using a subroutine. Instead of repeating the function

=SELECT(,"RC[1]")

eleven times in this macro, you can enter that function in a cell named *RIGHT*, then call RIGHT as a subroutine when you need to use it.

Let's look at how this works. To begin, select cell C2 in *Macro1* and enter the name *RIGHT*. Then, select cell C3 and enter the function

=SELECT(,"RC[1]")

While cell C3 is selected, use the Define Name... command to name this cell *RIGHT* and to identify the macro as a command macro. Now, enter the function =RETURN() in cell C4. Next, select cell B4 and replace the function in that cell

=SELECT(,"RC[1]")

with the function =*RIGHT()*.

Now, when you run the macro, Microsoft Excel first selects the relative range specified by the function in cell B2 and then enters the text *Jan* in the first cell in that range. The function in cell B4, RIGHT, then "calls" the subroutine in cell C2. The function in cell C3

=SELECT(,"RC[1]")

moves the active cell one cell to the right. When Excel encounters the RETURN function in cell C4, it jumps back to cell B5 and calculates the function in that cell.

Of course, if you were actually going to use this function, you would want to replace all of the SELECT functions in column B with RIGHT functions. But this one example shows how subroutines can be used to simplify your macros. (Excel also allows you to use the GOTO function to branch one macro to another macro. We describe this function in Chapter 18, "Macro Functions.")

This example also illustrates how easy it is to edit your macros. Because the entries in a macro are just like the entries in a worksheet, you can edit them using the same techniques you learned in Chapter 2, "Worksheet Basics."

Conclusion

In this chapter, we have shown you how to create and use command macros. In the next chapter, we cover the many Microsoft Excel macro-language functions in detail. Then, in the third chapter in this section, we show you how to build user-defined function macros.

18

Macro Functions

*I*n Chapter 17, "Macro Basics," we introduced you to the concept of macro functions and gave you a few examples of how they could be used in macros. In this chapter, we explain the form and purpose of most of the Microsoft Excel macro functions. We save a few specialized functions for Chapters 19 and 20. For example, in Chapter 19, "User-Defined Functions," we look at the ARGUMENT and RESULT functions, which appear only in user-defined functions. In Chapter 20, "Customizing Excel," we look at functions like DIALOG.BOX and ADD.MENU which allow you to customize your Excel applications.

Arguments

Most macro functions require one or more arguments; a few don't require any arguments. All macro functions must end with parentheses. Even functions that don't require arguments—like the worksheet functions PI and RAND—must end with parentheses. For example, to choose the Copy command from within a macro, you must enter the function in the following form:

=COPY()

In functions that do require arguments, one or more of the arguments may be optional. If you omit an optional argument, you must still enter the comma that separates the omitted argument from the next argument. The commas serve as placeholders to preserve the order in which the arguments are presented. If no additional arguments follow the omitted argument or if you include no arguments at all, a comma is not necessary.

Excel's macro functions use four types of arguments: *text values, numeric values, logical values,* and *references*. In the following sections, we explain the ins and outs of each type of argument.

Text arguments

Text arguments are usually entered as literal strings, enclosed in quotation marks. For example, you use the function

    =ACTIVATE("Worksheet1")

to activate a document named *Worksheet1*. You can also use formulas or functions that return text values as the argument. For example, the function

    =ACTIVATE("Worksheet"&A10)

activates *Worksheet1* if cell A10 of the macro sheet contains the value 1. The function would activate *Worksheet2* if cell A10 contained the value 2.

Numeric arguments

Numeric arguments are usually literal numeric values. For example, you use the function

    =COLUMN.WIDTH(15)

to set the width of the selected columns to 15. However, you could also use the function

    =COLUMN.WIDTH(10+5)

instead. Or you could use the function

    =COLUMN.WIDTH(10+B2)

if cell B2 of the macro sheet contains the value 5.

Logical arguments

When logical arguments are required, most people use the logical values TRUE and FALSE. For example, to choose the Data Find command from a macro, you use the function

    =DATA.FIND(TRUE)

To choose the Data Exit Find command, you use the function

=DATA.FIND(FALSE)

However, you can use the values 1 and 0, respectively, instead of TRUE and FALSE. For example, you could use the functions

=DATA.FIND(1)

and

=DATA.FIND(0)

to enter and exit the Find mode.

Reference arguments

Reference arguments are the most troublesome of the four types of arguments. In most cases, reference arguments can be in any of three forms: A1, "R1C1", or "R[1]C[1]". Note that two forms are enclosed in quotation marks.

You must preface an A1-style reference with an exclamation point to denote a cell in the active worksheet; if you omit the exclamation point, Excel assumes you mean a cell in the macro sheet. For example, the function

=FORMULA.GOTO(!A1)

selects cell A1 in the active worksheet. The function

=FORMULA.GOTO(A1)

activates cell A1 in the macro sheet containing the FORMULA.GOTO function.

In most cases, "R1C1" and "R[1]C[1]" references do not need to be prefaced with an exclamation point to denote the current worksheet; in fact, they usually cannot be. For example, the function

=FORMULA.GOTO("R1C1")

selects cell A1 in the active worksheet; the function

=FORMULA.GOTO("R[1]C?")

selects the cell below the active cell. The functions

=FORMULA.GOTO("!R1C1")

and

=FORMULA.GOTO("!R[1]C?")

cause macro errors.

To specify a cell in a worksheet other than the current worksheet, you must preface the reference with the name of that worksheet and an exclamation point.

For example, the functions

=FORMULA.GOTO(Worksheet1!A1)

=FORMULA.GOTO("Worksheet1!R1C1")

=FORMULA.GOTO("Worksheet1!R[1]C")

all select a cell in *Worksheet1*, no matter which document is active at the time.

The principal advantage of the "R1C1" and "R[1]C[1]" forms is that they can be calculated. For example, the function

=FORMULA.GOTO("R"&A1&"C"&A2)

selects cell B1 in the current worksheet, if cells A1 and A2 of the macro sheet contain the values 1 and 2, respectively. You can also use functions like OFFSET, ACTIVE.CELL, and SELECTION as reference arguments. However, you sometimes need to use the REFTEXT function to convert the results of these functions to text.

Unfortunately, there are exceptions to these rules about calculated references. We point out these exceptions later, in the discussions of the functions to which they apply.

Command-equivalent functions

Most commands available on the Excel menus can also be chosen from within a macro. For example, the OPEN function instructs Excel to choose the Open... command, the PASTE.SPECIAL function instructs Excel to choose the Paste Special... command, and so forth.

Most of the commands that use dialog boxes (that is, the commands that are followed by an ellipsis on the menus) can be duplicated in a macro in either of two ways: You can select the desired dialog-box options yourself by entering the appropriate arguments in the corresponding macro function, or you can add a question mark (?) after the function name to instruct Excel to display the dialog box and allow the user to select the desired options manually. For example, the function that corresponds to the Goto... command on the Formula menu can be represented as either FORMULA.GOTO(*reference*) or FORMULA.GOTO?.

If you do not use the question mark, you must include the function's mandatory arguments. For example, in the case of the FORMULA.GOTO function, you must specify which cell you want Excel to select. When Excel evaluates this form of a function, it carries out the indicated action without displaying a dialog box.

When Excel evaluates the question-mark form of a function, it displays the same dialog box that you see when you manually choose the command that corresponds to that function. For example, when Excel evaluates the function FORMULA.GOTO?, it displays the Goto dialog box and pauses the execution of the macro until you click OK or Cancel. During the pause, you can change any of the settings in the dialog box.

When you use the question-mark form of a function, you can usually include or exclude one or more of its arguments. If you exclude an argument, the dialog box contains the default entry—the one you set when you issued the corresponding command manually. If you include the argument, Excel sets the specified option in the dialog box but leaves the dialog box open so that you can change or confirm the selections. For example, when Excel evaluates the function =FORMULA.GOTO?(!A1:A5), it displays the Goto dialog box, enters the reference $A$1:$A$5 in the Reference box, and then pauses. At that point, you can accept Excel's "suggestion" by clicking OK, or you can change the reference.

The following macro functions can be entered using the question-mark form:

=ALIGNMENT?()	=GALLERY.AREA?()
=APPLY.NAMES?()	=GALLERY.BAR?()
=ATTACH.TEXT?()	=GALLERY.COLUMN?()
=AXES?()	=GALLERY.LINE?()
=BORDER?()	=GALLERY.PIE?()
=CALCULATION?()	=GALLERY.SCATTER?()
=CELL.PROTECTION?()	=GRIDLINES?()
=CHANGE.LINK?()	=INSERT?()
=CLEAR?()	=MAIN.CHART?()
=COLUMN.WIDTH?()	=MAIN.CHART.TYPE?()
=COMBINATION?()	=NEW?()
=COPY.CHART?()	=OPEN?()
=CREATE.NAMES?()	=OPEN.LINKS?()
=DATA.DELETE?()	=OPEN.MAIL?()
=DATA.SERIES?()	=OVERLAY.CHART.TYPE?()
=DEFINE.NAME?()	=PAGE.SETUP?()
=DISPLAY?()	=PARSE?()
=EDIT.DELETE?()	=PASTE.SPECIAL?()
=EXTRACT?()	=PRINT?()
=FILE.DELETE?()	=PROTECT.DOCUMENT?()
=FONT?()	=ROW.HEIGHT?()
=FORMAT.FONT?()	=RUN?()
=FORMAT.MOVE?()	=SAVE.AS?()
=FORMAT.NUMBER?()	=SAVE.WORKSPACE?()
=FORMAT.SIZE?()	=SELECT.SPECIAL?()
=FORMAT.TEXT?()	=SORT?()
=FORMULA.FIND?()	=STYLE?()
=FORMULA.GOTO?()	=TABLE?()
=FORMULA.REPLACE?()	=WORKSPACE?()

File-menu functions

Excel uses functions that correspond to the commands on its File menu to open documents, save documents, print documents, and so forth.

The NEW function

The NEW function is the macro equivalent of the New... command on the File menu. The NEW function creates a new document from within a macro. The NEW function has the following form:

=NEW(*type*)

The *type* argument is a numeric code that describes the type of document you want to create. The following table shows the possible *type* arguments:

If you use...	Excel creates a new...
1	Worksheet
2	Chart
3	Macro sheet

For example, the function

=NEW(1)

creates a new worksheet.

The OPEN function

The OPEN function is the macro equivalent of the Open... command on the File menu. This function instructs Excel to open an existing document. The OPEN function has the following form:

=OPEN("*document*",*update*,*read only*,*format*,"*password*")

The *"document"* argument must be a text string that specifies the name of the document you want to open. The *update* argument is a logical value that tells Excel whether to update references to any nonresident linked worksheets. If the *update* argument is omitted, it is assumed to be TRUE. The *read only* argument is also a logical argument. If the *read only* argument is TRUE, Excel selects the Read Only check box in the Open dialog box. (Also, if this argument is TRUE, documents in versions of Excel earlier than 1.03 will not open.) If the *read only* argument is omitted, it is assumed to be FALSE. The *format* argument should be used only if the file specified by the *"document"* argument is a text file. If the file is delimited with tabs, the *format* argument should be 1; if the file is comma-delimited, the *format* argument should be 2. The *"password"* argument is a text string that specifies the password that lets you open your document. Do not include this argument unless the document specified by the *"document"* argument was saved with a password.

For example, the function

=OPEN("Worksheet2")

opens the document named *Worksheet2*.

The FILE.CLOSE and CLOSE.ALL functions

The FILE.CLOSE macro function closes the active document. This macro function is equivalent to the Close command on the File menu. (The FILE.CLOSE and CLOSE functions are equivalent functions.) The FILE.CLOSE function has the following form:

=FILE.CLOSE(*save*)

The *save* argument tells Excel whether to save any changes that were made to the document since it was last saved, before closing the document. This argument is optional. If included, it must be a logical value: TRUE if you want Excel to save the changes before closing the document; FALSE if you don't want Excel to save the changes. If this argument is omitted, Excel presents the standard Save Changes? box when the document contains unsaved changes.

The CLOSE.ALL function is the macro equivalent of the Close All command on the File menu. (To access this command, you press the Shift key as you open the File menu.) The CLOSE.ALL function, which takes no arguments, closes all unprotected windows open in the workspace. Excel presents the Save Changes? dialog box when any document contains unsaved changes.

The OPEN.LINKS and CHANGE.LINK functions

The OPEN.LINKS and CHANGE.LINK macro functions correspond to the Open and Change... buttons in the dialog box Excel presents when you select the Links... command from the File menu.

The OPEN.LINKS function opens all the documents linked to the active document. The form of this function is

=OPEN.LINKS(*"document name 1","document name 2",...,read only*)

The *"document name"* arguments of this function are text strings that identify the documents you want to open. You can specify up to 14 document names in one OPEN.LINKS function. For example, the function

=OPEN.LINKS("Worksheet1","Worksheet2","Worksheet3")

opens three worksheets (*Worksheet1*, *Worksheet2*, and *Worksheet3*).

The final argument of this function, *read only*, specifies whether the documents should be opened in read-only mode. The *read only* argument is optional. If included, *read only* must be a logical value: TRUE if you want the documents to be opened in read-only mode; FALSE otherwise. If this argument is omitted, read-only mode is assumed.

The CHANGE.LINK function changes the external references in the active document from one supporting document to another. The CHANGE.LINK function is equivalent to choosing the Links... command from the File menu, selecting from the Links dialog box the supporting document to unlink, clicking the Change... button, and then selecting from the Change dialog box the name of the new supporting document.

The form of the CHANGE.LINK function is

=CHANGE.LINK(*"old link"*,*"new link"*)

The *"old link"* argument is a text string that specifies the supporting document you want to unlink; *"new link"* is a text string that specifies the document you want to link to the active document. Both arguments are required.

Like many other functions, CHANGE.LINK has a question-mark form: CHANGE.LINK?. Unlike the question-mark form of many functions, this question-mark form requires an argument: *"old link"*. When Excel evaluates this command, it selects for unlinking the document specified by the *"old link"* argument and then displays the same dialog box as when you choose the Links... command from the File menu and click the Change... button.

You will often use the LINKS macro function in conjunction with the OPEN.LINKS and CHANGE.LINK functions. As we explain in the "Informational functions" section later in this chapter, the LINKS function returns a vertical array of the names of all the documents linked to the active document.

The SAVE function

The SAVE function is the macro equivalent of the Save command on the File menu. This function has the form

=SAVE()

As you would expect, this function saves the document in the active window to disk. If the document is already stored on the disk, Excel overwrites the stored version with the document currently on the screen. If the document is new and you specify a filename that already exists on the disk, Excel saves the document with that title, overwriting any existing file with that name.

The SAVE.AS function

The SAVE.AS function is the macro equivalent of the Save As... command on the File menu. The SAVE.AS function names the document and then saves it in a specified file.

The form of the SAVE.AS function is

=SAVE.AS("*document*",*type*,"*password*",*backup*)

The *"document"* argument is a text string that names the document. The *type* argument is a numeric code that identifies the type of file in which you want to save the document. The following table shows the meaning of each of the nine *type* arguments:

If you use...	Excel uses file type...	If you use...	Excel uses file type...
1	Normal	6	CSV
2	SYLK	7	DBF2
3	Text	8	DBF3
4	WKS	9	DIF
5	WK1		

If you omit the *type* argument, Excel saves the document in the form in which it was saved previously. (If the file is being saved for the first time, Excel saves it in the Normal form.) The *type* argument does not apply if the document you are saving is a chart.

The optional *"password"* argument is a text string that assigns a password to the document. (This argument should be used only when Excel is saving the document in the Normal or the WK1 format.) The *backup* argument (also optional) controls whether Excel makes a backup of the previous version of the file before overwriting it. When included, this argument must be a logical value: TRUE if you want Excel to make a backup; FALSE if you don't. If this argument is omitted, Excel repeats what it did the last time you saved the document. (If you haven't saved the document since opening or creating it, Excel does not create a backup.)

For example, the functions

=SAVE.AS("Test1",1,,FALSE)

and

=SAVE.AS("Test1",1)

save the active document in a worksheet file named *Test1* without a password and without making a backup. The function

=SAVE.AS("Test1",1,"abracadabra",TRUE)

saves the active document in a worksheet file named *Test1* with the password *abracadabra*, after making a backup of the previous version of the file.

The SAVE.WORKSPACE function

The SAVE.WORKSPACE function is the macro equivalent of the Save Workspace… command on the File menu. This function saves a list of all windows and documents that are open at the time you run the macro and, optionally, saves any documents that you've changed since they were last saved.

The form of the SAVE.WORKSPACE function is

=SAVE.WORKSPACE(*"name"*)

The *"name"* argument is a text string that specifies the name you want Excel to assign to the document that will contain a description of the workspace. If you omit the *"name"* argument, Microsoft Excel uses either *RESUME* or the name of the last workspace document, if any, opened during the current session.

The FILE.DELETE function

The FILE.DELETE macro function corresponds to the Delete… command on the File menu. This function deletes files from disk from within a macro.

The form of this function is

=FILE.DELETE(*"document"*)

The *"document"* argument is a text string that specifies the name of the document you want to delete. For example, the function

=FILE.DELETE(*"Worksheet1"*)

deletes the file named *Worksheet1* from the current directory.

The PAGE.SETUP function

The PAGE.SETUP function is the macro equivalent of the Page Setup… command on the File menu. This function allows you to define print parameters such as headers, footers, margins, and so on.

This function has several forms. If you are printing a worksheet document on an Apple LaserWriter or ImageWriter, you should use this form of the PAGE.SETUP function:

=PAGE.SETUP(*"header"*,*"footer"*,*left,right,top,bottom,headings,gridlines*)

In this form of the PAGE.SETUP function, *"header"* and *"footer"* are arguments that define the header and footer you want to include in the printed document. These arguments, which must be text strings, can include the special header and footer symbols you learned about in Chapter 9, "Printing the Worksheet." The *left, right*, *top*, and *bottom* arguments are numbers that describe, in inches, the left, right, top, and bottom margins that you want to include in the document. The *headings* and *gridlines* arguments are logical values that determine whether row and column headings and gridlines are included in the printed document.

For example, the function

=PAGE.SETUP("This is a header","-&p-",1,1,2,1,FALSE,FALSE)

defines a report with the following characteristics:

Argument	Characteristic
"header"	This is a header
"footer"	Page number, surrounded by dashes
left	1 inch
right	1 inch
top	2 inches
bottom	1 inch
headings	Not included
gridlines	Not included

If you are printing a worksheet on a TTY printer, you should use this form of the PAGE.SETUP function:

=PAGE.SETUP(*"header","footer",left,width,top,length,headings,"message"*)   ·

In this form, the *"header"*, *"footer"*, *left*, *top*, and *headings* arguments are identical to the same arguments in the previous form. The *width* argument is a number that specifies the width, in inches, of the print area on each page; the *length* argument is a number that specifies the length, in inches, of the print area. The *"message"* argument allows you to send a message (a setup string) to the printer. This argument must be a text string.

Note that all the arguments of the PAGE.SETUP function are optional. If you exclude any argument, Excel does not alter the corresponding setting.

If you want Excel to display the Page Setup dialog box, you should use the question-mark form of this function. To set up the printing of a chart, you should use yet another form of the PAGE.SETUP function. We present this form later in this chapter in the "Command-equivalent functions for charts" section.

The PRINT function

The PRINT function is the macro equivalent of the Print... command on the File menu. This function instructs Excel to print a document.

The form of the PRINT function is

=PRINT(*range,from,to,copies,draft,preview,parts,color,feed*)

The *range* argument is a number: 1 for all pages or 2 for a subset of pages. The *from* and *to* arguments are numbers that specify the starting and ending pages to print. These two arguments are ignored unless *range* is equal to 2. The *copies* argument is a number that tells Excel how many copies of the selected pages to print. The *draft* and *parts* arguments are included only for compatibility with the PC version of Excel. Consequently, they should be omitted. However, if you use the *preview* argument, be sure to include a comma placeholder for the *draft* argument; if you use a *color* and/or *feed* argument, be sure to include comma placeholders for both the *draft* and *parts* arguments.

The *preview* argument is a logical value that indicates whether you want to preview the material before printing. Use TRUE to select the Preview option or FALSE to deselect it. The *color* argument is a logical value that corresponds to the Print Using Color check box. Use TRUE to select the check box or FALSE to deselect it. The *feed* argument is a number that indicates which type of paper feed you want to use: 1 for Continuous; 2 for Cut Sheet.

All of these arguments are optional. If you omit them, Excel uses the settings that were specified the last time it printed the current document.

The OPEN.MAIL function

The OPEN.MAIL function is the macro equivalent of the Open Mail... command on the File menu. This function can be used only when you are connected to a Microsoft Mail 2.0 server and are signed into your mailbox. The form of this function is

=OPEN.MAIL(*"subject"*,*comments*)

The *"subject"* argument is a text string that specifies the name of the message you want to open. The *comments* argument is a logical value: TRUE if you want comments to be displayed; FALSE if you don't want comments displayed. The *comments* argument is optional; if you omit it, Excel assumes it is FALSE.

The SEND.MAIL function

The SEND.MAIL macro function corresponds to the Send Mail... command on the File menu. The function can be used only when you are connected to a Microsoft Mail 2.0 server and are signed into your mailbox. The form of this function is

=SEND.MAIL(*"recipient"*,*"subject"*,*return*)

where *"recipient"* is a text value (or an array of multiple text values separated by commas enclosed in curly braces) that specifies the recipients of the message. Each name can include the server name in this form:

recipient name@server name

If a server name is left out and the user name is on more than one server, Excel displays an error message. If *"recipient"* is omitted, Excel displays a dialog box with a list of recipients for the user to choose from.

The *"subject"* argument gives the name of your message. The *return* argument is a logical value that indicates whether the return receipt check box is activated or turned off. If TRUE, Microsoft Mail activates the Return Receipt check box; if FALSE, it turns off the check box. If the *return* argument is omitted, it is assumed to be FALSE.

The QUIT function

The QUIT function is the macro equivalent of the Quit command on the File menu. When Excel evaluates this function, it ends the current session. The form of this function is simply

    =QUIT()

The QUIT function accepts no arguments. If any of the documents that are open in the workspace contain unsaved changes, Excel asks if you want to save them before quitting.

Any macro functions that follow a QUIT function will not be executed.

Edit-menu functions

Excel uses functions that correspond to the commands on its Edit menu to cut information to the Clipboard, to clear cells, to insert and delete rows and columns, and so forth.

The UNDO function

The UNDO macro function corresponds to the Undo command on the Edit menu. When Excel evaluates this function, it reverses the effect of the previous editing command. The form of this function is simply

    =UNDO()

The function accepts no arguments.

The CUT function

The CUT function is the macro equivalent of the Cut command on the Edit menu. When Excel evaluates this function, it cuts to the Clipboard whatever is selected at the time. The form of this function is simply

    =CUT()

The function accepts no arguments.

You'll usually precede a CUT function with a function that selects one or more cells—for example, the SELECT or FORMULA.GOTO function. (We examine these functions later in this chapter in the "Action-equivalent functions" section.) Once you have used the CUT function, you usually use a PASTE or PASTE.SPECIAL function to paste the cut range somewhere else in the worksheet. We discuss these two functions, which correspond to the Paste and Paste Special... commands on the Edit menu, later in this chapter.

The COPY function

The COPY function is the macro equivalent of the Copy command on the Edit menu. When Excel encounters this function in a macro, it copies the current selection to the Clipboard. Like the CUT function, the COPY function does not take any arguments; its form is simply

    =COPY()

Also, like the CUT function, the COPY function usually is used in conjunction with the SELECT, FORMULA.GOTO, PASTE, and PASTE.SPECIAL functions.

The COPY.PICTURE function

The COPY.PICTURE function is the macro equivalent of the Copy Picture command on the Edit menu. (To access this command, you must hold down the Shift key while you select the Edit menu.) When Excel encounters this function in a macro, it copies the selected range to the Clipboard as a picture, instead of as a row/column range. The form of the COPY.PICTURE function is

    =COPY.PICTURE(*appearance,size*)

where both the *appearance* and *size* arguments are numbers: for both arguments, 1 displays the picture as shown on the screen, and 2 displays the picture as shown when printed. Omitting the *appearance* argument is equivalent to specifying the value 2; omitting the *size* argument is equivalent to specifying the value 1. If a worksheet or macro sheet is active, omit the *size* argument.

The PASTE function

The PASTE function is the macro equivalent of the Paste command on the Edit menu. When Excel encounters a PASTE function in a macro, it pastes the contents of the Clipboard into the current selection. Like CUT and COPY, the PASTE function does not take any arguments; its form is simply

    =PASTE()

You usually precede a PASTE function with a cell-selecting function such as SELECT or FORMULA.GOTO.

The CLEAR function

The CLEAR function is the macro equivalent of the Clear... command on the Edit menu. The form of this function is

=CLEAR(*parts*)

The *parts* argument is a numeric code representing the part of the selected entries you want to delete. The following table shows the available *parts* options:

If you use...	Excel clears...
1	All
2	Formats only
3 (or omitted)	Formulas only
4	Notes

For example, the function

=CLEAR(2)

clears the formats from whatever cells are selected at the time the macro evaluates this function.

The PASTE.SPECIAL function

The PASTE.SPECIAL function is the macro equivalent of the Paste Special... command on the Edit menu. The PASTE.SPECIAL function has three forms, depending on whether you're using the function in a worksheet or a chart. We cover the first form here; we cover the other two forms later in this chapter when we examine the chart functions.

When you are working in a worksheet, the PASTE.SPECIAL function allows you to paste the contents of the cut or copied cells into the selected paste range using special parameters. The worksheet form of this function is

=PASTE.SPECIAL(*parts,operation,skip blanks,transpose*)

The *parts* argument is a numeric value that tells Excel what to paste into the selected range; the *operation* argument is a numeric value that describes how you want the contents of the cut or copied cells to interact with any existing contents of the selected paste range. The following tables show the possible *parts* and *operation* values.

For the *parts* argument:

If you use...	Excel pastes...
1	All
2	Formulas only
3	Values only
4	Formats only
5	Notes only

For the *operations* argument:

If you use...	Excel performs this operation...
1	None
2	Addition
3	Subtraction
4	Multiplication
5	Division

The last two arguments, *skip blanks* and *transpose*, control the Skip Blanks check box and the Transpose check box. Both arguments must be logical values: TRUE if you want the check box to be turned on; FALSE (or omitted) if you want the check box to be turned off.

For example, if Excel evalutes the function

=PASTE.SPECIAL(3,2)

after cutting cells A1:B2 of a worksheet to the Clipboard and selecting cell C3, it adds the values of cells A1:B2 to the values of cells C3:D4. The function

=PASTE.SPECIAL(4,1)

simply assigns the formats of cells A1:B2 to cells C3:D4.

The PASTE.LINK function

The PASTE.LINK macro function corresponds to the Paste Link command on the Edit menu. The form of this function is simply

=PASTE.LINK()

It accepts no arguments.

When Excel encounters a PASTE.LINK function in a macro, it pastes a reference to the cell or range on the Clipboard into the selected cells. For example, suppose a macro has selected cell A1 in a worksheet named *Worksheet1*, chosen the Cut command, and then activated a worksheet named *Worksheet2* and selected cell B5.

At that point, PASTE.LINK causes Excel to enter the formula =Worksheet1!$A$1 into the current cell of the current worksheet—in this case, cell B5 of *Worksheet2*.

The EDIT.DELETE function

The EDIT.DELETE macro function corresponds to the Delete... command on the worksheet Edit menu. This function allows you to delete cells from the worksheet from within a macro.

The form of the EDIT.DELETE function is

=EDIT.DELETE(*direction*)

where *direction* is a number that tells which direction you want to shift the cells in the worksheet to fill the space left by the deletion. If *direction* is 1, Excel shifts cells left; if *direction* is 2, Excel shifts cells up. If you omit the *direction* argument, Excel "guesses" which direction it should shift the cells, based on the range you select. For example, suppose Excel encounters the function

=EDIT.DELETE()

while cells A1:E1 are selected. Because this range is wider than it is tall, Excel shifts cells A2:E16384 up one row. If you want Excel to shift the cells F1:IV1 five cells to the left, you use the function

=EDIT.DELETE(1)

instead.

If one or more entire columns or rows are selected when Excel encounters an EDIT.DELETE function, it ignores the argument (if any) specified by that function.

The INSERT function

The INSERT function is the macro equivalent of the Insert... command on the worksheet Edit menu. The INSERT function tells Excel to insert cells into a worksheet. The form of the INSERT function is

=INSERT(*direction*)

The *direction* argument is a number that tells which direction you want Excel to shift the cells in the worksheet when it inserts new cells. If *direction* is 1, Excel shifts cells to the right; if *direction* is 2, Excel shifts cells down. If you omit the *direction* argument, Excel "guesses" which direction it should shift the cells, based on the range you select. For example, suppose Excel encounters the function

=INSERT()

while cells A1:A5 are selected. Because this range is taller than it is wide, Excel shifts cells A1:IU5 right one row.

If you want Excel to shift cells A6:A16379 five cells down, you use the function

=INSERT(2)

instead.

If one or more entire columns or rows are selected, Excel ignores the argument (if any) specified by the INSERT function.

The FILL functions

The FILL.RIGHT, FILL.DOWN, FILL.LEFT, and FILL.UP functions are the macro equivalents of the Fill Right, Fill Down, Fill Left, and Fill Up commands on the Edit menu. These functions allow you to copy an entry across, up, and down several adjacent cells from within a macro. None of these functions takes an argument; their forms are simply

=FILL.RIGHT()

=FILL.DOWN()

=FILL.LEFT()

=FILL.UP()

Like the commands to which they correspond, these functions copy the entries from the leftmost, topmost, rightmost, or bottommost column or row of the range selected at the time to the rest of the selected range. Consequently, you usually use a range-selecting function like SELECT or FORMULA.GOTO to select a range before issuing these commands.

Formula-menu functions

Excel provides a number of functions that correspond to commands on its Formula menu. However, there are no macro equivalents of the Paste Function... and Reference... functions, which are used when entering formulas and functions into a worksheet. To enter formulas and functions within a macro, you must use the FORMULA and FORMULA.ARRAY functions. We examine these functions when we discuss action-equivalent commands later in this chapter.

The LIST.NAMES function

The LIST.NAMES function is the macro equivalent of clicking the Paste List button in the dialog box Excel presents when you choose the Paste Name... command from the Formula menu. This function accepts no arguments. Its form is simply

=LIST.NAMES()

When Excel encounters this function in a macro, it enters in the current worksheet or macro sheet a two-column or four-column table, respectively, of all the named cells, ranges, values, and formulas in that document. In most cases, you use a function like SELECT or FORMULA.GOTO to select the location of the table before you use the LIST.NAMES function.

The DEFINE.NAME function

The DEFINE.NAME function is the macro equivalent of the Define Name... command on the Formula menu. This function allows you to create names in your worksheets from within a macro. The form of the DEFINE.NAME function is

=DEFINE.NAME(*"name"*,*refers to,type,key*)

The *"name"* argument is a text string that specifies the name you want to define. The *refers to* argument is the cell reference, formula, or value you want to name.

If you want to name a cell or range, the *refers to* argument should be a reference to that cell or range in either A1 or "R1C1" form. For example, you use the function

=DEFINE.NAME("Test",!B2)

or

=DEFINE.NAME("Test","R2C2")

to assign the name *Test* to cell B2 of the active worksheet. If you omit the *refers to* argument, Excel applies the name specified by the *"name"* argument to the current selection. For example, if cells A1:B2 are selected when Excel evaluates the function

=DEFINE.NAME("Test")

Excel assigns the name *Test* to that four-cell range.

If you want to name a numeric value, you should use that value as the second argument of the DEFINE.NAME function. For example, you use the function

=DEFINE.NAME("Count",1)

to assign the name *Count* to the value 1. If you want to assign a name to a text string, you should use that string as the second argument of the DEFINE.NAME function. For example, you use the function

=DEFINE.NAME("City","New York")

to assign the name *City* to the string *"New York"*.

You also can use the DEFINE.NAME function to name a formula or function. To do this, you use the text form of that formula or function—with the reference style R*x*C*y* or R[*x*]C[*y*]—as the second argument of the DEFINE.NAME function. For example, to assign the name *Formula* to the formula =$A$1+5, use the function

=DEFINE.NAME("Formula","=R1C1+5")

If cell A1 is the active cell, the function

=DEFINE.NAME("Formula","=R[1]C[1]+5")

assigns the name *Formula* to the formula =B2+5.

To name the *result* of a formula or function, you can use that formula or function—with references in A1 form—as the second argument of the DEFINE.NAME function. For example, you use the function

=DEFINE.NAME("Result",!A1+5)

to assign the name *Result* to the result of the function

=$A$1+5

If cell A1 of the current worksheet contains the value 100 when Excel evaluates this DEFINE.NAME function, Excel assigns the name *Result* to the value 105.

The *type* and *key* arguments apply only if the active worksheet is a macro sheet. In that case, *type* is a numeric code that defines the type of the name: 1 for function; 2 for command; 3 for None ("*name*" does not refer to a macro). The *key* argument is a single-letter text string that defines the Command-key equivalent you assign to the name (if any). For example, the function

=DEFINE.NAME("Sample",!A2,2,"s")

assigns the name *Sample* to cell A2 of the current macro sheet; it then defines the name as that of a command macro and links the name to the Option-Command-S key combination.

The DELETE.NAME function

The DELETE.NAME function is the macro equivalent of clicking the Delete button in the Define Name dialog box. The form of this function is

=DELETE.NAME("*name*")

The "*name*" argument is the name you want to delete. It must be a text string, enclosed in quotation marks. Excel assumes that "*name*" defines a name in the active worksheet or macro sheet.

The CREATE.NAMES function

The CREATE.NAMES function is the macro equivalent of the Create Names… command on the worksheet Formula menu. The CREATE.NAMES function allows you to use the labels in the top row, left column, bottom row, or right column of a selected range as names for the cells in the adjacent row(s) or column(s). The form of the CREATE.NAMES function is

=CREATE.NAMES(*top row,left column,bottom row,right column*)

The four arguments are logical values that correspond to the four check boxes in the Create Names dialog box: Top Row, Left Column, Bottom Row, and Right Column. The logical value TRUE turns on the corresponding check box; the logical value FALSE (or nothing at all) turns it off.

For example, if cells A1:B2 are selected, the function

=CREATE.NAMES(TRUE)

instructs Excel to use the text values in cells A1 and B1 as the names of cells A2 and B2. The function

=CREATE.NAMES(,TRUE)

instructs Excel to use the text values in cells A1 and A2 as the names of cells B1 and B2. The function

=CREATE.NAMES(TRUE,TRUE)

instructs Excel to use the text values from cells A1, A2, and B1 as the names of cell B2.

The APPLY.NAMES function

The APPLY.NAMES function is the macro equivalent of the Apply Names… command on the Formula menu. This function instructs Excel to search for references to a specified cell or range within the formulas in the entire worksheet (or, if more than one cell is selected, within that selection) and replace the reference with the name of that cell or range. The form of the APPLY.NAMES function is

=APPLY.NAMES(*"name array",ignore,use row/col,omit col,omit row,order,append*)

The *"name array"* argument specifies the names you want to apply. This argument can be a text string that specifies a single name (for example, *"Test"*) or an array that specifies the names of more than one range (for example, {*"Test","Sample","Temp"*}).

The remaining arguments are optional. The *ignore* argument corresponds to the Ignore Relative/Absolute check box. The argument is a logical value: TRUE or omitted turns the check box on; FALSE turns it off. The *use row/col* argument corresponds to the Use Row and Column Names check box. This argument is also a logical value: TRUE or omitted turns on the check box; FALSE turns it off.

The *omit col* and *omit row* arguments are logical values that correspond to the *Omit Column Name If Same Column* and *Omit Row Name If Same Row* check boxes. If these arguments are TRUE or omitted, the corresponding boxes are turned on; if these arguments are FALSE, the check boxes are turned off. (Of course, these arguments are meaningful only when the *use row/col* argument is TRUE or omitted).

The *order* argument tells Excel which name to list first: 1 (or omitted) for the Row Column option; 2 for the Column Row option.

The *append* argument is a logical value which, if TRUE, replaces the name definitions most recently created by the Define Name... or Create Names... command as well as those in the *"name array"* argument. If *append* is FALSE or omitted, Excel replaces the name definitions specified in the *"name array"* only.

The NOTE function

The NOTE function is equivalent to the Note... command on the Formula menu. It adds or edits notes attached to the cells of an Excel worksheet or macro sheet. The form of the NOTE function is

=NOTE(*"text",reference,start,count*)

The *"text"* argument is a text string (up to 255 characters long) that specifies the note you want to attach. The *reference* argument tells Excel which cell you want to work with. (If you omit this argument, Excel attaches the note to the active cell). The *start* argument specifies at which character to begin the change. If you omit the *start* argument, Excel starts at the beginning of the note. The *count* argument specifies how many characters to replace. If you omit the *count* argument, Excel replaces the remainder of the note—that is, all the characters from *start* to the end of the existing note. If you omit both *start* and *count*, Excel replaces the entire note.

For example, suppose you want to add the note *Call in June about car insurance* to cell G477 in your worksheet. To do this, you use the function

=NOTE("Call in June about car insurance",!G477,1)

If you later want to change the note to *Call in July about car insurance*, you can use the function

=NOTE("July",!G477,9,4)

You use the function

    =NOTE(,!G477,1)

if you want to delete the note entirely.

The FORMULA.GOTO function

The FORMULA.GOTO function is the macro equivalent of the Goto... command on the Formula menu. You use it to select any cell or range in a worksheet from within a macro. The form of the FORMULA.GOTO function is

    =FORMULA.GOTO(*ref*)

The *ref* argument is a reference that specifies the cell or range you want to select, in A1, "R1C1", or "R[1]C[1]" form. For example, the functions

    =FORMULA.GOTO(!A1)

and

    =FORMULA.GOTO("R1C1")

both select cell A1 of the active worksheet; the function

    =FORMULA.GOTO("R[–1]C[–1]")

selects cell A1 if cell B2 is currently the active cell.

To select a cell in a worksheet other than the current worksheet, you must preface the reference with the name of that worksheet, followed by an exclamation point. For example, you use the function

    =FORMULA.GOTO(Worksheet2!C3)

or

    =FORMULA.GOTO("Worksheet2!R3C3")

to select cell C3 in *Worksheet2*.

The FORMULA.FIND function

The FORMULA.FIND macro function corresponds to the Find... command on the worksheet Formula menu. This function instructs Excel to search for a specified text string throughout the worksheet (or, if more than one cell is selected, in the current selection). The form of the FORMULA.FIND function is

    =FORMULA.FIND(*"find text",look in,look at,look by*)

The *"find text"* argument is the text string you want to search for. This string can contain the wildcard characters ? and *. The next three arguments—*look in*, *look at*, and *look by*—are numeric codes that specify the parameters for the search.

If *look in* is 1, Excel looks for *"find text"* in formulas (the contents of the cells of the worksheet); if *look in* is 2, Excel looks for *"find text"* in displayed values. If *look at* is 1, Excel looks for exact matches between *"find text"* and the contents of the worksheet; and if *look at* is 2, Excel looks for any entry that contains *"find text"*. If *look by* is 1, Excel searches by rows; if *look by* is 2, Excel searches by columns. If you omit any of the FORMULA.FIND function arguments, Excel uses whatever setting you specified the last time you used the Find... or the Replace... command during the current Excel session.

For example, the function

    =FORMULA.FIND("=A1",1,2,1)

causes Excel to look for the argument *=A1* in the contents of the cells of the active worksheet. Excel finds any formula that includes *=A1*. The search is conducted by rows. If Excel finds the string, it selects the cell that contains the string and moves on to the next line in the macro. If it cannot find the string, it displays an alert box telling you so. When you click OK, Excel proceeds to the next line in the macro.

You'll often use the FORMULA.FIND.NEXT and FORMULA.FIND.PREVIOUS functions (the macro equivalents of the Command-H and Command-Shift-H key combinations) in conjunction with the FORMULA.FIND function. We examine these functions later in this chapter in the section titled "Action-equivalent functions."

The FORMULA.REPLACE function

The FORMULA.REPLACE function is the macro equivalent of the Replace... command on the Format menu. This function instructs Excel to find text and replace text in the cells of a worksheet.

The form of the FORMULA.REPLACE function is

    =FORMULA.REPLACE(*"find text"*,*"replace text"*,*look at*,*look by*,*current cell*)

where *"find text"* is the string you want to search for and *"replace text"* is the string you want to substitute. As with the FORMULA.FIND function, you can use the wildcard characters ? and * in the *"find text"* argument.

The *look at* and *look by* arguments are numeric codes that specify the parameters for the search. If *look at* is 1, Excel looks for exact matches between *"find text"* and the contents of the worksheet cells. If *look at* is 2, Excel looks for any entry that contains *"find text"*. The *look by* argument controls the direction of the search: 1 to search by rows; 2 to search by columns.

The *current cell* argument is a logical value that tells Excel where to put the replacement text. If *current cell* is TRUE, Excel puts *"replace text"* only in the active cell (the cell that is active when Excel evaluates the FORMULA.REPLACE function). If you want to put the replacement text in only the active cell, you would usually first use the FORMULA.FIND function to select the appropriate cell before using the FORMULA.REPLACE function. If *current cell* is FALSE (or omitted), Excel puts *"replace text"* in every matching cell in the selected range (or the entire worksheet, if only one cell is selected).

For example, the function

=FORMULA.REPLACE("Sales","Gross Sales")

replaces the string *Sales* with *Gross Sales* throughout a worksheet or selection.

If any of the arguments of the FORMULA.REPLACE function is omitted, Excel uses whatever setting was specified the last time you chose the Find... or the Replace... command.

The SELECT.SPECIAL and SELECT.LAST.CELL functions

The SELECT.SPECIAL function is the macro equivalent of the Select Special... command on the Formula menu. The form of this function is

=SELECT.SPECIAL(*type,value,levels*)

The *type* argument is a numeric code describing what you want to select. The allowable *type* values are shown in the following table:

If you use...	Excel selects...	If you use...	Excel selects...
1	Notes	7	Row differences
2	Constants	8	Column differences
3	Formulas	9	Precedents
4	Blanks	10	Dependents
5	Current region	11	Last cell
6	Current array		

The *value* argument, which is optional, applies only to *type* arguments 2 and 3. The *value* argument tells Excel what type of value to select:

If you use...	Excel selects...
1	Numbers
2	Text
4	Logicals
16	Error

These codes can be added to specify more than one data type; that is, you can use code 3 (code 1 and code 2) to select both numbers and text.

The *levels* argument, also optional, applies only to *type* arguments 9 and 10. A *levels* argument of 1 selects the Direct Only option; 2 selects the All Levels option.

For example, the statement

    =SELECT.SPECIAL(2,1)

selects all cells in the worksheet that contain constant numeric values.

The SELECT.LAST.CELL function is the macro equivalent of selecting the Last Cell option from the dialog box that Excel presents when you choose the Select Special... command. Consequently, it is identical in action to the function

    =SELECT.SPECIAL(11)

The form of this function is simply

    =SELECT.LAST.CELL()

The SELECT.LAST.CELL function accepts no arguments. This function is included for compatibility with Excel 1.5, which has a Select Last Cell command on its Formula menu.

The SHOW.ACTIVE.CELL function

The SHOW.ACTIVE.CELL function is the macro equivalent of the Show Active Cell command on the Formula menu. When Excel encounters this function in a macro, it shifts the worksheet within the current window so that the active cell is in view. The form of this function is simply

    =SHOW.ACTIVE.CELL()

The SHOW.ACTIVE.CELL function accepts no arguments.

Format-menu functions

Excel provides a number of functions that correspond to the commands on the Format menu. These functions allow you to assign and delete formats, alter the alignment of cells, change the width and height of rows and columns, and so forth.

The FORMAT.NUMBER and DELETE.NUMBER functions

The FORMAT.NUMBER function is the macro equivalent of the Number... command on the Format menu. This function allows you to assign a numeric format to any cell in the worksheet from within a macro. The form of the FORMAT.NUMBER function is

    =FORMAT.NUMBER("*format*")

The *"format"* argument is a text string that represents the format you want to assign to the selected range. The *"format"* argument can be any one of the 21 built-in Excel formats, or it can be a user-defined format. For example, the function

    =FORMAT.NUMBER("0")

assigns the 0 format to the cells in the selected range. The function

    =FORMAT.NUMBER("0.000")

creates a new format, the *0.000* format, and assigns it to the selected range.

The DELETE.FORMAT function is the macro equivalent of clicking the Delete button in the dialog box that Excel presents when you select the Number... command from the Format menu. This function allows you to delete any user-defined formats from the worksheet. The form of this function is

    =DELETE.FORMAT(*"format name"*)

where *"format name"* is the exact name of the format you have created.

For example, after you have created the format *0.000*, you can use the function

    =DELETE.FORMAT("0.000")

to delete the format.

The ALIGNMENT function

The ALIGNMENT function is the macro equivalent of the Alignment... command on the worksheet Format menu. This function causes Excel to change the alignment of the entries in a selected range. The form of the ALIGNMENT function is

    =ALIGNMENT(*type*)

The *type* argument is a numeric code that defines the alignment you want for the selected range. This argument is required. The following table shows the available *type* options:

If you use...	Excel uses this Alignment option...
1	General
2	Left
3	Center
4	Right
5	Fill

For example, the function

    =ALIGNMENT(2)

left aligns all the entries in the selected range.

The FORMAT.FONT and STYLE functions

The FORMAT.FONT macro function corresponds to the Font... command on the Format menu. It assigns a font to the entries in the current selection. The form of this function is

=FORMAT.FONT(*"name",size,bold,italic,underline,strike,color,outline,shadow*)

The *"name"* argument is a text string that names the font you want to use; the *"name"* argument must match one of the names in the font list that appears when you choose the Font... command on the Format menu. The *size* argument is a numeric value that specifies the point size for that font; it can be any value from 1 through 127. The *color* argument is a numeric value from 0 through 8. The value 0 tells Excel to choose the color automatically; the values 1 through 8 correspond to the eight colors in the Font dialog box. The *bold, italic, underline, strike, outline,* and *shadow* arguments are logical values that correspond to the Style check boxes in the Font dialog box.

For example, when Excel encounters the function

=FORMAT.FONT("New York",10,FALSE,TRUE,FALSE,FALSE,3,FALSE,TRUE)

in a macro, it changes the font to italic, shadowed New York; the type size to 10-point; and the color to red.

Note that any of the nine arguments can be omitted. When you omit arguments, the attribute controlled by that argument does not change. For example, the function

=FORMAT(,24)

changes the point size of the entries in the current selection to 24 without changing any other attributes.

Excel provides another form of the FORMULA.FONT function for use in the chart environment. We examine this function—along with the other functions that correspond to commands on the various menus in the chart environment—later in this chapter.

The STYLE function is a subset of the FORMULA.FONT function. The STYLE function lets you control the use of bold and italic type in the worksheet. The form of this function is

=STYLE(*bold,italic*)

The *bold* and *italic* arguments are logical values that tell Excel which style options to turn on or off. If the argument is TRUE, the option is turned on; if the argument is FALSE, the option is turned off. If an argument is omitted, the corresponding attribute does not change. This command is included for compatibility with Excel 1.5, which has a Style... command on its Format menu.

The BORDER function

The BORDER function is the macro equivalent of the Border... command on the Format menu; it allows you to add and remove borders around cells in the selected range. The form of this function is

=BORDER(*outline,left,right,top,bottom,shade*)

The *outline, left, right, top, bottom,* and *shade* arguments are logical values that tell Excel which Border options to use. The logical value TRUE turns on the specified attribute; FALSE turns it off. If you omit an argument, Excel does not alter the corresponding attribute.

For example, the function

=BORDER(,,,,TRUE)

causes Excel to draw a border line at the bottom edge of every cell in the selected range, without affecting other borders already assigned to the cells of that range. You must use the function

=BORDER(FALSE,FALSE,FALSE,FALSE,TRUE,FALSE)

to ensure that the cells in the range have only a bottom border.

The CELL.PROTECTION function

The CELL.PROTECTION function is the macro equivalent of the Cell Protection... command on the Format menu. The form of this function is

=CELL.PROTECTION(*locked,hidden*)

The *locked* and *hidden* arguments are logical values that tell Excel which protection attributes to use. If an argument is TRUE, Excel turns on that attribute; if an argument is FALSE, Excel turns off that attribute. If an argument is omitted, Excel does not alter the corresponding attribute.

For example, the function

=CELL.PROTECTION(TRUE,TRUE)

locks and hides the entries in the selected range. The function

=CELL.PROTECTION(TRUE,FALSE)

locks the selected range without hiding it. The function

=CELL.PROTECTION(,FALSE)

shows the selected range without locking or unlocking it (that is, without changing the current setting of the *locked* argument).

The ROW.HEIGHT function

The ROW.HEIGHT function is the macro equivalent of the Row Height… command on the Format menu. This function changes the height of selected rows in your worksheet or macro sheet from within a macro. The form of this function is

=ROW.HEIGHT(*height,reference,default height*)

The *height* argument tells Excel how high you want the rows to be. The *reference* argument identifies the rows to be changed; this argument can be in A1, "R1C1", or "R[1]C[1]" form. The *default height* argument is a logical value: If TRUE, Excel sets the row height according to the height of the fonts used in those rows (in this case, the *height* argument is irrelevant and can be omitted); if FALSE or omitted, the *default height* argument has no effect.

For example, the function

=ROW.HEIGHT(20)

changes the height of the currently selected row(s) to 20. The function

=ROW.HEIGHT(5,!A1)

sets the height of row 1 to 5;. The function

=ROW.HEIGHT(,"R2C1:R5C1",TRUE)

sets rows 2 through 5 to the default height.

The COLUMN.WIDTH function

The COLUMN.WIDTH function is the macro equivalent of the Column Width… command on the Format menu. It changes the widths of columns from within a macro. The form of this function is

=COLUMN.WIDTH(*width,ref*)

The *width* argument is a numeric value that specifies the column width. The *ref* argument specifies the column(s) whose width you want to adjust. The *ref* argument is optional; if you omit it, Excel alters the width of whatever columns are selected at the time.

For example, the function

=COLUMN.WIDTH(15)

changes the widths to 15 of whatever columns are selected at the time. The function

=COLUMN.WIDTH(20,!A:C)

changes the widths of columns A, B, and C in the active worksheet to 20.

Unlike the ROW.HEIGHT function, the COLUMN.WIDTH function does not accept a logical argument that resets the specified columns to the default width.

The JUSTIFY function

The JUSTIFY function is the macro equivalent of the Justify command on the Format menu. It arranges the text in each cell of the selected range so that each part of the text is approximately the same width. This function takes no arguments. Its form is simply

=JUSTIFY()

For example, suppose cell A1 in your worksheet contains the label *The rain in Spain falls mainly on the plain, except when it falls elsewhere*. Cells A1:A4 are selected and the width of column A is set to 18. In this case, the function

=JUSTIFY()

divides the label into the following four parts:

The rain in Spain falls
mainly on the plain,
except when it falls
elsewhere.

Data-menu functions

Excel also provides functions that correspond to the commands on the Data menu. These functions allow you to find criterion-matching records in a database, extract criterion-matching records from a database, sort records, and so forth, from within macros.

The DATA.FORM function

The DATA.FORM function is the macro equivalent of the Form... command on the Data menu. The form of this function is simply

=DATA.FORM()

This function accepts no arguments. When Excel encounters a DATA.FORM function in a macro, it creates and displays an entry form for the current database. After Excel displays the form, you can work with it until you click the Exit button. At that point, Excel closes the entry form and continues executing the macro.

The DATA.FIND function

The DATA.FIND function is the macro equivalent of the Find... command on the Data menu. The form of this function is

=DATA.FIND(*find*)

The *find* argument is a logical value: TRUE instructs Excel to enter Find mode and find the first criterion-matching record in the database. Excel remains in Find mode until it encounters a DATA.FIND(FALSE) function, which cancels the DATA.FIND function.

Once you've used the DATA.FIND(TRUE) function to enter Find mode, you can use the DATA.FIND.NEXT and DATA.FIND.PREV functions to select the next and previous matching records. These functions are the macro equivalents of the Command-F and Command-Shift-F key combinations.

The EXTRACT function

The EXTRACT function is the macro equivalent of the Extract... command on the Data menu. This function allows you to copy criteria-matching records from a database into an extract range from within a macro. The form of this function is

=EXTRACT(*unique*)

The optional *unique* argument is a logical value: TRUE instructs Excel to extract only the unique records from the database. If *unique* is FALSE or omitted, Excel extracts all records that match the specified criteria.

The DATA.DELETE function

The DATA.DELETE function is the macro equivalent of the Delete command on the Data menu. It deletes the criteria-matching records from the database. The form of this function is simply

=DATA.DELETE()

It accepts no arguments.

The SET.DATABASE function

The SET.DATABASE function is the macro equivalent of the Set Database command on the Data menu. It assigns the name *Database* to the current selection. This function has the form

=SET.DATABASE()

It accepts no arguments. The function

=DEFINE.NAME("Database")

has the same effect.

The SET.CRITERIA function

The SET.CRITERIA function is the macro equivalent of the Set Criteria command on the Data menu. It assigns the name *Criteria* to the current selection. The form of this function is simply

=SET.CRITERIA()

It accepts no arguments. The function

=DEFINE.NAME("Criteria")

does the same thing.

The SORT function

The SORT function is the macro equivalent of the Sort... command on the Data menu. This function allows you to sort a selected database range from within a macro. The form of the SORT function is

=SORT(*sort by,1st key,order,2nd key,order,3rd key,order*)

The *sort by* argument specifies the orientation of the sort. This argument should be a numeric value: 1 to sort by rows; 2 to sort by columns. The *1st key*, *2nd key*, and *3rd key* arguments specify the sort keys. These arguments can be in reference forms A1, "R1C1", or "R[1]C[1]". The *order* arguments are numbers that tell Excel the order to sort in: 1 for ascending; 2 for descending.

For example, the function

=SORT(1,!$A$5,1)

sorts the rows of the current database into ascending order on the basis of the entries in the field in column A of the worksheet.

Interestingly, all of the arguments of the SORT function are optional. If you use the SORT function in its simplest form

=SORT()

Excel sorts the selected range by rows into ascending order based on the entries in the leftmost column of the range.

Because the SORT function operates on the currently selected range, you usually use a SELECT or FORMULA.GOTO function before each SORT function. We've already looked at the FORMULA.GOTO function; we examine the SELECT function in detail later in this chapter.

The DATA.SERIES function

The DATA.SERIES macro function corresponds to the Series... command on the Data menu. This function allows you to create series of evenly spaced numbers in your worksheets. The form of the DATA.SERIES function is

=DATA.SERIES(*series in,type,unit,step,stop*)

The *series in* argument is a number that defines the orientation of the series: 1 for Rows; 2 for Columns. The *type* argument is a number that describes the type of the series: 1 for Linear; 2 for Growth; 3 for Date. The *unit* argument is a number that describes the date unit you are working with: 1 for Day; 2 for Weekday; 3 for Month; 4 for Year. (This option is necessary only when you are creating a date series; that is, when the second argument is the value 3). The *step* argument is a number that describes the interval you want between each number in the series. The *stop* argument is the maximum value in the series.

For example, if cells A1:A10 are selected and cell A1 contains the value 2, the function

=DATA.SERIES(2,1,,2,16)

enters the values 4, 6, 8, 10, 12, 14, and 16 into cells A2:A8.

All DATA.SERIES-function arguments are optional. If you omit the *series in* argument, Excel uses the dimensions of the selected range to determine the fill direction: by rows if the selected range contains more columns than rows; by columns if the selection contains more rows than columns. If you omit the *type* argument, Excel creates a Linear series. If you omit the *unit* argument and the *type* argument is 3, Excel creates a Day series. If you omit the *step* argument, Excel uses a step value of 1. If you omit the *stop* argument, Excel stops the series at the rightmost (or, in the case of a by-column fill, bottommost) edge of the selected range.

The TABLE function

The TABLE function is the macro equivalent of the Table... command on the Data menu. It calculates "what-if" tables from within macros. The form of the TABLE function is

=TABLE(*row input,column input*)

The *row input* argument is a reference that specifies the row input cell. The *column input* argument is a reference that specifies the column input cell. These arguments can be in A1, "R1C1", or "R[1]C[1]" form. Only one argument is required if you are calculating a one-way table; both arguments are required for a two-way data-table calculation.

Before you use a TABLE function in a macro, you should have the macro set up and select the table range. To set up the table range, use the FORMULA function; to select the table range, use the FORMULA.GOTO or SELECT function. We've already looked at the FORMULA.GOTO function; we examine the SELECT and FORMULA functions in detail later in this chapter.

The PARSE function

The PARSE function is the macro equivalent of the Parse... command on the Data menu. It distributes the contents of a single column into multiple columns. This function is usually used on data imported from other applications. The form of this function is

=PARSE("*text*")

where "*text*" specifies how the text values in the leftmost column of the selected range should be parsed. The "*text*" argument should be identical to the entry you would make into the Parse Line field if you chose the Parse... command from the Data menu. For more information on the Parse... command, see Appendix A, "Linking to Other Programs."

Options-menu functions

Excel provides several functions that correspond to the commands on the Options menu. These functions make it possible for you to choose those commands from within a macro.

The SET.PRINT.AREA function

The SET.PRINT.AREA function is the macro equivalent of the Set Print Area command on the Options menu. It defines the current selection as the range Excel is to print when you choose the Print... command. The form of this function is simply

=SET.PRINT.AREA()

It does not accept any arguments.

You usually use a function like SELECT to select the range to print before you use the SET.PRINT.AREA function to define that range as the print area. We discuss the SELECT function later in this chapter.

The SET.PRINT.TITLES function

The SET.PRINT.TITLES function is the macro equivalent of the Set Print Titles command on the Options menu. The SET.PRINT.TITLES function ensures that the selected column(s) and/or row(s) will be printed on each page of the document. The SET.PRINT.TITLES function does not take any arguments. Its form is simply

=SET.PRINT.TITLES()

Before using the SET.PRINT.TITLES function in a macro, you should use a function like SELECT to select the rows or columns to use as the print titles. We show you how to do this later in this chapter.

The SET.PAGE.BREAK and REMOVE.PAGE.BREAK functions

The SET.PAGE.BREAK and REMOVE.PAGE.BREAK functions are the macro equivalents of the Set Page Break and Remove Page Break commands on the Options menu. They allow you to set and delete page breaks from within a macro. The forms of these functions are simply

    =SET.PAGE.BREAK()

and

    =REMOVE.PAGE.BREAK()

They accept no arguments.

Before using these functions, you should use a function like SELECT or FORMULA.GOTO to select the place where you want the page break inserted or removed. We've already discussed the FORMULA.GOTO function. We discuss the SELECT function later in this chapter.

The DISPLAY function

The DISPLAY function is the macro equivalent of the Display… command on the Options menu. It controls the display of gridlines, row and column headers, and zero values in the worksheet; it also lets you switch from viewing the values that are the results of formulas in the worksheet to viewing the formulas themselves.

The DISPLAY function has two forms. The first form is

    =DISPLAY(*formulas,gridlines,headings,zero,color*)

The *formulas, gridlines, headings,* and *zero* arguments are logical values that tell Excel which display options to turn on or off. If the argument is TRUE, the specified option is turned on; if the argument is FALSE, the specified option is turned off. The *color* argument is a numeric value from 0 through 8. A value of 0 corresponds to the Automatic setting; a value from 1 through 8 corresponds to the colors in the Display dialog box. If you omit any of these arguments, Excel does not alter the corresponding attribute.

For example, the function

    =DISPLAY(,FALSE)

turns off the display of gridlines in the worksheet. The function

    =DISPLAY(TRUE)

turns on the display of formulas.

The second form of the DISPLAY function lets you choose commands from the Info menu that appear when you choose the Show Info command from the Window menu. A detailed discussion of this form of the DISPLAY function is included with the discussion of the SHOW.INFO function, later in this chapter.

The STANDARD.FONT and FONT functions

The STANDARD.FONT function changes the default font in which your worksheet entries are displayed. It is the macro equivalent of the Standard Font... command on the Options menu. The form of the STANDARD.FONT function is

=STANDARD.FONT(*"name",size,bold,italic,underline,strikeout,color,outline,shadow*)

The arguments of this function are identical to those of the FORMAT.FONT function, which controls the display attributes of individual cells and ranges. The *"name"* argument is a text string that names the font you want to use. The *size* argument is a numeric value that specifies the point size for that font; it can be any value from 1 through 127. The *color* argument is a numeric value from 0 through 8: The value 0 tells Excel to choose the color automatically; the values 1 through 8 correspond to the colors in the Font dialog box. The *bold, italic, underline, strike, outline,* and *shadow* arguments are logical values that correspond to the Style check boxes in the Font dialog box.

Any of the arguments can be omitted. If the argument is TRUE, Excel turns on the option; if FALSE, it turns off the option. When you omit an argument, Excel does not change the corresponding attribute.

The FONT function is a subset of the STANDARD.FONT function. It allows you to select only the default font and type size for the worksheet. The form of this function is

=FONT(*"name",size*)

The *"name"* argument is the name of the font you want to use. The *size* argument is the point size you want to use. The *"name"* argument must match one of the names in the font list that appears when you choose the Font... command from the Format menu. The *size* argument can be any value from 1 through 127. Either of these arguments can be omitted. When you use the question mark form of this function, Excel displays the same dialog box it presents when you choose the Standard Font... command from the Format menu. This function is included for compatibility with earlier versions of Excel, which have a Font command on the Options menu.

The REPLACE.FONT function

The REPLACE.FONT function is included only for compatibility with Microsoft Excel for the IBM PC. You should not use it in macros designed for use with versions of Excel for the Macintosh.

The FREEZE.PANES function

The FREEZE.PANES function is the macro equivalent of the Freeze Panes and Unfreeze Panes commands on the Options menu. The FREEZE.PANES function freezes and unfreezes the top pane, the left pane, or both in the active document window from within a macro. The form of this function is

=FREEZE.PANES(*panes*)

The *panes* argument controls whether Excel freezes or unfreezes the panes. This argument is a logical value: TRUE freezes the horizontal motion of the leftmost pane of a vertical split or the vertical motion of the topmost pane of a horizontal split; FALSE unfreezes the active window's panes.

The PROTECT.DOCUMENT function

The PROTECT.DOCUMENT function is the macro equivalent of the Protect Document command on the Options menu. This function controls the global protection status of a document from within a macro. The form of this function is

=PROTECT.DOCUMENT(*contents,windows,"password"*)

The *contents* and *windows* arguments are logical values that determine whether protection is turned on or off for a document's contents or the position and size of the document. If the argument is TRUE, this function turns on protection; if the argument is FALSE, this function turns off protection. If you want to secure a document with a password or remove a password you have previously assigned, you must include the *"password"* argument.

The CALCULATION and PRECISION functions

The CALCULATION function is the macro equivalent of the Calculation... command on the Options menu. The form of this function is

=CALCULATION(*type,iteration,number of,change,update,precision,date*)

The *type* argument is a numeric code that represents the type of calculation you want: 1 is Automatic; 2 is Automatic Except Tables; 3 is Manual. The *iteration* argument is a logical value: TRUE turns on iteration; FALSE turns off iteration.

The next two arguments should be included only if the *iteration* argument is TRUE. The *number of* argument defines the maximum number of iterations Excel should perform each time the worksheet is calculated. It can be any value from 1 through 32,767. The *change* argument·is the maximum change that can occur from one iteration to the next without stopping the calculation.

The *update* argument is a logical value: TRUE activates the Update Remote References check box; FALSE turns it off. The *precision* argument is a logical value: TRUE activates the Precision As Displayed option; FALSE turns it off. The *date* argument is also a logical value: TRUE activates the 1904 Date System; FALSE activates the 1900 Date System. If an argument is omitted, Excel does not alter the corresponding setting.

The PRECISION function is the macro equivalent of choosing the Calculation... command from the Options menu and then selecting or deselecting the Precision As Displayed option. The form of this function is

=PRECISION(*displayed*)

If the *displayed* argument is TRUE or omitted, the Precision As Displayed option is turned off. If *displayed* is FALSE, Excel turns on the Precision As Displayed command. This function is included for compatibility with earlier versions of Excel, which have a Precision As Displayed command on the Options menu. This function duplicates the effects of the functions

=CALCULATION(,,,,,TRUE)

and

=CALCULATION(,,,,,FALSE)

The CALCULATE.NOW and CALCULATE.DOCUMENT functions

The CALCULATE.NOW function is the macro equivalent of the Calculate Now command on the worksheet Options menu. When Excel encounters this function in a macro, it immediately recalculates all documents that are active. The CALCULATE.NOW function has the form

CALCULATE.NOW()

It accepts no arguments.

The CALCULATE.DOCUMENT function is the equivalent of the Calculate Document command on the worksheet Options menu. (To access this command, you must hold down the Shift key while selecting the Options menu.) When Excel encounters this function in a macro, it immediately recalculates only the active document. The CALCULATE.DOCUMENT function has the form

CALCULATE.DOCUMENT()

Like the CALCULATE.NOW function, the CALCULATE.DOCUMENT function accepts no arguments.

The WORKSPACE and A1.R1C1 functions

The WORKSPACE function is the macro equivalent of the Workspace... command on the Options menu. The form of this function is

=WORKSPACE(*fixed,decimals,r1c1,scroll,status,formula,menu,remote,return,underlines*)

All arguments except *decimals*, *menu*, and *underlines* arguments are logical values. The *fixed* argument is a logical value that tells Excel whether to fix the decimal places: TRUE turns on the Fixed Decimal check box; FALSE turns it off. The *decimals* argument specifies the number of automatic decimal places to be fixed. If the *fixed* argument is FALSE, the *decimals* argument is ignored.

The *r1c1* argument tells Excel whether to use the R1C1- or A1-reference style: TRUE specifies the R1C1 style; FALSE specifies the A1 style. The *scroll*, *status*, and *formula* arguments are logical values that determine whether or not the scroll, status, and formula bars are displayed. If TRUE, Excel displays these structures; if FALSE, Excel hides them.

The *menu* argument is a text value that tells Excel which key you're using as an alternative menu key. The *remote* argument is a logical value that determines whether Excel ignores remote requests: TRUE for ignoring requests; FALSE for acknowledging the requests. The *return* argument is also a logical value. If TRUE, Excel moves the cell selector after you press the Return key; if FALSE, the cell selector does not move. The *underlines* argument is a numeric value that corresponds to the three underline options in the Workspace dialog box: 1 for On, 2 for Off, and 3 for Automatic.

Any of these arguments can be omitted. Excel does not alter the settings that correspond to omitted arguments.

The A1.R1C1 function provides another way to access the R1C1 option in the Workspace dialog box. This function allows you to change Excel's method of referencing cells from the A1 method to the R1C1 method and back again. The form of this function is

=A1.R1C1(*ref*)

If the *ref* argument is TRUE, Excel uses the A1 style; if *ref* is FALSE, Excel uses R1C1 style. If *ref* is omitted, Excel toggles the R1C1 setting to its opposite state. This function is included for compatibility with earlier versions of Excel, which have an R1C1 function on the Options menu. The effects of this function are identical to those of the functions

=WORKSPACE(,,TRUE)

and

=WORKSPACE(,,FALSE)

The SHORT.MENUS function

The SHORT.MENUS function is the macro equivalent of the Short Menus and Full Menus commands on the Options menu. These functions control whether Excel displays the short or full versions of its menus. The form of this function is

=SHORT.MENUS(*menu*)

The *menu* argument is a logical value. TRUE causes Excel to display short menus; FALSE causes Excel to display full menus.

Macro-menu functions

The RUN function is the only command from the Excel Macro menu that has a macro-function equivalent.

The RUN function

The RUN function starts the execution of one macro from within another. The form of the RUN function is

=RUN(*ref*)

The *ref* argument is a cell of a macro sheet—a cell that contains the first function in the macro you want to run. This reference can be in either the A1 or "R1C1" style. To specify a macro in a sheet other than the one that contains the macro with the RUN function, you must include the name of the macro sheet and an exclamation point at the beginning of the reference. For example, the functions

=RUN(Macro1!A15)

and

=RUN("Macro1!R15C1") ·

both run the macro that begins at cell A15 in the macro sheet *Macro1*.

Window-menu functions

Excel provides a number of functions that correspond to commands on the Window menu. These functions allow you to access those commands during the execution of a macro.

The NEW.WINDOW function

The NEW.WINDOW function is the macro equivalent of the New Window function on the Window menu. This function allows you to open a new window onto a worksheet. The form of this function is simply

=NEW.WINDOW()

It accepts no arguments. If you run a macro that contains the NEW.WINDOW function when the active window is a Chart window, Excel returns an error message.

The SHOW.CLIPBOARD function

The SHOW.CLIPBOARD function is the macro equivalent of the Show Clipboard command on the Window menu. The form of this function is simply

=SHOW.CLIPBOARD()

It accepts no arguments. When Excel encounters this function in a macro, it opens the Clipboard window onto the desktop. To close the Clipboard, you must use the FILE.CLOSE or CLOSE function.

The SHOW.INFO and DISPLAY functions

The SHOW.INFO function is the macro equivalent of the Show Info... command on the Window menu. The form of this function is

=SHOW.INFO(*enable*)

The *enable* argument is a logical value: TRUE reveals the Info window; FALSE activates the document linked to the Info window if the Info window is the active window.

While the Info window is open, you can use the following alternative form of the DISPLAY function

=DISPLAY(*cell,formula,value,format,protection,names,precedents,dependents,note*)

to control what information is displayed in the window. The nine arguments of this function correspond to the commands on the Info menu; all arguments except *precedents* and *dependents* are logical values. If TRUE, the item is turned on; if FALSE, the item is turned off; if omitted, the item's status does not change. The *precedents* and *dependents* arguments are numeric values that correspond to the options in the Precedents and Dependents dialog boxes: 0 for none; 1 for Direct Only; and 2 for All Levels.

The ARRANGE.ALL function

The ARRANGE.ALL function is the macro equivalent of the Arrange All command on the Window menu. The form of this function is simply

=ARRANGE.ALL()

It takes no arguments. When Excel encounters this function in a macro, it arranges all open document windows so they do not overlap.

The HIDE and UNHIDE functions

The HIDE and UNHIDE functions are the macro equivalents of the Hide and Unhide... commands on the Window menu. They conceal and redisplay document windows. The form of the HIDE function is simply

=HIDE()

It takes no arguments. When Excel encounters this function in a macro, it hides the active document.

The UNHIDE function redisplays, or "unhides," hidden windows. The form of this function is

=UNHIDE(*"window"*)

The *"window"* argument is the name of the window you want to redisplay. This argument is required.

Excel allows you to use the ACTIVATE function and perform other actions on hidden windows from within a macro. Thus, you can use the HIDE function to suppress the display of windows while a macro is running, eliminating the need for screen updating and thereby speeding macro processing.

The ACTIVATE function

The ACTIVATE function is the macro equivalent of selecting the name of a document from the list that appears at the bottom of the Window menu. The ACTIVATE function allows you to activate different windows from within a macro. The form of this function is

=ACTIVATE(*"window"*,*pane*)

The *"window"* argument is the name of the window you want to open; the *pane* argument is a numeric value that specifies which pane you want to work with. The following table shows the possible *pane* argument codes.

Code...	Refers to...
1	The top-left pane (the only pane, if the window is unsplit; the top pane, if the window is split only horizontally; the left pane, if the window is split only vertically).
2	The top-right pane (the right pane, if the window is split only vertically).
3	The bottom-left pane (the bottom pane, if the window is split only horizontally).
4	The bottom-right pane (the bottom pane, if the window is split only horizontally; the right pane, if the window is split only vertically).

If you have opened more than one window in a document and the *"window"* argument does not specify which window you want to work with, Excel activates the first window that displays that document. For example, suppose two windows are open in a document: *Worksheet1:1* and *Worksheet1:2*. The formula

=ACTIVATE("Worksheet1")

activates the *Worksheet1:1* window. If you want to work with the second window, you must use the argument *"Worksheet1:2"*.

If you omit the *"window"* argument, Excel activates the pane you request on the current document. If you omit the *pane* argument, Excel opens the window you request without changing the active pane.

Command-equivalent functions for charts

Excel provides a number of functions that correspond to the commands on the menus in its chart environment. Many of these functions are identical to functions that are available in other environments. The File, Edit, Gallery, Chart, and Format menus, however, contain commands that are unique to—or work differently in— the chart environment. We take a look at the macro equivalents of those commands in this section.

File-menu functions

The functions that correspond to most of the commands on the chart-environment File menu are identical to those that correspond to the same commands in other environments. However, the PAGE.SETUP function is different for the chart environment. Specifically, it has the form

=PAGE.SETUP(*"header"*,*"footer"*,*left*,*right*,*top*,*bottom*,*size*)

The first six arguments in this form are equivalent to the first six arguments of the worksheet form of this function. The *"header"* and *"footer"* arguments are text strings that define the header and footer you want to include in the report; *left*, *right*, *top*, and *bottom* are numeric values that describe, in inches, the left, right, top, and bottom margins that you want to include in the document.

The final argument, *size*, is unique to the chart form of the PAGE.SETUP function. This argument is a numeric value: 1 if Excel scales the document to screen size; 2 if Excel scales the document to fit the printed page; and 3 if Excel scales the document to fill the printed page.

All the arguments of the PAGE.SETUP function are optional. If you exclude any argument, Excel does not alter the corresponding setting.

Edit-menu functions

The functions that correspond to most of the commands on the chart-environment Edit menu are identical to those that correspond to the same commands in the worksheet and macro environments. However, one function, COPY.CHART, is unique to the chart environment, and another function, PASTE.SPECIAL, has a different form for charts.

The COPY.CHART function

The COPY.CHART function is the macro equivalent of the Copy Chart… command on the Edit menu in the chart environment of earlier versions of Excel. The form of this function is

=COPY.CHART(*as shown*)

The *as shown* argument is a number that determines how Excel copies the chart. If *as shown* is 1 (or omitted), Excel copies the chart to the Clipboard as it appears on the screen; if *as shown* is 2, Excel copies the chart to the Clipboard as it would appear when printed.

The effect of this function is identical to that of the COPY.PICTURE function with its *appearance* argument omitted. For example, the functions

=COPY.CHART(1)

and

=COPY.PICTURE(,1)

both copy the chart to the Clipboard as the chart appears on the screen.

The PASTE.SPECIAL function

The PASTE.SPECIAL function is the macro equivalent of the Paste Special… command on the Edit menu. When used with a chart, PASTE.SPECIAL has two forms.

The first form,

=PASTE.SPECIAL(*values in,series names,categories,replace*)

allows you to paste data series into a chart from a worksheet. The *values in* argument is a number that tells Excel how the values are organized: 1 for in rows; 2 for in columns. The *series names* argument tells Excel whether or not to use the entries in the first row of the selection as series names: TRUE for yes; FALSE for no. Similarly, the *categories* argument tells Excel whether to use the entries in the first column of the selection as category labels: TRUE for yes; FALSE for no. The *replace* argument tells Excel whether to use the categories from the original range as data-series categories: TRUE for yes; FALSE for no.

The second chart-environment form of the PASTE.SPECIAL function,

=PASTE.SPECIAL(*parts*)

pastes portions of one chart into another chart. This form of the PASTE.SPECIAL function emulates the action of the Paste Special... command after you have selected a chart and chosen the Copy command.

The single argument of this form of the PASTE.SPECIAL function is a numeric code that tells Excel which parts of the selected chart should be pasted into the active document. The following table shows the possible values for the *parts* argument:

If you use...	Excel pastes...
1 (or omitted)	Formats and formulas
2	Formats only
3	Formulas only

Gallery-menu functions

Excel provides a group of macro functions that correspond to the commands on the chart-environment Gallery menu. These functions allow you to change the type of a chart within the context of a macro.

The GALLERY.AREA, GALLERY.BAR, GALLERY.COLUMN, GALLERY.LINE, GALLERY.PIE, and GALLERY.SCATTER functions

The functions that correspond to the first six commands on the Gallery menu share the same form:

=GALLERY.*TYPE*(*number,delete overlay*)

where *TYPE* specifies the type of chart: AREA, BAR, COLUMN, LINE, PIE, or SCATTER. The *number* argument is a numeric value that represents one of the options in the gallery for the specified type of chart. The *delete overlay* argument is a logical value that specifies whether or not Excel is to delete the overlay chart, if there is one: TRUE to delete the overlay chart and apply the new format to the main chart; FALSE (or no value at all) to keep the overlay chart and apply the new format to the main or the overlay chart, whichever is selected.

For example, the function

=GALLERY.PIE(1,TRUE)

changes the type of the chart in the active window to the first pie-chart format in the gallery—a basic pie chart—and deletes the overlay chart. The function

=GALLERY.BAR(2,FALSE)

changes the type of the main or the overlay chart—whichever is selected—to the second format in the bar-chart gallery.

The COMBINATION function

The COMBINATION function is the macro equivalent of the Combination... command on the Gallery menu. The COMBINATION function sets the type of the active chart to one of the five Excel combination-chart types from within a macro. The form of this function is

=COMBINATION(*type*)

The *type* argument is a numeric code that represents one of the five combination-chart types in the Combination dialog box. For example, the function

=COMBINATION(1)

changes the type of the current chart to a combined column/line chart.

The PREFERRED and SET.PREFERRED functions

The PREFERRED macro function corresponds to the Preferred command on the Gallery menu. The form of this function is simply

=PREFERRED()

It accepts no arguments. When Excel evaluates this function, it changes the current chart to the preferred type—whatever type of chart was displayed the last time you chose the Set Preferred... command.

The SET.PREFERRED function is the macro equivalent of the Set Preferred... command on the Gallery menu. The form of this function is simply

=SET PREFERRED()

It accepts no arguments. When Excel evaluates this function, it makes the current type of chart the preferred type.

Chart-menu functions

Excel provides a number of macro functions that correspond to the items on the Chart menu. These functions allow you to choose Chart-menu commands from within a macro.

The ATTACH.TEXT function

The ATTACH.TEXT function is the macro equivalent of the Attach Text... command on the Chart menu. The ATTACH.TEXT function attaches text to various parts of a chart. The form of this function is

=ATTACH.TEXT(*attach to,series,point*)

The *attach to* argument is a numeric code that tells Excel where to attach the text:

If you use...	Excel attaches the text to...
1	Chart title
2	Value axis
3	Category axis
4	Series or data point

If the *attach to* argument is 4, you use the *series* and *point* arguments to tell Excel the numbers of the series and the data point within the series to work with.

Importantly, the ATTACH.TEXT function enters only default text (*Title, Y, X,* and so forth). To change this text, you must follow the ATTACH.TEXT function with a FORMULA function. As long as the text is selected when Excel evaulates the FORMULA function, the text specified by that function replaces the default text. We examine the FORMULA function later in this chapter.

The ADD.ARROW and DELETE.ARROW functions

The ADD.ARROW and DELETE.ARROW macro functions correspond to the Add Arrow and Delete Arrow commands on the Chart menu. The forms of these functions are simply

=ADD.ARROW()

=DELETE.ARROW()

These functions accept no arguments.

The ADD.ARROW function adds an arrow to a chart; the DELETE.ARROW function removes an arrow. Before using the DELETE.ARROW function, you must select the arrow to delete. To do this, you use the SELECT function, which we examine later in this chapter. After you've added an arrow to a chart, you can use the FORMAT.SIZE and FORMAT.MOVE functions to position it on the chart. We talk about these functions later in this section.

The LEGEND function

The LEGEND function is the macro equivalent of the Add Legend and Delete Legend commands on the Chart menu. The form of this function is

=LEGEND(*add*)

The *add* argument is a logical value: if TRUE, Excel adds a legend to the current chart; if FALSE, Excel removes the legend from the chart.

The AXES function

The AXES function is the macro equivalent of the Axes... command on the Chart menu. The AXES function tells Excel which axes to display in the current chart. The form of this function is

=AXES(*main category,main value,overlay category,overlay value*)

The *main category, main value, overlay category,* and *overlay value* arguments are logical values that correspond to the four choices in the Axes dialog box. The first two arguments apply to the main chart; the third and fourth arguments apply to an overlay chart. (The third and fourth options appear in the Axes dialog box only when you have an overlay chart.) A value of TRUE displays the appropriate axis; a value of FALSE hides the axis. Any of these arguments can be omitted. If you omit an argument, Excel does not change the display status of the axis controlled by that argument.

The GRIDLINES function

The GRIDLINES macro function corresponds to the Gridlines... command on the Chart menu. It controls whether Excel display gridlines in the current chart. The form of this function is

=GRIDLINES(*category major,category minor,value major,value minor*)

The *category major, category minor, value major,* and *value minor* arguments are logical values that represent the four choices in the Gridlines dialog box. The first two arguments apply to the category axis; the third and fourth arguments apply to the value axis. The logical value TRUE displays the appropriate gridline; the value FALSE hides that gridline. If you omit an argument, Excel does not change the display status of the gridline controlled by that argument.

The ADD.OVERLAY and DELETE.OVERLAY functions

The ADD.OVERLAY and DELETE.OVERLAY functions are the macro equivalents of the Add Overlay and Delete Overlay commands on the Chart menu. These functions control whether the current chart is a combination chart. The forms of these functions are simply

=ADD.OVERLAY()

=DELETE.OVERLAY()

Neither function accepts an argument. When Excel evaluates an ADD.OVERLAY function, it turns the current chart into a combination chart; when Excel evaluates a DELETE.OVERLAY function, it turns the chart back into one of the six single chart types.

The SELECT.CHART function

The SELECT.CHART function is the macro equivalent of the Select Chart command on the Chart menu. The form of this function is simply

=SELECT.CHART()

It accepts no arguments. When Excel encounters this function in a macro, it selects the entire active chart.

The SELECT.PLOT.AREA function

The SELECT.PLOT.AREA function is the macro equivalent of the Select Plot Area command on the Chart menu. The form of this function is simply

=SELECT.PLOT.AREA()

The SELECT.PLOT.AREA function accepts no arguments. When Excel evaluates this function, it selects the plot area of the current chart. In early versions of Excel, you must use the SELECT(*"plot"*) function to achieve this effect.

Format-menu functions

Microsoft Excel provides several macro functions that correspond to the commands on the Format menu in the chart environment. These functions allow you to choose the Format-menu commands from within a macro.

The PATTERNS function

The PATTERNS macro function corresponds to the Patterns... command on the chart-environment Format menu. It changes the patterns and colors of the selected chart object.

The PATTERNS function has five forms, depending on the object you select:

Object selected	Function form
Chart, plot area, legend, text label, area, or bar	=PATTERNS(*BAuto,BStyle,BColor,BWeight,shadow, AAuto,APattern,AFore,ABack,invert,apply*)
Axis	=PATTERNS(*LAuto,LStyle,LColor, LWeight,TMajor, TMinor,TLabel*)
Gridline, hi-lo line, or drop line	=PATTERNS(*LAuto,LStyle,LColor,LWeight*)
Arrow	=PATTERNS(*LAuto,LStyle,LColor,LWeight, HWidth, HLength,HType*)
Data line	=PATTERNS(*LAuto,LStyle,LColor,LWeight, MAuto, MStyle,MFore,MBack,apply*)

The following table explains the arguments of the PATTERNS function:

Argument	Controls	Code	Action
BAuto	Automatic border settings	0 1 2	Set by user. Automatic. Invisible.
BStyle	Border-style options	1–8	Selects one of eight line styles.
BColor	Border-color options	1–8	Selects one of eight color options.
BWeight	Border-weight options	1–3	Selects one of three weight options.
shadow	Shadow check box	TRUE	Turns on check box.
		FALSE	Turns off check box.
AAuto	Automatic area settings	0 1 2	Set by user. Automatic. Invisible.
APattern	Area patterns	1–16	Selects one of 16 area patterns. .
AFore	Area foreground color	1–8	Selects one of eight foreground colors.
ABack	Area background color	1–8	Selects one of eight background colors.
invert	Invert if Negative check box	TRUE FALSE	Turns on check box. Turns off check box (does not apply to area, pie, or scatter charts).

(continued)

Argument	Controls	Code	Action
apply	Apply to All check box	TRUE	Turns on check box.
		FALSE	Turns off check box.
LAuto	Automatic line settings	0 1 2	Set by user. Automatic. Invisible.
LStyle	Line-style options	1–8	Selects one of eight line styles.
LColor	Line-color options	1–8	Selects one of eight color options.
LWeight	Line-weight options	1–3	Selects one of three weight options.
TMajor	Major tick-mark type	1 2 3 4	Invisible. Inside. Outside. Cross.
TMinor	Minor tick-mark type	1 2 3 4	Invisible. Inside. Outside. Cross.
TLabel	Tick-mark position	1 2 3 4	None. Low. High. Next to axis.
HWidth	Arrowhead width	1 2 3	Narrow. Medium. Wide.
HLength	Arrowhead length	1 2 3	Short. Medium. Long.
HType	Arrowhead type	1 2 3	No head. Open head. Closed head.
MAuto	Automatic marker settings	0 1 2	Set by user. Automatic. Invisible.
MStyle	Marker style	1–7	Selects one of seven style options.

(continued)

Argument	Controls	Code	Action
MFore	Marker foreground color	1–8	Selects one of eight foreground colors.
MBack	Marker background color	1–8	Selects one of eight background colors.

If you omit any of these arguments, Excel does not alter the settings that correspond to that argument.

Because the PATTERNS function acts upon the chart object that is selected at the time, you usually precede it with a SELECT command. Due to the complexity of the PATTERNS function, we recommend that you record it, rather than entering it manually.

The FORMAT.FONT function

The FORMAT.FONT macro function corresponds to the Font... command on the Format menu in the chart environment. This function changes the display attributes of the selected chart object. The form of the FORMAT.FONT function is

=FORMAT.FONT(*color,background,apply,"name",size,bold,italic,underline, strike,outline,shadow*)

The *color* argument is a number from 0 through 8. When this argument is 0, Excel chooses the color automatically; when this argument is a number in the range 1 through 8, Excel chooses one of the corresponding eight colors in the Font dialog box.

The *background* argument is a numeric code that tells Excel what type of background to use. The following table lists the possible *background* values:

If you use...	Excel uses this background...
1	Automatic
2	Transparent
3	White Out

The *apply* argument is a logical value that corresponds to the Apply to All check box: TRUE turns it on; FALSE turns it off. This argument applies only when you format data labels. The *"name"* argument specifies the name of the font to use and must be entered as text enclosed in quotation marks. The *size* argument tells Excel the type size to use, in points. The *bold, italic, underline, strike, outline,* and *shadow* arguments are logical values that correspond to the Style check boxes in the Font dialog box: TRUE turns on the check box; FALSE turns it off. If you omit an argument, Excel does not change the setting controlled by that argument.

In most cases, you use the SELECT function to select a chart object before using the FORMAT.FONT function.

The FORMAT.TEXT function

The FORMAT.TEXT macro function corresponds to the Text... command on the Format menu in the chart environment. This function changes the appearance of any text in the selected chart object. The form of the FORMAT.TEXT function is

=FORMAT.TEXT(*x,y,vertical,text,size,value,key*)

The *x* argument tells Excel how to align the text horizontally: 1 for left; 2 for center; 3 for right. The *y* argument tells Excel how to align the text vertically: 1 for top; 2 for center; 3 for bottom.

The *vertical*, *text*, and *size* arguments are logical values that correspond to the Vertical Text, Automatic Text, and Automatic Size check boxes in the Text dialog box: TRUE turns on the corresponding option; FALSE turns it off. The *value* and *key* arguments are logical values that correspond to the Show Value and Show Key check boxes in the Text dialog box. The *value* and *key* arguments apply only when the selected text is an attached data label. If you omit an argument, Excel does not change the status of the setting controlled by that argument.

In most cases, you use the SELECT function to select a chart object before using the FORMAT.TEXT function.

The SCALE function

The SCALE macro function corresponds to the Scale... command on the Format menu in the chart environment. It has two forms: one for category axes and one for value axes. (In scatter diagrams, both axes are treated as value axes.)

To change the scale of a category axis, you should use this form of the SCALE function:

=SCALE(*cross,labels,marks,between,reverse,max*)

The *cross* argument is a numeric argument that specifies where the value axis should cross the category axis. The *labels* argument—also numeric—tells Excel how many categories to put between tick-mark labels. The *marks* argument tells Excel how many categories to put between tick marks.

The last three arguments—*between, reverse,* and *max*—are logical values. If the *between* argument is TRUE, the value axis crosses the category axis between categories. If *reverse* is TRUE, Excel displays the categories in reverse order. If *max* is TRUE, the value axis crosses the category axis at the maximum category. If any of the last three arguments are FALSE, the corresponding check boxes in the Scale dialog box are turned off. If you omit an argument, Excel does not change the setting controlled by that argument.

To change the scale of a value axis, you should use this form of the SCALE function:

=SCALE(*min,max,major,minor,cross,log,reverse,maximum*)

The first five arguments—*min, max, major, minor,* and *cross*—correspond to the first five options in the Scale dialog box. Each argument can be the value TRUE or a number. If you enter TRUE, Excel uses the automatic scale for that option. If you enter a number, the number is used for that option. There are no FALSE values. The *min* argument specifies the minimum point on the value-axis scale; the *max* argument specifies the maximum point. The *major* and *minor* arguments define the distances between the major and minor tick marks. The *cross* argument tells Excel where the category axis crosses the value axis.

The last three arguments—*log, reverse,* and *maximum*—are logical values. If *log* is TRUE, Excel uses the logarithmic scale. If *reverse* is TRUE, Excel lists the values in reverse order. If *maximum* is TRUE, the value axis crosses the category axis at the maximum category.

Any of these arguments can be omitted. If you omit an argument, Excel does not alter the setting controlled by that argument.

The FORMAT.LEGEND function

The FORMAT.LEGEND function is the macro equivalent of the Legend command on the Format menu in the chart environment. This function controls the position of the legend on a chart. The form of the FORMAT.LEGEND function is

=FORMAT.LEGEND(*position*)

The *position* argument is a numeric code that tells Excel where to display the legend. The following table shows the possible position arguments:

If you use...	Excel positions the legend...
1	Bottom
2	Corner
3	Top
4	Vertical

Before using this function, you must select the legend. In most cases, you use the SELECT function to do this.

The MAIN.CHART and MAIN.CHART.TYPE functions

The MAIN.CHART function is the macro equivalent of the Main Chart... command on the Format menu in the chart environment. It allows you to change the main chart type. The form of the MAIN.CHART function is

=MAIN.CHART(*type,stack,100,vary,overlap,drop,hilo,overlap%,cluster,angle*)

The *type* argument is a number that specifies the type of chart to use. The following table shows the various *type* options:

If you use...	Excel creates...
1	Area chart
2	Bar chart
3	Column chart
4	Line graph
5	Pie chart
6	Scatter diagram

The *stack*, *100*, *vary*, *overlap*, *drop*, and *hilo* arguments correspond to the check boxes in the Format group box. They are logical values. If an argument is TRUE, Excel turns on the corresponding option; if an argument is FALSE, Excel turns the option off; if an argument is omitted, the option does not change.

The *overlap%* argument is a number that specifies the percentage of overlap between markers in the chart. The *cluster* argument is a number that specifies the spacing between the clusters of bars or columns. The *angle* argument is a number that sets the angle of the first pie slice in a pie chart.

For example, the macro

=MAIN.CHART(5,FALSE,FALSE,FALSE,FALSE,FALSE,FALSE,0,0,20)

defines the chart type as a pie chart whose first slice is tilted at 20 degrees.

Not all of these arguments apply to every type of chart. Excel ignores arguments that don't apply to the current chart type.

The MAIN.CHART.TYPE function is included for compatibility with Excel macros written with Excel versions 1.0 through 1.5. This function is the macro equivalent of the Main Chart Type... command, which appears on the Chart menu in those versions of Excel. The form of this function is

=MAIN.CHART.TYPE(*type*)

The *type* argument is a numeric value that specifies the type of chart. The allowable values for this argument are the same as the values allowed for the *type* argument of the MAIN.CHART function. In fact, you can achieve the effect of the MAIN.CHART.TYPE function by using the MAIN.CHART function with only its *type* argument.

If you use the question-mark form of the MAIN.CHART.TYPE function, Excel displays the dialog box for the Main Chart... command.

The OVERLAY and OVERLAY.CHART.TYPE functions

The OVERLAY function is the macro equivalent of the Overlay... command on the Format menu in the chart environment. This function allows you to define the type of overlay chart to use with the current chart. You must have already added an overlay chart to your main chart before using the OVERLAY function. The form of the OVERLAY function is

=OVERLAY(*type,stack,100,vary,overlap,drop,hilo,overlap% ,cluster,angle,series,auto*)

The *type* argument is a number that specifies the type of chart you want to overlay on the active chart. The following table shows the various *type* options:

If you use...	Excel creates...
1	Area chart
2	Bar chart
3	Column chart
4	Line graph
5	Pie chart
6	Scatter diagram

The *stack, 100, vary, overlap, drop,* and *hilo* arguments correspond to the check boxes in the Format group box. They are logical values. If an argument is TRUE, Excel activates the corresponding option; if an argument is FALSE, Excel turns the option off; if an argument is omitted, the option is not affected.

The *overlap%* argument is a number that specifies the percentage of overlap between markers in the chart. The *cluster* argument is a number that specifies the spacing between the clusters of bars or columns. The *angle* argument is a number that sets the angle of the first pie slice in a pie chart. The *series* argument is the number of the first series in the overlay chart. The *auto* argument is a logical value that activates or turns off the Automatic Series Distribution check box. Excel ignores arguments that don't apply to the specified type of chart.

For example, the macro

=OVERLAY(4,FALSE,FALSE,FALSE,FALSE,TRUE,FALSE,0,50,0,2,TRUE)

defines the overlay chart type as a line chart with drop lines displayed. Cluster spacing for the line chart is ignored. The Automatic Series Distribution is activated (the default status).

The OVERLAY.CHART.TYPE function is included for compatibility with Excel macros written with Microsoft Excel versions 1.0 through 1.5. This function, which is the macro equivalent of the Overlay Chart Type... command on the Chart menu in those versions of Excel, allows you to change the type of the overlay chart. The form of the OVERLAY.CHART.TYPE function is

=OVERLAY.CHART.TYPE(*type*)

The *type* argument is a numeric value that specifies the overlay type. The possible values of this argument are shown below:

If you use...	Excel creates...
1	No chart
2	Area chart
3	Bar chart
4	Column chart
5	Line graph
6	Pie chart
7	Scatter diagram

Notice that these arguments differ from the ones for the *type* argument of the OVERLAY function. A value of 1 has the same effect as the DELETE.OVERLAY function; the values 2 through 7 correspond to values 1 through 6 for the *type* argument of the OVERLAY function.

If you use the question-mark form of the OVERLAY.CHART.TYPE function, Excel displays the dialog box that appears when you select the Overlay... command from the Format menu.

The FORMAT.MOVE function

The FORMAT.MOVE macro function corresponds to the Move command on the Format menu in the chart environment. This function allows you to move a selected chart object. The form of the FORMAT.MOVE function is

=FORMAT.MOVE(*x-position,y-position*)

The *x-position* argument specifies the horizontal position of the selected chart object; the *y-position* argument specifies the vertical position. The *position* arguments are measured in points ($\frac{1}{72}$ inch) and specify a distance from the lower-left corner of the active window to the "base" of the selected object. The base of a text label is the lower-left corner of the text rectangle; the base of an arrow is the end without the arrowhead; the base of a pie slice is its point. If you omit the *x-position* argument, Excel moves the object only in a vertical direction; if you omit the *y-position* argument, Excel moves the object only in a horizontal direction.

Before you use the FORMAT.MOVE function, use the SELECT function to select the object to move. If the object you select cannot be moved, the FORMAT.MOVE function returns the logical value FALSE. You will usually use the FORMAT.MOVE function in conjunction with the FORMAT.SIZE function.

The FORMAT.SIZE function

The FORMAT.SIZE function is the macro equivalent of the Size command on the Format menu in the chart environment. It allows you to change the size of a selected chart object. The form of the FORMAT.SIZE function is

=FORMAT.SIZE(*width,height*)

The *width* argument specifies the horizontal size of the selected chart object; the *height* argument specifies the vertical size. Both arguments are expressed in points ($\frac{1}{72}$ inch). If you omit the *width* argument, Excel does not alter the width of the object; if you omit the *height* argument, Excel does not alter the height.

Before you use the FORMAT.SIZE function, you should use the SELECT function to select the object you want to change. If the object you select cannot be sized, the FORMAT.SIZE function returns the logical value FALSE. You usually use the FORMAT.SIZE function in conjunction with the FORMAT.MOVE function.

Action-equivalent functions

The functions we've discussed so far have been menu-equivalent functions— functions that emulate the actions of the commands on various Excel menus. However, not all the things you do in Excel are done with commands; many things are done from the keyboard or with the mouse. For example, you enter formulas, functions, and values by typing on the keyboard; you select cells, ranges, and chart objects by using the mouse.

Fortunately, Excel provides macro functions that allow you to perform these tasks within macros. Because these functions emulate actions, we call them *action-equivalent functions*. We examine each of these functions in this section.

The ACTIVATE.NEXT and ACTIVATE.PREV functions

The ACTIVATE.NEXT and ACTIVATE.PREV functions are the macro equivalents of the Command-M and Shift-Command-M key combinations. Like those key combinations, these functions activate the next and previous windows in the "stack." The forms of these functions are simply

=ACTIVATE.NEXT()

=ACTIVATE.PREV()

These functions accept no arguments.

For example, suppose there are three documents on the desktop and that the names of these documents appear at the bottom of the Window menu in the following order: *Worksheet1*, *Chart1*, and *Macro1*. If *Chart1* is the active document, the function =ACTIVATE.NEXT activates the document *Macro1*; the function =ACTIVATE.PREV activates the document *Worksheet1*.

The CANCEL.COPY function

The CANCEL.COPY function clears the marquee after you copy or cut a cell or range. Its action is equivalent to pressing Command-. (period). The form of the CANCEL.COPY function is simply

    =CANCEL.COPY()

It takes no arguments.

The DATA.FIND.NEXT and DATA.FIND.PREV functions

After you have used the DATA.FIND function in a macro to select the first record in the database that matches the selection criteria you have defined, you can then use the DATA.FIND.NEXT and DATA.FIND.PREV functions to select the next and the previous matching records. These functions are the macro equivalents of the Command-F and Command-Shift-F key combinations. The forms of these functions are simply

    =DATA.FIND.NEXT()

    =DATA.FIND.PREV()

These functions take no arguments.

The DIRECTORY function

The DIRECTORY function changes the current drive and directory (or folder). (To do this manually, you must choose the objects in the Open dialog box). The form of the DIRECTORY function is

    =DIRECTORY("*path*")

The "*path*" argument is the drive and directory you want to make current. The "*path*" argument must be a text string, enclosed in quotation marks. If you omit the drive name from the "*path*" argument, Excel assumes you want to access a directory on the current drive.

When you include a drive name in the "*path*" argument, be sure to separate the drive name and directory name with colons. If you are referring to an internal or external floppy-disk drive, the drive name is the name of the disk in the drive that you want to activate. If you are using a hard disk, the drive name probably is something like *Hard Drive*.

For example, the formula

=DIRECTORY("Hard Drive:Excel:Stocks")

directs Excel to the folder named *Stocks*, which is stored inside the folder named *Excel*, which, in turn, is located on a hard disk named *Hard Drive*.

When you use the DIRECTORY function, Excel returns the name of the new directory, including the drive name. In the above example, Excel returns the text

Hard Drive:Excel:Stocks

The FORMULA function

The FORMULA function allows you to make entries in cells from within macros. As such, it is one of the most frequently used macro functions. The form of this function is

=FORMULA(*formula text,ref*)

The *formula text* argument specifies what you want to enter; the *ref* argument specifies where you want to enter it. If you omit the *ref* argument (as you often will), Excel places the entry in the active cell.

You can use the FORMULA function to enter values, formulas, functions, or the results of formulas or functions. To enter a numeric value, simply use that value as the first argument of the function. For example, the function

=FORMULA(100)

enters the value 100 in the active cell. To enter a text value, simply use that value—enclosed in quotation marks—as the first argument of the FORMULA function. For example, the function

=FORMULA("Test")

enters the text *Test* into the active cell.

To enter a formula or function, use the text form of that formula or function as the first argument of the FORMULA function. The references in this formula must be in "R1C1" or "R[1]C[1]" form. For example, to enter the function =SQRT($B$5) into the active cell, you use the function

=FORMULA("=SQRT(R5C2)")

If cell C6 is the active cell, the function

    =FORMULA("=SQRT(R[-1]C[-1])")

enters the same function.

To enter the *result* of a formula or function, rather than the formula or function itself, you should use that formula or function—not its text form—as the *formula text* argument of the FORMULA function. In this case, the references in the formula must be in A1 form (unless Excel is in R1C1 mode). For example, if cell B5 of the active worksheet contains the value 36, the function

    =FORMULA(SQRT(!B5))

enters the value 6 into the active cell. Notice that you do not include a second equal sign in this form of the FORMULA function.

If you use the FORMULA function's optional *ref* argument, Excel places the entry specified by the first argument of the function in the cell specifed by the *ref* argument, rather than in the active cell. This argument can be in A1, "R1C1", or "R[1]C[1]" form. For example, the function

    =FORMULA(123,!A1)

enters the value 123 into cell A1 of the active worksheet. The function

    =FORMULA("Test","Worksheet2!R2C2")

enters the text value *Test* into cell B2 of the worksheet named *Worksheet2*. The function

    =FORMULA("=1+2","R[1]C")

enters the formula =1+2 into the cell immediately below the active cell in the active worksheet.

The FORMULA function also provides the only way to enter attached or unattached text into a chart from within a macro. To enter unattached text, simply use the FORMULA function after making sure that none of the objects in the chart are selected. To modify attached or unattached text, use the SELECT function to select the text and then use the FORMULA function to replace it.

The FORMULA.ARRAY function

The FORMULA.ARRAY function allows you to enter an array formula into a range of cells from within a macro. (To do this manually, you first select the range, type the formula or function, and then press Command-Enter). The form of the FORMULA.ARRAY function is

    =FORMULA.ARRAY(*formula text,ref*)

The *formula text* argument represents the formula you want to assign to the selected range. The *ref* argument tells Excel where to enter the formula. If you omit the *ref* argument, Excel assigns the array formula to the current selection. The restrictions on the arguments of the FORMULA.ARRAY function are the same as those for the FORMULA function.

For example, suppose you want to use the FORMULA.ARRAY function to assign the array formula {=SQRT($A$1:$A$5)} to cells B1:B5 of the same worksheet. To do this, you could select cells B1:B5 and use the function

=FORMULA.ARRAY("=SQRT(R1C1:R5C1)")

or you could use the function

=FORMULA.ARRAY("=SQRT(R1C1:R5C1)",!B1:B5)

no matter which cells are selected.

The FORMULA.FILL function

The FORMULA.FILL function causes Excel to fill a range of cells with a value, formula, or function. This function is the macro equivalent of typing an entry and then pressing Option-Enter after selecting a multicell range. The form of the FORMULA.FILL function is

=FORMULA.FILL(*entry,ref*)

The *entry* argument is the entry you want to make. The *ref* argument identifies the cells in which you want to place that entry. If you omit the *ref* argument, Excel enters the value, formula, or function in the cells of the current selection. The rules for the arguments of the FORMULA.FILL function are the same as those for the FORMULA and FORMULA.ARRAY functions.

For example, suppose you want to enter the formulas =A1+1, =A2+1, and =A3+1 into cells A2:A4 of an Excel worksheet. To do this, you could use the function

=FORMULA.FILL("=R[–1]C+1")

after selecting cells A2:A4 and making sure that cell A2 is the active cell. Or you could use the function

=FORMULA.FILL("=R[–1]C+1",!A2:A4)

no matter which cells are selected.

The FORMULA.FIND.NEXT and FORMULA.FIND.PREV functions

The FORMULA.FIND.NEXT and FORMULA.FIND.PREV functions are the macro equivalents of the Command-H (Find Next) and Command-Shift-H (Find Previous) key combinations. Used in conjunction with the FORMULA.FIND function (the macro equivalent of the Find... command on the Formula menu), these functions cause Excel to search for the next or previous occurrence of the specified text. The forms of these functions are simply

    =FORMULA.FIND.NEXT()

    =FORMULA.FIND.PREV()

These functions take no arguments.
    For example, the macro

    =FORMULA.FIND("=A1",1,2,1)
    =FORMULA.FIND.NEXT()

causes Excel to look for the *"find text"* argument =A1 in the contents of the cells of the active worksheet. When Excel finds the first occurrence, the second line of the macro causes Excel to search for the next occurrence of =A1 in the worksheet.

The FULL function

The FULL function expands the active window to fill the screen. This macro function is the equivalent of double-clicking the title bar of the active window. The form of this function is

    =FULL(*window*)

The *window* argument is a logical value. If it is TRUE, Excel expands the active window to fill the screen. If it is FALSE, Excel returns the active window to its original size.

The HLINE, HPAGE, and HSCROLL functions

The HLINE, HPAGE, and HSCROLL functions allow you to manipulate the horizontal scroll bar from within a macro. They are the macro equivalents of clicking and dragging within the horizontal scroll bar.
    The HLINE function is the macro equivalent of clicking the arrow at the right or left end of the horizontal scroll bar. The form of this function is

    =HLINE(*number of columns*)

The *number of columns* argument is a numeric value that specifies the number of columns to scroll into view. Positive values shift the worksheet to the left; negative values shift it to the right. For example, the function

=HLINE(2)

is the macro equivalent of clicking the arrow at the right edge of the horizontal scroll bar twice. The function

=HLINE(–3)

is the macro equivalent of clicking the arrow at the left end of the horizontal scroll bar three times.

The HPAGE function is the macro equivalent of clicking within the horizontal scroll bar to the right or left of the scroll box. The form of this function is

=HPAGE(*number of screens*)

The *number of screens* argument specifies the number of screens of information to scroll. Again, positive values shift the worksheet to the left; negative values shift it to the right. For example, the function

=HPAGE(2)

is the macro equivalent of clicking the horizontal scroll bar to the right of the scroll box twice. The function

=HLINE(–3)

is the macro equivalent of clicking the horizontal scroll bar to the left of the scroll box three times.

The HSCROLL function is the macro equivalent of dragging the scroll box within the horizontal scroll bar. The form of this function is

=HSCROLL(*column,number*)

The *column* argument can be a column number (not letter) or a percentage or formula that represents the position of the column you want to view, relative to all the columns in the worksheet. The *number* argument is a logical value that determines which type of *column* argument you are using. A TRUE logical argument indicates that the *column* argument is a column number. Therefore, Excel scrolls to the specified column. If the *number* argument is FALSE or omitted, Excel treats the *column* argument as a relative position. In that case, a *column* argument of 0 represents column A, and a *column* argument of 1 represents column IV.

The HLINE, HPAGE, and HSCROLL functions are the horizontal equivalents of the VLINE, VPAGE, and VSCROLL functions. We discuss those functions later in this section.

The MOVE function

The MOVE function allows you to change the position of a window in the workspace from within a macro. The MOVE function is the macro equivalent of dragging a window by its title bar. The form of the MOVE function is

=MOVE(*x-number,y-number,"window"*)

The *x-number* and *y-number* arguments identify the new position of the upper-left corner of the window. Both arguments specify a number of points ($\frac{1}{72}$ inch). The *x-number* argument specifies the distance between the left edge of the window and the left edge of the screen; the *y-number* argument specifies the distance between the top edge of the window and the bottom of the formula bar (or the bottom of the menu bar if you've used the Workspace... command to hide the formula bar).

The *"window"* argument is a text string, in quotation marks, that identifies which window you want to move. If *"window"* specifies a window other than the active window, the MOVE function changes that window's size but does not activate the window. If you omit the *"window"* argument, Excel moves the active window. If you use the name *"Clipboard"* as the *"window"* argument, Excel moves the Clipboard window, if it is open.

The SELECT function

The SELECT function allows you to select ranges in the worksheet and macro documents and select objects in chart documents from within a macro. Because most commands act upon a selected range or object, you use the SELECT function before using most menu-equivalent functions.

The SELECT function has two forms. The first form

=SELECT(*ref,active cell*)

allows you to select cells and ranges within worksheets and macro sheets. The *ref* argument is a reference to the cell or range you want to select; the *active cell* argument is a single cell in the *ref* range. If you omit the *active cell* argument, Excel selects the cell at the upper-left corner of the range specified by the *ref* argument. Both arguments can be in A1, "R1C1", or "R[1]C[1]" form.

For example, the function

=SELECT(!A1)

selects cell A1 in the active worksheet. The function

=SELECT("R1C1:R2C2")

selects cells A1:B2 in the active worksheet and makes cell A1 the active cell.

The function

=SELECT("R1C1:R2C2",!B2)

selects cells A1:B2 in the active worksheet and makes cell B2 the active cell. The function

=SELECT("R[1]C")

selects the cell immediately below the active cell in the active worksheet.

The second form of the SELECT function

=SELECT(*"object"*)

allows you to select objects in chart documents. The *object* argument is a text value that specifies which object to select. The following table shows the possible values for the *object* argument:

If you use...	Excel selects...
"Chart"	Entire chart
"Plot"	Plot area
"Legend"	Legend
"Axis 1"	Main-chart value axis
"Axis 2"	Main-chart category axis
"Axis 3"	Overlay-chart value axis
"Axis 4"	Overlay-chart category axis
"Title"	Chart title
"Text Axis 1"	Label for main-chart value axis
"Text Axis 2"	Label for main-chart category axis
"Text n"	Nth floating (unattached) text item
"Arrow n"	Nth arrow
"Gridline 1"	Major gridlines of value axis
"Gridline 2"	Minor gridlines of value axis
"Gridline 3"	Major gridlines of category axis
"Gridline 4"	Minor gridlines of category axis
"Dropline 1"	Main-chart drop lines
"Dropline 2"	Overlay-chart drop lines
"Hiloline 1"	Main-chart hi-lo lines
"Hiloline 2"	Overlay-chart hi-lo lines
"SnPm"	Data for point m in series n
"Text SnPm"	Text for point m in series n
"Text Sn"	Series-title text for series n of area chart

You must select a chart object before using most command-equivalent chart functions.

The SELECT.END function

The SELECT.END function moves the active cell to the edge of the next block of entries in your worksheet or macro sheet. Its action is the macro equivalent of pressing the Command key in conjunction with one of the arrow keys. The form of the SELECT.END function is

=SELECT.END(*direction*)

The *direction* argument is a numeric code that specifies the direction in which to move the active cell. Here are the possible values for this argument:

If you use...	Excel moves the cell...
1	Left
2	Right
3	Up
4	Down

The SIZE function

The SIZE function makes it possible to change the size of a window from within a macro. This function is the macro equivalent of dragging the size box at the lower-right corner of a window. The form of the SIZE function is

=SIZE(*x-number,y-number,"window"*)

The *x-number* and *y-number* arguments are the width and height you want the window to be. Both the *x-number* and *y-number* arguments are given in points ($\frac{1}{72}$ inch). The SIZE function moves only the lower-right corner of the window to achieve the desired width and height; it does not move the upper-left corner.

The *"window"* argument is a text string that specifies the name of the window you want the function to affect. If *"window"* describes a window other than the active window, the SIZE function changes that window's size but does not activate the window. If you omit the *"window"* argument, Excel changes the size of the active window. If you use the name *"Clipboard"* as the *"window"* argument, Excel changes the size of the Clipboard window, if it is open.

The SPLIT function

The SPLIT function allows you to divide a worksheet or a macro sheet window vertically, horizontally, or both. Its action is equivalent to dragging the split bars in the active window. The SPLIT function takes the form

=SPLIT(*column,row*)

The *column* argument is a numeric argument that tells Excel where to split the window vertically, with the leftmost column in the current window numbered 1. The *row* argument is a numeric argument that tells Excel where to split the window horizontally, with the topmost row numbered 1.

To remove a split window, enter 0 as the *column* or *row* argument. If you omit an argument, Excel does not change the split in that direction. If you attempt to use the SPLIT function in a window with frozen panes, Excel returns an error message and halts the macro.

For example, the formula

=SPLIT(,3)

produces a horizontal split just below the third row of the active window. If you have already split the window vertically, the vertical split remains unchanged. Similarly, the formula

=SPLIT(1,0)

creates a vertical split to the right of the first column in the active window. Any existing horizontal split is removed.

After splitting a window into panes, you can use the FREEZE.PANES function to freeze the top and left window panes.

The UNLOCKED.NEXT and UNLOCKED.PREV functions

The UNLOCKED.NEXT and UNLOCKED.PREV functions select either the next or the previous unlocked cell in a protected worksheet. Their actions are equivalent to pressing Tab or Shift-Tab. The forms of these functions are simply

=UNLOCKED.NEXT()

=UNLOCKED.PREV()

These functions take no arguments.

The VLINE, VPAGE, and VSCROLL functions

The VLINE, VPAGE, and VSCROLL functions allow you to manipulate the vertical scroll bar from within a macro. They are the macro equivalents of clicking and dragging within the vertical scroll bar.

The VLINE function is the macro equivalent of clicking the arrow at the top or bottom of the vertical scroll bar. The form of this function is

=VLINE(*number of rows*)

The *number of rows* argument is a numeric value that specifies the number of rows to scroll into view. Positive values shift the worksheet upward; negative values shift the worksheet downward.

For example, the function

=VLINE(2)

is the macro equivalent of clicking the arrow at the bottom of the vertical scroll bar twice. The function

=HLINE(–3)

is the macro equivalent of clicking the arrow at the top of the vertical scroll bar three times.

The VPAGE function is the macro equivalent of clicking within the vertical scroll bar above or below the scroll box. The form of this function is

=VPAGE(*number of screens*)

The *number of screens* argument specifies the number of screens of information to scroll. Again, positive values shift the worksheet upward; negative values shift it downward.

For example, the function

=VPAGE(2)

is the macro equivalent of clicking the vertical scroll bar below the scroll box twice. The function

=VLINE(–3)

is the macro equivalent of clicking the vertical scroll bar above the scroll box three times.

The VSCROLL function is the macro equivalent of dragging the scroll box within the vertical scroll bar. The form of this function is

=VSCROLL(*row,number*)

The *row* argument can be a row number or it can be a percentage or formula that represents the position of the row you want to view, relative to all the rows in the worksheet. The *number* argument is a logical value that determines which type of *row* argument you are using. A TRUE *number* argument indicates that the *row* argument is a row number. Therefore, Excel scrolls to the specified row. If the *number* argument is FALSE or omitted, Excel treats the *row* argument as a relative position. In that case, a *row* argument of 0 represents row 1, and a *row* argument of 1 represents row 16384.

The VLINE, VPAGE, and VSCROLL functions are the vertical equivalents of the HLINE, HPAGE, and HSCROLL functions, which we discussed earlier in this section.

Informational functions

As you have seen, many of the Microsoft Excel macro functions correspond to menu commands; others correspond to mouse and keyboard actions. A third group of functions returns information about the workspace—references, values, document names, and so forth. We present these functions—which we call *informational functions*—in this section.

Because macro sheets are typically set to display formulas and functions rather than their results, you usually won't see the results of these informational functions. You can use the results, however, simply by referencing the cells that contain them or by embedding the functions directly within other functions. If you want to see the result of an informational function, you activate the macro document, choose the Display... command from the Options menu, turn off the Formulas check box, and then click OK.

The ABSREF function

The ABSREF function returns the absolute reference of a cell that is offset by the amount you specify from another cell. The form of this function is

=ABSREF(*"ref text"*,*ref*)

The *"ref text"* argument is a relative reference, in "R[1]C[1]" form, that specifies the row and column offset from *ref*. The *ref* argument is a reference to a particular cell, in A1 form.

For example, the function

=ABSREF("R[–1]C[–1]",B2)

returns a reference to cell A1—the cell one column to the left and one row above cell B2. You can use the ABSREF function anywhere a reference argument is expected.

The ACTIVE.CELL function

The ACTIVE.CELL function returns an external reference to the active cell in the active worksheet. The form of this function is simply

=ACTIVE.CELL()

It takes no arguments.

For example, if *Worksheet1* is the active worksheet and cell B2 is the active cell, the macro function

=ACTIVE.CELL()

returns the reference *Worksheet1!B2*. Like the ABSREF function, this function can be used anywhere a cell reference is required.

The CALLER function

The CALLER function returns the reference of the cell that contains the function that called the currently running macro. (For more information on subroutine calls, see Chapter 17, "Macro Basics.") The form of this function is simply

=CALLER()

It takes no arguments.

For example, suppose you have two macros in a macro sheet: *TEST* and *TEST1*. Cell A10, which is a part of the macro *TEST*, contains the function

=TEST2()

If *TEST2* contains the function

=CALLER()

that function returns the reference R10C1.

The DEREF function

The DEREF function returns the value of the cell or the array of values in the cell range identified by its argument. The form of the DEREF function is

=DEREF(*ref*)

The *ref* argument is a reference to a cell or range in the macro sheet. For example, the function

=DEREF(A1)

returns 100 if cell A1 contains the value 100.

In most Excel functions, there is no difference between using a value and using a reference to a cell that contains that value. For example, if A1 contains the value –100, the functions =ABS(A1) and =ABS(–100) return the same result. In some cases, however, there is a big difference between using the reference and using the value. For example, the function

=SET.NAME("Test",C13)

stores the formula =$C$13 under the name *Test*. If you want to use the SET.NAME function to store the *value* from cell C13 under the name *Test*, you must include the DEREF function as follows:

=SET.NAME("Test",DEREF(C13))

The DOCUMENTS function

The DOCUMENTS function returns a horizontal array that contains an alphabetical listing of the names of all documents open on the workspace. The form of this function is simply

=DOCUMENTS()

It takes no arguments.

For example, suppose there are four windows on the desktop: *Worksheet1:1*, *Worksheet1:2*, *Worksheet2*, and *Chart1*. Before you enter the function, select a horizontal range that allows one cell for each open worksheet. When you enter the DOCUMENTS function, press Command-Enter. The function

=DOCUMENTS()

returns the horizontal array {"Chart1","Worksheet1","Worksheet2"}. Notice that only *Worksheet1* is included in the list, because although two windows are open into the document, the document itself is opened only once.

Typically, you use the DOCUMENTS function with the SET.NAME or the SET.VALUE function. For example, the function

=SET.NAME("Documents",DOCUMENTS())

stores the list of document names as a horizontal array under the name *Documents*. The function

=SET.VALUE(C1:Z1,DOCUMENTS())

enters the list of document names into cells C1:Z1 in the macro sheet. We examine the SET.NAME and SET.VALUE functions in greater detail later in this chapter.

After you have created an array of document names, you can use the INDEX function to select one of them from the list. For example, the macro

=SET.NAME("Documents",DOCUMENTS())
=SET.NAME("DocName",INDEX(Documents,2))

stores the array of document names under the name *Documents*, then stores the name of the second document in the array under the name *DocName*.

694 *Section Five: Macros*

The FILES function

The FILES function returns a horizontal array that contains the names of all files stored in a specified directory. The form of the FILES function is

=FILES(*"directory"*)

The *"directory"* argument is the name of the disk (and folders, if any) that contains the files you want to list. The *"directory"* argument must be a text string; it can include the ? and * wildcard characters. (You'll recall that the ? wildcard represents any single character in a directory name; the * wildcard represents any sequence of characters.)

If you omit the *"directory"* argument, Excel refers to the current directory. If you omit the disk name in the *"directory"* argument, Excel assumes that you are referring to the currently active disk.

For example, suppose you have stored three files (*Earnings*, *Analysis*, and *Buy/Sell*) in a folder named *Reports*, which is stored inside a folder named *Stocks* on the disk named *Excel*. If you select a three-cell horizontal range, type the formula

=FILES("Excel:Stocks:Reports:")

and press Command-Enter, Excel returns the names *Earnings*, *Analysis*, and *Buy/Sell* in the three cells of the array. The number of file names Excel can return depends on the size of the array you select. In the preceding example, if the *Reports* folder contained more than three files, Excel would return only the names of the first three files in the current path. Be sure to include the colon after the path name.

The GET.CELL function

The GET.CELL function returns information about a cell's formatting, location, or contents. The form of the GET.CELL function is

=GET.CELL(*type,reference*)

The *type* argument is a numeric code that specifies the information you want. The *reference* argument can be a cell reference or range name. If the *reference* argument refers to a range of cells, Excel returns information about the upper-left cell in that range. If you omit the *reference* argument, Excel refers to the current selection. The following table lists the possible *type* arguments and their results.

If you use...	Excel returns...
1	A reference to the first cell in the range specified in the *reference* argument. The reference is returned as text.
2	The row number of the top cell in the range specified in *reference*.
3	The column number of the leftmost cell in the range specified in *reference*.
4	A code that represents the type of value in *reference*. The possible type codes are:

Code	Type
1	Number
2	Text
4	Logical
16	Error
64	Array

If you use...	Excel returns...
5	The value of *reference*.
6	The formula in *reference* as text.
7	The number format of *reference* as text.
8	A numeric code that represents the alignment of *reference*. The possible alignment codes are:

Code	Type
1	General
2	Left
3	Center
4	Right
5	Fill

If you use...	Excel returns...
9	A TRUE value if *reference* has a left border; a FALSE value if not.
10	A TRUE value if *reference* has a right border; a FALSE value if not.
11	A TRUE value if *reference* has a top border; a FALSE value if not.
12	A TRUE value if *reference* has a bottom border; a FALSE value if not.
13	A TRUE value if *reference* is shaded; a FALSE value if not.
14	A TRUE value if *reference* is locked; a FALSE value if not.
15	A TRUE value if *reference* is hidden; a FALSE value if not.
16	The width of the column that contains *reference*.
17	The row height of *reference* cell, in points.
18	The name of the font used to display *reference*.
19	The size of the font used to display *reference*.

(continued)

If you use...	Excel returns...
20	A TRUE value if *reference* is displayed in bold type; a FALSE value if not.
21	A TRUE value if *reference* is displayed in italic type; a FALSE value if not.
22	A TRUE value if *reference* is displayed in underlined type; a FALSE value if not.
23	A TRUE value if *reference* is displayed in strikeout type; a FALSE value if not.
24	The font color of *reference*.
25	A TRUE value if *reference* is displayed in outline type; a FALSE value if not.
26	A TRUE value if *reference* is displayed in shadow type; a FALSE value if not.

The GET.CHART.ITEM function

The GET.CHART.ITEM function returns the horizontal or vertical position of a selected object in a chart. The form of this function is

=GET.CHART.ITEM(*x-y,point,"item"*)

The *"item"* argument is a text string that identifies the object you want to select. The possible values for this argument are the same ones allowed by the chart form of the SELECT function. For a list of those arguments, see the discussion of the SELECT function earlier in this chapter.

The *x-y* argument is a numeric code that tells Excel which coordinate to select: 1 for the horizontal coordinate; 2 for the vertical coordinate. The *point* argument identifies the position on the chart object. If you've selected a rectangle or an area in an area chart, use these values for the *point* argument:

If you use...	Excel positions the object...
1	Upper left
2	Upper middle
3	Upper right
4	Right middle
5	Lower right
6	Lower middle
7	Lower left
8	Left middle

If you select an arrow, use these values for the *point* argument: 1 for the base; 2 for the head. If you select a slice of a pie chart, use the following values for the *point* argument:

If you use...	Excel positions the slice...
1	Counterclockwise point furthest outside
2	Outer center point
3	Clockwise point furthest outside
4	Midpoint of most clockwise radius
5	Center point
6	Midpoint of most counterclockwise radius

If you select a point, the *point* argument must be 1. If you select any line except a data line, the *point* argument must be 1 for lower left or 2 for upper right.

The GET.DEF function

The GET.DEF function returns the name of a cell, range, value, or formula. The form of this function is

=GET.DEF(*"definition"*,*"document"*)

The *"definition"* argument is the description of the location or value for which the name is sought. The *"document"* argument is the name of the document in which *"definition"* occurs. Both arguments must be entered as text with quotation marks. References for the *"definition"* argument must be in "R1C1" form. If Excel finds more than one name for the *"definition"* argument, it returns the first name found.

For example, if cell A1 in *Worksheet1* is defined as *Test*, the function

=GET.DEF("R1C1","Worksheet1")

returns *Test*.

The GET.DOCUMENT function

The GET.DOCUMENT function returns information about a document. The GET.DOCUMENT function takes the form

=GET.DOCUMENT(*type*,*"name"*)

The *type* argument is a numeric code that defines the information you want. The *"name"* argument is a text string that specifies the name of the document you want information about; the document must be open in the workspace. If you omit the *"name"* argument, Excel assumes you are referring to the active document. The following table lists the available *type* arguments.

If you use...	Excel returns...
1	The name of the document, as text, without any drive or directory specifications.
2	The directory path name of the document as text. If the document has not been saved, Excel returns the #N/A! error value.
3	The type of document. The possible document types are:

Code	Type
1	Worksheet
2	Chart
3	Macro

4	A TRUE value if the document has been changed since it was saved; a FALSE value if not.
5	A TRUE value if the document was opened with the Read Only option selected; a FALSE value if not.
6	A TRUE value if the document is file-protected; a FALSE value if not.
7	A TRUE value if the document contents are protected; a FALSE value if not.
8	A TRUE value if the document windows are protected; a FALSE value if not.
9	0 if the document is empty; otherwise, 1. If the document is a chart, this argument returns the main chart type. The possible chart type codes are:

Code	Type
1	Area
2	Bar
3	Column
4	Line
5	Pie
6	Scatter

10	The number of the last row used; 0 if the document is empty. If the document is a chart, this argument returns the overlay chart type, as described for 9 above. If no overlay chart exists, Excel returns the #N/A! error value.
11	1 if the document is a worksheet or a macro sheet containing data; 0 if the worksheet or the macro sheet is empty. If the document is a chart, this argument returns the number of data series in the main chart.
12	If the document is a worksheet or a macro sheet, the number of the last column in the active area; 0 if the worksheet or the macro sheet is empty. If the document is a chart, this argument returns the number of data series in the overlay chart.

(continued)

If you use...	Excel returns...
13	The number of windows open on the document.
14	A numeric code for the document's calculation mode. The possible codes are:

Code	Type
1	Automatic
2	Automatic except tables
3	Manual

If you use...	Excel returns...
15	A TRUE value if iteration is turned on; a FALSE value if not.
16	The Maximum Iterations setting.
17	The Maximum Change Between Iterations setting.
19	A TRUE value if the Precision As Displayed setting is turned on; a FALSE value if not.
20	A TRUE value if the 1904 Date System option is turned on; a FALSE value if not.
21	A horizontal text array of the numbers of the fonts in the documents.
22	A horizontal numeric array of the document's font sizes.
23	A horizontal logical array indicating the document's bold fonts.
24	A horizontal logical array indicating the document's italic fonts.
25	A horizontal logical array indicating the document's underlined fonts.
26	A horizontal logical array indicating the document's strikeout fonts.
27	A horizontal numeric array indicating the document's font colors, from 0 through 8.
28	A horizontal logical array indicating the document's outlined fonts.
29	A horizontal logical array indicating the document's shadowed fonts.

The GET.FORMULA function

The GET.FORMULA function returns the contents of the cell in the upper-left corner of a specified range, in string form. The form of the GET.FORMULA function is

=GET.FORMULA(*ref*)

The *ref* argument is the reference of a cell or range.

For example, if cell A1 in the current worksheet contains the value 100, the function

=GET.FORMULA("R1C1")

returns the text value 100. If cell B3 contains the formula =B2, the function

=GET.FORMULA(!B3)

returns the string

="=R[–1]C"

If you want to retain the result of a GET.FORMULA function, you can use the SET.NAME function to store the result under a name or the SET.VALUE function to store the result in a cell.

The GET.NAME function

The GET.NAME function returns the definition of a specified name. The form of this function is

=GET.NAME(*"name"*)

The *"name"* argument is the name of a cell, value, or formula. The *"name"* argument can describe a name on the macro sheet (*"name"*), a name on the active worksheet (*"!name"*), or a name in a specific worksheet (*"Worksheet1!name"*). In all cases, *"name"* must be a text string enclosed in quotation marks.

If *"name"* describes a cell or range, the result of the function is the reference of that cell or range. If *"name"* describes a value or formula, the result of the function is a string containing that value or formula. If *"name"* describes a formula or a range, the result is presented in R1C1 notation.

For example, if *Test* is a name that has been assigned to cell A1 in the active worksheet, the function

=GET.NAME("!Test")

returns the string "=R1C1". If *Database* is a name that describes the range A1:H2000 in the worksheet *Worksheet2*, the function

=GET.NAME("Worksheet2!Database")

returns the string "=R1C1:R2000C8". If *Number* is a name that describes the value 100 in the macro sheet, the function

=GET.NAME("Number")

returns the string "=100".

The GET.NOTE function

The GET.NOTE function returns the text from a note attached to a cell. This function takes the form

=GET.NOTE(*reference,start,count*)

The *reference* argument is a reference to the cell whose note you want to work with. The *start* argument tells Excel where in the text string of the note to start reading. The *count* argument, which must be less than or equal to 255, tells Excel how many characters to return. If you omit the *reference* argument, Excel uses the active cell. If you omit the *start* argument, Excel begins with the first character in the note. If you omit the *count* argument, Excel returns the remainder of the note; that is, it returns all the characters from *start* to the end of the note.

The GET.WINDOW function

The GET.WINDOW function returns information about a window. The form of the GET.WINDOW function is

=GET.WINDOW(*type,"name"*)

The *type* argument is a numeric code that defines the information you want. The following table lists the available values for the *type* argument:

If you use...	Excel returns...
1	The document name as text.
2	The window number.
3	The distance from the left edge of the screen to the left side of the window, in points.
4	The distance from the top of the screen to the top of the window, in points.
5	The width, in points.
6	The height, in points.
7	A TRUE value if the window is hidden; a FALSE value if not.
8	A TRUE value if formulas are displayed; a FALSE value if not.
9	A TRUE value if gridlines are displayed; a FALSE value if not.
10	A TRUE value if row and column headings are displayed; a FALSE value if not.
11	A TRUE value if zeros are displayed; a FALSE value if not.

(continued)

If you use...	Excel returns...
12	A numeric code indicating gridlines and header color: 0 for automatic; 1 through 8 for the colors in the Display dialog box from the Options menu.
13	The leftmost column of each pane, as a horizontal numeric array.
14	The top row of each pane, as a horizontal numeric array.
15	The rightmost column of each pane, as a horizontal numeric array.
16	The bottom row of each pane, as a horizontal numeric array.

Codes 13 through 16 instruct Excel to return horizontal numeric arrays indicating which rows or columns appear at the edges of a window's panes. Therefore, to use these codes, you must select a horizontal group of cells in the macro sheet, type the formula, and press Command-Enter to enter it as an array.

The *"name"* argument is the name of the window you want to work with. This argument must be entered as text enclosed in quotation marks. If you omit the *"name"* argument, Excel refers to the active document window.

The GET.WORKSPACE function

The GET.WORKSPACE function returns information about the workspace. The form of the GET.WORKSPACE function is

=GET.WORKSPACE(*type*)

The *type* argument is a numeric code that defines the information you want. The following table lists the available values for the *type* argument and their results:

If you use...	Excel returns...
1	The name of the work environment and system number as text ("Macintosh 6.03").
2	The version number of Excel, as text.
3	The number of decimals; 0 if Fixed-Decimal is set.
4	A TRUE value if R1C1 mode is active; a FALSE value if A1 mode is active.
5	A TRUE value if scroll bars are active; a FALSE value if not.
6	A TRUE value if status bar is active; a FALSE value if not.
7	A TRUE value if formula bar is active; a FALSE value if not.
8	A FALSE value. Included for compatibility with Microsoft Excel for the IBM PC.
9	The alternate key, as text, if TRUE; #N/A if no alternate key is set.

(continued)

If you use...	Excel returns...
10	A number that corresponds to any special modes currently being used. Possible special mode codes are:

Code	Type
0	No special modes set
1	Data find
2	Copy
3	Cut

13	The width of the usable screen, in points.
14	The height of the usable screen, in points.
16	The amount of memory free, in kilobytes.
17	The total amount of memory, in kilobytes.
18	A TRUE value if a math coprocessor is being used; a FALSE value if not.
19	A TRUE value; checks for mouse presence.

The LINKS function

The LINKS function returns a list of all worksheets that serve as external references for a specified document. The form of this function is

=LINKS(*"document"*)

The *"document"* argument is a text value that specifies the name of the document for which the links are sought. If you omit the *"document"* argument, Excel refers to the active document. If Excel can't find any worksheets serving as external references for a document, it returns #N/A!.

For example, suppose the active worksheet is a chart named *Chart1*, developed from data in worksheets named *Profits* and *Losses*. The function

=LINKS("Chart1")

returns the array {"Profits","Losses"}.

Typically, you use the LINKS function with the SET.NAME or SET.VALUE function. For example, the function

=SET.NAME("Profits",LINKS())

stores the list of worksheets with external references as an array under the name *Profits*. The function

=SET.VALUE(F1:J1,LINKS())

enters the array into cells F1:J1 in the macro sheet.

The NAMES function

The NAMES function returns, as a horizontal array, all names defined in a document. The form of this function is

=NAMES(*"document"*)

The *"document"* argument is a text value that specifies the name of the document you want to refer to. If you omit the *"document"* argument, Excel returns the names defined in the active document.

The OFFSET function

The OFFSET function returns a reference to a range—usually the same size as the one you specify—but offset by a specified number of rows and columns. The form of this function is

=OFFSET(*ref,row offset,column offset,height,width*)

The *ref* argument is a reference to a cell or a range in the macro sheet; *row offset* and *column offset* are numbers that specify where the new range will be in relation to the one specified by the *ref* argument. The *height* and *width* arguments determine the height and width of the resulting range. If the *height* or *width* argument is omitted, Excel returns a reference to a range that has the same dimensions as the one specified by *ref*.

For example, if *Worksheet1* is the active worksheet and cell A1 of that worksheet is named *Test*, the function

=OFFSET(!Test,2,2)

returns the reference *Worksheet1!R3C3*. The function

=OFFSET(!A1:C5,2,3)

returns the reference *Worksheet1!R3C4:R7C6*.

The *row offset* and *column offset* arguments can be negative numbers. For example, the function

=OFFSET(!B2,–1,–1)

returns the reference *Worksheet1!R1C1* (assuming *Worksheet1* is the name of the active worksheet).

If *row offset* and *column offset* push *ref* off the worksheet, the function returns the value #REF!. For example, the function

=OFFSET(!B2,–2,–2)

returns #REF!.

You can use the *height* and *width* arguments to extend or contract a selection when it is offset. For example, suppose you want to change a three-column-by-two-row range (A1:C2) to a two-column-by-five-row range when offset. If *Worksheet1* is the current worksheet and cells A1:C2 are named *Temp*, the function

=OFFSET(!Temp,0,2,5,2)

returns the reference *Worksheet1!R1C3:R5C4*.

Although the actual result of the OFFSET function is a reference, in most cases, the practical result of the function is the contents of the cell or range described by that reference. This means that you can use the OFFSET function to "look up" information from tables that a macro might create on a worksheet.

The REFTEXT function

The REFTEXT function changes a reference to an absolute reference in the A1 or R1C1 text form. The function takes the form

=REFTEXT(*ref,a1*)

The *ref* argument is the reference you want to convert, in A1 form. The *a1* argument is a logical value that specifies the type of reference you want to create. If *a1* is TRUE, Excel returns the address in A1 form. If this argument is FALSE or omitted, Excel returns the address in R1C1 form.

For example, if *Worksheet1* is the active document, the function

=REFTEXT(!A1,TRUE)

returns the text value *Worksheet1!$A$1*. The functions

=REFTEXT(!A1,FALSE)

and

=REFTEXT(!A1)

return the text value *Worksheet1!R1C1*.

Generally, you embed the REFTEXT function in other functions that require that cell and range reference arguments be presented in text form. The TEXTREF function, which we discuss later in this chapter, performs the opposite conversion.

The RELREF function

The RELREF function returns the text form of a relative reference that describes the relationship between two cells. The form of this function is

=RELREF(*ref1,ref2*)

The *ref1* and *ref2* arguments are cell references in A1 form. The result of the function is a relative reference, in R[1]C[1] form, that describes the relationship of *ref1* to *ref2*.

For example, because cell A1 is one column to the left and one row above cell B2, the function

=RELREF(!A1,!B2)

returns the relative reference R[–1]C[–1]. Similarly, the function

=RELREF(!D5,!C3)

returns the relative reference R[2]C[1].

The SELECTION function

The SELECTION function returns an R1C1-style reference to whatever cells are selected at the time. The form of the SELECTION function is simply

=SELECTION()

It accepts no arguments.

For example, if the active window is named *Worksheet1*, and if cells A1:A10 in that document are selected, the function

=SELECTION()

returns the reference *Worksheet1!R1C1:R10C1*. Typically, the value in the reference cell is displayed. To see the actual reference, you can convert it to text by using the REFTEXT function, as follows:

=REFTEXT(SELECTION())

The TEXTREF function

The TEXTREF function converts references in A1 or R1C1 text form to standard references. The form of this function is

=TEXTREF("*text*",*a1*)

The "*text*" argument is the text reference, in quotation marks, that you want to convert to standard-reference form. The *a1* argument is a logical value that specifies the type of reference you're converting. If *a1* is TRUE, Excel treats "*text*" as an A1-style reference. If *a1* is FALSE or omitted, Excel treats "*text*" as an R1C1-style reference. When the arguments don't correspond, Excel returns a #REF error value.

For example, the function

=TEXTREF("Worksheet1!A1",TRUE)

returns the standard reference *Worksheet1!A1*. The functions

=TEXTREF("Worksheet1!R2C2",FALSE)

and

=TEXTREF("Worksheet1!R2C2")

return the standard reference *Worksheet1!R2C2*.

The WINDOWS function

The WINDOWS function returns a horizontal array that contains the names of all windows that are open at the time Excel interprets the function. The first name in the list is the name of the active window; the names of the remaining windows appear in the list in the same order in which the windows are "stacked" on the desktop. The form of this function is

=WINDOWS()

It takes no arguments.

For example, suppose three windows are stacked on the desktop in the following order: *Worksheet1:2*, *Worksheet1:1*, and *Worksheet2*. Before you enter the function, select a horizontal range that allows one cell for each open worksheet. When you enter the WINDOWS function, press Command-Enter. The function

=WINDOWS()

returns the horizontal array {"Worksheet1:2","Worksheet1:1","Worksheet2"}.

Typically, you use WINDOWS with the SET.NAME or SET.VALUE function. For example, the function

=SET.NAME("Windows",WINDOWS())

stores the list of window names as a horizontal array under the name *Windows*. The function

=SET.VALUE(C1:Z1,WINDOWS())

enters the array into cells C1:Z1 in the macro sheet. If there are not enough window names to fill the array, #N/A! appears in the empty cells.

After you have created a list of window names, you can select the name of the window you want to use with the INDEX function. For example, the macro

=SET.NAME("Windows",WINDOWS())
=ACTIVATE(INDEX(Windows,2))

stores the array of window names under the name *Windows* and then activates the second window in the array.

Macro-control functions

So far, we've covered three categories of macro functions: menu-equivalent functions, action-equivalent functions, and informational functions. The final group of macro functions covered in this chapter control the flow of the execution of the macro. For that reason, we refer to them as *macro-control functions*.

The ALERT function

The ALERT function allows you to create and use your own alert boxes The form of the ALERT function is

=ALERT(*"message",type*)

The *"message"* argument is the message you want Excel to display in the alert box. The *"message"* argument must be a text string enclosed in quotation marks.

The *type* argument is the type of alert box you want Excel to display. There are three possible *type* arguments: 1, 2, or 3.

Type 1 displays a caution alert with OK and Cancel buttons. For example, the function

=ALERT("Are you sure?",1)

displays the alert box shown in Figure 18-1. Notice the exclamation point in the balloon at the left side of the box. You use this kind of ALERT function to give users a "second chance" before the macro executes a destructive command.

FIGURE 18-1. *This is a type 1 alert box.*

Type 2 displays a note alert box with only an OK button. For example, the function

=ALERT("Argument must be W or R",2)

displays the alert box shown in Figure 18-2. Notice the profile with a speech balloon in the balloon at the left side of the box. You use this kind of alert box to inform users that they have made an error.

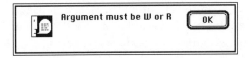

FIGURE 18-2. *This is a type 2 alert box.*

Type 3 displays a stop alert box with an OK button. For example, the function

=ALERT("Cannot activate closed window",3)

displays the alert box shown in Figure 18-3. Notice the raised-palm icon in the balloon at the left side of the box. This icon is the only difference between this type of alert box and a type 2 alert box.

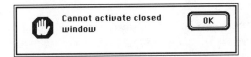

FIGURE 18-3. *This is a type 3 alert box.*

The BEEP function

The BEEP function instructs Excel to sound a beep. The form of this function is

=BEEP(*number*)

The *number* argument is a value from 1 through 4. Microsoft Excel for the Macintosh sounds the same tone no matter which argument you specify; different arguments cause the PC version of Excel to sound different tones.

The BREAK function

The BREAK function allows Excel to escape from FOR-NEXT loops or WHILE-NEXT loops and continue with the macro statement immediately after the NEXT function. The BREAK function takes no arguments. We talk about the FOR, WHILE, and NEXT functions later in this chapter.

The CANCEL.KEY function

The CANCEL.KEY function continues a disrupted macro or tells Excel which macro to run when a macro is disrupted. This function takes the form

=CANCEL.KEY(*enable,ref*)

The *enable* argument is a logical value. If *enable* is TRUE, Excel lets the Command-. (period) key combination interrupt a macro. If *enable* is FALSE or omitted, Excel doesn't allow the interruption of a macro by pressing Command-. (period). The *ref* argument, when combined with a TRUE *enable* argument, specifies the macro to be run when Command-. (period) is pressed. If the *ref* argument is omitted, the current macro simply halts when interrupted. If *ref* is included, the macro located at *ref* runs when the current macro is interrupted.

The ECHO function

The ECHO function allows you to control the updating of the screen while a macro is calculating. This function has the form

=ECHO(*updating*)

The *updating* argument sets screen updating. If *updating* is TRUE, the screen is updated as the macro runs; if *updating* is FALSE, Excel turns off screen updating. Turning off screen updating increases the speed of most macros. It does not prevent Excel from displaying dialog boxes on the screen.

There is no need to include an ECHO(TRUE) function at the end of your macro. When the macro stops running, Excel automatically turns screen updating back on. Excel also resumes screen updating after a macro is interrupted by an error message.

The ERROR function

Excel usually displays an alert box when it encounters an error while calculating a macro. This alert box contains three buttons—Halt, Step, and Continue—that allow you to decide what happens next. If you click Halt, the macro stops. If you click Step, the macro begins single-step calculation from the point of the error. If you click Continue, the macro continues without regard to the error.

The ERROR function allows you to use a more advanced form of error checking in your macros. This function has the form

=ERROR(*branch,ref*)

The *branch* argument causes the macro to branch to another cell when an error occurs. The *ref* argument specifies a cell that contains a macro subroutine that can deal with the error. If *branch* is TRUE, the macro branches to the cell indicated by *ref*. If you omit *ref*, Excel displays the standard error-alert box and does not branch to any cell. If *branch* is FALSE, Excel does not display an error message. If Excel encounters an error in this situation, it ignores the error and continues executing the macro.

The FOR and NEXT functions

The FOR and NEXT functions allow you to set up FOR-NEXT loops in an Excel macro. A FOR function marks the beginning of the loop; a NEXT function marks the end of the loop. A FOR-NEXT loop causes Excel to repeat a calculation or action a specified number of times before continuing with the remainder of the macro. You designate a "counter" name, a starting value, an ending value, and, if desired, a step value to increment the counter. After each pass through the loop, Excel adds the step value to the current value of the "counter." If the "counter" value is smaller than or equal to the ending value, Excel goes through the loop again. When the "counter" value is greater than the ending value, Excel stops the loop and continues processing the macro with the statement following the NEXT statement.

The form of the FOR function is

=FOR(*"counter",start,stop,step*)

The form of the NEXT function is simply

=NEXT()

The FOR function's *"counter"* argument is the name of the variable Excel uses to keep track of repetitions of the loop. The *start* argument specifies the initial value of the *"counter"* argument. The *stop* argument specifies the ending value of *"counter"*; the *step* argument determines the increment Excel adds to *"counter"* each time it executes the loop. If you omit *step*, Excel assumes it is 1.

You need not use the Define Name… command to define the *"counter"* variable before running the macro; Excel creates it automatically as it executes the FOR function and resets it to its initial start value each time you run the macro.

For example, this series of statements

```
=FOR("Test",1,10,1)
=SET.VALUE(B1,B1*2)
=NEXT()
```

doubles the value in cell B1 of the macro sheet 10 times. Suppose cell B1 initially contains the value 2. On the first loop through these statements, Excel sets that cell to 4 and adds 1 to the *"counter"* value, which is named *"Test"*. Then, the program doubles the value in cell B1 again, setting that cell to 8, and increases the *"counter"* value to 3. This process continues until the *"counter"* value, *Test*, is greater than 10. In fact, if you choose the Define Name… command after this loop is completed, you see that *Test* equals 11. (At this point, B1 contains 2048.) The next time you run the macro, *Test* is reset to its start value, 1.

The GOTO function

The GOTO function allows you to redirect the execution of a macro. The GOTO function can be used to branch from one macro to another or to create a loop within a macro. The GOTO function has the form

=GOTO(*ref*)

The *ref* argument is the reference or name of the cell in the macro sheet that contains the next macro function you want Excel to compute. After it computes *ref*, Excel continues to process the functions in the cells below *ref*, one after another, until it encounters a RETURN, HALT, or another GOTO function.

For example, suppose you have created two macros in one macro sheet. The first one is in the range A2:A10, and the second is in the range C2:C5. You want Excel to run the second macro as soon as it completes the first one. To link these macros, you enter the function

=GOTO(C2)

in cell A10—the last cell in the first macro. You do not need a RETURN function in the first macro in this case.

The GOTO function is also used frequently to create loops. A loop is a section of a macro that is computed over and over a specified number of times. In Chapter 19, "User-Defined Functions," we show you several examples of looping macros.

It is a good idea to name the cells that are referred to by GOTO functions and to include those names as labels in the macro sheet.

The ref *function*

The *ref* function tells Excel where to go to execute a subroutine macro. This function does not have a name in the usual sense and takes no arguments; instead, you simply enter an equal sign and the cell reference, followed by a set of parentheses. For example, to route macro processing to cell B20, you enter the statement

=B20()

If *ref* is a range, Excel begins executing in the upper-left corner of the referenced range. After Excel reaches the end of the macro subroutine, it does not stop; it jumps back to the macro that contains the subroutine call and continues executing that macro with the function that follows that call.

The HALT function

The HALT function stops the execution of a macro. This function has the form

=HALT()

It takes no arguments.

For example, the function

=IF(Test>100,HALT())

stops the macro immediately if the value of *Test* is greater than 100. If the macro that contains this function is embedded in another macro, the calling macro halts.

The INPUT function

The INPUT function allows you to solicit information from the user while a macro is executing. The form of this function is

=INPUT(*"prompt",type,"title"*)

When Excel evaluates an INPUT function, it displays a custom dialog box that contains a single text box. For example, the function

=INPUT("Please enter a date",,"Input 1")

creates the dialog box shown in Figure 18-4.

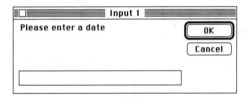

FIGURE 18-4. *This is the Input dialog box.*

The *"prompt"* argument defines a prompt that appears in the dialog box. The *"title"* argument describes the title of the dialog box. (If you omit the *title* argument, Excel supplies the name *Input*.) The *type* argument allows you to specify the type of information to be entered. The following table shows the possible values of the *type* argument:

If you use...	Excel expects the input to be...
0	Formula
1	Number
2	Text
4	Logical
8	Reference
16	Error
64	Array

Interestingly, you can also use the sum of any two or more of these codes as the *type* argument. Excel then allows the input to be any of the types specified by the compound codes. For example, if you use the number 3 (codes 1+2), Excel allows the input to be either type 1 (number) or type 2 (text). In fact, the default *type* argument is 7, the sum of codes 1 (number), 2 (text), and 4 (logical).

The MESSAGE function

The MESSAGE function lets you display messages in the status bar while your macros are running. This function has the form

=MESSAGE(*location,"text"*)

The *location* argument is a logical value that tells Excel whether to display the message specified by the *"text"* argument. If *location* is TRUE, Excel does display the message; if *location* is FALSE, Excel erases the message instead. The *"text"* argument must be a text string, enclosed in quotation marks. If you omit *"text"* argument, but *location* is TRUE, Excel displays a blank message line.

For example, the function

=MESSAGE(TRUE,"This is a message")

displays the message shown in Figure 18-5.

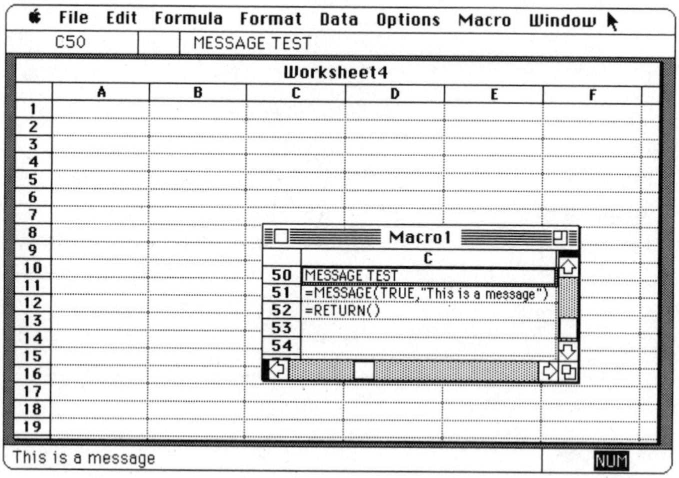

FIGURE 18-5. *This is a message displayed as a result of a MESSAGE function.*

The MESSAGE function is most useful when one of your macros is about to perform a lengthy calculation and you want to inform the user about what is happening. Messages can also be useful for telling the user that a macro is running, even if the macro is relatively brief.

The NEXT function

The NEXT function ends FOR-NEXT loops and WHILE-NEXT loops. The form of this function is

=NEXT()

It takes no arguments. For more on this function, see the discussions of the FOR and WHILE functions elsewhere in this chapter.

The ON.KEY function

The ON.KEY function runs a macro when you press a specific key. The form of this function is

=ON.KEY("*key*","*macro*")

The "*key*" argument identifies the key that the user must press in combination with the Command and Shift keys to run the macro specified by the "*macro*" argument. If you omit the "*macro*" argument, the key specified in this function returns to its normal use. Be sure the macro sheet that contains the macro specified by "*macro*" is open. If the macro sheet is closed, Excel returns an error when the user presses the specified Command-Shift key combination.

The ON.TIME function

The ON.TIME function runs a macro at a specified time. The form of the ON.TIME function is

=ON.TIME(*time*,"*macro*",*tolerance*,*insert*)

The *time* argument is a serial value of the time at which you want to run the macro specified by the "*macro*" argument. The "*macro*" argument is an R1C1-style text reference to the macro you want to run. The macro sheet that contains the macro must be open. The *tolerance* argument, another serial time value, tells Excel how long you're willing to wait for the *insert* argument to be TRUE. If you omit *tolerance*, its value is assumed to be infinite. The *insert* argument determines whether Excel runs the macro. If *insert* is TRUE or omitted, Excel runs the macro at the specified time. If *insert* is FALSE, Excel ignores all prior instructions to execute the macro.

Under some circumstances, Excel may not respond to the ON.TIME function as expected. If the macro sheet containing the macro specified by *"macro"* is not open when the correct time is reached, Excel ignores the request. Similarly, if Excel is not in Ready mode at the specified time or during the *tolerance* period (for example, if Excel is calculating a worksheet), it waits until the *tolerance* period has elapsed and then cancels the macro's run. If you create two ON.TIME functions, Excel executes the first and ignores the second, returning the #N/A error value.

The ON.WINDOW function

The ON.WINDOW function runs a macro when a user activates a specified window. The form of this function is

=ON.WINDOW(*"window"*,*"macro"*)

The *"window"* argument is the name of the window that, when activated, starts the macro specified by the *"macro"* argument. If you omit the *"window"* argument, Excel executes the specified macro when the user activates any window except those included in other ON.WINDOW statements. Omitting the *"macro"* argument breaks the link between the window and the macro.

The RESTART function

The RESTART function terminates a branched (nested) macro and enables you to return control to any macro level. This function takes the form

=RESTART(*level*)

When you include this function without a *level* argument in a macro subroutine and Excel subsequently encounters a RETURN function, the macro simply stops and does not return control to the parent macro. The *level* argument is a numeric value that specifies which of the macros preceding the initiating macro should receive control.

For example,

=RESTART(1)

returns control not to the macro that initiated the current macro, but to the macro preceding the initiating macro.

Note that the RESTART function does not take the place of a HALT or RETURN function.

The RETURN function

The RETURN function is used most commonly to stop the execution of a macro. This function has the form

=RETURN()

It takes no arguments.

If the macro that contains this function is embedded in another macro, the calling macro stops.

The SET.NAME function

The SET.NAME function allows you to create a name on the macro sheet from within a macro and to assign a value to that name. The form of this function is

=SET.NAME(*"name"*,*value*)

The *"name"* argument is the name you want to create. The *value* argument is the value you want to store under that name. The *"name"* argument is always a string enclosed in quotation marks.

For example, the function

=SET.NAME("Test",100)

stores the value 100 under the name *Test*. If you choose the Define Name... command from the Formula menu after running the macro that contains this line, you see the name *Test* in the list in the Define Name dialog box. If you select this name, you see that it applies to the value 100.

The *value* argument is usually a number, but it can also be a formula, text string, array, or cell reference. For example, if you have already created the name *Test* and assigned it the value 100, the function

=SET.NAME("Test",Test+1)

increases the value of *Test* by 1. Because *Test* is currently assigned the value 100, this macro function stores the number 101 under the name *Test*.

The function

=SET.NAME("Test","Text")

stores the text value *"Text"* under the name *Test*. The function

=SET.NAME("Test",{1;2;3;4;5})

stores the vertical array {1;2;3;4;5} under the name *Test*.

Finally, the function

=SET.NAME("Test",C1:C5)

assigns the name *Test* to the range C1:C5.

If you want to assign a name to a value that currently resides in a cell in the macro sheet, you must use the DEREF function as the SET.NAME function's *value* argument, because the SET.NAME function does not convert a referenced cell into the value contained in that cell. For example, if cell C1 contains the value 100, the function

=SET.NAME("Test",DEREF(C1))

stores the value 100 under the name *Test*.

You may have noticed that SET.NAME is very similar to DEFINE.NAME. They are very close in function, but whereas DEFINE.NAME creates a name in the active worksheet, SET.NAME creates a name in the current macro sheet. The SET.NAME function is best used for storing temporary values that result when the macro is executing.

The SET.VALUE function

The SET.VALUE function allows you to assign a value to a cell in the macro sheet from within a macro. The form of this function is

=SET.VALUE(*reference,value*)

The *reference* argument is the cell or range where you want to enter *value*. For example, the function

=SET.VALUE(C1,100)

enters the number 100 in cell C1 on the macro sheet. As in this example, *value* is usually a number, but it can also be a text string, a formula, or an array.

For example, the function

=SET.VALUE(C2,"Text")

enters the text value *"Text"* in cell C2. The function

=SET.VALUE(C1,C1+1)

increases the value in cell C1 by 1. If C1 contains the value 100, this macro function enters the number 101 in cell C1. The function

=SET.VALUE(C1:C5,{1;2;3;4;5})

enters the value 1 into cell C1, the value 2 into cell C2, and so on. If the *value* argument specifies an array that does not fit in the selected range, the function fills the specified range with as much of *value* as does fit.

The STEP function

The STEP function activates the Excel Step mode. This function has the form

=STEP()

It takes no arguments.

When Excel encounters this function in a macro, it immediately turns on the Step mode and begins executing the current macro, one step at a time. For more on the Step mode, see Chapter 17, "Macro Basics."

The WAIT function

The WAIT function suspends the execution of a macro until a specified time. The WAIT function takes the form

=WAIT(*time*)

The *time* argument is a serial time value. When Excel encounters this function, it suspends the macro's execution until the time indicated. For example, to have Excel pause until 2 P.M., you use the formula

=WAIT(0.583)

To pause execution for a specified amount of time, you can include an embedded NOW function in the *time* argument. Keeping in mind that one second is equal to about 0.00001, one minute to about 0.0007, and one hour to about 0.042, you could use a formula like

=WAIT(NOW()+0.00005)

to suspend execution of a macro for about five seconds.

After a WAIT function pauses execution of a macro, you can resume macro execution by pressing the Command-. (period) key combination.

The WHILE and NEXT functions

The WHILE and NEXT functions together make up the second of Excel's looping capabilities. A WHILE-NEXT loop repeats a set of calculations until a specified condition is met. The form of the WHILE function is

=WHILE(*execute*)

and, as you know, the form of the NEXT function is

=NEXT()

The WHILE function's *execute* argument is a logical value that determines whether Excel executes the macro again. Generally, this argument is an embedded logical test that results in a TRUE or FALSE value. The WHILE-NEXT loop tells Excel to repeat a calculation or action while a specified logical test is TRUE. Excel continues its repetition until the logical test is FALSE and then continues the macro with the statement after the NEXT function.

When *execute* is TRUE, Excel executes all statements up to a NEXT statement. When *execute* becomes FALSE, Excel executes the statements after the NEXT statement. If *execute* is FALSE the first time the macro reaches the WHILE statement, Excel skips the loop entirely and continues the macro by processing the first statement after the NEXT function.

For example, consider this simple macro loop:

```
=WHILE(B1<2048)
=SET.VALUE(B1,B1*2)
=NEXT()
```

This looping routine works much like a FOR-NEXT loop. It doubles the value in cell B1 of the macro sheet. This time, however, the macro continues until the value in cell B1 is greater than or equal to the test value. In this example, the loop terminates when the value in cell B1 is 2048. However, if the WHILE statement had used 2050 as the test value, the value of B1 would be 4096 when the WHILE-NEXT loop terminated (the next iteration).

You can use the BREAK function to stop either a FOR-NEXT loop or a WHILE-NEXT loop before completion. Often, you will embed the BREAK function in your loops to avoid error conditions. For example, in the series of statements

```
=WHILE(B1<2048)
=IF(TYPE(B1)<>1,BREAK())
=SET.VALUE(B1,B1*2)
=NEXT()
```

we used a logical function to ensure that cell B1 contains a numeric value. If cell B1 contains a text value, an error value, or any other type of nonnumeric entry, Excel breaks the loop and continues the macro with the statement that occurs immediately after the NEXT function.

Conclusion

In this long chapter, we have examined four groups of macro functions: menu-equivalent functions, action-equivalent functions, informational functions, and macro-control functions. In the next chapter, we show you how to use Excel's macro functions to create user-defined function macros. In Chapter 20, "Customizing Excel," we examine the remaining macro functions.

19

User-Defined Functions

*A*lthough Microsoft Excel includes a multitude of built-in functions, there are probably other calculations that you perform regularly that are not available as functions. For example, suppose your company uses a complex mathematical formula for computing salespeople's commissions. Wouldn't it be convenient if Excel had a function called *COMMIS* that would perform this calculation for you? Or suppose your company has a stepped discount schedule. Wouldn't it be easy if there were a function called *DISC* that could automatically compute the discount on any order for you?

In Microsoft Excel, it is possible to create functions like the ones we have just described. Called *user-defined functions*, these functions are possibly the most exciting and innovative calculation tools offered by Microsoft Excel. The types of tasks that can be simplified, generalized, or streamlined with user-defined functions are nearly unlimited.

To create a user-defined function, you must write a special macro, called a *function macro*, that accepts information from the worksheet, performs calculations, and then returns the result to the worksheet. Most user-defined functions are quite simple. Some, however, can be pretty complicated. In this chapter, we look at examples of both simple and complex user-defined functions.

Function macro basics

As we have said, user-defined functions are a special type of macro. To create a user-defined function, you need only two macro commands: ARGUMENT and RETURN. The ARGUMENT function allows you to define the arguments your user-defined function will use. The RETURN function returns the result of the user-defined function to the worksheet.

The best way to see how these functions work is to build a simple example. Suppose your company pays a commission of 10 percent on all sales. Each week, the payroll department has to compute the commission on each salesperson's sales for that week. The worksheet in Figure 19-1 shows the weekly sales of four salespeople. You need to compute their commission for this week. Let's create a user-defined function to perform this task.

```
 File  Edit  Formula  Format  Data  Options  Macro  Window
    C3
================= Weekly Sales =================
        A         B          C       D     E     F
  1
  2            Weekly Sales Commission
  3  Al          $12,000
  4  Joey         $4,500
  5  Terry       $15,200
  6  Tom         $11,500
  7
```

FIGURE 19-1. *This is the* Weekly Sales *worksheet.*

To begin, choose the New… command from the File menu and double click the Macro Sheet option. Like all other macros, user-defined functions are created and stored on macro sheets.

When the new macro sheet appears, type *COMMIS* in cell A1. (This first step is not absolutely required, but it is a good idea. We show you why in just a paragraph or two.) Next, select cell A2 and enter the function

    =ARGUMENT("Sales")

Now, select cell A3 and enter the formula

    =Sales*0.1

Finally, enter the function

    =RETURN(A3)

ir cell A4. Figure 19-2 shows the macro sheet at this point.

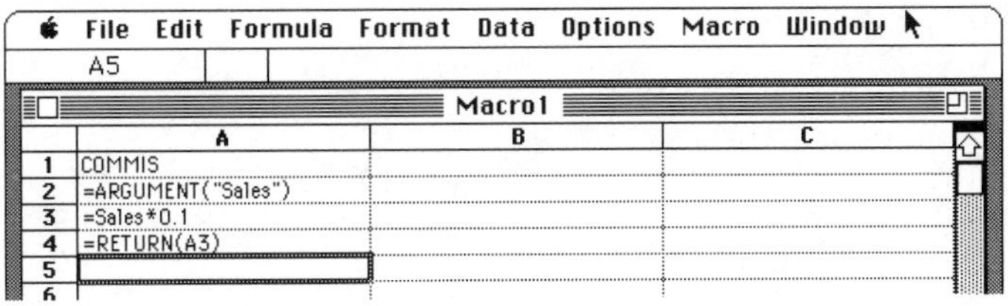

FIGURE 19-2. *This is the macro sheet after entering a function macro that calculates salespeople's commissions.*

Next, you must give this function macro a name. Like all other macros, the name of a function macro is a range name you assign to the first cell in the macro. In this case, the first cell is A2. (Technically, the name in cell A1 isn't a part of the macro.) To name this cell, click the cell to select it and then choose the Define Name... command from the Formula menu. Notice that the Refers To field contains the coordinates of the selected cell, $A$2, and that the Name field contains the label from cell A1, *COMMIS*. To tell Excel that the macro you are naming is a function macro, click the Function button. Then, to accept the default name, *COMMIS*, click the OK button.

You may recall from Chapter 2, "Worksheet Basics," that Excel always offers you the option of using the label in the cell above or to the left of the cell that you are naming as the name for that cell. Thus, by entering the label *COMMIS* in cell A1, you killed two birds with one stone: You made the job of naming the function easier, and you created a visual reminder of the name in the macro sheet. We recommend that you always enter the name of your function macro in the cell above the first cell in the macro.

Now, you are ready to use the function you've defined. To do this, select the worksheet, click cell C3, then enter the function

=Macro1!COMMIS(B3)

in that cell. Notice that the name of this user-defined function includes two parts: *Macro1!* identifies the macro sheet containing the function that is identified by the second part of the name, *COMMIS*; the function's argument, B3, identifies the cell you want the function to operate on. When you press Enter to lock in this function, it calculates and returns the correct commission for the sales amount in cell B3: $1,200. To complete the job, select the range C3:C6 and use the Fill Down command to copy the user-defined function in cell C3 into cells C4:C6. Because the reference to cell B3 in the original function is a relative reference, it changes as this formula is copied into the new cells. The formula in cell C4 is

=Macro1!COMMIS(B4)

and the formula in cell C5 is

=Macro1!COMMIS(B5)

When you perform this copy, Excel calculates the function macro once for each cell in the fill range. Figure 19-3 shows the result. (Notice that we've formatted for dollar values with no decimals.)

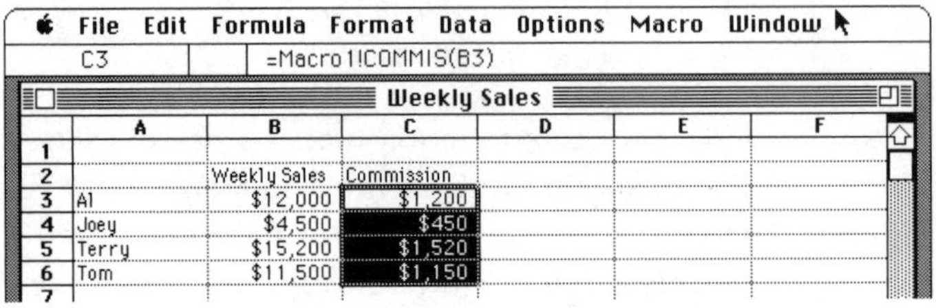

FIGURE 19-3. *This figure shows the result of using the Fill Down command to enter the COMMIS function into cells C4:C6.*

Let's consider what happens when you enter this function in the worksheet. When you press Enter, Excel immediately looks at the macro sheet *Macro1* for a cell named *COMMIS* (A2). Then, it processes the statements in cells A2, A3, and A4 of the macro sheet, one at a time. The ARGUMENT statement in cell A2 assigns the name *Sales* to the value in cell B3, $12,000. (Remember that cell B3 is the cell you used as the argument in cell C3.) In effect, Excel "passes" the value from cell B3 to the macro sheet *Macro1*, where it is stored under the name *Sales*. If you now select the macro sheet and choose the Define Name... command from the Formula menu, the name *Sales* appears in the list of names. If you select *Sales*, Excel displays the value 11500—the last value in the *Weekly Sales* column of the worksheet—in the Refers To field.

Next, the formula in cell A3 of the macro sheet multiplies the value of *Sales* by 0.1. Finally, the RETURN statement in cell A4 passes the value of the formula in cell A3, $1,200, back to C3, the worksheet cell that contains the *COMMIS* function.

Now, suppose you need to change the values in cells B3:B6. As you might expect, Excel automatically updates the commission calculations in cells C3:C6 as you enter the new sales figures.

Obviously, this first example is trivial, but when the computations become more complex, user-defined functions can be real time savers. In a page or two, we expand on this example to make the advantages of user-defined functions clear.

Function macro rules

Although the example we have just looked at is very simple, it illustrates many of the characteristics of all function macros. First, every function macro must include at least one ARGUMENT function and a RETURN function. Most function macros also include one or more formulas, like the one in cell A3 in the example, that perform computations using the arguments.

The order of the functions in a user-defined function macro is very important. The formulas that actually do the work of the function must be between the ARGUMENT functions and the RETURN function. If these formulas are below the RETURN function, the user-defined function does not calculate properly.

Often, you will begin your function macro in cell A1 in a blank macro sheet, as we did in the example. However, there is no restriction on the location of the macro in the macro sheet. You could just as easily enter this macro in cells Z100 to Z103 and assign the name *COMMIS* to cell Z101.

You can only use macros that are located on open macro sheets. If you close a macro sheet that contains a function macro that is referred to by user-defined functions in open worksheets, the value of those functions changes to #REF!. To recompute the functions, you must reopen the macro sheet.

Naming macro sheets

You must specify the name of a macro sheet every time you use a user-defined function, so we suggest that you get in the habit of using very short, descriptive names for your macro sheets. For example, you might want to use a name like *UD1* (for User-Defined 1) for the first macro sheet in which you create user-defined functions, *UD2* for the second such sheet, and so on.

Alternatively, you can use short macro-sheet names to describe the user-defined functions in the sheet. For example, you might name a macro sheet that contains depreciation functions *DEP*, or a sheet that contains tax functions *TAX*. Then, you can assign names to the functions that describe the particular purpose of that function within the general group. To change the name of a macro sheet, use the Save As... command on the File menu. When you choose this command, Excel offers you an opportunity to supply a new name for the sheet. To save the sheet with a new name, type the name and click the OK button. You can then delete the original worksheet, which was saved with a different name.

If you have used any of the user-defined functions on the macro sheet that you are saving in a worksheet, the names of those functions change automatically when you save the macro sheet. For example, suppose a cell contains the function

=Macro1!COMMIS(C5)

If you use Save As... to change the name of *Macro1* to *Sales*, the name of the function changes to

=Sales!COMMIS(C5)

We think you'll find that short, descriptive names are preferable to the default names that Excel gives to macro sheets: *Macro1*, *Macro2*, and so on.

Naming user-defined functions

As a general rule, you should give a user-defined function the shortest name that sufficiently describes the function's purpose, yet sets it apart from other functions. For example, you might call a function that computes federal income taxes *FEDERALINCOMETAX*, but you would be better off shortening that long name to *FEDINCTAX*, *FEDTAX*, or *FEDTX*. Using this same rule, you might call a function that computes Accelerated Cost Recovery System depreciation *ACRS*, a function that computes Social Security tax withholdings *FICA* (for Federal Insurance Contributions Act), and a function that computes the interest paid to date on a loan *TODATEINT*.

Be sure you don't make the names of your user-defined functions so short that they are not descriptive. For example, you probably wouldn't want to call your federal income tax function *TAX*, because this name doesn't tell you what kind of tax the function computes. Similarly, you probably wouldn't want to call the *ACRS* function *DEP* (for DEPreciation), since that name doesn't tell you what type of depreciation the function computes.

You also should not give your functions names that conflict with the names of Excel's built-in functions, such as PV, SUM, LINEST, or IF. If you do give a user-defined function one of these reserved names, Excel returns an *Error in formula* message when you attempt to use the user-defined function in a worksheet.

The Paste Function... command

Once you have created a user-defined function, Excel adds the name of that function to the list you see when you choose the Paste Function... command from the Formula menu. User-defined functions always appear at the end of the list, as shown in Figure 19-4.

You can use the Paste Function... command to make user-defined functions easier to use. Instead of typing the macro-sheet name and function name, you can simply select from the list the user-defined function you want to use. To do this, double click the name you want. Excel enters the macro-sheet name and the function name in the formula bar. Then, all you have to do is supply the arguments (by typing or pasting) and click the entry box to lock in the function.

The Paste Function list always includes the names of all the user-defined functions contained in the open macro sheets. When you open a new macro sheet, Excel automatically adds the names of any user-defined functions in that sheet to the list. When you close a macro sheet, all the names in that sheet are removed from the list.

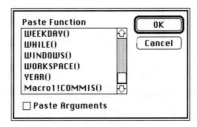

FIGURE 19-4. *This Paste Function dialog box shows a user-defined function at the end of the list.*

Making a change

Let's expand the simple commission calculation to see how function macros can be edited. Suppose your company uses a more complex commission formula: Salespeople receive a 10-percent commission if they sell under $5,000-worth of goods, an 11-percent commission if they sell more than $5,000-worth but less than $15,000-worth, and a 12-percent commission if they sell more than $15,000-worth. Let's modify the simple function to perform this new calculation.

To do this, select the macro sheet Macro1, select cell A3 (the cell that contains the commission calculation), and enter the formula

    =IF(Sales>15000,Sales*0.12,IF(Sales>5000,Sales*0.11,Sales*0.1))

That's all there is to it: The user-defined function now computes commissions using the new formula.

If you switch back to the *Weekly Sales* worksheet, however, you'll see that the values in cells C3 through C6 have not changed. Excel does not update the user-defined functions in your worksheet when you make a change to the macro that computes the function. To update the results in the *Weekly Sales* worksheet, you have to "re-enter" the user-defined functions in cells C3:C6.

Of course, you could re-enter the functions manually by selecting each of the cells and retyping the function. Fortunately, there is an easier method. You can select each of the cells in the range, one by one, and, while the cell is selected, click in the formula bar, then click the enter box. "Editing" each cell in this way updates the functions. Figure 19-5 shows the worksheet after the functions have been updated.

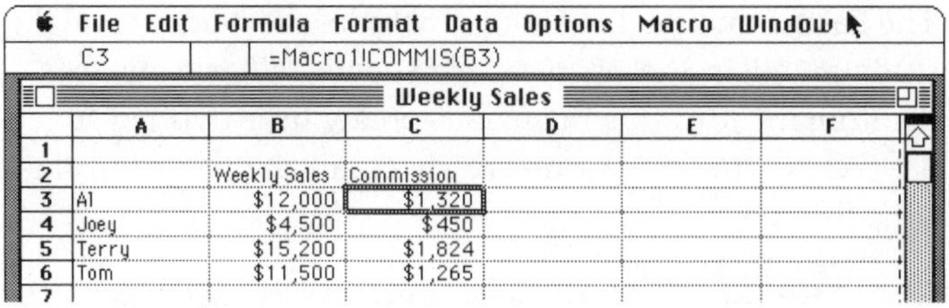

FIGURE 19-5. *You have recalculated the commissions using the revised function macro.*

Notice that cell A3 in this function macro contains a complicated IF function. Excel allows you to use all of the functions you learned about in Chapter 6, "Built-in Functions," in macro sheets. These functions behave exactly the same way in a macro sheet as they do in a worksheet, and you can use them to perform calculations or make decisions in your function macros. In a few pages, we look at a complex user-defined function that uses the VLOOKUP function.

Function macros with more than one argument

Now, let's consider a more complex example. Suppose your company sells three products, and each product carries a different discount schedule. Salespeople earn a flat 10-percent commission on all sales of *Product 1* and a flat 8 percent on sales of *Product 2*. They earn a commission on *Product 3* of 10 percent on sales up to $5,000, and 12 percent on sales of more than $5,000. In addition, any salesperson who sells more than $25,000 of products in a period earns an additional 1-percent bonus commission.

Let's create a new function macro to make this computation. To do this, move to cell A6 in the macro sheet, and enter the name *COMMIS2*. Then, enter the macro shown in Figure 19-6 into cells A7:A16. When you have entered this macro into the macro sheet, select cell A7 and choose the Define Name… command from the Formula menu. When you choose this command, Microsoft Excel suggests the name *COMMIS2* for the selected cell. To accept this name, first click the Function button, then click OK.

Obviously, this new function macro is more complex than the other two you've built. First, notice that it includes four ARGUMENT functions. When you use this user-defined function in the worksheet, it has the form

=Macro1!COMMIS2(*Prod1,Prod2,Prod3,Total*)

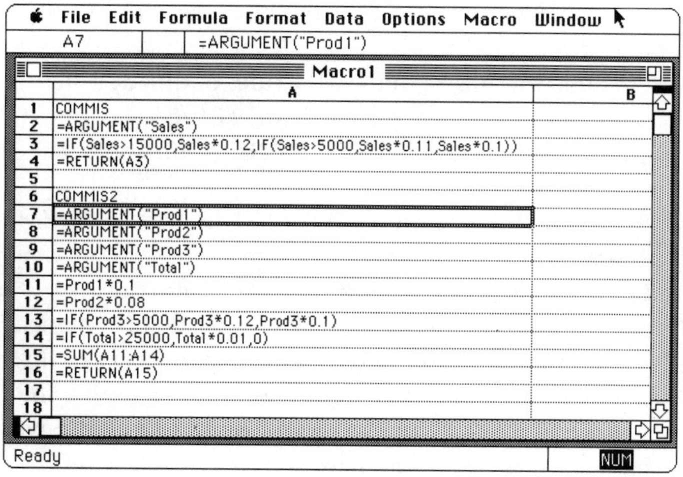

FIGURE 19-6. *This is a more complex function macro for calculating commissions.*

where *Prod1* is the sales of *Product 1*, *Prod2* is the sales of *Product 2*, *Prod3* is the sales of *Product 3*, and *Total* is the total sales. The four ARGUMENT functions store the values you specify for these four arguments under the names *Prod1*, *Prod2*, *Prod3*, and *Total*.

Notice that the order of the arguments in the user-defined function matches the order of the ARGUMENT functions in the macro. This is critical: If the arguments in the function are in a different order, the function does not compute the correct result. The order of the arguments in a user-defined function must always match the order of the ARGUMENT functions in the macro that defines the function.

Of course, you are free to define the order of the arguments in any way you wish. For example, you can reverse the arguments in the function macro. In that case, the corresponding worksheet formula has the form

=Macro1!COMMIS2(*Total,Prod3,Prod2,Prod1*)

Also, notice that the *COMMIS2* macro includes five formulas, in cells A11 through A15, while the earlier examples included only one formula. The first three formulas compute the commissions on sales of *Product 1*, *Product 2*, and *Product 3*. The formula in cell A14 computes the bonus commission on sales of over $25,000, and the formula in cell A15 computes the total commission by summing the results of the first four formulas.

The RETURN statement in cell A16 returns the result of the formula in cell A15 in the macro sheet to the cell in the worksheet that contains the user-defined function.

Notice that this macro follows the rules outlined earlier regarding the order of the terms in a function macro: ARGUMENT functions first, followed by the computing formulas, followed by the RETURN function. This order is absolutely required.

You've called this function *COMMIS2* instead of *COMMIS*. You cannot have two user-defined functions with the same name on the same macro sheet. Excel would have allowed you to name this new macro *COMMIS*, but it would have removed the name from cell A2 at the same time that it assigned the name to cell A7.

Now, let's put this user-defined function to work. To do this, first modify the *Weekly Sales* worksheet as shown in Figure 19-7, entering the *Commission* column header in cell F2, but leaving the rest of column F blank. Save the worksheet with the name *Commissions*. In the new worksheet, select cell F3 and enter the user-defined function

=Macro1!COMMIS2(B3,C3,D3,E3)

When you press Enter to lock in the function, Excel computes the *COMMIS2* macro and displays the correct commission for Al in cell F3, as shown in Figure 19-7. (We have formatted cells F3:F6 for dollar values without decimal places.) To complete the job, use the Fill Down command to copy the formula from cell F3 into cells F4:F6.

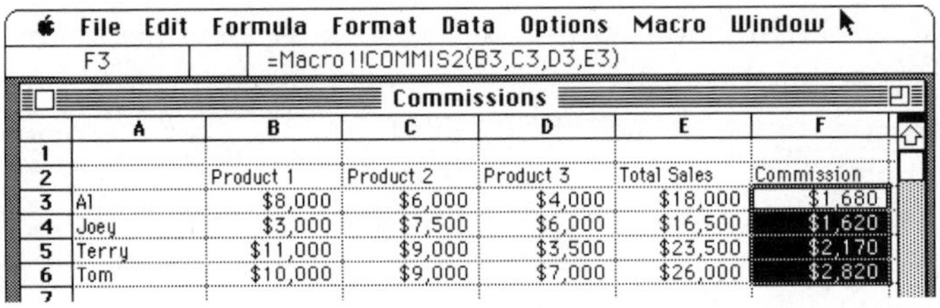

```
 File  Edit  Formula  Format  Data  Options  Macro  Window
      F3                  =Macro1!COMMIS2(B3,C3,D3,E3)
```

	A	B	C	D	E	F
1						
2		Product 1	Product 2	Product 3	Total Sales	Commission
3	Al	$8,000	$6,000	$4,000	$18,000	$1,680
4	Joey	$3,000	$7,500	$6,000	$16,500	$1,620
5	Terry	$11,000	$9,000	$3,500	$23,500	$2,170
6	Tom	$10,000	$9,000	$7,000	$26,000	$2,820
7						

FIGURE 19-7. *You have entered the* COMMIS2 *user-defined function in cells F3:F6.*

Here's how the function works. As soon as you lock in the formula, Excel calculates the macro. The four ARGUMENT functions store the values from cells B3, C3, D3, and E3 under the names *Prod1*, *Prod2*, *Prod3*, and *Total*. (Now you see why the order of the arguments in the function must match the order of the ARGUMENT functions in the macro.) The formulas in cells A11:A14 in the macro sheet then compute the commissions on all three products and the bonus commission (if any). Then, the formula in cell A15 computes the total commission. Finally, the RETURN function in cell A16 returns the value from cell A15 in the macro sheet to cell F3 in the worksheet, which contains the user-defined function.

A compound-interest function

Suppose you are contemplating investing $100,000 in an account that pays 10 percent interest—guaranteed—for as long as you want to hold the investment. You want to know what the value of the investment will be at any given time in the future. Let's build a user-defined function that makes this computation for you.

To begin, set up a worksheet like the one shown in Figure 19-8. Cell C2 in this worksheet contains the guaranteed rate of interest, cell C3 the amount you want to invest, and cell C4 the term of the investment. We use these three variables as the arguments in our function.

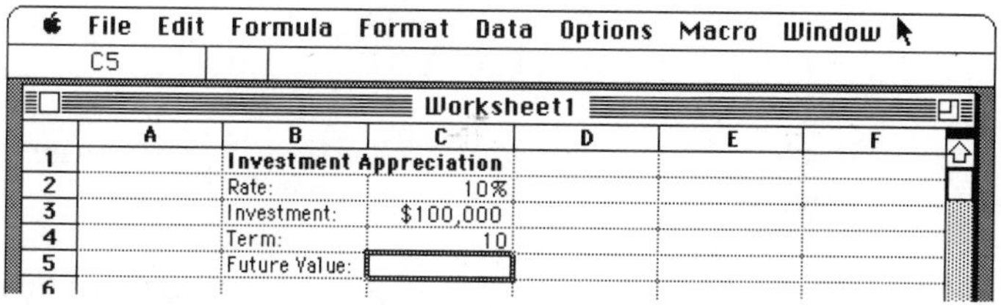

FIGURE 19-8. *This is the worksheet in which you will calculate the future value of an investment.*

Now, let's create a new macro sheet to hold the macro. To do this, choose the New... command from the File menu and double click the Macro Sheet option. After a moment, Excel presents you with a new macro sheet—in this case named *Macro2*. Now, select cell A1 and enter the text *COMPOUND*. This text entry will become the name of the function. Next, enter the function macro shown in Figure 19-9 into cells A2:A6 in the macro sheet.

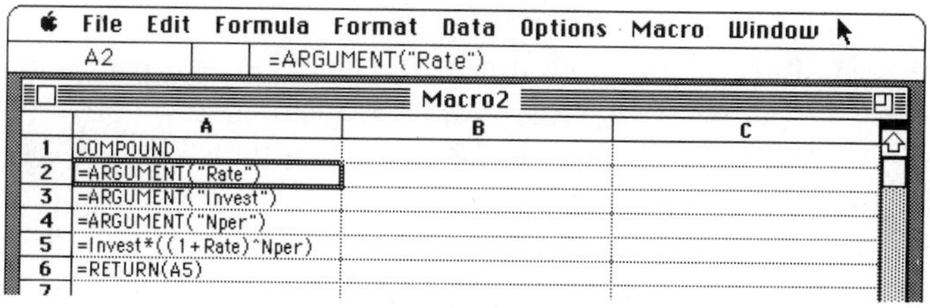

FIGURE 19-9. *This is our COMPOUND function macro.*

When you have finished entering the macro, select cell A2, choose the Define Name... command from the Formula menu, click Function to tell Excel that this is a function macro, and click OK to accept the default name *COMPOUND*.

Now, select your worksheet again, select cell C5, and type

=Macro2!COMPOUND(

As with Excel's built-in functions, you can paste arguments into user-defined functions. So now, instead of typing the references to cells C2, C3, and C4, click cell C2, type a comma, click cell C3, type another comma, and click cell C4. Finally, type a close parenthesis to finish the function and press Enter. Figure 19-10 shows the result, which we formatted for dollars.

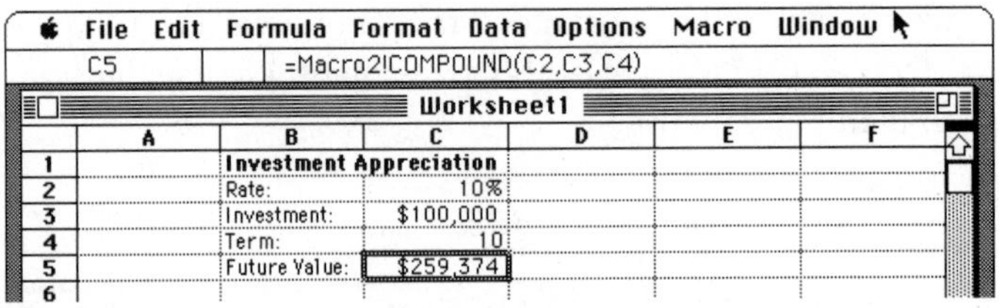

FIGURE 19-10. *The COMPOUND function macro has computed the future value of an investment.*

Here's how the function works. The three ARGUMENT functions in cells A2, A3, and A4 of the macro sheet store the values from cells C2, C3, and C4 of the worksheet under the names *Rate, Invest,* and *Nper*. Then, the formula in cell A5

=Invest*((1+Rate)^Nper)

computes the future value of the investment *Nper* number of periods into the future. Finally, the RETURN function in cell A6 returns the result of the computation from cell A5 to the worksheet.

As with the other user-defined functions that you have created, if you change the values of the arguments in cells C2, C3, and C4, the value of the function in cell C5 also changes. Once the user-defined function is in place, it behaves almost like one of Excel's built-in functions.

Again, this is a simple example of a user-defined function. You might be able to perform this particular computation faster using conventional formulas. As before, though, our purpose is to demonstrate the form and operation of user-defined functions. In a few pages, we expand on this example to create a more complex function macro.

Interest and principal paid-to-date functions

As you learned in Chapter 6, "Built-in Functions," Excel offers several financial functions, like PV, FV, and IRR, that allow you to make complex financial computations simply and easily. Among the most useful of these functions is PMT, which computes the period payment that is required to amortize a loan. However, although PMT is a very helpful tool, there are several other loan repayment calculations that are also useful.

Figure 19-11 shows a worksheet that includes all of the data you need to compute the periodic payment on a loan. (We widened column A to hold the long entries we typed there.) Cell B3 in this worksheet contains the amount that you have borrowed: $10,000. Cell B4 contains the periodic interest rate: 1.00%. (We're assuming that this loan requires monthly payments.) The term of the loan in months, 60, appears in cell B5. Finally, cell B6, formatted to show dollars and cents, contains the function

=PMT(B4,B5,–B3)

which computes the monthly payment on the loan: $222.44. (We've formatted cell B6 for a dollar value.) Notice that we made the last argument in the PMT function negative. Normally, the result of the PMT function is a negative number because it represents a cash outflow. However, we find the use of negative numbers for payments confusing. By changing the sign of the last argument, we make the result of the PMT function positive instead of negative.

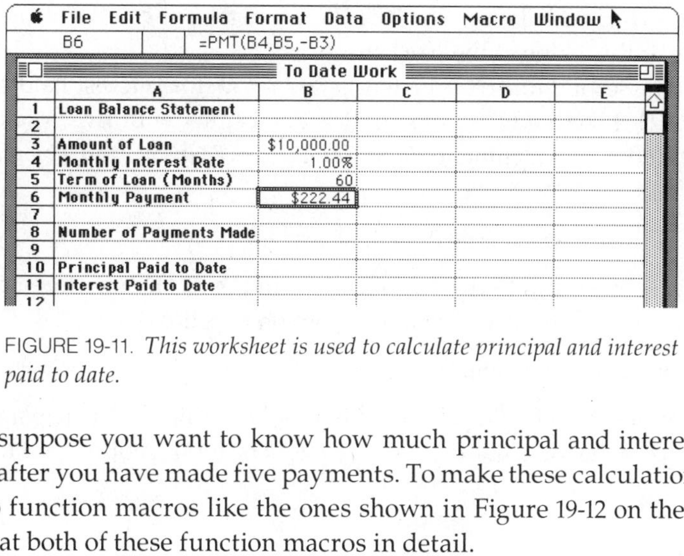

FIGURE 19-11. *This worksheet is used to calculate principal and interest paid to date.*

Now, suppose you want to know how much principal and interest you will have paid after you have made five payments. To make these calculations, you can create two function macros like the ones shown in Figure 19-12 on the next page. Let's look at both of these function macros in detail.

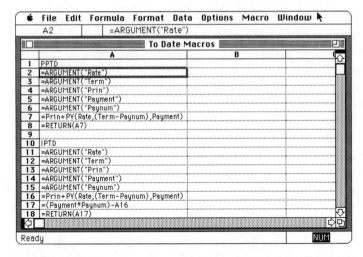

FIGURE 19-12. *These function macros compute principal and interest paid to date.*

The first macro, which is called *PPTD* (for Principal Paid To Date), begins with five ARGUMENT functions that define the arguments *Rate, Term, Prin, Payment*, and *Paynum*. The formula in cell A7

=Prin+PV(Rate,(Term−Paynum),Payment)

computes the principal paid to date by computing the present value of the remaining payments, then adding that value (which is a negative number) to the beginning principal balance. The RETURN function in cell A8 of the macro sheet then returns this value to the worksheet.

The second macro, which is called *IPTD* (for Interest Paid To Date), begins in cell A11. Like the PPTD macro, this one begins with five ARGUMENT functions that define the arguments *Rate, Term, Prin, Payment*, and *Paynum*. The formula in cell A16

=Prin+PV(Rate,(Term−Paynum),Payment)

which is identical to the one in cell A7 in the PPTD function macro, computes the principal paid to date. Then, the function in cell A17

=(Payment∗Paynum)−A16

computes the interest paid to date by subtracting the principal paid to date in cell A16 from the total amount paid to date. The total amount paid to date is computed by multiplying *Payment*, the monthly payment, by *Paynum*, the number of payments that have been made. After this computation is made, the RETURN function in cell A18 returns this value to the worksheet.

Of course, before you can use these functions, you must assign the name *PPTD* to cell A2 and the name *IPTD* to cell A11.

Let's see how these functions work. Return to the worksheet and enter the number 5 in cell B8. Now, enter the function

='To Date Macros'!PPTD(B4,B5,B3,B6,B8)

in cell B10 and the function

='To Date Macros'!IPTD(B4,B5,B3,B6,B8)

in cell B11. Figure 19-13 shows the result. The number in cell B10 (formatted to display dollars and cents), $624.59, is the amount of principal paid in the first five monthly payments, while the number in cell B11 (formatted to display dollars and cents), $487.63, is the amount of interest paid during the same period.

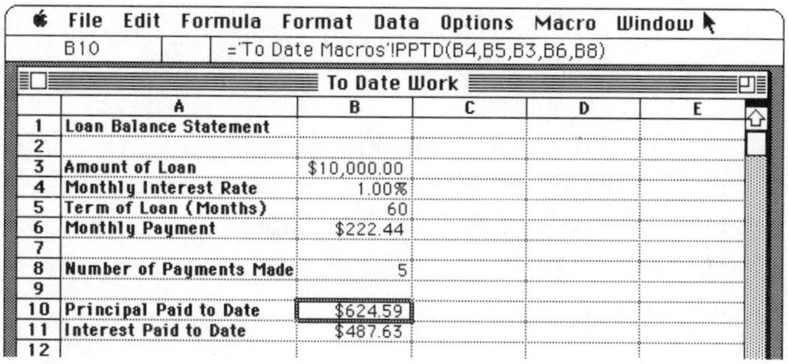

FIGURE 19-13. *This worksheet shows the result of entering the user-defined functions PPTD and IPTD in cells B10 and B11.*

Omitting arguments

Some of Excel's built-in functions allow you to omit certain arguments. For example, you can omit the *type* and *fv* arguments from a PV function, and Excel still computes the result of the function.

If you omit an argument from a user-defined function, however, Excel assigns that argument the value #N/A. As you learned in Chapter 2, "Worksheet Basics," any formula that refers to a cell or a name that contains the value #N/A generally assumes the value #N/A. Thus, if you omit an argument, the function will probably return the value #N/A. You can get around this problem by using the IF function to test the value of each of the arguments in the function that you might omit, to see if they have the value #N/A.

For example, suppose you want to create a function, called *TRIANGLE*, that uses the Pythagorean theorem to compute the length of any side of a right triangle, given the lengths of the other two sides. The function macro shown in Figure 19-14 does the trick. Note that we've doubled the size of column A for display purposes.

File	Edit	Formula	Format	Data	Options	Macro	Window

A8	=RETURN(IF(ISNA(Long),A5,IF(ISNA(Short1),A6,A7)))

Tri Macro

	A	B
1	TRIANGLE	
2	=ARGUMENT("Long")	
3	=ARGUMENT("Short1")	
4	=ARGUMENT("Short2")	
5	=IF(ISNA(Long),SQRT((Short1^2)+(Short2^2)))	
6	=IF(ISNA(Short1),SQRT((Long^2)-(Short2^2)))	
7	=IF(ISNA(Short2),SQRT((Long^2)-(Short1^2)))	
8	=RETURN(IF(ISNA(Long),A5,IF(ISNA(Short1),A6,A7)))	
9		

FIGURE 19-14. *This function macro computes the length of any side of a right triangle, given the lengths of the other two sides.*

The first three lines in this macro include three ARGUMENT functions that define the arguments *Long*, *Short1*, and *Short2*. The next three lines all contain IF functions that test the values of the arguments for possible #N/A errors. The formula in cell A5

=IF(ISNA(Long),SQRT((Short1^2)+(Short2^2)))

tests the value of *Long*. If *Long* contains the value #N/A, the formula computes the square root of the sums of the squares of the lengths of the two short sides. If not, Excel calculates the formula in cell A6

=IF(ISNA(Short1),SQRT((Long^2)-(Short2^2)))

which tests the value of *Short1*. If *Short1* contains the value #N/A, the formula computes the square root of the difference of the squares of the length of the long side minus the square of the length of the other short side. If not, Excel calculates the formula in cell A7

=IF(ISNA(Short2),SQRT((Long^2)-(Short1^2)))

which tests the value of *Short2*. If *Short2* contains the value #N/A, the formula computes the square root of the difference between the square of the length of the long side minus the square of the length of the other short side.

Finally, the formula in cell A8

=RETURN(IF(ISNA(Long),A5,IF(ISNA(Short1),A6,A7)))

returns the value from cell A5, A6, or A7 to the worksheet.

To name this function, select cell A2, choose the Define Name... command from the Formula menu, click the Function button, and click OK to accept the default name, *TRIANGLE*.

Now, let's see how the function works. The function

='Tri Macro'!TRIANGLE(5,4,)

returns the value 3, the length of the missing short side. Similarly, the function

='Tri Macro'!TRIANGLE(5,,3)

returns 4. The function

='Tri Macro'!TRIANGLE(,4,3)

returns 5, the length of the long side.

In this case, you were able to avoid using the omitted argument in any calculations. For this reason, you didn't have to worry about an #N/A value being passed from formula to formula in the macro. If you must use an omitted argument in a calculation, you can use the SET.NAME function to assign that argument the value 0 or 1 so that it has no effect on the calculation.

A lookup function

Suppose your company uses the following discount schedule for the products it sells to wholesalers and retailers:

Quantity purchased	Wholesale discount (%)	Retail discount (%)
0 to 5	0	0
6 to 10	0	40
11 to 20	50	41
21 to 50	51	43
over 51	52	45

You want to create a user-defined function that returns the correct discount for the type of customer you are selling to and the quantity purchased.

Figure 19-15 shows an invoice worksheet (with some special formatting for legibility). Cell B4 contains a code that describes the type of customer: *W* for wholesale; *R* for Retail. Cell C14 contains the total quantity ordered by the customer. The values in these cells will be the arguments to the function macro we are going to define.

To create the function macro, create a new macro sheet (call it *Discount Macro*), then enter the macro shown in Figure 19-16. Let's walk through this macro together so that you can see how it works. Notice that we've altered the column widths so we can display the macro in the figure.

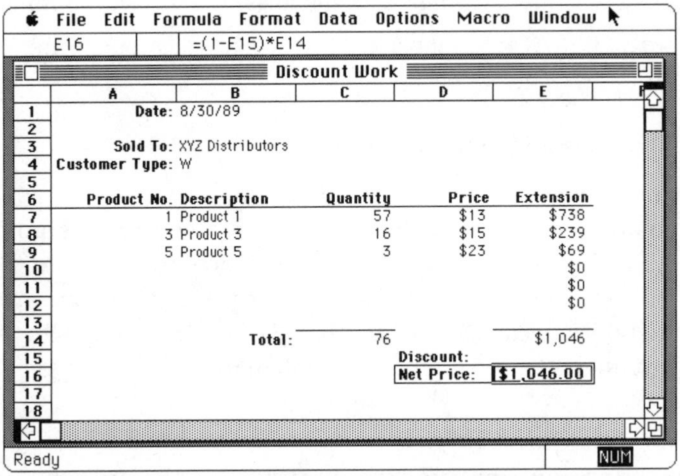

FIGURE 19-15. *This worksheet is used to calculate the correct discount for the type of customer and the quantity ordered.*

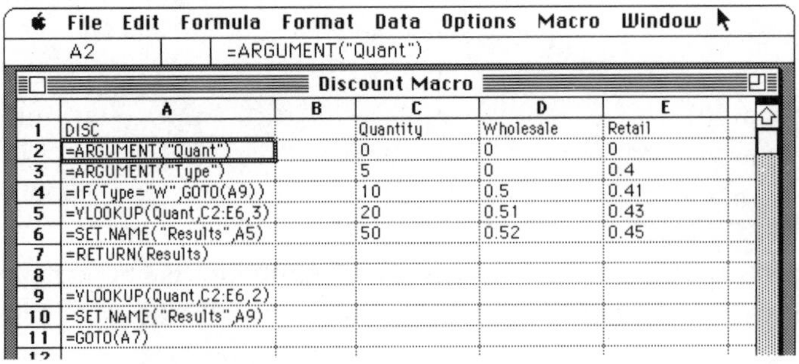

FIGURE 19-16. *This is the DISC function macro.*

Cell A1 of the macro sheet contains the text entry *DISC*, which becomes the name of the macro. Cells A2 and A3 contain ARGUMENT functions that define the arguments *Quant* and *Type*. Notice that you don't have to do anything special to define *Type* as a text argument. The ARGUMENT function can accept either numeric or text arguments.

The formula in cell A4

=IF(Type="W",GOTO(A9))

tests the value of *Type*. If *Type* is *W*, the GOTO function tells Excel to jump to cell A9 and execute the formula it finds there. The formula in cell A9

=VLOOKUP(Quant,C2:E6,2)

uses the value of *Quant* to look up the appropriate discount from the second column of the lookup table in the range C2:E6. The function in cell A10 stores the result from the formula in cell A9 under the name *Results*. Next, the formula in cell A11

=GOTO(A7)

sends the macro back to cell A7. The RETURN function in cell A7 then returns the value of *Results* to the worksheet.

If *Type* is not equal to *W*, the macro continues with the formula in cell A5

=VLOOKUP(Quant,C2:E6,3)

instead of branching to cell A9. This function uses the value of *Quant* to look up the appropriate discount from the third column of the lookup table in the range C2:E6. The function in cell A6 then stores the result from the formula in cell A5 under the name *Results*. The RETURN function in cell A7 in the macro sheet returns the value of *Results* to the worksheet.

Once you have created this function, you need to select cell A2 and choose the Define Name... command from the Formula menu. When you choose this command, Microsoft Excel suggests the name *DISC* for the selected cell. To accept this name, simply click Function and then click OK.

Now, let's use the function. Activate your worksheet, select cell E15, and enter the function

='Discount Macro'!DISC(C14,B4)

Figure 19-17 on the next page shows the result. As you can see, Excel has looked up the correct discount from the table in the macro sheet and returned that value to cell E15. (We've formatted the discount figure to be a whole number followed by a percent sign.) The formula in cell E16

=(1–E15)∗E14

uses this result to compute the net price of the order. Of course, if you change either the entry in cell B4 or the total in cell C14, the result of the function changes.

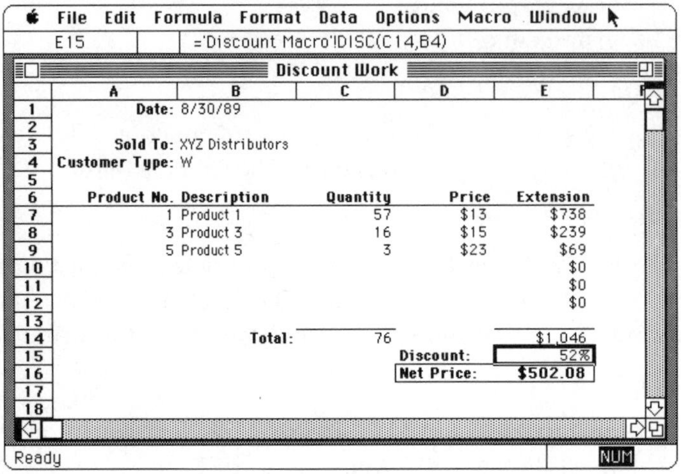

```
 File   Edit   Formula   Format   Data   Options   Macro   Window ▸
    E15                   ='Discount Macro'!DISC(C14,B4)
```

FIGURE 19-17. *This figure shows the results of using the DISC function macro to calculate the discount.*

A modification

Suppose the user makes an entry other than *W* or *R* in cell B4. The way the macro is structured, the function returns the retail discount no matter what is entered in cell B4. The IF function in cell A4 tests to see if *Type* is equal to *W*. If *Type* is not equal to *W*, the macro assumes that it is equal to *R*, and uses the first VLOOKUP function to compute the discount.

To overcome this problem, you can modify the macro as shown in Figure 19-18. To make this change, select row 7, choose the Insert... command from the Edit menu to insert a new row, then enter the function

=IF(AND(Type<>"R",Type<>"W"),SET.NAME("Results",#VALUE!))

in the new cell A7.

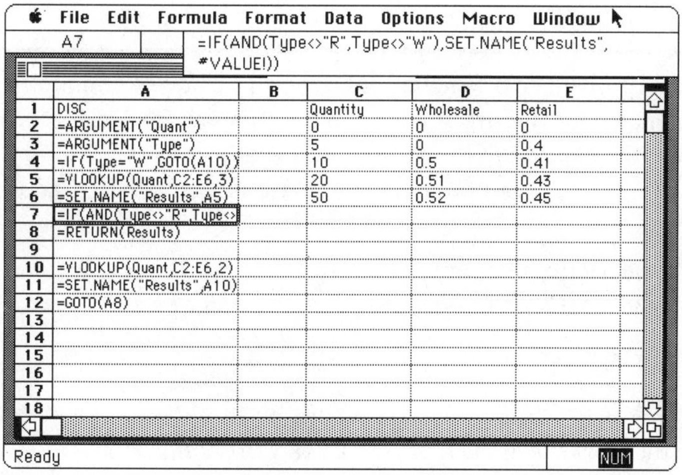

FIGURE 19-18. *You have modified the DISC function macro to trap erroneous entries.*

These two changes prevent the kind of error we described. The new macro tests the value of *Type* just before it returns *Results* to the worksheet. If *Type* is not equal to *R* or *W*, the formula in cell A7 changes the value of *Results* to the error value #VALUE!, so that the function returns #VALUE! to cells E15 and E16 instead of an erroneous value.

The basic concept presented in this macro—storing a lookup table on a macro sheet and using a function macro to look up values from that table—can be applied to many different types of user-defined functions. For example, you can use this technique to create functions that perform complicated tax computations based on tax tables that you store in a macro sheet.

The ARGUMENT function

The full form of the ARGUMENT function is

=ARGUMENT(*"name",type,cell reference*)

where *"name"* is the name of the argument, *type* is a number that specifies the type of the argument, and *cell reference* is the cell in which you want Excel to store the argument's value (more about this later). The *type* and *cell reference* arguments are optional.

The "name" argument

Each argument in a function macro should have a unique name. If you use the same name for two arguments in a function macro, Excel replaces the first definition of the name with the second definition.

For example, suppose you write a macro named *QUIZ* that begins with the lines

    =ARGUMENT("Test")
    =ARGUMENT("Test")

When you enter the formula

    =QUIZ(A1,A2)

into the worksheet, the first ARGUMENT function stores the value from cell A1 in the worksheet under the name *Test*, then the second function stores the value from cell A2 under the same name. Clearly, it doesn't work to use an identical name for two arguments within one macro.

For the same reason, you must be sure that you don't use the SET.NAME function to define range names in the macro sheet that conflict with your argument names. If you do, the value of the argument is replaced with the value defined by SET.NAME.

It is permissible to have two different function macros on one macro sheet that have arguments with the same names. Because Excel calculates each function separately, the names do not come into conflict.

The type argument

The *type* argument allows you to use different types of entries as arguments in your user-defined functions. The following table shows the possible values of the *type* argument and the meaning of each of those values:

If you use...	Excel expects *type* to be...
0	Formula
1	Number
2	Text
4	Logical
8	Reference
16	Error
64	Array

Interestingly, you can also use the sum of any two or more of these codes as the *type* argument, in which case Excel accepts any of those codes as the argument. For example, if you use the number 3, which is the sum of codes 1 and 2, as the *type* argument in an ARGUMENT function, Excel allows the argument to be of either type 1 (number) or type 2 (text). In fact, the default *type* argument is 7, which is the sum of codes 1 (number), 2 (text), and 4 (logical).

You will rarely, if ever, need to specify any *type* except the default, 7. In fact, about the only time you'll use the *type* argument is when you want to use an array as an argument in one of your user-defined functions. We look at an example of a function that uses array arguments in the next section. You will almost never use *reference* or *error* arguments in your functions either, so we won't dwell on those *type* arguments.

Array arguments

Many of Excel's built-in functions operate on ranges of cells. For example, the SUM function is used to sum the values in a range of cells. There will also be times when you'll want to use ranges as arguments in your user-defined functions. To do this, you must set the type argument in the ARGUMENT function to 64.

Let's consider an example of a user-defined function that uses array arguments. The worksheet in Figure 19-19 includes the semester grades in Business 101 for Joe Jones. Column B in this worksheet shows Joe's scores for the semester, and column C shows the weights that the professor has assigned to each of those scores. You need to compute Joe's weighted average score for the semester.

🍎	File	Edit	Formula	Format	Data	Options	Macro	Window	▶

| | F18 | | | |

≡			Grades				

	A	B	C	D	E	F	
1	Business 101						
2	Semester Grades: Joe Jones						
3		Grade	Weight				
4	Quiz	72	10				
5	Quiz	92	10				
6	Paper	87	30				
7	Final Exam	95	50				
8							

FIGURE 19-19. *This worksheet is used to compute weighted average scores.*

You can compute the weighted average score in one of three ways. For one method, you first enter the formula

=B4*C4

into cell D4 and copy that formula into cells D5, D6, and D7. Then, you enter the formula

    =SUM(C4:C7)

in cell C8 and copy that formula into cell D8. Finally, you enter the formula

    =D8/C8

in cell D10 to obtain the weighted average.

Alternatively, you can enter the array formula

    =SUM(B4:B7*C4:C7)/SUM(C4:C7)

in cell D10. (Remember, to make this function an array formula, you have to press the Command and Enter keys simultaneously to lock the formula in.) This formula tells Excel to compute the sum of the products of the values in cells B4:B7 and C4:C7, and then to divide that result by the sum of the values in the range C4:C7.

Instead of using either of these methods, you can create a user-defined function, called *WAVG*, that computes the weighted average of any list of values. To do this, you first create a macro sheet (or open an existing sheet). Then, you enter the macro shown in Figure 19-20. Let's walk through this macro one line at a time.

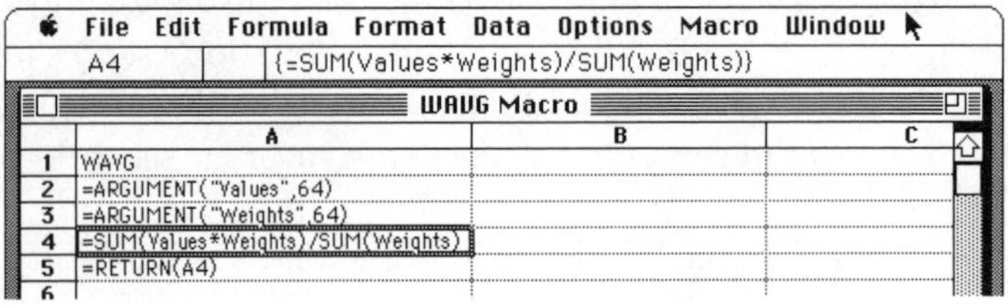

FIGURE 19-20. *This macro calculates weighted averages.*

The entry in cell A1 of this macro sheet, *WAVG*, is the name of the new function. The formula in cell A2

    =ARGUMENT("Values",64)

defines the *Values* argument and informs Excel that *Values* is an array. Similarly, the third line

    =ARGUMENT("Weights",64)

defines the *Weights* array argument. The formula in cell A4

    =SUM(Values*Weights)/SUM(Weights)

is very similar to the array formula you would have created had you used the second method we described for calculating weighted averages. This formula tells

Excel to compute the sum of the products of the values in the *Values* array and the *Weights* array and to divide that result by the sum of the values in the *Weights* array. Notice that this formula is an array formula. To make it an array formula, you need to press Command and Enter simultaneously to lock it in.

The last line in the macro

=RETURN(A4)

returns the result of the formula in cell A4 to the cell in the worksheet that contains the user-defined function.

After you have entered the macro in the macro sheet, you select cell A2 and choose the Define Name... command from the Formula menu. When you choose this command, Excel presents a Define Name dialog box proposing *WAVG* as the name for cell A2. Since this is the name you want to assign to the function, simply click Function to define the macro as a function macro and click OK to accept the default name.

Now, to use the function you've just defined, go back to the worksheet, select cell D10, and enter the formula

='WAVG Macro'!WAVG(B4:B7,C4:C7)

When you enter this function in the worksheet, Excel calculates the macro named *WAVG* in the macro sheet called *WAVG Macro,* beginning with cell A2 and continuing through cell A5. The two ARGUMENT functions store the arrays B4:B7 and C4:C7 (the argument ranges that you specified) under the names *Values* and *Weights.* The array formula in cell A4 then uses these arrays to compute the weighted average, and the RETURN function returns the result from cell A4 to D10, the cell in the worksheet that contains the function. Figure 19-21 shows the result. Notice that we've added a label to cell C10.

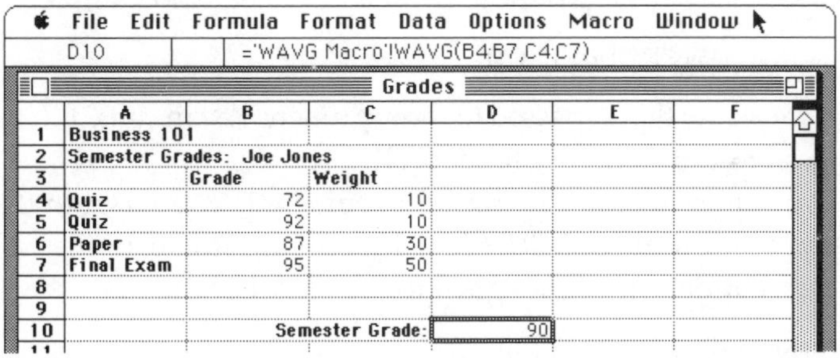

	A	B	C	D	E	F
1	Business 101					
2	Semester Grades: Joe Jones					
3		Grade	Weight			
4	Quiz	72	10			
5	Quiz	92	10			
6	Paper	87	30			
7	Final Exam	95	50			
8						
9						
10			Semester Grade:	90		

FIGURE 19-21. *This worksheet shows the result of computing a weighted average score with the user-defined WAVG function.*

It is important that you understand how much more flexible this user-defined function is than either of the two formulas it replaces. Both of the first two methods were limited to computing the weighted average of the four values that are in cells B4:B7. The WAVG function, however, can be used to compute the weighted average of a virtually unlimited list of values stored anywhere in the worksheet. For example, you could enter the function

='WAVG Macro'!WAVG(D1:D15,E1:E15)

in any blank cell in any worksheet to compute the weighted averages of values stored in cells D1:D15. The flexibility of this function is what makes it so superior to either of the other methods of computing the weighted average.

Determining the type of an argument

If you want to determine the type of an argument, you can use the TYPE function. For example, suppose you have defined an argument named *Test* in one of your function macros. The function

=TYPE(Test)

lets you know what type of argument *Test* was the last time the function macro containing it was calculated. The result of the TYPE function is not valid until after you have used the function macro. For example, if *Test* was 100 the last time the macro was calculated, the function returns the value 1 (number).

You must enter the TYPE function into one of the cells of the macro sheet that contains the function macro.

The cell reference argument

The *cell reference* argument allows you to tell Excel which cell it should use to store the value that will be passed to the macro sheet. For example, the function

=ARGUMENT("Test",7,C1)

stores the value that is passed to the argument *Test* in cell C1 in the macro sheet and then assigns the name *Test* to that cell.

You can even omit the *"name"* argument if you wish. In that event, the value that is passed to the ARGUMENT function is stored in the cell indicated by *cell reference*, but no name is assigned to that cell. For example, the formula

=ARGUMENT(,,C1)

stores the value that is passed from the worksheet in cell C1 of the macro sheet, but it does not assign a name to that cell.

To see how this works, let's go back to the weighted-average macro and make a few changes to it. Figure 19-20 shows the original macro. Change the first ARGUMENT function to

=ARGUMENT("Values",64,B1:B5)

and change the second ARGUMENT function to

=ARGUMENT("Weights",64,C1:C5)

Now, create another worksheet similar to the one in Figure 19-21, but this time enter the formula

='WAVG Macro'!WAVG(B4:B7,C4:C7)

in cell D10. When you press Enter, this function returns the result 90. Now, switch back to the macro sheet. Figure 19-22 shows the sheet after the macro has run. As you can see, Excel has entered the values from cells B4:B7 in the worksheet into cells B1:B4 in the macro sheet and has entered the values from cells C4:C7 in the worksheet into cells C1:C4 in the macro sheet. In addition, Excel has assigned the name *Values* to the range B1:B4 and the name *Weights* to the range C1:C4.

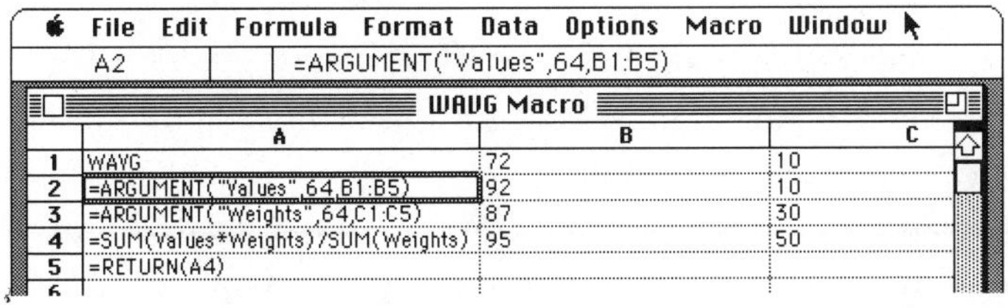

🍎 File Edit Formula Format Data Options Macro Window ▶		
A2	=ARGUMENT("Values",64,B1:B5)	
WAVG Macro		
A	B	C
1 WAVG	72	10
2 =ARGUMENT("Values",64,B1:B5)	92	10
3 =ARGUMENT("Weights",64,C1:C5)	87	30
4 =SUM(Values*Weights)/SUM(Weights)	95	50
5 =RETURN(A4)		
6		

FIGURE 19-22. *This is the macro sheet after the revised macro has run.*

If you use the *cell reference* argument to enter an array of entries into the macro sheet, you must be sure that *cell reference* defines a range of cells that is large enough to accommodate the array. Otherwise, only as many elements of the array as can fit in the defined space are passed to the macro sheet. If you want to be safe, you can use a *cell reference* argument that defines a range that you know is larger than the array. When you define a large range of cells, Excel assigns the designated name only to those cells in the range that are used, not to the entire range.

Most of the time, you won't want to store the values you pass to a macro sheet in the cells of that sheet. It is just as easy and effective, and much neater, simply to assign names to the values you pass to the function macro, although there are exceptions to this rule. For example, this capability comes in handy when you are debugging your function macros. If you enter each value that is passed to the function macro into one of the cells in the macro sheet, you can tell at a glance if all of the values have been received correctly.

The RESULT function

Just as a function macro can accept different types of arguments, it can also return different types of results. The type of result that a function macro returns is determined by the RESULT function. This function has the form

where *type* is a numeric code that specifies the type of the function's result. The numeric codes for RESULT are the same as those for ARGUMENT, and as with the ARGUMENT function, the *type* argument of the RESULT function can be the sum of two or more codes. Also like ARGUMENT, the default type is 7, which allows for number, text, and logical results.

As you might have guessed, you do not have to include the RESULT function in your function macros unless you want the function to return a result that is not text, a number, or a logical value. Since the vast majority of your functions return numbers or text, you probably won't use the RESULT function very often. But if you want to create a function that returns an array, you need to use this function.

Array results

Just as some of Excel's built-in functions return arrays, you can also create user-defined functions that return arrays. As you might expect, creating a user-defined function that returns an array is quite a bit more complex than the examples we've considered up to now. Let's look at a relatively simple example of a user-defined function that returns an array.

An example

Suppose you have $100,000 to invest in an interest-bearing account. You want to know what the value of that investment will be, including interest, at the end of each of the next five years. Figure 19-23 shows a worksheet set up to solve this problem. Cell C2 contains the rate of interest, 10 percent, that you expect to earn across the next few years. Cell C3 contains the amount you plan to invest, $100,000, and cell C4 contains the term of the investment, 5 years. You want to create a user-defined function that computes the value of the investment at the end of year 1, year 2, year 3, and so on, and enters those values in cells C8 through C12.

```
  ♦  File  Edit  Formula  Format  Data  Options  Macro  Window ▶
       C8
```

	A	B	C	D	E	F
1						
2		Rate:	0.1			
3		Amount:	$100,000			
4		Term:	5			
5						
6						
7		Year	Amount			
8		1				
9		2				
10		3				
11		4				
12		5				
13						
14						
15						
16						
17						
18						

```
 Ready                                                      NUM
```

FIGURE 19-23. *This worksheet is used to calculate the value of an investment at the end of each of the next five years.*

Since the result of this function occupies several cells, it must be an array function. Figure 19-24 shows a function macro called *PFV* (for Periodic Future Value) that does the trick. Let's walk through this macro one step at a time to see how it works.

```
  ♦  File  Edit  Formula  Format  Data  Options  Macro  Window ▶
       A2              =RESULT(64)
```

	A	B	C
1	PFV		
2	=RESULT(64)		
3	=ARGUMENT("Rate")		
4	=ARGUMENT("Invest")		
5	=ARGUMENT("Nper")		
6	=SET.NAME("Period",1)		
7	=SET.NAME("Results",C1:C5)		
8	=Invest*((1+Rate)^Period)		
9	=SET.VALUE(INDEX(Results,Period),A8)		
10	=SET.NAME("Period",Period+1)		
11	=IF((Period<=Nper),GOTO(A8))		
12	=RETURN(Results)		
13			
14			
15			
16			
17			
18			

```
 Ready                                                      NUM
```

FIGURE 19-24. *This is the PFV function macro.*

The first formula in the macro, RESULT(64), tells Excel that this function returns an array. As we have said, any function macro that you expect to return an array must begin with a RESULT(64) statement.

The next three lines in the macro contain the ARGUMENT functions that define the three arguments the function passes to the macro: *Rate* (the interest rate), *Invest* (the amount invested), and *Nper* (the term of the investment).

The next two lines use the SET.NAME function to define two names, *Period* and *Results*. The first of these

=SET.NAME("Period",1)

stores the value 1 under the name *Period*. This name is used as a counter by the macro. The second function

=SET.NAME("Results",C1:C5)

assigns the name *Results* to the range C1:C5. The macro stores the results of each calculation in the cells of this range. (Notice that the names in the SET.NAME function are, as always, enclosed in quotation marks.)

The next line

=Invest*((1+Rate)^Period)

actually performs the future-value calculation, using the *Invest* and *Rate* arguments and the named value *Period*.

The formula in cell A9

=SET.VALUE(INDEX(Results,Period),A8)

is a bit tricky. This function says: *Store the result of the formula in cell A8 in the cell at location* Period *in the range* Results. The INDEX function uses the variable *Period* to select a cell reference from the range *Results*, and the SET.VALUE function stores the value from cell A8 in that cell.

The function in cell A10

=SET.NAME("Period",Period+1)

increases by 1 the value stored under the name *Period*.

The next function

=IF((Period<=Nper),GOTO(A8))

creates a loop in the function macro. This function says: *If the value of* Period *(which was just increased by 1 in the previous line of the macro) is less than or equal to the value of* Nper *(which is passed to the macro by the user-defined function), then GOTO (or begin executing the function in) cell A8*. This function causes Excel to repeat the functions in cells A8, A9, and A10 for all values of *Period* from 1 to the number of periods specified by *Nper*. Finally, the function

=RETURN(Results)

in cell A12 returns the result in the range *Results.*

Once you have entered these functions in the macro sheet, you select cell A2 and choose the Define Name... command. To tell Excel that the macro you are naming is a function macro, click the Function button. Then, to accept the default name, *PFV*, simply click the OK button.

Here's how this function works: When you run the macro, Excel processes the functions in cells A2:A7 as you would expect. The function in cell A6 sets the value of *Period* to 1. When Excel calculates the function in cell A8, it uses 1, the current value of *Period*, to compute the future value of the investment at the end of the first period. Then, the function in cell A9 stores the result of that calculation in the first cell of the range *Results*. Next, the function in cell A10 increases the value of *Period* from 1 to 2. Because the value of *Period* (2) is less than the value of *Nper* (5) when Excel computes the function in cell A11, the macro branches to cell A8.

Now, because *Period* is 2, the function in A8 computes the future value of the investment at the end of the second period and the function in cell A9 stores the computed result in the second cell in the range *Results*. Next, the function in cell A10 increases the value of *Period* to 3, which is still less than 5, so the function in cell A11 then loops the macro back to cell A8.

This process repeats five times. When *Period* is equal to 6, the function in cell A11 breaks the loop and allows the RETURN function in cell A12 to return the results from the range *Results* to the cell that contains the function.

Now that you know how this macro works, let's go back to the worksheet and watch it in action. To begin, select the range C8:C12 and then type the formula

='PFV Macro'!PFV(C2,C3,C4)

To lock in this function as an array function, press Command and Enter together. Figure 19-25 on the next page shows the result. As you can see, Excel has entered the PFV function as an array formula in cells C8:C12 and has returned the values from the range *Results* to those cells.

If you switch back to the *PFV* macro after using this function macro, your screen looks like Figure 19-26, also on the next page. Notice that cells C1:C5 in the macro sheet, to which the macro assigned the name *Results*, contain the results of each computation. The RETURN function in cell A12 returns these values from the macro sheet to the worksheet.

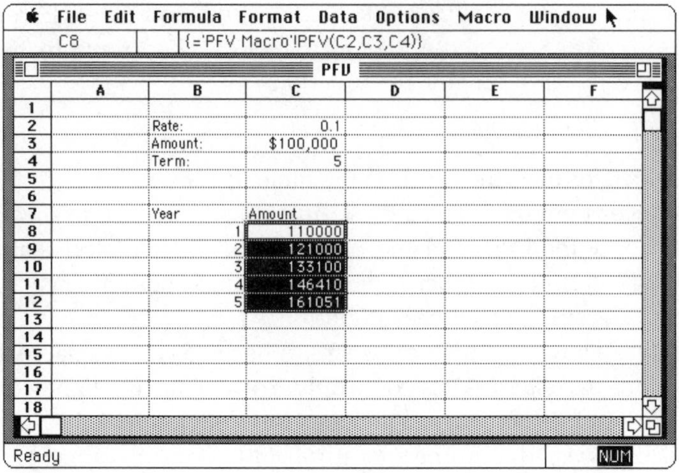

FIGURE 19-25. *This figure shows the results of the PFV function.*

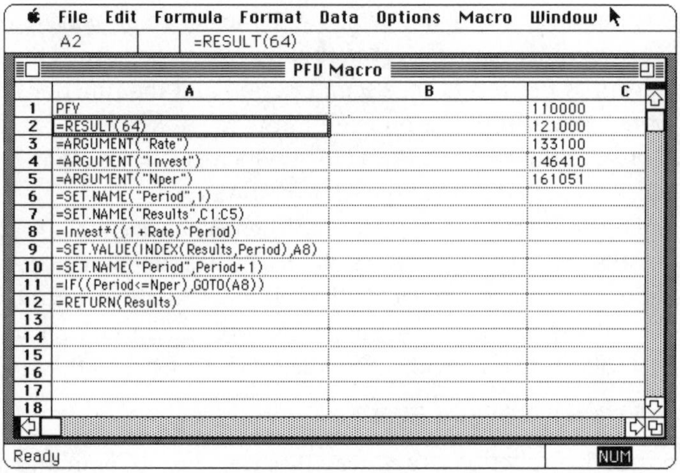

FIGURE 19-26. *This is the macro sheet after the PFV function macro has run.*

A modification

The macro shown in Figure 19-26 is a useful tool, but it is not very flexible. As it stands, it can only compute the future value of an investment five years into the future, because cell A7 contains an explicit reference to a cell range. To make the function open-ended so that it can compute the future value for any number of periods, you can change the function in cell A7, which defines the range *Results*, to

=SET.NAME("Results",C1:INDEX(C1:C600,Nper))

This function assigns the name *Results* to the range from cell C1 to the cell in column C determined by *Nper*. If *Nper* is 10, the name *Results* is assigned to the range C1:C10. If *Nper* is 100, the name is assigned to the range C1:C100.

Because the INDEX function uses the range C1:C600 as its *table* argument, the *Results* range is limited to the range C1:C600. This means that the function is not truly open-ended: It can compute the future value only 600 periods into the future. However, because 600 periods is 600 years if each period is a year, or 50 years if each period is a month, you'll probably not encounter this limitation very often.

An error trap

Now, suppose someone enters the value 601 as the *Nper* argument. When Excel tries to process the macro, it displays the alert box shown in Figure 19-27, warning that an error has occurred in cell A9 of the macro. Select Halt to stop the macro, then select the *PFV* macro sheet. The problem occurs because the *Nper* argument, 601, exceeds the number of cells in the *table* argument of the INDEX function in cell A7. As a result, the name *Results* is assigned to the #REF! error value.

FIGURE 19-27. *This is the Macro Error alert box.*

To overcome this problem, you can include an error trap within the *PFV* function macro. To do this, select row 7 and use the Insert... command on the Edit menu to insert a new, blank row in the macro sheet. Now, enter the function

=IF(Nper>600,GOTO(A15))

Next, select cell A15 and enter the function

=SET.NAME("Results",#VALUE!)

Then, select cell A16 and enter the function

=GOTO(A13)

When you have made these changes, your macro sheet looks like Figure 19-28 on the next page. Now, move back to the *PFV* worksheet and re-enter the user-defined formula, *='PFV Macro'!PFV(C2,C3,C4)*, into the range C8:C12, pressing Command-Enter to lock the formula into the range. Then, change the value in cell C4 to some value greater than 600. Figure 19-29 shows the result. This time, instead of displaying an alert box, Excel simply returns the error message #VALUE! into all of the cells that contain the function.

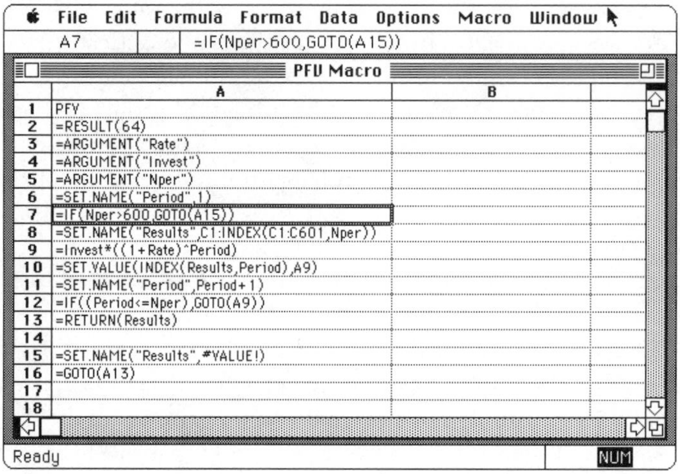

FIGURE 19-28. *This is the modified PFV function macro.*

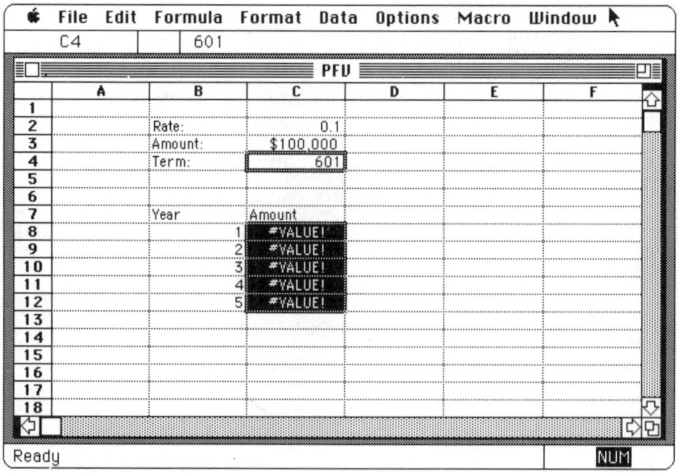

FIGURE 19-29. *The modified PFV function returns a #VALUE! error when the term of the loan exceeds 600.*

Here's how the trap works: The ARGUMENT function in cell A5 stores the value from cell C4 in the macro sheet under the name *Nper*. If *Nper* is greater than 600, then the function in cell A7 branches the macro to cell A15. The function in cell A15 assigns the error value #VALUE! to the name *Results*, and then the command in cell A16 branches the macro to cell A13. The RETURN function in this cell returns the value of *Results* to the worksheet.

This function macro returned the error value #VALUE! to the worksheet without any problem, even though the type of result specified by the RESULT function was 64 (array). Because arrays can themselves be of any type, this function has no difficulty returning an error value.

Although you could probably accomplish this same task just as easily using conventional formulas, this example does demonstrate the techniques you must use to create a function that returns an array. Every array function that we've seen works like this one: The function macro repeats a calculation a specified number of times, storing the results in a range of the macro sheet, then the RETURN function returns the contents of that range to the worksheet.

In the example, all of the variables but one were fixed: You changed only the value of *Period* and computed the equation repeatedly. You'll find that array functions are particularly handy when more than one variable changes across time. For example, when you perform a double-declining-balance depreciation calculation, both the period and the asset's undepreciated balance change from calculation to calculation. Problems like this one take longer to set up in the worksheet and lend themselves well to user-defined functions.

Conclusion

There is almost no limit to the types of tasks that can be simplified, generalized, or streamlined with user-defined functions. Now that you are familiar with the form and purpose of function macros and have seen both simple and complex examples of these macros, you're ready to begin creating your own functions.

20

Customizing Excel

One of the most significant advantages you gain by using Microsoft Excel is the ability to create custom menus and dialog boxes. You can use these capabilities to do something as simple as add a command to one of the Excel built-in menus or create a dialog box with a single OK button. You can also use custom menus and dialog boxes to build a complete application with one or more custom menu bars and complex dialog boxes that can accept a variety of information.

If you've written macros in Microsoft Excel, you'll probably find that it's fairly easy to create your own commands, menus, dialog boxes, and custom help files. In this chapter, you'll learn a handful of new macro functions, and you'll learn how to edit a definition table that describes your custom menus and dialog boxes. Even though Excel's Dialog Editor streamlines the process of creating a dialog box, we suggest you experiment to become familiar with the customizing procedures described in this chapter.

We begin by showing you how to create custom commands, menus, and menu bars and then we discuss using the Microsoft Excel Dialog Editor to create dialog boxes and data forms.

Creating custom menus

Microsoft Excel allows you to add new commands to its built-in menus and to build your own menus of custom commands. You can even create your own menu bar consisting entirely of menus of custom commands you design. A *custom command* is simply a macro that you create. You can simplify the process of invoking macros by using custom commands and custom menus; you simply run the macro by choosing its name from a command menu.

In the next few pages, we discuss the macro functions you use to create custom commands and menus. We also show you how these new functions work.

Menu-function arguments

Before we explore the individual functions you use to create custom menus, you need to be familiar with three common menu-function arguments: *bar id*, *menu id*, and *command id*. We describe these menu-function arguments briefly and then put each function to work with some of Excel's menu functions.

Many of the Microsoft Excel custom-menu functions require a *bar id* argument that identifies the menu bar you want to work with. The program's built-in menu bars—worksheet and macro sheet (with short and full menus), chart (with short and full menus), null, and info—are numbered from 1 through 6. (The null menu bar contains the File, Edit, and Window menus only. It appears only when no documents are open. The info menu bar contains the File, Info, Macro, and Window menus only. It appears when you choose the Show Info command from the Window menu.) The following table lists the *bar id* values and the menu bar each value refers to:

This value...	Refers to this menu bar...
1	Worksheet and macro sheet (full menus)
2	Chart (full menus)
3	Null
4	Info
5	Worksheet and macro sheet (short menus)
6	Chart (short menus)

When you add custom menu bars, they are numbered sequentially, beginning with 7. Thus, the first custom menu bar you add during an Excel session carries a *bar id* value of 7, the second carries a *bar id* value of 8, and so forth.

Many custom-menu functions also require that you identify the menu you want to work with, using the *menu id* argument. You can identify a menu by number or by name. Menus are numbered from left to right. For example, in the worksheet environment, a *menu id* value of 3 refers to the Formula menu. (Note that the ⌘ menu, which always appears at the leftmost position on the menu bar, is not included in this count.) Alternatively, you can use the text argument *"Formula"* to specify that you want to work with the Formula menu. When you use the menu name, you must enclose the argument in quotation marks.

Finally, some functions require a *command id* argument. This argument, enclosed in quotation marks, can be either a number that reflects the position of the command on the menu or the command name. When expressing the *command id* argument as a number, you must count the dividing lines that often appear between commands or groups of commands. Because these lines occupy space on the menu, Excel includes them in its count. For example, the Column Width... command on the worksheet Format menu (in full-menus mode) carries a *command id* value of 8 because this command is preceded by six commands and one dividing line. We show you how to determine the correct arguments for custom menu bars, custom menus, and custom commands when we show you how to add those elements.

Custom-menu functions

Now that you are familiar with the three main arguments you need to create custom-menu functions, we explore the macro functions themselves. We begin with the ADD.COMMAND function, which allows you to create custom-menu commands.

Creating a new command

The ADD.COMMAND function lets you add a new command to a menu. This new command always appears immediately below the last existing commands. When Microsoft Excel carries out the ADD.COMMAND function, it adds the command to the appropriate menu and returns the new command's position number. This position number serves as the *command id* argument in subsequent macro functions that refer to the newly created command. If you add more than one command to a menu, the commands appear in the order in which you add them. Thus, a command's position number might differ from one Excel session to another, depending on other commands you add to the same menu and the order in which you add them.

When you add a command to a menu, that command remains on the menu for the current Excel session unless you use the DELETE.COMMAND function to remove the command or you close all documents, activating the null menu bar. Each time you start Excel, you must run the macro containing the ADD.COMMAND function to place your custom command on a menu.

The ADD.COMMAND function takes the form

=ADD.COMMAND(*bar id,menu id,ref*)

We've already discussed the *bar id* and *menu id* arguments. The *ref* argument locates a definition table that defines the new command. This table can be located on either a worksheet or a macro sheet. Let's take a closer look at the structure of this definition table.

The definition table

The definition table you use to define a new command consists of two or three adjacent cells in a row in a macro sheet or worksheet. These cells contain the command name, the location of the macro that Microsoft Excel carries out when the command is chosen, and, optionally, the name of the key the user can press along with the Command key to invoke the command from the keyboard. We refer to these cells as the *command-name* cell, the *command-reference* cell, and the *command-key* cell, respectively.

You can use any name you want in the *command-name* cell. In most cases, you want the command name to be descriptive, indicating the purpose of the command. Of course, you should avoid using the name of one of the Microsoft Excel built-in commands.

The *command-reference* cell contains a reference to the first cell of the command macro you want to run when the command is issued. This reference must be entered in the form of text (for example, *F4, R[1]C[2]* or the range name *SalesReport*). If the macro that controls the command is located on a separate macro sheet, you can enter an external reference in the command-reference cell. For example, suppose you want to refer to a macro named *SalesReport* that's located on the macro sheet named *Reporter*. You enter *Reporter!SalesReport* in the command-reference cell of your command-definition table.

The third cell of the definition table, the *command-key* cell, is optional. If you want to assign a command-key shortcut for the command, simply enter the letter that you want the user to press. For example, if you enter *J* in this column, the user can choose the custom command by pressing Command-J. This letter appears as an uppercase letter next to the command name on the menu as a helpful reminder to the user.

When you add a command to a built-in menu, be sure you don't assign a command-key letter that's already used for one of the Microsoft Excel built-in commands. If you do, you can't control which command is invoked when the user presses that key combination.

Excel limits you to 26 command-key shortcuts on any menu bar. On the worksheet and macro sheet menu bars, all of the letters of the alphabet are already used. If you create your own menu bar, however, you can use any letters you want for your command-key shortcuts, because only one menu bar is active at a time. (You learn more about custom menu bars later in this chapter.)

An example

Suppose you want to create a command that assigns bold formatting to entries in the worksheet without having to open the Font dialog box. Figure 20-1 shows a macro for adding a command named *Boldface* to the Format menu. In the ADD.COMMAND function in cell A2, the *bar id* argument is 1, indicating that you want to use the worksheet or macro-sheet full-menus menu bar. The *menu id* argument is 4, indicating that you want to use the Format menu. The *ref* argument is C2:E2, indicating the location of the definition table that defines the new command. Notice that column B contains a command-option key combination to invoke the macro, as well as comments on each line of the macro.

	A	B	C	D	E	F
1	AddBold	Option-Command-a	Command Name	Reference	Key	BoldFormat.m
2	=ADD.COMMAND(1,4,C2:E2)	Add Boldface command to Format menu	Boldface	BoldFormat.m		=STYLE(TRUE,FALSE)
3	=RETURN()	End of macro				=RETURN()

FIGURE 20-1. *The macro in column A creates a new command on the Format menu.*

In the definition table (shown in Figure 20-1) for the new command, the command name *Boldface* appears in cell C2. Cell D2 contains a named reference to the macro to run when the command is invoked. This macro, which appears in column F of the macro sheet, is assigned the name *BoldFormat.m*. Because you chose not to assign a command-key shortcut to the new command, cell E2 in the definition table is blank.

When you run the macro containing the ADD.COMMAND function, Excel places a command named *Boldface* on the Format menu, as shown in Figure 20-2. When a user chooses the *Boldface* command, Excel runs the macro that appears in cells F2:F3 of the macro sheet, which assigns the bold style to the current selection.

FIGURE 20-2. *The Format menu now contains a new command called* Boldface.

When a user chooses a command that's been added to a menu, the macro sheet containing both the definition table and the macro that controls the command must be open. If the definition table and the controlling macro are on separate sheets, both sheets must be open. If Excel cannot locate both the definition table and the controlling macro, an alert message appears when a user chooses the new command.

Renaming a command

If you want to change the name of a command you have created, you can use the RENAME.COMMAND function. (You cannot rename one of Excel's built-in commands.) The RENAME.COMMAND function is handy when you want to create a toggle command—such as Excel's built-in Protect Document.../Unprotect Document... command—that alternates between two names each time a user chooses the command.

The RENAME.COMMAND function takes the form

=RENAME.COMMAND(*bar id,menu id,command id,"name"*)

We've already explained the *bar id*, *menu id*, and *command id* arguments. The *"name"* argument is the new name you want to assign to the command. You must enclose this argument in quotation marks.

For example, suppose you want to rename the *Boldface* command that you just created. You can change the name of the command to *Bold* by using a macro that contains the function

=RENAME.COMMAND(1,4,11,"Bold")

In this function, the *command id* argument is 11. We arrived at this number by counting all the commands that appear above the *Boldface* command on the Format menu (Number..., Alignment..., Font..., Border..., Cell Protection..., Row Height..., Column Width..., and Justify) and the dividing lines following the Cell Protection... and Column Width... commands.

Instead of the number 11, we could have used the text argument *"Boldface."* Using a text argument makes it less likely that you will accidentally rename a command other than the one you want to change. Another way to avoid unintentional changes is to refer to the cell of the macro sheet that contains the ADD.COMMAND function that created the command you want to change. For example, if the RENAME.COMMAND function appears on the macro sheet shown in Figure 20-1, you could refer to cell C2 as the *command id* argument like this:

=RENAME.COMMAND(1,4,C2,"Bold")

Figure 20-3 shows the Format menu after the *Boldface* command name has been changed to *Bold*.

FIGURE 20-3. *You used the RENAME.COMMAND function to rename the* Boldface *command. It is now called the* Bold *command.*

When you rename a command, you do not affect the command's name in the command-definition table. The next time you start Microsoft Excel and run the ADD.COMMAND macro, the old command name appears on the menu.

Disabling and enabling a command

Under certain conditions, you may want to disable a command. The Microsoft Excel ENABLE.COMMAND function lets you enable and disable your custom commands. The ENABLE.COMMAND function takes the form

=ENABLE.COMMAND(*bar id,menu id,command id,state*)

You are already familiar with the *bar id*, *menu id*, and *command id* arguments; *state* is a logical argument that serves as a switch that turns commands on and off. If the *state* argument is TRUE, Excel makes the command available; if *state* is FALSE, Excel dims the command name and makes the command unavailable to the user.

For example, suppose you want to disable the new *Bold* command on the Format menu. You could run a macro that contains the function

=ENABLE.COMMAND(1,4,11,FALSE)

to accomplish this. Figure 20-4, on the next page, shows how this disabled command appears on the menu.

To enable the *Bold* command, you can change the *state* argument of the ENABLE.COMMAND function to TRUE, like this:

=ENABLE.COMMAND(1,4,11,TRUE)

This reinstates the *Bold* command on the menu. The name is no longer dimmed.

FIGURE 20-4. *After you disable a command, the command name is dimmed.*

Deleting a command

You can use the DELETE.COMMAND function to remove a custom command from a menu. This function takes the form

=DELETE.COMMAND(*bar id,menu id,command id*)

For example, to delete the *Bold* command from the Format menu, you run a macro containing the function

=DELETE.COMMAND(1,4,11)

When you delete a command, the *command id* values of any commands below it on the menu are reduced by 1.

Placing a check mark by a command name

You can use the CHECK.COMMAND function to add or remove a check mark next to a command name on a menu. Check marks are often used with commands that function as toggle switches—turning certain features on or off. The CHECK.COMMAND function takes the form

=CHECK.COMMAND(*bar id,menu id,command id,state*)

The *state* argument is a logical value that acts as a switch that turns the check mark on and off. If the *state* argument is TRUE, Excel places a check mark next to the specified command name on the menu. As you might expect, when the *state* argument is FALSE, Excel removes the check mark.

Creating new menus

You've seen how to add a command to an existing menu. Now, we show you how to create a custom menu to display your custom commands. To add a custom menu to an existing menu bar or to a custom menu bar, you use the ADD.MENU function. This function takes the form

=ADD.MENU(*bar id,ref*)

You are already familiar with the *bar id* argument. The *ref* argument locates a definition table on a macro sheet or worksheet that defines the new menu. When Excel carries out this function, it adds the new menu to the right of the existing menus and returns the position number of the new menu to the macro sheet. A custom menu, like a custom command, remains available throughout the current Excel session unless you delete that menu using a macro that contains the DELETE.MENU function.

The simple macro shown in Figure 20-5 adds a menu named *Report* to the worksheet or macro-sheet menu bar. The ADD.MENU function in this macro refers to the definition table in cells C2:E5 of Figure 20-5.

	A	B	C	D	E
1	AddReportMenu	Option-Command-m	Command Names	Reference	Key
2	=ADD.MENU(1,C2:E5)	Build Report menu	Report		
3	=RETURN()	End of macro	Sales Report	Reporter!Sales	
4			Inventory Report	Reporter!Inventory	
5			Cash Report	Reporter!Cash	

FIGURE 20-5. *The macro in column A creates a new menu named* Report.

The definition table you use to define a new menu is similar to the one you use to create a new command. The only difference is that you enter the menu name in the upper-left cell of the command names column, above the menu command names (cell C2 in Figure 20-5). This menu name appears on the menu bar when you run the macro that creates the menu.

In the second and subsequent rows of the menu-definition table, you define the commands you want to appear on the new menu. Each of these command definitions is identical to the one you use with the ADD.COMMAND function to create a new command. Each command definition must include the command name, a reference to the location of the macro that Excel carries out when the command is chosen, and the name of the key that the user can press along with the Command key to choose the command from the keyboard.

For example, in rows 3 through 5 of column C of the definition table shown in Figure 20-5 we define commands named *Sales Report, Inventory Report*, and *Cash Report*. Column D contains references to the command macros that are invoked when the user chooses these commands. Notice that each of these macros is located on a macro sheet named *Reporter*. If you want to assign Command-key shortcuts to a name, enter these as letters in column E.

When building a menu-definition table, keep in mind that the commands appear in the order in which they are defined. If you want to include a dividing line between two commands, insert an extra row between the commands that you want to separate in the menu-definition table. Then, enter a hyphen in the command-name cell of that row.

When you run the macro shown in Figure 20-5, Excel adds the *Report* menu to your worksheet or macro-sheet menu bar, as shown in Figure 20-6.

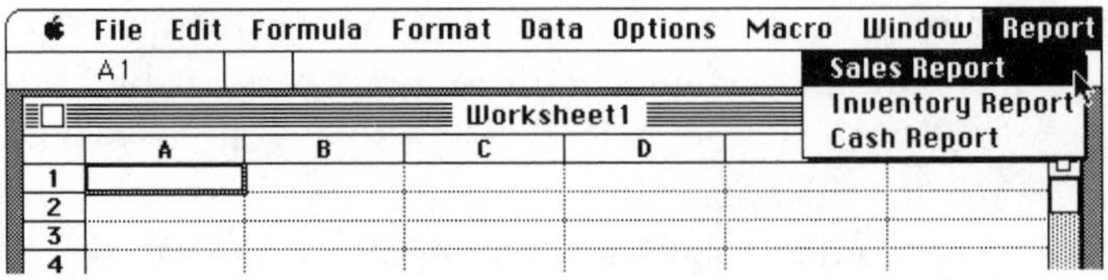

FIGURE 20-6. *The worksheet menu bar now contains the new* Report *menu.*

As you can see in Figure 20-6, adding even one menu to the worksheet menu bar crowds the edge of your screen. To avoid this problem, you can create a custom menu bar to display your menus. (We show you how, shortly.)

Deleting a menu

As you might expect, the DELETE.MENU function removes a menu. This function takes the form

    =DELETE.MENU(*bar id,menu id*)

and uses the *bar id* and *menu id* arguments to specify the location of the menu. For example, to delete the *Report* menu described in the previous example, you can run a macro that contains the function

    =DELETE.MENU(1,9)

If you have added more than one menu to a menu bar, removing one of those menus decreases by 1 the menu-position numbers for all menus to the right of the deleted menu. If you try to delete a nonexistent menu, the DELETE.MENU function returns the macro error dialog box.

Creating new menu bars

If you want to develop an application within Excel, you may want to create a custom menu bar for the menus and commands you'll use in the application. You can create as many as nine custom menu bars using the ADD.BAR, ADD.MENU, and SHOW.BAR functions. (Including the six built-in menu bars, Excel allows 15 menu bars to be defined at one time.)

The ADD.BAR function creates a menu bar. This function takes no arguments. The ADD.BAR function returns the bar number of the new menu bar to the functions that fill in the bar. If more than 15 menu bars are defined at one time, the ADD.BAR function returns the macro error dialog box. The ADD.BAR function, by itself, does not display the menu bar. To display the menu bar, you must use the SHOW.BAR function. First, however, you need to use one or more ADD.MENU functions to fill in your new menu bar. You can use the result of the ADD.BAR function as the *bar id* argument in your ADD.MENU functions.

After creating a menu bar and the commands you want to include on it, you use a SHOW.BAR function to display your menu bar and new menus. The SHOW.BAR function takes the form

=SHOW.BAR(*bar id*)

Again, to enter the *bar id* argument, you can refer directly to the cell that contains the ADD.BAR function.

Microsoft Excel can display only one menu bar at a time. When you use the SHOW.BAR function to display a custom menu bar, the default menu bar is temporarily hidden. To redisplay a built-in menu bar, you can run a macro that contains the SHOW.BAR function with a *bar id* argument for one of Excel's default menu bars—1 through 6. If you omit the *bar id* argument from the SHOW.BAR function, the default menu bar for the current window type is displayed. Before running any macro that displays a custom menu bar, we recommend that you use the SHOW.BAR function to create a simple macro for redisplaying the default menu bar and then assign that macro an Option-Command-key shortcut. That way, you can access Excel's built-in commands at any time.

Figure 20-7 shows a sample macro and definition table for creating a three-menu custom menu bar. The menu names (located in cells C2, C8, and C14) are *Dollar Sales, Unit Sales,* and *Net Income.* Each of these menus contains commands for creating summary reports by region, by product, and by account, and for creating a report of totals.

	A	B	C	D	E
1	**AddMenuBar**	**Option-Command-b**	**Command/Menu Name**	**Reference**	**Key**
2	=ADD.BAR()	Create new menu bar	Dollar Sales		
3	=ADD.MENU(A2,C2:E6)	Build Dollar Sales menu	Region	Summary.m!RSales	R
4	=ADD.MENU(A2,C8:E12)	Build Unit Sales menu	Product	Summary.m!PSales	P
5	=ADD.MENU(A2,C14:E18)	Build Net Income menu	Account	Summary.m!ASales	A
6	=SHOW.BAR(A2)	Display new menu bar	Total .	Summary.m!TSales	T
7	=RETURN()	End of macro			
8			Unit Sales		
9			Region	Summary.m!RUnits	E
1 0			Product	Summary.m!PUnits	O
1 1			Account	Summary.m!AUnits	C
1 2			Total	Summary.m!TUnits	L
1 3					
1 4			Net Income		
1 5			Region	Summary.m!RIncome	G
1 6			Product	Summary.m!PIncome	D
1 7	.		Account	Summary.m!AIncome	U
1 8			Total	Summary.m!TIncome	I

FIGURE 20-7. *This macro creates and displays a custom menu bar and defines the menus and commands that appear on it.*

As you can see, after entering the ADD.BAR function in cell A2, we entered three ADD.MENU functions that use the reference A2 as their *bar id* arguments. The ADD.MENU functions also refer to the definition tables in cells C2:E6, C8:E12, and C14:E18. These definition tables are set up in exactly the same way as the one shown in Figure 20-5.

Finally, to display the menu bar on the screen, we used the SHOW.BAR function in cell A6. To identify which custom menu bar to display, we used a reference to the ADD.BAR function in cell A2. Figure 20-8 shows the resulting menu bar.

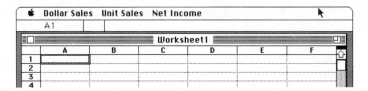

FIGURE 20-8. *This is the custom menu bar that results from the macro and the menu-definition table in Figure 20-7.*

Deleting a menu bar

To eliminate a custom menu bar, you use the DELETE.BAR function. This function takes the form

=DELETE.BAR(*bar id*)

The *bar id* argument must be a number of a menu bar returned by the ADD.BAR function. You cannot delete a built-in menu bar (bars 1 through 6), and you cannot delete the currently displayed menu bar. Before deleting a custom menu bar that is displayed on your screen, you must use the SHOW.BAR function to display another menu bar.

When you delete a menu bar, Excel does not renumber the other bars created during the work session. Each bar you create retains the bar number it was initially assigned. Keep in mind, however, that the *bar id* numbers may vary from one session to the next because Excel numbers them in the order created. If this order is apt to vary from one session to the next, be sure to use a reference to the ADD.BAR function as your *bar id* argument in all new functions. If you use a constant value as your *bar id* argument, you may inadvertently alter or delete the wrong menu bar.

The GET.BAR function

The GET.BAR function returns the number of the active menu bar. This function takes no arguments.

The GET.BAR function comes in handy when you are creating a custom menu bar and need to include its *bar id* number as an argument in a function. For example, the ADD.MENU function requires a *bar id* argument. To add a menu to the currently displayed menu bar, you can use an embedded GET.BAR function to supply this argument.

=ADD.MENU(GET.BAR(),C2:E6)

Creating custom dialog boxes

One of the powerful advantages of using Microsoft Excel is that it lets you create dialog boxes that store information specific to your needs. For example, if you need to organize customer or employee data, you can create a dialog box complete with specialized edit fields, option buttons, list boxes, check boxes, scroll boxes, and so forth to help you record that information.

Creating a dialog box with the Dialog Editor

You'll find the Dialog Editor program on your Microsoft Excel program disk. This program, which is run outside of Excel, allows you to create a custom dialog box using techniques you are already familiar with: cutting, pasting, dragging, and sizing. After creating a dialog box using the Dialog Editor, you use the Clipboard to copy the dialog box into an Excel macro sheet. Excel automatically translates the visual dialog box into a definition table with all the correct coordinates, labels, and other data. In fact, the Dialog Editor is so easy and intuitive, we recommend that you use it as a starting place for creating custom dialog boxes and that you also use it when you need to make major changes to an existing custom dialog box.

Even with the Dialog Editor, however, it is important to have a good grasp of the components of a definition table in your macro sheet. There are a few characteristics of a custom dialog box you cannot create accurately using the Dialog Editor. For example, you can't create list-box items using the Dialog Editor. You must enter any items that appear in a list box directly into your macro sheet. By understanding the structure of a definition table, you can make minor changes to a custom dialog box right on your macro sheet, without running the Dialog Editor program. Minor changes to a dialog box—for example, changing the order of options or specifying a default selection in an option group—may have to be made directly on your macro sheet. Finally, you must understand the basic structure of the definition table in order to retrieve the information and selections a user makes in a dialog box. We discuss methods for altering the definition table later in this chapter, but first, we discuss the Dialog Editor.

Getting started

You run the Dialog Editor by double clicking the program's icon at the Finder
level, or you can load the Dialog Editor using MultiFinder. We recommend using
MultiFinder to load the Dialog Editor and Microsoft Excel at the same time so that
you can quickly copy any dialog box you create directly into an Excel macro sheet.
After loading the Dialog Editor, you'll see a screen like the one in Figure 20-9.

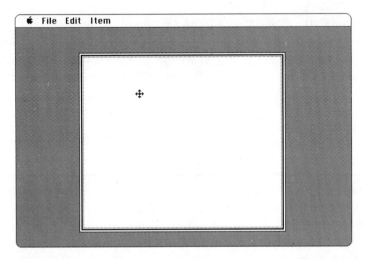

FIGURE 20-9. *This is the screen you see when you first load the Dialog
Editor.*

As shown in Figure 20-9, a blank dialog box is the first thing you see when you
load the Dialog Editor. You can move, resize, and add items (text, edit bars, options, and so on) to this dialog box. When you have added an item, you can move it,
resize it, copy it, or delete it. We discuss how to do this later in this chapter in the
section entitled "Editing a dialog box."

Because the Dialog Editor does not offer a Save command for saving your dialog box on disk, you must copy the dialog box to a Microsoft Excel macro sheet via
the Clipboard to save your work. All the physical characteristics of the dialog box
are then converted to commands on the macro sheet. Then you can save that macro
sheet on disk.

The New command on the Dialog Editor's File menu wipes out any work
you've done, returning you to the blank dialog box you saw when you first ran the
program. However, when you choose the New command from the File menu, as
shown in Figure 20-10, the Dialog Editor displays the message *Save changed dialog to
clipboard?* with the options Yes, No, and Cancel. You also see this message when
you choose the Quit command from the File menu without first copying your dialog box to the Clipboard.

FIGURE 20-10. *The Dialog Editor displays this message when you choose the New or Quit commands from the File menu without first copying your dialog box to the Clipboard.*

Sizing and moving the dialog box

While working in the Dialog Editor, you can resize or move the dialog box at any time. To change the size of the dialog box, just place the pointer on the border of the dialog box and drag. You'll notice that the pointer changes shape to a horizontal or vertical bar with an arrowhead on each side of it indicating in which direction you can move the dialog box border. When the pointer is on the left or right border of the dialog box, you can change the width of the box. Similarly, when the pointer is on the top or bottom border of the dialog box, you can change the height. If you want to change the width and height simultaneously, place the pointer on one of the corners and drag that corner. When the pointer is placed on one of the corners, it becomes a diagonal two-headed arrow slanting in the direction you can move the dialog-box corner.

You can change the position of the dialog box on the screen by pointing within the dialog box (except on a border or on an item) and dragging the entire box. Here, the pointer reverts to its most common four-headed arrow shape. If you want to center the dialog box on the screen, first select the dialog box by clicking a blank area inside the box or by choosing the Select Dialog command from the Edit menu. (This step is unnecessary if you have not added any items to the dialog box. In this case, the dialog box automatically remains selected.) Then, choose the Info... command from the Edit menu. In the Info dialog box, click the Auto check boxes that appear next to the X and Y fields, then click the OK button. Once you've activated the Auto check boxes for the X and Y position coordinates, the Dialog Editor centers the dialog box on your screen; you cannot move the dialog box to a different position until you deselect the Auto check boxes. We discuss the Info dialog box in more detail later in this chapter.

Creating a title bar

To create a movable dialog box (one with a title bar), select the dialog box and choose the Info... command from the Edit menu (or double click the dialog box to open the Info box). In the Text field of the Info dialog box, type the title you want to use for your dialog box. When you click OK to close the Info box, the title bar does not appear. However, when you copy the dialog box to an Excel macro sheet, your

entry in the Text field is transferred to the Text field of the first row of the definition table. When you display the dialog box in Excel, the title bar appears.

Creating dialog-box items

To add an item to a dialog box, choose one of the commands on the Item menu. In
some cases, you see a dialog box in which you must make further selections before
the item appears. (We talk about creating specific types of items in a moment.)

When a new item first appears in the dialog box, it is surrounded by a dotted-
line border. This dotted-line border indicates that the item is active, or selected.
Any item you add appears immediately below the item that was active when you
added the new item (or immediately below the item that was most recently
selected). Keeping this in mind, you may want to activate a particular item before
you add a new item. You activate an item by clicking it.

While an item is active or selected, you can perform a number of actions that
affect it, including moving it to a different location in the dialog box. To move an
item, simply point to the item and drag. (In a moment, we talk about some of the
other ways you can manipulate items.)

You can also edit the text of an item while it is active or selected. (The text
might be an option label, a button label, a group-box label, or a fixed-text item.) If
you haven't yet changed the text of an item, simply click it and begin typing. The
new text you type replaces the default text. If later you need to edit the text of an
item, use the Delete key to delete text, or open the Info dialog box for that item and
edit the contents of the Text field. (We tell you more about the Info dialog box later
in this section.)

Creating OK and Cancel buttons To create an OK button or a Cancel button,
choose the Button... command from the Item menu. When you see the Button
Type dialog box, shown in Figure 20-11, select the OK or Cancel option and then
click OK. The first time you add an OK or Cancel button to a dialog box, the Dialog
Editor activates the Default check box so that the button you create appears as a
default button. You'll recall that a default OK or Cancel button is displayed with a

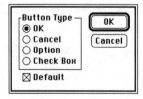

FIGURE 20-11. *When you choose the Button... command from the
Item menu, this dialog box appears.*

heavy black border. When you press Return or Enter while the custom dialog box is open, Excel carries out the default OK or Cancel button.

If you do not want the button to be a default OK or Cancel button, you can deselect the Default option by clicking the Default check box in the Button Type dialog box. Once your dialog box contains one default OK or Cancel button, the Dialog Editor does not allow you to create another default button of either type. However, you can create two or more nondefault OK or Cancel buttons.

Creating and editing fixed text To create fixed text, such as labels and instructions, simply choose the Text command from the Item menu. The word *Text* appears in the dialog box, surrounded by a dotted-line border, indicating that the text item is active. While the text item is active, you can change it to read anything you want. Simply type up to 255 characters. The characters you type overwrite the word *Text*.

Later, if you want to edit the text item (instead of replacing it entirely), select the item you want to edit and choose the Info... command from the Edit menu. In the Info dialog box, you see the text you created in the Text field. You can edit the contents of this field using standard editing techniques; then click OK to lock in your changes.

Creating edit boxes To create an edit box, choose the Edit Box... command from the Item menu. The Dialog Editor presents a dialog box with five options: Text, Integer, Number, Formula, and Reference. The Text option allows you to type an entry. The Integer option accepts integer values from –32,768 to 32,767. The Number option accepts decimal or integer values. The Formula option accepts cell references of formulas in A1 or R1C1 style. The Reference option accepts cell and range references.

When you select the type of edit box you want to create and click OK, the edit box appears in your dialog box; the edit box contains text that indicates its type. You see the placeholder words *Edit Text*, *Edit Integer*, *Edit Number*, *Edit Formula*, or *Edit Reference* in the edit box in dimmed type. This placeholder text does not appear in your final dialog box.

To create a default entry for an edit box, select that edit box and choose the Info... command from the Edit menu. In the Info dialog box, type the default entry in the Init/Result field and click OK. Your default entry does not appear in the edit box while you're in the Dialog Editor. However, when you copy the dialog box to your Excel macro sheet, your default entry is transferred to the Initial/Result column of the definition table. Then, when you display the dialog box in Excel, you see the default edit box contents. We explain the definition table and its parts later in this chapter.

Creating option buttons To create an option button, choose the Button...
command from the Item menu and, in the Button dialog box, select Option. When
you click OK, an option button with the words *Option Button* next to it appears in
your dialog box. (When the new option button is active, you can duplicate it by
pressing Return or Enter. To create a series of four option buttons, simply choose
the Button... command from the Item menu, select Option, and click OK. Then,
press Enter three times. You've created four option buttons, one above another.)

To name the option button, simply type the name you want while the button is
active. The Dialog Editor replaces the words *Option Button* with the text you type.

You can edit the text for an option button at any time by using the Delete key or
by selecting that button and choosing the Info... command from the Edit menu. In
the Info dialog box, you change the option-button label by editing the text that appears in the Text field.

Creating a group box for option buttons The Dialog Editor automatically
creates an option-button-group definition for you and assigns the first button in
the group as the default selection. To change this default, you must enter a new
number in the Initial/Result field of the option-button-group definition in the
definition table. A word of caution here: The first button is not determined by the
position of the buttons in the dialog box. It is determined by the order in which you
create the buttons. The first option button you create is considered the first button
of a group; its definition appears in your definition table before the definitions of
the other buttons. Similarly, the second button you create in the Dialog Editor is the
second button defined in the definition table. You must keep this in mind if you
rearrange the position of the option buttons while working in the Dialog Editor. As
we explain later in this chapter, the order of the button definitions in the definition
table determines how you specify a default selection and how Microsoft Excel
records which option a user chooses. We show you how to change the default
selection later in this chapter.

If you want more than one group of option buttons in your dialog box, you
must create group boxes to set apart each group of options. (We soon explain how
to create group boxes.) Otherwise, Excel assumes that all the option buttons belong
in the same group, even if they're not clustered together in the dialog box. Excel
uses the first group box you create to tie together all the option buttons in your dialog box. After you create a second group box, Excel assumes that all subsequent
option buttons you create belong to a new group.

For example, suppose you've added two option buttons to a dialog box. You
then create a group box to surround these options. If you create more option buttons, Excel assumes they belong with the first group. Suppose you create another
group box. Excel considers any option buttons you create after the second box to be
part of a new group.

To surround a set of options with a box, choose the Group Box command from the Item menu. A box with the label *Group* appears in the dialog box. You'll probably need to move and resize the group box so that it surrounds the options you want to group. To move the group box, point to a blank area in the box and drag. Resizing the group box is exactly like resizing the dialog box: Place the pointer on one of the borders or corners of the group box and drag.

While a group box is active—as indicated by a dotted-line border—you can change its label by typing a new label (assuming you have not edited the label previously). You can also edit the group-box label by using the Delete key or by choosing the Info... command from the Edit menu and editing the contents of the Text field.

While the group box is active, you can place option buttons in it by pressing Return or Enter. Each time you press Enter, Excel places an option button in the group box. If you press Enter four times, you see four option buttons, stacked one above another.

Creating check-box options Use the Button... command on the Item menu to create new check-box options. In the Button dialog box, choose Check Box, then click OK or press Enter. The Dialog Editor places a new check box with the words *Check Box* next to it in the dialog box. While the check-box option is active, you can change its label by typing a new one. The text you type replaces the default label. You can also edit the check-box label by choosing the Info... command from the Edit menu, then editing the contents of the Text field.

While the check box you just created is still active, you can press Return or Enter to create another check box. For example, to create a series of four check boxes, you create the first one by choosing the Button... command on the Item menu, selecting the Check Box option, and clicking OK. Then, press Enter three times to create three more check boxes.

If you want a particular check-box option to be active when a user first opens your custom dialog box, select that option, open the Info dialog box, and type *TRUE* in the Init/Result field.

Creating a list box To create a list box, choose the List Box... command from the Item menu. In the resulting dialog box, you can select the Standard or Combination option. A combination list box has an attached edit box in which your list-box selection is displayed. A standard list box has no attached edit box.

You use the Dialog Editor to position a blank list box in your dialog box. Creating the contents of that list box is done on the macro sheet. You cannot create the items in a list box using the Dialog Editor. If you place a Text item in your List Box, you cannot highlight that text. It is unalterable, just like a label. The items in a list box must be taken from a list of entries in your macro sheet outside the range of the definition table. Thus, after you transfer the dialog box to your Excel macro sheet, you must enter the list of items you want to appear in the list box, then type a reference to that list in the Text field of the list-box definition in the definition table.

Editing a dialog box

The Dialog Editor is an especially valuable tool when you want to edit a custom dialog box. With the Dialog Editor, you can quickly and easily change the size, position, and text of any item in the dialog box. You can also copy, cut, paste, and clear items.

Selecting items To edit an item, you must first select the item by clicking it. A dotted-line border appears around that item, indicating that it is selected.

You can also select different items in the dialog box by pressing the Tab key. Each time you press Tab, an item is selected (in the order in which the items were created). Pressing Shift-Tab selects items in the reverse order of their creation.

If you want to select two or more items at the same time, you can press the Shift key as you click each item. The Select Group command on the Edit menu allows you to select all of the items within a group box, as well as the box. This command makes it easy to move or clear a group of options. To select a group of options, first click one of the items in a group box or select the box itself. Then, choose Select Group from the Edit menu.

The Select All Items command selects all items in the dialog box, but not the dialog box itself. You can use this command to reposition all the items in a dialog box without changing the size or position of the dialog box.

Copying and deleting items There are two ways to copy an item. You can select the item and then choose the Duplicate command from the Edit menu. An identical item appears immediately below the original item. Or, you can select the item, choose the Copy command from the Edit menu, and then choose Paste from the Edit menu. This causes an identical item to appear on top of the copied item. In order to see the original item, you must first drag the new item out of the way.

To delete an item from the dialog box, select it and choose the Clear command from the Edit menu. Unlike the Cut command, the Clear command does not allow you to paste an item back into the dialog box after it has been removed.

A note of warning here: The Undo command is disabled for all the Edit-menu commands. You cannot undo a copy-and-paste or cut-and-paste procedure. This is important to keep in mind, because you must save your work in the Dialog Editor by copying it to an Excel macro sheet.

Moving items As mentioned earlier, you can move an item in a dialog box simply by pointing to it and dragging it to another location. If you press the Shift key while you drag an item, the Dialog Editor lets you move only horizontally or vertically. This Shift-key restriction proves handy when you've aligned some dialog-box items and you want to move one or more of them without losing the horizontal or vertical alignment. The direction in which you begin dragging is the only direction allowed.

To move two or more items at once, select the items you want to move, point to any one of the selected items, and drag; this moves the group of items. The Info... command allows you to place items more precisely by specifying a horizontal position, a vertical position, or both a horizontal and a vertical position. We discuss positioning in a moment.

Changing the size of items To change the size of an item, place the pointer on the edge or corner of the item and drag. For example, if you want to make a list box wider, place the pointer on the left or right border of the list box and drag the border outward. If you want to make the list box both wider and longer, place the pointer on one corner; the pointer changes to a diagonal double-headed arrow. Then, drag the box to expand both its length and width.

If you cannot change the size of an item, look at its Info dialog box. Chances are, the Auto setting has been activated for the item's width, height, or both. For example, the Auto setting initially is active for the height setting of edit boxes and text items.

Although you can increase the height of an edit box, there really is no point in doing so because Microsoft Excel does not wrap entries to more than one line in an edit box of a custom dialog box. Excel scrolls the text in the edit box until you finish the entry. Similarly, changing the height setting of a text item does not affect the size of the text.

Let's take a closer look at the Info... command and how you can use the settings in the Info dialog box.

The Info... command

The Info... command gives you precise control over the height, width, and position of a dialog box or an item within a dialog box. It also allows you to change the text associated with an item, create default settings, and insert explanatory messages about your dialog box in a macro sheet. When you choose the Info... command from the Edit menu, you see a dialog box like the one shown in Figure 20-12, on the next page. This Info dialog box is associated with a check-box option, as indicated by the words *Check Box Info* in the upper-left corner of the dialog box.

Another way to access the Info dialog box is to double click the item associated with the Info dialog box you want to see. If you want to see the Info dialog box for the dialog box (as opposed to an item in the dialog box), double click a blank area of the dialog box or click its border.

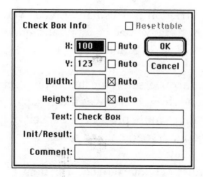

FIGURE 20-12. *This is the Info dialog box for the check-box option.*

As you have already seen, the X and Y fields in the Info dialog box contain the horizontal- and vertical-position coordinates of the item. You can change the values in these fields to obtain precise placement of items in the dialog box. (You can also wait to alter these settings in the definition table after you copy the dialog box to a macro sheet.) For example, if you want the left edges of two items to line up horizontally, be sure that they have the same value in the X field. The values in the X and Y fields correspond to settings in screen units—a unit of measure equal to approximately 1/72 of an inch. (A setting of 25 in the X field means the item will be positioned 25 screen units from the top of the dialog box.)

The Auto check boxes that appear next to the X and Y fields allow you to freeze an item in its current horizontal position, its current vertical position, or both. For example, suppose you were to open the Info dialog box for an OK button, enter the value 100 in the X field, and click the Auto check box next to the Y field. After you close the Info dialog box, the Dialog Editor allows you to drag the OK button horizontally, but it does not allow you to change its vertical position.

The Width and Height fields in the Info dialog box contain the width and height measurements of the item. You can change the width of an item, the height of an item, or both the width and height by entering a new value in these fields. (The values in the Width and Height fields correspond to settings in screen units, just as the values in the X and Y fields do.)

To return to the default width of an item, select the Auto check box next to the Width field. Similarly, to return to the default height of an item, select the Auto check box next to the Height field. Once you've selected the Auto check box, the Dialog Editor does not allow you to change an item's width or height by dragging its corner or border.

In some cases, the Auto check box is selected as the default. For example, if you examine the Info dialog box for a Text item, you see that the Auto setting is turned on for Width and Height. You can change this automatic setting if you want; it doesn't affect the size of the text. However, if you specify a setting that is less than the default, the text appears truncated.

You can use the Text field to alter a text item or to edit the text associated with an item. For example, suppose you've labeled a group box with the word *Design* and you want to change that label to *Design Options*. Double click the group box to open its Info dialog box. Then, click after the word *Design* in the Text field and type a space and *Options*. When you click OK in the Info dialog box, the Dialog Editor automatically changes the label on your group box. The Text field in the Info dialog box corresponds to the Text column of the definition table. Any text you enter in the dialog box's Text field appears in the definition table's Text column when you transfer the dialog box to a macro sheet.

You can enter the default status of some items in the Init/Result field. For example, if you're working in the Info dialog box for a list box, you can enter *#N/A* in the Init/Result field to indicate that no item in the list box should be selected when the dialog box appears, or you can enter the number of the list-box item to be selected when you open the dialog box. In the Check Box Info dialog box, you can enter *TRUE* or *FALSE* in the Init/Result field to indicate whether an item should be selected. If you enter *TRUE*, the check box is selected. In the Group Info dialog box for a group box containing option buttons, you can enter the number of the button to be activated when you open the dialog box.

The last field in the Info dialog box is the Comment field. This is the only part of the Info dialog box that does not correspond to one of the seven columns in a definition table. You can use the Comment field to enter explanatory text about an item. When you copy the dialog box from the Dialog Editor to a macro sheet, the contents of the Comment field are transferred to the column immediately to the right of the definition table. You can use the Comment field to create labels for the macro sheet to which you'll copy your dialog box. These labels appear in column J if you paste the dialog-box definition table into columns C through I.

The Info dialog box also includes a check-box option labeled *Resettable*. This option is available only for a group box surrounding option buttons or check-box options. The Dialog Editor makes an option-button group resettable by default. Check-box options are not resettable. When opening a dialog box, a user can reset the option buttons to their original settings by clicking the group-box name. If you do not want a group of option buttons to be resettable, open the Info dialog box for the group box surrounding those options and deselect the Resettable option. Unfortunately, if you select the Resettable option for a group box surrounding check-box options, the box appears to be checked, but nothing happens. You cannot reset these options when you use the dialog box.

Transferring the dialog box to Excel

After you've created a dialog box in the Dialog Editor, you can transfer the box to your Microsoft Excel macro sheet by using the Copy and Paste commands. First, select the dialog box by choosing the Select Dialog command from the Edit menu or clicking a blank area in the dialog box or clicking its border. (You can tell that the dialog box is selected by the dotted line that appears around its border.) After selecting the dialog box, choose the Copy command from the Edit menu and switch to Excel (if you're using MultiFinder) or quit the Dialog Editor and load Excel. In Excel, open a macro sheet and click the upper-left corner of the range in which you want your definition table to appear. Then, choose the Paste command from the Edit menu. All seven columns of the definition table (or eight, if you included comments in the Info boxes) appear in the macro sheet. You can now modify the table directly on the macro sheet. You can also add descriptive labels and change your column widths to make the table easier to read.

One of the first things to do after copying a dialog box from the Dialog Editor to a macro sheet is to create a simple macro that allows you to display the dialog box on the screen. This macro will tell Excel where the definition table is located. For example, Figure 20-13 shows a macro that displays the dialog box defined in cells C2:I31 of Figure 20-14 (shown later). As you can see, this macro consists of a *DIALOG.BOX* function that uses the argument C2:I31, the range of the definition table. The DIALOG.BOX function takes only one argument

=DIALOG.BOX(*ref*)

The *ref* argument is a reference to the range in the macro sheet that contains the dialog-box definition table. This argument can be a range reference or a range name. You can edit a dialog box from the Dialog Editor or from the definition table.

	A
1	DescriptionMacro
2	=DIALOG.BOX(C2:I31)
3	=RETURN()

FIGURE 20-13. *This macro activates the dialog box governed by the definition table shown later in Figure 20-14.*

Returning to the Dialog Editor

After you create a definition table in a macro sheet or copy a dialog box from the Dialog Editor into a macro sheet, you can if necessary transfer the definition table back to the Dialog Editor and make further changes. Again, you use the Copy and Paste commands to transfer the definition table on a macro sheet to the visual dialog box in the Dialog Editor.

Begin by selecting the entire table in Excel. (Be sure you select only the seven columns of the definition table and all the correct rows. An incorrect selection can lead to unpredictable results in the Dialog Editor.) Next, choose the Copy command from the Edit menu. Then, switch to the Dialog Editor using MultiFinder, or quit Excel and load the Dialog Editor program.

Once you're in the Dialog Editor, choose the Paste command. You see a dialog box that represents the contents of the definition table. Initially, all the items in the dialog box are selected. You can click any item and begin moving or modifying it.

If you're switching back and forth between Excel and the Dialog Editor in MultiFinder, keep in mind that when you paste a definition table in the Dialog Editor, a complete dialog box overwrites whatever is currently displayed in the Dialog Editor.

Working with definition tables

When you first look at a dialog box you have created in the Dialog Editor, you'll be amazed at how "built-in" the dialog box appears. It looks just like the box you've been using in the Dialog Editor, although you'll probably see certain adjustments that need to be made. Commonly, the alignment of group boxes, check boxes, option buttons, and edit boxes is a bit askew. You can expect this type of problem, because it's difficult, at first, to move items small distances when you are making final adjustments to the box in the Dialog Editor. After some experience with the Dialog Editor, though, you'll find it's easy to "fine tune" custom dialog boxes from the definition table.

Trying to create a dialog box in a definition table from scratch is an exercise in tenacity, but understanding how Excel stores information in a definition table allows you to make quick adjustments in your dialog box without having to load the Dialog Editor.

Understanding the structure of the dialog-box definition table

A definition table contains exactly seven columns and at least two rows. In it, you specify the item type (fixed text, edit box, OK button, and so forth) for each item in the dialog box, the horizontal and vertical positions of each item, the heights and widths of those items, and the dialog-box text you want to display. You also specify some of the overall characteristics of the dialog box, including its size and position on the screen. If you enter any text in the Comment field of an Info dialog box, it appears in an eighth column, which is technically not part of the definition table.

Figure 20-14, on the next page, shows the definition table of a dialog box created in the Dialog Editor. A user can use this dialog box for entering student information. The definition table resides in a macro sheet you keep active in your current Excel session. A DIALOG.BOX command macro invokes the dialog box from the definition table. The actual table in Figure 20-14 fills the range C2:I31. We've added labels in column B and row 1 to make the definition table easier to read. Figure 20-15 shows the dialog box as it will appear on the screen.

	B	C	D	E	F	G	H	I
1	Description	Item	X	Y	Width	Height	Text	Initial/Result
2	Dialog box size and title				509	269	Student Info	
3	First Name edit bar	6	94	7	126			
4	ID edit bar 1	8	100	41	36			
5	ID field divider	5	142	48			-	
6	ID edit bar 2	8	154	40	29			
7	ID field divider	5	184	44			-	
8	ID edit bar 3	8	198	40	50			
9	ID edit bar label	5	8	44			SID Number:	
10	First Name edit bar label	5	8	10			First Name:	
11	School list box label	5	164	80			School:	
12	GPA edit bar label	5	287	44			GPA:	
13	Last Name edit bar label	5	239	10			Last Name:	
14	Last Name edit bar	6	325	7	171			
15	GPA edit bar	8	325	41	70			
16	Year group	11	10	91	148	134	Year	4
17	Freshman button	12	14	109			Freshman	
18	Sophomore button	12	14	127			Sophomore	
19	Junior button	12	14	145			Junior	
20	Senior button	12	14	163			Senior	
21	Post-Grad button	12	14	181			Post-Grad	
22	Graduate button	12	14	199			Graduate	
23	Status group box	14	334	91	168	125	Status	
24	School list box	15	166	99	162	127		2
25	Honors check box	13	338	118			Honors	FALSE
26	Independent Study check box	13	338	136			Independent Study	FALSE
27	Foreign Study check box	13	338	154			Foreign Study	FALSE
28	Special Project check box	13	338	172			Special Project	FALSE
29	Teaching Assistant check box	13	338	190			Teaching Assistant	FALSE
30	Default OK button	1	348	232	64		OK	
31	Cancel button	2	428	232	64		Cancel	

FIGURE 20-14. *This definition table determines the placement of items in the dialog box shown in Figure 20-15.*

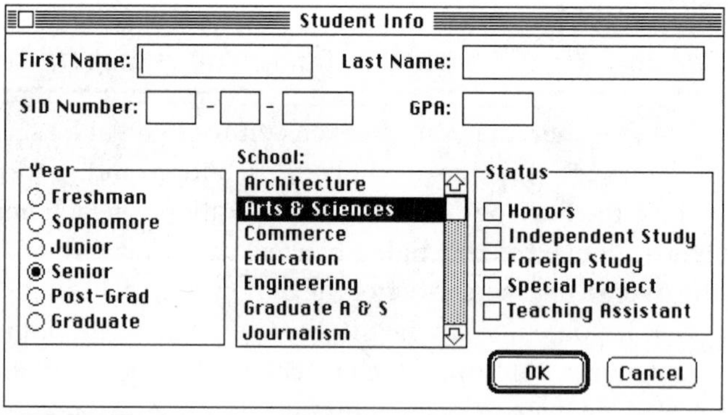

FIGURE 20-15. *This is how you want the Student Info dialog box to look after you adjust the definition table in Figure 20-14.*

When it was first created in the Dialog Editor, the Student Info dialog box looked like the box shown in Figure 20-16. As you can see, there are some minor problems with this dialog box. The GPA edit box is wider than it needs to be, the two hyphens separating the SID Number edit boxes are misaligned, and the list box has no items in it. We tell you the solution to these problems after we discuss the entries in the definition table.

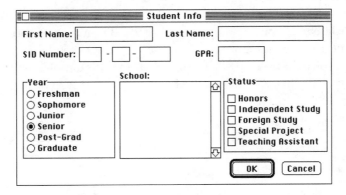

FIGURE 20-16. *This is a dialog box with minor problems.*

Definition-table entries

Figure 20-14 lists 30 dialog-box items. We discuss each of these items in the following sections.

Overall dimensions The first row of the definition table (row 2 in this example) defines the height and width of the dialog box, as well as its position on the screen. If there are no entries in this row, Excel centers the dialog box on the screen and adjusts its size to accommodate the contents of the dialog box.

If you want to define a specific screen position for your dialog box, enter a horizontal-position value in the X (or second) column of the first row and enter a vertical-position value in the Y (or third) column. In a definition table, the horizontal position is expressed in screen units from the left edge of the screen to the left edge of the dialog box. Similarly, the vertical position is measured in screen units from the top edge of the screen to the top edge of the dialog box. The actual size of a screen unit depends on the resolution of the monitor you are using. For example, a screen unit on a standard, built-in monitor is one point ($\frac{1}{72}$ inch), but on a monitor with a resolution of 144 dots per inch (twice that of a standard Macintosh monitor), a screen unit is half a point.

The widths for the items in your dialog box are recorded in the Width (or fourth) column of the first row of the definition table. Width is measured in horizontal screen units; horizontal screen units are approximately $\frac{1}{8}$ the width of the characters in the dialog box. Similarly, the height of your dialog box items is recorded in the Height (or fifth) column. Height is measured in vertical screen units; these units are $\frac{1}{12}$ the height of the characters in the dialog box.

If, for some reason, you erase the X, Y, Width, and Height field settings, Excel automatically sizes the dialog box for you. You may find, however, that Excel's automatic sizing does not result in a well-proportioned dialog box. Now, you see the freedom the Dialog Editor offers you from the difficulty of building a dialog box from scratch.

Title bar If you decide your dialog box doesn't need a title bar or, as in the Student Info box in Figure 20-15, your dialog box is too large to move across the screen, you can erase the title (from cell H2 in this example) in the definition table. When you do this, your dialog box becomes static. It can't be moved and looks like the one in Figure 20-17.

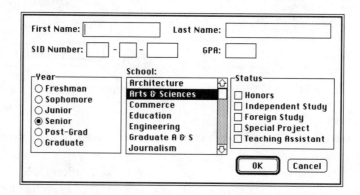

FIGURE 20-17. *This dialog box has no title bar and cannot be moved.*

Item type An Excel dialog box can have 17 different item types. Each dialog box can contain as many as 64 items, 32 of which can take or return arguments. You can include as many as four list boxes in each dialog box. Excel represents each item type by a code in the Item column (column C of Figure 20-14). The table at the top of the next page lists each item code and its purpose.

For example, if you use the Dialog Editor to create a dialog box with a default OK button and then decide you want the dialog box to display a default Cancel button instead, simply change the item-type settings—for the default OK button, change the type to 3, and for the Cancel button, change the type to 4. In Figure 20-14, this means changing the 1 in cell C30 to 3 and the 2 in cell C31 to 4.

To define the type of item that you want to create (edit box, OK button, option button, text, and so forth), you enter into the Item column of the definition table one of the 17 codes Excel provides for you.

Code	Item	Code	Item
1	Default OK button	10	Reference edit box
2	Cancel button	11	Option-button group
3	OK button	12	Option button
4	Default Cancel button	13	Check box
5	Fixed text	14	Group box
6	Text edit box	15	List box
7	Integer edit box	16	Combination list box
8	Number edit box	17	Icon
9	Formula edit box		

Item position The Horizontal column contains a numeric value that defines the horizontal (X) position of each item within the dialog box. Although your definition table must contain a Horizontal column, you do not need to make any entries into this field. If you omit the horizontal-position value from an item description, Excel positions that item in the dialog box automatically. However, if you want to specify the horizontal position of an item, enter the number of screen units from the left edge of the dialog box to the left edge of the item.

Like the Horizontal column, the Vertical column also contains numeric values. These values determine the vertical (Y) position in screen units of each item in the dialog box. The vertical-position values are optional. If you omit the vertical value from an item description, Excel positions the item in the dialog box automatically. To specify the vertical position of an item, enter the number of screen units from the top of the dialog box to the top of the item.

Item size The Width column contains a numeric value that defines the width of each item in the dialog box in horizontal screen units. The Height column is similar to the Width column. It contains a numeric value that defines the height of each item in the dialog box in vertical screen units.

Like the entries in the Horizontal and Vertical columns, the entries in the Height and Width columns are optional. If you omit these values for a particular item, Excel determines the size of that item automatically.

Text column The Text column in the definition table displays the fixed text you created in the Dialog Editor. You can correct misspellings or add text to an item. For example, you can change the text of your default OK button to read *Enter*. To do this, simply select the cell that contains the default OK button text. Then, type *Enter* and press Return or Enter. In the table shown earlier in Figure 20-14, you select cell H30, type *Enter*, then press Return or Enter.

Initial/Result column The last column in the definition table is the Initial/ Result column. Here, you enter codes and text to specify the entries and selections that appear the first time the dialog box is opened. When the user clicks the OK button, the current selections and entries overwrite any default entries specified in the Initial/Result column. The next time the dialog box is displayed, the user's most recent entries and selections appear. To reset some or all of the values in the Initial/Result column each time you run the dialog box macro, you can include one or more SET.VALUE functions in your macro, placing them immediately before the DIALOG.BOX function. (We discuss the SET.VALUE function in Chapter 18, "Macro Functions.")

The Initial/Result column also allows you to specify which edit box in the dialog box is active when the dialog box is initially displayed. The number you specify in the Initial/Result column of the first row of the table tells Excel which row contains the definition of the edit box you want to activate. Excel begins counting the rows with the second row of the definition table. Thus, in the table in Figure 20-14, you would type 13 in cell I2 if you wanted the GPA box to be active when the dialog box appears. If you leave the Initial/Result column in the first row of the definition table blank, Excel activates the first edit box in the dialog box when the dialog box appears.

You can use the values in the Initial/Result column to link a custom dialog box back to the macro that opened the dialog box. You can also use a function such as the FORMULA function after the DIALOG.BOX function to retrieve the user's dialog-box selections from the Initial/Result column. We cover this topic in greater detail at the end of this chapter.

List boxes The contents of a list box cannot be created in the Dialog Editor. To create the entries that appear in a list box, you must enter a text reference in the Text column to a range on your macro sheet containing the items that are to appear in the list box. This reference must be either a range name or an R1C1-style text reference. In the table in Figure 20-14, you would enter this reference in cell H24.

For example, to create the list-box items in Figure 20-17, you need to enter the items that appear in that box in cells J2:J11 of the macro sheet and then assign the range name *school* to this list. Then, you define the list-box item in row 24 of the definition table by entering the range-name reference *R2C10:R11C10* in the Text field. You'll see this added to the definition table in Figure 20-19 later in this chapter.

You can determine the default list-box selection by entering the option number in the Initial/Result column. The options of a list box are numbered sequentially, beginning with the first row of the list range. If you do not make an entry in the Initial/Result column, the first list item is initially selected. If you enter #*N/A*, no list item is selected. The number of the list item the user selects appears in the Initial/ Result column. Only one item in a list box can be selected at a time.

Icons Excel allows you to display three different types of icons in a dialog box. To change the display of an icon, type the appropriate icon code in the Text field. These icons are identical to the ones that appear when you use the ALERT function to create an alert box. The following table shows which type of icon each code generates:

FIGURE 20-18. *These are the dialog-box icons.*

Editing a dialog box from the definition table

When we first looked at the dialog box defined by the definition table shown in Figure 20-14, it resembled the one in Figure 20-16. We saw that we needed to make a few minor adjustments in the definition table: The two hyphens separating the SID number edit boxes were misaligned, the GPA edit box was wider than it needed to be, and the list box had no items in it.

To align the hyphens, we changed the vertical placement of the first hyphen in cell E5 of the definition table from 47 to 44, which matches the setting of the second hyphen.

We were dissatisfied with the size of the GPA edit box. It was too wide for the four-character values we would enter into it. When we discovered that a setting of 50 in cell F8 of the definition table provided the proper width for the values we would enter there, we changed cell F15 to match F8.

To create the list box of schools shown in Figure 20-16, we entered the items that appear in that box in cells J2:J11 of the macro sheet, outside the range of the definition table. Figure 20-19, on the next page, shows the definition table with the adjacent column J containing the list box items. We assigned the range name *school* to this list. Then, in row 24 of the definition table where the list-box item information is, we entered the reference *R2C10:R11C10*. (Instead of the range location, we could have used the range-name reference *school* in the Text field.) We also entered a value of 2 in row 24 of the Initial/Result column. This value highlights the second item, *Arts & Sciences*, as the default item in the School list box.

	B	C	D	E	F	G	H	I	J
		Item	X	Y	Width	Height	Text	Initial/Result	School
1	Description								
2	Dialog box size and title				509	269	Student Info		Architecture
3	First Name edit bar	6	94	7	126				Arts & Sciences
4	ID edit bar 1	8	100	41	36				Commerce
5	ID field divider	5	142	44			-		Education
6	ID edit bar 2	8	154	40	29				Engineering
7	ID field divider	5	184	44			-		Graduate A & S
8	ID edit bar 3	8	198	40	50				Journalism
9	ID edit bar label	5	8	44			SID Number:		Law
10	First Name edit bar label	5	8	10			First Name:		Medicine
11	School list box label	5	164	80			School:		Nursing
12	GPA edit bar label	5	287	44			GPA:		
13	Last Name edit bar label	5	239	10			Last Name:		
14	Last Name edit bar	6	325	7	171				
15	GPA edit bar	8	325	41	50				
16	Year group	11	10	91	148	134	Year	4	
17	Freshman button	12	14	109			Freshman		
18	Sophomore button	12	14	127			Sophomore		
19	Junior button	12	14	145			Junior		
20	Senior button	12	14	163			Senior		
21	Post-Grad button	12	14	181			Post-Grad		
22	Graduate button	12	14	199			Graduate		
23	Status group box	14	334	91	168	125	Status		
24	School list box	15	166	99	162	127	R2C10:R11C10	2	
25	Honors check box	13	338	118			Honors	FALSE	
26	Independent Study check box	13	338	136			Independent Study	FALSE	
27	Foreign Study check box	13	338	154			Foreign Study	FALSE	
28	Special Project check box	13	338	172			Special Project	FALSE	
29	Teaching Assistant check box	13	338	190			Teaching Assistant	FALSE	
30	Default OK button	1	348	232	64		OK		
31	Cancel button	2	428	232	64		Cancel		

FIGURE 20-19. *This definition table shows the information for the School list box in the Student Info custom dialog box.*

Using a custom dialog box

Now that you've seen how to create and edit a custom dialog box, let's consider how you can use a dialog box in a macro. As mentioned earlier, to display a custom dialog box, all you do is include the DIALOG.BOX function in your Excel command macro. After you've defined the items you want to appear in the dialog box, you can create a simple two-line macro, like the one in Figure 20-13, that allows you to see the dialog box as you're refining it.

After a user makes selections in a dialog box and clicks the OK button, Microsoft Excel records the new dialog box settings in the Initial/Result column of the definition table. Excel then continues macro processing with the first statement after the DIALOG.BOX function. Thus, in the macro statements that follow the DIALOG.BOX function, you can access the information entered by a user by referring to the contents of the Initial/Result column.

If you want to return the dialog-box selections to the macro sheet, you can use the FORMULA function. For example, suppose you want to return to the macro sheet the contents of the First Name edit box in the sample dialog box. You can do this by following the DIALOG.BOX function with the macro statement

=FORMULA(I3)

That's all you do to return an edit box entry to the active cell in the macro sheet.

Retrieving other dialog-box information is a little more complex—but not at all difficult. Figures 20-20, 20-21, and 20-22 show three simple macros; each one returns a different type of information from the example dialog box. The macro in Figure 20-20 returns the result of the selection made in the option-button group. Using a series of IF statements, this macro examines the contents of the Initial/ Result field for the option-button-group definition in row 16. Based on the contents of that field, this macro returns one of the text entries in cells H17:H22. (Of course, these same text entries are used to label the option buttons in the dialog box.)

	K	L
1	ReturnYear	Option-Command-y
2	=FORMULA(IF(I16=1,H17,))	If Result=1, return label in H17, otherwise,...
3	=FORMULA(IF(I16=2,H18,))	If Result=2, return label in H18, otherwise,...
4	=FORMULA(IF(I16=3,H19,))	If Result=3, return label in H19, otherwise,...
5	=FORMULA(IF(I16=4,H20,))	If Result=4, return label in H20, otherwise,...
6	=FORMULA(IF(I16=5,H21,))	If Result=5, return label in H21, otherwise,...
7	=FORMULA(IF(I16=6,H22,))	If Result=6, return label in H22
8	=RETURN()	End of macro

FIGURE 20-20. *This simple macro returns the name of the option button a user has selected.*

Figure 20-21 shows a macro that returns the result of a user's selection in the School list box. As you can see, a CHOOSE function is embedded in the FORMULA function. The *index* argument of this CHOOSE function is taken from cell I24—the Initial/Result field of the list-box definition. Recall that the entry in this field tells Excel which item in the list in cells J2:J11 was chosen by the user.

	K	L
10	ReturnSchool	Option-Command-s
11	=IF(ISNA(I24),GOTO(K13),)	If Result=NA, go to cell K13, otherwise,...
12	=FORMULA(CHOOSE(I24,J2,J3,J4,J5,J6,J7,J8,J9,J10,J11))	Use number in I24 to choose item from J2:J11
13	=RETURN()	End of Macro

FIGURE 20-21. *You can use a macro like this one to return a user's selection from a list box.*

If cell I24 contains #N/A—as it does when nothing has been selected from the list box—the CHOOSE function returns an error value. To make sure that this error does not stop the macro, we have included an IF statement in the first line of the macro. This IF statement evaluates the contents of cell I24; if the cell contains #N/A, the macro loops to the RETURN statement, bypassing the CHOOSE function.

Finally, Figure 20-22 shows a macro that returns to the macro sheet any of the check-box options selected by the user. Each IF statement in this macro examines the Initial/Result field of one of the check-box items. If the entry in that field is TRUE, Excel returns to the worksheet the contents of the Text field for that item.

(Recall that the Text field contains the name of the check-box option.) If the entry in the Initial/Result field is FALSE, Excel returns nothing to the macro sheet.

	K	L
15	ReturnStatus	Option-Command-t
16	=IF(I25=TRUE,,GOTO(K19))	If I25=TRUE, continue with cell K17, otherwise go to K19
17	=FORMULA(H25)	Return label in H25
18	=SELECT("R[1]C")	Select cell below active cell in same column
19	=IF(I26=TRUE,,GOTO(K22))	If I26=TRUE, continue with cell K20, otherwise go to K22
20	=FORMULA(H26)	Return label in H26
21	=SELECT("R[1]C")	Select cell below active cell in same column
22	=IF(I27=TRUE,,GOTO(K25))	If I27=TRUE, continue with cell K23, otherwise go to K25
23	=FORMULA(H27)	Return label in H27
24	=SELECT("R[1]C")	Select cell below active cell in same column
25	=IF(I28=TRUE,,GOTO(K28))	If I28=TRUE, continue with cell K26, otherwise go to K28
26	=FORMULA(H28)	Return label in H28
27	=SELECT("R[1]C")	Select cell below active cell in same column
28	=FORMULA(IF(I29=TRUE,H29,))	If I29=TRUE, return label in H29
29	=RETURN()	End of macro

FIGURE 20-22. *This macro returns a user's check-box selections.*

Because check-box options are not mutually exclusive, the name of each selected option is entered into a separate cell of the macro sheet using the SELECT function. After Microsoft Excel examines the Initial/Result field for one of the check-box options, the SELECT function selects a new cell in the same column of the macro sheet.

Chances are, when you create a custom dialog box, you want to do more than simply return the user's selections and entries to a macro sheet. For example, you might want the user's selections to be fed into calculations, or you might want the selections to determine which of several macro subroutines are carried out. These sample macros in Figure 20-20, Figure 20-21, and Figure 20-22 show how you can access the information you gather with a dialog box. The ways you can use this information are infinite.

Adding a custom help file

When you create a custom dialog box, you can easily write your own help information that will be displayed when you request context-sensitive help for a dialog box. This information will also be displayed when you press Command-Shift-? or press the Help key.

The HELP function

You can use a text editor of your choice (such as Microsoft Word) to write help information. You simply type the form of a help file into your text editor and save it as a text file in your current folder on your hard drive. If the custom help file is not in the current folder, Excel asks you to locate the file. The format of a help file is

number,personal comments
One or more lines of help text.

The *number* can be an integer from 0 through 32,767. This integer helps you to keep track of your help files in case you keep all of your custom help files in the same text document. The numbers do not have to be in consecutive order, but they do need to follow an asterisk.

The *personal comments* are optional notes you make to yourself to identify topics in the file. No *personal comments* are displayed when you request a custom help file. Excel displays only the help text you entered.

For example, if you want to create a custom help file for our example Student Info dialog box, you could create a text file in Microsoft Word that says

*1, Help file for Student Info
This dialog box tracks a student's status for the Registrar's files.

To use this help file, save it as a text file, called *Helptext* for example, in your current folder and close the file. Now, you need to open the definition table in Excel and enter a help reference in the dialog-box definition table's upper-left corner.

In Figure 20-19, the example definition table shows the cell C2 to be empty. In this cell, enter the help reference in the following form:

filename!topic number

The *filename* argument is the name of the text file in which you have saved the custom help file, and the *topic number* argument is the number in the text file that corresponds to the help file you want to attach to the custom dialog box. (You can store several help files in one text document, each with a different number.)

To call the help file to the screen when the dialog box is open, you can press the Help key or press Command-Shift-? to see a Help screen like the one in Figure 20-23, on the next page. This Help screen displays the message *This dialog box tracks a student's status for the Registrar's files*. Notice, however, that the only active button on a custom Help screen is the Cancel button.

You can add a HELP function to a macro that calls your custom dialog box to the screen so that your help file is available whenever the dialog box is opened. The form of this function is

=HELP("*filename!topic number*")

The arguments are identical to those we explained above. When you include the HELP function in a macro, the custom help file appears when the macro processes the cell in the macro that contains the HELP function. If you omit the custom help file argument from the function, the HELP function displays the Microsoft Excel Help screen.

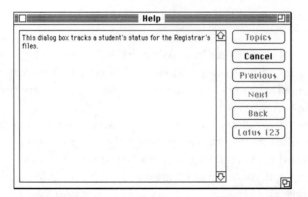

FIGURE 20-23. *This Help screen displays information about the custom dialog box shown in Figure 20-16.*

Building custom data forms

As we mentioned in Chapter 14, "Excel Database Management," you can replace Excel's built-in data form with a custom data form. To create your own data form, you work with the Dialog Editor that you use to create custom dialog boxes. A custom data form contains only the following items: static text and edit fields for text, integers, numbers, formulas, and references. You need not include items to create the standard buttons that appear in a data form (New, Delete, Restore, Find Prev, Find Next, Criteria, and Exit); Excel creates these buttons automatically. In addition, Microsoft Excel creates the record-number designation in the upper-right corner of the data form (such as *1 of 10*) and the data-form scroll bar you use to move among records.

When you finish creating the data form, copy the form from the Dialog Editor and paste it to a definition range in the same worksheet that contains your database. This definition range is set up with seven columns, like the definition table shown in Figure 20-14. Select the range and choose the Define Name… command. The range reference appears in the Refers To field. Type the name *Data_Form* in the Name field and click OK. When you either activate a cell in the top row of the definition range or select the entire definition range (cell B14:H27 in this example) and then choose the Form… command from the Data menu, your custom data form appears. If you activate a single cell within the range, Excel presents an error dialog box when you choose the Form… command. If you activate a cell in the database range, you'll see an unpredictably altered version of your dialog box. Figure 20-24 shows the custom data form we created. Figure 20-25 shows the definition range for that custom data form. We added headings to each column of information in the definition range.

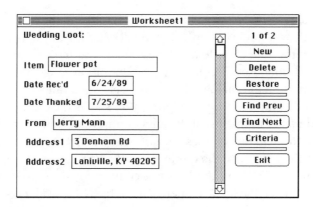

FIGURE 20-24. *This figure shows our custom data form.*

	A	B	C	D	E	F	G	H
12								
13		Item	X	Y		Width	Height	Text	Initial/Result
14			60	35	320	281		
15		5	9	5			Wedding Loot:	
16		8	116	81	72			Date Rec'd
17		8	116	113	73			Date Thanked
18		5	12	151			From	
19		6	59	146	171			From
20		6	88	178	142			Address1
21		6	88	210	142			Address2
22		5	13	215			Address2	
23		5	13	182			Address1	
24		5	10	87			Date Rec'd	
25		5	10	116			Date Thanked	
26		5	9	55			Item	
27		6	50	50	177			Item
28								
29								

FIGURE 20-25. *This figure shows the definition range for the data form in Figure 20-24.*

The data form you create in the Dialog Editor generates only the left half of the data form you see on the screen. The right half displays all of the items Excel automatically includes in the data form. When you create a centered data form in the Dialog Editor and then copy the form to Excel, it appears misaligned on the screen. Excel centers on the screen the part of the data form you exported from the Dialog Editor. The part of the data form that Excel provides is partially obscured by the lower-right corner of the screen. To center the entire data-form dialog box on the screen, you need to adjust the Horizontal (X) and Vertical (Y) settings for the dialog box. For example, in Figure 20-24 we changed the X and Y settings for the dialog box in cell C14 from 105 to 60 and in cell D14 from 58 to 35.

Even though you can type information into the fields of the new custom data form, the information is not linked automatically to your database range. To link each field in the data form to a database field, you must enter the database field name in the Initial/Result column of the definition range. (When you first copy the data form from the Dialog Editor to the definition range in your worksheet, the Initial/Result column is empty. Figure 20-25 shows the definition range after we added field names to the Initial/Result column.) You enter each field name in the same row as the item that defines the edit field where the field data will be entered. (Remember the rows with the number 5 in the *Item* column define text entries, so don't enter names in the Initial/Result column for those rows.) The field name must exactly match the name that appears in the field-header row of the database; otherwise, Microsoft Excel will not transfer the contents of the form window to your database correctly.

Although the field names in the Initial/Result column must exactly match the field names in the field-header row of the database, the field names that label each field or edit field in the data form need not match the database field names. For example, your database might contain a field called *Name*, but in your custom data form you can label the edit field *First Name*. In addition, the fields in your custom data form need not appear in the same order as the fields in your database; however, every field you create in the data form must correspond to one of the fields in your database range.

If you paste your definition range below the database range, be sure to leave plenty of space in your database above the definition range to record your entries from the data form. Excel does not automatically expand the database when it runs out of rows.

You aren't required to include all the database fields in the data form. If you include locked or calculated fields, the contents of these fields appear in the form window without boxes and are not available for editing.

Conclusion

In this chapter, we've explained the basics of four of the most impressive features of Microsoft Excel: custom menus, custom dialog boxes, the custom HELP function, and custom data forms. These features can greatly enhance your macro applications by making them more flexible and easier to use. With a little imagination, you're sure to find a variety of ways to put these new and powerful features to work.

SECTION SIX

BEYOND EXCEL

A

Linking to Other Programs

As you work with Microsoft Excel, you may sometimes need to transfer information to or receive information from another program. For example, you may want to exchange worksheets with Lotus 1-2-3, or you may import a macro from Microsoft Excel for the IBM PC. Or you may want to transfer a chart or a table from Excel to a report you're writing in Microsoft Word.

Excel offers several methods for exchanging data with other programs. Using the Save As... command, you can save a file in a format that other programs can read. Using the Clipboard, you can share data with other Macintosh programs.

In this appendix, we show you how to exchange information between Microsoft Excel and other programs, including Microsoft Excel for the IBM PC, Lotus 1-2-3, Microsoft Multiplan, dBASE, Microsoft Word, Microsoft Write, and Microsoft File. We discuss the Data menu's Parse... command, which allows you to separate data in database fields into individual columns. Finally, we show you some macro functions you can use to communicate with other programs.

The Save As… command

You can share data with other programs by saving the file in a format other programs can read. To save a file in a readable file format, use the Save As… command on the File menu. If you click the Options button in the Save As dialog box, a File Format dialog box appears with nine file-format choices: Normal, Text, CSV, SYLK/Excel 1.5, WKS, WK1, DIF, DBF 2, and DBF 3. The last two file-format choices, DBF 2 and DBF 3, appear dimmed unless you have defined a database in your document. As Figure A-1 shows, the default choice in the File Format dialog box is Normal. This is the standard format you use to save Excel worksheets, macro sheets, and charts.

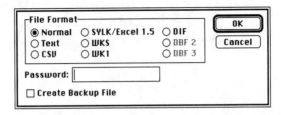

FIGURE A-1. *When you click the Options button in the File Format dialog box, a second dialog box appears, showing nine file-format choices.*

Note, however, that all Microsoft worksheet programs can produce SYLK (symbolic link format) files. The SYLK option is Microsoft's "generic" worksheet file format. You'll want to save Excel worksheets in the SYLK format when you plan to share data with other Microsoft worksheet programs, such as Microsoft Multiplan or Microsoft Excel for the IBM PC.

As you see later in this chapter, the WKS and WK1 file formats let you share data with Lotus 1-2-3 and Symphony. The DBF 2 and DBF 3 formats let you transfer a database range to dBASE, and the Text and CSV formats let you convert Excel documents to a text format for exchange with a variety of word-processing and spreadsheet programs.

When you use the Save As… command to save your worksheet in a format another program can read, attributes such as text and numbers, functions and formulas, formats, and calculation options are converted to the format the other program can read. However, window attributes, such as size, position, panes, and the position of the active cell, are not converted. In addition, none of your print settings are converted.

As you might guess, other programs won't be able to read some data in your Excel worksheet. For example, the program to which you're exporting may not have an equivalent for one of Excel's built-in functions. In that case, the Excel formula or function is generally converted to a constant value. Suppose a worksheet you're exporting to Lotus 1-2-3 contains a formula that returns the number 100. If Lotus 1-2-3 can't interpret this formula, it uses the current *value* of the formula, 100. (When you save a file in Text format, only the current values are stored. All underlying formulas are lost.)

Similarly, when you're importing data from another program, you may run into a formula or a function that Excel doesn't recognize. When Excel can't translate a formula into or out of a different file format, it pauses and displays the alert box shown in Figure A-2. This alert box displays two messages: *Can't read record (Cell: A1)* and *Continue reporting each error?* If you click Yes, Excel displays this dialog box each time it can't convert a formula. If you click No, Excel does not pause until it has converted the entire worksheet. When Excel finishes converting the data, it displays an alert box, like the one in Figure A-3, that shows the total number of formulas it could not convert. If you click Cancel, Excel stops the procedure.

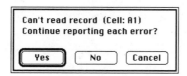

FIGURE A-2. *This alert box appears when Excel can't read a formula imported from another program.*

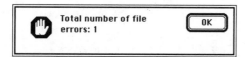

FIGURE A-3. *Excel keeps track of file conversion errors.*

Whether you click Yes or you click No depends on the type of worksheet you're converting. If the worksheet contains many formulas that Excel can't convert, you might want to click No to avoid seeing the dialog box again and to speed up the conversion process. If you think the worksheet contains only a few formulas that can't be converted, click Yes so that you can note the location of each problem. Excel assigns a value of 1 to each formula Excel can't convert.

Communicating data from a PC to a Macintosh

To obtain a Macintosh-readable diskette from a PC, there are a few approaches you can take. You can use a special null modem cable that has the proper configuration to connect a PC and a Macintosh through their communication ports. Your hardware dealer can provide you with such a cable and the communications software you need for both computers. If your PC and your Macintosh aren't in the same location, you can use a modem to transfer files.

If you plan to transfer files frequently from a PC to a Macintosh, you may want to invest in some additional hardware to quicken the data exchanges. For example, you can purchase a board for your PC that allows you to plug a Macintosh disk drive directly into a PC. Then, using special software, you can copy files from your PC drive to your Macintosh drive.

You can also buy a special disk drive that plugs directly into your Macintosh and allows you to format, read, and write PC disks. Additionally, the Macintosh SE/30 and the Macintosh IIcx are shipped with a SuperDrive that can read from and write to 3.5-inch PC disks.

If you're connected to a network that supports both a PC and a Macintosh, you're in luck. You can probably transfer files from one computer to another without any extra equipment or software.

From the network, Excel users can share and print the same documents. There are three ways you can gain access to shared Excel documents. First, you can open a document and specify "read-only" access (that is, you can read the document but not edit it). Second, you can open a document and specify "read-write" access (that is, you can read and edit the document). Note that only one person at a time can open a document specifying "read-write" access. Finally, you can link your active Excel document to another document on the network. This ensures that your document is updated along with any shared documents.

When you create documents that can be shared by other users in a network, don't forget that Excel allows you to save your documents with passwords so that unauthorized users can't open them. You can also lock all the cells in your document or hide certain ones so that other users cannot edit those cells or see them. You can choose the Cell Protection... command from the Format menu then the Protect Document... command from the Options menu to assign a password to the document. (We described this procedure in detail in Chapter 8, "Other Worksheet Topics.") To ensure only authorized use of your files, give the password to only those persons you want to have access to your document.

To open a document with "read-only" access, choose the Open... command from the File menu, select the document you want to open, click the Read Only check box, and then click Open or press Enter. If you open a file with "read-write" access while someone else is using that file, Excel only lets you "read" the file. In a network environment, it's a good idea to open a document as a "read-only" file unless you are certain you will edit that file.

Sharing data between a PC and a Macintosh is relatively commonplace today. There are fine products you can purchase in the marketplace to make this transfer of data easy. Your hardware dealer can help you choose the best transfer method for your needs.

Sharing files with Excel for the IBM PC

The Macintosh and IBM PC versions of Microsoft Excel can share data very easily. All numbers and text values and most formulas and cell formats convert without problems. A document's protection status, calculation and iteration settings, and display settings also convert. To exchange data between the two versions of Excel, you begin by saving a document in the SYLK/Excel 1.5 file format. Then, you transfer the file from one computer to the other.

Importing files from Excel for the IBM PC

As we just mentioned, the first step in importing a PC Excel file is to save the document in the SYLK Excel 1.5 format. To do this, load Excel for the IBM PC, then open the document you want to transfer. Choose the Save As... command from the File menu, click the Options button, and choose the SYLK file-format option in the File Format dialog box. After saving the file, transfer it to the Macintosh using cable, modem, network, or disk.

Next, start the Macintosh version of Excel, choose the Open... command from the File menu, and select the name of the document you want to open. Because Excel for the IBM PC automatically adds a filename extension when you save a file, you can easily find the PC Excel file by looking for a file with a filename extension (such as SLK).

Exporting Macintosh files

Transferring data from the Macintosh version of Excel to the PC version is just as easy. Simply open the document you want to transfer, choose the Save As... command from the File menu, and specify the name under which you want to save the file. Then, click the Options button, choose the SYLK/Excel 1.5 file format, and click OK or press Enter. After transferring the file to the IBM PC, start Excel for the IBM PC and choose the Open... command to load the SYLK file.

Adjusting date values

Although the Macintosh and PC versions of Excel share many characteristics and abilities, they do not share the same date system. In Excel for the IBM PC, the base date is January 1, 1900. In Excel for the Macintosh, the base date is January 1, 1904. Whether you transfer a Macintosh file to the PC or you transfer a PC file to the Macintosh, the date is adjusted automatically. Excel 2.2 for the Macintosh automatically deselects the 1904 Date System option in the Calculation dialog box when it opens the worksheet.

Sharing files with Microsoft Multiplan

Until Microsoft Excel came along, the best spreadsheet program for the Macintosh was Microsoft Multiplan. Many Excel users are former Multiplan users who may need to transfer their Multiplan worksheets to Excel. Fortunately, Excel makes importing Multiplan worksheets quick and easy.

Importing Microsoft Multiplan files

To import into Excel a Multiplan file saved as a SYLK file, choose the Open... command from the File menu, select the Multiplan file you want to import, and click OK. Excel automatically recognizes the file as a Multiplan file and, when it is loading, converts it into an Excel worksheet.

Most of the basic data on the Multiplan worksheet, including all value and text entries, names, formats, and so on, convert correctly. As you might expect, however, most worksheet properties, such as window settings and print settings, are not transferred. If Excel encounters a formula it cannot convert, it displays a #NAME? error.

In most respects, the Excel worksheet and the Multiplan worksheet are very similar. There are a few important differences between them, however, that are worth mentioning.

Cell references

In Multiplan, both columns and rows are identified by numbers, and cell addresses are always stated in R1C1 form. As you know, Excel can use either R1C1 or A1 cell references, but defaults to A1-style references. When you transfer a worksheet from Multiplan to Excel, R1C1 cell references are converted to A1-style references. If you are familiar with the R1C1 style and want to use this type of reference in Excel, simply choose the Workspace... command from the Options menu and select the R1C1 option.

Format conversion

In Excel, you assign formats to numbers by setting options with the Number... command on the Format menu. In Multiplan, the number-format options are commands on the Format menu: General, Dollar, Percent, No Decimal, Decimal, Scientific, and Bar Graph. Excel offers a format that corresponds to each of these options except Bar Graph.

Figure A-4 shows the complete list of Multiplan formats and their equivalent Excel formats. If the Multiplan worksheet contains formats with other than zero or two decimals, Excel creates a format using the number of decimals in the Multiplan format.

Multiplan	Excel
General	General
No Decimal	0
Decimal, 2 decimals	0.00
Scientific, 0 decimals	0E+00
Scientific, 2 decimals	0.00E+00
Dollar, 0 decimals	$0; ($0)
Dollar, 2 decimals	$0.00 ;($0.00)
Dollar, 0 decimals, comma	$#,##0 ;($#,##0)
Dollar, 2 decimals, comma	$#,##0.00 ;($#,##0.00)
Percent, 0 decimals	0%
Percent, 2 decimals	0.00%
No Decimal, comma	#,##0
Decimal, comma, 2 decimals	#,##0.00

FIGURE A-4. *Multiplan formats and their equivalent Excel formats.*

Calculation differences

In Multiplan, worksheets are calculated in strict linear order: column 1 first, then column 2, then column 3, and so on. Excel uses natural-order calculation instead.

In most cases, this difference does not cause problems. In a few cases, however, a Multiplan worksheet may not calculate properly after being imported. In that event, you may want to move the converted worksheet into a macro sheet. Because macro sheets use linear, column-by-column calculation, there is a good chance that the converted worksheet will compute properly in a macro sheet.

Both Excel and Multiplan allow you to use iterative calculation. However, the method for controlling iterative calculation in the two programs is different. In Multiplan, iterative calculation is controlled by two functions: DELTA and ITERCNT. The DELTA function measures the change in a given value in the worksheet from one iteration to another. The ITERCNT function counts the number of iterations. These functions are used in a completion-test formula that you enter into a cell of the worksheet and define using the Set Completion Test command. Iteration continues until the value of the completion-test formula changes from TRUE to FALSE.

In Excel the DELTA and ITERCNT functions are replaced with the Maximum Change and Maximum Iterations settings in the Calculation dialog box. These settings determine the number of iterations that occur when Excel calculates the worksheet.

If you import into Excel a Multiplan worksheet that uses iterative calculation, you must replace the completion-test formula with the proper Maximum Change and Maximum Iterations settings. Most of the time, the worksheet calculates properly in Excel after you make this change.

Function conversion

Excel supports every Multiplan function except the DELTA and ITERCNT functions. Excel does not convert formulas that contain either of these functions.

Sharing files with Lotus 1-2-3

Microsoft Excel has the ability to read and write Lotus 1-2-3 worksheets. This means that you can exchange worksheets with your friends and coworkers who use 1-2-3. If you are currently a 1-2-3 user, this capability also means that you can upgrade to Excel with a minimum of difficulty.

Communicating your worksheets

Before you can import 1-2-3 files into Excel or export Excel files into 1-2-3, you must communicate those files from one computer to another. (We discussed transferring files from the Macintosh to the PC, and vice versa, earlier in this appendix.)

Importing Lotus 1-2-3 files

Once you have transferred a 1-2-3 file to the Macintosh, importing that file into Excel is easy. All you do is load Excel, choose the Open… command from the File menu, and double click the name of the file you want to import. Excel automatically identifies the selected file as a 1-2-3 file and converts the file when loading it.

Excel does a good job of importing 1-2-3 worksheets. All the values and labels in the 1-2-3 worksheet are converted properly into number and text values. Most of the formulas in the 1-2-3 worksheet can also be converted into Excel formulas.

If Excel can't translate a formula (which does not happen very often), it pauses and displays an alert box that identifies the location of the cell that contains the error, asks if Excel should continue reporting each error, and offers three buttons: Yes, No, and Cancel. If you click Yes, Excel displays this dialog box each time it cannot convert a formula. If you click No, Excel does not pause until it has converted the entire worksheet. Then, Excel displays a dialog box that shows the total number of formulas that could not be converted. If you click Cancel, Excel stops the procedure.

When Excel cannot convert an incoming formula, it changes that formula to a constant value, if possible. For example, suppose a 1-2-3 worksheet contains a formula that returns the number 300. If Excel cannot convert this formula, it instead imports the current value of the formula, 300.

Formula differences

The Microsoft Excel range operator (:) is different from the 1-2-3 range operator (..). When Excel encounters the range operator in a formula, it converts that operator from its 1-2-3 form to its Excel form.

There is also a slight difference in the precedence of mathematical operators in Excel and 1-2-3. In Excel, the negation operator takes precedence over the exponentiation operator. In 1-2-3, the exponentiation operator takes precedence. This means that the formula =–2^2 returns 4 in Excel, and it returns –4 in 1-2-3. You can overcome this difference by careful use of parentheses. The formula =(–2)^2 returns 4 in both programs, and the formula =–(2^2) returns –4 in both programs.

Format conversion

Most 1-2-3 formats have counterparts in Excel. When you import 1-2-3 worksheets into Excel, Excel converts the formats according to the relationships shown in Figure A-5.

If your 1-2-3 worksheet contains a format other than the ones listed in Figure A-5 (for example, currency with three decimal places), Excel creates a format that matches the incoming one.

1-2-3	Excel
Fixed, 0 decimals	0
Fixed, 2 decimals	0.00
Exponential, 0 decimals	0E+00
Exponential, 2 decimals	0.00E+00
Currency, 0 decimals	$#,##0 ;($#,##0)
Currency, 2 decimals	$#,##0.00 ;($#,##0.00)
Percent, 0 decimals	0%
Percent, 2 decimals	0.00%
Comma, 0 decimals	#,##0 ;(#,##0)
Comma, 2 decimals	#,##0.00 ;(#,##0.00)
+/−	General
D1 (dd-mmm-yy)	d-mmm-yy
D2 (dd-mmm)	d-mmm
D3 (mmm-yy)	mmm-yy
Text	General
General	General
Hidden (version 2.0 or later)	;

FIGURE A-5. *Lotus 1-2-3 formats and their equivalent Excel formats.*

Function conversion

All Lotus 1-2-3 functions have counterparts in Microsoft Excel. When Excel translates a function that has an Excel counterpart, such as @SUM, @ABS, or @LN, the conversion works fine. For example, Excel converts the 1-2-3 function

@SUM(C1..C10)

into the Excel function

=SUM(C1:C10)

Some functions have slightly different names in Excel than in 1-2-3, but they are otherwise identical. For example, the function that computes the average of a set of values is =AVERAGE in Excel and @AVG in 1-2-3. When you convert one of these functions, Excel automatically changes the name of the function.

There are few cases in which an Excel function and its 1-2-3 equivalent don't work in the same way. In most of these cases, Excel overcomes the differences during translation. Some of these transformations are quite sophisticated. For example, both Lotus 1-2-3 and Microsoft Excel have a CHOOSE function. In Excel, this function has the form

=CHOOSE(*index,value1,value2,...*)

In 1-2-3, this function has the form

@CHOOSE(*offset,value0,value1,...*)

The difference between these functions is that the first value in the Excel function has an index value of 1, while the first value in the 1-2-3 list has an offset of 0. In other words, the function

=CHOOSE(1,100,200,300)

returns 100 in Excel, while the function

@CHOOSE(1,100,200,300)

returns 200 in 1-2-3.

Excel overcomes this difficulty by subtracting 1 from the index value when it converts an Excel @CHOOSE function to 1-2-3 or by adding 1 to the offset when it loads a 1-2-3 worksheet into Excel. The same thing happens when you convert the VLOOKUP and HLOOKUP functions or any database statistical function (DSUM, DAVERAGE, and so on).

Another example of this type of difference relates to the PV, FV, and PMT functions. In Excel, the payment and principal arguments of these functions are negative. In 1-2-3, the same arguments in these functions are positive. For this reason, when Excel translates one of these functions from Excel to 1-2-3 or from 1-2-3 to Excel, it changes the sign of the payment and principal arguments.

Here's another interesting translation. The 1-2-3 @IRR function has the form

@IRR(*guess,values*)

The Excel IRR function has the form

=IRR(*values,guess*)

To account for this difference, Excel always transposes the *values* and *guess* arguments when it translates the IRR and @IRR functions.

Excel's statistical functions (AVERAGE, COUNT, and so on) treat cells that contain nonnumeric values differently from the way the 1-2-3's statistical functions treat these cells. If you include in the argument of a 1-2-3 statistical function a cell that contains a label, the function assigns a value of 0 to that label. The Excel version of the function ignores the label. This small difference can make a big difference in the result of the function. You must watch for this difference when you translate statistical functions.

In addition, Excel's STDEV and VAR functions compute *sample* standard deviation and variance, while 1-2-3's STD and VAR functions compute *population* standard deviation and variance. (In Excel, you use the STDEVP and VARP functions to compute population standard deviation and variance.) Again, this is a difference you must watch for when you import these functions.

Also, Excel's INT function is different from 1-2-3's @INT function. In 1-2-3, @INT always rounds toward 0. In Excel, INT always rounds down. As a result, the function

@INT(–3.65)

returns –3 in 1-2-3, while the function

=INT(–3.65)

returns –4 in Excel.

This difference also causes the MOD and @MOD functions to return different answers if the arguments of both functions are negative.

Excel's DATE function accepts year arguments from 4 through 178 (if you don't turn off Excel's 1904 date system); 1-2-3's date function accepts year arguments from 1 through 199. As long as the year argument of a 1-2-3 @DATE function that you are importing is less than 179 and greater than 3, the function is converted correctly. If the year argument of a 1-2-3 @DATE function is outside this range, Excel changes the function into a constant value when converting it.

Other conversion problems

Most other attributes of your 1-2-3 worksheet are lost when you import the worksheet into Excel. For example, window attributes are not converted. Also, none of the print settings you have defined in 1-2-3 are transferred.

If the 1-2-3 worksheet contains a data table, the table formula, all the input values (variables), and the results of the table are converted, but the table definition is not. You must redefine the table range and the input cell(s) before you can use the data table.

If your 1-2-3 worksheet contains macros, they are converted into Excel intact. However, these macros are useless in Excel because the Excel command structure and macro language are completely different from those of 1-2-3. The graphs in your 1-2-3 worksheets, however, are automatically converted to Excel charts.

Exporting files to Lotus 1-2-3

Microsoft Excel also has the ability to save worksheets as Lotus 1-2-3 files. To save a worksheet as a 1-2-3 file, choose the Save As... command, specify a filename, click WK1, click OK, click the Options button, and then click Save. When you save the file with the WK1 option, Excel automatically converts the worksheet into a 1-2-3 (version 2.0 or later) file.

Excel does as good a job exporting 1-2-3 files as it does importing 1-2-3 files. All the numbers and text entries in the worksheet are converted correctly, as are most of the formulas in the worksheet.

Some formulas, however, cannot be translated correctly. As you might expect, there are many more obstacles to translating Excel formulas to 1-2-3 than there are to moving in the other direction. For example, because 1-2-3 does not support arrays, any Excel formula that involves arrays is not converted. In addition, because 1-2-3 does not support references to cells in other worksheets, any Excel formula that contains an external reference is not converted.

Excel offers several operators—union (,), intersection (space), and concatenation (&)—that 1-2-3 does not support. Any formula that contains a union, intersection, or concatenation (1-2-3, version 1A only) operator is changed to a constant value as the worksheet is converted. If the formula concatenates two or more text strings, Excel enters the text string that results from the concatenation as a simple label in the 1-2-3 (version 1A) worksheet.

The Excel worksheet can include up to 16,384 rows; the 1-2-3 (version 1A) worksheet can include up to only 2048 rows and the 1-2-3 (version 2.0) worksheet can include up to only 8192 rows. Excel does not convert any formula that refers to a cell in a row below the last row in a 1-2-3 worksheet. Instead, Excel changes the formula to a constant value during conversion.

In Excel, you can assign names to cells or ranges in the worksheet or to constant values and formulas not entered in cells. On the other hand, 1-2-3 allows you to assign only names to cells or ranges. Any formula that contains a reference to a named cell or range converts properly from Excel to 1-2-3. If you convert a worksheet that contains formulas that use named constants or formulas, however, those named constants and formulas are converted into constant values. For example, suppose you have assigned the name *Test* to the constant 100 in an Excel worksheet, then you used that name in the formula

    =Test*A1

When this function is converted to 1-2-3, the name *Test* is changed to the value 100.

    When Excel cannot translate a formula, it pauses and displays a dialog box. After you have made your selections (the Show Total and Show All options have the same meaning whether you export or import), Excel changes the formula to a constant value, if possible.

Function conversion

Most Excel functions have equivalents in 1-2-3. When Excel translates a function that has a 1-2-3 equivalent, the conversion works fine. Some functions have a slightly different name in Excel than they have in 1-2-3, but are otherwise identical. For example, as we said earlier, the function that computes averages is AVERAGE in Excel and @AVG in 1-2-3. Whenever you convert one of these functions, Excel automatically changes its name.

    There are few cases in which an Excel function and its 1-2-3 equivalent don't work in the same way. In most of these cases, Excel overcomes the differences during translation. In a few cases, however, the conversion may not always work. For example, Excel's PV, FV, and PMT functions can take as many as five arguments; 1-2-3 does not support the fourth (future value) and fifth (type) arguments. If you translate an Excel worksheet that contains one of these functions, the function is converted properly as long as it has no more than three arguments. If you translate a PV, FV, or PMT function that has more than three arguments, Excel changes that function to a constant value during translation.

    Excel's NPV function is similar to 1-2-3's @NPV function, except that Excel's function accepts up to 14 cash flow arguments, while 1-2-3's accepts only 1. As long as your Excel NPV function has only one argument, the function converts properly. If it has more than one cash flow argument, it is changed to a constant value during conversion.

    Some functions in Excel do not have a 1-2-3 counterpart. For example, there is no 1-2-3 function equivalent to the Excel GROWTH function. Figure A-6 lists the Excel functions that do not have a 1-2-3 equivalent; these functions are changed to constant values when converted to 1-2-3.

Array functions	Matrix functions	Database functions
COLUMNS	MDETERM	DCOUNT
INDEX	MINVERSE	DPROD
ROWS	MMULT	DSTDEV
TRANSPOSE	TRANSPOSE	DVAR
Statistical functions	*Text functions*	*Other functions*
COUNT	DOLLAR	AREAS
GROWTH	TEXT	COLUMN
LINEST		ISBLANK
LOGEST	*Lookup functions*	ISERROR
STDEV	LOOKUP	ISLOGICAL
TREND	MATCH	ISNUMBER
VAR	*Date and time functions*	ISREF
	WEEKDAY	ROW
Mathematical functions	*Financial functions*	SEARCH
FACT	INT	SUBSTITUTE
LOG	IPMT	TYPE
PRODUCT	MIRR	
SIGN	PPMT	

FIGURE A-6. *These Microsoft Excel functions have no Lotus 1-2-3 equivalents.*

Lotus 1-2-3 offers three operators not directly supported by Excel: #AND#, #OR#, and #NOT#. The Excel equivalents of these operators are the functions AND, OR, and NOT. When you transfer an Excel worksheet to 1-2-3, all AND, OR, and NOT functions are changed to the operators #AND#, #OR#, and #NOT#. When you transfer a 1-2-3 worksheet to Excel, the operators are changed into the functions. For example, the Excel function

=AND(A1>100,A1<200)

is converted to the 1-2-3 function

(A1>100#AND#A1<200)

Excel supports seven error values—#VALUE!, #REF!, #DIV/0!, #NAME?, #N/A, #NULL!, and #NUM!; 1-2-3 supports only two error values—ERR and NA. When you convert a 1-2-3 worksheet to Excel, any NA value is translated into the #N/A error constant. Any ERR value is translated into the #VALUE! error constant. When you export an Excel worksheet to 1-2-3, the error value #N/A is converted into the error value N/A. Any other error value is translated into ERR.

Alignment, styling, and format conversion

In 1-2-3, all number entries are right-aligned in cells, while label entries can be right-aligned, left-aligned, centered, or repeated to fill the cell. In Excel, you can control the alignment of both number and text entries. When you convert an Excel worksheet to 1-2-3, only cells that contain text entries retain their alignment attributes. All numbers are converted to right-aligned format.

Because 1-2-3 does not support bold, italic, or any of the other type styles found in Excel, all style attributes are removed when you export an Excel worksheet into 1-2-3.

All standard Excel numeric formats have 1-2-3 counterparts and are converted properly, according to the relationships shown previously in Figure A-5. If you have defined your own formats in a worksheet, Excel attempts to convert those formats to 1-2-3 formats. For example, the Excel format $#,##0.000 ;($#,##0.000) is converted to currency with three decimal places in 1-2-3.

If Excel cannot convert the format, the cell is unformatted in the 1-2-3 worksheet. For example, the format

dddd, mmmmm d, yyyy

displays dates in the form Tuesday, January 1, 1904. This format has no counterpart in 1-2-3. If you attempt to convert a cell with this format from Excel to 1-2-3, the resulting cell in the 1-2-3 worksheet is unformatted.

Protection differences

Excel and 1-2-3 both support cell protection. In Excel, however, a cell can be both locked (protected from accidental change) and hidden. In 1-2-3, cells can only be protected. When you convert a 1-2-3 worksheet to Excel, all cells that are protected in the 1-2-3 worksheet are locked in Excel. When you convert an Excel worksheet to 1-2-3, all locked cells are protected in the 1-2-3 worksheet; however, cells hidden in Excel are not hidden in 1-2-3.

Calculation differences

Excel and 1-2-3 both support Manual and Automatic calculation. However, Excel also supports a third method: Automatic Except Tables. Whenever you convert an Excel worksheet that has Automatic Except Table calculation, the resulting 1-2-3 worksheet has Automatic recalculation.

Excel supports only natural-order calculation (according to dependent formulas). In addition to natural-order calculation, 1-2-3 also supports by-row and by-column calculation. When you convert a 1-2-3 worksheet to Excel, recalculation is set to Natural.

Other conversion problems

Most other attributes of your Excel worksheet are lost when you save the worksheet as a 1-2-3 file. For example, even if you have created several windows on a single Excel worksheet, the resulting 1-2-3 worksheet has only one window. In addition, none of the print settings you have defined in Excel are transferred.

If the Excel worksheet contains a data table, the table formula and the input values (variables) are usually converted properly. The results in an Excel data table are array formulas. These formulas are changed to current values during conversion. In addition, you must redefine the table range and the input cell(s) before you can use the table.

You cannot convert Excel charts into 1-2-3 graphs. In addition, although you can convert Excel macro sheets into 1-2-3 worksheets, there is no point in doing so—Excel macros are completely useless in 1-2-3.

Sharing files with dBASE

Microsoft Excel also has the ability to read and write files that dBASE II and dBASE III can read. This means that you can exchange Excel worksheets with people who use dBASE II or dBASE III. If you are currently a dBASE user, this capability means that you can upgrade to Excel with a minimum of difficulty.

Importing dBASE files

To import a dBASE file into Excel, you must transfer the dBASE file to your Macintosh using one of the methods we discussed earlier in this appendix. After you do this, simply choose the Open… command from Excel's File menu and double click the name of the file you want to open.

Excel places the dBASE field names in the first row of a new Excel worksheet, then uses them as field names in the Excel database. Each dBASE field appears in a different Excel column. The dBASE records appear in rows immediately under the field-names row. Excel sets the worksheet column width to match the width of the dBASE fields. Columns that contain data from dBASE character and numeric fields are the same width as their corresponding fields in dBASE.

Exporting Excel files to dBASE

Before you save an Excel document in the DBF format, be sure you've set the database range. This range does not need to start in the first column or first row of the worksheet. (When you reopen the file after saving it, you'll see that Excel has moved the saved range to the first column and first row.) Next, to convert the file, choose the Save As... command from the File menu, click the Options button, and then choose the appropriate file format: DBF 2 if you are transferring an Excel database range to dBASE II, DBF 3 if you are transferring an Excel database range to dBASE III.

Excel saves the file in the appropriate dBASE format, retaining column-width settings but discarding any other formatting. Be sure to add the file extension DBF to the file name when you save the file in DBF format.

Working with text files

The Text option in the Save As dialog box saves your worksheet and macro-sheet files as text files. When you save a document as text, Excel saves the text and values as they appear in the worksheet cells. The underlying formulas in the worksheet or macro sheet aren't saved. The Text option is commonly used to convert an Excel worksheet into a form usable by a word-processing program such as Microsoft Write or Microsoft Word. Many other programs can also read and write text files.

Saving a document as a text file, of course, strips the document of all formatting. When you save an Excel document as a text file, columns are separated by tabs and rows are separated by paragraph markers; the file is exported into Microsoft Write or Microsoft Word as tabular data. When you save data from Write or Word, make sure the values you are saving are separated by tabs and that each line of data ends with a paragraph marker.

To save a worksheet in the Text file format, first choose the Save As... command. When the Save As dialog box appears, click the Options button, then select the Text option. Next, click OK in the Options dialog box and then click Save in the Save As dialog box. Excel saves the file as text.

For example, suppose you want to use the Excel worksheet shown in Figure A-7 in a Microsoft Word document. To do this, first choose the Save As... command from the File menu. When Excel displays the Save As dialog box, click the Options button and then select the Text option to save the worksheet as a text file. Click OK in the Options dialog box and then click the Save button.

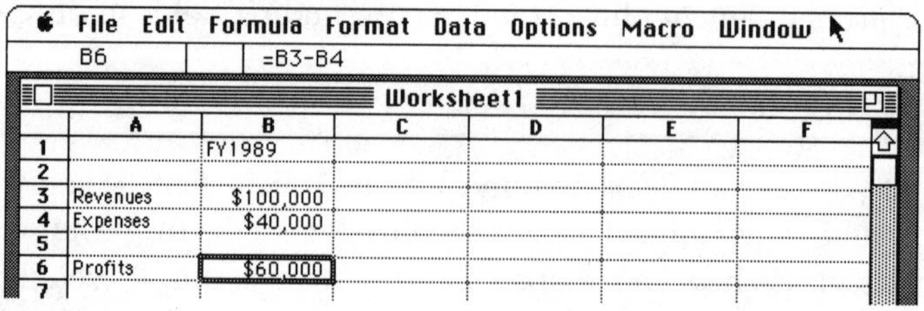

Figure A-7. *Save this worksheet in Text file format.*

To use this text file in Microsoft Word, load Word and then use the Open... command from the File menu to load the text file. As you can see in Figure A-8, only the text and values have been transferred into the Word document. Each column of data is separated by a tab, and each row appears as a separate paragraph. Each blank row appears as a single paragraph mark. (Of course, you must configure Word to show hidden characters if you want to see the tabs and paragraph marks.) You can now use Word's character and paragraph formatting commands to format this data, just as you would format any other Word document.

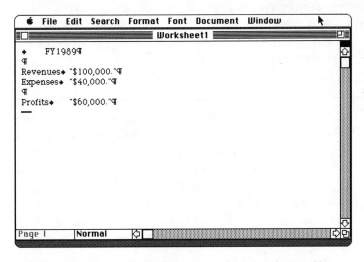

FIGURE A-8. *When you transfer a worksheet saved in the Text file format, tabs separate the columns and paragraph marks separate the rows.*

Notice that quotation marks appear around each piece of numeric text in the Word document. This is because Word can accept either tab-separated or comma-separated values. Because the numbers contain commas, the quotation marks prevent Word from treating the number as two separate entries. Unless you plan to use the transferred text as a data document for a form letter, which would require that values be separated by tabs or commas, you can use the Change command to eliminate the quotation marks.

The CSV file format

The CSV (Comma-Separated Values) file format is similar to the Text file format. Instead of tabs, the CSV format uses commas to separate columns or fields.

Whether you use the Text or the CSV file format depends on the program with which you're sharing data. Some programs can accept files saved in either file format; others accept only one of these formats.

If you open a CSV file in Excel, Excel begins a new column whenever it reads a comma. The contents of any cell containing a literal comma character is enclosed in double quotation marks.

Transferring information via the Clipboard and the Scrapbook

In many cases, the simplest way to exchange information between Microsoft Excel and other Macintosh programs is to copy and paste (or cut and paste) that information via the Clipboard or the Scrapbook. Cell values are transferred as text (numbers and letters). The underlying formulas are not transferred—only the displayed values. In addition to transferring values, you can take a "picture" of your worksheet and use the Clipboard or Scrapbook to transfer it into another document as a graphic. As you would expect, images of charts are always transferred as graphics. (We discuss using the Scrapbook later in this appendix.)

When to use the Clipboard

As you already know, when you cut or copy data in Excel, you place that data on the Clipboard to store it. That data remains on the Clipboard until you cut or copy something else or until you turn off your computer. When you're running Excel and another program simultaneously under MultiFinder, the Clipboard offers a quick and easy way to transfer information. You simply select the data you want to transfer and then choose the Copy or Cut command to place it on the Clipboard. Next, switch to the other program, click where you want the information to appear, and then choose the Paste command. You can always see what is on the Clipboard by choosing the Show Clipboard command from the Window menu.

You can also use the Clipboard to transfer information—even if you have insufficient memory to load both Excel and another program. When you have copied the information to the Clipboard, choose Quit from the File menu to exit Excel. If you have cut or copied a great deal of information, Excel displays a dialog box asking, *Save large clipboard from 'Document.Name'?* Click Yes to continue. When you are back on the Finder desktop, you can load the program into which you want to transfer the information you copied from Excel. Next, open the document into which you want to paste the copied information. Click where you want the information to appear. Finally, choose the Paste command from the Edit menu. Because you have not turned off your Macintosh, the Clipboard to which you copied the information from Excel is still active. The Paste command places the information you copied earlier from Excel into the new application.

If you want to return to Excel after you have copied information into the new application, save your work and choose Quit to exit the application and return to the Finder. When you are back on the Finder desktop, reload Excel.

Transferring information from Excel to Word

In this section, we discuss the transfer of Microsoft Excel data into Microsoft Word 3.0. Although we note some differences between the transfer of Excel data to Word 3.0 and to Word 4.0 as we go along, we save our discussion of Microsoft Word 4.0 until later in this appendix in the section called "Linking Excel documents to Word 4.0 documents."

If you want, you can save an Excel worksheet as a text file and then open it in Word. You can also use the Clipboard or Scrapbook to transfer values or pictures from Excel to Word. When you transfer cell values (numbers and text) to Word, that information can be manipulated just like the numbers and letters you type directly into a Word document. Pictures—including images of worksheet ranges as well as charts—are transferred to Word as graphics; their content cannot be edited. You can, however, resize and change the proportions of graphics imported into Word.

When to use the Scrapbook

The Scrapbook, unlike the Clipboard, stores information on your hard disk, rather than in RAM. Therefore, anything you paste into the Scrapbook remains there until you remove it. The information is not lost when you copy or cut another selection or when you shut down your computer. The Scrapbook allows you to extend the copy-and-paste procedure from one Excel session to the next without losing the information you've copied.

Because the Scrapbook stores information indefinitely, you should use it when you think you'll need to paste the same information into different documents at different times. The Scrapbook also offers an excellent way to transfer multiple data if you do not have enough memory to load Excel and another program simultaneously. By storing the data in the Scrapbook, you don't need to quit Excel and start the other program each time you want to copy a particular piece of information.

To place information in the Scrapbook, simply select the information and choose the Copy or Cut command. Next, choose Scrapbook from the Ú menu to open the Scrapbook; then select Paste from the Edit menu to place the selected information in the Scrapbook. (New information that you paste into the Scrapbook does not overwrite any existing information stored there.) After pasting data into the Scrapbook and closing it, you can quit Excel and start the application into which you want to paste that information.

To retrieve the data from the Scrapbook, choose the Scrapbook desk accessory from the Ú menu, scroll to the data you want to cut or copy, choose the Cut or Copy command from the Edit menu to place the data in the Clipboard, and then paste the data into the document of your choice. Remember, if you cut the information from the Scrapbook, you remove it permanently.

Transferring values

Suppose you want to copy the simple financial model shown in cells A1:B6 of the worksheet in Figure A-7 into a Word document. Most of these cells contain values. Cell B6, however, contains a formula.

To copy this section of the worksheet, drag across cells A1:B6 to select them, choose the Copy command from the Edit menu, and then quit Excel and load Microsoft Word.

When you are in the Word window, click where you want to insert the cell values and choose Paste Cells from the Edit menu. When you finish these steps, your Word document looks like the one in Figure A-8 for Word 3.0 or Figure A-9 for Word 4.0.

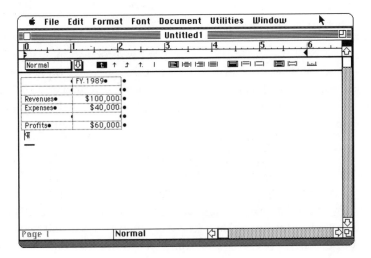

FIGURE A-9. *This is a Word 4.0 document with imported Excel data.*

The contents of cells A1:B6 from the Excel worksheet have been transferred to the Word document, but the formula in cell B6 has not been transferred as a formula. Instead, Excel has copied the current value of the formula into the Word document. Whenever you copy a formula or function into Word, only the current value of that formula is transferred.

If you copy the data into a Word 3.0 document, the data is imported in the same way an Excel document is imported as a text file, except there are no quotation marks around numeric values. If you copy your Excel data into a Word 4.0 document, the data is imported in tabular form and set up neatly in a Word 4.0 table. You don't need to do anything to arrange the imported Excel data. (By the way, the gridlines that appear in the Word 4.0 table are simply screen markers. They do not appear when you print the Word document.) Finally, the formats you assign to your Excel worksheet (except for colors) transfer into Word documents. Then, after your Excel data appears in Word, a Paste Cells command replaces the Paste command on Word's Edit menu.

Transferring a picture

You can also transfer a picture of a block of cells from an Excel worksheet to a Word document. In this example, we create a picture of cells A1:B6. To copy a picture of a block of cells to the Clipboard, drag across the block to select it, hold down the Shift key, and then choose the Copy Picture... command from the Edit menu (this command appears only when you press the Shift key). A dialog box like the one in Figure A-10 appears.

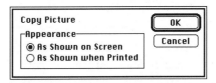

FIGURE A-10. *You can use the Copy Picture dialog box to control the appearance of a "snapshot" of selected cells.*

The As Shown on Screen and As Shown when Printed options let you control the appearance of the snapshot. If you want your worksheet or macro-sheet picture to look exactly as it is displayed on the screen, choose the As Shown on Screen option. If you want your snapshot to resemble more closely the way your document will look when printed, choose the As Shown when Printed option.

For example, let's use the As Shown on Screen option to copy the data in cells A1:B6 of Figure A-7. Click OK, quit Excel, load Word, and then activate a Word document and choose the Paste command. As you can see in Figure A-11, a snapshot of the selected range, complete with cells, gridlines, and row and column headers, appears in our report. (You can eliminate the gridlines and row and column headers by deselecting the Gridlines and Row & Column Headings settings in the Excel Options menu Display dialog box before copying the worksheet.)

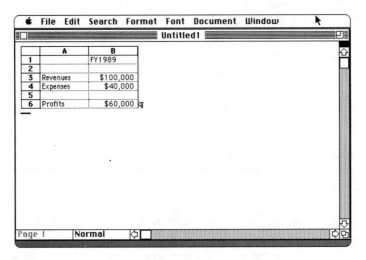

FIGURE A-11. *A snapshot of cells A1:B6 appears in our Word 3.0 document.*

Transferring a chart

Transferring an Excel chart to a Word document is a lot like transferring a picture of a worksheet range. For example, suppose you want to copy the chart shown in Figure A-12 to a Word document. To copy this chart to the Clipboard, first select it and then press the Shift key and choose the Copy Picture... command from the Edit menu. From within the Copy Picture dialog box, as shown in Figure A-13, you can select from two sets of As Shown on Screen or As Shown when Printed options to control the appearance and the size of the chart Excel copies to the Clipboard. If you select the first Appearance option, As Shown on Screen, the chart on the Clipboard appears exactly as you see it in the Excel window. If you select the second Appearance option, As Shown when Printed, the copied picture looks like it would if you printed it. However, when you do print the picture, different printers may produce different results.

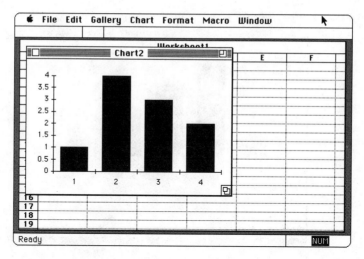

FIGURE A-12. *This is a simple chart created in Excel.*

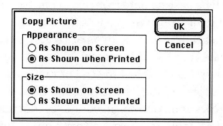

FIGURE A-13. *This is the Copy Picture dialog box for the Chart environment.*

If you select the first Size option, As Shown on Screen, Excel copies the picture in the size of the window shown on the screen. You can adjust the size of the chart by dragging its size box before you choose the Copy Picture… command. If you select the second Size option, As Shown when Printed, Excel makes the chart on the Clipboard as big as it would appear if you printed it. The picture varies according to the window's shape, your printer, and the settings in the Page Setup dialog box. In this and most other cases, you'll want to choose As Shown on Screen.

After you quit Excel and load Word, click the position at which you want to paste the chart and then choose the Paste command from Word's Edit menu. Figure A-14 shows the results of pasting this Excel chart into a Word document. Because we selected the As Shown on Screen size option, the chart we pasted into Word is the same size as the one that we copied from Excel. If you're working with a color monitor, notice that all colors are lost when transferring charts to Word. All patterns, however, are kept.

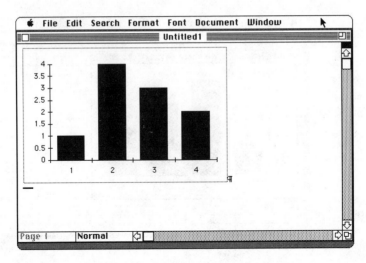

FIGURE A-14. *This is the Excel chart we pasted into Word.*

For the most part, you'll be pasting data from Excel into Microsoft Word. However, if you want to paste data from Word into Excel, make sure the values are separated by tabs and that each line ends with a paragraph mark. After you copy the data in Word and activate your Excel document (either by using MultiFinder or by quitting Word and loading Excel), select the cell or range into which you want to copy the Word data. Then, choose the Paste command from the Edit menu. Your data appears arranged in rows and columns in your Excel document. You can also transfer data from a Word 4.0 table into Excel. When you do this, Excel arranges your data in cells corresponding to the shape of your Word 4.0 table.

Linking Excel documents to Word 4.0 documents

If you are using Excel with MultiFinder and Microsoft Word (version 4.0 or later), you can link data you copied from a source worksheet in Excel into Word. After altering the information in the source Excel worksheet, you can issue one command in Word to update the data.

For example, suppose we want to copy a three-column by three-row range from an Excel worksheet into a Microsoft Word 4.0 document. We want to update this information in Word each time we change the Excel worksheet. By using Word 4.0's Paste Link and Update Link commands, we can keep the data in the Word document current with the Excel worksheet without having to copy and paste the data over and over. Figure A-15 shows an Excel worksheet with values we want to paste into a Word 4.0 document.

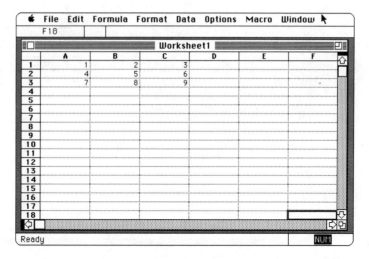

FIGURE A-15. *We want to link this Excel data to a Word 4.0 document.*

To transfer this information to a Word 4.0 document, begin by selecting the range A1:C3 in this Excel worksheet and then choosing the Copy command from the Edit menu. Next, use MultiFinder to switch to Word 4.0. (If you don't use Multi-Finder, simply quit Excel and load Word 4.0.) After the new Word 4.0 document appears on the screen, choose Paste Link from the Word 4.0 Edit menu. The data copied from Excel is pasted into the Word 4.0 document as a table, preceded by an identifier paragraph that gives the location of the worksheet from which the data was copied. The identifier paragraph maintains the link between the source document and the target document. Figure A-16, on the next page, shows the result of the Paste Link command.

If you need to change the information in the source Excel document, you can easily update the Word document to reflect those changes without recopying the entire worksheet range. For example, suppose you need to reverse the values in row 2 of the source Excel worksheet. After making this change in Excel, you would select the entire table in the Word 4.0 document and choose the Update Link command from Word's Edit menu. In a few moments, the outdated table becomes current again. The values corresponding to row 2 in the Excel worksheet are updated in the Word document to match those in the source Excel worksheet. Figure A-17 shows the result of the Update Link command.

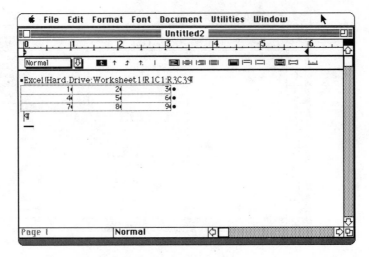

FIGURE A-16. *This Word 4.0 document shows the copied Excel data and the identifier paragraph that links the two documents.*

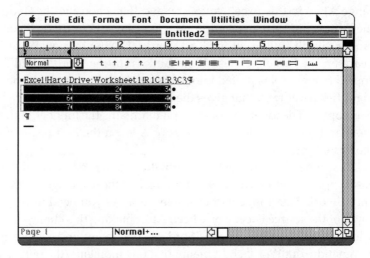

FIGURE A-17. *The Update Link command keeps the values current between two linked documents.*

Sharing data with Microsoft File

You may find it useful to transfer your Microsoft Excel databases to a Microsoft File datafile. The procedure for this transfer is similar to the one you used when transferring Excel files to Microsoft Word. First, you must save your Excel database as a text file using the Save As... command. Then, you quit Excel, load Microsoft File, and create a new datafile. Before you can open the Excel text file in Microsoft File, you need to create fields in the datafile form to match the number of fields in your Excel database. Next, choose the Open Datafile... command from the File menu to open the Excel text file into Microsoft File. Your Excel data is entered in the following way: Each tab-delimited value becomes a field within a Microsoft File record, and each line is a different record. Microsoft File ignores any values outside the database.

Of course, you can also use the Clipboard to copy Excel data into Microsoft File. If you use MultiFinder, this method is especially handy. However, you must still set up the datafile form in Microsoft File before you paste Excel data to Microsoft File from the Clipboard.

You can copy Excel charts to Microsoft File as easily as you copy values from an Excel worksheet. Before you paste an Excel chart, you must format the datafile as a Picture field. The entire process is easy to perform. With the Excel chart open, select the entire chart. Then, hold down the Shift key and choose the Copy Picture... command from the Edit menu. When the Copy Picture dialog box appears, select the As Shown on Screen option in both the Appearance and the Size boxes, then click OK. Next, quit Excel and open Microsoft File (or use MultiFinder to switch to Microsoft File), select the Picture field in the datafile window, and choose Paste from the Edit menu.

Sharing files with Excel 1.5

Even though you can use Microsoft Excel 1.5 documents in Microsoft Excel 2.2, some changes in Excel 2.2 affect users of Excel 1.5. You will have no problem when you open an Excel 1.5 document in Excel 2.2; however, after you save that document in Excel 2.2, you can open it successfully only in Excel 2.2. The Excel 1.5 document is reformatted to the specifications of Excel 2.2. If you want to reopen the document in Excel 1.5 after you've saved it in Excel 2.2, you must resave the document in SYLK/Excel 1.5 file format.

There are a few more Excel 2.2 characteristics you should be aware of. Excel 2.2 can open charts created in Excel 1.5, but it can't save them in a form Excel 1.5 can use. Excel 1.5 files are converted to the Excel 2.2 standard font settings when those files are opened in Excel 2.2. If you are going to reuse an Excel 1.5 file in 1.5 after you open it in Excel 2.2 (or create a new Excel 2.2 file that you can use in Excel 1.5), make sure the 1904 Date System in the Calculation dialog box is activated.

When you save an Excel 2.2 file as a SYLK/Excel 1.5 file for use in Excel 1.5, certain changes occur: All row heights are displayed at default height; all fonts are displayed in the Excel 1.5 single font (bold and italic styles are retained); all cell shading is removed; and all access to cell notes is lost.

The Parse... command

Occasionally, when you transfer information from another program into Microsoft Excel, several columns of incoming data are crammed together in a single cell. This problem is particularly common with database programs that don't use a compatible method of separating field entries. Of course, before the data can be used effectively in your Excel worksheet, you must divide it into more manageable portions. The Parse... command from the Data menu lets you separate the data so that each field is contained in a separate cell.

For example, Figure A-18 shows an imported file that contains five fields. You can see that all these field entries are strung together in column A. The first step in breaking this data into usable form is to select the entries you want Excel to parse. Excel places no limit on the number of rows it can parse, but your selection must be only one column wide. In our example, we want to parse all the records in column A, so we select the cells A4:A9.

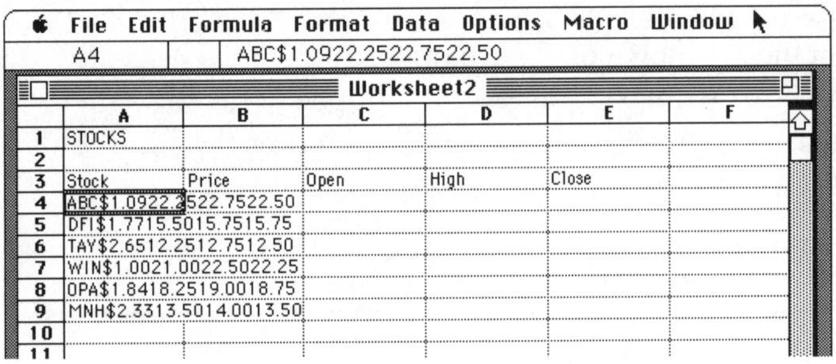

FIGURE A-18. *All five data fields in this sample worksheet are lumped together in column A.*

A word of warning: When Excel parses the records, it places each piece of information (after the first one) in a separate cell to the right of the selected column. Before you begin, be sure your worksheet has room to expand the records. In our example, the data will be redistributed into columns A through E.

When you've selected the range of entries to parse (A4:A9 in Figure A-18), choose the Parse... command from the Data menu. You see the dialog box shown in Figure A-19. As you can see, the contents of the first selected cell (A4) appear in the Parse Line edit box in the dialog box. You use the Parse Line edit box to indicate how the field entries should be divided.

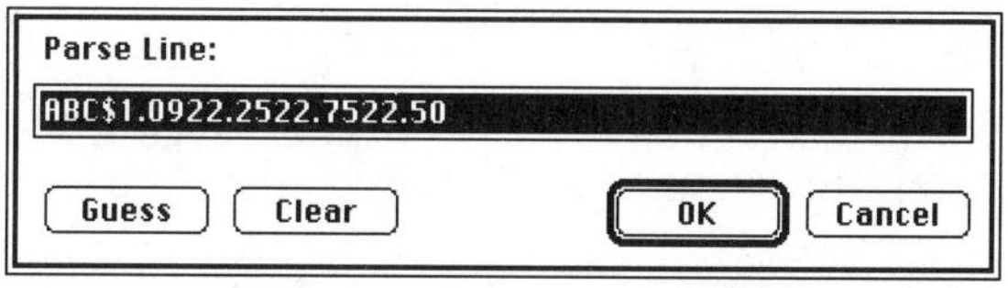

```
┌─────────────────────────────────────────────────────────┐
│ Parse Line:                                              │
│ ┌───────────────────────────────────────────────────┐   │
│ │ ABC$1.0922.2522.7522.50                           │   │
│ └───────────────────────────────────────────────────┘   │
│ ( Guess )  ( Clear )          (  OK  )  ( Cancel )       │
└─────────────────────────────────────────────────────────┘
```

FIGURE A-19. *You can use the Parse dialog box to break entries into separate fields.*

You use brackets ([]) to indicate the number of fields to create and the number of characters in each field. The left, or opening, bracket ([) marks the beginning of a field and the right, or closing, bracket (]) marks the end. You can insert as many pairs of brackets as you want. (If you omit an opening or closing bracket, Excel warns you with an *Error in parse line* message.) If you want to exclude some of the data from your worksheet when you parse, simply don't include that data in brackets.

To specify the length of each field, position the insertion point at the spot at which you want to insert a bracket or use the Left and Right arrow keys to move through the parse line. Then, insert the brackets into the parse line.

If you want to remove all the brackets from the parse line and make a fresh start, click the Clear button to remove these characters. To remove individual brackets, use your mouse or the Left and Right arrow keys to position the insertion point. Then, press the Delete key.

The Guess button at the bottom of the dialog box tells Excel to guess at the division of the selected entries. Excel bases its guess on the type of data it finds in the parse line—text or numbers, for example—and on the position of blank characters. When you click the Guess button, Excel inserts brackets in the parse line at locations at which it thinks the data should be separated. If necessary, you can adjust the position of the brackets Excel inserts by using standard editing techniques.

Figure A-20 shows the position of the brackets in our sample parse line. When you click OK or press Return or Enter, Excel separates all the selected entries into the five fields you delineated with the brackets. Figure A-21 shows the results. Notice that if you need to display formats as well as values in the cells that the entries are parsed to, you need to add the formatting manually.

```
┌─────────────────────────────────────────────────────────┐
│ Parse Line:                                              │
│ ┌───────────────────────────────────────────────────┐   │
│ │ [ABC][$1.09][22.25][22.75][22.50]                 │   │
│ └───────────────────────────────────────────────────┘   │
│ ( Guess )  ( Clear )          (  OK  )  ( Cancel )       │
└─────────────────────────────────────────────────────────┘
```

FIGURE A-20. *We have separated the parse line into five fields.*

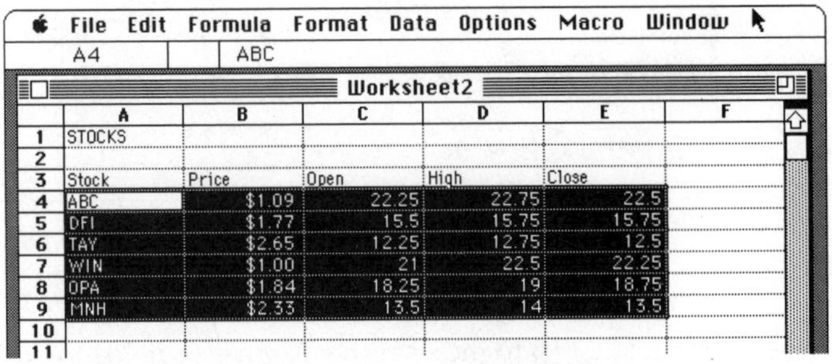

FIGURE A-21. *Using the brackets as its guide, Excel divides the entries in column A among five fields.*

Obviously, the Parse... command is most useful for fixed-length entries. If the fields in the parse selection vary in length, they will not be divided correctly. In that case, you must parse each record individually.

Using macros to communicate with other programs

You can create a Microsoft Excel macro that loads another Macintosh application (if you are using MultiFinder). You start the application by using the EXEC function to activate the application.

The EXEC function

To start another Macintosh program from within a macro, use the EXEC function. This function takes the form

    =EXEC("*program name*")

The *"program name"* argument is a text argument, enclosed in quotation marks, that identifies the application you want to load. Be sure that you direct the EXEC function to the correct folder and that you use the exact name of the program as your text argument. Separate the folder name and program name by a colon. For example, to load Microsoft Word 4.0 manually, you must first quit Excel and then double click the Word icon on the Finder desktop. To load Word 4.0 from within a macro, you use the formula

    =EXEC("Word 4.0")

The EXEC function returns a TRUE value to the macro sheet if the application is launched successfully. The EXEC function returns a FALSE value if the application is not found, if there is not enough memory to run the application, or if you are not using MultiFinder.

The EXEC function is used in an Excel macro to retrieve information from or export information to another program on your Macintosh. Used in conjunction with the functions we discuss in the next few pages (FOPEN, FCLOSE, FPOSE, and so forth), the EXEC function can retrieve specific information from files in another program.

Working with text files

Microsoft Excel offers a set of macro functions you can use to work with text files. These functions let you open, read, and write text files, as well as determine the size of the file and control your position in the file.

The FOPEN and FCLOSE functions

The FOPEN function lets you open an existing text file or create a new text file. This function takes the form

=FOPEN(*"file", access*)

The *"file"* argument, which is the name of the text file you want to open or create, must be a text value enclosed in quotation marks. Excel assumes the text file you're opening or creating is located in the current folder.

The *access* argument is a numeric code that specifies the type of access you want to allow to the document. The following table lists the types of access allowed:

Code	Type of access
1	Read file and write to it.
2	Read file but do not write to it.
3	Create a new file with read and write access.

If the file you specify doesn't exist and you specify an *access* argument of 1 or 2, Excel displays a macro error dialog box and the FOPEN function returns the #N/A error value.

When Excel carries out the FOPEN function, it returns a document ID value that you use to refer to the text file in subsequent macro functions.

When you're finished working with a file, you must use the FCLOSE function to close the file. This function takes the form

=FCLOSE(*id*)

The *id* argument is the document identification number that Excel returns when you use the FOPEN function to open or create the text file. This argument can be a constant value or a reference to the cell that contains the FOPEN function.

The FPOS function

The FPOS function lets you specify a character position in a text file. For example, before you use the FWRITE function to write a series of characters to a text file, you can use the FPOS function to specify the location at which you want those characters to be inserted.

The FPOS function takes the form

=FPOS(*id,position*)

where *id* is the file identification number Excel returns when you open the file using the FOPEN function. If the *id* argument is not valid, Excel shows a macro error dialog box and returns the #VALUE! error value.

The *position* argument is a numeric value that specifies your character position in a file. The first character in a file is numbered 1, the second is numbered 2, and so forth. You use this value in conjunction with the FREAD and FREADLN functions. The *position* argument specifies the character position from which the FREAD function reads. If you omit *position*, Excel uses the current position.

The FSIZE function

The FSIZE function returns the number of characters, including spaces, in a text file. This function takes the form

=FSIZE(*id*)

where *id* is the file identification number Excel returns when you open the file using the FOPEN function. If the *id* argument is not valid, Excel shows a macro error dialog box and returns the #VALUE! error value.

The FREAD and FREADLN functions

The FREAD and FREADLN functions let you retrieve data from a text file opened using the FOPEN function. The FREAD function lets you read a specified number of characters. This function takes the form

=FREAD(*id,number of characters*)

where *id* is the file identification number Excel returns when you open the file using the FOPEN function. If the *id* argument is not valid, Excel shows a macro error dialog box and returns the #VALUE! error value.

Excel begins reading the file at the current position and returns the specified number of characters to the macro sheet. (You can use the FPOS function, described above, to specify your starting position.)

The FREADLN function is similar to FREAD, except that it reads an entire line of text rather than a specified number of characters.

The FREADLN function takes the form

=FREADLN(*id*)

This function returns to the macro sheet all the characters from the current position up to but not including the carriage-return or linefeed character at the end of the line. If the *id* argument is not valid, Excel displays a macro error dialog box and returns the #VALUE! error value.

The FWRITE and FWRITELN functions

The FWRITE function lets you write text to a text file that an FOPEN function has opened. The FWRITE function takes the form

=FWRITE(*id,text*)

where *id* is the file identification number Excel returns when you open the file using the FOPEN function. If the *id* argument is not valid, Excel shows a macro error dialog box and returns the #VALUE! error value.

Excel begins writing the text at the current position. (You can use the FPOS function, described previously, to specify your starting position.) If Excel can't write to the file, it returns the #N/A! error value.

The FWRITELN function is similar to FWRITE. This function also writes text to a text file, beginning at the current position. However, FWRITELN adds a carriage-return or linefeed character at the end of the text string. The FWRITELN function takes the form

=FWRITELN(*id,text*)

If carried out successfully, the FWRITE and FWRITELN functions return to the macro sheet the number of characters written to the text file.

The REGISTER, CALL, and UNREGISTER functions

The REGISTER, CALL, and UNREGISTER functions are powerful but dangerous functions. Although Excel includes them in its macro function directory for sophisticated programmers to use, the average Excel user will have little reason to consider using these three functions. If you use these functions incorrectly, you can cause errors in your system's operation, or you can alter the codes beneath the visible part of your files.

These functions give you the ability to design custom functions for macros using Macintosh code resources that exist as separate files. Linking Excel to libraries of outside code resources connects Excel to outside databases or sound effects. The code resources can be in any standard Macintosh compiled language, such as Lightspeed C or MPW Pascal.

The forms of these functions are

=REGISTER(*"module text","procedure text","argument text"*)

=CALL(*"call text",argument1,...*)

=UNREGISTER(*"register text"*)

Conclusion

In this appendix, we have shown you how to exchange information between Microsoft Excel for the Macintosh and other programs, including Microsoft Excel for the IBM PC, Microsoft Multiplan, Lotus 1-2-3, dBASE, Microsoft Word, Microsoft Write, and Microsoft File. We discussed the Parse... command from the Data menu. We introduced you to some macro functions you can use to communicate with other programs. These macro functions let you bring into Excel information from other memory-resident programs. Finally, we mentioned three macro functions included in Excel primarily for the use of programmers.

B

Keyboard Shortcuts

Choosing commands

Activate next window	Command-M
Activate previous window	Command-Shift-M
Calculate Now	Command-=
Cancel	Command-. (period)
Clear…	Command-B
Close window	Command-W
Copy	Command-C
Copy Picture	Command-Shift-C
Cut	Command-X
Define Name…	Command-L
Delete…	Command-K
Extract…	Command-E
Fill Down	Command-D
Fill Right	Command-R
Find… (Formula menu)	Command-J
Find next (Data menu)	Command-F
Find next (Formula menu)	Command-H

(continued)

CHOOSING COMMANDS *continued*

Find previous (Data menu)	Command-Shift-F
Find previous (Formula menu)	Command-Shift-H
Goto…	Command-G
Help…	Command-/ or Command-?
Insert…	Command-I
New…	Command-N
Note…	Command-Shift-N
Open…	Command-O
Paste	Command-V
Paste Special…	Command-Shift-V
Print…	Command-P
Quit	Command-Q
Reference	Command-T
Repeat	Command-Y
Save	Command-S
Save As…	Command-Shift-S
Select all cells	Command-A
Select Chart	Command-A
Undo	Command-Z

Choosing dialog-box options directly

Format Border

Bottom	Command-Option-Down arrow
Left	Command-Option-Left arrow
Outline	Command-Option-0 (zero)
Right	Command-Option-Right arrow
Top	Command-Option-Up arrow

Format Number

General	Command-Option-~
h:mm AM/PM	Command-Option-@
$#,##0.00 ;($#,##0.00)	Command-Option-#
0%	Command-Option-%
0.00	Command-Option-!
0.00E+00	Command-Option-^

(continued)

CHOOSING DIALOG-BOX OPTIONS DIRECTLY *continued*

Select Special

Column Differences	Command-Shift-\
Current Region	Command-*
Dependents: All Levels	Command-Shift-]
Dependents: Direct Only	Command-]
Display Formulas (toggles between formulas and values)	Command-` (backquote)
Notes	Command-Shift-O (letter O)
Precedents: All Levels	Command-Shift-[
Precedents: Direct Only	Command-[
Row Differences	Command-\

Formatting commands

Bold	Command-Shift-B
Italic	Command-Shift-I
Plain	Command-Shift-P
Underline	Command-Shift-U
Shadow	Command-Shift-W
Bottom border	Command-Option-Down arrow
Left border	Command-Option-Left arrow
Right border	Command-Option-Right arrow
Top border	Command-Option-Up arrow

Editing the formula bar

Activate formula bar	Command-U
Cancel entry	Command-.
Enter formula as array formula	Command-Enter or Command-Return
Fill selection with formula	Option-Enter or Option-Return
Insert current date into formula bar	Command-- (hyphen)
Insert current time into formula bar	Command-;
Insert formula of above cell into formula bar	Command-' (apostrophe)
Insert value of above cell into formula bar	Command-"

Navigational commands

Down one block	Command-Down arrow
Left one block	Command-Left arrow
Right one block	Command-Right arrow
Up one block	Command-Up arrow
Cell A1	Command-Home
Last cell	Command-End
Down one cell	Down arrow
Left one cell	Left arrow
Right one cell	Right arrow
Up one cell	Up arrow
Next class (in charts)	Up arrow
Next item in a class (in charts)	Left arrow
Previous class (in charts)	Down arrow
Previous item in a class (in charts)	Right arrow
End of row	End
Start of row	Home
Down one screen	Page down
Left one screen	Command-Page up
Right one screen	Command-Page down
Up one screen	Page up

Numeric-keypad shortcuts

These commands work only when Numlock is toggled off.

Numlock	Shift-Clear (toggles on and off)
Down one cell	2
Left one cell	4
Right one cell	6
Up one cell	8
First cell in column	Command-8
Last cell in column	Command-2
Beginning of line	7
End of line	1
First cell in row	Command-4
Last cell in row	Command-6
Down one screen	3

(continued)

NUMERIC-KEYPAD SHORTCUTS *continued*

Left one screen	Command-9
Right one screen	Command-3
Up one screen	9
First cell in worksheet	Command-7
Last cell in worksheet	Command-1

Extended-keyboard function-key shortcuts

Activate menu bar	F10
Add to selection	Shift-F8
Calculate Document command	Shift-F9
Calculate Now command	F9
Close command (active window)	Command-F4
Copy command	F3
Create Names… command	Command-Shift-F3
Cut command	F2
Define Name… command	Command-F3
Extend selection (toggles on and off)	F8
Find… command (Formula menu)	Shift-F5
Find next command (Formula menu)	F7
Find previous command (Formula menu)	Shift-F7
Goto… command	F5
Help (context-sensitive)	Shift-F1
Move active document window	Command-F7
New chart	F11
New macro sheet	Command-F11
New worksheet	Shift-F11
Next pane	F6
Next window	Command-F6
Note… command	Shift-F2
Open… command	Command-F12
Paste command	F4
Paste Function… command	Shift-F3
Previous pane	Shift-F6
Previous window	Command-Shift-F6

(continued)

EXTENDED-KEYBOARD FUNCTION-KEY SHORTCUTS *continued*

Print... command	Command-Shift-F12
Restore window size	Command-F5
Save As... command	F12
Save command	Shift-F12
Show Info command	Command-F2
Undo command	F1
Zoom (maximize) active document window	Command-F10

Other keyboard actions

Cancel action	Esc
Select column	Command-Spacebar
Select row	Shift-Spacebar

C

Microsoft Mail
and Excel

One of the most exciting features of Microsoft Excel 2.2 is its ability to work with Microsoft's popular electronic mail program, Microsoft Mail 2.0. If you've installed Microsoft Mail 2.0 on your Macintosh along with Excel 2.2, you can use Excel to compose and send messages (in the form of worksheets, charts, and macro sheets) to other people on your Microsoft Mail network. Similarly, if someone sends you a Microsoft Mail message, you can read, edit, save, or print that message just as you would any other Excel document.

In addition, Microsoft Mail 2.0 can be integrated powerfully with Excel 2.2: If you are part of a team of Excel users connected to a Microsoft Mail server, you can create and transfer information as a team. Excel users are no longer merely individuals working alone, printing their work to share with other Excel users. Because you don't need to quit Excel to send or receive Excel files as Microsoft Mail messages, you can work with other users to create dynamic documents—sharing information until all the information your team needs is recorded in one active Excel document.

The Excel 2.2 macro language includes functions that automate the sending and receiving of information through Microsoft Mail. (To learn how to operate the OPEN.MAIL and SEND.MAIL macro functions, see Chapter 18, "Macro Functions.") For example, you can use Microsoft Mail and Excel together to automate the budgetary process and consolidate widespread financial information from several departments or companies. And you can carry out elaborate record-keeping procedures through a Microsoft Mail network without using hard copy or transferring disks.

In this appendix, we cover the mechanics of working with Microsoft Mail and Excel. We assume that you've already installed Microsoft Mail 2.0 on your computer and that you have a pretty good understanding of how to send and receive messages using Microsoft Mail. If you have not yet installed Microsoft Mail, version 2.0 or later (earlier versions of Microsoft Mail do not work .with Excel 2.2), spend some time with your Microsoft Mail manual first. If you need additional information or help with Microsoft Mail, you can call the Microsoft Product Support Department at (206) 454-2030.

Opening Excel messages

To open and send messages in Microsoft Excel, you use the Open Mail... and Send Mail... commands from the Excel File menu. These commands work only if your Macintosh is connected to a Microsoft Mail 2.0 server and you are signed into your mailbox. (For information on installing and signing into the Microsoft Mail system, refer to your Microsoft Mail manual.)

To open the Excel messages found in your Microsoft Mail mailbox, choose the Open Mail... command from the File menu. When you do this, a Mail Documents window similar to the one shown in Figure C-1 appears.

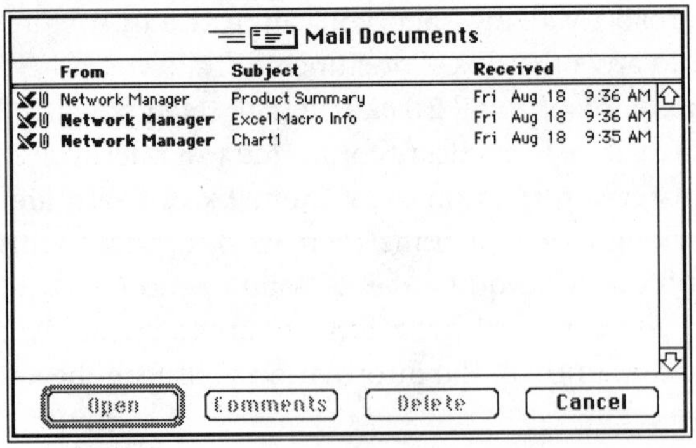

FIGURE C-1. *Excel's Open Mail... command lets you open Excel messages that reside in your Microsoft Mail mailbox.*

As you can see, the Mail Documents window in Figure C-1 indicates that messages entitled *Product Summary*, *Excel Macro Info*, and *Chart1* can be found in the mailbox. The "message," in this context, is the Excel file represented by the title shown in the Mail Documents window. The "message" also includes comments the sender may have attached to the file. To open any message listed in the window, double-click the title of the message you want to read, or click the title and then click the Open button. (When the sender's name appears in boldface, the message has not yet been read.)

If you want to read more than one message, press the Shift key while you click each title, then click the Open button to open all the selected messages at one time. As you might expect, Excel places each open message into its own window. All the windows are the same size, and Excel opens them one on top of another. When you close a window, the window underneath the closed one appears.

After you open a message in Excel, you can edit, save, or print the message like any other Excel document. The document you see in Excel, however, is a duplicate of the message in your Microsoft Mail mailbox. No matter what you do with the message you've opened in Excel, the original message remains unaltered in your mailbox until you delete it.

You can also delete a message from your mailbox by using the Open Mail… command. Choose the Open Mail… command from the File menu, click the title of the message you want to delete, then click the Delete button. To delete multiple messages, press the Shift key while you click each title, then click the Delete button.

Sending Excel messages

Before sending a message, you can customize your Send Document dialog box in Microsoft Mail. Simply choose the Microsoft Mail 2.0 desk accessory from the menu, and then select the Preferences… command from the Mail menu. For our example, we selected the Simpler User List option from the Preferences dialog box to customize the Send Document dialog box.

To send a message you've created in Excel to another person's mailbox, create the message as an Excel document, then choose the Send Mail… command from the File menu. When you choose the Send Mail… command, Excel displays a Send Document window, similar to the one shown in Figure C-2 on the next page, listing all the people on the Microsoft Mail network.

In the Send Document window, click the names of the people to whom you want to send your message. As soon as you click a name in the list, Excel places a check mark next to that name. If you accidentally click the wrong name, simply click it again to remove the check mark and to remove the name from the list of recipients.

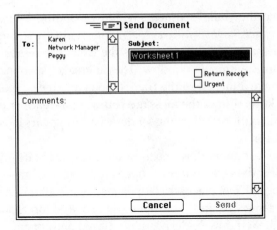

FIGURE C-2. *You use Excel's Send Mail... command to send an Excel document to someone else's Microsoft Mail mailbox.*

By default, Excel places the title of the document you are sending in the Send Document window's Subject field. The text in the Subject field becomes the message title the recipients see when they open their mail. As you'd expect, you can accept the default message title, or you can type a different title for the currently open document.

Selecting the Return Receipt check box in the Send Document window tells Microsoft Mail to notify you when each recipient reads your message. Figure C-3 shows the Return Receipt dialog box that appears when you activate the Return Receipt check box. The Return Receipt dialog box appears automatically on your screen when your message is read. If you do not want to be bothered with notification, do not select the Return Receipt check box.

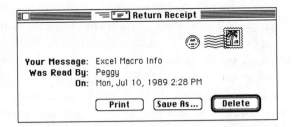

FIGURE C-3. *The Return Receipt dialog box appears when you activate the Return Receipt check box.*

You can activate the Urgent check box in the Send Document window when you want recipients to see your message immediately. To see your Urgent message, recipients must activate the default check box (Display urgent messages immediately) in their Microsoft Mail Preferences dialog box.

When you are satisfied with all the settings in the Send Document window, type any comments you want to add to your document and then click the Send button to send your Excel message to each recipient's mailbox. As soon as you click the Send button, the Send Document window disappears and the message *Sending file to the Microsoft Mail Server...* appears.

Conclusion

If your network is equipped with Microsoft Mail, version 2.0 or later, you can use Microsoft Excel 2.2 to take advantage of the Microsoft Mail capabilities. In this appendix, we've shown you how to use Excel's Open Mail... and Send Mail... commands to read and send messages directly from within Microsoft Excel. Together, Microsoft Mail and Microsoft Excel provide a dynamic way to share worksheets, macros, and charts among different Excel users.

Index

DOUGLAS COBB

Douglas Cobb is the president of The Cobb Group, Inc., a company that specializes in writing and publishing high-quality books, journals, and workbooks that support business software products. He is coauthor of *Using 1-2-3*, perhaps the most successful computer book ever published. His most recent books published by Microsoft Press include the bestselling PUTTING MICROSOFT WORKS TO WORK and RUNNING MICROSOFT EXCEL, both written for the IBM PC, PS/2, and compatibles. Doug Cobb is also a columnist for *PC Magazine*.

ALLAN McGUFFEY

Allan McGuffey is a writer and editor for the Cobb Group. He coauthored the WORD 4 COMPANION and the WORKS 2 COMPANION (distributed by Microsoft Press) and coordinated editing efforts on the original WORKS COMPANION. He has shared editing duties for the Cobb Group's nine journals, including *1-2-3 User's Journal*, *Symphony User's Journal*, *Paradox User's Journal*, and *Inside Word*.

The manuscript for this book was prepared and submitted to Microsoft Press in electronic form. Text files were processed and formatted using Microsoft Word.

Cover design by Thomas A. Draper
Interior text design by Craig A. Bergquist & Associates
Principal typography by Lisa Iversen
Color separations by Rainier Color Corporation

Text composition by Microsoft Press in Palatino with display in Palatino Italic, using the Magna composition system and the Linotronic 300 laser imagesetter.

Printed on recycled paper stock.

OTHER TITLES FROM MICROSOFT PRESS

MICROSOFT® EXCEL BUSINESS SOURCEBOOK
More Than 100 Practical Business Applications Created with Microsoft Excel Version 2.2
Macintosh Version
Charles W. Kyd

At last! Here is a valuable, one-of-a-kind resource to save you hours of time as it helps you create useful, error-free spreadsheets and reports with Microsoft Excel for the Apple Macintosh. These timesaving applications, created with the increased formatting capabilities of Microsoft Excel version 2.2, are also functionally compatible with version 1.5. Packed with more than 100 practical applications, the MICROSOFT EXCEL BUSINESS SOURCEBOOK addresses real business needs. Designed to be used by anyone with a basic understanding of Microsoft Excel, the applications cover basic financial statements, spreadsheet accounting systems, accounts payable and accounts receivable systems, business loan reports, sales and expense forecasts, management reports, and more. Also included are illustrations of the final, printed spreadsheets along with instructions for creating and customizing the spreadsheets.
608 pages, softcover 7⅜ x 9¼ $24.95 Order Code EXBUSM

MICROSOFT® EXCEL MONEY MANAGER
Macintosh® Version
Stephen L. Nelson

This easy-to-use book/disk package provides you with a complete and inexpensive personal financial-planning tool. On disk and certain to save you hours of development time, the ready-to-use templates help you with tax planning and preparation, checkbook balancing, fixed rate and variable rate loan amortization, debt analysis, real estate investment analysis, savings planning for education or retirement, personal financial statements, life insurance planning, and more. The book also explains financial alternatives and provides clear examples so that you understand the financial contexts of the forms as well as the mechanics of using them. Each chapter includes a detailed description of the formulas and macros behind the templates.
282 pages, softcover, with one 3.5-inch disk 7⅜ x 9¼ $34.95 Order Code EXMOMA

WORKING WITH WORD, 2nd ed.
The Definitive Guide to Microsoft® Word on the Apple® Macintosh®
Chris Kinata and Gordon McComb

"The best book for getting inside Microsoft's word processor. Geared for users of all levels and includes extensive tips and shortcuts on increasing productivity with Word." MacWEEK

For those who are ready to go beyond simple word processing with Microsoft Word for the Macintosh, WORKING WITH WORD is *the* book of choice. Now updated for version 4, it's filled with insider's advice, detailed information, and tutorials on every software feature. Scores of tips—many not included in the documentation that comes with the program—add power and range to your use of Microsoft Word, no matter what kinds of printed documents you want to create. Topics include desktop publishing with Word (integrating graphics into a Word document and wrapping text around them, working with lists and multiple columns, and creating spreadsheetlike tables); customizing menus and retrieving lost files; linking Word with other applications; programming conditional print merging instructions; including PostScript instructions in Word documents; and memory management for optimum Word performance. Also included are blueprints for correspondence and for multicolumn newsletters, brochures, and reports. WORKING WITH WORD is the most complete and up-to-date book on Microsoft Word available.
752 pages, softcover 7⅜ x 9¼ $22.95 Order Code WOWO2

QUICK REFERENCE GUIDE TO MICROSOFT® WORD FOR THE APPLE® MACINTOSH®
Version 4
Lisa Ann Jacobs

This great little alphabetic guide offers you a handy action-oriented reference to Microsoft Word through version 4. You can look up specific tasks—such as customizing menus, indexing, and underlining text—without knowing the specific Word commands. It's a practical, fast way to understand and use Microsoft Word. Also included are an index to commands and a summary of keyboard shortcuts.
144 pages, softcover   4¾ x 8 $5.95   Order Code QRWOMA

DESKTOP PUBLISHING BY DESIGN — Aldus® PageMaker® Edition
Three books in one: Elements of Design, Desktop Publishing Portfolio, and Hands-on Projects
Ronnie Shushan and Don Wright

"One of the most useful and attractive books on desktop publishing and design...400 pages full of ideas and inspiration."   The New York Times

Brochures. Newsletters. Promotional flyers. Projects that need effective design. But you're not a graphic designer by trade. Do you need some basic training? Some design ideas to get you going? DESKTOP PUBLISHING BY DESIGN is filled with how-to information, layout ideas, and inspiration for anyone new to design, publishing, or computers. The authors offer a primer on the use of basic design elements—typeface, page layout, and graphics. And they provide a wide-ranging and imaginative portfolio of promotional flyers and brochures, newsletters and magazines, catalogs, data sheets, and forms that demonstrate good design and constitute a sourcebook of inventive ideas. You'll also find a series of PageMaker projects (Aldus PageMaker version 3 for the IBM PC or Apple Macintosh) that provide hands-on experience and build confidence while they teach you how to produce exciting, professional-looking printed pieces. DESKTOP PUBLISHING BY DESIGN is a fact-filled, designed-oriented resource you'll turn to again and again.
408 pages, softcover   8½ x 11 $24.95   Order Code DEPUDP

THE APPLE® MACINTOSH® BOOK, 3rd ed.
Cary Lu

"The one Macintosh book you'd choose if you could have only one. Virtually anything you might want to know at any level is here."   The MACazine

Quoted by industry experts, recommended in classrooms, passed around in user groups, and relied upon by everyday Macintosh users, THE APPLE MACINTOSH BOOK is the bible of the Macintosh world. Updated to include information on the Mac II, Mac SE, and Mac Plus, this classic book provides an authoritative and comprehensive look at the Mac's design philosophy, architecture, and hardware and software options and explores significant user issues. Learn about how the Mac works and about its video screen, keyboard and mouse, disks and disk drives, data pathways and memory, and printers. Find out what's currently available and what is soon to be available in word processing, graphics, business software, communications, and desktop publishing for the Mac. Cary Lu covers selecting the right Mac, uses for the Mac, internal hardware expansion, mass-storage options, local area networks, and more. If you currently use a Mac or expect to use one, you need this book. Your Apple Macintosh library is incomplete without it.
416 pages, softcover   7⅜ x 9¼ $21.95   Order Code APMAB3

Microsoft Press books are available wherever quality computer books are sold. You can place credit card orders by calling 1-800-MSPRESS.